S0-ACR-936

University Textbook Series

May, 1985

Especially Designed for Collateral Reading

HARRY W. JONES
Directing Editor
Professor of Law, Columbia University

ADMINISTRATIVE LAW AND PROCESS (1985)
Richard J. Pierce, Jr., Dean and Professor of Law, University of Pittsburgh.
Sidney A. Shapiro, Professor of Law, University of Kansas.
Paul R. Verkuil, President and Professor of Law, College of William and Mary.

ADMIRALTY, Second Edition (1975)
Grant Gilmore, Professor of Law, Yale University.
Charles L. Black, Jr., Professor of Law, Yale University.

ADMIRALTY AND FEDERALISM (1970)
David W. Robertson, Professor of Law, University of Texas.

AGENCY (1975)
W. Edward Sell, Dean of the School of Law, University of Pittsburgh.

BUSINESS ORGANIZATION AND FINANCE (1980)
William A. Klein, Professor of Law, University of California, Los Angeles.

CIVIL PROCEDURE, BASIC, Second Edition (1979)
Milton D. Green, Professor of Law Emeritus, University of California, Hastings College of the Law.

COMMERCIAL TRANSACTIONS, INTRODUCTION TO (1977)
Hon. Robert Braucher, Associate Justice, Supreme Judicial Court of Massachusetts.
Robert A. Riegert, Professor of Law, Cumberland School of Law.

CONFLICT OF LAWS, COMMENTARY ON THE, Second Edition (1980)
Russell J. Weintraub, Professor of Law, University of Texas.

CONSTITUTIONAL LAW, AMERICAN (A TREATISE ON) (1978) with 1979 Supplement
Laurence H. Tribe, Professor of Law, Harvard University.

CONTRACT LAW, THE CAPABILITY PROBLEM IN (1978)
Richard Danzig.

CORPORATIONS, Second Edition (1971)
Norman D. Lattin, Professor of Law, University of California, Hastings College of the Law.

CORPORATIONS IN PERSPECTIVE (1976)
Alfred F. Conard, Professor of Law, University of Michigan.

UNIVERSITY TEXTBOOK SERIES—Continued

CRIMINAL LAW, Third Edition (1982)

Rollin M. Perkins, Professor of Law, University of California, Hastings College of the Law.

Ronald N. Boyce, Professor of Law, University of Utah College of Law.

CRIMINAL PROCEDURE (1980) with 1984 Supplement

Charles H. Whitebread, II, Professor of Law, University of Virginia.

ESTATES IN LAND & FUTURE INTERESTS, PREFACE TO, Second Edition (1984)

Thomas F. Bergin, Professor of Law, University of Virginia.

Paul G. Haskell, Professor of Law, University of North Carolina.

EVIDENCE: COMMON SENSE AND COMMON LAW (1947)

John M. Maguire, Professor of Law, Harvard University.

EVIDENCE, STUDENTS' TEXT ON THE LAW OF (1935)

The late John Henry Wigmore, Northwestern University.

JURISPRUDENCE: MEN AND IDEAS OF THE LAW (1953)

The late Edwin W. Patterson, Cardozo Professor of Jurisprudence, Columbia University.

LEGAL CAPITAL, Second Edition (1981)

Bayless Manning.

LEGAL RESEARCH ILLUSTRATED, Third Edition (1985) with 1985 Assignments Supplement

J. Myron Jacobstein, Professor of Law, Law Librarian, Stanford University.

Roy M. Mersky, Professor of Law, Director of Research, University of Texas.

LEGAL RESEARCH, FUNDAMENTALS OF, Third Edition (1985) with 1985 Assignments Supplement

J. Myron Jacobstein, Professor of Law, Law Librarian, Stanford University.

Roy M. Mersky, Professor of Law, Director of Research, University of Texas.

PROCEDURE, THE STRUCTURE OF (1979)

Robert M. Cover, Professor of Law, Yale University.

Owen M. Fiss, Professor of Law, Yale University.

THE PROFESSION OF LAW (1971)

L. Ray Patterson, Professor of Law, Emory University.

Elliott E. Cheatham, Professor of Law, Vanderbilt University.

PROPERTY, Second Edition (1975)

John E. Cribbet, Dean of the Law School, University of Illinois.

TAXATION, FEDERAL INCOME, Fourth Edition (1985)

Marvin A. Chirelstein, Professor of Law, Columbia University.

TORTS, Second Edition (1980)

Clarence Morris, Professor of Law, University of Pennsylvania.

C. Robert Morris, Professor of Law, University of Minnesota.

TRUSTS, PREFACE TO THE LAW OF (1975)

Paul G. Haskell, Professor of Law, University of North Carolina.

WILLS AND TRUSTS, THE PLANNING AND DRAFTING OF, Second Edition (1979) with 1982 Supplement

Thomas L. Shaffer, Professor of Law, University of Notre Dame.

LEGAL RESEARCH ILLUSTRATED

THIRD EDITION

An Abridgment of

FUNDAMENTALS

OF

LEGAL RESEARCH

THIRD EDITION

By

J. MYRON JACOBSTEIN

Professor of Law and Law Librarian
Stanford University

and

ROY M. MERSKY

Elton M. Hyder, Jr. and Martha Rowan Hyder Centennial
Professor of Law and Director of Research
University of Texas, Austin

Mineola, New York
THE FOUNDATION PRESS, INC.
1985

Reprinted from
Jacobstein and Mersky's Fundamentals of Legal Research, Third Edition
COPYRIGHT © 1985 THE FOUNDATION PRESS, INC.
All rights reserved

Library of Congress Catalog Card Number: 85–80952

ISBN 0–88277–304–6

PREFACE

This is an Abridgment of the Third Edition of *Fundamentals of Legal Research*. We noted in its Preface that perhaps nothing reflects the ever-changing patterns and growth of law better than the changes required in preparing a new edition of a text on legal research. The preparation of this edition has required substantial changes in nearly every Chapter—brought about by the publication of works in new fields of law, new editions of older titles, new titles for established fields of law, and the elimination of titles that have ceased publication.

Since the publication of the Second Edition, the use of machine-readable databases have become more widely available and such databases are described, when appropriate, throughout this edition. In addition, we have revised and expanded Chapter 20, which describes the use of computers in legal research.

This Abridgment is again designed to accomplish two purposes. The first objective is to introduce the fundamentals of legal resources to those law schools which do not have a formal course in legal research but attempt to integrate the techniques of legal research through a legal writing or other substantive law course. The Abridgment enables the law student to grasp the basic fundamental concepts of the materials in legal research in precise, readily comprehensive format.

Its second objective is to provide an introduction to legal resources for law-related courses and problems in the undergraduate or graduate curriculum. Dealing with the effective utilization of legal research and reference tools in a manner designed to meet the needs of the student in a non-law field, the Abridgment is a thorough guide to the scholar in interdisciplinary use of legal materials.

Law is a central concept in human society. Indeed, without law there would be no society. In our society, law is commonly defined in terms of the decisions of our various courts. It is the courts which fill out the bare bones of the statutes by specific applications and which fill in gaps in the statutory rules by creative judging. Especially since the 1954 decision by the Supreme Court of the United States in the now landmark case of *Brown vs. Board of Education of Topeka*,[1] popularly known as the School Segregation Case, our courts have been increasingly active in attacking social problems. As

---

[1] 347 U.S. 483 (1954).

a result, an understanding of legal rules is a necessary requirement for scientists, technologists, as well as other professions.

This fact is part of a general trend toward interdisciplinary studies. With each passing year, our civilization increases in complexity. As an inevitable result, research in all fields becomes more interdisciplinarian in nature. Legal research, for example, has been substantially affected in recent years by the continued expansion of technological innovation and by a greater tendency to use legal solutions for a wide range of social problems. As these interdisciplinarian scholars have discovered that legal studies add valuable materials to their programs of instruction, a guide is needed to provide these non-lawyers who feel the impact of law upon their disciplines with an introduction to the essentials of legal research.

Chapters in this Abridgment on international law, legislative histories, administrative law, and computers and the law, are but a few of the subjects covered which will provide the interdisciplinarian professions an indispensable understanding of the legal duties and liabilities inherent in their practice.

Law is a well-indexed, well-organized body of materials, confusing and complex to the uninitiated, but easily accessible with the aid of a knowledgeable guide. This Abridgment is designed to be that guide.

But we wish to emphasize that this work is intended to provide only a bird's-eye view of legal research. For more intensive information on the use of law books, the parent work, *Fundamentals of Legal Research* should be consulted.

In most instances, the summary of each chapter has been omitted in the Abridgment. The full edition should also be consulted for information on Court Rules and Procedures, Federal Tax Research, Municipal Legislation, English Legal Research, and for the Table of Legal Abbreviations.

J. MYRON JACOBSTEIN
Stanford University School of Law

ROY M. MERSKY
University of Texas at Austin
School of Law

May 1985

SUMMARY OF CONTENTS

*

CONTENTS

TABLE OF CONTENTS

TABLE OF CONTENTS

TABLE OF CONTENTS

TABLE OF CONTENTS

*

GLOSSARY OF TERMS USED
IN LEGAL RESEARCH

This glossary of terms* is limited in scope, and the definitions of words are restricted in meaning to their legal or legal research context. Words whose meanings conform to general usage and are obvious are omitted from the list, e.g., Index.

ACQUITTAL—

the verdict in a criminal trial in which the defendant is found not guilty.

ACT—

an alternative name for statutory law. When introduced into the first house of the legislature, a piece of proposed legislation is known as a *bill*. When passed to the next house, it may then be referred to as an *act*. After enactment the terms law and act may be used interchangeably. An act has the same legislative force as a joint resolution but is technically distinguishable, being of a different form and introduced with the words *Be it enacted* instead of *Be it resolved*.

ACTION—

the formal legal demand of one's rights from another person brought in court.

ADJUDICATION—

the formal pronouncing or recording of a judgment or decree by a court.

ADMINISTRATIVE LAW—

law that affects private parties, promulgated by governmental agencies other than courts or legislative bodies. These administrative agencies derive their power from legislative enactments and are subject to judicial review.

ADVANCE SHEETS—

current pamphlets containing the most recently reported opinions of a court or the courts of several jurisdictions. The volume and

* Revised for this edition by Fred R. Shapiro, Head of Reference Services and Adjunct Professor, New York Law School; Contributor, *Oxford English Dictionary Supplement.*

page numbers usually are the same as in the subsequently bound volumes of the series, which cover several numbers of the advance sheets.

ADVISORY OPINION—

an opinion rendered by a court at the request of the government or an interested party and indicates how the court would rule on a matter should adversary litigation develop. An advisory opinion is thus an interpretation of the law without binding effect. The International Court of Justice and some state courts will render advisory opinions; the Supreme Court of the United States will not.

AFFIDAVIT—

a written statement or declaration of facts sworn to by the maker, taken before a person officially permitted by law to administer oaths.

AMICUS CURIAE—

means, literally, friend of the court. A party with strong interest in or views on the subject matter of the dispute will petition the court for permission to file a brief, ostensibly on behalf of a party but actually to suggest a rationale consistent with its own views.

ANNOTATIONS—

(1) Statutory: brief summaries of the law and facts of cases interpreting statutes passed by Congress or state legislatures which are included in codes, or (2) Textual: expository essays of varying length on significant legal topics chosen from selected cases published with the essays.

ANSWER—

the pleading filed by the defendant in response to plaintiff's complaint.

APPEAL PAPERS—

the briefs and transcripts of records on appeal filed by attorneys with courts in connection with litigation. A brief consists of a summary of the facts and circumstances or legal propositions as presented by a party to a pending action.

APPELLEE—

the party against whom an appeal is taken (usually, but not always, the winner in the lower court). It should be noted that a party's status as appellant or appellee bears no relation to his status as plaintiff or defendant in the lower court.

ARBITRATION—

the hearing and settlement of a dispute between opposing parties by a third party. This decision is often binding by prior agreement of the parties.

ASSAULT—

an unlawful, intentional show of force or an attempt to do physical harm to another person. Assault can constitute the basis of a civil or criminal action. See also BATTERY.

ASSAULT AND BATTERY—

See BATTERY.

ATTORNEY GENERAL OPINIONS—

opinions issued by the government's chief counsel at the request of some governmental body interpreting the law for the requesting agency in the same manner as a private attorney would for his client. The opinions are not binding on the courts but are usually accorded some degree of persuasive authority.

AUTHORITY—

that which can bind or influence a court. Legislation, case law, administrative regulations and decisions, and writings about the law are all legal authority. See PRIMARY AUTHORITY; SECONDARY AUTHORITY; MANDATORY AUTHORITY; PERSUASIVE AUTHORITY.

AUTO–CITE—

the computerized citation verification service of Lawyers Cooperative Publishing Company and Bancroft-Whitney Company. AUTO–CITE provides parallel citations and case-history information.

BAIL—

security given, in the form of a bail bond or cash, as a guarantee that released prisoners will present themselves for trial. This security may be lost if the released person does not appear in court at the appointed time.

BATTERY—

an unlawful use of force against another person resulting in physical contact (a tort); it is commonly used in the phrase *assault and battery*, assault being the threat of force, and battery the actual use of force. See also ASSAULT.

BILL—

a legislative proposal introduced in the legislature. The term distinguishes unfinished legislation from directly enacted law.

BLACK LETTER LAW—

an informal term indicating the basic principles of law generally accepted by the courts and/or embodied in the statutes of a particular jurisdiction.

BLUE BOOK—

a popular name for *A Uniform System of Citation*, which is published and distributed by the Harvard Law Review Association et al., and which is bound in a blue cover.

BOOLEAN LOGIC—

a form of search strategy used in databases such as LEXIS and WESTLAW. In a Boolean search, *connectors* such as AND, OR and NOT are used to construct a complex search command. The LEXIS command *fungible and gasoline* for example, retrieves documents in which the term *fungible* and the term *gasoline* both appear.

BREACH OF CONTRACT—

the failure to perform any of the terms of an agreement.

BRIEF—

(1) in American law practice, a written statement prepared by the counsel arguing a case in court. It contains a summary of the facts of the case, the pertinent laws, and an argument of how the law applies to the facts supporting counsel's position; (2) a summary of a published opinion of a case prepared for studying the opinion in law school.

BRIEFS AND RECORDS—

See APPEAL PAPERS.

CALENDAR—

can mean the order in which cases are to be heard during a term of court. *Martindale-Hubbell Law Directory* contains calendars for state and federal courts, and includes the name of the court, the name of the judge, and the date of the term's beginning.

CALR—

an acronym for Computer-Assisted Legal Research. LEXIS and WESTLAW are CALR systems.

CAPTION—

See STYLE OF A CASE.

CASE IN POINT—

a judicial opinion which deals with a fact situation similar to the one being researched and substantiates a point of law to be asserted. (Also called *Case on All Fours.*)

CASE LAW—

the law of reported judicial opinions as distinguished from statutes or administrative law.

CASEBOOK—

a textbook used to instruct law students in a particular area of law. The text consists of a collection of court opinions, usually from appellate courts, and notes by the author(s).

CAUSE OF ACTION—

a claim in law and in fact sufficient to bring the case to court; the grounds of an action. (Example: breach of contract.)

CERTIORARI—

a writ issued by a superior to an inferior court requiring the latter to produce the records of a particular case tried therein. It is most commonly used to refer to the Supreme Court of the United States, which uses the writ of certiorari as a discretionary device to choose the cases it wishes to hear. The term's origin is Latin, meaning *to be informed of.*

CHARTER—

a document issued by a governmental entity which gives a corporation legal existence.

CHATTEL—

any article of personal property, as opposed to real property. It may refer to animate as well as inanimate property.

CHOSE—

any article of personal property. See PROPERTY.

CITATION—

the reference to authority necessary to substantiate the validity of one's argument or position. Citation to authority and supporting references is both important and extensive in any form of legal writing. Citation form is also given emphasis in legal writing, and early familiarity with *A Uniform System of Citation* will stand the law student in good stead.

CITATORS—

a set of books which provide, through letter-form abbreviations or words, the subsequent judicial history and interpretation of reported decisions, and lists of cases and legislative enactments construing, applying or affecting statutes. In America, the most widely used set of citators is *Shepard's Citations*.

CITED CASE—

a case which is treated by other cases.

CITING CASE—

the case which operates on the cited case.

CIVIL LAW—

(1) Roman law embodied in the *Code of Justinian* which presently prevails in most countries of Western Europe other than Great Britain and which is the foundation of Louisiana law; (2) the law concerning noncriminal matters in a common law jurisdiction.

CLAIM—

(1) the assertion of a right, as to money or property; (2) the accumulation of facts which give rise to a right enforceable in court.

CLASS ACTION—

a lawsuit brought by a representative party on behalf of a group, all of whose members have the same or a similar grievance against the defendant.

CODE—

in popular usage, a compilation of statutes. Technically, in a code the laws in force, and judicial decrees having the force of law, are rewritten and arranged in classified order. Repealed and temporary acts are eliminated and the revision is reenacted.

CODIFICATION—

the process of collecting and arranging systematically, usually by subject, the laws of a state or country.

COMMON LAW—

the origin of the Anglo-American legal systems. English common law was largely customary law and unwritten, until discovered, applied, and reported by the courts of law. In theory, the common law courts did not create law but rather discovered it in the customs and habits of the English people. The strength of the judicial system in pre-parliamentary days is one reason for the continued emphasis in common law systems on case law. In a narrow sense, common law is the phrase still used to distinguish case law from statutory law.

COMPILED STATUTES—

in popular usage, a code. Technically, it is a compilation of acts printed verbatim as originally enacted but in a new classified order. The text is not modified; however, repealed and temporary acts are omitted.

COMPLAINT—

the plaintiff's initial pleading. Under *Federal Rules of Civil Procedure*, it is no longer full of the technicalities demanded by the common law. A complaint need only contain a short and plain statement of the claim upon which relief is sought, an indication of the type of relief requested, and an indication that the court has jurisdiction to hear the case.

CONNECTOR—

See BOOLEAN LOGIC.

CONSIDERATION—

something to be done, or abstained from, by one party to a contract in order to induce another party to enter into a contract.

CONSOLIDATED STATUTES—

in popular usage, a code. Technically, it is a compilation of acts rewritten, arranged in classified order and reenacted. Repealed and temporary acts are eliminated.

CONSTITUTION—

the system of fundamental principles by which a political body or organization governs itself. Most national constitutions are written; the English and Israeli constitutions are unwritten.

CONVERSION—

the wrongful appropriation to oneself of the personal property of another.

CONVEYANCE—

the transfer of title to property from one person to another.

COUNT—

a separate and independent claim. A civil petition or a criminal indictment may contain several counts.

COUNTERCLAIM—

a claim made by the defendant against the plaintiff in a civil lawsuit; it constitutes a separate cause of action.

COURT DECISION—

the disposition of the case by the court. See OPINION.

COURT RULES—

rules of procedure promulgated to govern civil and criminal practice before the courts.

DAMAGES—

monetary compensation awarded by a court for an injury caused by the act of another. Damages may be *actual* or *compensatory* (equal to the amount of loss shown), *exemplary* or *punitive* (in excess of the actual loss given to punish the person for the malicious conduct which caused the injury), or *nominal* (a trivial amount given because the injury is slight or because the exact amount of injury has not been determined satisfactorily).

DATABASE—

(1) a collection of information organized for rapid retrieval by computer. In legal research, it usually refers to a commercial service searched *on-line* by a user at a terminal connected to a communications network. A *full-text database* provides the complete text of documents such as court decisions or newspaper articles. LEXIS and WESTLAW are full-text databases. A *bibliographic database* provides citations or abstracts of articles, books, reports, or patents. DIALOG is an example of a primarily bibliographic database.

(2) in WESTLAW, a collection of documents that can be searched together.

DECISION—

See COURT DECISION.

DECREE—

a determination by a court of the rights and duties of the parties before it. Formerly, decrees were issued by courts of equity and distinguished from judgments which were issued by courts of law. See EQUITY.

DEFENDANT—

the person against whom a civil or criminal action is brought.

DEMURRER—

a means of objecting to the sufficiency in law of a pleading by admitting the actual allegations made, but disputing that they frame an adequate legal claim.

DIALOG—

the information retrieval service of DIALOG Information Services, a subsidiary of Lockheed Corporation. DIALOG is composed of hundreds of individual databases providing indexing and abstracting of publications relating to a wide range of academic, business, current affairs, and law-related subjects.

DICTUM—

See OBITER DICTUM.

DIGEST—

an index to reported cases, providing brief, unconnected statements of court holdings on points of law, which are arranged by subject and subdivided by jurisdiction and courts.

DOCKET NUMBER—

a number, sequentially assigned by the clerk at the outset to a lawsuit brought to a court for adjudication.

DUE CARE—

the legal duty one owes to another according to the circumstances of a particular case.

DUE PROCESS OF LAW—

a term found in the Fifth and Fourteenth Amendments of the Constitution and also in the constitutions of many states. Its exact meaning varies from one situation to another and from one era to the next, but basically it is concerned with the guarantee of every person's enjoyment of his rights (e.g., the right to a fair hearing in any legal dispute).

EN BANC—

a session in which the entire bench of the court will participate in the decision rather than the regular quorum. In other countries, it is common for a court to have more members than are usually necessary to hear an appeal. In the United States, the Circuit Courts of Appeal usually sit in groups of three judges but for important cases may expand the bench to nine members, when they are said to be sitting *en banc*.

ENCYCLOPEDIA—

a work containing expository statements on principles of law, topically arranged, with supporting footnote references to cases in point.

EQUITY—

justice administered according to fairness as contrasted with the strictly formulated rules of common law. It is based on a system of rules and principles which originated in England as an alternative to the harsh rules of common law and which were based on what was fair in a particular situation. One sought relief under this system in courts of equity rather than in courts of law.

ESTATE—

(1) the interest or right one has in real or personal property;

(2) the property itself in which one has an interest or right.

EXECUTIVE AGREEMENT—

an international agreement, not a treaty, concluded by the President without senatorial consent on his authority as Commander-in-Chief and director of foreign relations. The distinction between treaty and executive agreement is complicated and often of questionable constitutionality, but the import of such agreements as that of Yalta or Potsdam is unquestionably great.

EXECUTIVE ORDERS—

an order issued by the President under specific authority granted to him by Congress. There is no precise distinction between presidential proclamations and executive orders; however, proclamations generally cover matters of widespread interest, and executive orders often relate to the conduct of government business or to organization of the executive departments. Every act of the President authorizing or directing the performance of an act, in its general context, is an executive order. See PRESIDENTIAL PROCLAMATIONS.

FICHE—

See MICROFICHE.

FORM BOOKS—

include sample instruments which are helpful in drafting legal documents.

FORMS OF ACTION—

that governed common law pleadings, which were the procedural devices used to give expression to the theories of liability recognized by the common law. Failure to analyze the cause of the action properly, to select the proper theory of liability and to choose the appropriate procedural mechanism or forms of action could easily result in being thrown out of court. A plaintiff had to elect his remedy in advance and could not subsequently amend his pleadings to conform to his proof or to the court's choice of another theory of liability. According to the relief sought, actions have been divided into three categories: real actions were brought for the recovery of real property; mixed actions were brought to recover real property and damages for injury to it; personal actions were brought to recover debts or personal

property, or for injuries to personal, property, or contractual rights. The common law actions are usually considered to be eleven in number: trespass, trespass on the case, trover, eject-ment, detinue, replevin, debt, covenant, account, special assump-sit, and general assumpsit.

FRAUD—

a deception which causes a person to part with his property or a legal right.

FULL TEXT—

See DATABASE.

GRAND JURY—

a jury of six to twenty-three persons which hears criminal accusations and evidence, and then determines whether indict-ments should be made. Compare with PETIT JURY.

HEADNOTE—

is a brief summary of a legal rule or significant facts in a case, which, among other headnotes applicable to the case, precedes the printed opinion in reports.

HEARINGS—

proceedings extensively employed by both legislative and admin-istrative agencies. Adjudicative hearings of administrative agen-cies can be appealed in a court of law. Investigative hearings are often held by congressional committees prior to enactment of legislation, and are important sources of legislative history.

HOLDING—

the declaration of the conclusion of law reached by the court as to the legal effect of the facts of the case.

HOLOGRAPH or OLOGRAPH—

a will, deed, or other legal document that is entirely in the handwriting of the signer.

HORNBOOK—

the popular references to a series of treatises published by West Publishing Company which reviews a certain field of law in summary, textual form, as opposed to a casebook which is designed as a teaching tool and includes many reprints of court opinions.

INDEMNITY—

a contractual arrangement whereby one party agrees to reim-
burse another for losses of a particular type.

INDICTMENT—

a formal accusation of a crime made by a grand jury at the
request of a prosecuting attorney.

INFORMATION—

an accusation based not on the action of a grand jury but rather
on the affirmation of a public official.

INJUNCTION—

a judge's order that a person do or, more commonly refrain from
doing, a certain act. An injunction may be preliminary or temporary, pending trial of the issue presented, or it may be final if the
issue has already been decided in court.

INSTA–CITE—

the computerized citation verification service of West Publishing
Company. This service, which is available through WESTLAW,
provides parallel citations and case-history information.

INTESTATE—

not having made a valid will.

JURISDICTION—

the power given to a court by a constitution or a legislative body
to make legally binding decisions over certain persons or property, or the geographical area in which a court's decisions or
legislative enactments are binding.

JURISPRUDENCE—

(1) the science or philosophy of law; (2) a collective term for case
law as opposed to legislation.

KEY NUMBER—

a building block of the major indexing system devised for American case law, developed by West Publishing Company. The key
number is a permanent number given to a specific point of this
case law.

LAW REVIEW or LAW JOURNAL—

a legal periodical. The term *law review* usually describes a scholarly periodical edited by students at a law school.

LEGISLATIVE HISTORY—

that information embodied in legislative documents that provides the meanings and interpretations (intent) of statutes. Citations and dates of legislative enactments, amendments, and repeals of statutes are sometimes imprecisely identified as legislative histories. More accurate designations of these citations of legislative changes, as included in codes, are historical notes or amendatory histories.

LEXIS—

the computerized legal research system of Mead Data Central. LEXIS is a database providing the full text of court decisions, statutory provisions, administrative materials, law review articles, Supreme Court briefs, and other items. Documents are organized into *libraries* which are subdivided into *files*. *Keyword searches* and *segment searches* are available.

LIABILITY—

the condition of being responsible either for damages resulting from an injurious act or for discharging an obligation or debt.

LIBEL—

(1) written defamation of a person's character. Compare with SLANDER; (2) in an admiralty court, the plaintiff's statement of the cause of action and the relief sought.

LIEN—

a claim against property as security for a debt, under which the property may be seized and sold to satisfy the debt.

LITIGATE—

to bring a civil action in court.

LOOSELEAF SERVICES AND REPORTERS—

contain federal and state administrative regulations and decisions or subject treatment of a legal topic. They consist of separate, perforated leaves in special binders, simplifying frequent substitution and insertion of new leaves.

MALPRACTICE—

professional misconduct or unreasonable lack of skill. This term is usually applied to such conduct by doctors and lawyers.

MANDATORY AUTHORITY—

authority which a given court is bound to follow. Mandatory authority is found in constitutional provisions, legislation and court decisions. Compare with PERSUASIVE AUTHORITY.

MEMORANDUM—

(1) an informal record; (2) a written document which may be used to prove that a contract exists; (3) an exposition of all the points of law pertaining to a particular case; (referred to as a *memorandum of law*); (4) an informal written discussion of the merits of a matter pending in a lawyer's office, usually written by a law clerk or junior associate for a senior associate or partner. (Referred to as an *office memorandum*.)

MICROFICHE—

a sheet of film, usually 4 x 6 inches or 3 x 5 inches in size, containing miniaturized photographic images of printed text. The term *fiche* is synonymous with *microfiche*. *Ultrafiche* is a type of microfiche containing images that are reduced by a factor of 90 or more.

MICROFILM—

a film containing miniaturized photographic images of printed text. This is usually in a reel, but may also be in a cartridge or cassette form.

MICROFORM—

a general term describing miniaturized reproduction of printed text on film or paper. *Microfilm* and *microfiche* are specific types of microform.

MODEL CODES—

codes formulated by various groups or institutions to serve as model laws for legislatures, intended to improve existing laws or unify diverse state legislation.

MOOT POINTS—

points which are no longer subjects of contention and which are raised only for purposes of discussion or hypothesis. Many law

schools conduct moot courts where students gain practice by arguing hypothetical or moot cases.

MOTION—

a formal request made to a judge pertaining to any issue arising during the pendency of a lawsuit.

NATIONAL REPORTER SYSTEM—

the network of reporters published by West Publishing Company, which attempt to publish and digest all cases of precedential value from all state and federal courts.

NEGLIGENCE—

the failure to exercise due care.

NEXIS—

the general and business news database of Mead Data Central. NEXIS provides the full text of newspaper, magazine and newsletter articles, wire-service stories, and other items.

NISI PRIUS—

generally, a court where a case is first tried, as distinguished from an appellate court.

NOTER–UP—

the term used in the British Commonwealth countries for a citator.

OBITER DICTUM—

an incidental comment, not necessary to the formulation of the decision, made by the judge in his or her opinion. Such comments are not binding as precedent.

OFFICIAL REPORTS—

court reports directed by statute. Compare with UNOFFICIAL REPORTS.

OPINION—

an expression of the reasons why a certain decision (the judgment) was reached in a case. A *majority opinion* is usually written by one judge and represents the principles of law which a majority of his or her colleagues on the court deem operative in a given decision; it has more precedential value than any of the following. A *separate opinion* may be written by one or more

judges in which he, she, or they concur in or dissent from the majority opinion. A *concurring opinion* agrees with the result reached by the majority, but disagrees with the precise reasoning leading to that result. A *dissenting opinion* disagrees with the result reached by the majority and thus disagrees with the reasoning and/or the principles of law used by the majority in deciding the case. A *plurality opinion* (called a *judgment* by the Supreme Court) is agreed to by less than a majority as to the reasoning of the decision, but is agreed to by a majority as to the result. A *per curiam opinion* is an opinion *by the court* which expresses its decision in the case but whose author is not identified. A *memorandum opinion* is a holding of the whole court in which the opinion is very concise.

ORDINANCE—

the equivalent of a municipal statute, passed by the city council and governing matters not already covered by federal or state law.

PAMPHLET SUPPLEMENT—

a paperbound supplement to a larger bound volume usually intended to be discarded eventually.

PARALLEL CITATION—

a citation reference to the same case printed in two or more different reports.

PER CURIAM—

literally, by the court. Usually a short opinion written on behalf of the majority of the court. It may be accompanied by concurring or dissenting opinions.

PERIODICAL—

a publication appearing at regular intervals. Legal periodicals include law school publications, bar association publications, commercially published journals, and legal newspapers.

PERMANENT LAW—

an act which continues in force for an indefinite time.

PERSONAL PROPERTY—

See PROPERTY.

PERSUASIVE AUTHORITY—

that law or reasoning which a given court is likely but not bound to follow. For example, decisions from one jurisdiction may be persuasive authority in the courts of another jurisdiction. Compare with MANDATORY AUTHORITY.

PETIT JURY—

a group of six, nine, or twelve persons which decides questions of fact in civil and criminal trials. Compare with GRAND JURY.

PETITION—

a formal, written application to a court requesting judicial action on a certain matter.

PETITIONER—

the person presenting a petition to a court, officer, or legislative body; the one who starts an equity proceeding or the one who takes an appeal from a judgment.

PLAINTIFF—

the person who brings a lawsuit against another.

PLEA BARGAINING—

the process whereby the accused and the prosecutor in a criminal case work out a mutually satisfactory disposition of the case. It usually involves the defendant's pleading guilty to a lesser offense or to only one or some of the counts of a multi-count indictment in return for a ligher sentence than that possible for the graver charge.

PLEADINGS—

technical means by which parties to a dispute frame the issue for the court. The plaintiff's complaint or declaration is followed by the defendant's answer; subsequent papers may be filed as needed.

POCKET SUPPLEMENT or POCKET PART—

a paper-back supplement to a book, inserted in the book through a slit in its back cover. Depending on the type of publication, it may have textual, case, or statutory references keyed to the original publication.

POPULAR NAME TABLE—

a table listing popular names by which some cases and statutes have become known, and identifying for each popular name the official name and citation of the case or statute.

POWER OF ATTORNEY—

a document authorizing a person to act as another's agent.

PRECEDENT—

See STARE DECISIS.

PRELIMINARY PRINTS—

the name given to the advance sheets of the official *United States Reports*.

PRESENTMENT—

in criminal law, a written accusation made by the grand jury without the consent or participation of a prosecutor.

PRESIDENTIAL PROCLAMATIONS—

a declaration issued under specific authority granted to the President by Congress. Generally, they relate to matters of widespread interest. Some proclamations have no legal effect but merely are appeals to the public, e.g., the observance of American Education Week. See EXECUTIVE ORDERS.

PRIMARY AUTHORITY—

statutes, administrative regulations issued pursuant to enabling legislation and case law. Primary authority may be either *mandatory* or *persuasive*. All other legal writings are *secondary authority* and are never binding on courts. See MANDATORY AUTHORITY; PERSUASIVE AUTHORITY.

PRIVATE LAW—

is an act which relates to a specific person.

PROCEDURAL LAW—

that law which governs the operation of the legal sytem, including court rules and rules of procedure, as distinguished from substantive law.

PROPERTY—

ownership or that which is owned. *Real property* refers to land; *personal property* refers to moveable things or chattels; *chose in action* refers to a right to personal property of which the owner does not presently have possession but instead has a right to sue to gain possession (e.g., a right to recover a debt, demand, or damages in a contractual action or for a tort or omission of a duty).

PUBLIC LAW—

an act which relates to the public as a whole. It may be (1) general (applies to all persons within the jurisdiction), (2) local (applies to a geographical area), or (3) special (relates to an organization which is charged with a public interest).

RATIO DECIDENDI—

the point in a case which determines the result—the basis of the decision.

REAL PROPERTY—

See PROPERTY.

RECORDS AND BRIEFS—

See APPEAL PAPERS.

REGIONAL REPORTER—

a unit of the *National Reporter System* which reports state court decisions of a defined geographical area.

REGULATIONS—

rules or orders issued by various governmental departments to carry out the intent of the law. Agencies issue regulations to guide the activity of their employees and to ensure uniform application of the law. Regulations are not the work of the legislature and do not have the effect of law in theory. In practice, however, because of the intricacies of judicial review of administrative action, regulations can have an important effect in determining the outcome of cases involving regulatory activity. United States Government regulations appear first in the *Federal Register*, published five days a week, and are subsequently arranged by subject in the *Code of Federal Regulations*.

REMAND—

to send back for further proceedings, as when a higher court sends back to a lower court.

REPORTS—

(1) *court reports*—published judicial cases arranged according to some grouping, such as jurisdiction, court, period of time, subject matter or case significance; and (2) *administrative reports or decisions*—published decisions of an administrative agency.

RESOLUTION—

a formal expression of the opinion of a rule-making body adopted by the vote of that body.

RESPONDENT—

the party who makes an answer to a bill in an equity proceeding or who contends against an appeal.

RESTATEMENTS OF THE LAW—

systematic restatements of the existing common law in certain areas, published by the American Law Institute since 1923. The Restatements are valuable secondary research sources, but are not binding as law.

REVISED STATUTES—

in popular usage, a code. Technically, it is a compilation of statutes in the order and wording originally passed by the legislature, with temporary and repealed acts deleted.

RULES OF COURT—

the rules regulating practice and procedure before the various courts. In most jurisdictions, these rules are issued by the individual courts or by the highest court in that jurisdiction.

SANCTION—

(1) to assent to another's actions; (2) a penalty for violating a law.

SCOPE NOTE—

a notation appearing below a topic heading in a publication, that delimits and identifies the content of the topic and appears below the topic's heading in a publication.

SECONDARY AUTHORITY—

See PRIMARY AUTHORITY.

SECTION LINE—

the subject of a key number in West's key number digests, printed after the key number.

SESSION LAWS—

laws of a state enacted that are published in bound or pamphlet volumes after adjournment of each regular or special session.

SHEPARDIZING—

a trade-mark of Shepard's Citations, Inc., descriptive of the general use of its publications.

SLANDER—

oral defamation of a person's character. Compare with LIBEL.

SLIP LAW—

a legislative enactment published in pamphlet or single sheet form immediately after its passage.

SLIP OPINION—

an individual court decision published separately soon after it is rendered.

SQUIB—

a very brief rendition of a single case or a single point of law from a case. Compare with HEADNOTE.

STAR PAGINATION—

a scheme in reprint editions of court reports, that is used to show where the pages of the text of the official edition begins and ends.

STARE DECISIS—

the doctrine of English and American law that states that when a court has formulated a principle of law as applicable to a given set of facts, it will follow that principle and apply it in future cases where the facts are substantially the same. It connotes the decision of present cases on the basis of past precedent.

STATUS TABLE—

gives the current status of a bill or court decision.

STATUTES—

are acts of a legislature. Depending upon its context in usage, a statute may mean a single act of a legislature or a body of acts which are collected and arranged according to a scheme or for a session of a legislature or parliament.

STATUTES AT LARGE—

the official compilation of acts passed by the Congress. The arrangement is currently by Public Law number, and by chapter number in pre-1951 volumes. This is the official print of the law for citation purposes where titles of the United States Code have not been enacted into positive law.

STATUTES OF LIMITATIONS—

laws setting time limits after which a dispute cannot be taken to court.

STATUTORY INSTRUMENTS—

English administrative regulations and orders. The term applies especially to the administrative rules published since 1939, supplementing the English administrative code, Statutory Rules and Orders.

STATUTORY RULES AND ORDERS—

English administrative regulations and orders.

STYLE OF A CASE—

the parties to a lawsuit as they are written in the heading at the beginning of a written case. Also known as the *caption* of a case.

SUBPOENA—

a court order compelling a witness to appear and testify in a certain proceeding.

SUBSTANTIVE LAW—

that law which establishes rights and obligations, as distinguished from procedural law, which is concerned with rules for establishing their judicial enforcement.

SUMMONS—

a notice delivered by a sheriff or other authorized person informing a person that he or she is the defendant in a civil action, and specifying a time and place to appear in court to answer to the plaintiff.

SUPERSEDE—

to displace or to supplant one publication or its segment with another.

SUPREME COURT—

(1) the court of last resort in the federal judicial system. (the United States Supreme Court also has original jurisdiction in some cases); (2) in state judicial systems, except New York and Massachusetts, the highest appellate court or court of last resort.

SYLLABUS—

See HEADNOTE.

TABLE OF CASES—

a list of cases, arranged alphabetically by case names, with citations and references to the body of the publication where the cases are treated.

TABLE OF STATUTES—

a list of statutes with references to the body of the publication where the statutes are treated or construed.

TEMPORARY LAW—

an act which continues in force for a limited period of time.

TERM OF COURT—

signifies the space of time prescribed by law during which a court holds session. The court's session may actually extend beyond the term. The October Term of the Supreme Court of the United States is now the only term during which the Court sits, and lasts from October to June or July.

TORT—

a civil wrong which does not involve a contractual relationship. The elements of a tort are a duty owed, a breach of that duty, and the resultant harm to the one to whom the duty was owed.

TRANSCRIPT OF RECORD—

the printed record as made up in each case of the proceedings and pleadings necessary for the appellate court to review the history of the case.

TREATISE—

an exposition, which may be critical, evaluative, interpretative, or informative, on case law or legislation. Usually it is more exhaustive than an encyclopedia article, but less detailed and critical than a periodical article.

TREATY—

an agreement between two or more sovereign nations.

TRESPASS—

an unlawful interference with one's person, property, or rights. At common law, trespass was a form of action brought to recover damages for any injury to one's person or property or relationship with another.

ULTRAFICHE—

See MICROFICHE.

UNIFORM LAWS—

statutes drafted for adoption by the several states in the interest of uniformity. A considerable number of uniform laws on various subjects have been approved by the National Conference of Commissioners on Uniform State Laws, and have been adopted in one or more jurisdictions in the United States and its possessions. The Uniform Commercial Code is now the law in forty-nine states.

UNIFORM SYSTEM OF CITATION—

See BLUE BOOK.

UNOFFICIAL REPORTS—

court reports published without statutory direction. They are not distinguished from official reports on grounds of varying quality or accuracy of reporting.

VENUE—

the particular geographical area where a court with jurisdiction may try a case.

WAIVER—

the voluntary relinquishment of a known right.

WESTLAW—

the computerized legal research system of West Publishing Company. WESTLAW is a database providing the full text of court decisions, administrative materials, the United States Code, law review articles, and other items. Documents are organized into *databases. Key-word searches, field searches* and *key-number searches* are available.

WRIT—

a written order, of which there are many types, issued by a court and directed to an official or party, commanding the performance of some act.

WRONGFUL DEATH—

a type of lawsuit brought by or on behalf of a deceased person's beneficiaries, alleging that the death was attributable to the willful or negligent act of another.

LEGAL RESEARCH
ILLUSTRATED

*

Chapter 1

THE LEGAL PROCESS

SECTION A. SOURCES OF THE LAW

1. Introduction

The American legal system, along with those of most English-speaking countries, is part of the common law tradition. The term *common law* is used here in the sense that distinguishes it from Roman law, modern civil law, canon law, and other systems of law.

The common law has been defined as that body of law which originated and developed in England and is in effect among those countries which were originally settled by or controlled by England. It consists of those principles and rules of action applicable to the government and security of persons and property which do not rest for their authority upon the positive declarations of the will of the legislature.[1]

In the early history of English law, the custom developed of considering the decisions of the courts as precedents. This was interpreted as *furnishing an example or authority for an identical or similar case afterwards arising or for a similar question of law*.[2] This, in turn, led to the development of the doctrine of *stare decisis* which has been defined as:

> * * * [T]hat when [a] court has once laid down a principle of law as applicable to a certain state of facts, it will adhere to that principle, and apply it to all future cases where facts are substantially the same.[3]

Under the doctrine of *stare decisis* the law became embodied in the written decisions of the English courts and was to be found in the decisions of the courts rather than in a codified body of law as in other countries of Europe with legal systems based on the Roman law. It is in this sense that the common law became known as the *unwritten* law. The doctrines of *precedent* and *stare decisis* necessarily require access to the decisions of the courts and resulted in

---

[1] BLACK'S LAW DICTIONARY 250–51 (5th ed. 1979). [Hereinafter cited as BLACK'S.]

[2] *Id.* at 1059. For a succinct and scholarly treatment of the development of case law, *see* J. DAWSON, THE ORACLES OF THE LAW 1–80 (1968).

[3] Moore v. City of Albany, 98 N.Y. 396, 410 (1885). *See also* West, *The Doctrine of Stare Decisis*, 21 WAYNE L.REV. 1043 (1975).

1

their publication under the generic term of *law reports*. To *find the law*, then, a lawyer has to search the law reports for opinions of the courts that arose from a similar fact situation to the one at hand and then determine if the cases located can serve as a precedent for the present case.

While the development of case law was predominant, the role of statutes cannot be ignored. The earliest statutes were enacted by the King with the concurrence of his Council, and then gradually the role of statute-making was assumed by Parliament. It was not until after the passage of the *Reform Act of 1832* that statutes played a significant role in the English legal system. The real growth of statutory law reflected the impact of the industrial revolution on society as it became apparent that a jurisprudence based only on judicial decisions could not meet the needs of a growing dynamic society. Situations soon developed where answers were needed that were not found in the court reports, or the answers found no longer met current needs, or resulted in actions that were felt to be unjust. To remedy this, Parliament began to pass statutes which changed the prior rules for circumstances not found in any decisions of the court. A statute has been defined as:

> An act of the legislature declaring, commanding, or prohibiting something; a particular law established by the will of the legislative department of government * * * according to the forms necessary to constitute it the law of the state.[4] The word is used to designate the written law in contradistinction to the unwritten law.[5]

Therefore, the sources of law in common law jurisdictions originate from the enactments of their legislative bodies and from the decisions of their courts.[6] The authorities of law in all common law jurisdictions [7] are separated into two divisions—primary and secondary.

    a. *Primary Law.* Primary law is found in: (1) written constitutions and the enactment of legislatures (and in those adopted in some jurisdictions through the vote of their electorates); (2) rulings and regulations issued by authorized administrative bodies; and (3) the body of law found in the written opinions of the courts.

Mandatory primary laws or sources consist of either constitutions, legislation, or decisions of the highest court of a jurisdiction.

---

[4] BLACK'S, *supra* note 1, at 1264.

[5] *Id.*

[6] For a more detailed discussion of the common law, *see* R. JACKSON, THE MACHINERY OF JUSTICE IN ENGLAND 9–17 (7th ed. 1977). *See also* L. FRIEDMAN, A HISTORY OF AMERICAN LAW 17–25 (1975).

[7] *Jurisdiction* in this sense is used to describe the territory over which a government or subdivision thereof has control.

These decisions, as well as the provisions of the constitution and the laws passed by the legislature, must be followed by all lower courts within the jurisdiction. Appellate court opinions of other common law jurisdictions are persuasive but not mandatory. Constitutions and legislation are published in statute books; court opinions are published in sets of court reports.

b. *Secondary Sources of the Law.* In addition to the primary sources of the law, lawyers refer to many other types of law books such as treatises, periodicals and journals, form books and citators. All such written expressions of the law, however, are known as secondary sources.

2. The Literature of the Law

It is axiomatic to describe law libraries as containing the literature of the law. This material includes statutes, administrative rules, judicial decisions, digests of case law, treatises, encyclopedias, and other publications.

American law libraries contain large, diffuse collections since, pursuant to the common law, much of our law is *found* or *made* by judicial decisions.[8] Determining the decisions of present cases on the basis of precedents results in legal literature accumulating and assuming large proportions. Another factor resulting in the growth of American legal collections is the multiple system of state and federal laws which makes necessary the acquisition and maintenance of primary sources for fifty states, as well as those of the federal government. Moreover, American law school libraries should also contain at least the court decisions of England, and many contain the decisions of Canada, Australia, New Zealand, and other common law jurisdictions.

3. The Authoritative Organ of the State

The officials or bodies of officials whose acts give validity to the law are descriptive of another meaning of its source. In the democratic countries, there are two types of officials with such authority. They are legislators and judges. The former include legislators and administrative rule-makers. These officials produce two authoritative forms of law: legislation and case law. The latter group includes ordinary judges and administrative hearing officials.

4. The Derivation of Legal Concepts

The third meaning given to the sources of the law relates to the derivation of the concepts contained in the body of law. This meaning indicates intellectual sources for the legal concepts which are

---

[8] For an indication of the size of large law libraries, *see* Jacobstein & Mersky, *An Analysis of Academic Law Library Growth Since 1907*, 75 LAW LIB.J. 212 (1982).

ultimately reflected in statutes or court decisions. For example, the source of the modern law of vicarious liability is considered by some as having its origin in the slave law of the Romans.[9] The source of the doctrine in American law of the right to privacy is attributed to an article first published in *Harvard Law Review*.[10] The ideas as expressed in the writings of Chancellor Kent and Justice Story also contributed significantly to the early development of American law.

However, we use the term *source of law* throughout this book to mean source as contained in the literature of the law.

SECTION B. THE LEGAL SYSTEM OF THE UNITED STATES: SOURCES

As a result of our federal system, any particular legal transaction may be governed solely by state law, or solely by federal law, or perhaps by both. Although the question of determination of jurisdiction is beyond the scope of this book, its significance cannot be overlooked in determining the answer to a legal question, and knowledge is needed of both federal and state law.

As previously indicated, the United States is a common law jurisdiction. The federal system of government in this country, however, has made its legal system extremely complex. Under our federal constitution, each state, except for those powers delegated to the federal government, is a sovereign state. This means, in effect, there is not one legal system in this country, but there are fifty-one, including the federal system.

1. Federal Government

The primary sources of the United States Government are found in its Constitution,[11] in the Acts of Congress, and in the decisions of the Supreme Court of the United States and other lower federal courts.

2. States

In addition to the above, the primary sources for each of the fifty states are found in each state's constitution as adopted by the people, in the enactments of the legislature (and those initiated and enacted

[9] O. HOLMES, COMMON LAW 16–17 (1881).

[10] Warren & Brandeis, *The Right to Privacy*, 4 HARV.L.REV. 193 (1890).

[11] To date, there have been 26 amendments proposed, ratified, and incorporated into the Constitution. Seven amendments proposed by Congress have not been ratified by the states. Texts of the proposed amendments may be located in the Constitution volumes of the *United States Code Annotated*. For more information on proposed and unratified amendments, *see* THE CONSTITUTION OF THE UNITED STATES OF AMERICA, AS AMENDED THROUGH JULY 1971: ANALYTICAL INDEX, UNRATIFIED AMENDMENTS, H.R. DOC. NO. 94–539, 94th Cong., 2d Sess. (1976).

directly by the electorate), in the written decisions of its highest court of appeal, and in the law of England as delineated in its reception statute.[12]

SECTION C. THE LEGAL SYSTEMS OF OTHER COUNTRIES

The doctrine of judicial precedent is not recognized by the European countries,[13] whose legal systems are derived from the Roman law, to the degree followed by common-law countries. Justinian, in codifying the law for the Roman state, declared that his code was to be the exclusive source of the law *on penalty of forgery,*[14] thus attempting to discourage reference to earlier sources. Codification as a legal tool was later adopted by the countries that followed the Roman law. However, in recent years, on the continent of Europe, judicial decisions are assuming a more significant authoritative role, claiming recognition with commentaries in interpreting the civil law. Modern European codes also recognize that no codification scheme can be all-inclusive and complete; thus, courts may be required to go outside the code, when its text is silent, obscure or deficient, for the solution to controversies.

The Latin American courts have followed a modified procedure. If a rule has been applied several times in different cases by the highest court, it is considered as binding. The French practice is also a compromise between the rule of *stare decisis* and the civil law concept. A single decision by a court is not binding on it or on subordinate courts. While another lower court in a comparable case is not bound to follow the highest court's twice-told precedent, in practice the lower courts are prone to follow the precedent. Further, a uniform pattern of decisions is considered as binding in all courts in a manner similar to that of the highest courts in the United States.[15]

Other legal systems or conceptions that should be mentioned here are: Socialist law, based on the theories and writings of Marx, Engels and Lenin, adopting and building upon the civil law systems;

[12] All states except Louisiana (whose legal system is based on the civil law) have adopted the English common law as the basis of their jurisprudence. *See* 1 POWELL ON REAL PROPERTY § 45 (1969). For representative statutes adopting the English common law as part of their law, *see* SMITH–HURD, ILL.ANN.STAT. Ch. 28, § 1 (1969); TEX.REV.CIV.STAT. Art. 1 (1969).

[13] For articles on judicial precedent in Europe, *see* Von Mehren, *Judicial Process: A Comparative Analysis*, 5 AM.J.COMP.L. 197 (1956); Dietze, *Judicial Review in Europe*, 55 MICH.L.REV. 539 (1957).

[14] A. KOCUREK, AN INTRODUCTION TO THE SCIENCE OF LAW 162 (1930).

[15] Goodhart, *Precedents in English and Continental Law*, 50 LAW Q.REV. 40 (1934). *See also* J. DAWSON, *supra* note 2, at 100; J. MERRYMAN, THE CIVIL LAW TRADITION: AN INTRODUCTION TO THE LEGAL SYSTEMS OF WESTERN EUROPE AND LATIN AMERICA (1969).

Muslim, Hindu, and Hebrew conceptions of law, with strong religious principles; and African law, which, although based upon local customs, has been influenced by the laws of colonial powers.[16]

SECTION D.   LEGAL RESEARCH

The short summary thus far presented on the structure of the legal system must be understood before one can approach the methods of doing legal research. What is involved in this process is a search for authorities. When engaged in legal research (more properly, legal search), lawyers are seeking to find those authorities in the primary sources of the law that are applicable to a particular legal situation. In short, they are seeking to find applicable statutes or court decisions (or both) [17] from the particular jurisdiction wherein the legal situation has occurred or will occur. The search is always first for mandatory primary sources, that is, constitutional or statutory provisions of the legislature, and court decisions of the jurisdiction involved. If these cannot be located, then the search focuses on locating persuasive primary authorities, that is, decisions from courts of other common law jurisdictions. Statutes of other jurisdictions are never considered persuasive authority. When in the legal search process primary authorities cannot be located, the searcher will seek for secondary authorities. These usually are considered to be the writings of lawyers as found in treatises or law reviews, or the publications of law reform organizations such as the American Law Institute and the law revision commissions of the various states.

1.   Professional Responsibility

Rule One of the *Model Rules of Professional Conduct* of the American Bar Association states that:

> A lawyer shall provide competent representation to a client.
> Competent representation requires the legal knowledge,
> skill, thoroughness, and preparation reasonably necessary
> for the representation.

For such representation, it is clear that a lawyer must be able to research the law, and all lawyers are expected to know "those plain and elementary principles of law which are commonly known by well-informed attorneys, *and to discover the additional rules which, although not commonly known, may readily be found by standard*

---

[16] For more information on the subject of this section, *see* R. DAVID & J. BRIERLEY, MAJOR LEGAL SYSTEMS IN THE WORLD TODAY: AN INTRODUCTION TO THE COMPARATIVE STUDY OF LAW (1978).

[17] The place of administrative regulations and rulings will be covered in Chapter 12.

research techniques." [18] (Emphasis ours.) The ability to find the law, to locate the applicable ruling authorities, and to ascertain their current status must become part and parcel of every lawyer's training if he/she is to uphold the standards of the legal profession.

2. Legal Book Publishing

To engage in legal research, one must have an understanding, not only of the organization of the legal system, but also of how law books are published and organized. In the American colonial period law books were extremely scarce and consisted mostly of English law reports. The most extensive law collections of attorneys numbered from fifty to one hundred volumes.[19]

The situation did not prevail for long. As the economy of the country changed from agrarian to industrial, and greater demands were made upon the courts and the legislatures, the repositories of the law grew proportionately.

Over the years, there have been various statistics used by legal authorities on quoting the tremendous volume of reported decisions in the American legal system. The preface to the *Century Edition of the American Digest System* states that the courts made 500,000 decisions during the period 1658–1896.[20]

In trying to determine the number of cases reported since the *Century Edition*, the authors of this book in cooperation with the editors of West Publishing Company determined that up to 1980 there were over 3,000,000 reported decisions in the United States.

It is estimated that over 50,000 cases are now reported annually in the various court reporting services. In 1950 there were 21,000 cases published. Congress and the various state legislatures produce about 50,000 pages of statutory law per year, and the *Federal Register* annually publishes thousands of pages of federal administrative regulations.[21] To this must be added the regulations promulgated each year by the administrative agencies of the states.

[18] Smith v. Lewis, 13 Cal.3d 349, 530 P.2d 589, 118 Cal.Rptr. 621 (1975). In this case the plaintiff received a judgment of $100,000 in a malpractice action based on the negligence of the defendant lawyer in researching the applicable law.

[19] A. HARNO, LEGAL EDUCATION IN THE UNITED STATES 19 (1953); L. FRIEDMAN, *supra* note 6, at 538–46. The first law book written by an American was printed in Virginia in 1736. This was G. WEBB, THE OFFICE AND AUTHORITY OF A JUSTICE OF PEACE, AND ALSO THE DUTY OF SHERIFFS, CORONERS, CHURCH–WARDENS, SURVEYORS OF HIGHWAYS, CONSTABLES AND OFFICERS OF THE MILITIA. For a thorough discussion of early law book publishing, *see* Parrish, *Law Books and Legal Publishing in America, 1760–1840*, 72 LAW LIB.J. 355 (1979).

[20] 1 CENTURY DIGEST iii (1897).

[21] *E.g.*, in 1983, 57,703 pages were published. Because of the growth of this and other government publications, Congress passed the Paperwork Reduction Act of

This flood of court decisions has from early times caused concern to the legal profession.[22] But despite all efforts to control the ever increasing number of court opinions, they continue to proliferate. Moreover, all fifty states as well as the federal government publish their own statutes and administrative regulations. To help lawyers cope with this multitude of primary sources, private publishers publish numerous types of secondary sources, such as treatises, periodicals, citators, digests, and annotations to assist lawyers in finding and understanding the law. A short discussion of the law book publishing industry will be helpful in understanding the use of law books, the subject of the remaining chapters.

The largest law book publisher is the West Publishing Company of St. Paul, Minnesota. This company primarily publishes court reports and statutes but also offers many secondary sources. The next largest law book publishing company is the Lawyers Co-operative Publishing Company of Rochester, New York, and its affiliate, the Bancroft-Whitney Company of San Francisco, California. Both emphasize the publication of primary sources. The Commerce Clearing House Company, the Bureau of National Affairs, Research Institute of America, and the Prentice-Hall Company are publishers of looseleaf publications which emphasize areas of law requiring frequent updating. The Matthew Bender Company and Callaghan Law Book Publishing Company specialize in publishing treatises for practicing lawyers. Many other smaller companies also publish legal materials most useful in legal research.[23]

When engaged in legal research, searching for the law may involve statutes and court reports of many states as well as countless numbers of secondary sources. The important point to remember, however, is that both legal finding aids and primary repositories of the law are predominantly products of the private law book publishing industry.

SECTION E. SUMMARY

The sources of American law for the purpose of legal research are found in the United States Constitution, the constitutions of the fifty states, the statutes of the United States Congress and of the

1980, Pub.L. No. 96–511, 94 Stat. 2812 (Dec. 11, 1980). As a result, the number of pages in the *Federal Register* began to decline. For example, the issues published in 1983 contained 57,703 pages. The 1984 issues contained 50,997 pages.

[22] For a discussion of the problem of excessive court reporting, *see* Jacobstein, *Some Reflections on the Control of the Publication of Appellate Court Opinions*, 27 STAN.L.REV. 791 (1975).

[23] The reliance of lawyers on private law book publishers led the Federal Trade Commission to promulgate standards for the law book trade. *See* 16 C.F.R. § 256 (1984).

fifty state legislatures, the regulations promulgated by federal and state administrative agencies, and the appellate court decisions of the various federal and state courts.

Constitutions, statutes, regulations, and court decisions are primary sources of the law. Other law books are secondary sources of the law.

Chapter 2

PRELIMINARY PROCEDURE IN LEGAL RESEARCH

Let us begin our study by surveying the procedure which is preliminary to the actual use of research publications. This entails three steps: (1) the determination and integration of facts; (2) the determination of the legal issues; and (3) the procedure to be applied in searching for the law.

To understand a legal problem clearly, carefully screen and ascertain the relevant facts. Though the legal principle may be constant, its application to different facts may result in different conclusions. Thus, incisive interrogation of the parties and resourceful investigation to derive the facts frequently determine the results of a problem.

SECTION A. DETERMINATION AND INTEGRATION OF FACTS

After assembling the facts, screen, integrate, and evaluate the information. Though these are not distinct processes, each possesses distinguishing characteristics. Screening entails the eliminating of nonessential facts; integration is the process of assembling the pertinent data; and evaluation gives direction to the research.

To appraise the relevant issues factually, recognize and weigh the following factors:

T—*Thing* or subject matter

A—Cause of *Action* or ground of defense

R—*Relief* sought

P—*Persons* or parties involved

1. *Thing or subject matter.* The place or property involved in a problem or controversy may be a significant element. Thus, where a passenger is injured in a skidding automobile, the personal property, the automobile, becomes an essential factor in the dispute.

2. *Cause of action or ground of defense.* A claim is asserted or a defense is made. The action centers around a point of controversy or a circumstance relating to the problem. The cause of action may be a breach of contract, neligence, or some other claim.

3. *Relief sought.* This relates to the purpose of the lawsuit. It may be a civil suit (as opposed to criminal) where the party bringing the suit (plaintiff) is seeking monetary damages for an injury suffered, or a matter wherein the plaintiff is seeking the court to order

the other party (defendant) to do a specific act or to refrain from doing an act; or it may be criminal action being brought by the state.

4. *Persons or parties involved in the problem; their factual and legal status and relationship to each other.* The parties or persons may be individuals, or may be a group which is significant to the solution of the problem or the outcome of the lawsuit. Thus, whether or not some of the parties involved are minors or mentally incompetent may have an important bearing on the outcome of the suit. Similarly, the relationship between parties may be of special importance, such as exists between husband and wife or employer and employee.

Factual analysis using the TARP rule should suggest headings to be examined during the research.

SECTION B. DETERMINATION OF THE LEGAL ISSUES

When the facts are ascertained and integrated, determine the legal issues. Legal controversies frequently involve more than one point of law. In such cases, the issues should be interrelated, not merged, and should be given separate treatment.

As the methods of research vary greatly with the problems and the subject matter, no single example can illustrate adequately all phases of research methodology. However, to facilitate the present study, an example case is analyzed below.

Example Case

The XYZ Auto Sales Company placed an advertisement in a local newspaper advertising a sports model Studecar ZZ–88 for $4,988.00. Through an inadvertent error, the advertisement listed the price as $4,088.00. A customer entered the salesroom and told a salesperson that she wanted to purchase a Studecar ZZ–88 for $4,088.00 as advertised. After checking with the Sales Manager, the salesperson told the customer that the advertisement was a mistake and that the car could not be sold for less than $4,988.00. The customer consults a lawyer.

Let us analyze this case.

a. *Thing or subject matter.* Here the subject matter is an automobile, but this is not the essential matter. The same rules of law would apply for an erroneous advertisement in a newspaper for nearly any type of consumer goods. The matter in question here is whether the advertisement was a valid offer which upon acceptance created an enforceable contract.

b. *Cause of action or ground of defense.* The cause of action is an alleged breach of contract; the defense is the lack of a binding contract.

c. *Relief sought.* Customer seeks delivery of auto at the advertised price, or the difference between this price and the price customer actually paid for similar model.

d. *Persons or parties involved.* The parties include customer and XYZ Auto Sales Company, and perhaps all others who want to purchase a Studecar ZZ–88 at the advertised price.

This problem now has to be researched to find the law on the following issues and perhaps others that will become apparent during the research.

Does an advertisement in a newspaper constitute a valid offer? Can an action be maintained against the XYZ Auto Sales Company for specific performance? That is, can it be made to deliver a ZZ–88 to the customer at the advertised price? If not, what other remedies does customer have? Is it possible to make this into a *class action* suit?

Do the facts of this case apply only to state law, or are there elements which could bring this case under the jurisdiction of a federal court?

During the research for the law, the researcher will first determine whether state or federal law is applicable. Under the facts presented, state law will apply as there are no federal issues present. Next, the researcher should ascertain if the state where this transaction occurred has a statute controlling this type of newspaper advertising. If it does, the next step is to determine if there are any court decisions that interpret the statute. If there is no statute, the researcher will search first for appellate court decisions in the state where the transaction occurred, then for appellate court decisions in other states. The search will be for cases with fact situations as similar as possible to the one being researched.

The remaining chapters of this book will be devoted to demonstrating how this research is accomplished and the different methods which may be used in finding the law.

Chapter 3

COURT REPORTS

SECTION A. THE REPORTING OF COURT DECISIONS

1. Introduction

The editing and publishing of court decisions have assumed special characteristics in American law. These manifestations were influenced significantly by the doctrine of judicial precedent or *stare decisis.* Since past decisions play such an important role in our law, the tremendous growth and inclusiveness of court reports are quite understandable. However, this extensive development in turn has created problems for the legal profession—problems relating to the informational content of case law, publication costs, absorption of office space and related issues.

As indicated in Chapter 1, Section D-2, there are over 3,000,000 reported judicial opinions in the United States, and over 50,000 American cases are published each year. These mostly include decisions of federal and state appellate courts. As a general rule, decisions of trial courts are not reported. A few states, such as New York, Ohio and Pennsylvania, do publish some trial court opinions but those so selected are few in number and represent only a very small proportion of the total cases heard by the trial courts. Moreover, opinions of trial courts do not serve as mandatory precedents and they do not play an important role in legal research.

Not all appellate court opinions, however, are necessarily published and the publication procedures differ in the various appellate courts.[1] Many judges and lawyers believe that far too many opinions are written and reported which do not merit the treatment of permanent publication. It is claimed that a significant number of reported decisions relate merely to prosaic problems and make no doctrinal advancements. Although of value to the parties involved in the litigation, these cases add little or nothing to the existing law.

Despite Justice Holmes' observation that, "It is a great mistake to be frightened by the ever-increasing number of reports. The reports of a given jurisdiction in the course of a generation take up pretty much the whole body of the law, and restate it from the present point of view. We could reconstruct the corpus from them if

---

[1] Chanin, *A Survey of the Writing and Publication of Opinions in Federal and State Appellate Courts,* 67 LAW LIB.J. 362 (1974).

13

all that went before were burned," [2] the tremendous growth of recent decisions has increased the attempts to restrict the number of reported court decisions.[3]

2. Court Organization

Each jurisdiction has its own system of court organization, and although there may be differences in detail, the general structure is the same. In general, there are trial courts and appellate courts. The former are the courts where the trial is first held (courts of the first instance). It is here the parties appear, witnesses testify, and the evidence is presented. The trial court usually determines any questions of fact that may be in dispute and then applies the applicable rules of law.

Once the trial court reaches its decision, the losing party has a right of appeal to an appellate court. Generally, the appellate court can only decide questions of law and its decision in each case is based on the record made below. Appellate courts do not receive new testimony or decide questions of fact, and in most jurisdictions only the appellate courts issue written opinions.

Each state has a final court of appeal (usually called the Supreme Court). Additionally, thirty states have intermediate courts of appeal.[4] [See Illustration 1.]

3. Methods of Reporting Court Opinions

When a case has been appealed to an appellate court, both parties submit written briefs which contain a summary of the facts and arguments on the points of law involved, and the court may hear oral arguments by the attorneys. The court then writes an opinion in which it states the reasons for its decision. Technically speaking, the decision of a court only indicates the action of the court and is

---

[2] Holmes, *The Path of the Law*, in COLLECTED LEGAL PAPERS 167, 169 (1975).

[3] A full discussion of this may be found in Jacobstein, *Some Reflections on the Control of the Publication of Appellate Court Opinions*, 27 STAN.L.REV. 791 (1975). *See also* Landes & Posner, *Legal Precedent: A Theoretical and Empirical Analysis*, 19 J. LAW & ECON. 249–307 (1976); Merryman, *Toward a Theory of Citations: An Empirical Study of the Citation Practice of the California Supreme Court in 1950, 1960, and 1970*, 50 S.CAL.L.REV. 381–428 (1977). The Constitution of the State of California directs the publication of appellate opinions "as the Supreme Court deems appropriate" and "as it may deem expedient." The California Supreme Court has been making increasing use of this provision, known as depublication or decertification, to deal with caseloads. This practice has engendered substantial debate in the literature. *See, e.g.*, Grodin, *The Depublication Practice of the California Supreme Court*, 72 CALIF.L.REV. 514 (1984); Gerstein, *Law by Elimination: Depublication in the California Supreme Court*, 67 JUDICATURE 292 (1984).

[4] NATIONAL CENTER FOR STATE COURTS, COURT STATISTICS AND INFORMATION MANAGEMENT PROJECT (1984).

indicated by the words *Affirmed,* or *Reversed,* or *Remanded,* or similar words and phrases. The reasons for this action are then stated in the opinion of the court. However, in actual practice, the terms *opinion* and *decision* have become interchangeable.[5]

SECTION B. THE SEGMENTS OF COURT DECISIONS

The segments of an American court decision are as follows:

1. Name or Title of the Case

Cases generally are identified by the names of the parties to a lawsuit:

Payne v. Green—in table of cases as *Payne v. Green.*

In re Payne—in table of cases as *Payne, In re.* Judicial proceedings in which there are no adversary parties. Such designations usually denote a bankruptcy case, a probate case, a guardianship matter, a contempt case, a disbarment, or a habeas corpus case.

Ex parte Payne—in table of cases as *Payne, Ex parte.* This is a special proceeding.

State on the relation of Payne v. Green—in table of cases as *State ex rel. Payne v. Green.* These cases involve the extraordinary legal remedies, viz.: Mandamus, prohibition, certiorari, quo warranto, or habeas corpus.

State v. Payne—in table of cases as *State v. Payne.* Suit by the state in its collective capacity as the party wronged by a criminal deed. In some sets the criminal cases are arranged in alphabetical order under the names of the respective states. *People* or *Commonwealth* are used in some states instead of *State.*

In maritime law, a suit may be brought against the ship, e.g., *The Caledonia.*

Cases involving the seizure of commodities are brought in their names, e.g., *United States v. 45 Barrels of Whisky.*

Usually, the plaintiff-defendant names remain in that order when cases are appealed by a defendant; however, in some states, they are reversed, and the defendant on appeal becomes the plaintiff in error.

2. Docket Number

A docket number is the numerical designation assigned to each case by a court. It is the means of identifying the case as the suit in progress. Also, it is a convenient method for filing briefs in cases in libraries.

---

[5] For a discussion of the difference between *decision of the court* and *opinion of the court, see* Rogers v. Hill, 289 U.S. 582, 587 (1933).

3. Date of Decision

This is the date on which the decision was rendered, and generally it appears after the docket number in the reported case.

4. Prefatory Statement

The prefatory statement explains the nature of the case, its disposition in the lower court, the name of the lower court and sometimes its judge, and the disposition of the case in the appellate court as being affirmed or reversed.

5. Syllabus or Headnote

Headnotes, or syllabi, are brief summaries of the rules of law or significant facts in a case. They are usually drafted by editors, although in a few states they are prepared by the judges who rendered the decisions. Each headnote represents a point of law extracted from the decision and the number of headnotes will vary from case to case.

The syllabi or headnotes are useful in allowing the reader to grasp quickly the legal issues discussed in the case. They also serve a very useful function in the process of locating cases on the same or similar points of law. This feature will be discussed in more detail in Chapter 5. [See Illustrations 3 and 4 for examples of headnotes.]

6. Names of Counsel

The names of counsel for both parties to a suit precede the opinion of the court.

7. Statement of Facts

A statement of the facts in the case usually follows the names of counsel.

8. Opinion of the Court

Although, as previously mentioned, a few trial court decisions are reported, most court opinions that are published are those of appellate courts. Every appellate court has at least three judges and in some jurisdictions the courts may have five, seven, or nine judges. The opinion of the court is the explanation of the court's decision, the latter being the conclusion or result in a controversy. The opinion is written by one member of the court after the majority has agreed to a decision. A member of the majority, while agreeing with a decision, may disagree with its reasoning; he or she then may write a concurring opinion which gives his or her reasons for the decision. The views of the minority generally are expressed by a dissenting opinion which is written by one of the dissenting judges. An opinion, in accord with the dissent, may be written by a dissenting judge when

he or she agrees with the conclusions and result of the dissent but disagrees with its reasoning. Or several dissenting opinions may be rendered independently by the judges, each expressing different views. A *per curiam* opinion is an opinion of the entire majority as distinguished from an opinion written by a specific judge. It may present a lengthy or a brief discussion of the issues in the case, e.g., New York Court of Appeals. In some courts, it may only give the conclusion without any reasoning, e.g., United States Supreme Court. A memorandum opinion is a brief holding of the whole court in which the opinion is limited or omitted.

Dissenting opinions are not the law in a case; nor are they binding as precedent. They assume the characteristics of *dicta* and serve merely as secondary authority. However, not infrequently the controlling opinion may later be overruled and the dissenting opinion is then accepted as the correct statement of the law.

There are two additional elements of a case which merit brief attention. The first is the *ratio decidendi*, or the point in a case which determines the result. In other words, it is the basis of the decision, explicitly or implicitly, stated in the opinion. The second is *obiter dictum*. The latter is a collateral statement contained in the opinion which does not relate directly to the issues raised in the case. *Dictum*, therefore, is an official, incidental comment, not necessary to the formulation of the decision, made by the judge in his opinion which is not binding as precedent.

9.   Decision, with Judgment or Decree

This refers to the actual disposition of the case by the court. Thus, a decision is noted by such terms as *affirmed, reversed, modified*, etc. Often the words *decision* and *judgment* are synonymously used. However, a judgment upon the verdict of a jury is the most common of the judgments upon facts found, and is for the party, i.e., plaintiff or defendant, obtaining the verdict.

SECTION C.   OFFICIAL AND UNOFFICIAL REPORTS

If the publication of the court reports is sanctioned by statute, they are called *official reports*. [See Illustration 2.] Those published without such authority are referred to as *unofficial reports*, i.e., commercial or private publications. Neither term reflects quality or accuracy, for both originate from the clerks and the judges.

1.   Unofficially Reported Cases as Authority

Since decisions of courts are not copyrighted,[6] numerous sets of court reports have been published by private firms, which either

---

[6] Wheaton v. Peters, 33 U.S. 591 (1834). *See also* Annotation, *Law Reports as Subject of Copyright*, 8 L.Ed. 1055 (1883); Banks v. Manchester, 128 U.S. 244 (1888).

duplicate the official reports or include decisions not officially published. Since the early nineteenth century legal scholars have warned against such uncontrolled proliferation of court reports. In the past, courts and legislatures have attempted to control the publication of court opinions by limiting the publication of opinions in the official reports to those decisions which (1) lay down a new rule of law or alter or modify an existing rule; (2) involve a legal issue of continuing public interest; (3) criticize existing law; or (4) resolve an apparent conflict of authority. But, inevitably, each such attempt has resulted in those opinions not appearing in the official reports being published in unofficial sets of reports. Only recently have some courts attempted to control this by prohibiting the citing of opinions not specifically marked *For Publication*.[7] This practice in turn has been severely criticized by some members of the bar. The final solution to the proliferation of court opinions has still not been found. It is reasonable to conclude that so long as precedent plays a dominant role in American law, the number of published court decisions will continue to grow. Care should be taken, however, to check the authority of unofficially reported decisions before citing them as authority.[8]

SECTION D. THE ELEMENTS OF JUDICIAL REPORTING

Several techniques are used in publishing court cases. Generally, the order of their release is determined by their decision dates and not by a logical arrangement, such as subject. Some decisions are published individually, when rendered by a court, and are called *slip* opinions. Usually, the *slip* opinions do not contain syllabi, nor are they indexed. Illustrations 3 and 4 show examples of the same case as reported in an official and unofficial set of reports. In some states, the official reports have ceased publication, and privately published reports have been adopted as the official reports for those states. This will be discussed in more detail in Chapter 5.

Advance sheets contain decisions of a court or the courts of several jurisdictions. They typically are published as quickly as they can be assembled after the decisions are rendered. Their format is that of a periodical pamphlet, and the emphasis is on speed of publication. The paging of the *advance sheets* ordinarily is the same as the bound cumulative volumes. This permits quick, permanent citations to cases. The features of the cases in the *advance sheets* are identical with those included in the bound volumes. Some jurisdictions do not publish *advance sheets*.

[7] CAL.SUP.CT. (Civ.) R. 977. The treatment of non-publication of opinions in the federal courts of appeals will be discussed in Chapter 4.

[8] For a historical survey of the selected publication of court opinions, *see* Jacobstein, *supra* note 3.

1. Features of Bound Volumes of Reports

As indicated above, the cases are finally cumulated in bound volumes. The bound volumes include most of the following significant features:

   a. A table of cases contained in the volume.

   b. A table of statutes interpreted by the decisions reported.

   c. The opinions are cumulated from advance sheets and have the same volume and page numbers as the advance sheets.

   d. The types of opinions are (1) written by a judge (majority, dissenting or concurring), (2) *per curiam* and (3) memorandum.

   e. Subject index or digest of the cases reported.

   f. Judicial definition of words and phrases used in the cases reported.

   g. Court rules.

   h. The various volumes of unofficial reports generally contain cross-reference tables to the official reports.

SECTION E.   ORGANIZATION OF COURT REPORTS

Court reports are organized in different ways.

1. By Jurisdiction

The opinions of a particular court are issued chronologically in a numbered series such as the *New York Reports* or the *Illinois Appellate Court Reports* or the *United States Reports*. In some instances, the reports of both the highest state court and its intermediate appellate court are published in the same set of reports, such as in the *California Reporter*.

2. By Geography

The opinions of a group of geographically adjacent states are published in one set of reports such as the *Northwestern Reporter* which includes opinions from the appellate courts of Iowa, Michigan, Minnesota, Nebraska, North Dakota, South Dakota, and Wisconsin.

3. By Subject

Standard sets of law reports contain opinions arranged chronologically and each volume may contain opinions on subjects ranging from abandonment to zoning. There are some sets of court reports which contain opinions on a particular subject. Examples of these are the *CCH Labor Law Reporter, Prentice-Hall Tax Court Memorandum Decisions* and the *United States Patents Quarterly*.

SECTION F. ILLUSTRATIONS

[Illustration 1]

THE UNITED STATES COURT SYSTEM

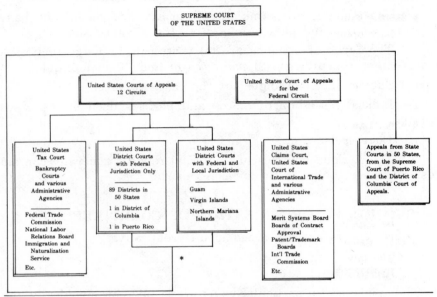

CALIFORNIA STATE COURT SYSTEM

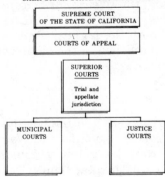

* Direct review by the Supreme Court of an order granting or denying an interlocutory or permanent injunction in a civil action to be heard and determined by a district court of three judges, and from an interlocutory or final judgment of a court of the United States holding an Act of Congress unconstitutional in any civil proceeding to which the United States or any of its agencies, or any officer or employee, is a party. (28 U.S.C.A. §§ 1252, 1253)

[Illustration 2]

TYPICAL STATUTORY PROVISIONS FOR PUBLICATION
OF COURT REPORTS

Excerpt from West's Ann.Calif. Gov't Code

§ 68902. Publication of reports: Supervision by Supreme Court.

Such opinions of the Supreme Court, of the courts of appeal, and of the appellate departments of the superior courts as the Supreme Court may deem expedient shall be published in the official reports. The reports shall be published under the general supervision of the Supreme Court.

Excerpts from McKinney Consol.Laws of N.Y. Judiciary Law

§ 430. Law reporting bureau; state reporter

There is hereby created and established the law reporting bureau of the state of New York. The bureau shall be under the direction and control of a state reporter, who shall be appointed and be removable by the court of appeals by an order entered in its minutes. The state reporter shall be assisted by a first deputy state reporter and such other deputy state reporters and such staff as may be necessary, all of whom shall be appointed and be removable by the court of appeals.

§ 431. Causes to be reported

The law reporting bureau shall report every cause determined in the court of appeals and every cause determined in the appellate divisions of the supreme court, unless otherwise directed by the court deciding the cause; and, in addition, any cause determined in any other court which the state reporter, with the approval of the court of appeals, considers worthy of being reported because of its usefulness as a precedent or its importance as a matter of public interest.

Each reported decision shall be published as soon as practicable after it is rendered. Added L.1938, c. 494, § 1, eff. July 1, 1938.

Excerpt from Vernon's Ann.Mo.Stat.

§ 477.231. Designation of private publication as official reports

The supreme court may declare the published volumes of the decisions of the supreme court as the same are published by any person, firm or corporation, to be official reports of the decisions of the supreme court, and the courts of appeals may jointly make a similar declaration with respect to published volumes of the opinions of the courts of appeals. Any publication so designated as the official reports may include both the opinions of the supreme court and the courts of appeals in the same volume.

[Illustration 3]

A TYPICAL CASE AS REPORTED IN AN OFFICIAL SET OF COURT REPORTS
(39 Or.App. 311)

Argued November 20, 1978, affirmed in part;
reversed in part and remanded for new trial on the
issue of damages for loss of use March 19, reconsideration
denied April 16, petition for review denied June 6, 1979

GRAF, *Appellant*,
v.
DON RASMUSSEN COMPANY, *Respondent.*
(No. 424-151, CA 9935)
592 P2d 250

Owner of automobile brought action against garage, from which automobile had been stolen and damaged, to recover, for the cost of repairs, loss of use of the vehicle, and intentional infliction of emotional distress. The Circuit Court, Multnomah County, Jeff D. Dorroh, Jr., J. pro tem., entered judgment on the verdict in favor of the owner for the cost of repair but struck the cause of action for emotional distress and refused to submit to the jury the issue of compensation for loss of use of the automobile. Automobile owner appealed. The Court of Appeals, Richardson, J., held that: (1) owner's acceptance of payment of the judgment for the cost of repairs did not preclude her from pursuing her appeal with respect to other issues; (2) owner was entitled to recover for the loss of use of the vehicle during the time that it was being repaired, but not for the time during which she delayed authorizing repairs, and (3) complaint did not state a basis for recovery for emotional distress, either on the basis that it was the direct result of the garage's negligent storage of the automobile or on the theory that it was result of the intentional infliction of emotional distress.

Affirmed in part, reversed in part and remanded.

Schwab, C. J., dissented in part and filed an opinion.

1. Appeal and Error—Waiver of right to appeal

Party may waive the right to appeal by acquiescing in the order below or claiming the benefits of the judgment.

2. Appeal and Error—Maintaining an appeal

An appeal may be maintained when it is not inconsistent with the acceptance of the judgment.

3. Appeal and Error—Where judgment provisions divisible

If the provisions of the judgment are divisible and the appeal does not place those portions of the judgment accepted by the appellant in jeopardy, the appeal may continue.

4. Appeal and Error—Acceptance of payment of judgment on repair costs did not preclude appeal for damages, loss of use and emotional distress

Action of plaintiff, who had brought action against garage to recover for the cost of repair, compensation for loss of use of the vehicle, and damages for intentional infliction of emotional distress, in accepting payment of the judgment for the cost of repair did not preclude her from continuing her appeal from the denial of damages for loss of use of the vehicle and for emotional distress.

ILLUSTRATIONS

[Illustration 3–a]

SAMPLE PAGE FROM 39 Or.App. 311, 312

Graf v. Don Rasmussen Co.

5. Automobiles—Owner entitled to recover costs for loss of use of vehicle stolen from garqage

Subject to proof, owner of automobile was entitled to recover from garage damages to compensate her for the reasonable time the use of her vehicle was lost as a result of damage to the vehicle when it was stolen from the garage.

6. Automobiles—Owner not entitled to compensation for loss of use due to own delay in commencing repairs

Owner of automobile who had entrusted its care to a garage for storage was not entitled to compensation for loss of use of the vehicle during a period of unexcused or excessive delay on the part of the owner in commencing the repairs to damage which occurred when the vehicle was stolen from the garage.

7. Automobiles—Owner not entitled to recover for loss of use due to own delay in authorizing repairs

Owner of automobile who made no attempt to secure prompt repair of the vehicle while the vehicle was stored in a garage, and who showed no reason for the delay from October of 1975 to February of 1977 in authorizing repairs was not entitled to recover for the loss of use of vehicle, which was damaged when it was stolen from the garage, from October of 1975 to February of 1977.

8. Automobiles—Evidence supported claim for loss of use of vehicle

Evidence that automobile sustained considerable damage when it was stolen from the garage, evidence of the repairs which were undertaken and how long the work took, and evidence of uncontrollable delay in securing parts was sufficient to make a submissible case on the owner's claim against the garage from which that automobile had been stolen for loss of use of the vehicle during the time that it was being repaired.

9. Evidence—Recovery of damages for loss of use of vehicle stolen from garage

Even though person whose automobile was damaged when it was stolen from a garage did not rent another vehicle while her vehicle was being repaired, she was entitled to establish her damages for loss of use of the vehicle through the testimony of a person who, for 23 years, had been engaged in the business of leasing automobiles and other equipment and who testified that the regular charge for a nonpurchase lease which the lessee was free to terminate at any time would be three percent of the value of the vehicle per month.

10. Bailment—Determining fair measure of damages as result of damage to item while in possession of another

Although the rental expense of a replacement item would be material in ascertaining the fair measure of the owner's damages as a result of damage to an item while in the possession of another, the rental expense does not determine the owner's entitlement to damages for loss of use of the item.

[Illustration 3–b]

FIRST PAGE OF OPINION FROM 39 Or.App. 311, 313

Cite as 39 Or App 311 (1979)

RICHARDSON, J.

This appeal involves an action for damages resulting from the theft of and subsequent injury to plaintiff's automobile while it was in storage in defendant's garage. Alleging that defendant was negligent in its supervision of her vehicle, plaintiff sought to recover the cost of repair, compensation for loss of use of the vehicle, and damages for the intentional infliction of emotional distress. The trial court struck the latter claim for damages and refused to submit the claim for loss of use. The jury returned a verdict for the full amount of plaintiff's prayer for cost of repair. Plaintiff appeals the striking of her cause for emotional distress, the refusal to submit to the jury the issue of compensation for loss of use and the denial of her motion to examine certain of defendant's sales records. Defendant moved for dismissal of the appeal.

On June 17, 1975, plaintiff delivered her 1972 Mercedes Benz 280 SE automobile to defendant for minor repair and storage while she was in Europe. The vehicle was stolen from defendant's storage area and was later found wrecked. Defendant wrote to plaintiff, explained what had happened, and informed her that the repairs would probably be completed prior to her return. Plaintiff instructed defendant not to repair the car until she returned. In January, 1977, about 16 months after her return to Portland, plaintiff selected an automobile shop to repair her vehicle. The repairs were completed July 11, 1977, at a cost of $8,364.68.

Plaintiff filed notice of appeal on January 3, 1978. Defendant did not cross-appeal. On March 8, 1978, plaintiff demanded and received payment of the judgment for cost of repair. Plaintiff filed a partial satisfaction of judgment excepting those issues which were on appeal. Defendant then moved to dismiss the appeal on the basis that plaintiff waived her right to appeal by accepting payment of her judgment. The motion was denied with leave to renew in defendant's brief.

[Illustration 4]

A TYPICAL CASE AS REPORTED IN A SET
OF UNOFFICIAL REPORTS

250 Or.   **592 PACIFIC REPORTER, 2d SERIES**

This is the same case as shown in Illus. 3 as it appears in the Pacific Reporter, an unofficial set of court reports. The headnotes are prepared by the publisher's editorial staff. Note how they differ from the headnotes for this case in the Oregon Appellate Reports (Illus. 3).

Although the material preceding the opinion of the court varies in the unofficial reports from the official reports, the text of the opinion is exactly the same.

The difference between the official and unofficial reports and other features of court reports will be discussed in Chapters 4, 5, and 6.

39 Or.App. 311
Violet GRAF, Appellant,

v.

DON RASMUSSEN COMPANY, an Oregon Corporation, Respondent.

No. 424–151; CA 9935.

Court of Appeals of Oregon.

Argued and Submitted Nov. 20, 1978.

Decided March 19, 1979.

Owner of automobile brought action against garage, from which automobile had been stolen and damaged, to recover, for the cost of repairs, loss of use of the vehicle, and intentional infliction of emotional distress. The Circuit Court, Multnomah County, Jeff D. Dorroh, Jr., J. pro tem., entered judgment on the verdict in favor of the owner for the cost of repair but struck the cause of action for emotional distress and refused to submit to the jury the issue of compensation for loss of use of the automobile. Automobile owner appealed. The Court of Appeals, Richardson, J., held that:

(1) owner's acceptance of payment of the judgment for the cost of repairs did not preclude her from pursuing her appeal with respect to other issues; (2) owner was entitled to recover for the loss of use of the vehicle during the time that it was being repaired, but not for the time during which she delayed authorizing repairs, and (3) complaint did not state a basis for recovery for emotional distress, either on the basis that it was the direct result of the garage's negligent storage of the automobile or on the theory that it was result of the intentional infliction of emotional distress.

Affirmed in part, reversed in part and remanded.

Schwab, C. J., dissented in part and filed an opinion.

1. Appeal and Error ⟐154(1), 161
Party may waive the right to appeal by acquiescing in the order below or claiming the benefits of the judgment.

2. Appeal and Error ⟐161
An appeal may be maintained when it is not inconsistent with the acceptance of the judgment.

3. Appeal and Error ⟐161
If the provisions of the judgment are divisible and the appeal does not place those portions of the judgment accepted by the appellant in jeopardy, the appeal may continue.

4. Appeal and Error ⟐162(2)
Action of plaintiff, who had brought action against garage to recover for the cost of repair, compensation for loss of use of the vehicle, and damages for intentional infliction of emotional distress, in accepting payment of the judgment for the cost of repair did not preclude her from continuing her appeal from the denial of damages for loss of use of the vehicle and for emotional distress.

5. Automobiles ⟐372
Subject to proof, owner of automobile was entitled to recover from garage damages to compensate her for the reasonable

[Illustration 4–a]

FIRST PAGE OF OPINION FROM 592 P.2d 250

14. Damages ⇐149

Complaint which alleged that owner of automobile was a widow in her 60's and was of a sensitive and emotional nature, all of which was or should have been known to the garage which was storing her automobile and that, by reason of and the wrongful and unjustified conduct of the garage in misrepresenting amount of damage done to the vehicle when it was stolen from the garage, in refusing to repair the automobile in the absence of a release from liability, in later representing that the automobile was not repairable and in attempting to force a settlement on the automobile owner did not allege conduct which would support a cause of action for intentional infliction of emotional distress.

Ferris F. Boothe, Portland, argued the cause and filed the briefs for appellant.

Michael A. Lehner, Portland, argued the cause for respondent. With him on the brief were Wm. H. Mitchell and Hershiser, Mitchell, Mowery & Davis, Portland.

Before SCHWAB, C. J., and LEE, RICHARDSON and JOSEPH, JJ.

RICHARDSON, Judge.

This appeal involves an action for damages resulting from the theft of and subsequent injury to plaintiff's automobile while it was in storage in defendant's garage. Alleging that defendant was negligent in its supervision of her vehicle, plaintiff sought to recover the cost of repair, compensation for loss of use of the vehicle, and damages for the intentional infliction of emotional distress. The trial court struck the latter claim for damages and refused to submit the claim for loss of use. The jury returned a verdict for the full amount of plaintiff's prayer for cost of repair. Plaintiff appeals the striking of her cause for emotional distress, the refusal to submit to the jury the issue of compensation for loss of use and the denial of her motion to examine certain of defendant's sales records. Defendant moved for dismissal of the appeal.

On June 17, 1975, plaintiff delivered her 1972 Mercedes Benz 280 SE automobile to defendant for minor repair and storage while she was in Europe. The vehicle was stolen from defendant's storage area and was later found wrecked. Defendant wrote to plaintiff, explained what had happened, and informed her that the repairs would probably be completed prior to her return. Plaintiff instructed defendant not to repair the car until she returned. In January, 1977, about 16 months after her return to Portland, plaintiff selected an automobile shop to repair her vehicle. The repairs were completed July 11, 1977, at a cost of $8,364.68.

Plaintiff filed notice of appeal on January 3, 1978. Defendant did not cross-appeal. On March 8, 1978, plaintiff demanded and received payment of the judgment for cost of repair. Plaintiff filed a partial satisfaction of judgment excepting those issues which were on appeal. Defendant then moved to dismiss the appeal on the basis that plaintiff waived her right to appeal by accepting payment of her judgment. The motion was denied with leave to renew in defendant's brief.

On the Motion to Dismiss.

[1–3] It is the general rule that a party may waive the right to appeal by acquiescing in the order below or claiming the benefits of the judgment. *Pac. Gen. Contrs. v. State Const. Co.*, 196 Or. 608, 611, 251 P.2d 454 (1952); *West et al. v. Broadwell et al.*, 124 Or. 652, 653, 265 P. 783 (1928); *State of Oregon v. Wells, Fargo & Co.*, 64 Or. 421, 425, 126 P. 611, 130 P. 983 (1913). However, an appeal may be maintained when it is not inconsistent with acceptance of the judgment. *Schlecht v. Bliss*, 271 Or. 304, 309, 532 P.2d 1 (1975). If the provisions of the judgment are divisible and the appeal does not place those portions of the judgment accepted by appellant in jeopardy, the appeal may continue. *Schlecht, supra; Vaughan et ux. v. Wilson et al.*, 203 Or. 243, 246, 273 P.2d 991, 279 P.2d 521 (1955).

The test for divisibility was set out in *Pac. Gen. Contrs. v. State Const. Co., supra:*

SECTION G. ABBREVIATIONS AND CITATIONS
OF COURT REPORTS

Court reports are published in numbered sets [9] with the name of the set reflected in its title; for example, the *Illinois Reports* (the opinions of the Illinois Supreme Court) or the *Supreme Court Reporter* (the opinions of the Supreme Court of the United States) or the *Oil and Gas Reporter* (opinions from all U.S. jurisdictions dealing with the law of oil and gas). In all legal writing it is customary when referring to a court decision to give the name of the case and its citation in the appropriate court reports. But rather than citing to, for example, *Volume 132 of the Michigan Reports for the case starting at page 235*, a citation is given using a standard format and a standard abbreviation for the name of the set of reports, e.g., 132 Mich. 235, or 41 S.Ct. 191, or 18 OIL & GAS REP. 1289.

It is extremely important in any legal writing to give a complete citation to the source or sources relied on in reaching one's conclusions. Tables of abbreviations should be consulted for the proper method of abbreviation; and citation manuals, for proper form of citation.[10]

A Table of Abbreviations with reference to the full name of court reports is set forth in Appendix A, Jacobstein and Mersky, *Fundamentals of Legal Research*. 3d ed. (1985).

SECTION H. SUMMARY

To facilitate learning the essential features of the significant publications described in the following chapters, a summary of them is provided towards the end of the various chapters. The summaries are generally arranged with the following points in mind: (1) scope—indicating coverage by subject matter and chronology, if any; (2) arrangements—for example, alphabetically by subject, by names or titles, or by chronology (following a time sequence); (3) index; and (4) supplementation.

---

[9] The first American decisions were reported by private reporters and were cited to the name of the reporter. In Massachusetts, for example, the first volume of court reports was reported by Williams and is cited as 1 Will. Mass.; the next sixteen volumes were reported by Tyng and are cited as 1–16 Tyng. The practice of citing to named reporters ceased in most jurisdictions during the middle of the nineteenth century.

[10] There is no universally accepted table of abbreviations or manual of citations. In addition to those in Appendix A, tables of abbreviations may be located in law dictionaries and in other books on legal bibliography. A commonly used citation manual is *A Uniform System of Citation*, published by the Harvard Law Review Association, Columbia Law Review, University of Pennsylvania Law Review and the Yale Law Journal.

1. Segments of a Court Decision

  a. Name of the case.

  b. Docket number.

  c. Date of decision.

  d. Synopsis, or Summary, of case.

  e. Syllabus or headnote—brief summary of the legal rule or significant facts in a case.

  f. Names of counsel.

  g. Statement of facts.

  h. Opinion of the court—explanation of the court's decision.

  Concurring opinion—opinion of a judge which agrees with the decision of the majority but disagrees with the reasoning.

  Dissenting opinion—expressed disagreement of one or more judges of a court with the decision reached by the majority in a case before them.

  Per curiam opinion—opinion of the majority of the court as distinguished from an opinion written by a specific judge.

  Memorandum opinion—a brief holding of the whole court in which the opinion (explanation) is very concise or totally absent.

  Ratio decidendi—the point in a case which determines the result.

  Obiter dictum—incidental comment made by the judge in his opinion, which is not necessary to the formulation of the decision nor binding as precedent.

  i. Decision of the court—disposition of the case by the court.

2. Official and Unofficial Reports

  a. Official reports—court reports directed by statute.

  b. Unofficial reports—court reports published without statutory direction.

3. Elements of Judicial Reporting

  a. *Slip* opinion—an individual court decision published separately soon after it is rendered.

  b. Advance sheets—contain the decisions of a court or the courts of several jurisdictions decided just prior to publication and are in pamphlet format.

  c. Order of release of cases is determined by their decision dates and not by a logical arrangement, such as subject.

  d. A bound volume includes:

  (1) Table of cases contained in the volume.

(2) Table of statutes interpreted by the decisions reported.

(3) Opinions (comprised of cases from preceding advance sheets)—written, *per curiam* or memorandum.

(4) Subject index or digest of the cases reported.

(5) Judicial definitions of words and phrases used in the cases reported.

(6) Court rules.

(7) Unofficial reports generally contain cross-reference tables to the official reports.

4. Organization of Court Reports

a. By jurisdiction. Opinions of a specific court or several courts from the same state or jurisdiction. Opinions are generally reported in chronological order.

b. By geography. Opinions of the courts of adjacent states are reported in the same set of reports.

c. By subject. Contains only cases on a specific subject.

Chapter 4

FEDERAL COURT DECISIONS

Section 1 of Article III of the United States Constitution provides that "The judicial power of the United States shall be vested in one Supreme Court, and in such inferior courts as the Congress may from time to time ordain and establish." Since the adoption of the Constitution in 1789, Congress has provided for various arrangements of the lower federal courts.[1]

Since 1880 the federal court system can be described as consisting of three main divisions: the Supreme Court of the United States (the highest court), the courts of appeals (intermediate courts), and the district courts (courts of original jurisdiction or trial courts).[2]

All written opinions of the Supreme Court of the United States are published in the official and unofficial reports. Most *per curiam* decisions also are reported. All written opinions designated *for publication* by the courts of appeals are unofficially published. Memorandum opinions are not published. As for the district court decisions, only selected opinions of those courts are unofficially reported. Unreported cases of the district courts generally are available through the court clerks.

SECTION A. UNITED STATES SUPREME COURT REPORTS

The decisions of the United States Supreme Court are published in five current reports:

1. United States Reports (official edition), cited *U.S.*

2. United States Supreme Court Reports, Lawyers' Edition (Lawyers Co-operative Publishing Company), cited *L.Ed.* and *L.Ed. 2d.*

3. Supreme Court Reporter (West Publishing Company), cited *Sup.Ct.* or *S.Ct.*

4. United States Law Week (Bureau of National Affairs), cited *U.S.L.W.* or *U.S.L. Week.*

5. United States Supreme Court Bulletin (Commerce Clearing House), cited *S.Ct.Bull. (CCH).*

[1] C. WRIGHT, THE LAW OF THE FEDERAL COURTS 1–8 (4th ed.1983).

[2] For a more detailed description of the federal court system, *see* HOUSE COMM. ON THE JUDICIARY, 92D CONG., 1ST SESS., THE UNITED STATES COURTS: THEIR JURISDICTION AND WORK, by J. Spaniol (Comm. Print 1975).

1. United States Reports (Official Edition)

Prior to 1827, the *United States Reports* were published by private reporters. Since that date they have been published by official reporters. The reports were cited by the name of the reporters from Dallas through Wallace. The seven early reporters, with their abbreviations, are as follows:

Dallas (Dall.)	4 v.	v.	1– 4 U.S.	(1789–1800)
Cranch (Cranch)	9 v.	v.	5–13 U.S.	(1801–1815)
Wheaton (Wheat.)	12 v.	v.	14–25 U.S.	(1816–1827)
Peters (Peters)	16 v.	v.	26–41 U.S.	(1828–1842)
Howard (How.)	24 v.	v.	42–65 U.S.	(1843–1860)
Black (Black)	2 v.	v.	66–67 U.S.	(1861–1862)
Wallace (Wall.)	23 v.	v.	68–90 U.S.	(1863–1874)

The first ninety volumes, from Dallas through Wallace, were later numbered consecutively and beginning with volume 91 (1875) this method of numbering was adopted. 1 Dallas, although a volume of the *U.S. Reports*, contains only Pennsylvania decisions. The other volumes of Dallas contain Supreme Court of the United States and Pennsylvania decisions.[3]

It is the custom of the Supreme Court of the United States to have one term of court each year. The term starts in October and ordinarily adjourns in June or July. This is known as the October Term. The opinions of the Supreme Court are printed and sold by the United States Government Printing Office. They are initially issued separately as *slip* opinions and then subsequently published in advance sheets (called preliminary prints). The Reporter of Decisions of the Supreme Court provides a summary of facts, syllabus, and an index. After the end of the October Term each year, the advance sheets are replaced by bound volumes. There are usually three or four volumes per term.

Sample pages of an opinion are shown in Illustration 5.

2. Supreme Court Reporter (West Edition)

This set is published by the West Publishing Company, and it contains many of the editorial features common to the company's other sets of law reports. These will be discussed in detail in Chapter 5. This edition begins with volume 106 (1882) of the official

---

[3] Keefe, *More Than You Want to Know About Supreme Court Reports*, 62 A.B. A.J. 1057 (1976). For a descriptive bibliography of the first ninety volumes of the United States Reports, *see* Cohen & Hamby, *A Bibliography of the Early Reports of the Supreme Court of the United States*, 1 LEGAL REFERENCE SERVICES Q. 43 (Summer/Fall 1981); for a listing of the opinions by individual justices, *see* L. BLANDFORD, SUPREME COURT OF THE UNITED STATES, 1789–1980: AN INDEX TO OPINIONS ARRANGED BY JUSTICE (1983). This two-volume set lists opinions from all justices from 1789 through the 1979 term.

set; therefore, it does not contain the cases reported in volumes 1–105 of the official reports. The full text of the opinions is reported with the publisher adding its own editorial features and headnotes. Decisions are first issued in advance sheets biweekly during the term of Court; after the adjournment of the Court, the advance sheets are replaced by two or more bound volumes containing all of the decisions of the term. As does the *Lawyers' Edition of the U.S. Supreme Court Reports*, the *Supreme Court Reporter* uses smaller print than the official *U.S. Reports* and usually contains the opinions of a term in two volumes.

Sample pages from the *Supreme Court Reporter* are shown in Illustration 6.

3. United States Supreme Court Reports, Lawyers' Edition

This set of the reports of the Supreme Court of the United States is privately published by the Lawyers Co-operative Publishing Company and the Bancroft-Whitney Company. It is presently in two series. The first series contains all of the opinions that appear in 1 U.S. through 349 U.S. The second series commences with 350 U.S. As this set uses smaller type than the official reports, the opinions for each term are in fewer volumes. For example, the 1976 term required five volumes for the *United States Reports*, but only two for the *Lawyers' Edition*. The opinions in it are exactly the same as the opinions that appear in the official edition. The difference lies in the editorial treatment given to the opinions by the publishers, who prepare their own summary of cases and headnotes which precede the opinions. Additionally, an appendix to each volume contains, for selected important cases only, summaries of attorneys' briefs submitted to the Court and annotations written by the editorial staff of the publishers. Annotations are articles or essays on significant legal issues discussed in the reported cases. These are very useful in gaining an understanding of the impact and meaning of the decisions. Annotations will be discussed in more detail in Chapter 7. A separate volume supplements the annotations in Volumes 1–31 of the *Lawyers' Edition*, Second Series. Starting with Volume 32 of the Second Series, each volume is provided with pocket supplementation in the back of the volume. Pocket supplementation is in three parts: (1) *Citator Service*, consisting of brief summaries of the pertinent holdings from Supreme Court opinions subsequent to those reported in the volume, (2) *Later Case Service*, supplementing the annotations in the volume, and (3) *Court Corrections*, consisting of any corrections made by justices of the Supreme Court after the volume was printed.

In 1978, a *Desk-Book to the United States Supreme Court Reports, Lawyers' Edition*, was published. This volume contains (1)

a Table of Cases for all full decisions found in volumes 1–49 of *L.Ed. 2d*, (2) a Table of Justices of the Supreme Court of the United States since 1789, and (3) an index to all annotations in *L.Ed.2d* or in *ALR Federal*. An annual supplement is issued.

Current decisions are issued biweekly in advance sheets during the course of each term. The pagination of the advance sheets is the same as in subsequent bound volumes, but they do not contain annotations.

Sample pages from the *United States Supreme Court Reports, Lawyers' Edition* are shown in Illustration 7.

4. Other Publications

As the decisions of the Supreme Court of the United States become the *law of the land* and must be followed as precedent by all other American courts, both federal and state, it is rather obvious that lawyers, as well as lay persons, have a need for immediate access to the current decisions of the Supreme Court of the United States. Before opinions can be published in the advance sheets of the sets mentioned above, they must receive editorial treatment such as preparation of the summary and the headnotes, resulting in a delay of several weeks from the date a decision is rendered until it appears in advance sheets.

More rapid access to current Supreme Court of the United States decisions is available through one of the two following publications. Each receives the slip decisions on the day they are handed down, photocopies them, and mails them weekly to its subscribers. These sets of Supreme Court opinions have few editorial features added to them, but they do allow opinions to become available within a week after they have been released by the Supreme Court.

a. *United States Law Week.* This is published in two or more looseleaf volumes by the Bureau of National Affairs, Inc., in Washington, D.C. Volume One contains the Supreme Court of the United States opinions in complete text and is in looseleaf form. In addition to the current opinions, this volume contains the following features:

(1) Summary of Orders: This is a summary of cases finally acted upon as well as the lower court holdings that the Supreme Court consented to review with the questions presented for review.

(2) Journal of Proceedings: This contains the minutes of all sessions of the Court held during the week.

(3) Cases Docketed: This includes citations to opinions in the lower court, and the general subject matter of the case.

(4) Summary of Cases Recently Filed.

(5) Arguments Before the Court: A summary of the oral arguments of the more important cases argued each week.

(6) Table of Cases and the Case Status Report: Issued every three to four weeks. For most cases the user can determine the current status of a case by consulting this table.

(7) Topical Index: Issued seven times annually.

Volume Two deals with other matters not connected with the Supreme Court of the United States.

b. *Commerce Clearing House Supreme Court Bulletin.* This set is also in looseleaf format. In addition to photocopies of the current opinions, it includes an index to opinions, an index to docket numbers and a status table of cases pending before the Court.

5. Chamber Opinions of Supreme Court Justices

Each Supreme Court Justice is assigned at the beginning of each term the supervision of one or more federal judicial circuits. Frequently, when the Supreme Court is not in session, a petition may be directed to a Justice in his capacity as Circuit Justice. When an opinion is written on this, it is known as a *Chamber Opinion.* Before the 1970 Term, these chamber opinions appeared only in *Lawyers' Edition* and the *Supreme Court Reporter.* Starting with the 1970 Term, they also appear in the official *United States Reports.*[4]

6. Summary of United States Supreme Court Reports

The opinions of the Supreme Court of the United States are published in three sets: the official *United States Reports,* the *United States Supreme Court Reports, Lawyers' Edition,* and the *Supreme Court Reporter.* Each set first publishes the opinions in advance sheets. As proper citation practice calls for only citing to *United States Reports,* the two unofficial sets which have their own distinct pagination also show the pagination of the official reports so that the proper citation can be made to the *United States Reports.* This is sometimes denoted as *star-pagination.* [See Illustration 7–b.] Both the *Lawyers' Edition* and the *Supreme Court Reporter* have in each volume a cross-reference table listing the cases in the *United States Reports* and showing where they are reported in their volumes.

As the United States Government Printing Office is much slower in publishing its advance sheets, and as the two unofficial sets have editorial features facilitating their use, most lawyers and researchers prefer using them to the *United States Reports.*

[4] R. STERN & E. GRESSMAN, SUPREME COURT PRACTICE 811–913 (5th ed. 1978); Wiener, *Opinions of Justices Sitting in Chambers,* 49 LAW LIB.J. 2 (1956); Boner, *Index to Chambers Opinions of Supreme Court Justices,* 65 LAW LIB.J. 213 (1972).

United States Law Week and the *Commerce Clearing House Supreme Court Bulletin* are most useful for use during the current term of the Court. For older decisions, it is preferable to use one of the three other sets.

SECTION B. LOWER FEDERAL COURT REPORTS

Although the Supreme Court of the United States is the highest court in the country, it deals with only a small fraction of the total litigation within the federal court system. With certain exceptions, the Supreme Court selects only the cases it wishes to hear on appeal,[5] and these are relatively few in number. The bulk of the work of the federal courts occurs in the trial courts—the federal district courts— and in the appeals from them to the United States courts of appeals. These are divided geographically into twelve circuits, plus the United States Court of Appeals for the Federal Circuit.

In addition, there are federal courts with limited or specialized jurisdictions. The more important of these are the United States Claims Court, the United States Court of Appeals for the Federal Circuit (mentioned above),[6] and the United States Tax Court.[7]

1. Privately Published Editions of Lower Federal Court Reports

a. *Federal Cases.* Prior to 1880, the decisions of the district courts and the circuit courts of appeals were published in many different sets of law reports. In 1880, the West Publishing Company reprinted all of the previously reported lower federal court decisions in one set of 31 volumes called *Federal Cases.* This set contains 18,000 cases reported between 1789 and 1879. Unlike most sets of court reports, where the cases are arranged chronologically, the decisions in this set are arranged alphabetically by name of case and are numbered consecutively. Volume 31 is the Digest volume, and includes Blue Tables which cross-reference from the citations of the original volumes of reports to *Federal Cases.*

b. *Federal Reporter.* This set is published by the West Publishing Company and started in 1880. Until 1932 it included opinions from the courts of appeals and the federal district courts. The *Federal Reporter* consists of two series. The First Series stopped with Volume 300 and the Second Series started numbering anew from Volume 1. This scheme of starting a new series for the numbering

---

[5] Technically, cases reach the Supreme Court either by writ of certiorari or by appeal. *See* R. STERN & E. GRESSMAN, *supra* note 4, at Chapters 2 & 3.

[6] This Court was created by Public Law 97–164, 96 Stat. 25, effective on October 1, 1982. This Court is a merger of the Court of U.S. Customs and Patent Appeals and the appellate division of the U.S. Court of Claims.

[7] For a more detailed description of specialized federal courts, *see* HOUSE COMM. ON THE JUDICIARY, *supra* note 2.

of court reports is a common one, as it serves to avoid long and unmanageable numbers.

Until recently, nearly all written opinions of the courts of appeals were published in the *Federal Reporter*. The increasing caseload placed on the courts, however, has caused reconsideration of this practice,[8] and all circuits have now adopted rules restricting the number of published opinions.[9]

In order to let researchers know which cases were decided without written published opinions, most of the courts of appeals from time to time publish in the *Federal Reporter* a list of *Decisions without Published Opinions*. [See Illustration 8.]

The *Federal Reporter* contained the decisions of the United States Court of Patent Appeals, beginning with Volume 34 of the Second Series, until the court was abolished October 1, 1982.[10] The function of the court, as well as that of the appellate division of the former United States Court of Claims, has been transferred to the United States Court of Appeals for the Federal Circuit, whose opinions are included in the *Federal Reporter*. Also included in it are the decisions of the Temporary Emergency Court of Appeals.

    c. *Federal Supplement*. This set started publication in 1932 and is also published by the West Publishing Company. It contains selected opinions of the federal district courts. As these courts are the trial courts within the federal court system, they are exceptions to the general rule that only appellate court opinions are reported. It must be emphasized, however, that only a very small percentage of the cases heard in the federal district courts are ever reported in the *Federal Supplement*. The decision on whether or not to publish is determined by the judge writing the opinion. However, many cases not published in the *Federal Supplement* may be published in the subject reporters of other publishers. These will be discussed in Chapter 13. Additionally, some unreported cases may be located in the databases of LEXIS or WESTLAW, computerized legal retrieval services. These will be covered in Chapter 20.

From Volume 1 to Volume 181 the *Federal Supplement* contained the decisions of the United States Court of Claims; and, in Volume 135, it began to include the decisions of the United States Customs Court (now the Court of International Trade). Also included

---

[8] NLRB v. Amalgamated Clothing Workers, 430 F.2d 966, 971 (5th Cir.1970).

[9] *Unreported Decisions in the United States Courts of Appeals*, 63 CORNELL L.REV. 128 (1977); Reynolds & Richman, *The Non-Precedential Precedent—Limited Publication and No-Citation Rules in the United States Courts of Appeals*, 78 COLUMB.L.REV. 1167 (1978); Reynolds & Richman, *An Evaluation of Limited Publication in the United States Courts of Appeals: The Price of Reform*, 48 U.CHI.L.REV. 573 (1981).

[10] *See* note 6 *supra*.

are the decisions of the Special Court of the Regional Rail Reorganization Act and the rulings of the Judicial Panel on Multidistrict Litigation.

Since 1880 there have not been any officially published sets of reports for the federal courts of appeals and the federal district courts. The *Federal Reporter* and the *Federal Supplement* are relied on for these reports. Both of these sets are first issued in advance sheets and subsequently replaced by bound volumes.

d. *Federal Rules Decisions.* This set is discussed in Chapter 12, Jacobstein and Mersky, *Fundamentals of Legal Research*, 3rd ed. (1985).

e. *United States Claims Court Reporter.* This set, by the West Publishing Company, began publication in 1983 and contains the decisions of the United States Claims Court, a trial-level federal court created in 1982. It also includes reprints from the *Federal Reporter* and the *Supreme Court Reporter* of those cases which have reviewed decisions of the United States Claims Court. It is issued first in advance sheets and then in bound volumes.

2. Officially Published Reports of Special Federal Courts

Cases decided in the Court of Claims. Washington, Government Printing Office, 1863–1982. v. 1–231.

U.S. Court of International Trade. Reports. v. 1 et seq., 1980 to date. (This court was formerly the United States Customs Court, and its decisions were reported in U.S. Customs Court Reports, v. 1–85, 1938–1980.)

Tax Court of the United States. Reports. Washington, Government Printing Office, Oct. 1942 to date. v. 1 et seq. (now the United States Tax Court).

SECTION C. ILLUSTRATIONS

The opinion of *Board of Education v. Pico* [457 U.S. 853, 102 S.Ct. 2799, 73 L.Ed.2d 435] as it is published in:

5. **Advance Sheets (Preliminary Print) of the U.S. Reports (Official)**

6. **Volume 102 of the Supreme Court Reporter (West Publishing Company)**

7. **Volume 73 of the Lawyers' Edition of the United States Supreme Court Reports, 2d Series (Lawyers Co-operative Publishing Company)**

8. **Page from 722 Federal Reporter, 2d Series**

[Illustration 5]

BOARD OF EDUCATION v. PICO AS REPORTED IN THE ADVANCE SHEETS OF THE UNITED STATES REPORTS

BOARD OF EDUCATION *v.* PICO 853

Syllabus

BOARD OF EDUCATION, ISLAND TREES UNION FREE SCHOOL DISTRICT NO. 26, ET AL. *v.* PICO, BY HIS NEXT FRIEND, PICO, ET AL.

CERTIORARI TO THE UNITED STATES COURT OF APPEALS FOR THE SECOND CIRCUIT

No. 80–2043.   Argued March 2, 1982—Decided June 25, 1982

Petitioner Board of Education, rejecting recommendations of a committee of parents and school staff that it had appointed, ordered that certain books, which the Board characterized as "anti-American, anti-Christian, anti-Sem[i]tic, and just plain filthy," be removed from high school and junior high school libraries.   Respondent students then brought this action for declaratory and injunctive relief under 42 U. S. C. § 1983 against the Board and petitioner Board members, alleging that the Board's actions had denied respondents their rights under the First Amendment. The District Court granted summary judgment in petitioners' favor. The Court of Appeals reversed and remanded for a trial on the merits of respondents' allegations.

Held: The judgment is affirmed.

638 F. 2d 404, affirmed.

   JUSTICE BRENNAN, joined by JUSTICE MARSHALL and JUSTICE STEVENS, concluded:

   1. The First Amendment imposes limitations upon a local school board's exercise of its discretion to remove books from high school and junior high school libraries.   Pp. 863–872.

   (a) Local school boards have broad discretion in the management of school affairs, but such discretion must be exercised in a manner that comports with the transcendent imperatives of the First Amendment.

> This page is taken from the Advance Sheets to the U.S. Reports.   As customary, indication is given to the court from which the case is being appealed.
>
>   Note that docket number, date of argument, and date of decision are also given.

   (b) While petitioners might rightfully claim absolute discretion in matters of *curriculum* by reliance upon their duty to inculcate community values in schools, petitioners' reliance upon that duty is misplaced

[Illustration 5–a]

SAMPLE PAGE FROM 457 U.S.

854   OCTOBER TERM, 1981

Syllabus   457 U. S.

where they attempt to extend their claim of absolute discretion beyond the compulsory environment of the classroom into the school library and the regime of voluntary inquiry that there holds sway.   P. 869.

(c) Petitioners possess significant discretion to determine the content of their school libraries, but that discretion may not be exercised in a narrowly partisan or political manner.   Whether petitioners' removal of books from the libraries denied respondents their First Amendment rights depends upon the motivation behind petitioners' actions.   Local school boards may not remove books from school libraries simply because they dislike the ideas contained in those books and seek by their removal to "prescribe what shall be orthodox in politics, nationalism, religion, or other matters of opinion." *West Virginia Board of Education v. Barnette*, 319 U. S. 624, 642.   If such an intention was the decisive factor in petitioners' decision, then petitioners have exercised their discretion in violation of the Constitution.   Pp. 869–872.

Each opinion is preceded by a summary and syllabus prepared by the Reporter of Decisions.

---

from their school libraries.   Respondents' allegations, and some of the evidentiary materials before the District Court, also fail to exclude the possibility that petitioners' removal procedures were highly irregular and ad hoc—the antithesis of those procedures that might tend to allay suspicions regarding petitioners' motivation.   Pp. 872–875.

JUSTICE BLACKMUN concluded that a proper balance between the limited constitutional restriction imposed on school officials by the First Amendment and the broad state authority to regulate education, would be struck by holding that school officials may not remove books from school libraries for the *purpose* of restricting access to the political ideas or social perspectives discussed in the books, when that action is motivated simply by the officials' disapproval of the ideas involved.   Pp. 879–882.

JUSTICE WHITE, while agreeing that there should be a trial to resolve the factual issues, concluded that there is no necessity at this point for discussing the extent to which the First Amendment limits the school board's discretion to remove books from the school libraries.   Pp. 883–884.

BRENNAN, J., announced the judgment of the Court and delivered an opinion, in which MARSHALL and STEVENS, JJ., joined and in all but Part II–A(1) of which BLACKMUN, J., joined.   BLACKMUN, J., filed an opinion concurring in part and concurring in the judgment, *post*, p. 875.   WHITE, J., filed an opinion concurring in the judgment, *post*, p. 883.   BURGER, C. J., filed a

[Illustration 5–b]

SAMPLE PAGE FROM 457 U.S.

BOARD OF EDUCATION *v.* PICO   855

853   Opinion of BRENNAN, J.

dissenting opinion, in which POWELL, REHNQUIST, and O'CONNOR, JJ., joined, *post*, p. 885. POWELL, J., filed a dissenting opinion, *post*, p. 893. REHNQUIST, J., filed a dissenting opinion, in which BURGER, C. J., and POWELL, J., joined, *post*, p. 904. O'CONNOR, J., filed a dissenting opinion, *post*, p. 921.

George W. Lipp, Jr., argued the cause for petitioners. With him on the briefs was *David S. J. Rubin.*

Alan H. Levine argued the cause for respondents. With him on the brief were *Steven R. Shapiro, Burt Neuborne, Alan Azzara, Bruce J. Ennis, Jr.,* and *Charles S. Sims.* *

JUSTICE BRENNAN announced the judgment of the Court and delivered an opinion, in which JUSTICE MARSHALL and JUSTICE STEVENS joined, and in which JUSTICE BLACKMUN joined except for Part II–A–(1).

The principal question presented is whether the First Amendment [1] imposes limitations upon the exercise by a local

---

*Briefs of *amici curiae* urging reversal were filed by *Bruce A. Taylor* for Charles H. Keating, Jr., et al.; and by *David Crump* for the Legal Foundation of America.

The third page of the Pico opinion. Note the indication as to which Justice wrote the opinion, which Justices agreed with the opinion, and which dissented.

Note also how the names of the attorneys who were involved in the case before the Supreme Court are given.

James R. Sandner, Jeffrey S. Karp, and *Elizabeth A. Truly* for New York State United Teachers; and by *Jerry Simon Chasen* and *Marcia B. Paul* for P. E. N. American Center.

Briefs of *amici curiae* were filed by *Nathan Z. Dershowitz* and *Edward Labaton* for the American Jewish Congress et al.; and by *Whitney North Seymour, Jr.,* and *Martha L. Wolfe* for the Long Island Library Association Coalition.

[1] The Amendment provides in pertinent part that "Congress shall make no law . . . abridging the freedom of speech, or of the press." It applies to

[Illustration 5–c]

SAMPLE PAGE FROM 457 U.S.

BOARD OF EDUCATION *v.* PICO   885

853   BURGER, C. J., dissenting

CHIEF JUSTICE BURGER, with whom JUSTICE POWELL, JUSTICE REHNQUIST, and JUSTICE O'CONNOR join, dissenting.

The First Amendment, as with other parts of the Constitution, must deal with new problems in a changing world.   In an attempt to deal with a problem in an area traditionally left

---

First page of the dissenting opinion.

---

ing what books are to be in the school library is subject to federal-court review.[1] Were this to become the law, this Court would come perilously close to becoming a "super censor" of school board library decisions.   Stripped to its essentials, the issue comes down to two important propositions: *first*, whether local schools are to be administered by elected school boards, or by federal judges and teenage pupils; and *second*, whether the values of morality, good taste, and relevance to education are valid reasons for school board decisions concerning the contents of a school library.   In an attempt to place this case within the protection of the First Amendment, the plurality suggests a new "right" that, when shorn of the plurality's rhetoric, allows this Court to impose

---

[1] At the outset, the plurality notes that certain school board members found the books in question "objectionable" and "improper" for junior and senior high school students.   What the plurality apparently finds objectionable is that the inquiry as to the challenged books was initially stimulated by what is characterized as "a politically conservative organization of parents concerned about education," which had concluded that the books in question were "improper fare for school students." *Ante*, at 856.   As noted by the District Court, however, and in the plurality opinion, *ante*, at 859, both parties substantially agreed about the motivation of the school board in removing the books:

"[T]he board acted not on religious principles but on its conservative educational philosophy, and on its belief that the nine books removed from the school library and curriculum were irrelevant, vulgar, immoral, and in bad taste, making them educationally unsuitable for the district's junior and senior high school students."   474 F. Supp. 387, 392 (1979).

[Illustration 6]

BOARD OF EDUCATION v. PICO AS REPORTED IN 102 S.Ct.

BOARD OF EDUC., ISLAND TREES, ETC. v. PICO   2799
Cite as 102 S.Ct. 2799 (1932)

way connected with the statutory review structure set forth above [14], then there is no

> The first page of the Pico opinion as it appears in the Supreme Court Reporter, an unofficial set published by the West Publishing Company. The summary is prepared by its editors.

plain, and because this renders petitioners state actors for purposes of the Fourteenth Amendment, I dissent.

BOARD OF EDUCATION, ISLAND TREES UNION FREE SCHOOL DISTRICT NO. 26 et al., Petitioners,

v.

Steven A. PICO, by his next friend, Frances Pico et al.

No. 80–2043.

Argued March 2, 1982.

Decided June 25, 1982.

An action was brought seeking declaratory and injunctive relief with respect to removal by defendant board of education of certain books from school libraries. The United States District Court for the East-

ern District of New York, 474 F.Supp. 387, granted summary judgment in favor of defendants, and plaintiffs appealed. The United States Court of Appeals for the Second Circuit, 638 F.2d 404, reversed and remanded for trial, and certiorari was granted. The Supreme Court, Justice Brennan, held that: (1) local school boards may not remove books from school library shelves simply because they dislike the ideas contained in those books and seek by their removal to prescribe what shall be orthodox in politics, nationalism, religion or other matters of opinion, and (2) issues of fact precluding summary judgment existed as to whether school board exceeded constitutional limitations in exercising its discretion to remove the books from the school libraries.

Court of Appeals affirmed.

Justice Blackmun filed opinion concurring in part and concurring in the judgment.

Justice White filed opinion concurring in the judgment.

Chief Justice Burger, with whom Justice Powell, Justice Rehnquist and Justice O'Connor joined, filed a dissenting opinion.

Justice Powell and Justice O'Connor filed dissenting opinions.

Justice Rehnquist, with whom Chief Justice Burger and Justice Powell joined, filed a dissenting opinion.

1. Schools ⟫164

Local school boards must be permitted to establish and apply their curriculum in

14. The issue presented in this case—the issue that the Court decides presents a live controversy—concerns *facility-initiated* discharges or transfers. See *ante*, at 2784. Transfers initiated by the Utilization Review Committee are within the terms of the consent decree entered by the District Court below, and are not before the Court today. These transfers even more clearly show the State's hand in the transfer decision—indeed, it appears that the physicians on the Committees are reimbursed for their services by Medicaid. But there is absolutely no basis upon which to conclude that that decision to transfer a patient to a lower level of care can be made in any meaningful way inde-

pendent of the state regulatory standards described in text. Of course, we might hypothesize a decision of the resident's personal physician, not premised on the State's view of what constitutes an appropriate level-of-care for the patient, to remove the patient from the particular facility. In these circumstances, I would agree that the nursing home owner, in simply responding to the personal physician's request, is not a state actor. But it appears to me that the Court's decision sweeps more broadly than that, and clearly reaches transfers based directly upon and arising from the State's procedures and standards.

[Illustration 6–a]

SAMPLE PAGE FROM 102 S.Ct.

2800   **102 SUPREME COURT REPORTER**

such a way as to transmit community values, and there is legitimate and substantial community interest in promoting respect for authority and traditional values, be they social, moral or political. (Per Justice Brennan with two Justices concurring and two Justices concurring in the judgment.)

2. Constitutional Law ⟺82(12)

Discretion of state and local school boards in matters of education must be exercised in a manner that comports with the transcendent imperatives of the First Amendment. (Per Justice Brennan with two Justices concurring and two Justices concurring in the judgment.) U.S.C.A. Const.Amend. 1.

3. Constitutional Law ⟺82(12)

First Amendment rights, applied in the light of the special characteristics of the school environment, are available to students. (Per Justice Brennan with two Justices concurring and two Justices concurring in the judgment.) U.S.C.A.Const. Amend. 1.

4. Schools ⟺11

Courts should not intervene in the resolution of conflicts which arise in the daily operations of school systems unless basic constitutional values are directly and sharply implicated in those conflicts. (Per Justice Brennan with two Justices concurring and two Justices concurring in the judgment.)

5. Constitutional Law ⟺90(1)

Right to receive information and ideas is inherent corollary of the rights of free speech and press that are explicitly guaranteed by the Constitution. (Per Justice Brennan with two Justices concurring and two Justices concurring in the judgment.) U.S.C.A.Const.Amend. 1.

> Eleven headnotes have been prepared by the Publisher's editorial staff.
>
> The significance of headnotes will be discussed in Chapter 6.

the First Amendment rights of students. (Per Justice Brennan with two Justices concurring and two Justices concurring in the judgment.) U.S.C.A.Const.Amend. 1.

7. Schools ⟺164

School board might well defend its claim of absolute discretion in matters of curriculum by reliance on duty to inculcate community values, but reliance on that duty is misplaced where board attempts to extend claim of absolute discretion beyond the compulsory environment of the classroom and into the school library and the regime of voluntary inquiry that there holds sway. (Per Justice Brennan with two Justices concurring and two Justices concurring in the judgment.)

8. Schools ⟺76

Board of education rightly possesses significant discretion to determine the contents of school libraries, but that discretion may not be exercised in a narrowly partisan or political manner. (Per Justice Brennan with three Justices concurring and one Justice concurring in the judgment.)

9. Constitutional Law ⟺90.1(1)

Whether removal of books from school libraries by board of education denied students First Amendment rights depends upon motivation behind the board's actions; if the board intended by removal decision to deny students access to ideas with which board members disagreed, and if this intent was the decisive factor in the decision, then the board has exercised its discretion in violation of the Constitution. (Per Justice Brennan with three Justices concurring and one Justice concurring in the judgment.) U.S.C.A.Const.Amend. 1.

10. Schools ⟺76

Local school boards may not remove books from school library shelves simply because they dislike the ideas contained in those books and seek by their removal to prescribe what shall be orthodox in politics, nationalism, religion or other matters of opinion. (Per Justice Brennan with three Justices concurring and one Justice concurring in the judgment.)

[Illustration 6–b]

SAMPLE PAGE FROM 102 S.Ct.

2802   **102 SUPREME COURT REPORTER**

tioners exceeded constitutional limitations in exercising their discretion to remove the books at issue from their school libraries. Respondents' allegations, and some of the evidentiary materials before the District Court, also fail to exclude the possibility that petitioners' removal procedures were highly irregular and ad hoc—the antithesis of those procedures that might tend to allay suspicions regarding petitioners' motivation. Pp. 2810–2812.

Justice BLACKMUN concluded that a proper balance between the limited constitutional restriction imposed on school officials by the First Amendment and the broad state authority to regulate education, would be struck by holding that school officials may not remove books from school libraries for the *purpose* of restricting access to the political ideas or social perspectives discussed in the books, when that ac-

> This page shows the end of the syllabus as it appeared in the official U.S. Reports. The majority, concurring and dissenting opinions are then set forth exactly as in the official reports.

from the school libraries. Pp. 2816–2817.

George W. Lipp, Jr., Babylon, N. Y., for petitioners.

Alan H. Levine, for respondents.

Justice BRENNAN announced the judgment of the Court, and delivered an opinion in which Justice MARSHALL and Justice STEVENS joined, and in which Justice BLACKMUN joined except for Part II–A–(1).

The principal question presented is whether the First Amendment[1] imposes

limitations upon the exercise by a local school board of its discretion to remove library books from high school and junior high school libraries.

I

Petitioners are the Board of Education of the Island Trees Union Free School District No. 26, in New York, and Richard Ahrens, Frank Martin, Christina Fasulo, Patrick Hughes, Richard Melchers, Richard Michaels, and Louis Nessim. When this suit was brought, Ahrens was the President of the Board, Martin was the Vice-President, and the remaining petitioners were Board members. The Board is a state agency charged with responsibility for the operation and administration of the public schools within the Island Trees School District, including the Island Trees High School and Island Trees Memorial Junior High School. Respondents are Steven Pico, Jacqueline Gold, Glenn Yarris, Russell Rieger, and Paul Sochinski. When this suit was brought, Pico, Gold, Yarris, and Rieger were students at the High School, and Sochinski was a student at the Junior High School.

In September 1975, petitioners Ahrens, Martin, and Hughes attended a conference sponsored by Parents of New York United (PONYU), a politically conservative organization of parents concerned about education legislation in the State of New York. At the conference these petitioners obtained lists of books described by Ahrens as "objectionable," App. 22, and by Martin as "improper fare for school students," *id.*, at 101.[2] It was later determined that the High School library contained nine of the listed books, and that another listed book was in

---

1. The Amendment provides in pertinent part that "Congress shall make no law ... abridging the freedom of speech, or of the press." It applies to the states by virtue of the Fourteenth Amendment. *Gitlow v. New York,* 268 U.S. 652, 666, 45 S.Ct. 625, 629, 69 L.Ed. 1138 (1925); *Grosjean v. American Press Co.,* 297

U.S. 233, 244, 56 S.Ct. 444, 446, 80 L.Ed. 660 (1936).

2. The District Court noted, however, that petitioners "concede that the books are not obscene." 474 F.Supp. 387, 392 (1979).

[Illustration 6–c]

SAMPLE PAGE FROM 102 S.Ct.

2812   **102 SUPREME COURT REPORTER**

that in making their removal decision petitioners ignored "the advice of literary experts," the views of "librarians and teachers within the Island Trees School system," the advice of the superintendent of schools, and the guidance of "publications that rate books for junior and senior high school students." App. 128–129. Respondents also claimed that petitioners' decision was based solely on the fact that the books were named on the PONYU list received by petitioners Ahrens, Martin, and Hughes, and that petitioners "did not undertake an independent review of other books in the [school] libraries." *Id.,* at 129–130. Evidence before the District Court lends support to these claims. The record shows that immediately after petitioners first ordered the books removed from the library shelves, the superintendent of schools reminded them that "we already have a policy . . . designed expressly to handle such problems," and recommended that the removal decision be approached through this established channel. See n. 4, *supra.* But the Board disregarded the superintendent's advice, and instead resorted to the extraordinary procedure of appointing a Book Review Committee—the advice of which was later rejected without explanation. In sum,

> **This is the last page of the majority opinion. All cases in the S.Ct. Reporter are exactly the same as in the official U.S. Reports. Only the editorial material preceding the majority opinion differs.**
>
> **Note, however, the smaller typeface. This allows the unofficial reports to reproduce cases of each term in fewer volumes.**

evidence plainly does not foreclose the possibility that petitioners' decision to remove the books rested decisively upon disagree-

U.S. 415, 433, 83 S.Ct. 328, 338, 9 L.Ed.2d 405 (1963); *Keyishian v. Board of Regents,* 385 U.S. 589, 603–604, 87 S.Ct. 675, 683–684, 17 L.Ed.2d 629 (1966); *Blount v. Rizzi,* 400 U.S. 410, 417, 91 S.Ct. 423, 428, 27 L.Ed.2d 498 (1971). In the case before us, the presence of

ment with constitutionally protected ideas in those books, or upon a desire on petitioners' part to impose upon the students of the Island Trees High School and Junior High School a political orthodoxy to which petitioners and their constituents adhered. Of course, some of the evidence before the District Court might lead a finder of fact to accept petitioners' claim that their removal decision was based upon constitutionally valid concerns. But that evidence at most creates a genuine issue of material fact on the critical question of the credibility of petitioners' justifications for their decision: On that issue, it simply cannot be said that there is no genuine issue as to any material fact.

The mandate shall issue forthwith.

Affirmed.

Justice BLACKMUN, concurring in part and concurring in the judgment.

While I agree with much in today's plurality opinion, and while I accept the standard laid down by the plurality to guide proceedings on remand, I write separately because I have a somewhat different perspective on the nature of the First Amendment right involved.

I

To my mind, this case presents a particularly complex problem because it involves two competing principles of constitutional stature. On the one hand, as the dissenting opinions demonstrate, and as we all can agree, the Court has acknowledged the importance of the public schools "in the preparation of individuals for participation as citizens, and in the preservation of values on which our society rests." *Ambach v. Norwick,* 441 U.S. 68, 76, 99 S.Ct. 1589, 1594, 60 L.Ed.2d 49 (1979). See, also, *ante,* at 2806–2807 (plurality opinion). Because

such sensitive tools in petitioners' decisionmaking process would naturally indicate a concern on their part for the First Amendment rights of respondents; the absence of such tools might suggest a lack of such concern. See 638 F.2d, at 416–417 (Opinion of Sifton, J.).

[Illustration 7]

BOARD OF EDUCATION v. PICO AS REPORTED IN 73 L.Ed.2d

[457 US 853]

BOARD OF EDUCATION, ISLAND TREES UNION FREE SCHOOL DISTRICT NO. 26 et al., Petitioners

v

STEVEN A. PICO, by his next friend, FRANCES PICO et al.

457 US 853, 73 L Ed 2d 435, 102 S Ct 2799

[No. 80–2043]

Argued March 2, 1982. Decided June 25, 1982.

Decision: Federal District Court's entry of summary judgment in case challenging local school board's removal of library books as violative of First Amendment, held erroneous where material issue of fact remained as to board's justifications.

SUMMARY

A local school board, characterizing a number of books as "anti-American, anti-Christian, anti-Semitic, and just plain filthy," directed their removal from the libraries of a district high school and junior high school. The board then appointed a committee of parents and members of the school staff to make recommendations about the books, but it substantially rejected the committee's recommendations in deciding that nine books should be re-moved from elementary and secondary school libraries and from use in the

First page of the Pico decision as it appears in the bound volume of L.Ed.2d.

Summary is prepared by the publisher's editorial staff.

Note the citations to the other two sets of reports of opinions of the U.S. Supreme Court.

removal of the books and that, although the removal was content-based, there was no constitutional violation of the requisite magnitude (474 F Supp 387). The United States Court of Appeals for the Second Circuit reversed the judgment of the District Court and remanded the action for a trial on the students' allegations (638 F2d 404).

SUBJECT OF ANNOTATION

Beginning on page 1466, infra

First Amendment rights of free speech and press as applied to public schools

Briefs of Counsel, p 1464, infra.

435

[Illustration 7–a]

SAMPLE PAGE FROM 73 L.Ed.2d

U.S. SUPREME COURT REPORTS   73 L Ed 2d

HEADNOTES

Classified to U.S. Supreme Court Digest, Lawyers' Edition

Constitutional Law § 941; Summary Judgment and Judgment on Pleadings § 5 — District Court determination — remaining issues of material fact — school board's removal of library books — First Amendment

1a-1d. A Federal District Court errs in entering summary judgment in favor of a local school board in an action under 42 USCS § 1983 alleging that the school board's removal of several books from the school district's libraries denied students their rights under the First Amendment, where there remains a genuine issue of material fact as to the board's justification for the removal of the books. [Per Brennan, Marshall, Stevens, Blackmun and White, JJ. Dissenting: Burger, Ch. J., and Powell, Rehnquist, and O'Connor, JJ.]

[See annotation p 1466, infra]

Constitutional Law § 941 — freedom of speech — students

2a-2c. Students do not shed their rights to freedom of speech or expression at the schoolhouse gate. [Per Brennan, J., Marshall, J., Stevens, J., Burger, Ch. J., Powell, J., Rehnquist, J., and O'Connor, J.]

[See annotation p 1466, infra]

SYLLABUS BY REPORTER OF DECISIONS

Petitioner Board of Education, reject-

The headnotes are prepared by the Publisher's editorial staff and differ from the headnotes in the Supreme Court Reporter.

L.Ed. also reprints the syllabus as it appears in the U.S. Reports.

---

the Board's actions had denied respondents their rights under the First Amendment. The District Court granted summary judgment in petitioners' favor. The Court of Appeals reversed and remanded for a trial on the merits of respondents' allegations.

Held: The judgment is affirmed.

638 F2d 404, affirmed.

Justice Brennan, joined by Justice Marshall and Justice Stevens, concluded:

1. The First Amendment imposes limitations upon a local school board's exercise of its discretion to remove books from high school and junior high school libraries.

(a) Local school boards have broad discretion in the management of school affairs, but such discretion must be exercised in a manner that comports with

the transcendent imperatives of the First Amendment. Students do not "shed their Constitutional rights to freedom of speech or expression at the schoolhouse gate," Tinker v Des Moines School Dist., 393 US 503, 506, 21 L Ed 2d 731, 89 S Ct 733, 49 Ohio Ops 2d 222, and such rights may be directly and sharply implicated by the removal of books from the shelves of a school library. While students' First Amendment rights must be construed "in light of the special characteristics of the school environment," ibid., the special characteristics of the school *library* make that environment especially appropriate for the recognition of such rights.

(b) While petitioners might rightfully claim absolute discretion in matters of *curriculum* by reliance upon their duty to inculcate community values in schools, petitioners' reliance upon that duty is misplaced where they attempt to extend their claim of absolute discretion beyond the compulsory environment of the classroom into the school library and the regime of voluntary inquiry that there holds sway.

(c) Petitioners possess significant discretion to determine the content of their school libraries, but that discretion may not be exercised in a narrowly partisan or political manner. Whether petitioners'

[Illustration 7–b]

SAMPLE PAGE FROM 73 L.Ed.2d

U.S. SUPREME COURT REPORTS   73 L Ed 2d

shelves, the Superintendent of Schools reminded them that "we already have a policy . . . designed expressly

→ [457 US 875]

to handle such problems," and recommended that the removal decision be approached through this established channel. See n 4, supra. But the Board disregarded the Superintendent's advice, and instead resorted to the extraordinary procedure of appointing a Book Review Committee—the advice of which was later rejected without explanation. In sum, respondents' allegations and some of the evidentiary materials presented below do not rule out the possibility that petitioners' removal procedures were highly irregular and ad hoc—the antithesis of those procedures that might tend to allay suspicions regarding petitioners' motivations.

The last page of the majority opinion.

Note the references to the pages of the U.S. Reports. These cross-references are also given in the bound volumes of the Supreme Court Reporter.

---

stitutionally protected ideas in those books, or upon a desire on petitioners' part to impose upon the students of the Island Trees High School and Junior High School a political orthodoxy to which petitioners and their constituents adhered. Of course, some of the evidence before the District Court might lead a finder of fact to accept petitioners' claim that their removal decision was based upon constitutionally valid concerns. But that evidence at most creates a genuine issue of material fact on the critical question of the credibility of petitioners'

justifications for their decision: On that issue, it simply cannot be said that there is no genuine issue as to any material fact.

The mandate shall issue forthwith.

Affirmed.

Justice **Blackmun,** concurring in part and concurring in the judgment.

[1c] While I agree with much in today's plurality opinion, and while I accept the standard laid down by the plurality to

[457 US 876] ◄

guide proceedings on remand, I write separately because I have a somewhat different perspective on the nature of the First Amendment right involved.

I

To my mind, this case presents a particularly complex problem because it involves two competing principles of constitutional stature. On the one hand, as the dissenting opinions demonstrate, and as we all can agree, the Court has acknowledged the importance of the public schools "in the preparation of individuals for participation as citizens, and in the preservation of the values on which our society rests." Ambach v Norwick, 441 US 68, 76, 60 L Ed 2d 49, 99 S Ct 1589 (1979). See, also, ante, at 863–864, 73 L Ed 2d, at 444–445 (plurality opinion). Because of the essential socializing function of schools, local education officials may attempt "to promote civic virtues," Ambach v Norwick, 441 US, at 80, 60 L Ed 2d 49, 99 S Ct 1589, and to "awake[n] the child to cultural values." Brown v Board of Education, 347 US 483, 493, 98 L Ed 873, 74 S Ct 686, 53 Ohio Ops 326, 38 ALR2d 1180 (1954). Indeed, the Constitution presupposes the ex-

[Illustration 7–c]

FIRST PAGE OF ANNOTATION FOR BOARD OF EDUCATION v. PICO

BOARD OF EDUCATION v PICO
Reported p 435, supra
ANNOTATION

FIRST AMENDMENT RIGHTS OF FREE SPEECH AND PRESS AS APPLIED TO PUBLIC SCHOOLS—SUPREME COURT CASES

by

Kenneth May, J.D.

I. PRELIMINARY MATTERS

§ 1. Introduction:
    [a] Scope
    [b] Related matters
    [c] Constitutional provision
§ 2. Summary

II. FIRST AMENDMENT PRINCIPLES AS APPLIED TO PUBLIC SCHOOLS, GENERALLY

§ 3. Violations of academic freedom
§ 4. Demonstrators on or near school grounds
§ 5. First Amendment interests as balanced against interest of local self-government represented by local school boards

III. FIRST AMENDMENT PRINCIPLES AS APPLIED TO PUBLIC SCHOOL TEACHERS

§ 6. Generally

    Lawyers' Edition of the U.S. Supreme Court Reports includes in its bound volumes annotations on selected cases which bring together and analyze previous Supreme Court cases on a particular topic. Annotations are explained in more detail in Chapter 7.

[Illustration 7–d]

SAMPLE PAGE OF ANNOTATION FOR 73 L.Ed.2d 435

§ 2   BOARD OF EDUCATION v PICO
Reported p 435, supra

reason to anticipate that the wearing of the armband would substantially interfere with the work of the school or impinge upon the rights of other students (§ 13, infra). On the other hand, the court, in a case dealing with demonstrators near a school who were not all students, held that a municipal antinoise ordinance, which prohibited disturbing the school session by willfully making a noise while on adjacent public or private grounds, was neither unconstitutionally vague nor unconstitutionally overbroad in restricting First Amendment freedoms (§ 4, infra). The court, in another case, upheld a nonstudent's right to picket a school on equal protection grounds, and noted that because picketing involves expressive conduct within the protection of the First Amendment, discrimination among pickets must be tailored to serve a substantial governmental interest. The court noted that the First Amendment means that government has no power to restrict expression because of its message, its ideas, its subject matter, or its content, but that reasonable time, place, and manner regulations of picketing may be necessary to further significant governmental interests (§ 4, infra).

II. First Amendment principles as applied to public schools, generally

§ 3. Violations of academic freedom

The Supreme Court has stated that the First Amendment does not tolerate laws that cast a pall of orthodoxy over the classroom.

In Epperson v Arkansas (1968) 393 US 97, 21 L Ed 2d 228, 89 S Ct 266, the court stated that the First Amendment does not tolerate laws that cast a pall of orthodoxy over the classroom. The case dealt with a public school biology teacher in Arkansas, faced with the dilemma that if she used a new textbook she would presumably teach a chapter therein on the Darwinian theory of evolution and thus would be subject to dismissal for committing a criminal offense in violation of an Arkansas statute prohibiting any teacher in the state schools from teaching that theory. She instituted an action in state court seeking a decla-

ration that the statute was void and enjoining the state officials from dismissing her for violating the statute. A parent of children attending the public schools intervened in support of her action. The Supreme Court of Arkansas sustained the statute as an exercise of the state's power to specify the curriculum in public schools. On appeal, the United States Supreme Court reversed, holding that the statute was contrary to the mandate of the First Amendment as conflicting with the constitutional prohibition of state laws respecting an establishment of religion or prohibiting the free exercise thereof.

☆ COMMENT: The court in Keyishian v Board of Regents (1967) 385 US 589, 17 L Ed 2d 629, 87 S Ct 675, a college case cited in Epperson v Arkansas (1968) 393 US 97, 21 L Ed 2d 228, 89 S Ct 266, stated that academic freedom is a special concern of the First Amendment, which does not tolerate laws that cast a pall of orthodoxy over the classroom. The court noted that the classroom is peculiarly the marketplace of ideas and that the nation's future depends upon leaders trained through wide exposure to that robust exchange of ideas which discovers truth out of a multitude of tongues, rather than through any kind of authoritative selection.

◆

In Meyer v Nebraska (1923) 262 US 390, 67 L Ed 1042, 43 S Ct 625, the court struck down a state law which forbade the teaching of foreign languages in public or private schools prior to the completion of eighth grade as a violation of the liberty guaranteed by the Fourteenth Amendment. In the course of the opinion, the court noted that the state "may do much, go very far, indeed, in order to improve the quality of its citizens, physically, mentally, and morally," but the individual has certain fundamental rights which must be respected. The protection of the Constitution extends to all, the court noted, including those who speak other languages as well as to those born with "English on the tongue." Perhaps, the court stated, it would be highly

[Illustration 8]

PAGE FROM 722 FEDERAL REPORTER, 2d SERIES

DECISIONS WITHOUT PUBLISHED OPINIONS   **727**

UNITED STATES COURT OF APPEALS

Second Circuit

DECISIONS WITHOUT PUBLISHED OPINIONS

Title	Docket Number	Date	Disposition	Appeal from and Citation (if reported)
Abraham v. Bender	82–7712	2/8/83	AFFIRMED	D.Conn.
Anselmo v. Mecca & Son Trucking Corp.	82–7778	2/18/83	AFFIRMED	E.D.N.Y.
Barbarosa v. Anagel Dilgence Ship Inc.	82–7755	2/25/83	AFFIRMED	S.D.N.Y.
Batista v. U.S.	82–6216	2/28/83	AFFIRMED	S.D.N.Y.
Bende and Sons, Inc. v. Crown Recreation, Inc., Kiffe Products Div.	82–7793	2/18/83	AFFIRMED	E.D.N.Y., 548 F.Supp. 1018
Bigg v. U.S. Army	82–6158	2/18/83	AFFIRMED	E.D.N.Y.
Capobianco v. Brink's Inc.	82–7647	2/14/83	AFFIRMED	E.D.N.Y., 543 F.Supp. 971
Christenson v. Headley	82–2289	2/18/83	AFFIRMED	S.D.N.Y.
Clementi v. Scully	81–2393	2/8/83	AFFIRMED	S.D.N.Y.
Connecticut State Employees Ass'n (CSEA) v. State of Conn.	82–7801	2/10/83	AFFIRMED	D.Conn.
Conte v. C.I.R.	82–4110	2/10/83	AFFIRMED	U.S.T.C.
Corbett v. M.S.P.B.	81–4169	2/7/83	PETITION FOR REVIEW DENIED	M.S.P.B.
Desvaux v. Farrell Lines, Inc. ...	82–7705	2/24/83	AFFIRMED	S.D.N.Y.

> **A chart illustrating how cases without published opinions decided in a Federal Court of Appeals are reported in the Federal Reporter.**

Title	Docket Number	Date	Disposition	Appeal from and Citation (if reported)
Authority	82–7378	2/2/83	AFFIRMED	E.D.N.Y.
Eng v. Coughlin	83–3005	2/2/83	MANDAMUS DENIED	W.D.N.Y.
Engel v. New York State Human Rights Appeal Bd.	82–7571	2/24/83	AFFIRMED	N.D.N.Y.
Forman v. International Harvester Co.	82–7414	2/8/83	AFFIRMED	N.D.N.Y.
Foster v. Harris	82–2298	2/17/83	AFFIRMED	S.D.N.Y.
General Establishment For Cereal Processing and Trade v. Gemini Shipping, Inc.	82–7781	2/10/83	AFFIRMED	S.D.N.Y.
Gorjan v. U.S. Dept. of Commerce	82–6014	2/18/83	AFFIRMED	E.D.N.Y.
Greene v. Edwards	82–7343	2/8/83	AFFIRMED	E.D.N.Y.
Harris v. Quinlan	82–2282	2/17/83	AFFIRMED	S.D.N.Y.
Hiss v. U.S.	82–6196	2/16/83	AFFIRMED	S.D.N.Y., 542 F.Supp. 973

Chapter 5

STATE COURT DECISIONS AND THE NATIONAL REPORTER SYSTEM

SECTION A. STATE COURT REPORTS

As has been indicated previously, the laws of the several states generally provide for the method of publishing state court decisions. Opinions published in accordance with such legislation are called *official* reports. [See Illustration 2.] Private companies also publish judicial decisions, with or without legislative directives. The private publications that are not legislatively endorsed are called *unofficial* reports, although they are no less accurate than the official reports. The unofficial reports may duplicate official reports or may be the only source of publication. The unofficial reports fall into three categories. The first consists of those sets that were or are published to compete directly with the officially published state reports. These reports are published chronologically as issued and usually have more useful editorial features and faster publication than the official reports. In most states, the unofficial sets are units of the *National Reporter System*, which is discussed later in this chapter. The other two categories are annotated reports and special or subject reports. These will be discussed in subsequent chapters.

At one time, all states published their judicial decisions in bound volumes of reports such as the *Michigan Reports*.[1] Those states having intermediate courts of appeals [2] may also have separately bound sets of reports, such as the *Illinois Appellate Reports*. The decisions are published chronologically by terms of court. An increasing number of states, however, have discontinued publishing

[1] For additional references to early law reporting in America *see*:

1. C. EVANS, AMERICAN BIBLIOGRAPHY vols. I, II, III (1893).

2. I. THOMAS, HISTORY OF PRINTING IN AMERICA vol. VI (1874).

3. AMERICAN ANTIQUARIAN SOCIETY, PROCEEDINGS (1874).

4. C. WARREN, HISTORY OF THE HARVARD LAW SCHOOL AND OF EARLY LEGAL CONDITIONS IN AMERICA vol. I., Ch. X (1908).

5. CONNECTICUT ACTS AND LAWS 1784, at 267.

6. M. CHAPMAN, BIBLIOGRAPHICAL INDEX TO THE STATE REPORTS PRIOR TO THE NATIONAL REPORTER SYSTEM (1977).

[2] NATIONAL CENTER FOR STATE COURTS, COURT STATISTICS AND INFORMATION MANAGEMENT PROJECT (1984).

their official reports and are relying solely on the *National Reporter System.*[3]

Advance sheets or slip opinions precede the publication of the official reports in several states. The unofficial publications generally include advance sheets for the state cases.

A court or its reporter may have the power to select the decisions for publication in the official state reports. In the exercise of that power some less important cases may be eliminated from the official reports.[4]

In a general survey, such as this, it would be inappropriate to present a detailed study of the reporting systems of each state.[5]

SECTION B. NATIONAL REPORTER SYSTEM

The *National Reporter System,* published by the West Publishing Company, consists of three main divisions: (1) opinions of state courts, (2) opinions of federal courts, and (3) opinions of two special courts. This system of court reporting was initiated in 1879 with the *North Western Reporter.* The state reporting units consist of seven regional reporters each containing the opinions of several adjacent states. Additionally, there are two units which only contain the opinions of single states, namely, the *California Reporter* and the *New York Supplement.* There are four units which cover the various federal courts and two that report the opinions of special federal courts: *Bankruptcy Reporter* and the *Military Justice Reporter.* Additionally, the West Publishing Company has started publication of the *Education Law Reporter.* This set, however, consists only of cases reprinted from other units of the *National Reporter System.*

The full texts of the decisions of the courts are provided by this service. The editors prepare headnotes, which then are Key Numbered to the *American Digest* classification system. This is a very significant and helpful feature, the nature of which is described in Chapter 6. However, because it was not developed until the turn of the century, cases in the early volumes of the units of the *National Reporter System,* although headnoted, are not integrated into the *Key Number System.*

The development of the *National Reporter System* had a profound impact on the method of finding court opinions and indeed

[3] *See* Appendix C for a list of states discontinuing their state reports and for a Table showing the year of the first case decided for each state or territory.

[4] Chanin, *A Survey of the Writing and Publication of Opinions in Federal and State Appellate Courts,* 67 LAW LIB.J. 362 (1974).

[5] For an article discussing these various guides, *see* Snyder, *State Legal Research Guides,* 4 LEGAL REFERENCE SERVICES Q. 3 (Spring 1984).

on the development of American law. By 1887, nearly all federal and state court opinions were being reported by the West Publishing Company with each opinion receiving similar editorial treatment. As will be described in the next chapter, this made possible a relatively simple method for researchers to find cases on the same points of law for all of the states as well as those decided in the federal courts. The development of the various regional reporters of the *National Reporter System* also provided a much faster method of making available the opinions of the state courts. The opinions of several adjacent states could be published quickly in the advance sheets which usually contained the same pagination as in the subsequent bound volumes.[6]

In addition to the opinions and the headnotes, the volumes of the *National Reporter System* contain many other useful editorial features. These include tables of cases reported in the volumes and a list of words and phrases as defined in the opinions. Each advance sheet and bound volume also includes a digest section containing the Key Numbered headnotes of the cases covered.[7] The sole exception is the *Bankruptcy Reporter* bound volumes, which do not have digest sections.

The publishers note that the *National Reporter System* contains over 90,000 cases which are not in the official state reports.

The decisions of all state intermediate appellate courts are now included in the *National Reporter System*. For each intermediate court, the inclusion of its cases in the *National Reporter System* began at different times. For example, Missouri appellate cases are included in the *South Western Reporter*, beginning with 93 Mo.App. (1902); Illinois appellate decisions are contained in the *North Eastern Reporter*, beginning with 284 Ill.App. (1936). Variations also exist between the *Reporters* as to general inclusion of state trial court

---

[6] Occasionally after an opinion has been published in an advance sheet, the judge who wrote the opinion may, for one reason or another, recall the opinion and not publish it. In such instances, another opinion is published in the appendix of a subsequent advance sheet with the same pagination as the withdrawn case. By this means, the original pagination is preserved in the bound volume. An unusual event occurred with respect to the case of U.S. v. Kilpatrick. A controversial opinion by Judge Winner of the U.S. District Court of Colorado was published in an advance sheet of the *Federal Supplement* (505 F.Supp. 570, Nov. 7, 1983). In an unprecedented ruling, a federal panel barred West Publishing Company from publishing the opinion in the bound volume. After numerous outcries from First Amendment advocates, the order was vacated and the case was ultimately published in 575 F.Supp. 325 (1983).

[7] In volumes which it reprints, West Publishing Company may not include all of the tables mentioned in this section. Since tools such as the digest section are primarily current awareness devices, and are repeated in the cumulations of digests on the state, regional, and national levels, West has elected not to reproduce them when reprinting older volumes.

cases, and the trial courts which are covered have different starting dates in each set.

See Illustration 9 for a map of the *National Reporter System* and Appendix D for a chart showing the coverage of the *National Reporter System.*

[Illustration 9]

MAP OF THE NATIONAL REPORTER SYSTEM

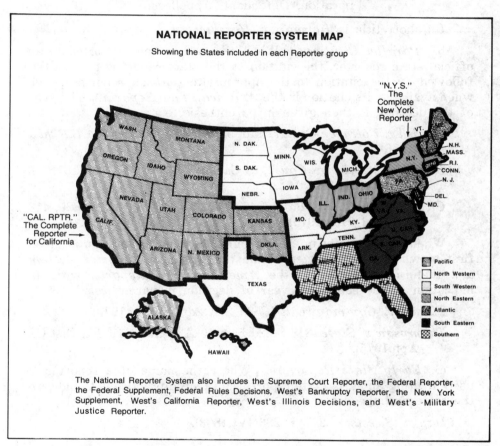

NATIONAL REPORTER SYSTEM MAP

Showing the States included in each Reporter group

"N.Y.S."
The Complete New York Reporter

"CAL. RPTR."
The Complete Reporter for California →

Pacific
North Western
South Western
North Eastern
Atlantic
South Eastern
Southern

The National Reporter System also includes the Supreme Court Reporter, the Federal Reporter, the Federal Supplement, Federal Rules Decisions, West's Bankruptcy Reporter, the New York Supplement, West's California Reporter, West's Illinois Decisions, and West's Military Justice Reporter.

SECTION C. METHODS OF CITATION

1. State Opinions

a. *Name of Case.* When an opinion is cited, it should contain the name of the case and the citation to the case in the official reports, if available, and in the corresponding unit or units of the *National Reporter System.* The full name of the case appears at

the beginning of each opinion, and then there is usually a short form used as a *running title* at the top of each subsequent page of the opinion.   It is the short form that is used in the citation, e.g.:

Harvey HERMAN, Plaintiff-Appellant,

v.

Michael J. HAMBLET; Herrick, McNeill, McElroy & Peregrine; Thomas H. Miner; AMH Industries, Inc., an Illinois Corpora- tion; AMH Industries of Nevada, Inc., a Nevada Cor- poration, Defendants-Appellees.

Its short title is *Herman v. Hamblet.*

b.   *Parallel Citations.*   When a case has been reported in an official state reporter, the citation to the state report is given first, followed by the citation to the appropriate regional reporters, and, when available, its citation in the *American Law Reports.*[8]   The year of the decision is then given in parenthesis, e.g.:

Menish v. Polinger Co., 277 Md. 553, 356 A.2d 233, 95 *A.L.R.3d* 1 (1976)

Barber v. Municipal Court, 24 Cal.3d 742, 598 P.2d 818, 157 Cal. Rptr. 658 (1979)

City of New York v. Baker, 46 N.Y.2d 790, 386 N.E.2d 825, 413 N.Y.S.2d 913 (1979).

When a case is not in the official state reports, citation is given first to where it is reported within the *National Reporter System* and then, if available, to the *American Law Reports*, with an indication of the court and year of decision in parenthesis.

Tussey v. Commonwealth, 589 S.W.2d 215 (Ky.1979)

Thompson v. State, 318 So.2d 549, 90 *A.L.R.3d* 641 (Fla.Dist.Ct. App.1975).

c.   *Early State Reporters.*   Where the name of a reporter is used in citing an early state report, the favored practice is to indicate the state and the date.

Day v. Sweetser, 2 Tyl. 283 (Vt.1803).

2.   Federal Court Opinions

a.   *Supreme Court of the United States.*   Since both the *Su- preme Court Reporter* and the *United States Supreme Court Reports, Lawyers' Edition* give cross-references to the pages of the official *United States Reports*, it is customary to cite only to that set, e.g.: *University of California Regents v. Bakke*, 438 U.S. 265 (1978).

[8] The *American Law Reports* will be discussed in Chapter 7.

b. *Courts of Appeals and District Courts.* As there are no official reports for the opinions of these courts, citations are given to the appropriate unit of the *National Reporter System,* e.g.:

United States v. Five (5) Coin-Operated Gaming Devices, 248 F.Supp. 115 (W.D.Va.1965)

In re Irving, 600 F.2d 1027 (2d Cir.1979).

SECTION D. CROSS–REFERENCE TABLES

1. State Court Citations

Frequently, a researcher has only the citation to the official state reports or to the regional unit of the *National Reporter System* and will need to find the parallel citation.

a. *State Citation* to *National Reporter Citation.* When only the state citation is available, refer to one of the following:

(1) *National Reporter Blue Book.* This set is presently in six bound volumes and is kept current by an annual cumulative pamphlet. It lists all state citations, alphabetically by state, and gives for each state citation its parallel citation in the appropriate unit or units of the *National Reporter System.* [See Illustration 10.]

(2) *Shepard's Citations* for the state.

(3) The *Table of Cases* in the appropriate state or regional digest.

b. *National Reporter Citation to State Citation.* When only the *National Reporter* citation is available, refer to one of the following:

(1) *[State] Blue and White Book.* This volume is provided to subscribers by the West Publishing Company. It is only sent to subscribers for the state in which the subscriber is located. The blue pages repeat for the state the information available in the *National Reporter Blue Book* described *supra.* The white pages give the citations from the regional reporter or reporters to the official state reports. [See Illustration 10.] It is only useful in locating state citations for the state where the research is taking place.

(2) *Shepard's Citations* for the appropriate regional reporter.

(3) *Table of Cases* in the appropriate state or regional digest, or *Table of Cases* volumes in the appropriate unit of the *American Digest System.*

2. Federal Citations

a. *United States Supreme Court.* As the two unofficial sets of the U.S. reports give citations to the official U.S. reports [see Illustration 7], it is the general practice to cite only to the official reports. When, however, the only citation available is the *Supreme*

Court Reporter or the *United States Supreme Court Reports, Lawyers' Edition,* the citation to the other two sets may be obtained by referring to:

(1) *Shepard's United States Citations: Case Volumes.*

(2) *Table of Cases* in one of the digests for federal cases.

Tables of Cases and the *American Digest System* are discussed in Chapter 6. *Shepard's Citations* are discussed in Chapter 14.

3.   AUTO–CITE and INSTA–CITE

AUTO–CITE is the trade name of an automated system of citations of the Lawyers Co-operative Publishing Company. INSTA–CITE is also an automated system of case citations and is available on the West Publishing Company automated legal retrieval system called WESTLAW. Both of these systems will be discussed in more detail in later chapters.

Each can be used to locate a parallel citation when only the official or unofficial citation is at hand. [See Illustration 11.]

[Illustration 10]

AN EXCERPT FROM THE NATIONAL REPORTER BLUE BOOK

20 CALIFORNIA REPORTS, THIRD SERIES

Cal.3d Page	Vol.	Parallel Citation Page	Cal.3d Page	Vol.	Parallel Citation Page	Cal.3d Page	Vol.	Parallel Citation Page	Cal.3d Page	Vol.	Parallel Citation Page
1.	141 CalRptr	28	232.	142 CalRptr	171	457.	143 CalRptr	215	679.	143 CalRptr	885
	569 P2d	133		571 P2d	628		573 P2d	433		574 P2d	1237
10.	141 CalRptr	20	238.	142 CalRptr	279	476.	143 CalRptr	205	➤694.	144 Cal.Rptr.	751
	569 P2d	125		571 P2d	990		573 P2d	423		576 P.2d	466
25.	141 CalRptr	315	251.	142 CalRptr	414	489.	143 CalRptr	212	708.	144 CalRptr	133
	569 P2d	1303		572 P2d	28		573 P2d	430		575 P2d	285
55.	141 CalRptr	146	260.	142 CalRptr	411	500.	143 CalRptr	240	717.	144 CalRptr	214
	569 P2d	740		572 P2d	25		573 P2d	458		575 P2d	757
73.	141 CalRptr	169	267.	142 CalRptr	418	512.	143 CalRptr	247	725.	144 CalRptr	380
	569 P2d	763		572 P2d	32		573 P2d	465		575 P2d	1162
90.	141 CalRptr	157	285.	142 CalRptr	429	523.	143 CalRptr	609	765.	144 CalRptr	758
	569 P2d	751		572 P2d	43		574 P2d	425		576 P2d	473
109.	141 CalRptr	177	300.	142 CalRptr	286	550.	143 CalRptr	253	788.	144 CalRptr	404
	569 P2d	771		571 P2d	997		573 P2d	472		575 P2d	1186
130.	141 CalRptr	447[2]	309.	142 CalRptr	439	552.	143 CalRptr	408	798.	144 CalRptr	408
	570 P2d	463[2]		572 P2d	53		573 P2d	852		575 P2d	1190
142.	141 CalRptr	542	317.	142 CalRptr	443	560.	143 CalRptr	625	813.	144 CalRptr	905
	570 P2d	723		572 P2d	57		574 P2d	441		576 P2d	945
150.	141 CalRptr	698	327.	142 CalRptr	904	567.	143 CalRptr	542	844.	143 CalRptr	695
	570 P2d	1050		572 P2d	1128		573 P2d	1369		574 P2d	711

The **National Reporter Blue Book** consists of a main bound volume, **bound volume** supplements, and an annual cumulative pamphlet. This **Blue Book** contains tables showing volume and page of the **National Reporter** volume for every case found in the corresponding state reports.

In this example, if one had only the citation to 20 Cal.3d 694, the table may be used to locate the citation of this case in the **California Reporter** and the **Pacific Reporter**.

AN EXCERPT FROM THE WHITE TABLES IN CALIFORNIA BLUE AND WHITE BOOK

1190	20 Cal.3d 798
	144 Cal.Rptr. 408

576 P.2d

Page		Parallel Citation
92 [1]		
	Not officially published	
92 [2]		20 Cal.3d 878
		144 Cal.Rptr. 609 [2]
93		20 Cal.3d 888
		144 Cal.Rptr. 610
➤466		20 Cal.3d 694
		144 Cal.Rptr. 751
473		20 Cal 3d 765
		144 Cal.Rptr. 758
945		20 Cal.3d 813
		144 Cal.Rptr. 905
963		20 Cal.3d 893
		145 Cal.Rptr. 1
971		20 Cal.3d 906
		145 Cal.Rptr. 9
1342		21 Cal.3d 1
		145 Cal.Rptr. 176

579 P.2d

Page		Parallel Citation
1		21 Cal.3d 337
		146 Cal.Rptr. 352
7		21 Cal.3d 471
		146 Cal.Rptr. 358
441		21 Cal.3d 322
		146 Cal.Rptr. 550
449		21 Cal.3d 386
		146 Cal.Rptr. 558
476		21 Cal.3d 431
		146 Cal.Rptr. 585
495		21 Cal.3d 349
		146 Cal.Rptr. 604
505		21 Cal.3d 497
		146 Cal.Rptr. 614
514		21 Cal.3d 482
		146 Cal.Rptr. 623
1043		21 Cal.3d 513
		146 Cal.Rptr. 727
1048		21 Cal.3d 542
		146 Cal.Rptr. 732
1053		21 Cal.3d 523
		146 Cal.Rptr. 737

[Illustration 11]

USING AUTO–CITE AND INSTA–CITE
AUTO–CITE

Auto—Cite

457 US 853 [Input]

Board of Education v. Pico*1 (1982) 457 US 853, 73 L Ed 2d 435, 102 S Ct 2799, 8 Media L R 1721

Print-Out   Annotations citing the case(s) indicated above with asterisk(s):

*1 First Amendment rights of free speech and press as applied to public schools—Supreme Court cases, 73 L Ed 2d 1466, secs. 5, 11, 12.

To search for collateral annotations referring to the annotation(s) above, type the citation and press the TRANSMIT key.

INSTA–CITE

457 N.E.2d 392 [Input]

CITATION: 457 N.E.2d 392   INSTA–CITE   ONLY PAGE

1. FRIED V. JACOBSON, 107 ILL.APP.3d 780, 63 ILL.DEC. 564, 438 N.E.2d 495 (ILL.APP. 1 DIST, JUN 23, 1982) (NO. 80–1793) JUDGMENT VACATED BY

Print-Out

2. FRIED V. JACOBSON, 99 ILL.2d 24, 75 ILL.DEC. 398, 457 N.E.2d 392 (ILL.DEC 01, 1983) (NO. 57279)

CASE HISTORY INFORMATION FOR CASES AFFECTED BY DECISIONS PUBLISHED AFTER 1971

SECTION E. SUMMARY

1. State Court Reports

a. Official reports are court reports published by statutory authority.

b. Unofficial reports are court reports published without statutory authority.

c. Advance sheets and slip opinions are published in several states—most states rely on unofficial advance sheets, e.g., *National Reporter System* or other private publication.

2. National Reporter System

a. Opinions of state appellate courts, arranged geographically into seven regional reporters and two state reporters.

b. Opinions of the federal courts in four reporters plus two special subject reporters.

3. Cross-Reference Tables

a. *National Reporter Blue Book* refers the user from the official citation to the unofficial *National Reporter* citation.

b. White Tables in *[State] Blue and White Book* refer the user from the unofficial *National Reporter* citation to the official citation.

4. AUTO–CITE and INSTA–CITE

Computerized tables of cases that provide citations in different sets of court reports.

Chapter 6

DIGESTS FOR COURT REPORTS

SECTION A. DIGESTS: IN GENERAL

As our system of law follows the doctrine of *stare decisis*, the location of past cases in the various sets of court reports described in the previous chapters is an essential requirement to legal research. It has been noted that cases are published in the law reports in chronological order rather than by subject. Each volume of reports may contain cases dealing with diverse subjects ranging from *Abatement* to *Zoning*. It is evident that there must be a method of searching for cases by subject or else locating cases with the same or similar points of law would become unwieldy and unmanageable. For example, assume the following problem:

> *A* parked her car in an unfenced and unlit outdoor parking lot. There was an attendant who handed her a claim ticket. When *A* returned at about 10:30 p.m., she discovered that the roof of her convertible had been slashed and her expensive FM radio and cassette player had been taken. Additionally, she noticed that severe damage had been done to the leather seats of the automobile. *A* now wishes to know if she can make the parking lot owner pay for the losses she has incurred.

Before being able to answer this inquiry, the researcher must first determine the important issues involved in this fact situation, one of which may be whether operators of parking lots are negligent in not providing security for cars left in their possession. Another may be whether the act of parking a car in a parking lot creates a legal situation known as a bailment between the operator and the person parking the car. In order to find the law applicable to this situation, the researcher must search for appellate court decisions with the same or similar facts. From these cases, the rules of law should be determined. If this accident had happened, for example, in Ohio, and all that were available to the researcher were the volumes containing the opinions of the Ohio appellate courts, it would be necessary to examine the individual indexes to hundreds of volumes of the Ohio reports in order to determine if there were any cases on point. To alleviate this laborious task, sets of law books known as *digests* have been developed that rearrange cases by subject. Instead, however, of reprinting the entire opinions, only abstracts or

digests are given. Digests are one method by which cases may be located by subject.

There are various kinds of digests available, each with different coverage. Some include only cases for a single state, court or system of courts; others include cases from a group of neighboring states; some, only federal cases; and one includes cases from all appellate courts, federal and state.

In this chapter we shall describe primarily digests published by the West Publishing Company. Other digests, as well as different techniques for locating cases, will be discussed in subsequent chapters.

SECTION B. THE AMERICAN DIGEST SYSTEM

1. Key Number System

The *American Digest System* is a subject classification scheme whereby decisions reported chronologically in the various units of the *National Reporter System* are rearranged by subject, bringing together all cases on a similar point of law. Instead, however, of rearranging complete decisions, it rearranges digests (abstracts) of decisions. The West Publishing Company has developed its own classification of law and classifies the digests of all cases to its system of classification. The system divides the subject of law into seven main classes. Each class is divided into subclasses and each subclass into topics. There are over 435 topics, each of which corresponds to a legal concept. The topics are then divided into subdivisions of the topic, and each subdivision is given a paragraph number called a *Key Number*. The Key Numbers vary from topic to topic from a few to many hundred. [See Illustrations 12–13.]

With this outline in mind, it is necessary to examine the actual steps involved in the making of the *American Digest System*. Essentially, it all starts with a slip decision. After a decision is written, a copy of it goes to the West Publishing Company and is assigned to an editor. Keep in mind that all the editor has is the decision with no other information except the name of the case, the name of the judge who wrote it, and the name of the court. The editor reads the case and determines the headnotes. In theory, each headnote represents a particular point of law. The editor takes each point of law that is about to be made into a headnote and assigns to it a Topic and Key Number.

The editor decides that a particular headnote deals with, for example, automobiles, and then, turning to the *Table of Key Numbers* [Illustrations 13–13–a] under *Automobiles*, further decides it specifically is involved with *Garage Keepers, Repairmen, Auto Liverymen, and Filling Stations* and thus assigns to this headnote the

Topic *Automobiles* and the specific Key Number 372. Frequently, a headnote will deal with two different points of law and will receive two different Key Numbers.

2. Units of the American Digest System

The next step is found in a publication called the *General Digest*. This is issued in bound volumes, with a new volume being issued approximately once a month. Each volume will consist of *all* the headnotes taken from *all* of the units of the *National Reporter System*. These again are arranged alphabetically by Topic, and then under each Topic numerically by Key Number. Thus, in each volume of the *General Digest*, by looking under a particular Topic and Key Number, digests of all cases that dealt with a particular point of law reported for the time period covered by the volume can be located.

From this point on, the digest building becomes mechanical. This process has been going on since 1897. If no further cumulation had taken place, digests of all the cases, arranged topically, would be in all the bound volumes of the *General Digest*. In order to find all the cases dealing with a particular Topic, it would be necessary to examine each one of hundreds of bound volumes. As this was not practical, the publishers in 1906 cumulated all the Topics from all of the volumes from 1897 to 1906 into one alphabet. This is called the *First Decennial*. Now, by examining the volume containing a particular Topic and Key Number, all of the cases decided on that point during the years 1897–1906 may be located. This process has taken place since 1897 with a new *Decennial* every ten years. The latest one is the *Ninth, Part 1*,[1] covering the years 1976–1981. All of the digests of cases since 1981 are in the *General Digest, 6th Series*. Thus, given a Topic and Key Number, one can start with the *First Decennial* and then proceed through the *Ninth Decennial, Part 1* and the available volumes of the *General Digest*, and thereby locate all cases on a point of law under a particular Topic and Key Number from 1897 to several weeks ago.

It is actually possible to find all cases from 1658, as cases from 1658 to 1896 are in the *Century Digest*. However, the *Century Digest* did not use Key Numbers. This means that the numbering in the *Century* is different from that of the *Decennials*. For example, the Topic *Damages* Key Number 51 in the *Decennials* stands for *Mental Suffering Caused by Injury to the Person of Another*, whereas in the *Century*, Damages 51 stands for *Damages Flowing Directly From Intervening Agency of Third Person*, and cases dealing with mental suffering caused by injury to a third person are

---

[1] Starting with the *Ninth Decennial*, the publisher decided to issue it in two parts: Part 1 covering the years 1976–81; part 2, the years 1982–86. One advantage of this new arrangement will be the need to examine fewer volumes of the *General Digest*.

digested under Paragraph Numbers 103, 255, and 256.   In both the second and third *Decennials*, cross-references are made from the *Decennial* paragraph or Key Numbers to the paragraph number or numbers used in the *Century Digest*.

Should the search be started in the *Century Digest*, a means of transfer from the *Century* paragraph number to the equivalent Key Number is needed.   This is accomplished by using the *Table of Key Numbers Section for Century Digest*, located in the Table of Cases volume of the *First* and *Second Decennials*.

The *American Digest System* consists of the following sets:

	Chronological Coverage	No. of Vols.
Century Digest	1658–1896	50 vols.
First Decennial	1897–1906	25 vols.
Second Decennial	1907–1916	24 vols.
Third Decennial	1916–1926	29 vols.
Fourth Decennial	1926–1936	34 vols.
Fifth Decennial	1936–1946	49 vols.
Sixth Decennial	1946–1956	36 vols.
Seventh Decennial	1956–1966	38 vols.
Eighth Decennial	1966–1976	50 vols.
Ninth Decennial, Part 1	1976–1981	38 vols.
General Digest (6th Series)	1981–1986	

Several volumes of the *General Digest* are published each year. From 1906 through 1976, a new *Decennial* appeared every ten years and superseded the *General Digest* that had been published during the previous ten years.   Starting with the *Ninth Decennial*, each *Decennial* will be issued in two parts.   Part 1 will cover the first five years of a *Decennial* and supersede the *General Digest* volumes.   It can be anticipated that a new series of the *General Digest* will commence in 1986, and then those volumes will be cumulated into the *Tenth Decennial, Part One*, in 1991.

3.   Keeping Key Number System Current

Law, of course, is constantly expanding or changing.   It is obvious that when the original Key Number classification was prepared in 1897, no provisions were made for cases dealing with damages resulting from a jet plane breaking the sound barrier or for the control and regulation of nuclear energy.   Consequently, in order to keep abreast of the law, new topics have to be added and at times older ones expanded.   Thus, in the *Eighth Decennial Digest* the following titles were added or expanded: *Arbitration, Civil Rights, Drugs and Druggists, Federal Courts, Pretrial Procedure, Products Liability, Public Contracts, Securities Regulation, Social Se-*

curity, Public Welfare, and *Taxation*. As additional new titles are required, or revisions to older titles needed, they will be incorporated into the volumes of the *General Digest, 6th*, and then eventually in the *Ninth Decennial.*

One example of how the *Key Number System* expands may be illustrated by examining the headnotes to *Garlock v. Multiple Parking Services, Inc.* at Illustration 14–a. Note how Headnotes 3–6 have been assigned the Key Number 372, and then examine this Key Number in Illustration 13–a. Note how it has been subdivided. When this case was decided in 1980, Key Number 372 had not been subdivided. In the *Ninth Decennial, Part 1*, the publisher, in view of the increasing number of decisions on this Topic, decided to subdivide Key Number 372. Thus, headnotes similar to those in the *Garlock* case, but decided after 1980, will be assigned the Key Number 372(1).

4. Table of Key Numbers

After one has searched through the *Ninth Decennial Digest*, it is necessary to start examining the digest paragraphs under the same Topics and Key Numbers in the individual volumes of the *General Digest, 6th Series*. This series will contain digests of cases decided after 1981. As each volume contains cases only for a short period, there may be as many as thirty individual volumes to search before the publication of the *Ninth Decennial, Part 2*. To avoid the necessity of examining a volume of the *General Digest* that may not include any cases for a particular Key Number, the publisher includes a *Table of Key Numbers* in the volumes of the *Descriptive-Word Index* to the *General Digest*. This table indicates in which volumes of the *General Digest* there are cases digested for a particular Key Number. [See Illustration 16.]

Illustrations in Section C show the development of headnotes from reported cases, the assignment of Topics and Key Numbers to headnotes, and how the headnotes become part of the various units of the *American Digest System.*

The methods of finding what Topics and Key Numbers to search under are described in Sections D & E *infra.*

SECTION C. ILLUSTRATIONS: KEY NUMBER CLASSIFICATION AND UNITS OF THE AMERICAN DIGEST SYSTEM

[Illustration 12]

SAMPLE PAGE FROM ALPHABETICAL LIST OF DIGEST TOPICS
USED IN KEY NUMBER SYSTEM

DIGEST TOPICS

See, also, Outline of the Law by Seven Main Division of Law, Page VII

Abandoned and Lost Property	Attachment	Compositions with Creditors
Abatement and Revival	Attorney and Client	Compounding Offenses
Abduction	Attorney General	Compromise and Settlement
Abortion and Birth Control	Auctions and Auctioneers	Condominium
Absentees	Audita Querela	Confusion of Goods
Abstracts of Title	Automobiles	Conspiracy
Accession	Aviation	Constitutional Law
Accord and Satisfaction	Bail	Consumer Credit
Account	Bailment	Contempt
Account, Action on	Bankruptcy	Continuance
Account Stated	Banks and Banking	Contracts
Accountants	Bastards	Contribution
Acknowledgment	Beneficial Associations	Conversion
Action	Bigamy	Convicts
Action on the Case	Bills and Notes	Copyrights and Intellectual
Adjoining Landowners	Blasphemy	Property
Administrative Law and	Bonds	Coroners
Procedure	Boundaries	Corporations
Admiralty	Bounties	Costs

There are over 435 Topics in the American Digest System. Each Topic is subdivided into "Key Numbers." See next illustration.

Ambassadors and Consuls	Cancellation of Instruments	Crops
Amicus Curiae	Carriers	Curtesy
Animals	Cemeteries	Customs and Usages
Annuities	Census	Customs Duties
Appeal and Error	Certiorari	Damages
Appearance	Champerty and Maintenance	Dead Bodies
Apprentices	Charities	Death
Arbitration	Chattel Mortgages	Debt, Action of
Armed Services	Chemical Dependents	Debtor and Creditor
Arrest	Citizens	Declaratory Judgment
Arson	Civil Rights	Dedication
Assault and Battery	Clerks of Courts	Deeds
Assignments	Clubs	Depositaries
Assignments for Benefit of	Colleges and Universities	Depositions
Creditors	Collision	Deposits and Escrows
Assistance, Writ of	Commerce	Deposits in Court
Associations	Common Lands	Descent and Distribution
Assumpsit, Action of	Common Law	Detectives
Asylums	Common Scold	

[Illustration 13]

FIRST PAGE OF TOPIC: AUTOMOBILES, FROM NINTH DECENNIAL
DIGEST, PART 1

AUTOMOBILES

SUBJECTS INCLUDED

Regulation and licensing of motor vehicles and motor carriers

Licensing and regulation of drivers

Rights in and use of highways and other public places

Injuries to highways, to motor vehicles, and to occupants of private vehicles

Injuries from defects in, or negligent or wrongful use of, motor vehicles, other than
   as public carriers, or to employees

Injuries from defects in, or obstruction of, highways or other public places

Liabilities for such injuries and actions to enforce such liabilities, including statutory
   and punitive damages

Accident indemnity funds

Violation of regulations as offenses, and prosecution and punishment thereof

Filling stations, garages, repairmen, and rental agencies

SUBJECTS EXCLUDED AND COVERED BY OTHER TOPICS

Compensatory damages for injuries, see DAMAGES

Employers' rights, duties and liabilities as to their employees, see EMPLOYERS'
   LIABILITY, WORKERS' COMPENSATION

General contractual rights, duties and liabilities, and consideration of motor vehicles
   as property, see BAILMENT, CARRIERS, CHATTEL MORTGAGES, EXEMP-
   TIONS, INSURANCE, SALES, SECURED TRANSACTIONS, TAXATION and other
   specific topics

Manufacturers and sellers, liability of, see PRODUCTS LIABILITY

Motor carriers' rights, duties, and liabilities as to passengers and freight, see
   CARRIERS

Particular offenses not involving motor vehicle regulations nor direct injuries from
   negligent or wrongful use of motor vehicles, see CUSTOMS DUTIES, INTOXICAT-

ecific

**In each unit of the Decennial Digests and in the special Key
Number digests, each Topic has a list of subjects excluded and an** ecif-
analysis of the Key Number classification for the Topic.

BAN

For detailed references to other topics, see Descriptive-Word Index

---

Analysis

I. CONTROL, REGULATION, AND USE IN GENERAL, ⟜1–20.

II. LICENSE AND REGISTRATION OF PRIVATE VEHICLES, ⟜21–57.

II. PUBLIC SERVICE VEHICLES, ⟜58–128.
   (A) CONTROL AND REGULATION IN GENERAL, ⟜58–64.
   (B) LICENSE AND REGISTRATION, ⟜65–108.
   (C) REGULATION OF OPERATION AND MANAGEMENT, ⟜109–128.

IV. LICENSE AND REGULATION OF CHAUFFEURS OR OPERATORS, ⟜129–145.

[Illustration 13–a]

SAMPLE PAGE OF TOPIC: AUTOMOBILES, FROM NINTH DECENNIAL DIGEST, PART 1

3–9th D Pt 1—641 **AUTOMOBILES**

VII. OFFENSES AND PROSECUTIONS.—Cont'd

(B) PROSECUTION AND PUNISHMENT.—Cont'd

350. Jurisdiction and venue.
351. Indictment, information, or complaint.
352. —— Issues, proof, and variance.
353. Presumptions and burden of proof.
354. Admissibility of evidence.
355. Weight and sufficiency of evidence.
    (1). In general.
    (2). License and registration.
    (3). Equipment.
    (4). Reckless operation.
    (5). Excessive speed, lack of control, and racing.
    (6). Driving while intoxicated.
    (7). Stopping, standing, and parking.

   (8). Neglect of duty after accident.
   (9). Frightening or injuring animals.
   (10). Taking and using without consent of owner.
   (11). Identification marks altered or removed.
   (12). Movement of stolen cars in interstate commerce.
   (13). Homicide.
   (14). Assault and battery.
   (15). Malicious mischief.
356. Questions for jury.
357. Instructions.
358. Verdict and findings.
359. Judgment and sentence.
360. Appeal and error.
361. Costs.

VIII. GARAGE KEEPERS, REPAIRMEN, AUTO LIVERYMEN, AND FILLING STATIONS.

362. Power to regulate.
363. Statutory and local regulations.
364. Who are garage keepers.
365. Licenses and taxes.
366. Buildings.
367. Garage as nuisance.
368. Repairs and other services and supplies.
369. Storage of vehicles; parking facilities.
370. —— In general.
371. —— Compensation.
372. —— Injury to or loss of vehicle or contents.
    (1). In general; nature of relation.
    (2). Limitation of liability.
    (3). Actions.
    (4). —— Evidence and fact questions.
373. Lien.
374. —— In general.
375. —— Consent or agreement of owner.
376. —— Contract with conditional buyer.

377. —— Contract with infant.
378. —— Possession by lienor.
379. —— Services or supplies for which allowed.
380. —— Assignment or transfer.
381. —— Waiver or loss.
382. —— Reinstatement.
383. —— Priorities.
384. —— Proceedings to perfect.
385. —— Enforcement.
386. Renting out of vehicle by auto liverymen.
387. —— In general.
388. —— Injuries to person of hirer.
389. —— Liability of hirer in general.
390. —— Injuries to vehicle.
391. —— Injuries to third persons.
392. Penalties for violation of regulations.
393. Offenses by garage keepers.
394. Offenses by persons dealing with garage keepers.
395. Filling stations.

For detailed references to other topics, see Descriptive-Word Index

> Immediately following the analysis, there appears a detailed listing of the Key Numbers, each representing a minute point of law. Each time a headnote deals with garages or parking lots and there has been loss of or injury to a vehicle, it will receive the Topic Automobiles and the Key Number 372(1).

[Illustration 14]

SAMPLE PAGE FROM NEW YORK SUPPLEMENT

678   **427 NEW YORK SUPPLEMENT, 2d SERIES**

"The distinctions which the common law draws between licensee and invitee were inherited from a culture deeply rooted to the land, a culture which traced many of its standards to a heritage of feudalism. In an effort to do justice in an industrialized urban society, with its complex economic and individual relationships, modern common-law courts have found it necessary to formulate increasingly subtle

stolen auto, under a finding of bailment, but where it was clear that the gravamen was lack of reasonable care.

One of the reasons in applying the *Basso* rationale is that we are unable to perceive any logical reason why property left on the real property of another should be treated by the law any differently than persons on other persons' real property.

> This is a typical page from a case reported in a unit of the National Reporter System. It illustrates how headnotes are developed. The bracketed numbers are inserted by the editors. Each paragraph so bracketed has been rewritten into a headnote. See next illustration.

conflict. As new distinctions have been spawned, older ones have become obscured. Through this semantic morass, the common law has moved, unevenly and with hesitation, towards 'imposing on owners and occupiers a single duty of reasonable care in all the circumstances.'" (358 U.S. 625, at 630–31, 79 S.Ct. 406, at 410).

The same tortured reasoning in the evolution of jurisprudential thought on the question of responsibility for automobiles left with others can be found in comparison to that outlined above in regard to persons or property. The citation at 7 A.L.R.3d 927 is ample proof of the absurd state of the law as to the liability for damaged or stolen autos left in commercial parking lots.

The unarticulated conclusion that this annotation and many others lead to is that the concept of bailment is no longer a viable theory in application to a very real modern problem. Therefore, this Court need not decide whether a bailment was created in the instant case. The measure we will apply is that of the *Basso* case (*supra*): "reasonable care under the circumstances whereby foreseeability shall be a measure of liability" (40 N.Y.2d 233, at 241, 386 N.Y.S.2d 564, at 568, 352 N.E.2d 868, at 872). In doing thus, this Court is not making new law. We are only stripping away the excusatory verbiage from those cases where liability was found for a damaged or

of a passenger vehicle, plus its financing costs; the ravages of depreciation; the cost of repair; the costs of insurance and license fees; the wear and tear of potholes and salt corrosion, and costs of parking itself, it is a small thing to ask that a parking lot owner at least keep it from being stolen or damaged.

[3] This Court finds that the defendant failed to properly protect the plaintiff's vehicle from damage through the acts of a vandal. The possibility of such acts were clearly foreseeable considering the parking lot's location, size, and general accessibility. The failure to fence or provide a guard, or to at least direct the patron to a location close to the attendant's booth are acts of omission which, as a matter of law, constitute negligence.

[4, 5] The Court further finds that the attendant's failure to observe the acts of vandalism—which, by nature of the damage caused, had to be overt and observable—was also negligence, attributable to the defendant. This is true, whether the attendant was officially on duty or not, since the defendant cannot establish when the damage took place. Even though the plaintiff has the burden of proof, since he was not present and the defendant's employee was, the burden of coming forward with those facts shifts to the defendant.

[Illustration 14–a]

SAMPLE PAGE FROM NEW YORK SUPPLEMENT

670 **427 NEW YORK SUPPLEMENT, 2d SERIES**

paragraphs 1(g) and 3 of the "wherefore" clause of the complaint, and in all other respects shall be denied, without costs.

---

103 Misc.2d 943

Harold GARLOCK, Plaintiff,

v.

MULTIPLE PARKING SERVICES, INC., Defendant.

Buffalo City Court, Erie County.

Jan. 15, 1980.

Acts were instituted for damages sustained by plaintiff's automobile while

> Note how the wording of Headnotes 3–5 is paraphrased from the opinion. See previous illustration.

while parked on premises, notwithstanding whether a bailment was created, where operator failed to properly protect vehicle from damage through acts of a vandal in that possibility of such acts was clearly foreseeable, considering parking lot's location, size, and general accessibility, and failure to fence or provide a guard or to at least direct owner to a location close to attendant's booth were acts of omission which, as a matter of law, constituted negligence.

Motion of plaintiff granted, and cross motion of defendant denied.

1. Bailment ⟳14(1)

The "bailment theory" as a basis for recovery in parking lot cases is no longer appropriate.

2. Bailment ⟳14(1)

The new standard for recovery in parking lot cases is that of reasonable care under the circumstances and of foreseeability.

3. Automobiles ⟳372

Operator of parking lot was liable to owner of automobile for damage sustained when vehicle was burglarized and vandalized while parked on premises, notwithstanding whether a bailment was created, where operator failed to properly protect vehicle from damage through acts of a vandal in that possibility of such acts was clearly foreseeable, considering parking lot's location, size, and general accessibility, and failure to fence or provide a guard or to at least direct owner to a location close to attendant's booth were acts of omission which, as a matter of law, constituted negligence.

4. Automobiles ⟳372

Failure of parking lot attendant to observe acts of vandalism which, by nature of damage caused, were overt and observable constituted negligence which was attributable to operator of lot since, whether attendant was officially on duty or not, operator could not establish when damage took place.

5. Automobiles ⟳372

Even though plaintiff had burden of proof with respect to damage to his vehicle while parked in parking lot operated by defendant, where plaintiff was not present at time of damage and defendant's employee was, burden of coming forward with facts on issue of negligence shifted to defendant.

6. Automobiles ⟳372

Burden of plaintiff with respect to damages sustained by his automobile while parked in a parking lot operated by defendant was met by showing that defendant failed to exercise reasonable care under circumstances and that possibility of damages through acts of a vandal was foreseeable.

Dixon & DeMarie, Daniel L. Schoenborn, Buffalo, of counsel, for plaintiff.

[Illustration 15]

SAMPLE PAGE FROM NINTH DECENNIAL DIGEST, PART 1

⬅372 AUTOMOBILES   3–9th D Pt 1—1272

ville Central School v. Herb's Dodge Sales & Service, Inc., 435 N.Y.S.2d 179, 79 A.D.2d 1049.

⬅372(1). In general; nature of relation.

Fla. 1979. Where automobile driver stopped his car in front of public lounge and waved to lounge attendant, who waved back, where driver then entered lounge, leaving lights on and motor running, but no lounge attendant parked the car, and where car was then stolen, lounge employees were in no way negligent, and lounge could not be held liable for personal injuries caused by thief while driving stolen car.—Almeida v. Trushin, 368 So.2d 346.

Ga.App. 1976. Construing evidence most favorably to officer of corporate owner of automobile from which plaintiff officer's personal property was taken while automobile was parked in defendant's lot, a jury question was presented as to whether defendant, in whose presence officer had allegedly opened trunk many times, had actual knowledge of contents of trunk thereby creating a bailment as to contents of trunk.—White v. Atlanta Parking Service Co., 228 S.E.2d 156.

Ill.App. 1977. Once bailment for hire is created, garage operator as bailee is liable to car owner for damages caused by his employees, and bailor who does not retain control of vehicle is not responsible to third persons for negligent use of car by bailee.—Great Central Ins. Co. v. Harris, 4 Ill.Dec. 776, 360 N.E.2d 1151, 46 Ill.App.3d 542.

Ind.App. 1980. Automobile insurer, which had initiated action against parking lot owner to recover amounts paid to insured under automobile policy after automobile was stolen from lot, was entitled to recover all natural, direct and proximate consequences of owner's acts and omissions and thus rental value of substitute vehicle was properly considered in m...

porarily on his premises was nothing more than business courtesy, and fact that repairman allegedly agreed to help owner look for automatic transmission parts was ambiguous and was not commitment to resume responsibility for truck.—Hutchinson v. Aime, 392 So.2d 143.

Statute, which provides that voluntary deposit can only be regularly made by owner, or with his consent expressed or implied, was applicable when issue concerned initial establishment of deposit relationship through delivery, and thus contention of truck owner, suing automobile repairman because truck, which had previously been wrecked and towed to repairman's premises for tire repair, was damaged from fire which occurred after owner paid for tire repairs and unsuccessfully attempted to drive truck away, that under such statute, repairman had given his implied consent to be depositary by allowing truck, to remain temporarily on his premises, provided no basis for relief. LSA–C.C. art. 2933.—Id.

La.App. 1979. Where wrecked automobile was towed to storage facility at request of state police and automobile owner never made any arrangements either to pay for storage of automobile or to pick it up for a long period of time, owner abandoned automobile and storage facility was not liable for subsequent loss of automobile. LSA–C.C. arts. 2937 et seq., 2938.—Swain v. Hymel, 377 So.2d 888.

La.App. 1978. Fact that parking garage attendant got into insureds' car and started the car before a thief jumped into the car and drove it away did not warrant charging the operator of the parking garage and its insurer with constructive knowledge of the car's contents where the insured owners had already left and the automobile had been received by the time the attendant entered the car, so that any contract of deposit was already confected. LSA–C.C. art. 2926.—Insurance Co. of North America v. Solari Parking, Inc., 367 ...23, re...

case the operator of the lot has no right to exclude the owner of the car or anyone else who comes with the keys, and same rule would apply to owner or lessor of rented tie down space for aircraft.—State ex rel. Mather v. Carnes, 551 S.W.2d 272.

N.Y.City Civ.Ct. 1979. No bailment was created when owner parked his car in garage of defendant.—Linares v. Edison Parking, Inc., 414 N.Y.S.2d 661.

N.Y.City Civ.Ct. 1979. When a fee is paid for storage of an automobile, under circumstances that do not give rise to a bailment, lot or garage owner is liable upon proof of failure to exercise reasonable care under those circumstances.—Linares v. Edison Parking, Inc., 414 N.Y.S.2d 661, 97 Misc.2d 831.

Removal of wheels and tires from automobile parked in garage of defendant, in manner it was accomplished, created sufficient noise to put defendant's cashier on notice of an occurrence so that failure to act was a failure to exercise reasonable care under the circumstances and, thus, garage owner would be liable.—Id.

No bailment was created when owner parked his car in garage of defendant.—Id.

N.Y.City Civ.Ct. 1978. Private garage corporation was negligent in failing to take adequate precautions and safeguards to protect automobile parked in garage by officer of automobile owner with whom garage corporation maintained landlord/tenant relationship pursuant to contract, in that set of ignition keys in possession of corporation were in clear and open view on pegboard in unlocked and unattended office, and thus independent act of thief in stealing automobile and damaging it did not exonerate garage owner from liability for damage to automobile. General Obligations Law § 5–325.—Motors Ins. Corp. v. American Garages Inc., 404 N.Y.S.2d 803, 94 Misc.2d 338, affirmed 414 N.Y.S.2d 841, 98 Misc.2d 887.

N.Y.City Ct. 1980. Operator of parking lot was liable to owner of automobile for damage sustained when vehicle was burglarized and vandalized while parked on premises, notwithstanding whether a bailment was created, where operator failed to properly protect vehicle from damage through acts of a vandal in that possibility of such acts was clearly foreseeable, considering parking lot's location, size, and general accessibility, and failure to fence or provide a guard or to at least direct owner to a location close to attendant's booth were acts of omission which, as a matter of law, constituted negligence.—Garlock v. Multiple Parking Services, Inc., 427 N.Y.S.2d 670, 103 Misc.2d 943.

Failure of parking lot attendant to observe acts of vandalism which, by nature of damage caused, were overt and observable constituted negligence which was attributable to operator of lot since, whether attendant was officially on duty or not, operator could not establish when damage took place.—Id.

> When the Topic and Key Number are known, the digest paragraphs are consulted to select cases in point with the problem under research. For those so selected, the full cases should be read. Note how citation is given to where the case is reported.
>
> Note also how the digest paragraphs are reprinted as they originally appeared as headnotes in the reported decisions.

...uld not ...e when ...re was ...leet at ...r knew -Wash-S.W.2d

...ny of ...recau-...omobile ...radict-...r-sub-...nt paid ...utomo-...did not ...e stan-...ailee so ...ligence. Motor

the garage was liable for loss of the stolen automobile's contents.—Insurance Co. of North America v. Solari Parking, Inc., 370 So.2d 503.

La.App. 1980. Automobile repairman was not depositary when truck, which had previously been wrecked and towed to repairman's premises for tire repair, was damaged by fire after owner had paid for tire repairs and unsuccessfully attempted to drive truck away, and thus repairman was not responsible for such damage, where deposit terminated when owner paid for repairs and attempted to drive truck away, fact that repairman then allowed truck, which required towing, to remain tem-

Mo.App. 1977. Garage keeper is liable for loss by theft of motor vehicle stored in his garage where he failed to use ordinary care to prevent theft.—Toston v. McCracken, 555 S.W.2d 48.

Fact that bailor's motorcycle was stolen from premises of bailees where bailor had taken motorcycle for repairs was not defense as matter of law to bailor's action against bailees for loss of motorcycle.—Id.

Mo.App. 1977. Parking lot owner who rents parking space to owner who keeps keys to his car does not become bailee of vehicle because there is no delivery of possession to him from the owner of the car and in such

Tex.Civ.App. 1978. Bailee was negligent where he left bailed property, a pickup truck, on car lot unlocked, he had no security service that served lot, he did not check lot at night himself, he did not put pickup in one of his lock sheds, move it to another location, or attempt to render vehicle incapable of moving on its own power, and pickup truck was stolen.—Wilson v. Hooser, 573 S.W.2d 601, ref. n.r.e.

Tex.Civ.App. 1977. Absent a bailment, person who parked his car in fenced lot at airport, leaving the machine receipt ticket above the sunvisor, failed to prove affirmative negligence on the part of parking lot operator with respect to theft of the car.—Allright

For references to other topics, see Descriptive-Word Index

[Illustration 15–a]

SAMPLE PAGE FROM THE EIGHTH DECENNIAL DIGEST

🔑371 AUTOMOBILES 4–8th D—2040

vehicle found wrecked, abandoned or parked in violation of state law, thus, ordinance was not authority to impound vehicle and charge owner with storage and towing charges where vehicle was seized because marijuana was allegedly found therein. 11 Del.C. § 2322.—Thompson v. Danvir Corp., 264 A.2d 361.

Ky. 1970. Where state police seized a truck and placed the truck in a garage, garageman was agent of the Commonwealth and/or the state police and whatever arrangement was made with him could not impose a liability on owner for towing and storage charges nor impair his right to possession under court order.—Robey v. Winn, 453 S.W.2d 763.

La.App. 1976. Auto repair shop could not recover for storage of truck which had been brought to shop for repairs, where no contract for storage was established and there was testimony that truck was left on auto shop's property for a long period because of the auto shop's previous poor workmanship and its refusal to release truck to its owner.—Lindsay

> **This illustrates how a search may be continued from one Decennial to another under the same Topic and Key Number.**
>
> **In all of the Decennial Digests, cases under a Key Number are arranged alphabetically by jurisdiction with those of the federal courts given first.**

town ordinance, owner was not liable on basis of implied contract to towing company for cost of towing and storage of the automobile.—Pollina v. Bergh, 346 N.Y.S.2d 318, 74 Misc.2d 896.

While, in proper case, a towing company can recover cost of towing and storage of automobile pursuant to order of police for reasonable length of time, it cannot be allowed to hold car indefinitely and allow the charges to add up. Lien Law §§ 184, 187, 200 et seq.—Id.

Tex.Civ.App. 1973. Statute providing that storage charges accruing while vehicle is stored at request of seizing officer of Department of Public Safety, pending outcome of forfeiture suit, shall be paid by Department, if vehicle shall be returned to owner by action of court, rendered state liable for storage charges on vehicle seized but ordered to be returned, even though seizing officer was not a member of Department of Public Safety, inasmuch as the seizing officer acted legally and within purview of applicable statute. Vernon's Ann.P.C. arts. 725b, § 22, 725d, §§ 2, 3, 8A(b).—Brandes v. State, 503 S.W.2d 318.

Tex.Civ.App. 1967. Plaintiff was entitled to recover reasonable storage charges upon an implied contract for storage of an automobile.—Eddie v. Ladwig, 412 S.W.2d 811, citing 61 C.J.S. Motor Vehicles §§ 725, 868.

🔑372. —— Injuries to or loss of vehicle.

Ark. 1972. Doctrine of res ipsa loquitur was applicable with respect to burning of plaintiff's automobile in defendant's automobile repair shop, where there was no evidence of arson, nor was there any evidence of an electrical storm, but proof did reflect that the area where fire occurred contained flammable fluids, rags, paint, and there were automobiles stored in building which contained gasoline, and it was admitted that pilot light on top of oven in paint department was left on.—Megee v. Reed, 482 S.W.2d 832, 252 Ark. 1016.

Evidence, in action by automobile owner against automobile repairer for damages to automobile when repair shop burned, supported finding that repairer was negligent and that this was proximate cause of the fire.—Id.

Fla.App. 1971. Where bailor's automobile had been left with bailee for repair and was stored by bailee on its premises overnight with the keys in the ignition, and where vehicle was stolen and recovered some days later with personal property of bailor missing from trunk of vehicle, finding that bailee had actual or constructive knowledge of personal property being located in the trunk was supported by substantial evidence.—Crippen Oldsmobile, Inc. v. Brabec, 244 So.2d 554.

nted space
g, on each
lation was
that driver
oon depar-
ned risk of
l not read
de, § 12-
ng Center,

in defend-
suming risk
recover on
absence of
ul miscon-

ny, against
nt of theft
rose out of
s was fair
op at time
and place of loss.—Id.

Plaintiff in action against parking garage proprietor on account of theft of plaintiff's battery could not recover exemplary damages or attorney's fees, although proprietor refused to settle claim and defended action.—Id.

Ga.App. 1970. The question of whether bailee-garage, which had placed bailor's repaired automobile in padlocked, fenced-in parking area in back of garage, from which it was stolen over weekend and had left keys in ignition switch of unlocked automobile was negligent was for jury in bailor's suit for value of automobile. Code, § 12–403.—Cordell Ford Co. v. Mullis, 173 S.E.2d 120, 121 Ga.App. 123.

Value of automobile which was stolen from garage after being repaired by garage was either value at time it was turned over to garage, or value at time of loss, in which event garage would be entitled to amount of repair bill as evidence of amount by which value of automobile had been increased due to its furnishing of labor and materials.—Id.

When bailor left his automobile at garage for repairs, contract of bailment created imposed upon bailee an implied obligation to return automobile to bailor free from injury and in same condition it was in when bailee received it. Code, § 12–403.—Id.

Where plaintiff, in suit against garage to which plaintiff had turned over automobile for repairs and from which repaired automobile had been stolen, recovered value of automobile, not as turned over by him to repairman, but after repair, garage was entitled to deduct contract price of repairs by which value had been enhanced.—Id.

Ga.App. 1967. Allegations that for consideration owner stored automobile in garage and that automobile was lost or destroyed during pendency of bailment were sufficient to allege breach of bailment contract, even though they may have been subject to special demurrer requiring more specific allegations of acts of negligence of garage operator. Code, § 12–403.—Bunn v. Broadway Parking Center, Inc., 156 S.E.2d 464, 116 Ga.App. 85.

Idaho 1972. In suit arising out of disappearance of transmission from plaintiff's automobile while it was stored by defendant garage owner in unfenced area between garage and adjacent street, evidence as to custom regularly observed by other service garages in the area was properly admitted and where plaintiff bailor failed to introduce any evidence to overcome inference of reasonable care arising from bailee's evidence and there was nothing in common experience to lead to conclusion that bailee's conduct was negligent, even though burden of persuasion was on bailee, it proved by preponderance of the evidence its freedom from negligence.—Low v. Park Price Co., 503 P.2d 291, 95 Idaho 91.

Where court refused to allow bailor to ask one of bailee-garage owner's witnesses what his profits amounted to for the preceding year and by making the inquiry bailor sought to disprove witness' assertion that he could not afford to hire a night watchman, whether garage owner could afford to hire night watchman was immaterial to question of whether ordinary care required a night watchman and court's refusal was proper.—Id.

Ind.App. 1968. Where printed work order authorizing specified work to be done on semi-tractor relieved owner of garage from any liability for theft due to negligence, and owner of garage negligently permitted semi-tractor with ignition keys in it to stay in unguarded and unfenced lot, and semi-tractor was stolen during night, owner of garage was liable to owner of semi-tractor for loss, even though in previous bailments owner of semi-tractor had received same or similar work order, which it did not read.—General Grain, Inc. v. International Harvester Co., 232 N.E.2d 616, 142 Ind.App. 12.

Iowa 1968. Evidence in automobile owner's action against garage keeper, in whose possession automobile had been damaged, for breach of bailment contract did not support finding that it would have been futile for owner to demand possession.—Halferty v. Hawkeye Dodge, Inc., 158 N.W.2d 750.

Garage keeper's failure to offer to return automobile, which had been damaged in garage keeper's possession and been repaired, was immaterial with respect to garage keeper's liability for breach of bailment contract, where garage keeper had earlier offered to return automobile and owner did not then pick it up but sued for its value.—Id.

Automobile owner, whose automobile was damaged while in possession of garage keeper, did not make demand sufficient to sustain recovery for loss of use where he accepted offer of loaned automobile pending repair and never demanded automobile in its damaged condition but refused to take it in repaired condition and apparently wanted only replacement with new automobile.—Id.

Conduct of garage keeper, in whose care automobile was damaged, in proceeding with repairs without owner's consent was not conversion such as would relieve owner of necessity of making demand before seeking damages for loss of use.—Id.

For references to other topics, see Descriptive-Word Index

[Illustration 16]

TABLE OF KEY NUMBERS FROM THE DESCRIPTIVE-WORD INDEX TO THE GENERAL DIGEST, 6th SERIES, VOLUMES 1–10

TABLE OF KEY NUMBERS
GENERAL DIGEST, VOLUMES 1–10 6th SERIES

A Time Saver for Locating The Latest Cases

1400

AUTOMOBILES—Cont'd	AUTOMOBILES—Cont'd	AUTOMOBILES—Cont'd	AUTOMOBILES—Cont'd
243(7)—4, 8	245(72)—1, 3, 4, 6, 9	256—1, 2, 3, 4, 5, 6, 7, 8, 9, 10	341—5, 7
243(11)—2, 8	245(74)—2, 9	257—1, 2, 6, 7	342—2, 4, 5, 7, 9, 10
243(12)—8	245(78)—2, 3	258—7, 10	344—8, 10
243(14)—5, 10	245(80)—1, 2, 3, 4, 5, 7, 8, 10	259—1, 2, 8	347—7, 8
243(16)—5, 7	245(81)—2, 5, 6, 7	261—7, 9	349—1, 2, 3, 4, 5, 6, 7, 8, 9, 10
243(17)—8	245(82)—2, 3, 5, 6, 8	264—2, 4, 5, 10	350—3, 5, 6
244(1)—1, 7, 8, 9, 10	245(83)—2	265—1	351—1, 2, 3, 4, 5, 6, 7, 8, 9, 10
244(2)—1, 2, 3, 5, 6, 7, 8, 9, 10	245(85)—1, 5	266—6, 7, 10	352—5, 6, 7, 8, 9
244(5)—2	245(87)—1, 2, 7, 8, 10	269—7, 8	353—1, 2, 3, 5, 6, 7, 8, 9, 10
244(6)—1, 5, 8	245(88)—5, 8, 9	270—10	354—1, 2, 3, 4, 5, 6, 8, 9, 10
244(7)—7, 8, 10	245(90)—4, 5, 9	273—2, 3, 4, 6, 8, 9, 10	355(1)—1, 5, 6, 7, 10
244(10)—8, 9	245(91)—10	276—6, 10	355(2)—1, 2, 3, 4, 5, 6, 8, 9, 10
244(11)—1, 2, 4, 5, 6, 7, 8, 9, 10	246(2)—4, 5, 6, 7, 9	277—1, 3, 4, 5, 6, 7, 8, 9, 10	355(3)—1, 10
244(12)—1, 2, 3, 5, 6, 7, 8, 9, 10	246(3)—7	278—2, 4, 7, 8, 10	355(4)—1, 2, 4, 7, 8, 9
244(13)—4, 5, 10	246(4)—3, 6	279—1, 2, 3, 4, 5, 6, 7, 8, 9, 10	355(5)—1, 3, 9, 10
244(14)—2, 3, 5, 7, 9, 10	246(7)—4	282—1, 4, 5, 6, 7, 9, 10	355(6)—1, 2, 3, 4, 5, 6, 7, 8, 9, 10
244(20)—1, 3, 4, 6, 7, 9	246(9)—3, 9	283—6	355(7)—6, 8
244(22)—2, 10	246(10)—10	284—2, 3, 4, 6, 8, 9, 10	355(8)—1, 2, 3, 4, 7, 8, 10
			355(10)—1, 3, 6, 7, 8, 10
			355(11)—6, 7
			355(12)—5, 8, 9
			355(13)—1, 2, 3, 4, 5, 6, 7, 8, 9, 10
			355(14)—2, 5, 6, 7, 8, 10
			356—1, 2, 3, 4, 5, 6, 7, 8, 10
			357—1, 2, 3, 4, 5, 6, 7, 8, 9, 10
			358—1, 3, 5, 6
			359—1, 2, 3, 4, 5, 6, 8, 9, 10
			360—6
			363—1, 3, 9
			365—3, 6, 7, 9, 10
			368—1, 3, 4, 5, 6, 7, 8, 9, 10
			370—1
			372(1)—1, 3, 6, 10 ←
			372(3)—1
			372(4)—1
			374—8, 10
			375—5, 8

> This is an illustration from the Table of Key Numbers in the Descriptive-Word Index to the General Digest, 6th Series. This table allows a researcher to determine which of the 10 volumes may have digests from the Topics and Key Numbers under research. For the instant case, one would need only to examine volumes 1, 3, 6, and 10 for cases with the Topic: Automobiles Key Number 372(1).

245(2)—4, 5, 7, 8, 10	246(40)—4	305(7)—1	378—3
245(5)—2, 3	246(41)—7	306(1)—2, 3, 6, 7, 8, 10	379—10
245(6)—1, 3, 6, 9, 10	246(45)—10	306(2)—1, 2, 3, 6, 8, 10	381—3
245(8)—5, 9, 10	246(46)—4	306(4)—1, 2, 3, 5, 6, 7, 8, 9, 10	383—10
245(13)—2, 3, 7, 8	246(47)—3	306(5)—1, 3, 4, 6, 9	384—6
245(14)—2, 3, 4, 5, 7, 8, 10	246(48)—10	306(7)—1, 2, 4, 5, 8, 9, 10	385—8
245(15)—5, 6, 7, 8, 10	246(54)—9	306(8)—2, 3, 6, 8, 10	387—5, 6
245(16)—3, 4	246(55)—2	308(4)—2, 7, 8	388—6
245(17)—2, 8, 9	246(56)—3	308(6)—2	389—5
245(19)—2	246(57)—4, 6, 8	308(10)—4, 7, 9	391—7
245(21)—1, 8	246(58)—1, 2, 3, 4, 6, 7, 8, 10	308(11)—2, 7	392—4, 8
245(24)—2, 6, 7, 8, 9	246(60)—1, 2, 3, 4, 6, 7, 8	309(1)—1, 4, 8, 9	395—8
245(26)—6, 8	247—1, 2, 4, 5, 6, 8, 10	309(2)—5, 6, 7, 9	
245(28)—4, 8, 9	248—8	309(3)—1, 7, 9	AVIATION
245(30)—3, 4, 6, 10	249—5, 7, 8, 9, 10	309(4)—1, 7	
245(33)—1	251.1—1, 5, 7, 9	310—4, 8, 10	3—7
245(35)—10	251.2—3, 5, 8	311—10	9—1, 3, 5
245(38)—5, 8	251.3—1, 5, 7	313—10	10—6
245(39)—1, 2, 3, 4	251.5—1, 3, 6	316—1, 2, 3, 4, 5, 6, 7, 8, 9, 10	13—3, 5, 8, 9, 10
245(40)—3, 7, 8	251.6—4	318—4, 5, 10	14—1, 5, 10
245(41)—2	251.8—5	320—1, 2, 3, 5, 8, 9, 10	15—2
245(44)—8	251.11—1, 2, 4, 5	322—6	16—6, 8
245(48)—7	251.12—2, 3, 4, 8, 10	323—5	17—6
245(49)—5	251.13—2, 6, 10	324— ., ., 6, 9	31—3, 7, 10
245(50)—2, 5	251.14—1, 8, 10	326—1, 2, 4, 5, 6, 7, 8, 9, 10	32—3
245(51)—8	251.15—1, 4, 5, 6	327—1, 8	33—2, 6, 7
245(57)—7	251.16—4, 8, 9, 10	330—1, 2, 3, 4, 7, 10	35—2, 5
245(58)—6	251.17—1, 2, 4, 5, 6, 7, 8	331—3, 5, 6, 7, 8	101—6, 7, 8, 10
245(59)—2	251.18—4, 5, 7, 8, 9	332—1, 2, 3, 4, 5, 6, 7, 8, 9, 10	102—3, 4, 9
245(60)—5, 8	251.19—1, 4, 6, 8, 9, 10	333—7	107—4
245(61)—8	252—1, 2, 4, 5, 6, 7, 9, 10	336—1, 2, 3, 4, 8	122—10
245(62)—2, 4, 5, 8, 9	253—3, 10	337—1, 2, 6, 8	123—4, 7, 10
245(65)—1	254—4, 10	339—2, 3, 6, 8	124—7, 9
245(67)—1, 2, 3, 4, 5, 7, 8	255—2, 9	340—6, 7	141—2, 8, 9

[Illustration 17]

KEY NUMBER TRANSLATION TABLE FROM THE EIGHTH DECENNIAL DIGEST

FEDERAL COURTS

TABLE 1

KEY NUMBER TRANSLATION TABLE

COURTS AND APPEAL AND ERROR TO FEDERAL COURTS

The topic FEDERAL COURTS was formerly part of the topic COURTS. This table lists key numbers in the topic COURTS together with the corresponding key number(s) in the topic FEDERAL COURTS (or reference to another topic) where cases are now digested.

Federal cases formerly under certain key numbers of the topic APPEAL AND ERROR are also included in the topic FEDERAL COURTS. This table also lists key numbers of the topic APPEAL AND ERROR involved, with the key number(s) under FEDERAL COURTS where federal cases are now digested.

For present classification of a particular case, see the Table of Cases.

Courts Key Number	Federal Courts Key Number	Courts Key Number	Federal Courts Key Number
23 (selected pars.)	31	263(5)	15
101	742	263(6)	17
101.5(1)	991, 1008–1010	263(7)	16
101.5(2)	992, 998, 1002, 1008–1010	264(1)	20, 23, 24
101.5(3)	997	264(2)	21, 23, 24
101.5(4)	993–996, 998–1002, 1008–1010	264(3)	22
101.5(5)	1003–1006, 1008–1010	264(4)	21
101.5(6)	1007	264(5)	25
101.5(7)	1011	264.1	8

> This illustrates how the Key Number classification is kept current. In the Eighth Decennial Digest, Federal Courts was made a separate Topic. This Table, which precedes the Topic, allows one who has been searching in earlier Decennials under a Courts Key Number to translate into the new Federal Courts Key Number. While not shown, Table 2 translates Federal Court Key Numbers into Court Key Numbers.

Courts Key Number	Federal Courts Key Number	Courts Key Number	Federal Courts Key Number
262.1	7 (and specific topics)	274.2	93
262.2	(specific topics)	274.3	77
262.3	(specific topics)	274.4	91
262.4	6 (and specific topics)	274.5	86
262.5	(Injunction)	274.6	78
262.6	(Injunction)	274.7	77, 89
262.8	27 (and specific topics)	274.8–10	88
262.9	28 (and specific topics)	274.11	90
263(1, 2)	14	274.12	77, 92
263(3)	18	274.13	80
263(4)	19	274.14(1, 2)	79, 82, 87, 92

SECTION D.   FINDING TOPICS AND KEY NUMBERS

The *American Digest System* as classified to the *Key Number System* provides a means to locate all decisions on the same point of law.   Once it is determined to what Topic and Key Number a particular point of law has been classified, searching for cases can commence in the various units of the *American Digest System.*

The important matter is to learn how to find the Topic and Key Number.   There are three common methods provided for within the *American Digest Sytem.*

1.   The Descriptive-Word Index

The *Descriptive-Word Index* is arranged alphabetically and includes: (1) all topics of the digest classification; (2) all Key Number section lines and editorial reference lines in the *Decennial Digests*; (3) *catch words* or descriptive words relating to parties to the suits who are members of a class, occupation, or legal relation; (4) place names and physical objects; (5) questions of law; (6) constitutional and legislative provisions; and (7) legal principles which relate to the subject matter of the suit.

There is a separate *Descriptive-Word Index* to each of the *Decennial* units as well as to the *General Digest.*

Let us examine the problem described in Section A to see how the *Descriptive-Word Indexes* to the *Decennial* units of the *American Digest System* are used to locate Topics and Key Numbers for finding cases dealing with damages to an automobile left in a parking lot.

In starting the search, it is best to start in a recent *Decennial* or in the *General Digest.*   When using an index, the first entry looked under should be a specific word or phrase relevant to the fact situation under research.   In this instance, *Automobiles* would most likely be too general a term.   A more specific one would be *Parking Lot* or perhaps *Garage.*   If the use of specific words or phrases is not successful, it may be necessary to search a legal concept such as *bailment.*   At times, it may be necessary to consult the *Descriptive-Word Indexes* to other *Decennials.*   After a Topic and Key Number has been identified from the Index volumes, the volume or volumes containing the digests for this Topic should be consulted to locate cases analogous to the problem under research.   If deemed necessary, other units of the *American Digest System* may also be consulted under the same Topic and Key Number.

Illustration 18 demonstrates in detail the use of the *Descriptive-Word Index* as a means of locating Topics and Key Numbers.

2. Analysis or Topic Method

As the *American Digest System* is based on a classification system, it is possible to analyze a fact situation and to determine from this analysis which Topics and Key Numbers will be applicable to the problem being researched. In the problem used to illustrate the *Descriptive-Word Index* approach, *supra,* one could determine that the topic of law involved is *Automobiles.* Then check the *Analysis and Outline* that appears immediately after the Topic *Automobiles* in the *Ninth Decennial, Part 1* and locate the appropriate Key Numbers. [See Illustrations 13–13–a.]

The method requires a certain amount of legal sophistication and should not be used without having a fairly good knowledge of law. Moreover, there is always the danger inherent in this approach that the researcher may arrive at one analysis that leads to a specific Topic and Key Number, whereas the editors in their analysis assigned a different Topic and Key Number. Hence, it is recommended that this method be used with care and only after one has had considerable experience in legal research.

3. Table of Cases Method

Each *Decennial* unit and each volume of the *General Digest* has an alphabetical table of cases by plaintiff. Each case listing includes the citation and the Topics and Key Numbers under which the case has been digested. Thus, if one knew, for example, that the case of *Garlock v. Multiple Parking Services, Inc.* dealt with the question of liability for automobiles left in parking lots, the Topics and Key Numbers assigned to that case could easily be located by consulting the *Table of Cases* volumes. [See Illustration 19.]

This method is most useful when one knows the name of a case and wishes to find additional cases on the same points of law.

SECTION E. ILLUSTRATIONS: FINDING THE TOPICS AND KEY NUMBERS

18–18a. Sample pages from the Descriptive-Word Index to the Eighth Decennial Digest

19.   Sample page from Table of Cases Volumes of the Ninth Decennial Digest, Part 1

[Illustration 18]

SAMPLE PAGE FROM DESCRIPTIVE-WORD INDEX TO THE EIGHTH DECENNIAL DIGEST

46-8th D—1299   **GARBAGE**

GARAGES—Cont'd
Liability and indemnity insurance—Cont'd
  Excess or other insurance. Insurance 512.1(4)
  Excess or other insurance, primary liability, customer automobile loaned during repairs. Insurance 512.1(1)
  Other insurance clause, permissibility under statute. Insurance 512.1(1)
  Proprietor's personal injury liability—
    Judgment creditor proving use or maintenance of automobile. Insurance 457.1(3)
  Proration of loss, accident involving loaned automobile. Insurance 512.1(3)
  Teenage risks. Insurance 435.23(5)
Liability insurance—
  Ambiguous coverage. Evid 450(5)
Licenses and permits—
  Corporations, consolidation and merger, liabilities. Corp 569
  Denial of, interference with rights to liberty or pursuit of happiness. Licens 7(1)
Lien—
  Accident, disabled vehicle moved without hospitalized owners' consent. Autos 375
  Automobile storage charges, priority, finance company's security interest. Sec Tran 138
  Bad checks, relinquishment of property. Autos 363
  Bank's antecedent's security interest perfected, priority over garage owner's mechanic's lien. Sec Tran

GARAGES—Cont'd
Motor vehicle inspection station license, appeal from granting. Autos 365
Municipal garage, dumping operation equipment, refusal of injunction. Mun Corp 736
Municipal parking authority—
  Lease facilities or exclusive option to purchase—
    Taxpayers' challenge. Mun Corp 990
Night attendant, authority to contract bailment of property worth $23,000. Autos 370
Nuisance—
  Storage of codeine based cough syrup. Nuis 92
  Tenants, cause of action, apartment rendered partially uninhabitable from condition existing prior to taking occupancy. Nuis 44
Operator as compensated depository or bailee—
  Autos 370
  Bailm 3
  Depositaries 3
Parking—
  Unauthorized use. Autos 355(10)
Parking, limitation of liability for garage owner's negligence, validity of contract. Autos 370
Proximate cause, theft, automobile placed unlocked in lot, keys inside. Autos 365
Rent, 41 garages in complex of 424 apartments assigned from waiting list, amendment to maximum base rent orders. Land & Ten 200.45
Repairs and other services—
  Motor vehicle accident, starting while undergoing—

GARAGES—Cont'd
Workmen's compensation—
  Flat tire on own vehicle, using employer's equipment. Work Comp 665
  Watchman crushed by own car. Work Comp 1359
Wrongful sequestration, repaired automobile before warranty expired—
  Autos 368
  Sequest 21
Zoning—
  Federal housing regulations, not permitting expenditure for construction. Zoning 405
Zoning regulations—
  Garage for rubbish trucks in rural residential district. Zoning 418
  Home light, air and view restricted. Zoning 789
  Storage of city parks' trucks and tractors, single-family restriction. Zoning 237

GARBAGE
Abandonment, searches and seizures. Searches 3.3(9)
Army Corps of Engineers permit regulations, nonnavigable waters, ultra vires. Nav Wat 35
Assessment lien, foreclosure. Plead 354(33)
Bid for exclusive collection franchise, overestimation of value of described equipment, fraud. Counties 116
City truck, negligent operation, suit against city. Autos 187
Collection—
  Agreement by collector with city, claim that night trash pickups were extra work. Mun Corp 254
  Authorization for county commis-

> We can now start to illustrate how Topics can be located using the Descriptive-Word Index to a unit of the American Digest System. In this instance, we start with the Index to the Eighth Decennial. Note how there does not seem to be an entry precisely on point. This usually indicates that the search should continue under a more specific word or phrase. See next illustration.

Dealer's purchase money lien. Autos 374
Declaratory judgment. Judgm 181(15)
  Perfected security interest. Sec Tran 144
  With respect to seller's security interest. Sec Tran 144
Repairman's lien. Autos 374
Stolen automobile, removal to place of business on direction of deputy sheriff, storage and towing charges. Autos 375
Towage, police ordering, validity of statute giving service station lien. Autos 363
Loaned employee, driver of truck being tested after repairs. Insurance 457.1(4)
Location 15 feet from boundary, town ordinance requiring 20 foot distance unauthorized. Towns 15
Malicious mischief, repaired vehicles damaged by vandals in an unfenced lot. Autos 368
Mechanic, work on automobile accidentally starting and injuring another, omnibus coverage. Insurance 435.2(6)
Mechanic's action against another mechanic for injuries sustained as result of explosion when starting vehicle. Explos 7
Modified stock car racer, garage liability coverage, towing of driverless racer. Insurance 435.23(3)

Searches 7(12)
Search, rented garage without consent of landlady, necessity of search warrant. Searches 7(27)
Search of residential garage, authority of wife to consent in absence of husband. Searches 7(27)
Searches and seizures. Searches 7(10)
Sequestration repaired automobile before term of warranty expired—
  Autos 368
  Sequest 21
Spring gun, burglary prevention, boy attempting entry shot. Assault 69
Stock car racers, garage liability coverage, towing of driverless racer. Insurance 435.23(3)
Storage of vehicles—
  Bailor-bailee relationship. Statut 145
Suspension of license for two days, attempt to conceal damage from vehicle. Autos 365
Taxation, valuation. Tax 491
Theft of automobile—
  Liability of operator for damages—
    Autos 370
    Bailm 31(3)
Towing, stock car racer, garage liability coverage. Insurance 435.23(3)
Transmission, disappearance from vehicle stored in unfenced area. Autos 372
Trap gun, burglary prevention, boy attempting entry shot. Assault 69

61
Collection contracts exceeding $2,500, statute requiring bidding, implied repeal. Pub Contr 2, 6
Collection fees, nonpayment, municipal discontinuance of telephone and electric service. Mun Corp 807
Collection service charge by city. Mun Corp 807
Collectors, injury, earning losses. Work Comp 833
Collectors, ordinance giving township board of health power to control rates, ultra vires exercise of municipal authority. Towns 15
Commercial haulers, regulation imposing disposal charges on, authority to enact. Mun Corp 807
Counties, nonputrescible solid waste collection and removal, authority to regulate. Counties 21¼
Counties, ordinances, commissioners empowered to grant disposal certificates, ex post facto laws. Const Law 197
County dump by airport, jet crashing after ingesting birds flying over, immunity of county. Counties 206
County solid waste ordinance requiring deposit in landfill sites within county, invalidity—
  Const Law 296(2)
  Health & E 21
Curbside collection, municipality's determination to limit service, permissibility. Const Law 253(2)

[Illustration 18–a]

EXCERPTS FROM THE DESCRIPTIVE–WORD INDEX TO THE EIGHTH DECENNIAL DIGEST

PARKING LOTS　　47–8th D—**506**

PARKING LOTS—Cont'd
Liability, damage to engine caused by impact, engine repairs necessitated by loss of oil pressure—
　Balm 14(1)
　Damag 62(3)
Liability insurance, coverage for light pole damaged during installation.
　Insurance 435.23(6)
Lights and lighting. **Neglig 124(3)**
Light bulb burned out, constructive notice, building tenant's employee falling. **Land & T 165(4)**
Lights, laundromat, failure to maintain, eviction of tenant. **Land & Ten 172(3)**
Limitation of actions, improper design of ramps for parking deck. **Lim of Act 30**
Limitation of liability, negligence of lot owner, validity of contract. **Autos 370**
Limitation of liability, theft of vehicle due to ordinary negligence, validity of contract. **Balm 14(1)**
Littering, prevention, prohibiting distribution of union literature in during nonworking hours. **Labor 386**

PARKING LOTS—Cont'd
Ordinances, township, gross receipts tax, county's airport parking lot.
　Licens 19(3)
Parish police jury, expenditure for lot on industrial inducement project property, permissibility. **Counties 153½**
Parking lot garages, nature of contract with customer. **Autos 372**
Parks, joint use agreement giving university exclusive lot use at specified times, authorization. **Mun Corp 721 (3)**
Patrons, injuries to—
　Lane divider, trip over. **Neglig 56 (1.1)**
Patrons, injury from fellow patron's automobile, foresight of lot attendant, jury question. **Autos 17**
Pedestrian, injuries, work rule violation. **Work Comp 2168**
Personal injuries, patron falling in adjacent parking lot extended into unleased property. **Neglig 54**
Personal property in automobile, proprietor's responsibility, contract, knowledge or notice. **Balm 14(1)**
Presumption, negligence of lot owner

PARKING LOTS—Cont'd
Shopping centers, partial taking of property resulting in loss of parking spaces, consequential damages. **Em Dom 96**
Slope, employee's vehicle sliding into canal, drowning. **Work Comp 681**
Stealing and damaging automobile.
　Balm 31(3)
Stores, fall on ice, negligence of owner.
　Neglig 134(7)
Summary judgment, patron falling over metal plank, negligence. **Judgm 185.3(21)**
Supermarket, child's fall from shopping cart during nonbusiness hours, summary judgment precluded. **Judgm 181(33)**
Tax, invalid provision of ordinance, amendment of preamble. **Mun Corp 110, 111(4)**
Tax exemption—
　Church lot commercially used six days per week, establishment of religion—
　　Const Law 84
　　Tax 197

> Using the entry, "parking lots," note how we locate a more specific entry. The next step is to take the volume of the Eighth Decennial containing the Topic Automobiles and look first to the Analysis to see if this indicates a more specific Key Number. If not, examine the digest paragraphs under 372, and note citations of cases with facts closest to the problem under research. Then examine same Topic and Key Number in Ninth Decennial, Part I, and the General Digest volumes. If necessary, consult Seventh and earlier Decennials. Read there cases for which citations were noted.

Mun Corp 450(4)
Municipal parking lot, recovery for injuries precluded. **Mun Corp 733(1)**
Municipal taxes, authority for 10 percent tax on gross receipts of commercial lots. **Licens 6(13)**
Municipalities, population exceeding 60,000, proposed bill authorizing construction, constitutionality. **Mun Corp 266, 406(1), 722**
Musical equipment in trunk, owner not mentioning, loss when vehicle stolen.
　Balm 14(1)
Negligence—
　Parking vehicles facing up and down slope. **Neglig 28**
Negligence, presumption against lot operator. **Balm 31(1)**
Nightclub concession, licensor-licensee rather than landlord-tenant relationship. **Licens 44(2)**
Noncompetition agreements, reasonableness. **Contracts 117(3)**
Obligation to light parking area. **Neglig 38**
Obscenity, public indecency statute.
　Obscen 3
Off-line CBCT, status as branch.
　Banks 236
Operator, authorization to move automobiles, evidence. **Autos 244(22, 33)**
Operator as compensated depository or bailee—
　Autos 370
　Balm 2
　Depositaries 3

..........y, liability for injuries by robbers—
　Counties 143
　Schools 89.6
Security, open-air lot not providing adequately, license renewal denial. **Licens 25, 36**
Self-service parking lot, bailment of automobile. **Balm 2, 14(1)**
Service of process. **Partners 204**
Shoppers—
　Invitee status. **Neglig 32(2.8)**
Shopping center—
　Bank drive-in teller lane, landlord's right to grant. **Land & Ten 53 (1)**
　Declaratory judgment petition alleging landlord's taking of parking spaces. **Decl Judgm 316**
Driving vehicle while under influence of intoxicating liquors. **Autos 332**
Employee of tenant falling on ice.
　Neglig 32(1)
Pavement laying contract, substantial performance. **Contracts 322 (3)**
Automobile accidents, negligence.
　Autos 155, 201(1)
Shopping center, customer attacked by stranger in lot, liability of center owners and shopkeepers. **Neglig 48**
Shopping center, loss of parking space through eminent domain, severance damages. **Em Dom 107**
Shopping center, motorcycle striking debris pile in lot, vicarious liability of lessors. **Autos 290**

safe place. **Neglig 31**
Trespass—
　Piling debris and rocks on parking area. **Tresp 46(1)**
Two-inch verticle pavement rise, invitee tripping and falling over, status as dangerous condition, fair grounds.
　Agric 4(3)
Universities, rules, authority to establish penalties for breach. **Colleges 7**
Wall falling on parked vehicle, liability of lessor of parking lot for failure to maintain. **Land & Ten 165(1)**
Wearing apparel, disappearance from automobile unexplained by direct evidence. **Balm 31(3)**
Workmen's compensation—
　Attendant shot by jealous husband.
　　Work Comp 697
　Closing co-employee's automobile windows in case of adverse weather.
　　Work Comp 666, 669
　Collision in company-maintained lot—
　　Course of employment. **Work Comp 732, 2168, 2170**
　Collision in employer's parking lot, injury in course of employment.
　　Work Comp 732
　Constituting employer's operating premises. **Work Comp 732**
　Employee falling while enroute to work. **Work Comp 723, 756, 1716**
　Employee injured by automobile operated by fellow employee.
　　Work Comp 2168

[Illustration 19]

SAMPLE PAGE FROM THE TABLE OF CASES VOLUMES OF THE NINTH DECENNIAL DIGEST, PART 1

35–9th D Pt 1—1065 **GARONE**

References are to Digest Topics and Key Numbers

Garlic v. Mathews, DCVa, 423 FSupp 40.—Labor 13.

Garlick v. Workmen's Compensation Appeal Bd., PaCmwlth, 377 A2d 212, 31 PaCmwlth 570.—Work Comp 1818, 1912, 1949.

Garlock v. Multiple Parking Services, Inc., NYCity Ct, 427 NYS2d 670, 103 Misc2d 943.—Autos 372(1), 372(4); Bailm 14(1).

Garlock v. Penn Cent. Transp. Co., NYAD, 386 NYS2d 490, 53 AD2d 1006.—Courts 100(1); R R 382(1), 400(1), 400(11).

Garlor Associates v. Zoning Bd. of Appeals of Town of Huntington, Suffolk County, NYAD, 426 NYS2d 41. See Sokoloff v. Zoning Bd. of Appeals of Town of Huntington, Suffolk County.

Garlovsky, State ex rel., v. Eastmore, FlaApp, 393 So2d 567. See State ex rel. Garlovsky v. Eastmore.

Garman, Appeal of, PaSuper, 378 A2d 449. See Garman, In re.

Garman, In re, PaSuper, 378 A2d 449, 250 PaSuper 54.—Infants 131, 224.

Garman, Matter of, CAIll, 643 F2d 1252, cert den Garman v. Northern Trust Co.

487.—Divorce 208, 321½.

Garmon v. Johnson, Ga, 257 SE2d 276, 243 Ga 855.—Crim Law 273(2); Ind & Inf 5; Jury 29(2).

Garmond v. Kinney, NM, 579 P2d 178, 91 NM 646.—Ease 6, 8(1), 8(4), 9(2), 36(3); Evid 71.

Garnas v. American Farm Equipment Co., DCND, 502 FSupp 349.—Rem of C 77.

Garnas v. Milbank Mut. Ins. Co., DCND, 502 FSupp 349. See Garnas v. American Farm Equipment Co.

Garnatz v. Stifel, Nicolaus & Co., Inc., CAMo, 559 F2d 1357, cert den 98 SCt 1578, 435 US 951, 55 LEd2d 801.—Fed Civ Proc 2331; Fed Cts 631; Lim of Act 100(6); Sec Reg 121, 134, 147, 148, 154, 156.

Garnel v. Bunzel, CalApp, 137 CalRptr 627, 68 CA3d 999.—Colleges 8(1); Const Law 251.5, 255(1), 255(2), 277(1), 277(2), 278.5(2), 318(1).

Garner, Matter of, CAGa, 556 F2d 772.—Bankr 1106; Cons Cred 56, 57; Fed Cts 542.

Garner v. Atlantic Bldg. Systems, Inc., GaApp, 236 SE2d 183, 142 GaApp 517.—Work Comp 564, 1543, 1752, 1943, 2009.

Garner v. Chandler, Ga, 227 SE2d 256, 237 Ga 245.—Bound 41; New Tr 159.

Garner v. City of Michigan City, DCInd, 453 FSupp 33.—Mun Corp 723.

Garner v. Cruz, Mont, 567 P2d 40. See First Nat Bank of Circle v. Garner.

Garner v. Driver, GaApp, 270 SE2d 863, 155 GaApp 322.—Autos 245(2), 246(60); Damag 216(4); Evid 571(9), 588; Neglig 136(14), 136(25), 136(26), 136(31), 138(2), 138(4); Torts 15; Trial 252(21).

Garner v. East Texas Nat. Bank of Palestine, TexCivApp, 608 SW2d 939, ref nre.—Cons Cred 4, 33; Evid 461(1), 461(4).

Garner v. E. I. Du Pont De Nemours & Co., CASC, 538 F2d 611.—Civil R 31, 40.

Garner v. E. I. Du Pont De Nemours & Co., DCSC, 416 FSupp 682, rev 538 F2d 611.—Civil R 40.

Garner v. E. I. du Pont de Nemours and Co., Va, 248 SE2d 830, 219 Va 652.—Mast & S 78.1(6).

Garner v. Enright, DCNY, 71 FRD 656

Law 8.

Garner v. Johnson, Okl, 609 P2d 760.—Judgm 181(2), 181(27).

Garner v. Jones, MoApp, 589 SW2d 66.—App & E 1069.3, 1078(4); Autos 245(1), 246(9); Evid 483(1), 508, 519; Trial 312(2), 314(1).

Garner v. Memphis Police Dept., City of Memphis, Tenn., CATenn, 600 F2d 52.—Civil R 13.8(3), 13.8(4).

Garner v. Metropolitan Life Ins. Co., GaApp, 262 SE2d 544, 152 GaApp 242.—Contracts 143.5, 162; Ven & Pur 70.

Garner v. Missouri Division of Family Services, MoApp, 591 SW2d 27.—Admin Law 391; Social S 241; Statut 219(9).

Garner v. Skafar, IllApp, 4 IllDec 462, 360 NE2d 398, 45 IllApp3d 859.—Autos 171(8), 208, 242(8), 244(43), 245(80).

Garner v. Smith, Ga, 233 SE2d 797. See State Bd of Corrections v. Smith.

Garner v. State, AlaCrApp, 364 So2d 406, writ den Ex parte Garner, 364 So2d 411.—Crim Law 1036.2; Witn 246(2).

Garner v. State, GaApp, 269 SE2d 912, 154 GaApp 839.—Crim Law 394.6(4); Searches 3.2, 3.3, 7(10).

Garner v. State, Ind, 413 NE2d 584.—Crim Law 1170½(6), 1171.8(1); Rob 24.1(3); Witn 337(6).

Garner v. State, Miss, 359 So2d 764.—Homic 250.

Garner v. State, TexCrApp, 556 SW2d 332.—Game 9.

Garner v. State, TexCrApp, 552 SW2d 809.—Crim Law 1202(3).

Garner v. State, TexCrApp, 545 SW2d 178.—Const Law 270(5); Crim Law 982.9(4).

Garner v. State of Okl, CAOkl, 561 F2d 1351. See Bromley v. Crisp.

Garner v. State of Okl., DCOkl, 430 FSupp 692, aff Bromley v. Crisp, 561 F2d 1351, cert den 98 SCt 1458, 435 US 908, 55 LEd2d 499, appeal after remand Rutledge v. Sunderland, 671 F2d 377.—Crim Law 232; Hab Corp 45.2(4), 45.3(3), 45.3(4), 85.5(1), 85.5(7), 90; Infants 68.5.

Garner v. Tuckahoe Housing Authority, NYAD, 439 NYS2d 188, 81 AD2d 915.—Mun Corp 717.

Garner v. U. S., CATenn, 538 F2d 128, cert gr 97 SCt 1574, 430 US 942, 51 LEd2d 789.—Crim Law 991; Weap 4).

er v. Valley Sav. and Loan Ass'n, App, 580 P2d 493, 91 NM 725.— nt Ten 12, 14.

er Associates, Inc. v. Beauhall, La, 492 FSupp 1020. See Walt Garr Associates, Inc. v. Beauhall.

er Tool & Die v. Laux, Neb, 285 V2d 219, 204 Neb 717.—App & E (2); Mast & S 60, 66; Trade Reg).

et v. D'Alonzo, PaCmwlth, 422 A2d 11, 55 PaCmwlth 263.—Atty & C 77, (1).

ett, City of, v. Anderson, Kan, 625 d 491. See City of Garnett v. iener.

ett, City of, v. Chilson, Kan, 625 d 491. See City of Garnett v. iener.

ett, City of, v. Miller, Kan, 625 P2d l. See City of Garnett v. Zwiener.

ett, City of, v. Zwiener, Kan, 625 d 491. See City of Garnett v. iener.

ick v. Zoning Hearing Bd. of idgeton Tp., PaCmwlth, 427 A2d), 58 PaCmwlth 92.—Zoning 465,

ix Trucking Co, In re, DCAla, 455 FSupp 327. See Gardner, In re.

Garn L. Baum v. Gillman, CAUtah, 648 F2d 1292. See Baum v. Gillman.

Garnto v. State, Ga, 273 SE2d 608, 247 Ga 22.—Crim Law 939(1).

Garo v. Garo, Fla, 347 So2d 418.—Divorce 269(13).

Garo v. Garo, 327 So2d 845, quashed 347 So2d 418.

Garo v. Garo, FlaApp, 340 So2d 1226.—Divorce 285; Trial 23.

Garofalo v. Community Hospital of South Broward, FlaApp, 382 So2d 722.—Lim of Act 6(1).

Garofalo v. Malaysia Overseas Export Lines, Inc., DCNY, 470 FSupp 166.—Ship 84(1), 84(3¼); Work Comp 11.

Garofalo v. Public Emp Retirement System, State Dept of Treasury, Division of Pensions, NJSuperAD, 386 A2d 428. See Burkhart v. Public Emp Retirement System, State Dept of Treasury Division of Pensions.

Garofoli v. Town of Henniker, NH, 427 A2d 35, 121 NH 153.—Mun Corp 712.

Garone v. Joy, NYSup, 436 NYS2d 697, 107 Misc2d 1094.—Land & Ten 200.16, 200.83.

A page from the Table of Cases, Ninth Decennial Digest, Part 1.

When a case is known to deal with a topic of law, Key Numbers assigned to that Topic can be located by use of the Table of Cases. See, for example, the listing for the Garlock case.

Note also how a Table of Cases may be used to determine if a particular case has been appealed to a higher court and the results of the appeal. See Garner v. State of Oklahoma.

SECTION F. SPECIAL DIGESTS

As the *American Digest System* with its Key Number classification is made up from the headnotes from all of the units of the *National Reporter System*, it is all-inclusive and most useful when one is interested in locating decisions from all American jurisdictions. More typically, however, when engaged in legal research, one is primarily interested in locating decisions from a particular state or group of states, or in only those decisions reached in the federal courts. In such instances, it is better and easier to use a digest less comprehensive than that of the *American Digest System*.

1. State Digests

The West Publishing Company publishes for nearly every state a Key Number digest.[2] A typical state Key Number digest consists of digest paragraphs for all the cases of the particular state, including those that originated in the federal courts of the state. It is kept current through the issuing of annual cumulative pocket supplements for the set, and each state digest has its own *Descriptive-Word Index* and *Table of Cases* volumes. [See Illustrations 20–20–a for examples of a state digest.]

2. Regional Digests

There are regional digests corresponding to most of the regional reporters of the *National Reporter System*. These digests are arranged under the Key Number classification and include digests of cases for each of the states within the particular region. The digest paragraphs under each Key Number are arranged alphabetically by the states included within the digest. Each regional digest has its own volumes of the *Descriptive-Word Index* and its own volumes of *Tables of Cases*. These are kept current by the issuing of annual cumulative pocket supplements and interim pamphlet supplements. The regional digests are:

Atlantic Digest, First and Second Series

North Western Digest, First and Second Series

Pacific Digest, First, Second and Third Series

South Eastern Digest, First and Second Series

Southern Digest

---

[2] The West Publishing Company publishes Key Number digests for every state except Delaware, Nevada, and Utah. Additionally, a few states have digests available from other publishers.

3. Digests for Federal Court Opinions

a. *Federal Practice Digest, 3d.* This set is another Key Number digest and contains digests of opinions from 1976 to date for all of the federal courts. It is kept up to date by annual cumulative pocket supplements and interim pamphlet supplements. Other features are:

(1) Under each Key Number, cases are arranged first for the Supreme Court, then the courts of appeals, and then the district courts arranged alphabetically by jurisdiction.

(2) The digest paragraphs include information as to whether a case has been affirmed, reversed, or modified.

(3) *Table of Cases* volumes including a Defendant-Plaintiff table.

(4) *Words and Phrases* volumes.

(5) A complete numerical listing of all patents adjudicated is included under the Topic, *Patents*, Key Number 328.

(6) An alphabetical table of all *Trade-Marks and Trade-Names Adjudicated* is included in the *Trade Regulations* volume at Key Number 736.

b. *Earlier Federal Digests.* Federal cases prior to 1976 are available in the following:

(1) *Federal Practice Digest, 2d*, 1961–1975.

(2) *Modern Federal Practice Digest*, 1939–1960.

(3) *Federal Digest*, all cases prior to 1939.

Whenever a researcher is aware that the problem being researched is one under the jurisdiction of a federal court, it will be quicker and more accurate to confine the research to a federal digest.[3]

c. *Digests for the Supreme Court of the United States.* As the Supreme Court of the United States plays such a significant role within the American legal system, it is extremely useful to have digests that only contain its opinions. There are currently two such digests. One is published by Lawyers Co-operative Publishing Company, whose publications are described in more detail in Chapter 7. The other is a Key Number digest of the West Publishing Company.

(1) *U.S. Supreme Court Reports Digest* (Lawyers Co-operative Publishing Co.). This is a 20-volume digest, with cumulative annual pocket supplements, to all U.S. Supreme Court decisions. Since this set is not published by the West Publishing Company, it does not employ the *Key Number System* and follows the publisher's own distinct classification.

---

[3] Jurisdiction for some areas of law is restricted by the Constitution to the federal courts, e.g., U.S.CONST. art. 1, sec. 8, cl. 8 (Copyright) or U.S.CONST. art. 1, sec. 8, cl. 4 (Bankruptcy). For further information on the relationship between state courts and federal courts, *see* 1 MOORE'S FEDERAL PRACTICE ¶ 0.6 (2d ed. 1948).

(2) *U.S. Supreme Court Digest* (West Publishing Company). This 17-volume digest of all decisions of the Supreme Court of the United States is classified under the *Key Number System* and duplicates the Supreme Court cases in the *American Digest System*. It is kept up to date by cumulative annual pocket supplements.

d.   *Digests for Other Federal Courts*

(1) *West's Bankruptcy Digest.* This Key Number digest includes cases from *West's Bankruptcy Reporter* and selected Bankruptcy cases from the *Federal Reporter* and the *Supreme Court Reporter.*

(2) *Military Justice Digest.* This digests cases from the *Military Justice Reporter* and is a Key Number digest.

(3) *United States Claims Court Digest.* This is a Key Number digest that includes cases from the United States Claims Court since 1982, and cases appealed from it to the United States Court of Appeals for the Federal Circuit and the Supreme Court of the United States.

(4) *West's Federal Case News.* This is a weekly pamphlet that provides a summary of cases decided in all federal courts. It is arranged by court, with summaries printed under topics arranged alphabetically. As this pamphlet does not cumulate, it is only useful as a current awareness service.

SECTION G. CHART ILLUSTRATING THE AMERICAN DIGEST SYSTEM **

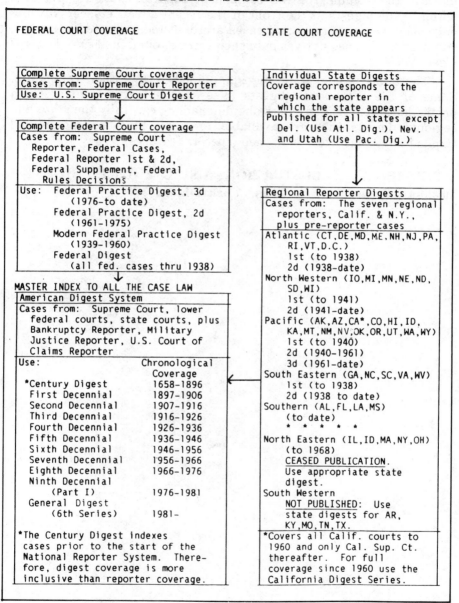

** Prepared by Professor Donald J. Dunn, Law Librarian, Western New England College, School of Law.

Once a particular digest is selected, it is important to update the search completely. Each pocket part and pamphlet supplement will indicate the volumes of the component reporter that are digested within. The digests at the front of the recent advance sheets are the only place where very recent cases are digested. For federal cases, summaries of cases not yet published can be found in *West's Federal Case News*.

There are some state digests published by other companies. Some of the West state digests have special features unique to a particular state. Researchers should examine carefully the state and regional digests that are available for their state or region and familiarize themselves with their special features.

SECTION H.   ILLUSTRATIONS USING A STATE DIGEST
20–20-a.   Pages from the New York Digest.

[Illustration 20]

SAMPLE PAGE FROM THE NEW YORK DIGEST, 3rd EDITION

PARDON   41 N Y D 3rd—4

References are to Digest Topics and Key Numbers

PARDON AND PAROLE—Cont'd
SEARCH and seizure. **Pardon 68**
SENTENCE, effect on computation. **Crim Law 1216.2**
SENTENCE provisions, parole eligibility. **Pardon 54**
Minimum sentence. **Pardon 50**
SEVERITY rating, parole. **Pardon 54**
SPEEDY trial. **Pardon 84**
STATUS of parolee. **Pardon 66**
SUPERVISION of parolee. **Pardon 68**
UNEXECUTED parole, rescission of retardation. **Pardon 63**
VALIDITY, parole conditions. **Pardon 64**
WAIVER of jurisdiction. **Pardon 79**
WARRANT, parole revocation. **Pardon 81**
Time for. **Pardon 83**

PARENS PATRIAE
STATE acting as "superparent". **Infants 2**

PARENT AND CHILD
RIGHT of child to visit parent. **Parent & C 1**

PARENTAL KIDNAPPING PREVENTION ACT OF 1980
PREEMPTION, state law. **States 4.10**

PARIMUTUEL BETTING
REGULATION. **Gaming 4**
REGULATION by Racing and Wagering Board. **Gaming 4**

PARKING
DEFAULT judgment for failure to pay parking violations, due process—
Autos 349
Const Law 315
DUE process, default judgment for failure to pay parking violations—
Autos 349
Const Law 315
MUNICIPAL contract for collection of parking meter revenues, limitation. **Contracts 129(1)**

→ **PARKING LOTS**
OPERATOR'S liability for loss of vehicle or contents.
Autos 372

PARTITION
COTENANCY—
See also, this index Tenancy in Common
Right to partition—
Generally. **Partit 13, 14**
TENANCY in common—
Right to partition—
Generally. **Partit 13, 14**

PARTNERSHIP
BANKRUPTCY—
Of general partner—
Causing dissolution—
Winding up affairs. **Partners 376**
DISSOLUTION—
Investors seeking accounting and share of moneys wrongfully obtained, defenses. **Partners 317**
EXCHANGES—
Members'. **Exchanges 9.20**

PARTY
INJURIES sustained at—
Dramshop Act. **Int Liq 288**

PASSENGERS
AIR carrier—
Bumping, liability. **Carr 236(2)**
Warn, duty to—
Of dangers of flying with head cold. **Carr 281**
AIRLINE—
Safeguarding hand baggage during security check at airport—
Breach of duty. **Carr 397**
"BUMPED" airline passenger—
Damages—
Elements of compensation. **Carr 236(2)**
BUMPING from aircraft, liability under tariff. **Carr 236(2)**
DAMAGES—
"Bumped" airline passenger—
Elements of compensation. **Carr 236(2)**
HAND baggage—
Airline's duty to safeguard during security check at airport. **Carr 397**
HEAD cold—
Airline's duty to warn of dangers of flying with. **Carr 281**

Frequently, when engaged in legal research, the researcher is interested in finding cases from the courts of a particular state. In such instances, it may be best to start the research in a state digest. As the illustration indicates, this is much less complex than using the Index to a *Decennial* as shown in Illustration 18.

State digests are kept current with annual pocket parts.

PART PERFORMANCE
MODIFICATION—
Fully executed. **Contracts 238(2)**

PARTIES
LIMITATION of actions—
Affected by defects. **Lim of Act 121**
Amendment of defects. **Lim of Act 121(2)**
NECESSARY or indispensable, see this index Joinder of Parties

ent agents. **Pat 178(1)**
FAILURE of others, affecting obviousness. **Pat 36.1(4)**
HINDSIGHT, determination of obviousness. **Pat 16(4)**
INCOME tax, deduction for depreciation. **Int Rev 3502**
LICENSES—
Diligence by licensee in exploiting process. **Pat 212(1)**
OBVIOUSNESS—
Generally. **Pat 16(2)–36.2**
PRIOR art—
Rings placed on sale by inventor. **Pat 80, 155**
PROCESSES—
Licensee's diligence in exploiting process. **Pat 212(1)**

[Illustration 20–a]

SAMPLE PAGE FROM THE NEW YORK DIGEST, 3rd EDITION

⟨⊙⟩372(1) AUTOMOBILES   4 N Y D 3rd—48

bile and retained the keys merely had a license to use space within parking lot and was not entitled to recover from defendant, on theory of breach of contract of bailment, when automobile was gone when he returned to place where he left it.—Silberman v. Olympic Parking Service, 302 N.Y.S.2d 194, 60 Misc.2d 68.

N.Y.City Civ.Ct. 1968. Where full time attendant was on duty at single point of ingress and egress to automobile parking lot, license number was placed on each ticket issued, return of customer's portion of ticket was required, proof of ownership and identification was required if customer's portion of ticket was not returned, and six-foot wire enclosure was provided as well as spaces for 3,500 vehicles for fixed daily rate, bailment for hire was intended. General Obliga-

put his automobile or whether he has turned its possession over to care and custody of another, thus creating a bailment, depends on the place, condition, and nature of the transaction.—Passero v. Diana Parking Station, 123 N.Y.S.2d 652.

Where automobile owner knew that parking lot was unguarded part of the time, continuing to park his automobile in such lot was assent to limited supervision.—Id.

Although parking lot operator requested patron to leave keys in ignition switch, where patron acquiesced in such procedure, and parking arrangement did not require issuance of ticket to patron and tender thereof before removal of automobile, even if request to leave keys was negligence contributing to theft loss, patron's acquiescence was like negligence and precluded recovery

---

When doing research for cases, it is frequently better to start the search in a special digest. This illustrates the search for parking lot cases using a state digest.

The search may be broadened by switching to other Key Number digests.

---

automobile, which patron left with night club employee to park, within view or some measure of observation for two hours constituted negligence on part of night club in that it failed to exercise that degree of care required of a reasonably prudent operator of a night club as to motor vehicles of type owned by patron.—Id.

N.Y.City Civ.Ct. 1962. One who operated automobile parking lot at La Guardia Airport under permit from Port of New York Authority was negligent in failing to fence lot and in keeping only a small area of lot and a short distance of unfenced part of lot under observation of attendant, and operator was liable for damage to automobile stolen from lot. Administrative Code, §§ B32–257.0, B32–259.0.—Nargi v. Parking Associates Corp., 234 N.Y.S.2d 42.

Even though plaintiff locked his automobile and took the key when he left his automobile in La Guardia Airport parking lot operated by defendant under permit from Port of New York Authority and even though fee was small and even though parking ticket stated that transaction was license and not bailment, defendant was responsible as bailee for hire for care and custody of automobile. —Id.

N.Y.City Ct. 1980. Operator of parking lot was liable to owner of automobile for damage sustained when vehicle was burglarized and vandalized while parked on premises, notwithstanding whether a bailment was created, where operator failed to properly protect vehicle from damage through acts of a vandal in that possibility of such acts was clearly foreseeable, considering parking lot's location, size, and general accessibility, and failure to fence or provide a guard or to at least direct owner to a location close to attendant's booth were acts of omission which, as a matter of law, constituted negligence.—Garlock v. Multiple Parking Services, Inc., 427 N.Y.S.2d 670, 103 Misc.2d 943, 13 A.L.R.4th 428.

Failure of parking lot attendant to observe acts of vandalism which, by nature of damage caused, were overt and observable constituted negligence which was attributable to operator of lot since, whether attendant was officially on duty or not, operator could not establish when damage took place.—Id.

N.Y.City Ct. 1953. Whether person in leaving automobile at parking lot simply hires place to

Owner of automobile left in parking lot under such circumstances as to create a bailment was entitled to surveillance over parking lot by proprietor or his employees to see that automobiles entering and leaving and while in parking area did no damage to other automobiles in the lot, and to assistance in every way possible to such end, and small fee charged did not lessen proprietor's duty in such respects.—Id.

Parking lot proprietor was not an insurer of parked automobiles.—Id.

N.Y.City Ct. 1939. Where patrons of automobile parking station were not assigned to a designated place but were permitted to park wherever there was vacant space with express understanding that station owner might move automobiles when necessary, station owner's right to exercise physical dominion at his discretion constituted him a "bailee" generally, rather than a mere "lessor".—Fire Ass'n of Philadelphia v. Fabian, 9 N.Y.S.2d 1018, 170 Misc. 665.

⟨⊙⟩372(2). Limitation of liability.

N.Y.Sup. 1979. Where garage attendant left keys to customer's automobile in clear and open view on a pegboard in an unlocked and unattended office, garage owner was liable for theft of automobile, notwithstanding that garage contract had specifically provided that the relationship between garage and customer was that of a landlord-tenant, and not bailor-bailee. General Obligations Law § 5–325.—Motors Ins. Corp. v. American Garages, Inc., 414 N.Y.S.2d 841, 98 Misc.2d 887.

Attempt to limit liability of garage owner for negligence to $100, unless an added payment equal to cost of theft insurance policy were paid, was an attempt to evade intent of statute and thus could not bar recovery for negligence for theft of automobile, even by automobile owner's subrogated insurer. General Obligations Law §§ 5–321, 5–323, 5–325.—Id.

N.Y.Sup. 1972. Parking lot owner could not free itself of liability for loss of automobile by virtue of statement on its ticket that no bailment was created. General Obligations Law, § 5–325.— Ellish v. Airport Parking Co. of America, 331 N.Y.S.2d 283, 69 Misc.2d 837, affirmed 345 N.Y. S.2d 650, 42 A.D.2d 174, appeal dismissed 350 N.Y.S.2d 411, 33 N.Y.2d 764, 305 N.E.2d 490,

SECTION I. POPULAR NAME TABLES AND WORDS AND PHRASES

1. Popular Name Tables

Frequently a case becomes known by a popular name rather than by its actual name. Examples of such cases are *Brown v. Board of Education* or *United States v. Nixon*. They are frequently cited by their popular names as the *School Desegregation Case* or the *Nixon Tapes Case*. When only the citation of the popular name of a case is at hand, it is necessary to consult a table of cases by popular name in order to obtain the actual name of the case. These tables may be located as follows:

a. *Sixth Decennial* of the *American Digest System*. The Table of Cases volume contains a cumulative *List of Popular Name Titles* in the *American Digest System*. This feature has been discontinued in the subsequent *Decennials*.

b. *Tables of Cases by Popular Names* in the various special digests.

c. *Shepard's Acts and Cases by Popular Names*. [See Illustration 21.]

2. Words and Phrases

Sometimes a problem in legal research involves the definition of certain words or phrases as, for example, *good faith* or *reasonable market value*. Courts constantly must define the meaning of such words and phrases. In cases reported in the units of the *National Reporter System*, such definitions are usually included as headnotes, as in the following example from 606 P.2d 1314 (1980).

---

2. Divorce ☞252.3(1)

In division of marital property, value of goodwill incident to husband's dental practice acquired during his marriage must be considered as "marital property." C.R.S. '73, 14–10–113(2).

See publication Words and Phrases for other judicial constructions and definitions.

All such headnotes are subsequently reprinted in a publication called *Words and Phrases*. This set contains 46 volumes and includes over 350,000 court definitions of legal and non-legal terms. They are arranged alphabetically by word or phrase defined. *Words*

and Phrases is kept up to date by annual cumulative pocket supplements, which are further supplemented by *Words and Phrases Tables* in the current volumes and advance sheets of the various units of the *National Reporter System.* Many of the special digests discussed in Section F also contain such tables. [See Illustration 22 for an example of a page from *Words and Phrases.*]

SECTION J. ILLUSTRATIONS

[Illustration 21]

AN EXCERPT FROM A PAGE OF SHEPARD'S ACTS AND CASES CITED BY POPULAR NAMES

FEDERAL AND STATE CASES CITED BY POPULAR NAMES   **Sch**

Schenectady Six Tickets for a Quarter Case
2 DeptR 284

Schenk Case
253 Fed 212; 249 US 47, 63 LE 470, 39 SC 247

Schiedam Schnapps Cases
18 HowPr 64
15 AbbPr 336

Schlesinger Cases
14 Fed 682; 120 US 109, 30 LE 607, 7 SC 442
14 Fed 687; 120 US 264, 30 LE 656, 7 SC 546
153 Minn 88, 189 NW 415
153 Minn 136, 189 NW 714

Schoharie Valley Railroad Case
12 AbbPr (NS) 394

School Board Cases
213 Ala 106, 104 So 273
221 Ala 217, 128 So 435

School Bus Case
132 NJL 98, 39 A2d 75; 133 NJL 350, 44 A2d
333; 330 US 1, 91 LE 711, 67 SC 504; 330
US 855, 91 LE 1297, 67 SC 962

School Cases
296 Fed 928; 268 US 510, 69 LE 1070, 45 SC
571
281 F2d 452
284 F2d 377; 163 FS 637
361 F2d 250
127 FS 591
141 FS 777
142 FS 916
152 FS 84
161 FS 409

372 US 901, 83 SC 715; 83 SC 869; 232 Md
368, 193 A2d 554
18 Misc2d 659, 191 NYSupp2d 453; 11
AppDiv2d 340, 206 NYSupp2d 183; 10
NY2d 174, 218 NYSupp2d 659, 176 NE2d
579; 370 US 421, 8 LE2d 601, 82 SC 1261;
12 NY2d 712, 233 NYSupp2d 766, 186
NE2d 124; 368 US 982, 82 SC 597; 369 US
809, 82 SC 686

School Segregation Cases
344 US 873, 97 LE 676, 73 SC 173; 345 US
972, 97 LE 1388, 73 SC 886; 347 US 497,
98 LE 884, 74 SC 693; 348 US 886, 75 SC
210; 349 US 294, 99 LE 1083, 75 SC 753
270 F2d 209
369 F2d 55
373 F2d 75
380 F2d 955
98 FS 529; 342 US 350, 96 LE 342, 72 SC 327;
345 US 972, 97 LE 1388, 73 SC 1118; 347
US 483, 98 LE 873, 74 SC 686; 348 US 886,
75 SC 210; 349 US 294, 99 LE 1083, 75 SC
753; 349 US 914, 75 SC 602
98 FS 797; 344 US 1, 97 LE 3, 73 SC 1; 344 US
141, 97 LE 152, 73 SC 124; 345 US 972, 97
LE 1388, 73 SC 1118; 347 US 483, 98 LE
873, 74 SC 686; 348 US 886, 75 SC 210;
349 US 294, 99 LE 1083, 75 SC 753
103 FS 337; 344 US 1, 97 LE 3, 73 SC 1; 345
US 972, 97 LE 1388, 73 SC 1118; 347 US
483, 98 LE 873, 74 SC 686; 348 US 886, 75
SC 210; 349 US 294, 99 LE 1083, 75 SC
753
32 DelCh 343, 87 A2d 862; 33 DelCh 144, 91
A2d 137; 344 US 891, 97 LE 689, 73 SC
213; 345 US 972, 97 LE 1388, 73 SC 1118;
347 US 483, 98 LE 873, 74 SC 686; 348 US
886, 75 SC 210; 349 US 294, 99 LE 1083

> A typical page of Cases Cited by Popular Names. This set
> is kept current by publication of a periodic pamphlet supple-
> ment.
>
> Other Tables of Popular Names appear in many of the state,
> regional, and other special digests.

371 US 807, 9 LE2d 52, 83 SC 25; 371 US
907, 83 SC 251; 371 US 944, 83 SC 499;
372 US 901, 83 SC 715; 374 US 203, 10
LE2d 844, 83 SC 1560; 83 SC 870
228 MD 239, 179 A2d 698; 374 US 203, 10
LE2d 844, 83 SC 1560; 371 US 809, 9 LE2d
52, 82 SC 21; 371 US 907, 83 SC 251; 371
US 944, 83 SC 498; 372 US 901, 83 SC 714;

Schwegmann Case
184 F2d 11; 340 US 928, 95 LE 669, 71 SC
491; 341 US 384, 95 LE 1035, 71 SC 745;
341 US 956, 95 LE 1377, 71 SC 1011

Schwimmer Case
27 F2d 742; 278 US 595, 73 LE 526, 49 SC 80;
279 US 644, 73 LE 889, 49 SC 448

[Illustration 22]

SAMPLE PAGE FROM VOLUME OF WORDS AND PHRASES

MARINE CAUSE   26 W & P—120

MARINE CAUSE

Action by seaman for wages and an additional sum for withholding of wages constituted a "marine cause" within New York City Court Act. Dooley v. Moore-McCormick Lines, Inc., 183 N.Y.S.2d 43, 44, 16 Misc.2d 534.

MARINE INSURANCE

The characterization of all-risk "Jewelers' Block Policy" as "marine insurance" by virtue of statutory definition is a mere label and has no effect on substantive rights. Woods Patchogue Corp. v. Franklin Nat. Ins. Co., of N. Y., 173 N.Y.S.2d 859, 864, 5 A.D.2d 577.

MARINE INSURANCE COMPANY

Company which issued public liability and prop_____

lege

cense

insur

tion

again

count

Pan

321 S

MAR

"M

storn   A page from Words & Phrases. The paragraphs

Treas   are essentially the same as they appeared as head-

and .   notes in the volumes of the National Reporter Sys-

F.2d   tem. The pocket supplement of the volumes of

Dat   Words & Phrases should always be checked.

auton

yacht

any "marine peril" within yacht policy. Hanover Ins. Co. v. Sonfield, Tex.Civ.App., 386 S.W. 2d 160, 162.

The test of "marine peril" as basis for recovery for salvage is not whether the peril is imminent; but whether it is reasonably to be apprehended, and vessel stranded so that it is subject to potential danger of damage or destruction may be a subject of salvage services. Fort Myers Shell & Dredging Co. v. Barge NBC 512, C.A.Fla., 404 F.2d 137, 139.

MARINER

See, Also, Negligence of a Mariner.
Negligence of Masters, Mariners or Pilots.

MARINE RAILWAY

"Marine railway" is a permanently fixed system of tracks or rails which extends from point on shore well above waterline to point off-shore well below waterline, along which tracks a cradle can move docked ship into or out of water; marine railway is to be distinguished from building way, for purposes of determining coverage under Longshoremen's and Harbor Workers' Compensation Act. St. Louis Shipbuilding Co. v. Director of the Office of Workers' Compensation Programs, U. S. Dept. of Labor, C.A.8, 551 F.2d 1119, 1123.

A permanent shipyard structure located entirely on land, designed and used exclusively for new ship construction did not constitute a "drydock" or "marine railway" within the act, and therefore the act did not apply to injuries sustained by a shipyard employee working on construction of a new ship on such structure, even though a portion of the structure extended into the water on an incline to facilitate launching of completed vessels. Puget Sound Bridge & Dry Dock Co. v. O'Leary, D.C.Wash., 224 F.Supp. 557, 559.

MARINE RULE

The so-called "marine rule" provides that if cost of restoration of leased premises is more than one-half of value of building just before fire, then there is total destruction. Old Line

Co. v. Getty Square Dept. Store, Inc., 322 N. Y.S.2d 149, 151, 66 Misc.2d 825.

MARITAL

See, Living in Marital Union.

MARITAL AGREEMENT

"Marital agreement", as term is used in statute pertaining to deportation of immigrants who used marital agreement to procure entry, means more than mere indulgence in marriage ceremony, and means that contracting parties at least begin in good faith to live together as husband and wife. Giannoulias v. Landon, C.A.Cal., 226 F.2d 356, 359.

MARITAL ASSETS

_____ the
_____ of a
_____ sent
_____ Ind.

_____ dis-
_____ lia-
_____ hich
_____ and
_____ hich
_____ lud-
_____ as-
_____ hich
_____ con-
_____ em-

MARITAL COMMUNICATIONS

"Marital communications", within statute providing privilege with respect to the same, connote confidential communications. State v. Benner, Me., 284 A.2d 91, 108.

MARITAL DEDUCTION BEQUEST

"Marital deduction bequest" defined. In re Rogers' Estate, Fla.App., 180 So.2d 167, 171.

Testamentary provision expressly recognizing specific bequest to daughter and bequeathing to widow full undivided one-half of residuary estate to be so computed as to entitle estate to full "marital deduction" used quoted phrase as referring to marital deduction for federal estate tax purposes and disclosed testamentary purpose to minimize estate taxes. Id.

Will, construed as a whole, bequeathing to testator's widow a full undivided one-half of residuary estate to be so computed as to entitle estate to full marital deduction disclosed testamentary intent and purpose to make a "marital deduction bequest" to widow. Id.

MARITAL DEDUCTION TRUST

See, Pecuniary Formula Marital Deduction Trust.
Percentage or Fraction Marital Deduction Trust.

MARITAL, FILIAL AND DOMESTIC CIRCUMSTANCES AND OBLIGATIONS

Employee who left work in order to care for her mother who was suffering from cancer had left for a "marital, filial or domestic circumstance or obligation" and not for "good cause" within Employment Security Law and was not entitled to unemployment benefits. Mississippi Employment Sec. Commission v. Stafford, 158 So.2d 55, 56, 248 Miss. 95.

For purposes of statutory provision stating that marital, filial and domestic circumstances and obligations shall not be deemed good cause for leaving work within meaning of statutory provisions conditioning right to receive unemployment compensation benefits upon having

SECTION K. CITING DIGESTS

Digests serve as a means of locating cases by subject. As they are merely finding aids with no legal authority, they are seldom, if ever, cited.

In connection with the use of digests, a further caveat is appropriate. Do not rely on the text of the digest-paragraphs for the theory of a case. They merely serve as a means of obtaining citations to the cases. Digest-paragraphs are necessarily brief and can be misleading, or can fail to suggest a nuance or shading of a case or may omit an element which may have a specific bearing on the problem being researched.

In all instances, the actual opinion from which the digest was obtained should be read.

SECTION L. COMPUTER–ASSISTED LEGAL RESEARCH

The use of the computer for legal research is becoming more prevalent. The two systems best suited for case law research are LEXIS and WESTLAW. When appropriate, mention will be made of these and other relevant computer-research systems, but full coverage will be given only in Chapter 20.

1. Digests and Computer-Assisted Legal Research

Both LEXIS and WESTLAW can be used for the finding of cases. In addition, WESTLAW has headnotes from all cases reported since 1971 online in its databases, which allow a user to locate all cases with specific Topics and Key Numbers.

Chapter 7

ANNOTATED LAW REPORTS

The *National Reporter System* with its *Key Number System* provides for the comprehensive publication of all reported decisions. Another private publishing company, the Lawyers Co-operative Publishing Company (and its related company, the Bancroft-Whitney Company) publishes court reports on a selective basis. Their theory is that only a small portion of the total number of cases handed down each year is of interest to most lawyers, as most cases deal with either strictly local matters, or cover an area of law so well settled that they add very little to an understanding of the law. What serves lawyers better, they claim, is reporting only significant court decisions: those that deal with points of law not previously decided, or indicate a change in the law, or indicate a new trend in legal thinking. By this manner of selective reporting lawyers could have all important decisions and not have to burden their bookshelves with thousands of cases that really add nothing to the corpus of the law.

Although selective law reporting was the basis for their first venture in publishing court reports, Lawyers Co-operative realized that lawyers would also have to be able to locate other decisions not reported in their publication and have a method of locating current decisions. To provide this service, they began to publish auxiliary sets, all related to each other, and all aimed to assist lawyers in finding answers to all of their legal questions through the use of these publications. These sets gradually grew into what they now call *The Total Client-Service Library*,[1] which consists of thirteen distinctive sets of law books. This chapter will discuss its annotated law reports.

SECTION A. AMERICAN LAW REPORTS

1. Introduction

The *American Law Reports* is a selective reporter of mostly appellate court decisions. Its editors scan all current decisions and select those that in their opinion have points of law of general interest. There are no advance sheets to this set, and several volumes are

---

[1] *The Total Client-Service Library* consists of: *American Jurisprudence 2d; American Jurisprudence Legal Forms 2d; American Jurisprudence Pleading and Practice Forms, Annotated, Revised; American Jurisprudence Trials; American Law Reports Annotated (A.L.R.; A.L.R.2d; A.L.R.3d; A.L.R.4th; A.L.R.Fed.); American Jurisprudence Proof of Facts; United States Code Service; United States Supreme Court Reports, Lawyers' Edition; Federal Procedural Forms, Lawyers' Edition; Federal Procedure, Lawyers' Edition; Bankruptcy Service, Lawyers' Edition; Federal Regulation of Employment Service;* and *Auto-Cite.*

published each year. *A.L.R.*, however, is significant, not for the decisions it reports, but for the editorial service that follows each reported decision, or what the publishers call *Annotations.* These are encyclopedic essays or memoranda on the significant legal topics from each case selected for publication in the *American Law Reports.*

The manner in which the *American Law Reports* are published and the role of annotations can best be made clear by example.

In the case of *Gumenick v. United States,* decided in the Supreme Court of Virginia,[2] the plaintiff had been sitting on the back porch of a friend's apartment. When he was leaving, plaintiff put his hand on the porch railing and then turned to talk to his friend. The railing collapsed, throwing plaintiff to the ground and severely injuring him. He then brought suit against the owners of the apartment building alleging their failure to exercise reasonable care in the maintenance of the hand rail. The editors decided that this case was suitable for publication in *A.L.R.;* in terms of legal research, this is not important, as this decision is also published in the official *Virginia Reports* and in the *South Eastern Reporter.* What is significant is what *A.L.R.* provides *in addition* to the decision, namely, a 222-page annotation that immediately follows the decision as printed in the *A.L.R.* volume. In legal research, *A.L.R.* is used not for the reported decisions, but for the subsequent annotations. The case of *Gumenick v. United States,* in common with most reported cases, involves more than one point of law. For instance, this case, in addition to the topic of landlord and tenant, dealt with the topics of evidence, damages, and trial procedure. It was chosen by *A.L.R.* for the issues involving the law of landlord and tenant, and it is these issues which are covered in the *Annotation.*

Although the decision itself consists only of ten pages, the *Annotation* is not restricted to its limited fact situation, but rather it is written on the generalized topic. The editor assigned to write the *Annotation* researched the entire area of law covered by the topic of the *Annotation* and located all previous decisions from all jurisdictions that dealt with this topic. The *Annotation* cites and summarizes the facts and holdings of all reported cases in point and presents an analysis and synthesis of the cases. What *A.L.R.* designates as an *Annotation* is in fact a legal memorandum on a particular aspect of the law that covers all sides of every question, presents general principles deduced from the cases, and gives their exceptions, qualifications, distinctions, and applications. [See Illustrations 23, 23–a, and 23–b.]

[2] 213 Va. 510, 193 S.E.2d 788, 65 A.L.R.3d 1 (1973).

SECTION B. ILLUSTRATIONS: A.L.R. ANNOTATIONS

23–23–b. Pages from Gumenick v. United States, 65 A.L.R.3d 1

[Illustration 23]

FIRST PAGE OF AN A.L.R.3d ANNOTATION

ANNOTATION

LANDLORD'S LIABILITY FOR INJURY OR DEATH DUE TO DEFECTS IN AREAS OF BUILDING (OTHER THAN STAIRWAYS) USED IN COMMON BY TENANTS

by

Allan E. Korpela, LL.B.

> This is the first page of the Annotation for 65 A.L.R.3d 14. Immediately preceding it is reprinted the case of Gumenick v. United States, 213 Va. 510, 193 S.E.2d 788, 65 A.L.R.3d 1 (1973). Although this case dealt specifically with the liability of a landlord for negligent maintenance of a porch railing, note how the Annotation deals with the many aspects of the liability of a landlord.

TO

49 AM

16 AM

403

2 AM J

6 AM JUR PROOF OF FACTS 527, Invitees; 7 AM JUR PROOF OF FACTS 239, Lights; 10 AM JUR PROOF OF FACTS 785, Slip and Fall

10 AM JUR TRIALS 255, Premises Liability—Trip and Fall

ALR DIGESTS, Landlord and Tenant §§ 174, 174.2, 174.4, 174.8

ALR QUICK INDEX, Landlord and Tenant; Premises Liability

Consult POCKET PART in this volume for later cases

14

[Illustration 23–a]

PAGE FROM 65 A.L.R.3d

---

65 ALR3d   LANDLORD'S LIABILITY — COMMON AREAS
                              65 ALR3d 14

§ 6. —Other areas:
     [a] Control retained
     [b] Control not retained
§ 7. Requirement of notice of defect; generally
§ 8. Actual notice charged
§ 9. Constructive notice charged; generally
§ 10. Duration of defect; years
§ 11. —Less than year but more than month
§ 12. —Less than month

III. LANDLORD'S BREACH OF DUTY AS TO PARTICULAR CONDITION

A. CONSTRUCTION AND STRUCTURAL MAINTENANCE

1. LOBBIES, HALLS, AND PASSAGEWAYS

§ 13. Floors:

                                                                r of
§ 1

An outline of the topics covered in the Annotation
is set forth. This is the second page of the outline.
Note how cases dealing with porch railings are cov-   r of
ered at § 17 within the Annotations. Thus, the re-
§ 1   searcher can immediately turn to this section to find
cases for the matter being researched.

§ 1

     [a] Finding of negligence held supported or supportable
     [b] Finding of no negligence held supportable or required as matter of
         law
§ 17. Railings and posts:
     [a] Finding of negligence held supported or supportable
     [b] Finding of no negligence held supportable or required as matter of
         law
§ 18. Other parts or appurtenances:
     [a] Finding of negligence held supported or supportable
     [b] Finding of no negligence held supportable or required as matter of
         law

3. ATTICS, BATHROOMS, BASEMENTS, AND CHAMBERS

§ 19. Floors:
     [a] Finding of negligence held supported or supportable
     [b] Finding of no negligence held supportable or required as matter of
         law
§ 20. Other areas or appurtenances:
     [a] Finding of negligence held supported or supportable
     [b] Finding of no negligence held supportable or required as matter of
         law

15

[Illustration 23–b]

PAGE FROM 65 A.L.R.3d

§ 16[b]　　　　Landlord's Liability — Common Areas　　　65 ALR3d
65 ALR3d 14

trolled by the landlord, a finding for defendant on the issue of defendant's negligence with respect to such condition was held required or supportable under the particular facts and circumstances of the case.[82]

§ 17 brings together and discusses all cases dealing with landlord's liability in reference to railings and posts.

a child of one of the defendant's tenants, who ventured upon the platform of the fire escape and was injured when a trap door in the platform, the hinges of which were defective, gave way.

Testimony by the plaintiff and his wife that they commonly used the fire escape on the defendant's building for the purpose of reaching the cellar was held in Aubrey v McCarthy (1926) 217 App Div 492, 217 NYS 161, not to justify a finding that it was a common passageway provided for this purpose, where there was an interior stairway provided from the ground floor into the cellar, and to reach it by the fire escape one had to climb through a window. It was therefore held that there could be no recovery for injuries to a tenant from a defect in a wooden platform which had been laid over a platform of the fire escape, where, at the time of the accident, the plaintiff tenant was using the fire escape to reach the ground to pick up a piece of clothing which had fallen from his apartment, the court pointing out that there was no claim of any defect in the fire escape itself.

§ 17. Railings and posts

[a] Finding of negligence held supported or supportable

In the following cases, where recovery was sought for injury or death allegedly caused by defective or improper mode of construction or a failure to perform proper structural maintenance of railings or posts of porches, balconies, fire escapes, and platforms used in common by tenants, or by a tenant and the landlord, and controlled by the landlord, a finding for plaintiff on the issue of defendant's negligence with respect to such condition was held supportable under the particular facts and circumstances of the case.

Allegations that the plaintiff, a tenant of part of the defendant's premises, was injured when a faultily constructed railing inclosing a rear stair landing used in common by the tenants and the defendant collapsed with the plaintiff when she was attempting to use a clothesline and pulley device attached to the railing for the joint use of the parties, and that the defect in the railing was a latent one not observable by the plaintiff in the exercise of due care, but known to the defendant at all the times in question, was held in Hassell v Denning (1927) 84 Cal App 479, 258 P 426, to state a cause of action as against general demurrer, either on the theory that the lessor through fraud or concealment allowed the lessee to occupy the premises in ignorance of a risk known to the landlord, or that the landlord reserved control of the part of the premises in question for the common use of himself and the tenants, or of different tenants, the court saying that liability under the latter theory might

82. For cases involving injuries suffered because of the allegedly rotten condition of the floors of porches, balconies, fire escapes, or platforms, see infra § 33.

SECTION C. A.L.R. AND ITS SERIES

The usefulness of locating an *A.L.R.* annotation should be evident, since it presents in an organized fashion a commentary and discussion of all previously reported decisions and saves the researcher the task of locating the cases and then analyzing and synthesizing them.

The *American Law Reports* are published in five series.[3]

First Series (cited *A.L.R.*) 1919–1948, 175 volumes.

Second Series (cited *A.L.R.2d*) 1948–1965, 100 volumes.

Third Series (cited *A.L.R.3d*) 1965–1980, 100 volumes.

Fourth Series (cited *A.L.R.4th*) 1980 to date.

Federal (cited *A.L.R.Fed.*) 1969 to date.

The last set started in 1969 and includes only court decisions from the federal courts. As mentioned in Chapter 3, the Lawyers Cooperative Publishing Company publishes an annotated set of the *U.S. Reports.* Although decisions from the federal courts of appeals previously have appeared in *A.L.R.*, litigation has been increasing in both amount and importance, and the publishers felt that federal cases now deserved special treatment.

A.L.R.Fed. is published in a format similar to *A.L.R.* Leading decisions of the federal courts are published followed by an annotation in the same manner as described *supra.*

SECTION D. FINDING A.L.R. ANNOTATIONS

In Chapter 6, we set forth the matter of liability of parking lot owners for damage done to automobiles left in their care. We explained how cases with similar fact situations could be located by using the *American Digest System* with its Key Number method of classification.

We will now demonstrate how cases on this subject can also be located by the use of the *American Law Reports Annotated.*

1. Index Method

The first step is to consult the indexes to the various *A.L.R.* series. These are:

> *Quick Index* to *A.L.R.3d* and *A.L.R.4th* (with cumulative pocket supplement kept inside front cover). Second edition.
>
> *Quick Index* to *A.L.R.2d.*

[3] The *American Law Reports Annotated* replaced the *Lawyers' Reports Annotated (L.R.A.).* For a description of the set and other earlier sets of annotated reports, *see* E. POLLACK, FUNDAMENTALS OF LEGAL RESEARCH 116 (3d ed. 1967).

Quick Index to *A.L.R.*

Quick Index to *A.L.R.Fed.*, 3d ed., 2 vol. (with cumulative pocket supplement inside front cover).[4]

A.L.R. Federal Tables Volume (with cumulative pocket supplement inside front cover). This volume includes a *Table of Cases* reported in *A.L.R. Federal*, an *A.L.R. Federal Annotation History Table*, and a *Table of Laws and Regulations* cited in *A.L.R. Federal.*

It is best to start with the *Quick Index* to *A.L.R.4th* and then, if necessary, to check the earlier ones.

In this example, by looking in the *Quick Index* to *A.L.R.4th* under either *Parking Lots* or *Garages, Liveries, Parking, and Filling Stations*, the following index entry would be located:

Parking lots

  • liability for damage to automobile left in parking lot or garage, 13 A.L.R.4th 442

If no entry on point was located, the earlier *Quick Indexes* should then be examined.

2. Table of Cases

If one knows of a case that has been or is likely to have been reported in *A.L.R.*, the citation to the annotation following the case can be located by using the Table of Cases to the various *A.L.R.* series.

It is important to note that these Tables list decisions reported in *A.L.R.* and not the cases cited in the *Annotations.*

3. Digest Method

A.L.R. and *A.L.R.2d* were both provided with additional sets entitled *A.L.R. Digests*. These are no longer provided for *A.L.R.3d* or *4th.*

4. American Jurisprudence and Shepard's Citations

The methods of using these sets for finding *A.L.R. Annotations* will be discussed in Chapters 14 and 15.

---

[4] This index is called *Federal Quick Index to the Total Client-Service Library*. It indexes *A.L.R.Fed.* as well as all matters on federal law in the other sets of *The Total Client-Service Library*. There are also published for the first and second series of *A.L.R.* separate indexes called *Word Indexes*. The *Annotations* were indexed in much greater depth in these indexes. The *Word Index* for the first series is in four volumes and in three volumes for the second series. These have now been replaced by the *Quick Indexes*.

SECTION E: ILLUSTRATIONS: FINDING A.L.R. ANNOTATIONS

[Illustration 24]

SAMPLE PAGE OF SUBJECTS ANNOTATED IN AN A.L.R. VOLUME

x   SUBJECTS ANNOTATED

LAUNDRIES OR DRY CLEANERS
Application of city ordinance requiring license for a laundry, to supplier of coin-operated laundry machines intended for use in apartment building—65 ALR3d 1296

LICENSES AND PERMITS
Application of city ordinance requiring license for a laundry, to supplier of coin-operated laundry machines intended for use in apartment building—65 ALR3d 1296

MALICIOUS PROSECUTION
May action for malicious prosecution be predicated on defense or counterclaim in civil suit—65 ALR3d 901

MALPRACTICE
Coverage and exclusions under hospital

PUBLIC OFFICERS
Validity of requirement that candidate or public officer have been resident of governmental unit for specified period—65 ALR3d 1048

PUNITIVE DAMAGES
Intoxication of automobile driver as basis for awarding punitive damages—65 ALR3d 656

RELEASE OR DISCHARGE
Validity and effect of agreement with one cotortfeasor setting aside his maximum liability and providing for reduction or extinguishment thereof relative to recovery against nonagreeing cotortfeasor—65 ALR3d 602

M

A.L.R. Annotations are written on many different topics.

MEDICAL TREATMENT OR CASE
Admissibility of evidence showing payment, or offer or promise of payment, of medical, hospital, and similar expenses of injured party by opposing party—65 ALR3d 932

MONEY ORDER
Falsifying of money order as forgery—65 ALR3d 1307

PARDON, PAROLE OR PROBATION
Propriety, in imposing sentence for original offense after revocation of probation, of considering acts because of which probation was revoked—65 ALR3d 1100

POLLUTION
Validity and construction of statute or ordinance allowing tax exemption for property used in pollution control—65 ALR3d 434

PREMISES LIABILITY
Landlord's liability for injury or death due to defects in areas of building (other than stairways) used in common by tenants—65 ALR3d 14

Propriety, in imposing sentence for original offense after revocation of probation of considering acts because of which probation was revoked—65 ALR3d 1100

SCHOOLS
What constitutes a private, parochial, or denominational school within statute making attendance at such school a compliance with compulsory school attendance law—65 ALR3d 1222

SENTENCE AND PUNISHMENT
Propriety, in imposing sentence for original offense after revocation of probation, of considering acts because of which probation was revoked—65 ALR3d 1100

STARE DECISIS
Binding effect upon state courts of opinion of United States Supreme Court supported by less than a majority of all its members—65 ALR3d 504

[Illustration 25]

PAGE FROM QUICK INDEX TO A.L.R.4th

QUICK INDEX   **Gas and Oil**

Civil Rights Act of 1871 (42 USCS § 1983), 55 ALR Fed 208

Grant or denial of furlough or work release to federal prisoner under 18 USCS § 4082(c), 64 ALR Fed

> **Note citation to the Annotation for the problem being researched.**

Attor

Drag

debts ("Dragnet Clause")—modern status, 3 ALR4th 690

False pretenses: modern status of rule that crime of false pretenses cannot be predicated upon present intention not to comply with promise or statement as to future act, 19 ALR4th 959

FUTURES CONTRACTS

"Security": commodity futures contract or account as included in meaning of "security" as defined in § 3(a)(10) of the Securities Exchange Act of 1934 (15 USCS § 78c(a)(10)), 58 ALR Fed 616

GAMBLING

§ 1. Generally.

Five or more persons: requirement of 18 USCS § 1955, prohibiting illegal gambling businesses, that such businesses involve five or more persons, 55 ALR Fed 778

Interstate travel as element of offense established by Travel Act (18 USCS § 1952), 69 ALR Fed 251

Modus operandi: admissibility of expert testimony as to modus operandi of crime—modern cases, 31 ALR4th 798

Racketeer Influenced and Corrupt Organizations: what is an "enterprise," as defined at 18 USCS § 1961(4), for purposes of the Racketeer Influenced and Corrupt Organizations (RICO) statute (18 USCS §§ 1961 et seq.), 52 ALR Fed 818

§ 2. Devices.

Delay between seizure of personal property by Federal Government and institution of proceedings for forfeiture thereof as violative of Fifth Amendment due process requirements, 69 ALR Fed 373

GARAGES, LIVERIES, PARKING, AND FILLING STATIONS

§ 1. Generally.

Franchise: termination or nonrenewal of franchise to sell motor fuel in commerce under Petroleum Marketing Practices Act (15 USCS §§ 2801 et seq.), 53 ALR Fed 348

Nuisance: carwash as nuisance, 4 ALR4th 1308

Supervisors: who are "supervisors" within meaning of National Labor Relations Act (29 USCS §§ 151 et seq.) in service operations, 49 ALR Fed 230

§ 2. Compensation and charges.

Unauthorized repairs
- liability of repairer for unauthorized, unnecessary, or fraudulent repairs of motor vehicle, 23 ALR4th 274
- liability to pay for allegedly unauthorized repairs on motor vehicle, 5 ALR4th 311

§ 3. Liability for injury, loss, or damage.

Incompetence: negligent entrustment: bailor's liability to bailee injured through his own negligence or incompetence, 12 ALR4th 1062

Owner: liability of owner of motor vehicle for negligence of garageman or mechanic, 8 ALR4th 265

Parking lots
- liability for damage to automobile left in parking lot or garage, 13 ALR4th 442
- liability for loss of automobile left at parking lot or garage, 13 ALR4th 362

Repairs and maintenance
- liability of owner of motor vehicle for negligence of garageman or mechanic, 8 ALR4th 265
- manufacturer's warranty: construction and effect of new motor vehicle warranty limiting manufacturer's liability to repair or replacement of defective parts, 2 ALR4th 576
- measure and elements of damages in action against garageman based on failure to properly perform repair or service on motor vehicle, 1 ALR4th 347
- repairman's duty to provide customer with information, estimates, or replaced parts, under automobile repair consumer protection act, 25 ALR4th 506

GARBAGE

Searches and seizures: reasonable expectation of privacy in contents of garbage or trash receptacle, 28 ALR4th 1219

GAS AND OIL

§ 1. Generally.

Abandonment of facilities: what constitutes abandonment of facilities or service, under § 7(b) of Natural Gas Act (15 USCS § 717f(b)), 61 ALR Fed 454

Cancellation, revocation, and automatic termination, under § 31 of Mineral Lands Leasing Act (30 USCS § 188), of lease entered into under terms of Act, for failure to comply with lease provisions, 62 ALR Fed 866

Environmental impact statement: necessity and sufficiency of environmental impact statements under § 102(2)(C)) of National Environmental Policy Act of 1969 (42 USCS § 4332(2)(C)), in cases involving power projects, 66 ALR Fed 395

Market value: meaning of, and proper method for determining, market value or market price in oil and gas lease requiring royalty to be paid on standard measured by such terms, 10 ALR4th 732

"Mine": what is "mine" under Federal Mine Safety and Health Act of 1977 (30 USCS §§ 801 et seq.), 63 ALR Fed 415

Sales or use tax: exemption, from sales or use tax, of water, oil, gas, other fuel, or electricity provided for residential purposes, 15 ALR4th 269

Secondary recovery: rights and obligations, with respect to adjoining landowners, arising out of secondary recovery of gas, oil, and other fluid minerals, 19 ALR4th 1182

Subdivided realty: production on one tract as extending term on other tract, where one mineral deed conveys oil or gas in separate tracts for as long as oil or gas is produced, 9 ALR4th 1121

Supervisors
- *who are "supervisors" within meaning of National Labor Relations Act (29 USCS §§ 151 et seq.)*

[Illustration 26]

FIRST PAGE OF ANNOTATION: 13 A.L.R.4th 442

ANNOTATION

LIABILITY FOR DAMAGE TO AUTOMOBILE LEFT IN PARKING LOT OR GARAGE

TOTAL CLIENT-SERVICE LIBRARY® REFERENCES

8 Am Jur 2d, Bailments §§ 132–155; 38 Am Jur 2d, Garages, and Filling and Parking Stations §§ 27–46

Annotations: See the related matters listed in the annotation, infra.

4 Am Jur Pl & Pr Forms (Rev), Bailments, Forms 104–106; 9 Am Jur Pl & Pr Forms (Rev), Garages, Parking Stations, and Filling Stations, Forms 9:811, 9:814, 9:814.05

3 Am Jur Legal Forms 2d, Bailments and Personal Property Leases § 36:223

4 Am Jur Proof of Facts 2d 673, Bailee's Failure to Adequately Care for Bailed Property

3 Am Jur Trials 637, Selecting the Remedy

US L Ed Digest, Bailment §§ 3–5

ALR Digests, Automobiles and Highway Traffic §§ 235, 237, 238

L Ed Index to Annos, Bailment; Contracts; Municipal Corporations

ALR Quick Index, Attendant;• Bailment; Brakes; Contracts; Garages, Liveries, Parking, and Filling Stations; Master and Servant; Municipal Corporations

Federal Quick Index, Bailment; Brakes; Contracts; Garages and Parking and Filling Stations; Municipal Corporations; Parking

---

First page of an A.L.R. Annotation has the subject of the Annotation. References are also given to where the topic of the Annotation is covered in the other sets of the Publishers.

Consult POCKET PART in this volume for later cases

[Illustration 27]

SECOND PAGE OF ANNOTATION: 13 A.L.R.4th 442

13 ALR4th   DAMAGE TO AUTOMOBILE—PARKING LOT
                              13 ALR4th 442
          Liability for damage to automobile left in parking lot or garage

§ 1. Introduction:
     [a] Scope
     [b] Related matters
§ 2. Summary and comment:
     [a] Generally
     [b] Practice pointers
§ 3. Disclaimer of liability
§ 4. Damage done by attendant—while driving automobile:
     [a] In parking lot
     [b] In parking garage
§ 5. —Other damage
§ 6. Damage done by third party:
     [a] Recovery allowed
     [b] Recovery denied

Each Annotation is preceded by an outline which indicates how the Annotation
has been organized. By scanning the outline the researcher can turn immediately
to the relevant part of the Annotation. As some Annotations may contain over 200
pages, the outline becomes extremely useful. In the instant case, one can turn
immediately to paragraph 6 and find discussion of cases with facts similar to the
problem under research.

Bent wheel, § 4[b]

"Blown up" and "burst" engine, § 5

Brakes, §§ 4, 5

Broken windshield, § 6[b]

Brother of vehicle owner, person claiming
     to be, § 6[a]

Bumper, damage to, § 4[b]

Burglarized automobile, § 6

"Burst" and "blown up" engine, § 5

Cable of elevator in wrong position, § 5

Carburetor defective, § 4[b]

Care and custody, automobile not left in
     operator's, § 6[b]

Cavities in ice and snow indicating rock-
     ing of automobile, § 4[a]

Ceiling and curb, automobile becoming
     lodged between, § 4[a]

Charger attached to battery, § 5

Claim check and ticket, §§ 3, 4[a], 5, 6

Clause of disclaimer of liability on face of
     claim check, § 3

Clutch sheered, § 5

Crest, wheels of automobile over, § 5

Crime area, lot located near, § 6[a]

Crushed automobile, §§ 4[a], 5

Curb and ceiling, automobile becoming
     lodged between, § 4[a]

Custody and care, automobile not left in
     operator's, § 6[b]

Cylinder, connecting rod going through,
     § 4[b]

Daily patron of parking garage, motorist
     as, § 4[b]

Defective accelerator and carburetor,
     § 4[b]

Delivering automobile to motorist, dam-
     age occurring while, § 4[b]

Directions to receive claim check, § 6[b]

Disclaimer of liability, § 3

Doors locked, § 6

Edge of ramp, attendant backing automo-
     bile over, § 4[b]

Elevator, §§ 4[b], 5

Emergency brake, § 4

Engine, §§ 4, 5, 6[a]

[Illustration 28]

THIRD PAGE OF ANNOTATION: 13 A.L.R.4th 442

**Immediately following the Outline to the Annotation, an Index listing the facts
of the various cases cited in the Annotation is set forth. This can be very useful in
finding citations to cases in point to the problem being researched.**

[Illustration 29]

FOURTH PAGE OF ANNOTATION: 13 A.L.R.4th 442

13 ALR4th	DAMAGE TO AUTOMOBILE—PARKING LOT	§ 1[a]
	13 ALR4th 442	

> **Immediately following the Index, there is a Table indicating which state cases are cited in the Annotation. § 1 always sets forth the scope of the Annotation.**

Third party, §§ 4[b], 6
Ticket and claim check, §§ 3, 4[a], 5, 6
Time of arrival, claim check stamped with,

Vandalized automobile, §§ 3, 6[a]
Wheels of automobile, §§ 4, 5, 6[a]
Windshield broken, § 6[b]

TABLE OF JURISDICTIONS REPRESENTED
Consult POCKET PART in this volume for later cases

Del: §§ 2[b]
DC: §§ 2[b], 4[b], 5, 6[a, b]
Ga: §§ 2[b], 3, 6[b]
Ill: §§ 4[b]
La: §§ 2[b], 4[a, b], 5
Mass: §§ 2[b], 4[b]
Mo: §§ 4[a, b], 6[b]
NJ: §§ 6[b]

NY: §§ 2[b], 3, 4[b], 5, 6[a, b]
NC: §§ 2[b]
Ohio: §§ 2[b], 4[a, b]
Okla: §§ 2[b], 4[a]
Pa: §§ 4[a]
Tenn: §§ 5
Tex: §§ 4[b], 5
Wash: §§ 2[b]

---

§ 1. Introduction

[a] Scope

This annotation[1] collects and analyzes the state and federal cases involving the question whether a parking lot or garage owner is liable for the damage done to a motorist's automobile which is parked in the lot or garage.[2] Included within this annotation are only those cases in which a customer's motor vehicle is physically damaged by either the parking lot or garage owner, his attendant, or a third party.[3] Furthermore, this annotation does not treat those cases where a motor vehicle is damaged in the parking lot or garage of a hotel or motel or similar establishment,[4] an automobile dealership or repair shop parking lot or garage, or a parking lot or garage which a landlord has provided for his tenant.

As used in this annotation, the term "parking lot" includes parking space furnished in conjunction with some other enterprise, such as a theater or restaurant, regardless of whether or

---

1. This annotation supersedes §§ 14–16 of the annotation at 7 ALR3d 927, entitled "Liability for loss of or damage to automobile left in parking lot or garage." The remainder of that annotation is superseded by the annotation at 13 ALR4th 362.

2. Cases involving damage done to an automobile as a result of its wrongful removal from a parking lot or garage are treated in the annotation at 13 ALR4th 362, entitled "Liability for loss of automobile left at parking lot or garage."

3. For a discussion of damage done to the contents of a parked motor vehicle, see the annotation at 78 ALR3d 1057, entitled "Liability of owner or operator of parking lot or garage for loss of or damage to contents of parked motor vehicle."

4. For a discussion of this topic, see the annotation at 52 ALR3d 433, entitled "Liability of hotel, motel, or similar establishment for damage to or loss of guest's automobile left on premises."

[Illustration 30]

FIFTH PAGE OF ANNOTATION: 13 A.L.R.4th 442

> **§ 1 always indicates related Annotations. § 2 gives a summary of the contents of the Annotations.**

but does not include permanent storage garages, warehouses, or service or repair facilities.

[b] Related matters

Liability for loss of automobile left at parking lot or garage. 13 ALR4th 362.

Elements and measure of damages recoverable from bailee for loss, destruction, or conversion of personal papers, photographs, or paintings. 9 ALR4th 1245.

Measure and element of damages in action against garageman based on failure to properly perform repair or service on motor vehicle. 1 ALR4th 347.

Bailee's liability as affected by bailment condition that bailor procure insurance. 83 ALR3d 519.

Bailee's liability for bailor's expense of recovering stolen subject of bailment. 80 ALR3d 264.

Liability of owner or operator of parking lot or garage for loss or damage to contents of parked motor vehicle. 78 ALR3d 1057.

Validity of regulation providing for reserved parking spaces or parking priority on publicly owned property for members of a designated group. 70 ALR3d 1323.

Bailor's right of direct action against bailee's theft insurer for loss of bailed property. 64 ALR3d 1207.

Liability of hotel, motel, or similar establishment for damage to or loss of guest's automobile left on premises. 52 ALR3d 433.

Application of warranty provisions Uniform Commercial Code to bailments. 48 ALR3d 668.

Presumption and burden of proof where subject of bailment is destroyed or damaged by fire. 44 ALR3d 171.

Presumption and burden of proof where subject of bailment is destroyed or damaged by windstorm or other meteorological phenomena. 43 ALR3d 607.

Liability for negligence of doorman or similar attendant in parking patron's automobile. 41 ALR3d 1055.

Liability of owner or operator of parking lot for personal injuries allegedly resulting from condition of premises. 38 ALR3d 10.

Bailee's duty to insure bailed property. 28 ALR3d 513.

Liability of garageman, service or repair station, or filling station operator for destruction or damage of motor vehicle by fire. 16 ALR2d 799.

Liability of owner or operator of parking lot or station for personal injuries. 14 ALR2d 780.

§ 2. Summary and comment

[a] Generally

The question of the liability of a parking lot or garage owner for the damage done to an automobile while parked on the premises has usually been decided by the courts according to the law of bailment.[5] Generally, the courts have stated that a bailment relation is a contractual arrangement, and may result from an express contract or from a contract implied in fact or in law. Accordingly, the courts have concluded that there must be a delivery by the bailor to the bailee, with the intention to surrender complete custody and control of the

---

5. See 8 Am Jur 2d, Bailments § 54.

[Illustration 31]

PAGE FROM ANNOTATION: 13 A.L.R.4th 442

13 ALR4th   DAMAGE TO AUTOMOBILE—PARKING LOT   § 6[b]
                            13 ALR4th 442

that the employee's negligence was the proximate cause of the damage.

Holding a parking lot operator liable for damages sustained by the motorist's vehicle when it was vandalized and burglarized, the court, in Garlock v Multiple Parking Services, Inc. (1980) 103 Misc 2d 943, 427 NYS2d 670, 13 ALR4th 428, concluded that the existence of a bailment was no longer the basis for recovery; instead, the controlling test was whether the operator had used reasonable care to protect the vehicle from foreseeable harm. Commenting that the lot was located on the edge of a "high crime area" and was not fenced in or guarded, and that the motorist had

bile whose windshield was broken while the vehicle was parked in a parking lot, a large sign fronting on an adjacent street invited motorists to "Park and Lock," and at the entrace to the lot were printed instructions directing the incoming party to remove a "claim check," stamped with the time of arrival from an automatic dispensing apparatus. The customer was then instructed to proceed onto the parking area and occupy any available space. The motorist's only contact with lot personnel was at the time of departure, when he drove to a cashier's booth by an exit and presented the check, by means of which the attendant computed the amount

---

A page containing § 6 of this Annotation that deals with all cases in which a third party has caused damage or stolen property from a car in a parking lot.

---

erly protect the vehicle from injury, had failed to exercise reasonable care under the circumstances.

[b] Recovery denied

In the following cases which involved injury to a motorist's vehicle, apparently caused by a third person, judgment was entered for the proprietor where the motorist's evidence was insufficient to show either unexplained damage concomitant with a contract of bailment, or an affirmative act of negligence by the operator or his employees.

In 1420 Park Road Parking, Inc. v Consolidated Mut. Ins. Co. (1961, Mun Ct App **Dist Col**) 168 A2d 900, an action for damage to an automo-

sufficient to rebut the presumption of negligence which arose from the return of the automobile in a damaged condition. Reversing the judgment, the appellate court held that the relationship of bailment had not been established, since the lot operator did not have the requisite control of the automobile necessary to create that relationship. The court held that in the absence of a bailment relationship the car owner was obliged to show affirmatively that the damage resulted from the lot operator's wrongful act.[32]

Holding that the owner of an automobile from which a battery had been stolen while parked in a garage could not recover from the garage operator, the court, in Brown v Five Points

---

32. It should be noted that in Parking Management, Inc. v Glider (1975, **Dist Col** App) 343 A2d 51, which is not within the scope of this annotation because it involved a hotel parking garage, the court held that the landlord-tenant theory was outmoded as applied to "park and lock"

arrangements, and that the operator of such a parking lot could under appropriate circumstances be held to his customer duty to exercise reasonable care to protect the customer's automobile from malicious mischief.

459

SECTION F.   HOW A.L.R. IS KEPT CURRENT

1.   Upkeep Service

Once an *A.L.R. Annotation* has been found in a volume, further steps must be taken to locate cases subsequent to those found in the *A.L.R. Annotation.* For example, after Volume 1 of *A.L.R.* was published in 1919, the publishers were immediately faced with the problem of providing their subscribers with a means of alerting them to cases that were handed down after Volume 1 was published and that related to the *Annotations* in it, and would have been cited had they been handed down before Volume 1 had been published. They accomplished this by providing their subscribers a supplementary set to *A.L.R.* Each of the *A.L.R.* series is now supplemented as follows.

a.   *A.L.R. (First Series).* Volume 1 of *A.L.R.* was published in 1919. The publishers then started a companion set to *A.L.R.*, which they called the *A.L.R. Blue Book of Supplemental Decisions.* This service is correlated to *A.L.R. Annotations* and lists citations to all decisions on the same topic as the *Annotations.* Thus, if one locates an *Annotation* in 117 *A.L.R.* 606–39, all that is necessary is to turn to that citation in *A.L.R. Blue Book of Supplemental Decisions* and find citations to all cases on that topic handed down after the *Annotation* in 117 *A.L.R.* 606–39 was written. The *A.L.R. Blue Book of Supplemental Decisions* is now in six volumes and is kept current by an annual cumulative pamphlet. [See Illustration 32.]

b.   *A.L.R.2d.* After the publication of 175 *A.L.R.* in 1948, the publishers decided to stop this series and the next volume published was *1 A.L.R.2d,* being the second series of the *American Law Reports.* Actually, each volume of the second series appears nearly the same as the first series. The most fundamental change was in the method of keeping *Annotations* published in *A.L.R.2d* up to date. For this purpose the publishers abandoned the use of the *A.L.R. Blue Book of Supplemental Decisions* (although still publishing it for use with *A.L.R. (First Series)*). In its place, a new set called *A.L.R.2d Later Case Service* was started. This provides the same service for *A.L.R.2d* that *A.L.R. Blue Book of Supplemental Decisions* does for the first series, but instead of merely listing citations to later cases, it provides digests of these cases and then keys them directly to each section of the *A.L.R.2d Annotations.* In using *A.L.R.2d,* then, after the *Annotation* has been read, the set of *A.L.R.2d Later Case Service* must be consulted. [See Illustration 33.]

c.   *A.L.R.3d and A.L.R.4th.* After 100 volumes of *A.L.R.2d* were published, the publishers again decided to change the method of upkeep. In 1965, *A.L.R.3d* began. The most significant difference from the previous two series is that it is no longer necessary to examine an auxiliary set, such as the *A.L.R. Blue Book of Supple-*

mental Decisions or *A.L.R.2d Later Case Service.* Rather, each volume of *A.L.R.3d* has an annual cumulative pocket supplement. When using *A.L.R.3d* and after reading the *Annotations,* it is only necessary to check the pocket supplement to locate later cases. *A.L.R.4th* continues this method of upkeep. [See Illustration 34.]

d. *A.L.R.Fed.* This is kept up to date by pocket supplements the same as *A.L.R.3d* and *A.L.R.4th.*

2. Supplementing and Superseding Annotations

a. *Superseding Annotations.* Frequently, a topic of law of an *A.L.R. Annotation* is completely changed by later decisions. For example, an *Annotation* in an early volume of *A.L.R.* may have dealt with the right to receive damages for emotional distress when there was no physical impact. Subsequently, this rule is changed and the courts start allowing damages in such instances. The editors may then decide to rewrite and publish in a later *A.L.R.* volume a superseding *Annotation.* Sometimes only a part of a previous *Annotation* will be superseded.

b. *Supplementing Annotations.* This method was used most frequently in *A.L.R. (First Series)* and *A.L.R.2d.* In such instances, a new *Annotation* was written which served as a supplement to the original one. Both had to be read and then the upkeep service used for the citation to the supplementing *Annotation.*

c. *Annotation History Table.* Whenever a researcher has a citation to an *A.L.R. Annotation,* whether obtained from the *A.L.R. Quick Index* or elsewhere, it is good practice to check first to see if the *Annotation* has been superseded. This may be done either by checking the citation in the appropriate *A.L.R.* upkeep service, or using the *Annotation History Table* located in the back of both the bound volume and pocket supplement of the *A.L.R.3d and 4th Quick Index* volume. The *A.L.R. Federal Annotation History Table* is located in a separate volume entitled *A.L.R. Federal Tables Volume.*[5] Its use may best be described graphically:

HISTORICAL TABLE

10 ALR 321–336 Superseded 75 ALR2d 633	**10 ALR 488–494** Superseded 92 ALR2d 570	**11 ALR 1401–1402** Superseded 24 ALR2d 194
10 ALR 409–410 Superseded 84 ALR2d 1017	**10 ALR 783–809** Supplemented 40 ALR2d 1407	**11 ALR 1405–1407** Superseded 20 ALR2d 1053
10 ALR 429–435 Superseded 17 ALR3d 705	**11 ALR 1325–1328** Superseded 50 ALR2d 143	**12 ALR 111–144** Supplemented 37 ALR2d 453

[5] These tables do not include supplementing or superseding *Annotations* published in the first series of *A.L.R.* To determine if an *Annotation* in 1–175 *A.L.R.* was supplemented or superseded in a subsequent volume of the first series, consult the *A.L.R. Blue Book of Supplemental Decisions.*

HISTORICAL TABLE—Continued

12 ALR 333	13 ALR 225–247	13 ALR 346–355
Superseded 7 ALR2d 226	Supplemented 43 ALR2d 1291	Superseded 19 ALR3d 1227

13 ALR 151–156	13 ALR 324–340	13 ALR 372–383
Superseded 46 ALR2d 1227	Superseded 8 ALR3d 235	Superseded 35 ALR2d 124

This means that 12 *A.L.R.* 111–44 and 37 *A.L.R.2d* 453 should be read together as if they were a single *Annotation*, and then searching for later decisions as previously outlined in *A.L.R.2d Later Case Service.*

Suppose, however, that the researcher had found a citation to 7 *A.L.R.3d* 937–91, an *Annotation* on the liability of owners of garages and parking lots for damages to automobiles left in their possession. By checking in the *Historical Table* in the pocket supplement in the *Quick Index to A.L.R.3d and 4th*, it would be noted that this *Annotation* has been superseded as indicated in the *Historical Table A.L.R.4th* that follows:

HISTORICAL TABLE

A.L.R.4th

89 ALR2d 150–173	98 ALR2d 325–329	7 ALR3d 663–669
Superseded 15 ALR4th 10	Superseded 90 ALR3d 222 and 1 ALR4th 1270	Superseded 26 ALR4th 967

90 ALR2d 211–252		7 ALR3d 937–991
Superseded 21 ALR4th 765	98 ALR2d 966–1036	Superseded 13 ALR4th 362 & 13 ALR4th 442

91 ALR2d 700–733	§ 19 Superseded 3 ALR4th 1057	
Superseded 19 ALR4th 192		

91 ALR2d 763–770	99 ALR2d 599–627	8 ALR3d 974–1065
Superseded 10 ALR4th 246	§§ 11–13 and 14[c] Superseded 8 ALR4th 464	Superseded 21 ALR4th 929

91 ALR2d 936–956		11 ALR3d 1377–1379
Superseded 11 ALR4th 774	99 ALR2d 1151–1155	Superseded 7 ALR4th 8

92 ALR2d 421–459	Superseded 23 ALR4th 230	
Superseded 80 ALR3d 1280 & 22 ALR4th 534		14 ALR3d 873–886
	100 ALR2d 1112–1121	Superseded 12 ALR4th 57

92 ALR2d 682–691	Superseded 2 ALR4th 859	
Superseded 26 ALR4th 455		14 ALR3d 1272–1276
	100 ALR2d 1128–1134	Superseded 28 ALR4th 647

92 ALR2d 838–861	Superseded 2 ALR4th 859	
Superseded 21 ALR4th 729		15 ALR3d 411–436
	100 ALR2d 1404–1421	§ 5 Superseded 11 ALR4th 1099

92 ALR2d 878–891	Superseded 14 ALR4th 121	
Superseded 1 ALR4th 1021		

92 ALR2d 1408–1449	100 ALR2d 1433–1454	17 ALR3d 1010–1149
§§ 22 and 23 Superseded 1 ALR4th 347	Superseded 31 ALR4th 798	§§ 3, 5, 6 Superseded 4 ALR4th 85
§ 11 Superseded 23 ALR4th 274		§ 4 Superseded 4 ALR4th 912
	1 ALR3d 6–117	§ 48 Superseded 26 ALR4th 294
	Superseded 28 ALR4th 786	§ 16.1 Superseded 30 ALR4th 396

98 ALR2d 318–322	1 ALR3d 123–202	17 ALR3d 1442–1444
Superseded 29 ALR4th 1230	Superseded 28 ALR4th 786	Superseded 14 ALR4th 170

SECTION G. ILLUSTRATIONS: A.L.R. UPKEEP SERVICES

32. Excerpts from A.L.R. Blue Book of Supplemental Decisions
33. Page from A.L.R.2d Later Case Service
34. Page from an A.L.R.4th Volume Pocket Supplement

[Illustration 32]

EXCERPTS FROM A.L.R. BLUE BOOK OF SUPPLEMENTAL DECISIONS

VOL. 1	VOL. 3	LATEST PAM. SUPPL.
117 A.L.R. 606–639. Richardson v. D. (Ala.) 187 So 176. Norgard v. N. 54 CalApp(2d) 82, 128 P(2d) 506. Morrison v. N. 311 IllApp 411, 36 NE(2d) 581. Loeser v. B. (Ind) 39 NE(2d) 945 Re Gollobit (Iowa) 8 NW(2d) 191. Crawford v. C (Iowa) 15 NW (2d) 633. Re Stephenson (Iowa) 14 NW (2d) 684. Simpson v. S. 276 Ky 223, 123 S W (2d) 816. Feltner v. G (Ky) 177 SW (2d) 903 Re Boese (Minn) 7 NW(2d) 355.	**117 ALR 583–599** General Motors Acceptance Corp v M. (Kan) 311 P2d 339. **117 ALR 606–639** Berendsen v Mel. 126 Cal App2d 347, 272 P2d 76 Serha v B (Fla) 86 So2d 432. Fuller v F. (Ga) 97 SE2d 306 Hays v I. I. H. (Ill) 147 NE2d 297. Re Guardianship of Anderson (Iowa) 78 NW2d 788. Rebllinger v A. (Mo) 266 SW2d 410. Grimm v G. (Mo) 303 SW2d 43. Ellison v S. (ND) 82 NW2d 85 Theadgill v A. (Okla) 303 P2d 297 Chandler v W. (Tex) 294 SW2d 801. Leach v C. E. (Tex Civ App) 279 SW2d 630 Chandler v W. (Tex Civ App) 282 SW2d 940 Chamberlain v R. (Tex Civ App) 305 SW2d 817.	**117 ALR 470–484** Supplemented 108 ALR 581+ **117 ALR 496–498** Superseded 95 ALR2d 585+ **117 ALR 522–538** Mo.—Swiastyn v S J L & P Co. (App) 459 SW2d 24 (citing anno) **117 ALR 563–565** Superseded 53 ALR2d 224+ **117 ALR 571–572** U. S.—Doyle v N. J. Const. Co. (CA Wis) 382 F2d 735 **117 ALR 606–639** Fla.—Roberts v R. (Ann) 201

VOL. 2	VOL. 4	
117 ALR 606–639 Livingston v. P. (Ala) 57 So2d 521. Cross v P. (Ark) 221 SW2d 24 Guyot v. F. (Ark) 243 SW2d 650. Black v B 91 Cal App2d 328, 204 P2d 950 Johnson v. B. (Ga App) 67 SE2d 189. Re Conner's Estate (Iowa) 36 NW2d 833 Boggess v. C. E. (Mo App) 207 SW2d 814 Re Haas' Estate, 10 NJ Super 581, 77 A2d 523. Santos v M (Tex Civ App) 195 SW2d 927 Logan v. T (Tex Civ App) 199 SW2d 210 error granted	**117 ALR 606–639** Ala.—Taylor v F. N. B. 189 So 2d 141 Alaska—Re Hewett's Estate. 358 P2d 579 Ky.—Cook v B. 346 SW2d 725 Neb.—Oliven v B 92 NW2d 531 N. J.—Moss v G (Co) 146 A2d 227 N. Y.—Lindsay v L. 22 Misc 2d 1071, 203 NYS2d 705 Tex.—Connor v P (Civ App) 360 SW2d 435 **117 ALR 649** Superseded 130 ALR 272+	Note how A.L.R. Blue Book of Supplemental Decisions also indicates when an Annotation has been supplemented or superseded. It is simpler to use the Historical Table.

After using an *Annotation* in *A.L.R. (First Series)*, later cases may be found in the *A.L.R. Blue Book of Supplemental Decisions*. There are six *Blue Books* that contain references decided after the original *Annotation* was written. Vol. 1 covers 1919–46; Vol. 2, 1946–52; Vol. 3, 1953–58; Vol. 4, 1959–67. Vol. 5 (not illustrated) covers the years 1968–75. Volume 6 (not illustrated) covers 1976–84. An annual pamphlet lists citations since 1984.

[Illustration 33]

PAGE FROM A.L.R.2d LATER CASE SERVICE

LATER CASE SERVICE　　　**90 ALR2d 1071–1105**

> When using Annotations in A.L.R.2d, a different method of locating later cases must be used, as A.L.R.2d did not use pocket supplements. Rather, a separate multi-volume set called A.L.R.2d Later Case Service is provided. This set should be used to update an A.L.R.2d citation. Be sure also to check the pocket supplement to the Later Case Service.

:ed by the Federal Rules of Evidence h became effective July 1, 1975. See 20 Supreme Court Digest, Lawyer's Edition; Jur 2d, Federal Rules of Evidence or S Lawyer's Edition, Title 28.

le that expressions of present pain are etent and original evidence which may stified to by lay witness who observed the ration or expression by another also sup- d by:

.waii—Cozine v Hawaiian Catamaran, (Hawaii) 412 P2d 669, reh den 414 P2d 354.

l.—Robinson v Lewis, 20 Md App 710 317

N.C.—Inman v Harper, 2 NC App 103, 162 SE2d 629 (quoting annotation).

Okla.—Southwestern Bell Tel. Co. v Nelson (Okla) 384 P2d 914; Gulf Oil Corp. v Harris (Okla) 425 P2d 957.

S.C.—Wright v Graniteville Co., Vaucluse Div., 266 SC 88, 221 SE2d 777.

Tenn.—Magnoofox Co. of Tennesee v Shep- erd, 214 Tenn 321, 379 SW2d 791 (dictum).

Tex.—Southern Pacific Transp. Co. v Pera- lez (1976, Tex Civ App) 546 SW2d 88, error ref n r e.

caused by the extension of the injury over the body, and a juror's speculation, if he indulged in it, would bring him to the same conclusion, whether the judge gave the instructions ob- jected to or left them out. Texas Employers' Ins. Asso. v Charles (**Tex** Civ App) 381 SW2d 664, error ref n r e.

§ 6. Rulings that error is nonprejudicial or harmless, p. 1054.

Although trial court erred by instructing jury as to effect of answers to special verdict interrogatories, error was harmless, where evidence overwhelmingly supported jury's an- swers. Richfield Bank & Trust Co. v Sjogren (**Minn**) 244 NW2d 648.

90 ALR2d 1071–1105

Admissibility in civil action, apart from res gestae, of lay testimony as to another's expressions of pain.

§ 1. Scope and related matters, p. 1072.

[b] Related matters.

Admissibility, in civil case, of expert evi- dence as to existence or nonexistence, or se- verity, of pain. 11 ALR3d 1249.

5 Am Jur Trials 921, 982, Showing Pain and Suffering.

8 Am Jur Trials 173, 247 Airline Passenger Death Cases.

9 Am Jur Trials 1, 50 Falls from Scaffolds.

18 Am Jur Trials 595, Medical Malpractice —Cosmetic Surgery.

§ 3. Generally; rule approving testimony relating to manifestations of present pain, p. 1074.

[a] Generally.

As to cases tried in federal courts, the subject matter of this annotation may be

§ 4. Inadmissibility of declarations as to pain suffered in the past, p. 1084.

As to cases tried in federal courts, the subject matter of this annotation may be affected by Federal Rules of Evidence which became effective July 1, 1975. See 20 U. S. Supreme Court Digest, Lawyer's Edition; Am Jur 2d, Federal Rules of Evidence or USCS Lawyer's Edition, Title 28.

⁵. Testimony as to involuntary or sponta- neous expressions, p. 1087.

As to cases tried in federal courts, the subject matter of this annotation may be affected by the Federal Rules of Evidence which became effective July 1, 1975. See 20 U. S. Supreme Court Digest, Lawyer's Edition; Am Jur 2d, Federal Rules of Evidence or USCS Lawyer's Edition, Title 28.

§ 6. Rule rejecting testimony as to declara- tive statements, p. 1090.

Also limiting admissibility to involuntary or spontaneous expressions, and holding or rec- ognizing that lay testimony of narrative dec- larations or complaints of another's pain or suffering is not admissible:

Ark.—Granite State Ins. Co. v Martin, 252 Ark 613, 480 SW2d 326.

357

[Illustration 34]

PAGE FROM POCKET SUPPLEMENT TO 13 A.L.R.4th

SUPPLEMENT   **13 ALR4th 442–460**

> **After reading an Annotation, a search should be made for cases handed down after the Annotation was written but relevant to the topic of the Annotation. In *A.L.R.3d–4th*, or *A.L.R.Fed.*, this is done by checking in the annual supplement in the back of the volume.**
>
> **Note how the pocket supplement is keyed to the paragraph numbers of the main Annotation.**

problems engendered by amputation including difficulty in maintaining stability, lifting objects, ascending staircase, and walking long distances; amputation led to continual back pain necessitating hospitalization and physical therapy which prevented prolonged sitting and standing. Mattox v Philadelphia (1982, Pa Super) 454 A2d 46.

—$102,479. See Johnson v Alexander (1982, La App) 424 So 2d 1269, § 7[a].

—$40,000; employee, while on job, suffered multiple fractures to foot, including fractures to fourth and fifth toes and displaced fracture to fourth metatarsal neck, when steel fell on right foot; emergency fasiectomy surgery was performed to preserve as much of foot as possible, however fifth toe was amputated as well; one month later, gangrenous fourth toe was amputated and ray resection was performed in order to remove metatarsal bones so as to provide plaintiff with better contour of feet; treating physician testified that there was 100 percent disability with respect to fourth and fifth toes and ten percent permanent physical impairment to entire lower extremity. Lee v State Farm Fire & Casualty Co. (1981, La App) 400 So 2d 330.

—$30,000; 13-year-old boy's foot struck exposed base of fire hydrant while riding dirt bike; sustained broken great toe which was set; hospitalized five weeks later for amputation of toe; eight days hospitalization; 75 percent disability of great toe, affecting balance, walking stamina, and ability to push off. Vega v St. Bernard Water District No. 1 (1981, La App) 398 So 2d 1248.

§ 27. Toes; other injuries:
[a] Not excessive
—$146,715. See American Nat. Watermat-

tress Corp. v Manville (1982, **Alaska**) 642 P2d 1330, § 25[a].

—$102,479. See Johnson v Alexander (1982, La App) 424 So 2d 1269, § 7[a].

[b] Damages fixed by court
—$45,000. See Bickford v Reliance Ins. Cos. (1982, La App) 415 So 2d 405, cert den (La) 420 So 2d 442, § 13[b].

13 ALR4th 362–427

§ 1. Introduction:
[b] Related matters
Liability for damage to automobile left in parking lot or garage. 13 ALR4th 442.

Auto-Cite®: Any case citation herein can be checked for form, parallel references, later history and annotation references through the Auto-Cite computer research system.

13 ALR4th 442–460

§ 1. Introduction:
[b] Related matters
Liability for loss of automobile left at parking lot or garage. 13 ALR4th 362.

Auto-Cite®: Any case citation herein can be checked for form, parallel references, later history and annotation references through the Auto-Cite computer research system.

§ 3. Disclaimer of liability
See Gauthier v Allright New Orleans, Inc. (1982, La App) 417 So 2d 375, cert den (La) 422 So 2d 156, § 6[a].

§ 6. Damage done by third party:
[a] Recovery allowed
In action by patron of unattended self-park lot for value of tires, wheels and hub caps stolen from his automobile while it was on lot, operator of lot was liable, notwithstanding notice on back of receipt that no bailment was created and that operator was not liable for loss of or damage to car or contents, where relationship between parties was that of deposit governed by statutory section providing that depositary is bound to use same diligence in preserving deposit that he uses in preserving his own property, and where operator failed in its burden to prove that it used requisite diligence; even if parking-lot operator could, as matter of law, limit its liability

31

SECTION H. AUTO–CITE

Auto-Cite is a computer-based research system of the Lawyers Co-operative Publishing Company. As discussed in Chapter 5, its database consists of citations for nearly all reported American court decisions. When a citation to a case is inputted, the system will print out parallel citations and the history of the case on appeal, with citations, and indicate if the case had been cited in an *A.L.R. Annotation*.

If an *A.L.R.* citation is inputted, the system will print out the titles of all related *Annotations*. An example is set forth below:

Auto-Cite

94 A.L.R.3d 486: [Input]

[Output]
```
Auto-Cite Service:

94 ALR3D 486:

Relationship between victim and plaintiff-witness as affecting right to recover
damages in negligence for shock or mental anguish at witnessing victim's injury
or death, 94 ALR3d 486

Collateral annotations citing 94 ALR3d 486:

    Bystander recovery for emotional distress at witnessing another's injury
    under strict products liability or breach of warranty, 31 ALR4th 162.

    Necessity of physical injury to support cause of action for loss of
    consortium, 16 ALR4th 537.

    Recovery for mental or emotional distress resulting from injury to, or
    death of, member of plaintiff's family arising from physician's or

    hospital's wrongful conduct, 77 ALR3d 447, supp.

    Right to recover damages in negligence for fear of injury to another, or
    shock or mental anguish at witnessing such injury, 29 ALR3d 1337, supp sec.
    1.

    Right to recover for emotional disturbance or its physical consequences, in
    the absence of impact or other actionable wrong, 64 ALR2d 100, supp sec. 1.

    Comment Note.--Recovery for mental shock or distress in connection with
    injury to or interference with tangible property, 28 ALR2d 1070, supp sec.
    1.
                                                                    [D3325]
```

SECTION I. SUMMARY

A.L.R. may be used to locate court decisions on a topic of law. If, through the indexes, an *A.L.R. Annotation* is located, in most cases it will cite all previous court decisions that its author found on the topic, and the upkeep services provided will locate cases subsequent in time to the writing of the *A.L.R. Annotation*.

It is important to keep in mind that *A.L.R.* is primarily a *case finding tool*, and all decisions located through its use should be read.

Summary of Finding A.L.R. Annotations

STEP 1.   Start search in *Quick Index* to *A.L.R.3d* and *A.L.R.4th.*

(a) If reference in index to an appropriate *Annotation* is located, proceed to Step 2; if not:

(1) search *Quick Index* to *A.L.R.2d;* if reference located, proceed to Step 2; if not,

(2) search *Quick Index* to *A.L.R. (1st);* if applicable reference found, proceed to Step 2; if not:

(b) subject being researched probably not covered by *A.L.R.;* start search for cases using other techniques outlined in Chapter 21.

STEP 2.   Check *Historical Table* in pocket supplement in *Quick Index* to *A.L.R.3d* and *4th* to determine if *Annotation(s)* located through Step 1 have been *superseded* or *supplemented:*

(a) if superseded, note superseding *Annotation*, ignore original, and proceed to Step 3;

(b) if supplemented, note supplementary *Annotation* and proceed to Step 3;

(c) if *Annotation* not listed in *Historical Table*, proceed to Step 3.

STEP 3.   Read *Annotation(s)* found through Steps 1 and 2.

After reading *Annotation(s)*, check for later cases:

(a) if *A.L.R. (1st)*, *Annotation* in *A.L.R. Blue Book of Supplemental Decisions;*

(b) if *A.L.R.2d*, *Annotation* in *Later Case Service* to *A.L.R.2d;*

(c) if *A.L.R.3d* or *A.L.R.4th*, *Annotation* in pocket supplement to that volume;

(d) if *A.L.R.Fed.*, *Annotation* in pocket supplement to *A.L.R. Fed.* volume.

Other methods of locating *A.L.R. Annotations* will be discussed in Chapters 14 and 15.

Chapter 8

CONSTITUTIONS

This chapter will discuss the role of constitutions for both the federal and state governments. As these documents are the charters adopted by the people, they are the highest primary authority.

SECTION A. FEDERAL CONSTITUTION

The Constitution of the United States, in a formal sense, is the written document which was drafted at Philadelphia in the summer of 1787 plus the amendments that have since been added. It was not the intention of the framers that the Constitution be static, but that rather, as noted by Chief Justice Marshall, it should "endure for ages to come, and, consequently, be adapted to various crises in human affairs." [1] More recently, a noted constitutional scholar commented that "[t]he proper point of view from which to approach the task of interpreting the Constitution is that of regarding it as a living statute, palpitating with the purpose of the hour, reenacted with every waking breath of the American people, whose primitive right to determine their institutions is its sole claim to validity as law and as the matrix of laws under our system." [2]

It follows from this that to research problems in federal constitutional law, one must not only consult the document itself, but all of the sources that will assist in the interpretation of the Constitution. Such sources will include the background and record of the Constitutional Convention, the interpretation of the Constitution by the Supreme Court of the United States in the over 450 volumes of its reports, and the commentaries on the Constitution which appear in treatises, legal periodicals and encyclopedias.

Lawyers, when faced with grave constitutional questions of interpretation, frequently refer to the sources of constitutional interpretation.[3] How to locate and use such sources will be discussed in this chapter.

---

[1] McCulloch v. Maryland, 17 U.S. (4 Wheat.) 316, 415 (1819).

[2] Edwin S. Corwin, quoted in LIBRARY OF CONGRESS, CONGRESSIONAL RESEARCH SERVICE, THE CONSTITUTION OF THE UNITED STATES OF AMERICA, S.DOC. NO. 92–82, 92d Cong., 2d Sess. VII (1973). This edition of the Constitution is supplemented biennially with pocket supplements, and new hardbound editions are issued every ten years. 2 U.S.C. § 168 (1982).

[3] United States v. Nixon, 418 U.S. 683, 705 at n. 15 (1974) (citing RECORDS OF THE FEDERAL CONVENTION OF 1787, M. Farrand ed. 1911); Federal Energy Reg. Comm'n v. Mississippi, 456 U.S. 742, 792 (1982) (citing ELLIOT'S DEBATES OF

1. Historical Sources

When faced with interpreting the meaning of a provision or clause of the Constitution, it is frequently useful to ascertain the meaning given to the words used by the "founding fathers." At times, it may be necessary to check into sources that preceded the adoption of the Constitution, such as documents of the Continental Congress or the Articles of Confederation. These may be easily located in *Documents Illustrative of the Formation of the Union of the American States.*[4]

While the Constitutional Convention did not keep official records of its secret sessions, several sources exist that provide an insight into the debates that took place and should be consulted when researching a historical interpretation of the Constitution.[5]

2. Judicial Interpretation: Annotated Editions of the Federal Constitution

When determining the meaning of the United States Constitution, it is also necessary to search for the interpretations of constitutional provisions by the courts, and especially for those of the Supreme Court of the United States. Some of the most useful sources for these are the various annotated editions of the United States Constitution, which set forth each article, section, and clause of the Constitution and provide digests (and, in some instances, commentary) on court decisions.

THE FEDERAL CONVENTION, 2d ed. 1863); Marsh v. Chambers, 463 U.S. 783, 786 (1983) (citing Farrand).

[4] LIBRARY OF CONGRESS, LEGISLATIVE REFERENCE SERVICE, DOCUMENTS ILLUSTRATIVE OF THE FORMATION OF THE UNION OF THE AMERICAN STATES, H.R.DOC. NO. 398, 69th Cong., 1st Sess. (1935). *See also* S. BLOOM, FORMATION OF THE UNION UNDER THE CONSTITUTION (1935). For background on the Articles of Confederation, *see* Swindler, *Our First Constitution: The Articles of Confederation*, 67 A.B.A.J. 166 (1981).

[5] J. MADISON, THE PAPERS OF JAMES MADISON (H. Gilpin ed. 1840); THE FEDERALIST (P. Ford ed. 1898) (This is one of several editions); U.S. BUREAU OF ROLLS AND LIBRARY OF THE DEPARTMENT OF STATE, DOCUMENTARY HISTORY OF THE CONSTITUTION OF THE UNITED STATES OF AMERICA, 1786–1870 (1894–1905); M. FARRAND, THE RECORDS OF THE FEDERAL CONVENTION OF 1787 (1934–1937); J. ELLIOT, THE DEBATES, RESOLUTIONS, AND OTHER PROCEEDINGS, IN CONVENTION, ON THE ADOPTION OF THE FEDERAL CONSTITUTION (1827) (This set has appeared in many editions with different titles and somewhat different content, all known generally as *Elliot's Debates*. The most complete edition appeared in 1937); THE DOCUMENTARY HISTORY OF THE RATIFICATION OF THE CONSTITUTION (to be completed in 12 volumes) (M. Jensen ed. 1976). When finished, the Jensen set will be the most complete and up to date source for the history of the United States Constitution. For evaluation of scholarship in this area since 1937, *see* Hutson, *Pierce Butler's Records of the Federal Constitutional Convention*, 37 Q.J.LIBR.CONG. 64 (1980).

a. *United States Code Annotated, Constitution of the United States Annotated (West Publishing Company).* The *United States Constitution volumes are a separate unit of the United States Code Annotated* and consist of several unnumbered volumes, including a separate index to the Constitution. After each article, section or clause of the Constitution, digest headnotes from all cases that have interpreted a constitutional provision are organized into *notes of decisions.* For example, Article I is followed by 103 notes while Article I, section 8, clause 3 is followed by 1,187 notes. To assist in the location of these notes, indexes to them are provided. The means of locating a constitutional provision and the annotations to it are shown in Illustrations 35–36.

b. *United States Code Service, Constitution Volume.* These volumes are a separate unit of the *United States Code Service,* which is published by the Lawyers Co-operative Publishing Company and the Bancroft-Whitney Company, and is part of their *Total Client-Service Library.*[6] It is organized similarly to the *United States Code Annotated* and is used in a like manner.

c. *The Constitution of the United States of America* (Library of Congress ed. 1973).[7] This one-volume edition of the annotated Constitution was prepared by the Congressional Research Service of the Library of Congress, as authorized by a Joint Congressional Resolution.[8] It sets forth each article, section, and clause of the Constitution; immediately following each of them, in smaller typeface, appear an analysis and commentary prepared by the editorial staff. Important decisions of the Supreme Court of the United States are discussed in the analysis, and citations to them are given in the footnotes. [See Illustrations 37–38.] Frequently, the commentary will quote from the proceedings of the Constitutional Convention, the opinions of dissenting justices, and other documents. This volume, unlike the ones discussed above, does not attempt to cite or comment on all decisions of the Supreme Court of the United States, but refers only to the significant ones. It has a detailed index and includes the following useful tables:

Proposed Amendments Pending Before the States.

Proposed Amendments Not Ratified by the States.

Acts of Congress Held Unconstitutional in Whole or in Part by the Supreme Court of the United States.

[6] *See* Chapter 7, Section A.

[7] For the complete citation of this *see* note 2 *supra.*

[8] 2 U.S.C. § 168 (1982).

State Constitutional and Statutory Provisions and Municipal Ordinances Held Unconstitutional on Their Face or As Administered (1789–1972).

Table of Cases.

This is a very useful volume, and it is often the preferred starting point for research on constitutional questions.

d. *Digests.* The following digests of federal cases provide additional judicial interpretations to the Constitution. These publications are discussed in detail in Chapter 6.

United States Supreme Court Reports Digest (Lawyers Cooperative Publishing Company)

Volume 17 includes the text of the Constitution with references to related sections in the *Digest*.

United States Supreme Court Digest (West Publishing Company)

Federal Digest, Modern Federal Practice Digest, and *West's Federal Practice Digest, 2d & 3d* (West Publishing Company)

e. *Annotations.* The *Annotations* in *A.L.R.Fed.* and the *U.S. Supreme Court Reports (L.Ed.)* may contain discussion, with case analysis, of a phase of the Constitution that is being studied.

3. Treatises and Periodical Literature

Voluminous literature has been written by legal scholars on the interpretation of constitutional provisions, and research in constitutional law can seldom be completed successfully without consulting the writings of constitutional scholars in either treatises or legal periodicals.[9]

[9] Useful titles include: P. BREST & S. LEVINSON, PROCESSES OF CONSTITUTIONAL DECISION MAKING (2d ed. 1983); G. GUNTHER, CASES AND MATERIALS ON CONSTITUTIONAL LAW (10th ed. 1980); L. TRIBE, AMERICAN CONSTITUTIONAL LAW (1978); K. HALL, A COMPREHENSIVE BIBLIOGRAPHY OF AMERICAN CONSTITUTIONAL AND LEGAL HISTORY (5 vols. 1983). For a list of older titles *see* NEW YORK UNIVERSITY, SCHOOL OF LAW LIBRARY, A CATALOGUE OF THE LAW COLLECTION AT NEW YORK UNIVERSITY (1953); ASSOCIATION OF AMERICAN LAW SCHOOLS, 2 LAW BOOKS RECOMMENDED FOR LIBRARIES: CONSTITUTIONAL LAW (1968). Periodical literature may be located through methods described in Chapter 16.

SECTION B. ILLUSTRATIONS: FEDERAL CONSTITUTION

Problem: What protection is given in the Constitution to speeches of the members of Congress?

Illustrations

35.   Page from Index to Constitution: U.S.C.A.
36.   Page from Constitution volume: U.S.C.A.
36–a.   Page showing Annotations: Constitution Volume: U.S. C.A.
37–37–a.   Pages from the Library of Congress Edition, Annotated Constitution

[Illustration 35]

PAGE FROM INDEX TO CONSTITUTION: U.S.C.A.

CONSTITUTION OF THE UNITED STATES

CONGRESS—Continued
►**Members**—Continued
    Discipline, Art. 1, § 5, cl. 2.
    Elections,
        Each House own judge, Art. 1, § 5, cl. 1.
        Power to regulate, Art. 1, § 4, cl. 1.
    Eligibility for other offices, Art. 1, § 6, cl. 2.
    Expulsion, Art. 1, § 5, cl. 2.
    Oath to support Constitution, Art. 6, cl. 3.
    Punishment for disorderly behavior, Art. 1, § 5, cl. 2.
    Qualifications, Art. 1, § 6, cl. 2.
    Salaries, Art. 1, § 6, cl. 1.
  ➤ Speeches, etc., immunity from questioning, <u>Art. 1, § 6, cl. 1.</u>
Powers,
    Abolition of slavery, enforcement, Am. 13, § 2.
    Acting President, designation, Art. 2, § 1, cl. 5.
    Admission of states, Art. 4, § 3, cl. 1.
    Amendments to Constitution, Art. 5.
    Army, government and regulation of, Art. 1, § 8, cl. 14.
    Bankruptcy laws, establishment, Art. 1, § 8, cl. 4.

    The first step in researching a problem involving the U.S. Constitution is to look in an index to the Constitution. For the problem under research, Article 1, Section 6, Clause 1 should be examined. See next illustration.

Full faith and credit clause, prescribing manner of proving state acts,
    records, etc., Art. 4, § 1.
General welfare, provision for, Art. 1, § 8, cl. 1.
Habeas corpus, suspension of writ, Art. 1, § 9, cl. 2.
Impost, levying, etc., Art. 1, § 8, cl. 1.
Incidental, Art. 1, § 8, cl. 18.
Income tax, levy without apportionment, Am. 16.
Inferior courts,
    Creation, Art. 1, § 8, cl. 9.
    Establishment, Art. 3, § 1.
Insurrections and invasions, calling militia, Art. 1, § 8, cl. 15.
Judge of elections, returns and qualifications of members, Art. 1, § 5, cl. 1.
Letters of marque and reprisal, granting, Art. 1, § 8, cl. 11.
Members, disciplining, Art. 1, § 5, cl. 2.
Militia,
    Calling forth, Art. 1, § 8, cl. 15.
    Organizing, governing, etc., Art. 1, § 8, cl. 16.
Money, coining and regulating value of, Art. 1, § 8, cl. 5.
Naturalization, uniform rule for, Art. 1, § 8, cl. 4.
Navy,
    Government and regulation of, Art. 1, § 8, cl. 14.
    Providing and maintaining, Art. 1, § 8, cl. 13.

597

[Illustration 36]

PAGE FROM CONSTITUTION: U.S.C.A.

1 § 5, cl. 3   CONSTITUTION

Section 5, Clause 3. Journal; publication; recording of yeas and nays

Each House shall keep a Journal of its Proceedings, and from time to time publish the same, excepting such Parts as may in their Judgment require Secrecy; and the Yeas and Nays of the Members of either House on any question shall, at the Desire of one fifth of those Present, be entered on the Journal.

Notes of Decisions

Entries 1
Evidence 2

_____

Library references
United States ⊕⊐18.
C.J.S. United States §§ 21, 23.

not expressly require bills that have passed Congress to be attested by the signatures of the presiding officers of the two houses, usage, the orderly conduct of legislative proceedings, and the rules under which the two bodies have acted since the organization of the government, require that mode of authenti-

Text of the constitutional provision covering speeches by members of the Congress as it appears in the Constitution volumes of the United States Code Annotated. This set and the United States Code Service are kept current by annual pocket supplements.

mode to that end which its wisdom sug-   Morgenthau, 1939, 106 F.2d 330, 70 App
gests. Although the Constitution does   D.C. 306.

Section 5, Clause 4. Consent of each house to adjournment

Neither House, during the Session of Congress, shall, without the Consent of the other, adjourn for more than three days, nor to any other Place than that in which the two Houses shall be sitting.

Section 6, Clause 1. Compensation of members; privilege from arrest

The Senators and Representatives shall receive a Compensation for their Services, to be ascertained by Law, and paid out of the Treasury of the United States. They shall in all Cases, except Treason, Felony and Breach of the Peace, be privileged from Arrest during their Attendance at the Session of their respective Houses, and in going to and returning from the same; and for any Speech or Debate in either House, they shall not be questioned in any other Place.

190

[Illustration 36–a]

PAGE SHOWING ANNOTATIONS: CONSTITUTION VOLUME: U.S.C.A.

COMPENSATION, ARREST, ETC. 1 § 6, cl. 1

Note 3

Notes of Decisions

Civil arrest or process 8
Construction 1
Determination of status of Congressman 10
Duration of privilege from arrest 6
Enforcement of privilege from arrest 5
Offenses within privilege from arrest 4
Privilege from arrest 3–7
  Duration of 6
  Enforcement of 5
  Offenses within 4
  Scope of 3
  Waiver of 7
Purpose 2
Scope of privilege from arrest 3
Status of Congressman 9, 10
  Determination 10
Waiver of privilege from arrest 7

Library references
United States ≐12.
C.J.S. United States § 18.

1. Construction

This clause that for any speech or debate in either House, Senators and Representatives shall not be questioned in any other place is to be interpreted liberally and not narrowly. U. S. v. Johnson, C.A.Md.1964, 337 F.2d 180, affirmed 86 S.Ct. 749, 383 U.S. 169, 15 L.Ed.2d 681, certiorari denied 87 S.Ct. 44, 134, 385 U.S. 846, 889, 17 L.Ed.2d 77, 117.

This clause will be read broadly to effectuate its purpose. Id.

This clause, providing that congressmen should, except for treason, felony, and breach of peace, be privileged from arrest, and that they should not be questioned for any speech in either House, is to be liberally construed to free congressman from fear of prosecutions for words spoken, votes cast, or actions taken in pursuit of their lawful functions but

lieved from absenting himself from his public duties during the session of Congress, for the purpose of defending his private suits in court, as that he should be exempt from imprisonment on execution. Doty v. Strong, 1840, 1 Pinn. (Wis.) 84.

2. Purpose

Purpose of this clause that for any speech or debate in either House, Senators and Representatives shall not be questioned in any other place, is to promote free expression on floor of each House by freeing Congressmen from fear of involvement in judicial proceedings. U. S. v. Johnson, C.A.Md.1964, 337 F.2d 180, affirmed 86 S.Ct. 749, 383 U.S. 169, 15 L.Ed.2d 681, certiorari denied 87 S.Ct. 44, 134, 385 U.S. 846, 889, 17 L.Ed.2d 77, 117.

Purpose of this clause giving to Senators and Representatives immunity from arrest, except in certain cases, during attendance at sessions and in going to and returning therefrom is not for benefit or even convenience of individual legislators but is to prevent interference with the legislative process, and it prevents judicial branch of government from effecting such interference by restricting power of courts. James v. Powell, 1966, 274 N.Y.S.2d 192, 26 A.D.2d 295, affirmed 277 N.Y.S.2d 135, 18 N.Y.2d 931, 223 N.E. 2d 562, motion granted 279 N.Y.S.2d 972, 19 N.Y.2d 813, 226 N.E.2d 705.

3. Privilege from arrest—Scope of

Where attention given in evidence is to substance of defendant congressman's speech on floor of House and his motivation in making it was not incidental part of government's prosecution under charge of conspiracy to defraud United States, since conspiracy theory depended on showing that speech was made

---

After the text of each clause, there are digests of all cases that have interpreted the clause, preceded by an index to the digests.

[Illustration 37]

PAGE FROM LIBRARY OF CONGRESS EDITION, ANNOTATED CONSTITUTION

116   ART. I—LEGISLATIVE DEPARTMENT

Sec. 6—Rights of Members   Cl. 1—Compensation, Privileges

This one-volume edition sets forth the text of each Section and Clause of the Constitution. Immediately following, in smaller type, is an analysis and commentary of the Clause.

SECTION 6. Clause 1. The Senators and Representatives shall receive a Compensation for their Services, to be ascertained by Law, and paid out of the Treasury of the United States. They shall in all Cases, except Treason, Felony and Breach of the Peace, be privileged from Arrest during their Attendance at the Session of their respective Houses and in going to and returning from the same; and for any Speech or Debate in either House, they shall not be questioned in any other Place.

Clause 2. No Senator or Representative shall, during the Time for which he was elected, be appointed to any civil Office under the Authority of the United States, which shall have been created, or the Emoluments whereof shall have been encreased during such time; and no Person holding any Office under the the United States, shall be a Member of either House during his Continuance in Office.

COMPENSATION, IMMUNITIES AND DISABILITIES OF MEMBERS

When the Pay Starts

A Member of Congress who receives his certificate of admission, and is seated, allowed to vote, and serve on committees, is *prima facie* entitled to the seat and salary, even though the House subsequently

---

* *Field* v. *Clark*, 143 U.S. 649 (1892) ; *Flint* v. *Stone Tracy Co.*, 220 U.S. 107, 143 (1911). A parallel rule holds in the case of a duly authenticated official notice to the Secretary of State that a state legislature has ratified a proposed amendment to the Constitution. *Leser* v. *Garnett*, 258 U.S. 130, 137 (1922) ; *see also Coleman* v. *Miller*, 307 U.S. 433 (1939).

[Illustration 37–a]

PAGE FROM LIBRARY OF CONGRESS EDITION, ANNOTATED CONSTITUTION

ART. I—LEGISLATIVE DEPARTMENT   117

Sec. 6—Rights of Members   Cl. 1—Privileges

declares his seat vacant. The one who contested the election and was subsequently chosen to fill the vacancy is entitled to salary only from the time the compensation of such "predecessor" has ceased.[1]

Analysis of the privilege of speech clause by the editors of the volume. Footnotes contain citations to cases mentioned in the analysis.

Privilege of Speech or Debate

Members.—This clause represents "the culmination of a long struggle for parliamentary supremacy. Behind these simple phrases lies a history of conflict between the Commons and the Tudor and Stuart monarchs during which successive monarchs utilized the criminal and civil law to suppress and intimidate critical legislators. Since the Glorious Revolution in Britain, and throughout United States history, the privilege has been recognized as an important protection of the independence and integrity of the legislature."[6] So Justice Harlan explained the significance of the speech and debate clause, the ancestry of which traces back to a clause in the English Bill of Rights of 1689[7] and the history of which traces back almost to the beginning of the development of Parliament as an independent force.[8] "In the American governmental structure the clause serves the additional function of reinforcing the separation of powers so deliberately established by the Founders."[9] "The immunities of the Speech or Debate Clause were not written into the Constitution simply for the personal or private benefit of Members of Congress, but to protect the integrity of the legislative process by insuring the independence of individual legislators."[10]

---

[1] *Pace v. United States*, 127 U.S. 67 (1888).
[2] *Long v. Ansell*, 293 U.S. 76 (1934).
[3] Id., 83.
[4] *United States v. Cooper*, 4 Dall. (4 U.S.) 341 (C.C. Pa. 1800).
[5] *Williamson v. United States*, 207 U.S. 425, 446 (1908).
[6] *United States v. Johnson*, 383 U.S. 169, 178 (1966).
[7] "That the Freedom of Speech, and Debates or Proceedings in Parliament, ought not to be impeached or questioned in any Court or Place out of Parliament." 1 W. & M., Sess. 2, c. 2.
[8] *United States v. Johnson*, 383 U.C. 169, 177–179, 180–183 (1966); *Powell v. McCormack*, 395 U.S. 486, 502 (1969).
[9] *United States v. Johnson*, 383 U.S. 169, 178 (1906).
[10] *United States v. Brewster*, 408 U.S. 501, 507 (1972). This rationale was approvingly quoted from *Coffin v. Coffin*, 4 Mass. 1, 28 (1808), in *Kilbourn v. Thompson*, 103 U.S. 168, 203 (1881).

SECTION C. STATE CONSTITUTIONS

Each of the fifty states has adopted its own constitution, and many states have adopted several different constitutions over the years. The procedure for adopting a new constitution is usually accomplished by the convening of a state constitutional convention.[10] The state constitution, except for those issues covered by the supremacy clause of the United States Constitution,[11] is the highest primary legal authority for the state.

When doing research involving a state constitution, it may also be necessary to check the historical documents that led to its adoption and to consult the state and federal court decisions interpreting it.

1. Texts of State Constitutions

a.   The most common source for the text of a state constitution is the constitution volume of the state code.[12] This ordinarily will contain the current text, the text of previously adopted versions, and annotations similar in format to those of the United States Constitution as described in Section A *supra*. The volume or volumes containing the state constitution should be examined carefully, and distinctive bibliographic features should be noted. Many states also print and distribute an unannotated edition of the state constitution in pamphlet form.

b.   Columbia University, Legislative Drafting Research Fund. *Constitutions of the United States: National and State* (2d ed. 1974).[13]

This multi-volume, looseleaf set collects the text of the Constitutions of all U.S. territories and fifty states and is kept current by supplements.

[10] A. STURM, A BIBLIOGRAPHY ON STATE CONSTITUTIONS AND CONSTITUTIONAL REVISION, 1945–1975 (1975).

[11] U.S. CONST. art. VI; Gibbons v. Ogden, 22 U.S. (9 Wheat.) 1 (1824); National Labor Relations Bd. v. Jones & Laughlin Steel Corp., 301 U.S. 1 (1937); United States v. Darby, 312 U.S. 100 (1941); Perez v. United States, 402 U.S. 146 (1971).

[12] State codes are discussed in Chapter 11.

[13] The following older titles are also useful in tracing the historical development of state constitutions: B. POORE, CHARTERS AND CONSTITUTIONS (1877); F. STIMSON, THE LAW OF THE FEDERAL AND STATE CONSTITUTIONS OF THE UNITED STATES (1908); F. THORPE, FEDERAL AND STATE CONSTITUTIONS (1909); C. KETTLEBOROUGH, STATE CONSTITUTIONS (1918); NEW YORK CONSTITUTIONAL CONVENTION COMMITTEE, 3 REPORTS: CONSTITUTIONS OF THE STATES AND UNITED STATES (1938). Although Thorpe and Poore are out of date, they are useful for their parallel study of state constitutions. The last item, although never brought up to date, is still useful for its index volume to the constitutions of all of the states.

2. Historical Sources of State Constitutions

The records, journals, proceedings, and other documents relating to state constitutional conventions provide valuable information on the intended meanings and interpretations given to state constitutions by their framers.[14] Some state codes also contain historical introductions to the constitutions printed therein. Local encyclopedias and treatises should also be consulted.

3. Judicial Interpretation of State Constitutions

In addition to consulting the annotations to the constitution in the appropriate volumes of the state code, the state digest should also be consulted, using the index to the constitution to locate the relevant sections of the digest.

4. Comparative Sources of State Constitutions

Frequently, a provision of a particular state constitution may not have received any judicial interpretation. In such instances, judicial decisions on similar provisions in other state constitutions may be useful. One method of locating which state constitutions have similar provisions is through the use of the following:

Index Digest of State Constitutions

This set is a companion to the *Constitutions of the United States: National and State*, discussed in Section 1–b *supra*. It is arranged alphabetically by subject and under each subject are listed the various constitutional provisions of the states. Although this set has not been kept current since 1971, it is still useful, as many provisions of state constitutions do not change with great frequency. The publisher has announced that a new edition is in preparation.

---

[14] *See* note 10 *supra*. The Congressional Information Service has made most of these materials available in their collection *State Constitutional Conventions, Commissions, and Amendments on Microfiche* (1972–1980), with accompanying hardcopy indexes.

Chapter 9

FEDERAL LEGISLATION

Article I, Section 8, of the United States Constitution enumerates the powers of Congress, and provides the authority for Congress to make all laws necessary and proper for carrying into execution the enumerated powers, as well as other powers vested in the Congress.

Congress meets in two-year periods, with each such period known as a *Congress*. The period in which Congress met, for example, during the years 1983–84, is known as the 98th Congress, the 1st Congress being 1789–91. Under the Constitution, Congress must meet at least once a year.[1]

SECTION A. THE ENACTMENT OF FEDERAL LAWS

Before discussing the various ways the laws of Congress are published, a brief description of the legislative process is necessary.[2] At the beginning of each Congress, Representatives or Senators may introduce legislation in their respective branch of Congress. Each proposed law is called a *bill* [3] when introduced. The first bill in the House of Representatives in each Congress is labeled *H.R. 1*, with all subsequent bills numbered sequentially. Similarly, the first bill introduced into the Senate is labeled *S. 1*. After a bill passes the house in which it was introduced, it is sent for consideration to the other house. If approved, it is then sent to the President for his signature. If he signs it, it then becomes a law. If the President vetoes it, it becomes law if approved by two-thirds of both houses of Congress.[4] Under the Constitution, a bill sent to the President also becomes law if the President does not either sign or veto it within ten

---

[1] U.S. CONST. art. I, § 4.

[2] For more detailed statements on the enactment of federal laws, *see* E. WILLETT, HOW OUR LAWS ARE MADE, H.R.DOC. NO. 97–120, 97th Cong., 1st Sess. (1982); ENACTMENT OF A LAW: PROCEDURAL STEPS IN THE LEGISLATIVE PROCESS, S.DOC. NO. 97–20, 97th Cong., 1st Sess. (1981). *See also* CONGRESSIONAL QUARTERLY SERVICE, GUIDE TO THE CONGRESS OF THE UNITED STATES, ORIGINS, HISTORY, AND PROCEDURE, Pt. III (2d ed. 1976).

[3] A *bill* is the form used for most legislation. *Joint resolutions* may also be used, but there is no practical difference between the two, and the two forms are used indiscriminately. *Concurrent resolutions* are used for matters affecting both houses, but are not legislative. *Simple resolutions* are used for matters concerning the operation of either house. The first three forms are published in the *Statutes at Large*, the latter in the *Congressional Record*. HOW OUR LAWS ARE MADE, *supra* note 2, at 6–8.

[4] U.S. CONST. art. I, § 7.

days of receiving it.[5]   Bills introduced, but not passed during a specific Congress, do not carry over to the next Congress. If the sponsors wish the bill to be considered by the new Congress, it must be submitted as a new bill.

After a bill has been approved in identical form by both houses and signed by the President (or approved over a Presidential veto,[6] or neither signed nor vetoed by the President within ten days), it becomes a law.   It is then sent to the Administrator of General Services, who is directed to publish all laws so received.[7]   The Administrator classifies each law as either a public law or a private law.   The former is one that affects the nation as a whole, or deals with individuals as a class and relates to public matters.   A private law benefits only a specific individual or individuals.   Such laws deal primarily with matters relating to claims against the government or with matters of immigration and naturalization.[8]

The first law to pass a Congress is designated as either Public Law No. 1 or Private Law No. 1.   Each succeeding public or private law is then numbered in sequence throughout the two-year life of a Congress.

SECTION B.   PUBLICATION OF FEDERAL LAWS

1.   Current Laws

During a session of Congress, each law as passed is first issued by the United States Government Printing Office as a *slip law*. [See Illustration 38.] This means that each law is separately published and may be one page or several hundred pages in length. There are four sources commonly consulted for the text of current laws.

a.   *Slip Laws.*   These are available at all libraries that are depositories for U.S. Government publications [9] and in certain law libraries.

b.   *United States Code Congressional and Administrctive News Service.*   This set is published by the West Publishing Company in connection with the *United States Code Annotated.*   During each session of Congress, it is issued monthly in pamphlet form and prints in full text all of the public laws.   Each issue contains a cumulative subject index and a cumulative *Table of Laws Enacted.*

[5] *Id.*

[6] For a list of Presidential vetoes, *see* U.S. CONGRESS, SENATE LIBRARY, PRESIDENTIAL VETOES, 1789–1976 (1978).

[7] 1 U.S.C. §§ 106(a), 112 (1982 ed.).

[8] For a complete discussion of private bills and laws, *see* CONGRESSIONAL QUARTERLY SERVICE, *supra* note 2, at 299–310.

[9] JOINT COMM. ON PRINTING, 98TH CONG., 1ST SESS., GOVERNMENT DEPOSITORY LIBRARIES (Comm.Print 1983).

After each session of Congress, the pamphlets are reissued in bound volumes.

c.   *Advance Sheets, United States Code Service, Lawyers' Edition.*   This is published by the Lawyers Co-operative Publishing Company in connection with the *United States Code Service, L.Ed.* It contains similar information to that described in b *supra.*

d.   *United States Law Week.*   This weekly looseleaf service, which is published by the Bureau of National Affairs, includes the text of selected laws passed during the week.

2.   United States Statutes at Large

At the end of each session of Congress, all of the slip laws are published in numerical order as part of the set called the *United States Statutes at Large.*   Thus, all of the laws enacted since 1789 are contained in the many volumes of this set.[10]

It is important to keep in mind that the laws are arranged in chronological order rather than by subject.   Moreover, amendments to a previously passed law will appear in different volumes from the law being amended.   For example, a law passed in 1900 is in volume 31 of the *Statutes at Large.*   If Congress amended it in 1905, the amendment will appear in the volume for that year.   Some laws have been amended many, many times and in order to obtain the full and current text of such a law, the *Statutes at Large* volume containing the original law must be examined in conjunction with subsequent volumes in which amendments to the law appear.

Each volume of the *Statutes at Large* has its own subject index and contains tables listing how each public law in it affects previous public laws.

SECTION C.   CODIFICATION OF FEDERAL LAWS

The chronological method of publication of Congressional laws creates obvious problems for the process of determining the statutory provisions on any given subject.   In order to better accomplish this, the laws passed by Congress have to be rearranged in a manner that will do three things: (1) collate the original law with all subsequently passed amendments by taking into consideration the deletion or addition of language changed by the amendments;   (2) bring all laws on the same subject or topic together;   and (3) eliminate all

---

[10] Until 1936, each volume of the *Statutes at Large* covered the two-year period for each Congress.   *See also* CHECKLIST OF U.S. SESSION LAWS, 1789–1873 (U.S. Library of Congress 1979).

repealed, superseded, or expired laws. This process is called codification.[11]

1. United States Revised Statutes

The first codification [12] of the *Statutes at Large* was authorized by the Congress in 1866 and resulted in the publication of the *Revised Statutes of 1875.*

The Commissioners authorized by Congress to prepare this revision began by extracting from the volumes of the *Statutes at Large* all public laws that met the following two criteria: (1) they were still in force, and (2) they were of a general and permanent nature. They eliminated all appropriation laws and those that did not have general applicability. The next step was to take each public law and all its amendments and rewrite the law in one sequence by incorporating amending language and eliminating deleting language. All of the laws were then arranged by topic in chapters, or *titles.* Title 35, for example, contained all legislation passed by Congress, and still in force, on taxation; Title 70, all legislation in force on criminal law. All of the titles were then bound in one volume, a subject index prepared, and the volume issued as the *Revised Statutes of 1875.*

This volume as prepared by the Commissioners was then submitted to Congress, introduced as a bill, and went through the legislative process of becoming a public law. Within the bill before Congress there was a section specifically repealing each previously passed public law that had been incorporated into the *Revised Statutes of 1875.*[13]

Thus, when it passed Congress and was signed by the President, all of the laws passed since 1789, in force and of a general and public nature, were codified in the *Revised Statutes of 1875.* Moreover, as the act of codification repealed all the previous *Statutes at Large* citations, the *Revised Statutes of 1875* became *positive law,* and it was no longer necessary to refer to the *Statutes at Large* volumes.

Unfortunately, this volume, known as the first edition, was subsequently discovered to contain many inaccuracies and unautho-

[11] For articles dealing with codification, *see* Tucker, *Tradition and Technique of Codification in the Modern World: The Louisiana Experience,* 25 LA.L.REV. 698 (1965); Zinn, *Revision of the United States Code,* 51 LAW LIB.J. 388 (1958); *A Code Odyssey, A Critical Analysis of the Alabama Recodification Process,* 10 CUM.L.REV. 119 (1979); Dowling, *The Creation of the Montana Code Annotated,* 40 MONT.L.REV. 1 (1979); McKenzie, *The Making of a New Code—The Official Code of Georgia Annotated: Recodification in Georgia,* 18 GA.ST.B.J. 102 (1982).

[12] Dwan and Feidler, *The Federal Statutes, Their History and Use,* 22 MINN.L. REV. 1008 (1938).

[13] Revised Statutes of the United States, 1873–1874, Act of June 22, 1874, tit. LXXIV, Repeal Provisions, §§ 5595–5601, at 1091–92 (1875).

rized changes in the law.[14]   In 1878, a second edition of the *Revised Statutes* was authorized to be published that would include legislation passed since 1873, delete sections that were repealed since 1873, and also correct the errors inadvertently incorporated into the first edition.

The second edition indicated changes to the text of the first edition by the use of brackets and italics.   It is important to note, however, that the second edition of the *Revised Statutes* was never reenacted by Congress, and all changes indicated in it are only *prima facie* evidence of the law.   There was no further codification of federal laws until 1926.

2.   United States Code (U.S.C.)

Prior to 1926, the positive law for federal legislation was contained in the one volume of the *Revised Statutes of 1875* and then in each of the twenty-four subsequent volumes of the *Statutes at Large*.   Although several attempts were made to adopt a new codification, nothing further officially occurred until the publication of the *United States Code*, prepared under the auspices of special committees of the House of Representatives and the Senate.   In this codification, all sections of the *Revised Statutes of 1875* not repealed were extracted, and then all of the public and general laws still in force from the *Statutes at Large* since 1873 were included.   These were then arranged into fifty titles and published as the *United States Code*, 1926 edition.[15]   Between 1927 and 1931 cumulated bound supplements were issued each year.   In 1932 a new edition was issued which incorporated the cumulated supplements to the 1926 edition, and this became the *United States Code*, 1932 edition. Every six years a new edition is published with cumulative supplements being issued during the intervening years.

The *U.S.C.* differs from the *Revised Statutes of 1875* in an important aspect.   It was never submitted to Congress and reenacted in its entirety.   Instead, Congress has created the Office of Law Revision Counsel[16] and directed it to revise the *U.S.C.* title by title. Each title is then submitted to Congress for enactment into law.   To date, twenty-three titles have been enacted into law.[17]   Thus, in using

[14] Dwan and Feidler, *supra* note 12.

[15] *See* Preface to Volume 44, Part One, *Statutes at Large* (1926).

[16] The principal duty of this Office is "to develop and keep current an official and positive codification of the laws of the United States" and "to prepare * * * one title at a time, a complete compilation, restatement and revision of the general and permanent laws of the United States * * * ."   1 U.S.C. § 204(a) (1982).

[17] These are 1, 3, 4, 5, 6, 9, 10, 11, 13, 14, 17, 18, 23, 28, 31, 32, 34, 35, 37, 38, 39, 44, 46, 49, and the Internal Revenue Code (Title 26).   Titles 46 and 49 were partial enactments.   The enactment of Title 31 repealed Title 6, Surety Bonds, which had been enacted previously.   A list of enacted titles may be found in the following

the *U.S.C.,* it is important to ascertain if the title being consulted has been enacted into positive law. Those titles not yet enacted are *prima facie* evidence of the law.[18] Should there be a conflict between the wording in the *U.S.C.* and the *Statutes at Large,* the latter will govern.[19]

3. Annotated Editions of the United States Code

The *U.S.C.* is designated as the official edition, and is printed and sold by the U.S. Government Printing Office. As is frequently the case with such publications, it is slow in being published, particularly in the issuance of the supplements, which are seldom available until several months after a session of Congress is over. Furthermore, the meaning of a law passed by a legislative body is not always clear and the language used must frequently be interpreted by a court. Consequently, access to the court decisions interpreting statutes is frequently as important as the text of the statute itself. This has led to the publication of annotated codes where digests of court decisions interpreting a code section are given. There are two privately published annotated editions of the *U.S.C.*

Both of these sets have many advantages over the official edition of the *U.S.C.* and are usually consulted in preference to it. These advantages are (1) each title is published in one or more separate volumes; (2) the entire set is kept up to date by annual cumulative pocket supplements and, when necessary, by recompiled volumes; (3) pamphlets are issued during the year bringing the pocket supplements up to date; (4) more detailed indexing is provided in both bound volumes and supplements; (5) each code section contains annotations of court decisions which have cited and interpreted it; (6) when applicable, citations to the *Code of Federal Regulations*[20] are given.

sources: (1) Preface to the volumes of the *U.S.C.;* (2) after Section 204(e) of title 1 in the *U.S.C.A.* and the *U.S.C.S.;* (3) inside front cover of the volumes of the *U.S.C.S.*

[18] 1 U.S.C. § 204(a) (1982) provides that "The matter set forth in the edition of the Code of Laws of the United States current at any time shall, together with the then current supplement, if any, establish *prima facie* the laws of the United States, general and permanent in their nature, in force on the day preceding the commencement of the session following the last session the legislation of which is included: *Provided, however,* that whenever titles of such Code shall have been enacted into positive law the text thereof shall be legal evidence of the laws therein contained in all the courts of the United States, the several States, and the Territories and insular possessions of the United States."

[19] *See* an interpretation of 1 U.S.C. § 204(a) (1982 ed.) in United States v. Welden, 377 U.S. 95, 98 n. 4 (1964). *See also* North Dakota v. United States, 460 U.S. 300, 103 S.Ct. 1095, 75 L.Ed.2d 77 (1983).

[20] This set is discussed in Chapter 12.

a. *United States Code Annotated (U.S.C.A.).* This set is published by the West Publishing Company. In addition to annotating relevant cases, the notes following each code section make reference to other West publications and frequently refer to the Topic and Key Numbers where additional cases may be located. In addition to a separate paperback eight-volume index which is issued every other year with an interim update pamphlet in alternate years, each title has an individual, detailed index.

b. *United States Code Service, Lawyers' Edition (U.S.C.S.).* This set is published by the Lawyers Co-operative Publishing Company and the Bancroft-Whitney Company and is a unit of their *Total Client-Service Library.*[21] It includes a multi-volume index and the multi-volume *United States Code Guide.* This volume is arranged by *U.S.C.* citation and indicates where the matter covered by a code section is discussed in the other units of their *Total Client-Service Library.* Two unnumbered volumes contain the rules of procedure governing practice before the federal administrative agencies, and Volume I includes the text of the Universal Copyright Convention, the Convention on Enforcement of Foreign Arbitral Awards, and the Warsaw Convention.

c. *Summary and Comparison: Annotated Editions of the United States Code.* Both the *U.S.C.A.* and the *U.S.C.S.* follow the same citation pattern as the official *U.S.C.*[22] Thus, a citation to *U.S.C.* may be located in either of the two annotated sets. Each of these contains exactly the same information as in the official *U.S.C.,* but, in addition, contains digests of decisions that have cited or interpreted a section of the *U.S.C.* Each set is kept up to date by annual pocket supplements, monthly pamphlets, and, when necessary, by the issuance of replacement volumes. Each has editorial matter that refers to other publications by the same publisher. The *U.S. C.A.* will usually contain more annotations than the *U.S.C.S.,* which makes frequent cross-references to *Annotations* in *A.L.R.Fed.* or in the *Lawyers' Editions* of the *United States Reports* for additional cases. Each set is simple to use, more current, and better indexed than the *U.S.C.* However, when only the text of the Code is needed, it may be simpler to consult the official unannotated edition. Illustrations 39–43 show the use of the various editions of the *U.S.C.*

As we noted in Section C–2, *supra,* only certain titles of the *U.S.C.* have been reenacted. The *U.S.C.A.* uses the text as it appears in the *U.S.C.,* while the *United States Code Service* follows the text as it appears in the *Statutes at Large.* Thus, when using the *U.S. C.A.,* it may be necessary at times to check the text in the *Statutes*

---

[21] *See* Chapter 7, note 1.

[22] For a discussion of these two sets, *see* Benioff, *A Comparison of Annotated U.S. Codes,* 4 LEGAL REFERENCE SERVICES Q. 37 (Summer 1984).

at Large for those titles that are still only *prima facie* evidence of the law.

SECTION D. ILLUSTRATIONS

[Illustration 38]

SLIP LAW—96TH CONGRESS

PUBLIC LAW 96-73—SEPT. 29, 1979 **[1]** ———▶ 93 STAT. 537

Public Law 96-73
96th Congress

An Act

To amend the Rail Passenger Service Act to extend the authorization of appropri-
ations for Amtrak for 2 additional years, and for other purposes. **[2]** ———▶
Sept. 29, 1979
[H.R. 3996]

*Be it enacted by the Senate and House of Representatives of the
United States of America in Congress assembled,*

Amtrak
Reorganization
Act of 1979

TITLE I—AMTRAK REORGANIZATION

SHORT TITLE

SECTION 101. This title may be cited as the "Amtrak Reorganization
Act of 1979"

45 USC 501 note.

PURPOSES

SEC. 102. Section 101 of the Rail Passenger Service Act (45 U.S.C.
502) is amended—

    (1) by inserting "(a)" immediately before "The Congress";
    (2) by striking out "and" after "this purpose;";
    (3) by striking out the period after "Railroad Passenger Corpo-
ration" and inserting in lieu thereof the following: "; and that
rail passenger service offers significant benefits in public transportation for the safe movement of passengers with minimum
energy expenditure and represents a significant national transportation asset in time of national emergency or energy shortage."; and
    (4) by adding at the end thereof the following new subsection:
"(b) The Congress further finds that—
    "(1) inadequately defined goals for the Corporation have
denied its board of directors an effective role in guiding the

45 USC 502.

This is a typical *slip* law. At the end of the year, laws are published in a bound
volume of the Statutes at Large.

Marginal notes are not part of the law but editorial aids. The code citations in
the margin indicate where the Statutes at Large citations in the text are found in
the United States Code.

Notes: 1.   Statutes at Large citation.
      2.   Bill number in House.

---

to justify additional expenditure of public funds.".

GOALS

SEC. 103. (a) GOALS FOR AMTRAK.—The Rail Passenger Service Act
(45 U.S.C. 501 et seq.) is amended by redesignating section 102 as

45 USC 502.

[Illustration 39]

PAGE FROM INDEX VOLUME TO THE U.S.C.A.

GRAZING   92

GRAZING—Cont'd
Resource Conservation, generally, this index
Sawtooth National Recreation Area, adminis-
    tration of in manner best providing for
    management, utilization and disposal of
    on federally owned lands, 16 § 460aa–1
Sequoia National Park, 16 § 45c
Set-aside acreage programs, wheat producers,

GRAZING DISTRICTS—Cont'd
Leases—Cont'd
    Disposition of moneys received, 43
        § 315m–4
    Isolated or disconnected tracts, 43 § 315m
Manufacturing rights, 43 § 315b
Mineral resources, development, 43 § 315e
Mineral title, application for, 43 § 315i

FINDING A FEDERAL STATUTE

Problem: Find the statutory section dealing with water rights in
grazing districts.

Step 1: Check index volumes to either U.S.C., U.S.C.A., or U.S.C.S.
This will indicate that this topic is covered at 43 U.S.C.
§ 315b.

Alaska, this index
Appeals, local hearings, 43 § 315h
Appropriation of money received, 43 §§ 315i,
    315j
Citizens, permits, 43 § 315b
Coal, use for domestic purposes, 43 § 315d
Contributions, 43 § 315h
Cooperation with,
    Governmental departments, 43 § 315k
    Local associations, 43 § 315h
Coordination of range administration, 43
    § 315k
Disposition of moneys received, 43 § 315i
Domestic purposes, grazing for, 43 § 315d
Drought, reduction or refund, 43 § 315b
Erosion, study, 43 § 315a
Establishment, 43 § 315
Federal land policy and management, public
    lands acquired by Interior Secretary, to
    become part of, 43 § 1715   ⟶
Fees for permits, 43 § 315b
Fences, 43 § 315c
Firewood, use for domestic purposes, 43
    § 315d
Flood control, 43 § 315a
Gravel, use for domestic purposes, 43 § 315d
Hearings,
    Creation of districts in States, notice, 43
        § 315
    On appeals, 43 § 315h
Homestead entries, 43 § 315f
Hunting or fishing rights, 43 § 315
Improvement, 43 §§ 315a, 315c, 315i
    Availability of moneys received from graz-
        ing district, 43 § 315i
Indian ceded lands, application of public land
    laws to, 43 § 315j
Indians, deposit of money to credit of, 43
    § 315j
Leases, 43 §§ 315m, 315m–1
    Administration of land leased, 43 § 315m–2
    Contributions available for, 43 § 315m–3

Restrictions, etc., concerning prior rights, 43
    § 315
Rights of way, 43 §§ 315, 315e
Roads, appropriation of money received, 43
    § 315j
Rules and regulations for protection, adminis-
    tration, etc., 43 § 315a
Schools, appropriation of money received, 43
    § 315j
Secretary of Interior, powers, duties, etc., 43
    § 315 et seq.
Soldiers' and sailors' civil relief, remission,
    etc., of grazing fees, 50 App. § 561
State police power, 43 § 315n
States,
    Appropriations of moneys received to State,
        43 § 315j
    Police power, 43 § 315n
Stone, use for domestic purposes, 43 § 315d
Water rights, 43 § 315b
Wells, 43 § 315c
Wildlife, cooperation in conservation or pro-
    pagation, 43 § 315h

GRAZING LANDS
Coos Bay Wagon Road grant lands, recon-
    veyed lands, 43 § 1181d
Field employees of Bureau of Land Manage-
    ment to furnish horses and equipment, 43
    § 315o–2
Grazing Districts, generally, this index
Inapplicability of law concerning Federal civil
    defense transactions to lease of Govern-
    ment realty for grazing, 50 App. § 2285
Lease of isolated or disconnected tracts, 43
    § 315m
Mining activities causing damage, liability, 30
    § 54
National defense, payment for use for national
    defense purposes, 43 § 315q
National Forest Administration land under,
    43 §§ 315k, 315l

[Illustration 40]

PAGE FROM UNITED STATES CODE, 1970 EDITION

Page 10775   TITLE 43.—PUBLIC LANDS   § 315b

which such person has stock-grazing rights. Neither this subchapter nor sections 291 to 301 of this title, commonly known as the "Stock Raising Homestead Act", shall be construed as limiting the authority or policy of Congress or the President to include in national forests public lands of the character described in section 471 of Title 16, for the purposes set forth in section 475 of Title 16, or such other pur-

---

Step 2: Locate the title and section referred to in the Index. Ordinarily one would consult the latest edition of the U.S.C. and its cumulative supplement or one of the two annotated editions.

This edition is shown to illustrate how this section of the Code appeared before its latest amendment.

---

permittee any right whatsoever to interfere with hunting or fishing within a grazing district. (June 28, 1934, ch. 865, § 1, 48 Stat. 1269; June 26, 1936, ch. 842, title I, § 1, 49 Stat. 1976; May 28, 1954, ch. 243, § 2, 68 Stat. 151.)

AMENDMENTS

1954—Act May 28, 1954, struck out of first sentence the provision limiting to one hundred and forty-two million acres the area which might be included in grazing districts.

Act June 26, 1936 increased the acreage which could be included in grazing districts from 80 million to 142 million acres.

SHORT TITLE

Sections 315—315g, 315h—315m, 315n and 315o–1, are from act June 28, 1934, and constitute the Taylor Grazing Act. See section 315m–2 of this title.

SECTION REFERRED TO IN OTHER SECTIONS

This section is referred to in sections 315a, 1425 of this title; title 30 section 601.

§ 315a. Protection, administration, regulation, and improvement of districts; rules and regulations; study of erosion and flood control; offenses.

The Secretary of the Interior shall make provision for the protection, administration, regulation, and improvement of such grazing districts as may be created under the authority of section 315 of this title, and he shall make such rules and regulations and establish such service, enter into such cooperative agreements, and do any and all things necessary to accomplish the purposes of this subchapter and to insure the objects of such grazing districts, namely, to regulate their occupancy and use, to preserve the land and its resources from destruction or unnecessary injury, to provide for the orderly use, improvement, and development of the range; and the Secretary of the Interior is authorized to continue the study of erosion and flood control and to perform such work as may be necessary amply to protect and rehabilitate the areas subject to the

provisions of this subchapter, through such funds as may be made available for that purpose, and any willful violation of the provisions of this subchapter or of such rules and regulations thereunder after actual notice thereof shall be punishable by a fine of not more than $500. (June 28, 1934, ch. 865, § 2, 48 Stat. 1270.)

CROSS REFERENCES

Petty offense defined, see section 1 (3) of Title 18, Crimes and Criminal Procedure.

SECTION REFERRED TO IN OTHER SECTIONS

This section is referred to in title 30 section 601.

§ 315b. Grazing permits; fees; vested water rights; permits not to create right in land.

The Secretary of the Interior is authorized to issue or cause to be issued permits to graze livestock on such grazing districts to such bona fide settlers, residents, and other stock owners as under his rules and regulations are entitled to participate in the use of the range, upon the payment annually of reasonable fees in each case to be fixed or determined from time to time, and in fixing the amount of such fees the Secretary of the Interior shall take into account the extent to which such districts yield public benefits over and above those accruing to the users of the forage resources for livestock purposes. Such fees shall consist of a grazing fee for the use of the range, and a range-improvement fee which, when appropriated by the Congress, shall be available until expended solely for the construction, purchase, or maintenance of range improvements. Grazing permits shall be issued only to citizens of the United States or to those who have filed the necessary declarations of intention to become such, as required by the naturalization laws, and to groups, associations, or corporations authorized to conduct business under the laws of the State in which the grazing district is located. Preference shall be given in the issuance of grazing permits to those within or near a district who are landowners engaged in the livestock business, bona fide occupants or settlers, or owners of water or water rights, as may be necessary to permit the proper use of lands, water or water rights owned, occupied, or leased by them, except that until July 1, 1935, no preference shall be given in the issuance of such permits to any such owner, occupant, or settler, whose rights were acquired between January 1, 1934, and December 31, 1934, both dates inclusive, except that no permittee complying with the rules and regulations laid down by the Secretary of the Interior shall be denied the renewal of such permit, if such denial will impair the value of the grazing unit of the permittee, when such unit is pledged as security for any bona fide loan. Such permits shall be for a period of not more than ten years, subject to the preference right of the permittees to renewal in the discretion of the Secretary of the Interior, who shall specify from time to time numbers of stock and seasons of use. During periods of range depletion due to severe drought or other natural causes, or in case of a general epidemic of disease, during the life of the permit, the Secretary of the Interior is authorized, in his discretion to remit, reduce, refund in whole or in part, or authorize postponement of payment

[Illustration 40–a]

PAGE FROM UNITED STATES CODE, 1970 EDITION

§ 315c   TITLE 43.—PUBLIC LANDS   Page 10776

of grazing fees for such depletion period so long as the emergency exists: *Provided further,* That nothing in this subchapter shall be construed or administered in any way to diminish or impair any right to the possession and use of water for mining, agriculture, manufacturing, or other purposes which has heretofore vested or accrued under existing law validly affecting the public lands or which may be hereafter initiated or acquired and maintained in accordance with such law. So far as consistent with the purposes and provisions of this subchapter, grazing privileges recognized and acknowledged shall be adequately safeguarded, but the creation of a grazing district or the issuance of a permit pursuant to the provisions of this subchapter shall not create any right, title, interest, or estate in or to the lands. (June 28, 1934, ch. 865, § 3, 48 Stat. 1270; Aug. 6, 1947, ch. 507, § 1, 61 Stat. 790.)

AMENDMENTS

1947—Act Aug. 6, 1947 provided for method to be used by the Secretary of the Interior in fixing the amount of grazing fees and by assessing a separate grazing fee and a range improvement fee...

§ 315e. Rights-of-way; development of mineral resources.

Nothing contained in this subchapter shall restrict the acquisition, granting or use of permits or rights of way within grazing districts under existing law; or ingress or egress over the public lands in such districts for all proper and lawful purposes; and nothing contained in this subchapter shall restrict prospecting, locating, developing, mining, entering, leasing, or patenting the mineral resources of such districts under law applicable thereto. (June 28, 1934, ch. 865, § 6, 48 Stat. 1272.)

SECTION REFERRED TO IN OTHER SECTIONS

This section is referred to in title 30 section 601.

§ 315f. Homestead entry within district or withdrawn lands; classification; preferences.

The Secretary of the Interior is authorized, in his discretion, to examine and classify any lands withdrawn or reserved by Executive order of November 26, 1934 (numbered 6910), and amendments thereto, and Executive order of February 5, 1935 (numbered 6964), or within a grazing district which

---

Note how at the end of § 315b (as is the case with all U.S.C. sections) citations are given to where the section originally appeared in the Statutes at Large. § 315b was first passed in 1934 and amended in 1947.

---

mitted livestock may be constructed on the public lands within such grazing districts under permit issued by the authority of the Secretary, or under such cooperative arrangement as the Secretary may approve. Permittees shall be required by the Secretary of the Interior to comply with the provisions of law of the State within which the grazing district is located with respect to the cost and maintenance of partition fences. No permit shall be issued which shall entitle the permittee to the use of such improvements constructed and owned by a prior occupant until the applicant has paid to such prior occupant the reasonable value of such improvements to be determined under rules and regulations of the Secretary of the Interior. The decision of the Secretary in such cases is to be final and conclusive. (June 28, 1934, ch. 865, § 4, 48 Stat. 1271.)

SECTION REFERRED TO IN OTHER SECTIONS

This section is referred to in title 30 section 601.

§ 315d. Grazing stock for domestic purposes; use of natural resources.

The Secretary of the Interior shall permit, under regulations to be prescribed by him, the free grazing within such districts of livestock kept for domestic purposes; and provided that so far as authorized by existing law or laws hereinafter enacted, nothing contained in this subchapter shall prevent the use of timber, stone, gravel, clay, coal, and other deposits by miners, prospectors for mineral, bona fide settlers and residents, for firewood, fencing, buildings, mining, prospecting, and domestic purposes within areas subject to the provisions of such subchapter. (June 28, 1934, ch. 865, § 5, 48 Stat. 1271.)

SECTION REFERRED TO IN OTHER SECTIONS

This section is referred to in title 30 section 601.

ance with such classification under applicable public-land laws, except that homestead entries shall not be allowed for tracts exceeding three hundred and twenty acres in area. Such lands shall not be subject to disposition, settlement, or occupation until after the same have been classified and opened to entry: *Provided,* That locations and entries under the mining laws including the Act of February 25, 1920, as amended, may be made upon such withdrawn and reserved areas without regard to classification and without restrictions or limitation by any provision of this subchapter. Where such lands are located within grazing districts reasonable notice shall be given by the Secretary of the Interior to any grazing permittee of such lands. The applicant, after his entry, selection, or location is allowed, shall be entitled to the possession and use of such lands: *Provided,* That upon the application of any applicant qualified to make entry, selection, or location, under the public-land laws, filed in the land office of the proper district, the Secretary of the Interior shall cause any tract to be classified, and such application, if allowed by the Secretary of the Interior, shall entitle the applicant to a preference right to enter, select, or locate such lands if opened to entry as herein provided. (June 28, 1934, ch. 865, § 7, 48 Stat. 1272; June 26, 1936, ch. 842, title I, § 2, 49 Stat. 1976.)

REFERENCES IN TEXT

The Act of February 25, 1920, as amended, referred to in the text, is classified to section 181 et seq. of Title 30, Mineral Lands and Mining.

AMENDMENTS

1936—Act June 26, 1936, amended section generally.

SECTION REFERRED TO IN OTHER SECTIONS

This section is referred to in title 30 sections 601, 704.

[Illustration 41]

PAGE FROM 90 STATUTES AT LARGE

PUBLIC LAW 94–579—OCT. 21, 1976   **90 STAT. 2773**

of all moneys received by the United States as fees for grazing domestic livestock on public lands (other than from ceded Indian lands) under the Taylor Grazing Act (48 Stat. 1269; 43 U.S.C. 315

---

43 U.S.C. § 315b was again amended in 1976 by Pub.L. No. 94–579. As is frequently the case, a public law may amend many different sections of the U.S.C.

---

range rehabilitation, protection, and improvements on such lands, and the remaining one-half shall be used for on-the-ground range rehabilitation, protection, and improvements as the Secretary concerned directs. Any funds so appropriated shall be in addition to any other appropriations made to the respective Secretary for planning and administration of the range betterment program and for other range management. Such rehabilitation, protection, and improvements shall include all forms of range land betterment including, but not limited to, seeding and reseeding, fence construction, weed control, water development, and fish and wildlife habitat enhancement as the respective Secretary may direct after consultation with user representatives. The annual distribution and use of range betterment funds authorized by this paragraph shall not be considered a major Federal action requiring a detailed statement pursuant to section 4332(c) of title 42 of the United States Code.

(2) The first clause of section 10(b) of the Taylor Grazing Act (48 Stat. 1269), as amended by the Act of August 6, 1947 (43 U.S.C. 315i), is hereby repealed. All distributions of moneys made under **43 USC 1751.** section 401(b)(1) of this Act shall be in addition to distributions made under section 10 of the Taylor Grazing Act and shall not apply to distribution of moneys made under section 11 of that Act. The **43 USC 315j.** remaining moneys received by the United States as fees for grazing domestic livestock on the public lands shall be deposited in the Treasury as miscellaneous receipts.

(3) Section 3 of the Taylor Grazing Act, as amended (43 U.S.C. **43 USC 315b.** 315), is further amended by—

(a) Deleting the last clause of the first sentence thereof, which begins with "and in fixing," deleting the comma after "time", and adding to that first sentence the words "in accordance with governing law".

(b) Deleting the second sentence thereof.

GRAZING LEASES AND PERMITS

SEC. 402. (a) Except as provided in subsection (b) of this section, **43 USC 1752.** permits and leases for domestic livestock grazing on public lands issued by the Secretary under the Act of June 28, 1934 (48 Stat. 1269, as amended; 43 U.S.C. 315 et seq.) or the Act of August 28, 1937 (50 Stat. 874, as amended; 43 U.S.C. 1181a–1181j), or by the Secretary of Agriculture, with respect to lands within National Forests in the eleven contiguous Western States, shall be for a term of ten years subject to such terms and conditions the Secretary concerned deems appropriate and consistent with the governing law, including, but not limited to, the authority of the Secretary concerned to cancel, suspend, or modify a grazing permit or lease, in whole or in part, pursuant to the terms and conditions thereof, or to cancel or suspend a grazing permit or

[Illustration 42]

PAGE FROM UNITED STATES CODE, 1982 EDITION

REFERENCES IN TEXT

The Stock Raising Homestead Act, referred to in text, is act Dec. 29, 1916, ch. 9, 39 Stat. 862, as amended, which is classified generally to subchapter X (§ 291 et seq.) of chapter 7 of this title. For complete classification of this Act to the Code, see Short Title note set out under section 291 of this title and Tables.

Section 471 of title 16, referred to in text, was repealed by Pub. L. 94–579, title VII, § 704(a), Oct. 21, 1976, 90 Stat. 2792.

AMENDMENTS

1954—Act May 28, 1954, struck out of first sentence the provision limiting to one hundred and forty-two million acres the area which might be included in grazing districts.

1936—Act June 26, 1936, increased the acreage which could be included in grazing districts from 80 million to 142 million acres.

SHORT TITLE

Act June 28, 1934, which enacted this subchapter, is popularly known as the Taylor Grazing Act.

SECTION REFERRED TO IN OTHER SECTIONS

This section is referred to in sections 315a, 1715 of this title.

§ 315a. Protection, administration, regulation, and improvement of districts; rules and regulations; study of erosion and flood control; offenses

The Secretary of the Interior shall make provision for the protection, administration, regulation, and improvement of such grazing districts as may be created under the authority of

> This illustrates how 43 U.S.C. § 315b appears in the current edition of the U.S.C. Note how the text contains the changes made by Pub.L. No. 94–579 and how the citations at the end of the section include the 1976 amendment. When using the U.S.C., always be sure to check the latest cumulative supplement. When using an annotated edition, be sure to check the pocket supplement.

chapter or of such rules and regulations thereunder after actual notice thereof shall be punishable by a fine of not more than $500.

(June 28, 1934, ch. 865, § 2, 48 Stat. 1270.)

CROSS REFERENCES

Petty offense defined, see section 1 of Title 18, Crimes and Criminal Procedure.

§ 315b. Grazing permits; fees; vested water rights; permits not to create right in land

The Secretary of the Interior is authorized to issue or cause to be issued permits to graze livestock on such grazing districts to such bona fide settlers, residents, and other stock owners as under his rules and regulations are entitled to participate in the use of the range, upon the payment annually of reasonable fees in each case to be fixed or determined from time to

time in accordance with governing law. Grazing permits shall be issued only to citizens of the United States or to those who have filed the necessary declarations of intention to become such, as required by the naturalization laws, and to groups, associations, or corporations authorized to conduct business under the laws of the State in which the grazing district is located. Preference shall be given in the issuance of grazing permits to those within or near a district who are landowners engaged in the livestock business, bona fide occupants or settlers, or owners of water or water rights, as may be necessary to permit the proper use of lands, water or water rights owned, occupied, or leased by them, except that until July 1, 1935, no preference shall be given in the issuance of such permits to any such owner, occupant, or settler, whose rights were acquired between January 1, 1934, and December 31, 1934, both dates, inclusive, except that no permittee complying with the rules and regulations laid down by the Secretary of the Interior shall be denied the renewal of such permit, if such denial will impair the value of the grazing unit of the permittee, when such unit is pledged as security for any bona fide loan. Such permits shall be for a period of not more than ten years, subject to the preference right of the permittees to renewal in the discretion of the Secretary of the Interior, who shall specify from time to time numbers of stock and seasons of use. During periods of range depletion due to severe drought or other natural causes, or in case of a general epidemic of disease, during the life of the permit, the Secretary of the Interior is authorized, in his discretion to remit, reduce, refund in whole or in part, or authorize postponement of payment of grazing fees for such depletion period so long as the emergency exists: *Provided further,* That nothing in this subchapter shall be construed or administered in any way to diminish or impair any right to the possession and use of water for mining, agriculture, manufacture, or other purposes which has heretofore vested or accrued under existing law validly affecting the public lands or which may be hereafter initiated or acquired and maintained in accordance with such law. So far as consistent with the purposes and provisions of this subchapter, grazing privileges recognized and acknowledged shall be adequately safeguarded, but the creation of a grazing district or the issuance of a permit pursuant to the provisions of this subchapter shall not create any right, title, interest, or estate in or to the lands.

(June 28, 1934, ch. 865, § 3, 48 Stat. 1270; Aug. 6, 1947, ch. 507, § 1, 61 Stat. 790; Oct. 21, 1976, Pub. L. 94–579, title IV, § 401(b)(3), 90 Stat. 2773.)

AMENDMENTS

1976—Pub. L. 94–579 substituted provisions authorizing fees to be fixed in accordance with governing law, for provisions authorizing fees to take into account public benefits to users of grazing districts over and above benefits accruing to users of forage resources and provisions requiring fees to consist of a grazing fee and a range-improvement fee.

1947—Act Aug. 6, 1947, provided for method to be used by the Secretary of the Interior in fixing the

[Illustration 43]

PAGE FROM TITLE 43 U.S.C.A.

Ch. 8A GRAZING LANDS 43 § 315b

to foliage on lands owned by deceased as well as lands on which he had held grazing privileges under regulations to the effect that a transfer of base property entitled transferee, if qualified, to so much of grazing privilege as was based thereon and that original license or permit would be terminated or decreased to the extent of such transfer, and fire occurred after deceased's death and before devisees applied for transfer or new grazing permit, original permit had terminated on death of decedent and there was no permit in effect at time of fire, and hence Government was not liable to either executors of deceased's estate or devisees under will for destruction of foliage on land on which decedent had held grazing privileges. Wilkinson v. U. S., D.C.Or.1900, 189 F.Supp. 413

§ 315b. Grazing permits; fees; vested water rights; permits not to create right in land

The Secretary of the Interior is authorized to issue or cause to be issued permits to graze livestock on such grazing districts to such bona fide settlers, residents, and other stock owners as under his rules and regulations are entitled to participate in the use of the range, upon the payment annually of reasonable fees in each case to be fixed or determined from time to time, and in fixing the amount of such fees the Secretary of the Interior shall take into account the extent to which such districts yield public benefits over and above those accruing to the users of the forage resources for livestock purposes. Such fees shall consist of a grazing fee for the use of the range, and a range-improvement fee which, when appropriated by the Congress, shall be available until expended solely for the construction, purchase, or maintenance of range improvements. Grazing permits shall be issued only to citizens of the United States or to those who have filed the necessary declarations of intention to become such, as required by the naturalization laws, and to groups, associations, or corporations authorized to conduct business under the laws of the State in which the grazing district is located. Preference shall be given in the issuance of grazing permits to those within or near a district who are landowners engaged in the livestock business, bona fide occupants or settlers, or owners of water or water rights, as may be necessary to permit the proper use of lands, water or water rights owned, occupied, or leased by them, except that until July 1, 1935, no preference shall be given in the issuance

The annotated codes (U.S.C.A. and U.S.C.S.) have the text the same as it appears in the official edition of the U.S.C.

[Illustration 43–a]

PAGE FROM TITLE 43 U.S.C.A.

43 § 315b   **PUBLIC LANDS**   Ch. 8A
Note 1

The important difference in the annotated codes is the digest of court decisions that appears after each section of the Code and assists in interpreting the meaning of the Code section.

---

validly affecting the public lands or which may be hereafter initiated or acquired and maintained in accordance with such law. So far as consistent with the purposes and provisions of this chapter, grazing privileges recognized and acknowledged shall be adequately safeguarded, but the creation of a grazing district or the issuance of a permit pursuant to the provisions of this chapter shall not create any right, title, interest, or estate in or to the lands. June 28, 1934, c. 865, § 3, 48 Stat. 1270; Aug. 6, 1947, c. 507, § 1, 61 Stat. 790.

Historical Note

1947 Amendment. Act Aug. 6, 1947, provided for method to be used by the Secretary of the Interior in fixing the amount of grazing fees and by assessing a separate grazing fee and a range-improvement fee.

Congressional Comment: For legislative history and purpose of Act Aug. 6, 1947, see 1947 U.S.Code Cong.Service, p. 1638.

Cross References

Disposition of moneys received, see section 315i of this title.

→ Notes of Decisions ←

Actions against 8–10
  Grantors 8
  Officers 9
  United States 10
Constitutional protection 3
Evidence 11
Grant of application in part 6
Grantors, action against 8
Judgment 12
Officers, actions against 9
Permit as contract 5
Privileges 1
Ratification of administrative action 7
Review 13
Rights and title of purchaser 2
State police power 4
United States, actions against 10

1. Privilege

Stock raisers qualifying for grazing permits under this chapter acquire rights which are something of real value and have their source in an enactment of Congress. McNeil v. Seaton, 1960, 281 F.2d 931, 108 U.S.App.D.C. 296.

Where rancher was engaged in stock grazing when this chapter was passed and qualified for grazing permit under the

Range Code as first promulgated, subject to such considerations as the orderly use of public lands, possibility of overgrazing, forage capacity of base property, available water and other pertinent factors, extent of rancher's grazing privileges was to be determined. Id.

A permit, granted owners of land in grazing district by district grazer, to graze additional number of cattle after they leased adjacent state land and two ranches, did not impliedly grant them exclusive right to graze livestock on public domain simply because it decreased lessor's grazing permit by equivalent number of sheep, in view of evidence that district grazer and advisory board did not intend to grant such owners exclusive grazing permit on any public land district, except land on which they already had exclusive grazing privileges, nor on public domain attached to leased ranches until range line agreements could be adjusted after investigation by committee. Oman v. U. S., C.A.Utah 1952, 195 F.2d 710.

Grazing permits are only a privilege withdrawable at any time for any use by the sovereign without payment of compensation. Oman v. U. S., C.A.Utah 1949, 179 F.2d 738. See, also, U. S. v. Cox,

[Illustration 43–b]

PAGE OF ANNOTATIONS FROM 43 U.S.C.A. § 315b

43 § 315b   **PUBLIC LANDS**   38
Note 2

not have compensable interest in such property, though holder's interest in such lands may have been subject to taxation by state. Placer County Water Agency v. Scarborough, 1969, 80 Cal.Rptr. 252, 275 C.A.2d 691.

Where county water agency's original application for federal power license for project within government lands in national forest was made in 1962 and license was received in 1963 and permit granting person grazing preference on part of such lands expired in 1965 and another permit was issued to person in 1966, permit issued in 1966 was subordinate to license. Id.

3. Constitutional protection

Grazing permits issued pursuant to this chapter created no interest or estate in public lands but only a privilege which might be withdrawn and no property rights would accrue to the licensee upon revocation which would be compensable in condemnation. Acton v. U.S., C.A.Ariz.1968, 401 F.2d 896, certiorari denied 89 S.Ct. 1003, 393 U.S. 1121, 22 L.Ed.2d 128.

4. State police power

Lease of tax exempt land for grazing and agricultural purposes pursuant to this chapter is taxable by the State as a "possessory interest". Board of Supervisors of the County of Modoc v. Archer, 1971, 96 Cal.Rptr. 379, 18 C.A.3d 717.

5a. Determination

Secretary of Interior properly granted grazing permit to extent of number of animal units based on grazer's 1929–34 ownership and use, plus number of animal units based on ownership of other land in the area not used for grazing during the priority period and such allowance was not inadequate on ground that it did not allow for increased productivity of the 1929–34 land. McNeil v. Udall, 1964, 340 F.2d 801, 119 U.S. App.D.C. 276, certiorari denied 85 S.Ct. 1448, 381 U.S. 904, 14 L.Ed.2d 285.

9. —— Officers

Mandamus was not available to review decision of Secretary of Interior affirming partial cancellation of grazing allotments. Mollohan v. Gray, C.A.Ariz.1969, 413 F.2d 349.

10. —— United States

As against the United States, a permittee can acquire no right or interest in federal grazing lands. Holland Livestock Ranch v. U.S., C.A. Nev.1981, 655 F.2d 1002.

11. Evidence

Finding of grazing trespass upon federal public land which resulted in reduction and revocation of certain grazing privileges under this chapter was adequately supported by evidence of actual trespasses. Holland Livestock Ranch v. U.S., C.A. Nev.1981, 655 F.2d 1002.

Even disregarding access trespass evidence, in view of ranch owner's inadequate employment of control staff, poor fence conditions, history of trespass and of ignoring conditions upon his grazing permits, and failure to remedy trespasses upon notification, record contained substantial evidence of ranch owner's willfulness in trespassing upon federal public lands to support administrative de-

cisions to revoke and reduce his grazing permits and to impose double damages. Id.

Substantial evidence supported finding of hearing examiner and of the Interior Board of Land Appeals that ranch's negligence in failing to instruct pilot not to spray government land was so gross as to be tantamount to willfulness. Diamond Ring Ranch, Inc. v. Morton, C.A.Wyo. 1976, 531 F.2d 1397.

The only relevance of evidence that ranch was ignorant of the fact that a permit is required for spraying government land was that such evidence might possibly affect the imposition of a sanction against the ranch for violating the terms and conditions of a lease to it of government land under this chapter. Id.

Speculative testimony that value of grazing leases, permits and improvements on lands was reduced some 60% as result of request of Indians for restoration of subsurface lands when based on fear that not merely subsurface but also surface rights would be restored did not show that holders of grazing permits and leases had any standing to sue the Secretary of the Interior for injunctive relief. Bowman v. Udall, D.C.D.C.1965, 243 F.Supp. 672, affirmed 364 F.2d 676, 124 U.S.App. D.C. 283.

11a. Jurisdiction

Federal district court did not lack jurisdiction, under "agency discretion" exception to reviewability of agency decisions, to review various administrative level determinations of willful trespass on federal lands by ranch copartnership which resulted in reduction and revocation of certain grazing privileges under this section. Holland Livestock Ranch v. U.S., C.A.Nev.1981, 655 F.2d 1002.

Fact that solicitor for Department of Interior expressed opinion that Secretary of Interior had discretionary power to return remaining undisposed portions of certain land to Indian tribe did not create justiciable controversy over which court had jurisdiction and did not give landowners or holders of grazing leases and permits standing to contest Secretary's authority to restore subsurface rights to Indians where restoration order protected rights of lease and permit holders. Bowman v. Udall, D.C.D.C.1965, 243 F.Supp. 672, affirmed 364 F.2d 676, 124 U.S.App.D.C. 283.

11b. Presumptions

Where there was evidence of actual trespasses upon in addition to unrestricted access to federal public land, Interior Board of Land Appeals could raise rebuttable presumption of trespass based upon existence of unrestricted access in making determinations of willful trespass on federal lands which resulted in reduction and revocation of certain grazing privileges under this chapter. Holland Livestock Ranch v. U.S., C.A.Nev.1981, 655 F.2d 1002.

11c. Estoppel

Where record failed to establish that government engaged in affirmative misconduct or had legal obligation either to fence its lands or to restrain wild horses and burros, Government was not estopped from alleging ranch owner's trespasses by permitting his cattle to graze upon federal

SECTION E.   POPULAR NAMES OF FEDERAL ACTS

It is common practice to refer to a federal act by a popular name. Generally, this is the name which the public or media gives the statute, and it may describe its subject matter (e.g., Gold Clause Act) or refer to its authors (e.g., the Taft-Hartley Act).

The tables of popular names of federal acts are designed to provide the citations to acts when only the popular names are known.

There are a number of such tables.   They are:

1.   *Shepard's Acts and Cases by Popular Names*, vol. 1, 1979 and Cumulative Supplement.   [See Illustration 44.]

2.   *U.S.C.A.* contains a table of acts cited by popular name in an index volume.   [See Illustration 45.]

3.   Many of the titles of the *U.S.C.A.* have in the first volumes of the title a *Popular Name Table* for the principal laws included in the title.   [See Illustration 46.]

4.   The popular names of federal acts still in force are also listed alphabetically in the general indexes to the *U.S.C.A.* and the *United States Code Service*.

5.   The *U.S.C.* has an *Index of Acts by Popular Name* in the *General Index* volume.

6.   *United States Code Service.*   Table volumes contain a *Table of Acts by Popular Name.*

7.   Beginning with the 77th Congress, 2d Session, 1942, the *United States Code Congressional and Administrative News* contains tables of *Popular Name Acts* for each session of Congress.

[Illustration 44]

PAGE FROM SHEPARD'S ACTS AND CASES BY POPULAR NAMES

FEDERAL AND STATE ACTS CITED BY POPULAR NAMES   Bon

Bond Act of 1915 (Improvement Bonds)
Cal. Streets and Highways Code §8500
et seq.

Bond Act of 1918
N. J. Rev. Stat. 1937, 2:60-207 to 2:60-211

Bond Act of 1935 (Revenue)
N. C. Public Laws 1935, Ch. 473

Bond Act of 1938 (Revenue)
N. C. Gen. Stat. 1943, §160-413 et seq.

> **All laws are listed in this volume by popular name.**

Cal. Military and Veterans Code §996
et seq.

Bond Act of 1962 (State Construction Program)
Cal. Statutes 1962 1st Ex. Sess., Ch. 23,
p. 193

Bond Act of 1962 (State School Building Aid)
Cal. Education Code 1959, §19591 et seq.

Bond Act of 1962 (Veterans)
Cal. Military and Veterans Code §996.87
et seq.

Bond and Coupon Collection Law
Cal. Government Code §16311

Bond and Coupon Registration Law
Cal. Statutes 1935, p. 994

Bond and License Act (Citrus Fruits)
Fla. Stat. 1965, 601.55 et seq.

Bond and Lien Collateral Act of 1949
Az. Rev. Stat. 1956, §30-191 et seq.

Bond and Mortgage Act
N. J. Rev. Stat. 1937, 2A:50-1 et seq.

Bond and Warrant Acts
N. J. Rev. Stat. 1937, 2:27-266 to 2:27-277, 22:
1-13
Tex. Rev. Civ. Stat. 1948, Art. 2368a

Bond Assumption Acts (Highways)
Tex. Rev. Civ. Stat. 1948, Arts. 6674q-1 to
6674q-11a

Bond Certification Law
Cal. Water Code §20000 et seq.

Bond Compromise Law (Municipal)
Cal. Statutes 1903, p. 164

Bond Curative Act (Municipalities)
Wis. Stat. 1965, 67.02

Bond for Deed Act
La. Rev. Stat. 1950, 9:2941 et seq.

Bond Guarantors Protection Law
Cal. Government Code §5100 et seq.

Bond Investment Act
Ohio Rev. Code 1953, 3949.01 et seq.

Bond Issue Acts (Roads)
Ill. Rev. Stat. 1965, Ch. 121, §6-510 et seq.

Bond Limitation Act
U. S. Code 1964 Title 31, §757b
May 26, 1938, c. 285, 52 Stat. 447
Kan. Stat. Anno. 10-301 et seq.

Bond Plan Enabling Act (Industrial Locations)
Ala. Code 1958, Title 37, §511(20)

Bond Purchase Act
U. S. Code 1964 Title 31, §741
Mar. 3, 1881, c. 133, §2, 21 Stat. 435

Bond Refinancing Act (Revenue)
W. Va. Code 1931, Ch. 13, Art. 2A, §1 et seq.

Bond Refinancing Act of 1937
Ark. Stat. 1947, 19-4301 et seq.

Bond Refunding Act
Ark. Pope's Digest 1937, §§11237-11367

Bond Refunding Act (Municipal)
Mich. Comp. Laws 1948, 136.1 et seq.

Bond Refunding and Special Assessment Law of 1939
Cal. Government Code §59100 et seq.

Bond Registration Act
Mo. Rev. Stat. 1959, 108.240 et seq.

Bond Registration Act (Municipal)
Kan. Stat. Anno. 10-601 et seq.
N. C. Gen. Stat. 1943, §160-406 et seq.

Bond Retirement Fund Act
Okla. Stat. 1961, Title 62, §217.1 et seq.

Bond Sinking Fund Law of 1943
Cal. Statutes 1943, Ch. 611, p. 2225

Bond Surrender Act
Okla. Stat. 1961, Title 62, §341 et seq.

Bond Trust Fund Act
Nev. Rev. Stat. 1957, 282.230 et seq.

Bond Validating Acts
Fla. Stat. 1965, 75.01 et seq.
Ida. Laws 1935, First Extra Session, Ch. 3
Ida. Laws 1937, Ch. 232

Continued

91

[Illustration 45]

PAGE FROM THE POPULAR NAME TABLE IN U.S.C.A.

POPULAR NAME TABLE   **616**

Legislative Reorganization Act of 1970
  Pub.L. 91–510, Oct. 26, 1970, 84 Stat. 1140 (Title 2, §§ 28, 29, 60–1,
    61–1, 72a, 88b–1, 166, 190a–190d, 190f, 190h–190k, 198, 281–
    281b, 282–282e, 331–336, 411–417, 2107, 8332; Title 5, §§ 2107,
    5533, 8332; Title 8, § 1106 note; Title 31, §§ 11, 1151–1157,
    1171–1176; Title 40, §§ 166 note, 166b–1a–166b–1f, 184a,
    193m–1, 851)
  Pub.L. 91–522, § 1(1), (3)–(5), Dec. 16, 1970, 84 Stat. 1440

Leprosy Act
  Mar. 3, 1905, ch. 1443, 33 Stat. 1009

Lesinski Pension Increase Act
  June 6, 1940, ch. 246, 54 Stat. 237

Lever Act (Food Control)
  Aug. 10, 1917, ch. 53, 40 Stat. 276
  Oct. 22, 1919, ch. 80, 41 Stat. 297

Liberty Loan Acts
  (First)
  Apr. 24, 1917, ch. 4, 40 Stat. 35 (Title 31, §§ 745, 746, 755, 755a,
    759, 764, 768, 774, 804)
  (Second)
  Sept. 24, 1917, ch. 56, 40 Stat. 288 (Title 31, §§ 745, 747, 752–754b,
    757, 757b–757e, 758, 760, 764–766, 769, 771, 773, 774, 801)
  (Third)
  Apr. 4, 1918, ch. 44, 40 Stat. 502 (Title 31, §§ 752, 752a, 754, 765,
    766, 771, 774)
  (Fourth)
  July 9, 1918, ch. 142, 40 Stat. 844 (Title 31, §§ 750, 752, 772, 774)
  (Supplement to Second)
  Sept. 24, 1918, ch. 176, 40 Stat. 965 (Title 12, §§ 84, 95a; Title 31,
    §§ 757, 774; Title 50 App., § 5)
  (Victory)
  Mar. 3, 1919, ch. 100, 40 Stat. 1309 (Title 31, §§ 750, 753, 754, 763,
    767, 774, 802, 803)
  Mar. 2, 1923, ch. 179, 42 Stat. 1427 (Title 31, § 767)

Library of Congress Police Act
  Aug. 4, 1950, ch. 561, §§ 1 to 11, 64 Stat. 411 (Title 2, §§ 167 to
    167j)
  June 17, 1970, Pub.L. 91–281, 84 Stat. 309 (Title 2, § 167j)

Library of Congress Trust Fund Board Act
  Mar. 3, 1925, ch. 423, 43 Stat. 1107 (Title 2, §§ 154–163)

Library Services Act

> This Popular Name Table is from the U.S.C.A.
>
> There is a similar Table in the U.S.C. and the U.S.C.S.

  3551–2, 3551–3, 3551–6, 3551–7, 358)
  Pub.L. 91–600, § 2(b), Dec. 30, 1970, 84 Stat. 1660–1669 (Title
    20, §§ 351–354, 355a–355c, 355e to 355e–2)

Library Services and Construction Act Amendments of 1966
  Pub.L. 89–511, July 19, 1966, 80 Stat. 313 (Title 20, §§ 351–353,
    355–355b, 355e to 355e–3, 355f to 355f–7, 356–358)

Library Services and Construction Amendments of 1970
  Pub.L. 91–600, Dec. 30, 1970, 84 Stat. 1660 (Title 20, §§ 351–354,
    355a–355c, 355e to 355e–2, 1204, 1211)

[Illustration 46]

POPULAR NAME TABLE FROM TITLE 29, U.S.C.A.

POPULAR NAME ACTS

This table lists the principal laws included in Title 29, designated as they are popularly known, and shows the classification of each within the title.

Popular Name	Sections
Age Discrimination in Employment Act of 1967	621–634
American Samoa Labor Standards Amendments of 1956	206, 213, 216
Anti-Injunction Act (Labor Disputes)	101–115
Barden-LaFollette Act (Vocational Rehabilitation)	31–41
Black-Connery Fair Labor Standards Act	201–216, 217–219
Child Labor Act (Fair Labor Standards)	212, 213
Clayton Act (Trusts)	52, 53
Combination and Conspiracies Acts	52, 53
Connery-Black Fair Labor Standards Act	201–216, 217–219
Connery-Wagner Labor Relations Act	151 et seq.
Cooper Labor Jurisdiction Amendment	164(c)
Department of Labor Acts	1 et seq.; 551 et seq.
Employment Service Act	49 et seq.
Equal Pay Act of 1963	206, 206 notes
Fair Labor Standards Act of 1938	201–216, 217–219
Fair Labor Standards Amendments of 1949	201 note, 202, 202 note, 203–208, 208 note, 211–216, 216 note, 216b, 217
Fair Labor Standards Amendments of 1955	204–206, 208, 210
Fair Labor Standards Amendments of 1961	203–208, 212, 213, 213 note, 214, 216, 217
Fair Labor Standards Amendments of 1966	203, 203 note, 206, 207, 213, 214, 216, 218, 255
Fess-Kenyon Act (Vocational Rehabilitation)	31–41
Fitzgerald Act (Apprentice Labor)	50, 50a, 50b
Griffin-Landrum Labor Reform Act	153, 158–160, 164, 186, 187, 401 et seq.
Gwynne Act (Portal to Portal)	216(b), 251–262
Hartley-Taft Act	141 et seq.
Hour-Wage Act	201–216, 217–219
Industrial Productivity and Labor Costs Act	2b
Injunction Act (Labor Disputes)	101–110, 113–115
Kennedy-Douglas Welfare and Pension Plans Disclosure Act	301–309
Kenyon-Fess Act (Vocational Rehabilitation)	31–41
Labor Disputes Acts	51, 101 et seq.
Labor Injunction Act	101–115
Labor Management Relations Act, 1947	141 et seq.
Labor-Management Reporting and Disclosure Act of 1959	153, 158–160, 164, 186, 187, 401 et seq.
Labor Standards Act	201–216, 217–219
LaFollette-Barden Act (Vocational Rehabilitation)	31–41

T. 29 U.S.C.A. §§ 1–157 XVII

SECTION F.　TABLES FOR FEDERAL STATUTES

As has been noted, federal laws are first published in chronological order in the volumes of the *Statutes at Large*. A particular law may be on one topic, or may include matters on several different topics. Another law may amend one or several previously passed laws. Some are public laws of a general and permanent nature and are codified in the *U.S.C.* This method of enacting and publishing laws makes it necessary to have tables so that a researcher may be able to trace each section of a law as it appears in the *Statutes at Large* and find out if it has been codified and, if so, its citation in the *U.S.C.* For example, assume a researcher has a citation to Section 103 of Public Law No. 96–73 and wishes to find out where this section is in the *U.S.C.* To do so, the appropriate table of statutes has to be consulted. [See Illustration 47.]

From time to time, a particular title in the *U.S.C.* is completely revised with entirely new section numbers. One having a citation to the old title must then consult a table to find out the section number in the new title. [See Illustration 48.]

Each of the three sets of *U.S.C.* described *supra* has a volume or volumes containing transfer tables of one kind or another. These include the following:

Revised Titles: These tables show where former section titles of the *U.S.C.*, which have been revised, are now incorporated within the Code.

Revised Statutes of 1878: This shows where *Revised Statutes* citations are found in the Code.

Statutes at Large: This table shows where the Acts of Congress as they appear in the *Statutes at Large* are found in the Code.

[Illustration 47]

PAGE FROM TABLES VOLUME—U.S.C.A.

STATUTES AT LARGE   1979

	1979–96th Cong.–93 Stat.			USCA		
Sept.	P.L.	Sec.	Page	Tit.	Sec.	Status
		1(g)	501	12	1715z-10	
		1(h)	501	12	1748h-1	
		1(i)	501	12	1748h-2	
		1(j)	501	12	1749bb	
		1(k)	501	12	1740aaa	
		2	501	12	1709-1	
		3	502	12	1723e nt	
		4	502	42	1452b	
		5(a)	502	42	1483	
		5(b)	502	42	1485	
		5(c)	502	42	1487	
		5(d)	501	42	1490c	
29	96-72	1	503	50 App.	2401 nt	
		2 to 19(a)	503	50 App.	2401 to 2418	
		19(b)(1)	535	50 App.	2409 nt	
		19(b)(2)	535	50 App.	2408 nt	
		20, 21	535	50 App.	2419, 2420	
		22(a)	535	22	2778	
		22(b)(1)	535	42	6212	
		22(b)(2)	535	42	6274	
		22(c)	535	26	993	
		23(a)	536	22	3108	
		23(b)	536	22	3108 nt	
		24	536	7	1732	
→	96-73	101	537	45	501 nt	
		102	537	45	501	
	→	103	537	45	[502]	
		103	538	45	501a	
		104	538	45	502	
		105 to 111(a)	539	45	545	
		111(b)	541	45	641	
		112	541	45	546	
		113	542	45	548	
		114 to 120(a)	542	45	562 to 565	
		120(b)	548	45	565 nt	
		121	548	45	566	
		122(a)	550	45	601	
		122(b)(1)	551	45	601	
		122(b)(2)	551	45	602	
		123 to 126	551	45	647 to 650	
		127	552	45	521 nt	
		128	553	49	1653	
		129	553	45	602 nt	

> **This Table lists the numbers of all Public Laws and indicates where each section has been codified in the U.S.C.**
>
> **For example, Section 103 of Pub.Law No. 96–73 may be located in Title 45, § 502 in the U.S.C., or the U.S.C.A., or the U.S.C.S.**

112	580	42	297b	
113	581	42	296 nt	
201	582	42	294b	
202(a), (b)	582	42	294u	

329

[Illustration 48]

PAGE FROM TABLES VOLUME—U.S.C.A.

23   **REVISED TITLES**   **Title 23**

TITLE 23. HIGHWAYS

This title was enacted into law by Pub.L. 85–767, § 1, August 27, 1958, 72 Stat. 885. This table shows where sections of former Title 23 have been incorporated in revised Title 23.

Title 23 Former Sections	Title 23 New Sections	Title 23 Former Sections	Title 23 New Sections	Title 23 Former Sections	Title 23 New Sections
1	Omitted	21c	311	101a	Omitted
2	101	21d	Omitted	102	Omitted
2a	101(a)	21e	122	103	Omitted
2b	101(a)	22	104(e)	104	Omitted
3	Omitted	23	101(a), 202(b),	105	Omitted
3a	Omitted		204(a), 204(b), 204(c),	106	210(a), 210(b)
3b	Omitted		205(a), 205(b), 205(c)	107	Omitted
4	Omitted	23a	Omitted	108	Omitted
5	Omitted	23b	Omitted	109	Omitted
6	103(b), 103(e), 105(c), 121(c)	23b–1	Omitted	110	Omitted
6–1	103(c)	23c	205(c)	111	Omitted
6a	103(d)	24	Omitted	112	Omitted
6a–1	105(d)	24a	109(e)	113	Omitted
6a–2	310	25	Omitted	114	210(e)
6b	Omitted	26	Omitted	115	308(a)
6c	Omitted	41	101(a), 105(e) (Rep.)	116	315
7	110(a)	41a	101(a), 103(b)	117	312
8	109(a)	41b	101(a), 103(b)	151	104(c), 117(a), 117(b), 117(c), 118(b)
8a	109(a), 112(a)	42	Omitted	152	204(f), 205(d)
9	301	43	Omitted	153	206(a), 207(a), 208 (a), 206(b)
9a	129(a)	44	Omitted	154	209(a)
9a–1	Omitted	45	Omitted	155	203
9b	129(a)	46	See T. 18, § 1020	156	101(b), 103(f) (Rep.), 104(b) (1), 116(d)
10	109(a)	47	Omitted		(Rep.), 119(a) (Rep.)
10a	Omitted	48	Omitted		
		49	See T. 40, §§ 483, 484		

> **Whenever a Title of the U.S.C. is revised with new section numbering a table similar to this is prepared and may be consulted in the Tables Volumes of the various editions of the U.S.C.**

Title 23 Former Sections	Title 23 New Sections	Title 23 Former Sections	Title 23 New Sections	Title 23 Former Sections	Title 23 New Sections
18	317(a) (b) (c)	62	318	165	318
19	315	63	109(d)	166	113(a), 113(b)
20	Omitted	64	320(a)	167	101(b), 128(a), 128(b), 304
20a	Omitted	65	320(b)	168	Omitted
21	104(a), 104(b) (1)	66	320(c)	169	Omitted
21–1	307(a), 307(b)	67	320(d)	170	305
21a	104(b), 105(a), 106 (a), 114(a), 118(a), 118(c)	68	320(e)	171	306
		69	320(f)	172	Omitted
		70	313	173	See § 120 note
21a–1	Omitted	71	303(a)	174	See § 307 note
21a–2	Omitted	72	See § 303 note	175	Omitted
21b	Omitted	73	303(a)		
		101	Omitted		

Chapter 10

FEDERAL LEGISLATIVE HISTORIES

SECTION A. LEGISLATIVE HISTORIES IN LEGAL RESEARCH

A law is the means by which a legislative body expresses its intent to declare, command, or prohibit some action. A legislative history is the term used to designate the documents that contain the information considered by the legislature prior to reaching its decision to enact a law. A legislative history of a statute is consulted in order to better understand the reasons for the enactment of the statute. Since an act of the legislature is usually prospective and is not always drafted with the most precise language, courts constantly look to extrinsic aids in determining the intent of a legislative body.[1]

This intent may be found in the language of the bill introduced into the legislature, the subsequent amendments to the bill, the reports of legislative committees to which the bill was assigned, and other legislative documents issued in consideration of the submitted bill.

There has been some difference of opinion as to the extent to which legislative histories should be used to determine the meaning of legislation.[2] But this conflict is more academic than it is practical, for the use of legislative histories is a very essential technique of contemporary litigation.

---

[1] *"But, while the clear meaning of statutory language is not to be ignored, 'words are inexact tools at best,' Harrison v. Northern Trust Co., 317 U.S. 476, 479 (1943), and hence it is essential that we place the words of a statute in their proper context by resort to the legislative history."* Tidewater Oil Co. v. United States, 409 U.S. 151, 157 (1972).

[2] *See, e.g.,* Schwegmann Bros. v. Calvert Distillers Corp., 341 U.S. 384, at 395–396, where Justice Jackson states that, "Resort to legislative history is only justified where the face of the Act is inescapably ambiguous, and I think we should not go beyond Committee reports ∗ ∗ ∗ ." In National Small Shipments Traffic Conference Inc. v. C.A.B., 618 F.2d 819, 828 (D.C.Cir.1980), the court warns against the recent tendency to place favorable statements in a legislative history so that a court can be persuaded to construe the statutory language in light of those statements. *But see* Schwenke v. Secretary of the Interior, 720 F.2d 571 (9th Cir.1983) where the court of appeals reversed the decision of the lower court because of its failure to consider the legislative history of a statute in question. *See also* F. DICKERSON, THE INTERPRETATION AND APPLICATION OF STATUTES (1975); Carro & Brann, *Use of Legislative Histories by the United States Supreme Court: A Statistical Analysis,* 9 J.LEGIS. 282 (1982).

154

Once the concept of what is contained in a legislative history is understood, the location and compilation of the history of a federal act becomes relatively simple. The techniques for locating legislative documents which assist in the interpretation of a statute or statutory provision will be discussed in the following sections of this chapter.

SECTION B. THE ELEMENTS OF A LEGISLATIVE HISTORY

Before compiling a legislative history, it is necessary to be familiar with the documents that are relevant to establishing the legislative intent of a federal law.[3]

1. Congressional Bills

Prior to its enactment as a law, a proposed piece of legislation is first introduced as a bill into either the House of Representatives, where it will be assigned an H.R. or H.J.R. number, or the Senate, where it will be assigned either an S. or S.J.R. number.[4] This number stays with the bill until it is passed or until the end of Congress. When a bill is amended, it is usually reprinted with the amending language, or the amendment or amendments are printed separately. The comparison of the language of the bill as introduced and its subsequent amendments, with the final language of the law as passed, may reveal legislative intent.[5]

Starting with the 97th Congress (1981/82), congressional bills have been distributed to depository libraries only in microfiche format. This may make it difficult to trace and to locate all amendments to a bill. Moreover, since April 1983, amendments to Senate bills are no longer printed separately and are printed only in the *Congressional Record*. The safest method to obtain all amendments to a congressional bill is to check the bill number in the *History of Bills and Resolutions* section in the *Congressional Record Index*. [See Illustration 52.]

2. Committee Reports

After a bill is introduced into either the House or the Senate, it is assigned to a committee which has jurisdiction over the subject matter of the bill. It is then the committee's obligation to consider the bill and to decide whether or not to recommend its passage. If passage is not recommended or if no action is taken during the life of

---

[3] As legislative histories consist primarily of documents produced during the consideration of the bill or law by Congress, the documents cited in Chapter 9, note 2, should be consulted.

[4] *See* note 3, Chapter 9.

[5] United States v. St. Paul M. & M.R. Co., 247 U.S. 310, 318 (1918). *See also* Donovan v. Hotel, Motel & Restaurant Employees, 700 F.2d 539, 543 (9th Cir.1983).

the Congress in which the bill was introduced, the latter "dies in committee." If the committee recommends passage, it does so in a written report which usually sets forth the rationale behind the recommendations. When the bill is approved by the house in which it was introduced, it is then sent to the other house and again assigned to an appropriate committee where it receives similar consideration. When a bill has been passed by both houses, but in different versions, a *conference* committee is appointed that consists of Representatives and Senators who must reconcile differing language in the respective versions of the bill. Its recommendation is issued in a conference report.

Committee reports are usually considered the most important documents in determining the legislative intent of Congress.[6]

3. Congressional Debates

After a bill has been reported out of the committees to which it had been assigned, it may be debated upon the floor of the House or Senate.[7] Some authorities claim that floor statements of legislators on the substance of a bill under discussion are not to be considered by courts as determinative of Congressional intent.[8] The courts, however, generally do give some weight to such statements, especially when they are made by the bill's sponsors, whose stated intention is to clarify or explain the bill's purpose.[9] Such statements are published in the *Congressional Record* and are usually included as an integral part of legislative histories.[10]

4. Committee Hearings

After a bill is assigned to a Congressional committee, a hearing is frequently scheduled. The primary function of a hearing is to

---

[6] G. FOLSOM, LEGISLATIVE HISTORY: RESEARCH FOR THE INTERPRETA-TION OF LAWS 33 (1972). *See also* Zuber v. Allen, 396 U.S. 168, 186 (1969); Stevenson v. J.C. Penney Co., 464 F.Supp. 945 (N.D.Ill.1979).

[7] Most public laws are passed without ever being debated on the floor of Congress. It is usually only bills of great public interest that receive such debate.

[8] S. & E. Contractors, Inc. v. United States, 406 U.S. 1, 13 and n. 9 (1971).

[9] Jacques Islar Corp. v. United States, 306 F.Supp. 452, 454 (Cust.Ct. 1st Div.1969). *But see* Northern Colo. Water Conservancy Dist. v. FERC, 730 F.2d 1509, 1518 (D.C. Cir.1984).

[10] Prior to 1978, the *Congressional Record* may not have reflected what was actually said on the floor of Congress as members had the right of correcting their remarks before publication. *See* Morehead, *Record Redux,* 4 SERIAL LIBR. 355 (1979). However, effective March 1, 1978, Congress changed its rules to provide that statements in the *Congressional Record* were to be identified when no part of them was spoken on the floor of Congress. In such instances, a *bullet* symbol (●) precedes and follows the statement. If, however, any part of a statement was delivered verbally, the entire statement appears without the symbol. 124 CONG.REC. 3852 (1978).

provide committee members with information which may be useful in their consideration of the bill. Interested persons or experts on the subject of the bill may be requested to express their opinions on the bill's purpose or effect and may suggest changes or amendments to its language. In most instances transcripts of the hearings are published. Committee hearings are technically not part of a legislative history since they do not contain Congressional deliberations but rather the views of non-legislators of what the bill under consideration should accomplish. But, in practice, hearings should be consulted when available because they frequently contain information helpful to understanding why Congress adopted or did not adopt certain language.

5. Other Documents

There are occasions when other documents are relevant to obtaining the legislative intent of a law. These may consist of presidential messages, committee hearings on other bills, or reports and documents of other federal agencies. The location and use of these, however, are beyond the scope of this chapter. Ordinarily, the documents discussed are sufficient to help determine the legislative intent of a federal statute. When not sufficient, the researcher must then pursue the matter further.[11]

SECTION C.   THE SOURCES OF LEGISLATIVE HISTORIES

A legislative history consists of all or some of the following documentary sources:

1. Bills

    a.   The bill as originally introduced in the House or Senate.

    b.   The bill, with any amendments.

    c.   The bill as it passed in the originating body and as introduced into the other. (At this point, it is called an *act*.)

    d.   The *act*, with any amendments.

    e.   The *act* as amended by a joint Conference Committee of the House and Senate.

2. Reports

    a.   The reports of the committee to which the bill was assigned.

    b.   The reports of the committee to which the "act" was assigned.

[11] G. FOLSOM, *supra* note 6.

c. The report of the Joint Conference Committee of the House and Senate. This is usually issued as a House report.[12]

3. Debates

The debates, if any, on the floor of Congress that appear in the *Congressional Record.*

4. Hearings

The hearings, if any, held by the committees to which the bill or *act* had been assigned.

5. The Public Law resulting from all of the above

SECTION D. COMPILED LEGISLATIVE HISTORIES

The process of identifying and then locating all of the various documents that are needed in compiling a legislative history can be a time-consuming and laborious task. As compiled legislative histories may be available for some public laws, researchers may save considerable time and effort by ascertaining if one is available for the statute or statutes involved in their research. This may now be easily accomplished by consulting the *Sources of Compiled Legislative Histories.*[13] This is a looseleaf publication that lists all the sources of compiled legislative histories. It also includes a chart of legislative histories for all public laws starting with the first Congress in 1789, with an indication of where they have been published. *Sources of Compiled Legislative Histories* should be carefully consulted before one attempts the task of compiling a legislative history.

Beginning with the 96th Congress, CCH has published *Public Laws—Legislative Histories Microfiche.* This service makes available the House or Senate bill as introduced; the reported House bill, Senate bill, or both; committee reports; conference reports, if any; and relevant legislative debate as reported in the *Congressional Record.* All enactments are indexed by subject, by public law number, and by bill number.

The Congressional Information Service (CIS) has available on microfiche selected legislative histories from the 61st Congress through the 82nd Congress. Starting with the 97th Congress, CIS has a *Legislative History Service* for all significant public laws.

---

[12] Under the rules of Congress, the Conference Report is also to be printed as a Senate Report. This requirement is frequently waived by the unanimous consent of the Senate. ENACTMENT OF A LAW: PROCEDURAL STEPS IN THE LEGISLATIVE PROCESS, S.DOC. NO. 97–20, 97th Cong., 1st Sess. (1982).

[13] N. JOHNSON, SOURCES OF COMPILED LEGISLATIVE HISTORIES (AALL Pub.Ser. No. 14, 1979 and latest supplement).

They may be ordered either in paper or microfiche format.[14] Some larger libraries also subscribe to this series.

SECTION E.   HOW TO COMPILE A LEGISLATIVE HISTORY

There are frequent occasions when a legislative history has to be compiled during the course of one's research. This may be necessary because the sources described in Section D are not available, or because the public law in question does not have a previously compiled history.   Moreover, it is also frequently necessary to examine the congressional documents for a bill considered by Congress but not enacted into a public law.

The method of compiling a legislative history of Congressional documents for enacted legislation is described in this section.

1.   Legislative Histories, since 1970

The publication of a set commencing in 1970 by the Congressional Information Service, Inc., has simplified the method of compiling legislative histories for enacted legislation. This service is first issued in monthly pamphlets and then each year is reissued in two cumulative bound volumes. Part (Volume) One contains abstracts of hearings, reports, committee prints,[15] and other congressional publications such as House and Senate documents. This part is cumulated annually.   Part (Volume) Two contains detailed indexes of the subjects of reports, documents, and hearings, lists of witnesses, official and popular names of laws, reports, and bills, and names of committee and subcommittee chairmen.   This index section is cumulated quarterly, annually, and quadrennially.

Each CIS annual volume has a section on legislative histories for the public laws passed during the year.   Each public law is listed and citations are given to the bill number, the committee reports, hearings, the *Congressional Record*, and other documents that may be relevant to a legislative history, such as committee prints, congressional documents and hearings held under related bills.[16]   References

[14] CIS, 4520 East-West Highway, Suite 800 LH, Bethesda, MD 20814.

[15] Special studies in specific subject areas are often prepared for congressional committees. These are known as committee prints. Often, only limited numbers, for the use of the committee members, are printed. Recently they have become more available through the Depository Program, though indexing is often incomplete. The Depository Program is a system whereby approximately 1,400 libraries throughout the country are issued a copy of selected U.S. government publications. For further information, *see* GOVERNMENT DEPOSITORY LIBRARIES, JOINT COMM. ON PRINTING, 98TH CONG., 1ST SESS. (Comm. Print 1983). Since 1970, committee prints have been made available on microfiche by the Congressional Information Service, Inc.

[16] In order to speed measures through, identical or similar bills are frequently introduced into both houses, so that House and Senate committees may work on the

are also given to the abstracts of these documents within CIS. Through the use of the indexes in Part Two, references to public laws may be found by the name or title of a public law, by the subject matter of the law, or by bill number.

Because of the frequency of publication, the thoroughness of the indexing and the citation to all relevant documents, the CIS, since 1970, is now the quickest and most efficient method of locating citations to documents that make up a legislative history.

2. Legislative Histories: Other Methods

When compiling legislative histories for legislation enacted prior to 1970, or when the CIS volumes described in Section E–1 *supra* are not available, or for bills that were not enacted into law, the key to locating citations of the various congressional documents is the bill number under which a law or proposed law was introduced in either the House of Representatives or the Senate. This bill number may be located by use of one of the following sources:

a. *Statutes at Large Volumes.* Since 1903, each volume of the *Statutes at Large* gives the bill number under which the law was introduced into Congress.[17] [See Illustration 64.]

b. *Guide to Legislative History of Bills Enacted Into Public Law.* From volume 77 (1963) through volume 88 (1974), each volume of the *Statutes at Large* contained this guide, which lists all laws passed during the year with corresponding bill number, report numbers, and citations to consideration and passage in the *Congressional Record.*

Starting with volume 89 (1975), this *Guide* has been discontinued, and citations to legislative history are given at the end of each public law.

c. *Daily Digest. Annual Cumulation.* The *Daily Digest* appears in each issue of the *Congressional Record* and highlights the daily activities of Congress. After each annual session of Congress, it is cumulated and contains a *History of Bills Enacted into Public Law,* arranged by public law number.

d. *Digest of Public General Bills and Resolutions.* This is published by the Library of Congress and contains brief summaries of public bills for each Congress. The *Digest* is normally issued in five cumulative issues during each session of Congress. Among its

measure at the same time. Ordinarily, at some point in the legislative process, one house agrees to drop its bill and the legislative process continues on the other bill.

[17] Bill numbers for laws passed prior to 1903 may be located in E. NABERS, LEGISLATIVE REFERENCE CHECKLIST, THE KEY TO LEGISLATIVE HISTORIES FROM 1789–1903 (1982).

many tables is a Public Law listing with corresponding bill numbers for each law.

e. *CCH Congressional Index.* This is a privately published looseleaf service which issues weekly supplements while Congress is in session and covers its legislative work. New volumes are issued for each Congress. One section contains a list of public laws passed and gives the bill number for each. This set lists all bills introduced, contains a history of all Senate and House bills introduced, and includes a detailed subject index. Because of its weekly supplements, this is the best set to use to obtain information about current laws.

It should be noted that the publications in a–d, *supra,* are government publications and thus do not give citations to committee hearings, as they are technically not part of a legislative history.

The *CCH Congressional Index,* a private publication, does indicate when congressional hearings are available, but it does not give citations to the *Congressional Record.*

After the bill number has been ascertained from one of the above, it is then necessary to check a status table, which presents a chronological history of the bill as it has moved through the various legislative steps toward enactment. From such tables, it is possible to determine if committee reports were issued, if debates on the bill took place in Congress, and if hearings were held and printed. Tables of histories of bills may be found in all of the publications listed *supra.*

SECTION F.   ILLUSTRATIONS

When compiling a legislative history for a congressional statute, there are ordinarily two different procedures to follow. The first is to identify those documents which are part of a legislative history. This is accomplished by consulting indexes or tables which indicate the steps taken during the consideration of a bill by Congress. The end result is a list of citations to bills, reports, hearings and other documents.

The second procedure is to actually locate the documents for the citations which were found from the indexes and tables consulted.

For purposes of demonstration, illustrations are shown in this Section for the procedures involved in compiling a legislative history for the Justice System Improvement Act of 1979, Pub.L. No. 96–157.

Illustrations of Indexes and Tables

Illustrations of Documents

Legislative History of Public Law 96–157

[Illustration 49]

PAGE FROM 1979 VOLUME—CONGRESSIONAL INFORMATION SERVICE (CIS)

PL96-157 JUSTICE SYSTEM IMPROVEMENT ACT OF 1979.
Dec. 27, 1979. 96-1. 57 p.
* CIS/MF/3 •Item 575.
93 STAT. 1167.

"To restructure the Federal Law Enforcement Assistance Administration, to assist State and local governments in improving the quality of their justice systems, and for other purposes."

Amends the Omnibus Crime Control and Safe Streets Act of 1968 to extend through FY83 and revise LEAA programs for State and local criminal justice system improvement. Also establishes within the Justice Dept a National Institute of Justice (NIJ) and a Bureau of Justice Statistics (BJS) for criminal justice research and statistics activities, and an Office of Justice Assistance, Research, and Statistics to coordinate NIJ, BJS, and LEAA programs.

Legislative history (S. 241 and related bills):
1979 CIS/Annual:
Senate Hearings: S521-51.
House Reports: H523-9 (No. 96-163, accompanying H.R. 2061); H523-22 (No. 96-655); H523-25 (No. 96-695, Conference Report).
Senate Report: S523-6 (No. 96-142).
Congressional Record Vol. 125 (1979):
May 21, considered and passed Senate.
Oct. 12, H.R. 2061 considered and passed House; passage vacated and S. 241, amended, passed in lieu.
Dec. 11, Senate agreed to conference report.
Dec. 13, House agreed to conference report.

PL96-158 LITTLE SISTERS OF THE POOR, D.C., land conveyance.
Dec. 27, 1979. 96-1. 1 p.
* CIS/MF/3 •Item 575.
93 STAT. 1224.

"To grant to the Little Sisters of the Poor all right, title, and interest of the United States in the land comprising certain alleys in the District of Columbia."

Volume 10, Number 1-12

expected to adversely impact wildlife, encourages international cooperation in the conservation of endangered and threatened plants, establishes an advisory commission to act as

amendment.
Dec. 28, 1979. 96-1. 1 p.
* CIS/MF/3 •Item 575.
93 STAT. 1232.

"To amend the District of Columbia Self-Government and Governmental Reorganization Act with respect to the borrowing authority of the District of Columbia."

Extends D.C. authority to obtain Treasury loans to cover FY81 capital projects for which funding is authorized or appropriated.

Legislative history: (H.R. 5537 and related bill):

Also amends the Federal Deposit Insurance Act, National Housing Act, Small Business Investment Act, Federal Reserve Act, and Federal Home Loan Bank Act to exempt financial insti-

in House amendment.
Weekly Compilation of Presidential Documents Vol. 15, No. 52 (1979):
Dec. 28, Presidential statement.

PL96-162 YAKIMA RIVER BASIN WATER ENHANCEMENT PROJECT, feasibility study.
Dec. 28, 1979. 96-1. 1 p.
* CIS/MF/3 •Item 575.
93 STAT. 1241.

"To authorize the Secretary of the Interior to engage in a feasibility study."

Locating Legislative History Documents Using CIS

The CIS/INDEX volumes have a section containing legislative histories for all public laws. For each law, citations are given to all related documents. The citations refer to the pages in CIS where they are abstracted. In most instances, the researcher will need to examine the full documents.

This set is only useful for public laws. For congressional bills considered but not enacted, the tables shown in subsequent illustrations should be consulted.

[Illustrations 50 and 51]

PAGES FROM CCH CONGRESSIONAL INDEX AND DIGEST OF
PUBLIC GENERAL BILLS AND RESOLUTIONS

Illustration 50

```
                    * 241
Hearing in S. ....................2/9/79
Reptd., amended, S. Rept. No.
  96-142 ..........................5/14/79
Amended on S. floor (Voice) .......5/21/79
Passed S. as amended (Roll-call) ...5/21/79
Amended to contain text of H. 2061 as
  passed (Voice) ....................10/12/79
Passed H. as amended (Voice) ......10/12/79
H. amends. rejected by S. .........10/18/79
Conferees appointed by S. .........10/18/79
Conferees appointed by H. .......10/19/79
Conf. Rept. filed, H. Rept. No.
  96-655 ..........................11/16/79
Conf. Rept. recommitted to Conference
  Committee (Voice) .............11/29/79
Conf. Rept. filed, H. Rept. No.
  96-695 ..........................12/10/79
Agreed to by S. (Voice) ..........12/11/79
Agreed to by H. (Roll-call) ........12/13/79
To President .....................12/17/79
Approved (P.L. 96-157 ) .........12/27/79
```

Locating Legislative History Documents Using CCH Congressional Index—96th Congress

The Status Tables in this Index list all bills and give citations to all relevant documents, including hearings, but not to the debates in the Congressional Record.

Illustration 51

5-14-79	Reported to Senate from the Committee on the Judiciary with amendment, S. Rept. 96-142
5-21-79	Measure called up by unanimous consent in Senat
5-21-79	Measure considered in Senate
5-21-79	Measure passed Senate, amended, roll call # 102 (67-8)
10-12-79	Measure called up by special rule in House
10-12-79	Measure considered in House
10-12-79	Measure passed House, amended, in lieu of H. R. 2061
10-18-79	Conference scheduled in Senate
10-19-79	Conference scheduled in House
11-16-79	Conference report filed in House, H. Rept. 96-65!
11-29-79	Conference report recommitted to the Committee of Conference
12-10-79	Conference report filed in House, H. Rept. 96-69! (Second Conference Report)
12-11-79	Senate agreed to conference report
12-13-79	House agreed to conference report, roll call # 730 (304-83)
12-17-79	Measure enrolled in House
12-17-79	Measure enrolled in Senate
12-17-79	Measure presented to President
12-27-79	Public Law 96-157

Locating Legislative History Documents Using the Digest of Public General Bills and Resolutions

This publication of the Library of Congress gives a substantive digest for public bills considered by Congress and then, as shown, gives citations to all relevant documents, except hearings.

[Illustration 52]

PAGE FROM 1979 CONGRESSIONAL RECORD INDEX

History of Bills and Resolutions

SENATE BILLS

S. 157—For the relief of Anibal Hadad, his wife Alicia Hadad, and his son Daniel Hadad.
Mr. Bumpers and Mr. Pryor; Committee on the Judiciary, S373.
Reported (S. Rept. 96–510), S19036.
Passed Senate, S19399.
Referred to Committee on the Judiciary, H12522.
S. 207—For the relief of Dr. Herman Sardjono and his wife, Erlanda Sardjono.
Mr. Danforth; Committee on the Judiciary, S555.
Reported (S. Rept. 96–511), S19036.
Passed Senate, S19399.
Referred to Committee on the Judiciary, H12522.
S. 219—To amend the Internal Revenue Code of 1954

Examined and signed, H12133, S18877.
Presented to the President, S18877.
S. 299—To amend sections 551 and 553 of title 5, United States Code, to improve Federal rulemaking by creating procedures for regulatory issuance in two or more parts, and for other purposes.
Mr. Culver, Mr. Nelson, Mr. Thurmond, Mr. Wallop, Mr. Baucus, Mr. Nunn, Mr. Tower, Mr. Pressler, and Mr. Leahy; Committee on the Judiciary, S854.
Cosponsors added, S1475, S2225, S2541, S3610, S4721, S13211, S14262, S16778, S19489.
S. 328—For the relief of Mr. Oliver O. Ratajczek and his wife, Christine Diane Ratajczek.
Mr. Hatch; Committee on the Judiciary, S987.
Reported (S. Rept. 96–451), S17853.
Passed Senate, S18580.

Senate concurs in House amendment with an amendment, S19119.
Examined and signed, H12500.
S. 493—To promote the orderly development of hard mineral resources in the deep seabed, pending adoption of an international regime relating thereto, and for other purposes.
Mr. Matsunaga, Mr. Jackson, Mr. Church, Mr. Long, Mr. Bumpers, Mr. Ford, Mr. Inouye, Mr. Melcher, Mr. Weicker, and Mr. Wallop; Committees on Energy and Natural Resources; Commerce, Science and Transportation; Foreign Relations; if and when reported, jointly to the Committee on Finance to consider title V only, and Committee on Environment and Public Works for not to exceed 60 calendar days; and that each latter committees be required to file separate

---

Locating Legislative History Documents Using History of Bills and Resolutions Table in the Congressional Record.

This Table gives the history of all Senate bills introduced into each session of Congress. It gives citations to all relevant documents, except hearings.

These Tables are located in the bound annual Index volumes of the Congressional Record, and in the bi-weekly indexes of the unbound issues.

Conference report (H. Rept. 96–606), submitted in House and agreed to, H10493, H11369.
Conference report submitted in Senate and agreed to, S16432.
Examined and signed, S17670, H11471.
Presented to the President, S17670.
Approved [Public Law 96–143 , S18599.
S. 241—To restructure the Federal Law Enforcement Assistance Administration, to assist State and local governments in improving the quality of their justice systems, and for other purposes.
Mr. Kennedy, Mr. Thurmond, Mr. DeConcini, Mr. Glenn, Mr. Javits, Mr. Leahy, Mr. Bayh, and Mr. Baker; Committee on the Judiciary, S763.
Cosponsors added, S1278.
Reported with amendments (S. Rept. 96–142), S5789.
Debated, S6196.
Amended and passed Senate, S6230.
Amended and passed House (in lieu of H.R. 2061), H9114.
Senate disagreed to House amendments and asked for a conference. Conferees appointed, S14802.
House insisted on its amendment and agreed to a conference. Conferees appointed, H9444.
Conference report (H. Rept. 96–655) submitted in House, H10988.
Senate recommitted report of conference the conference report, S17540.
Conference report (H. Rept. 96–695) submitted in House and agreed to, H11709, H11957.
Conference report submitted in the Senate and agreed to, S18272.

tional goal for the development and maintenance of effective, fair, inexpensive, and expeditious mechanisms for the resolution of consumer controversies, and for other purposes.
Mr. Ford, Mr. Kennedy, Mr. Danforth, Mr. Bayh, and Mr. Metzenbaum, S1429.
Ordered placed on the calendar, S1411.
Cosponsors added, S1593.
Amended and passed Senate, S4091.
Referred to Committee on Interstate and Foreign Commerce, H2150.
Reported with amendment (H. Rept. 96–492), H8786.
Reported with amendment (H. Rept. 96–492 pt II), H9586.
Made special order H. Res. 488, H10795.
Debated, H11695, H11806.
Amended and passed House, title amended, H11841.
House insisted on its amendments and asked for a conference, conferees appointed, H11858.
S. 440—To revise and extend the Comprehensive Alcohol Abuse and Alcoholism Prevention Treatment and Rehabilitation Act of 1970.
Mr. Riegle, Mr. Williams, and Mr. Hatch; Committee on Labor and Human Resources, S1578.
Reported with amendment (S. Rept. 96–103), S4926.
Debated, S5366, S5386.
Amended and passed Senate, S5392.
Referred to Committee on Interstate and Foreign Commerce, H2946.
Amended and passed House (in lieu of H.R. 3916), H9234.
House concurs in Senate amendment to House amendment, H12317.

Examined and signed, S17670, H11471.
Presented to the President, S17670.
Approved [Public Law 96–142 , S18599 .
S. 521—To provide for the payment of losses incurred as a result of the ban on the use of the chemical Tris in apparel, fabric, yarn, or fiber, and for other purposes.
Mr. Thurmond, Mr. Kennedy, and Mr. Hollings; Committee on the Judiciary, S1935.
Reported (S. Rept. 96–528), S19036.
Passed Senate, S19343.
Referred to Committee on the Judiciary, H12522.
S. 523—To amend chapter 5 of title 37, United States Code, to revise the special pay provisions for certain health professionals in the uniformed services.
Mr. Hart; Committee on Armed Services, S1935.
Cosponsors added, S2225, S3361, S11500, S17971.
Reported with amendment (S. Rept. 96–507), S18877.
Debated, S19359.
Indefinitely postponed (H.R. 5235 passed in lieu), S19364.
S. 525—To amend the Drug Abuse Office and Treatment Act of 1972, and for other purposes.
Mr. Riegle and Mr. Williams; Committee on Labor and Human Resources, S1935.
Cosponsors added, S2764.
Reported with amendment (S. Rept. 96–104), S4926.
Debated, S5418, S5424, S5426.
Amended and passed Senate, S5428.
Referred to Committee on Interstate and Foreign Commerce, H2946.

H.B. 1

[Illustration 53]

FIRST PAGE OF S. 241—96th CONGRESS, 1st SESSION

96TH CONGRESS
1ST SESSION **S. 241**

To restructure the Federal Law Enforcement Assistance Administration, to assist
State and local governments in improving the quality of their justice systems,
and for other purposes.

IN THE SENATE OF THE UNITED STATES

JANUARY 29 (legislative day, JANUARY 15), 1979

Mr. KENNEDY (for himself, Mr. THURMOND, Mr. DeCONCINI, Mr. GLENN, Mr.
JAVITS, Mr. LEAHY, Mr. BAYH, and Mr. BAKER) introduced the following
bill; which was read twice and referred to the Committee on the Judiciary ◄——

A BILL

To restructure the Federal Law Enforcement Assistance Administration, to assist State and local governments in improving
the quality of their justice systems, and for other purposes.

From the indexes or tables shown in previous illustrations the researcher
should now have citations to (1) Bill number, (2) Reports, (3) Hearings, (4)
Congressional Record. These must all be separately obtained and examined.

This illustration shows the first page of S. 241 as first introduced during
the 96th Congress.

---

  6 Streets Act of 1968, as amended, is amended to read as fol-

  7 lows:

    II—E●

[Illustration 54]

FIRST PAGE OF SENATE HEARINGS ON S. 241

LAW ENFORCEMENT ASSISTANCE REFORM

HEARINGS

BEFORE THE

COMMITTEE ON THE JUDICIARY
UNITED STATES SENATE

NINETY-SIXTH CONGRESS

FIRST SESSION

ON

S. 241

FEBRUARY 9, 15, 28, AND MARCH 7, 13, 1979

Serial No. 96–5

Printed for the use of the Committee on the Judiciary

The Committee to which a bill is referred will usually hold hearings in which interested parties are invited to testify. Hearings are usually (but not always) printed. In many instances, similar hearings are held by the other house either on a companion bill or on the same bill after it has passed the first house.

This volume of the hearings contains 880 pages. Frequently, hearings on a bill will be printed in multi-volume sets.

U.S. GOVERNMENT PRINTING OFFICE

44-116   WASHINGTON : 1979

[Illustration 55]

FIRST PAGE OF SENATE REPORT NO. 96–142 ON S. 241

96TH CONGRESS	SENATE	REPORT
1st Session		No. 96–142

LAW ENFORCEMENT ASSISTANCE REFORM ACT OF 1979

MAY 14 (legislative day, APRIL 9), 1979.—Ordered to be printed

Mr. KENNEDY, from the Committee on the Judiciary, submitted the following

REPORT

[To accompany S. 241]

The Committee on the Judiciary, to which was referred the bill (S. 241) to restructure the Federal Law Enforcement Assistance Administration, to assist State and local governments in improving the quality of their justice systems, and for other purposes, reports favorably thereon, with amendments, and recommends that the bill as amended do pass.

AMENDMENTS AND PURPOSE OF AMENDMENTS

The committee made a number of technical and substantive amendments to S. 241, as introduced.[1] These amendments are usually identified and discussed throughout this report. Among the more significant

---

After the Committee has held hearings and agrees to send the bill for consideration by the full Senate, it issues a report setting forth the purposes of the bill and why it reported favorably on it. This report consists of 68 pages.

---

be under the general authority and policy control of the Attorney General.

---

[1] In the interest of economy, the committee decided not to list and number the amendments. The amendments are described in the report, with exact language indicated in the bill as reported by inserts in italics and deletions by linetype.

(1)

[Illustration 56]

FIRST PAGE OF S. 241 AS AMENDED BY COMMITTEE

Calendar No. 150

96TH CONGRESS
1ST SESSION **S. 241**

[Report No. 96–142]

To restructure the Federal Law Enforcement Assistance Administration, to assist State and local governments in improving the quality of their justice systems, and for other purposes.

IN THE SENATE OF THE UNITED STATES

JANUARY 29 (legislative day, JANUARY 15), 1979

After a bill has been introduced, it may be amended several times. This is the bill reprinted with the amendments made by the Senate Committee on the Judiciary.

A BILL

To restructure the Federal Law Enforcement Assistance Administration, to assist State and local governments in improving the quality of their justice systems, and for other purposes.

1   *Be it enacted by the Senate and House of Representa-*

2 *tives of the United States of America in Congress assembled,*

[Illustration 57]

FIFTH PAGE FROM S. 241, AS AMENDED

When a bill is amended it is frequently reprinted with the new version indicating the new language added by the amendments in italics, and the deleted words indicated by the lines drawn through the amended language.

7   ment to reduce and prevent delinquency by developing and

8   implementing effective programs to improve the quality of

9   juvenile justice in the United States.

10   *"Congress further finds that the victims of crime should*

11 *be made a more integral part of the criminal justice system.*

12   "Congress further finds that there is an urgent need to

13 encourage basic and applied research, to gather and dissemi-

14 nate accurate and comprehensive justice statistics, and to

15 evaluate methods of preventing and reducing crime.

16   ~~"Congress further finds that although crime is essential-~~

17 ~~ly a local problem that must be dealt with by State and local~~

18 ~~governments, the financial and technical resources of the~~

19 ~~Federal Government should be made available to support~~

20 ~~such State and local efforts.~~ *"Congress further finds that*

21 *crime is essentially a State and local and community prob-*

22 *lem that must be dealt with by State and local governments.*

23 *Congress further finds that the financial and technical re-*

24 *sources of the Federal Government should be made available*

25 *to support such State and local and community-based efforts.*

[Illustration 58]

FIRST PAGE OF H.R. 2061, AS AMENDED

Union Calendar No. 88

96TH CONGRESS
1ST SESSION

H.R. 2061

[Report No. 96–163]

To restructure the Federal Law Enforcement Assistance Administration, to assist State and local governments in improving the quality of their justice systems, and for other purposes.

Frequently, when a bill is introduced in one house of Congress, a similar bill is introduced in the other and both start proceeding through the legislative process. Shown here is H.R. 2061 after it has been reprinted with the amendments made by the House Committee on the Judiciary.

[Strike out all after the enacting clause and insert the part printed in italic]

A BILL

To restructure the Federal Law Enforcement Assistance Administration, to assist State and local governments in improving the quality of their justice systems, and for other purposes.

1   *Be it enacted by the Senate and House of Representa-*

2 *tives of the United States of America in Congress assembled,*

[Illustration 59]

FIRST PAGE OF HOUSE OF REPRESENTATIVES REPORT NO. 96–
163 ON H.R. 2061

96TH CONGRESS | HOUSE OF REPRESENTATIVES | REPORT
1st Session | | No. 96–163

JUSTICE SYSTEM IMPROVEMENT ACT OF 1979

MAY 15, 1979.—Committed to the Committee of the Whole House on the
State of the Union and ordered to be printed.

Mr. RODINO, from the Committee on the Judiciary,
submitted the following

REPORT

together with

SEPARATE, SUPPLEMENTAL, ADDITIONAL, AND
DISSENTING VIEWS

[To accompany H.R. 2061]

The report of the House Committee on the Judiciary on H.R. 2061.
This report contains 128 pages.

The House Committee on the Judiciary also held hearings on this
bill.

H.R. 2061 would amend the Omnibus Crime Control and Safe
Streets Act of 1968, as amended (42 U.S.C. 3701 et seq.) to restructure
the Law Enforcement Assistance Administration (LEAA) and to
reauthorize LEAA for four years. The bill would restructure LEAA
by (1) eliminating the requirment that States submit an annual comprehensive plan for the use of the federal funds, substituting therefor
a requirement that a three-year application be submitted; (2) providing for a similar simplified application process by which local units
of government and state agencies receive federal funds from the State
administering agency; (3) modifying the formula by which each
State's share of formula grants (formerly called "block grants") is
computed by including, in addition to the population distribution factor used under present law, provision for an alternative formula tak-

[Illustration 60]

PAGE FROM DEBATES ON S. 241—CONGRESSIONAL RECORD

May 21, 1979　　　　**CONGRESSIONAL RECORD — SENATE**　　　　**S 6263**

tion" insert "under this title other than part L";

On page 133, line 19, strike "and";

On page 133, line 20, after "1983" insert "; and $780,000,000 for the fiscal year ending September 30, 1984";

On page 133, line 22, after the period, insert "There is authorized to be appropriated in each fiscal year such sums as may be necessary to carry out the purposes of part L.";

On page 134, beginning with line 7, strike through and including page 136, line 3;

On page 136, line 3, strike "1006" and insert "1005";

On page 136, line 8, strike "and";

On page 136, line 9, after "1983" insert "; and $25,000,000 for the fiscal year ending September 30, 1984";

On page 141, line 14, after "Puerto Rico," insert "the Virgin Islands, Guam, American Samoa, the Trust Territory of the Pacific Islands, the Commonwealth of the Northern Mariana Islands,";

On page 142, line 20, strike "—REPEALER";

On page 142, line 23, strike "and the National Institute of Corrections";

On page 142, line 3, strike "or";

On page 143, line 4, after "the" insert "Director of the";

On page 143, line 5, strike "and" and insert "or";

On page 143, line 14, after "Act," insert "and title II(o) of the Juvenile Justice and Delinquency Prevention Act,";

On page 143, line 16, strike "that Act" and insert "those Acts";

On page 143, beginning with line 19, strike through and including page 144, line 3;

On page 144, line 4, strike "(d)" and insert "(c)";

On page 144, line 6, strike "previously" and insert "funds";

On page 144, line 7, strike "unused or reversionary funds" and insert "for fiscal years prior to 1980";

On page 144, line 8, strike "the continuation of";

On page 144, line 11, strike "and the provisions of sections 4351 to 4353 of title 18, United States Code,";

On page 144, line 13, strike "these Acts" and insert "this Act";

On page 144, line 16, strike "(e)" and insert "(d)";

On page 144, line 20, strike "previously" and insert "funds";

On page 144, line 20, after "appropriated" insert "for fiscal years prior to 1980";

On page 144, line 21, strike "unused or reversionary funds or funds" and insert "and";

On page 144, line 22, strike "the continuation of" and insert "programs or";

On page 144, line 23, after "projects" insert "to be expended";

On page 144, line 24, strike "sections 4351 to 4353 of title 18, United States Code, and";

On page 145, line 4, strike "(f)" and insert "(e)";

On page 145, line 7, strike "(g)" and insert "(f)";

On page 145, line 13, strike "or under sections 4351 to 4353 of title 18, United States Code";

On page 145, line 18, strike "and sections 4351 to 4353 of title 18, United States Code,";

On page 145, line 22, strike "(h)" and insert "(g)";

On page 145, line 34, strike "and the National Institute for Corrections";

On page 146, line 6, after the period, strike through and including line 10;

On page 146, line 11, strike "(i)" and insert "(h)";

On page 146, line 17, strike "(j)" and insert "(i)";

On page 147, line 4, strike "(k)" and insert "(j)";

On page 147, line 9, strike the colon and "Provided, That they meet" and insert

under this Act."

Mr. KENNEDY. I yield myself such time as I may use.

Mr. President, S. 241, the Law Enforcement Assistance Reform Act of 1979, would reauthorize the Law Enforcement Assistance Administration for an additional 5-year period. But more importantly, it makes long overdue reforms in the structure and administration of the LEAA program. S. 241 constitutes the most ambitious effort yet undertaken by the U.S. Senate to reform an agency which has often been sharply criticized.

This program is of critical importance to the American people; LEAA remains the major Federal vehicle to assist localities in their struggle against crime. S. 241 has enjoyed broad bipartisan support, was unanimously reported out of the Senate Judiciary Committee, and has the personal endorsement of President Carter. Attorney General Bell, and this administration. A companion bill—sponsored by Chairman RODINO—was favorably reported out of the House Judiciary Committee last week.

S. 241 is the culmination of a decade of debate over the nature and scope of the LEAA program. This bill is designed to deal with the problems which have plagued the agency and limited its impact. Band-Aid reforms have been rejected; major surgery has been performed. I am convinced that S. 241 will go a long way in making LEAA the type of Federal agency contemplated by the Congress when it first enacted the LEAA program over 10 years ago.

The major reforms proposed in S. 241 include:

Reduced redtape.—Burdensome annual planning requirements are eliminated and replaced by simplified 3-year applications.

Greater local flexibility.—Earmarking of funds in all but a few areas is eliminated, thus allowing more flexibility in

dealing with unique State and local needs.

Strengthened role for local governments.—Large cities and counties are guaranteed a fixed allotment of funds and localities are granted greater control over the use of LEAA funds in their communities.

Elimination of match requirements.— Funds for criminal justice use no longer require any State or local matching contribution.

New grant formulas.—Designed to target LEAA funds to urban, rural and suburban areas of greatest need.

More effective use of funds.—Limita-

contract making authority, is established with new independence.

Improved Statistics.—A Bureau of Justice Statistics, with grant and contract-making authority, is established to collect, analyze and disseminate reliable and uniform statistics on criminal and civil justice.

National Priority Grant Program.— Provides an opportunity for States and localities to invest in programs which, on the basis of research and evaluation, have been shown to be particularly effective in improving and strengthening the administration of justice. Under this approach, the Federal Government suggests, but does not mandate, certain LEAA priorities; local governments are encouraged, but not forced, to participate in these programs.

Finally, Mr. President, the Judiciary Committee unanimously accepted an amendment of critical importance offered by Senator BIDEN. This amendment would mandate the type of careful evaluation and priority-setting that has for too long been absent from the LEAA program. The amendment is designed to focus LEAA spending practices on eighteen long-standing, measurable problems confronting our criminal justice systems. The Biden amendment goes a long way in answering widespread criticism that LEAA's grant activities have been excessively diffuse, misguided, and undirected. Although a straight-forward categorical grant program as a solution to these problems was considered by the committee to be too rigid to take into account the varying needs of different localities, the Biden amendment requires an evaluation, an explanation of the effectiveness of LEAA assistance in 18 specific problem areas itemized in the bill.

Mr. President, the Senate Judiciary Committee conducted 8 days of hearings on the reauthorization and reform of the LEAA program. S. 241 reflects the type of

[Illustration 61]

FIRST PAGE OF S. 241 AS PASSED BY THE SENATE

96TH CONGRESS
1ST SESSION
S. 241

IN THE SENATE OF THE UNITED STATES

MAY 21 (legislative day, APRIL 9), 1979

Ordered to be printed as passed

AN ACT

To restructure the Federal Law Enforcement Assistance Administration, to assist State and local governments in improving
the quality of their justice systems, and for other purposes.

After the house in which a bill has been introduced has voted to
enact the bill, it is reprinted with all amendments and labeled an "Act"
and sent to the other house for consideration.

In this instance, S. 241 was sent to the House of Representatives
for its consideration.

---

6 Streets Act of 1968, as amended, is amended to read as fol-

7 lows:

"TABLE OF CONTENTS

"Sec. 2. Title I—Justice system improvement.

[Illustration 62]

PAGE FROM HOUSE OF REPRESENTATIVES DEBATE ON H.R. 2061—CONGRESSIONAL RECORD

H 9114   CONGRESSIONAL RECORD — HOUSE   *October 12, 1979*

Sawyer	Stark	White
Schulze	Stockman	Whiteburst
Sharp	Stokes	Whitley
Shelby	Stratton	Whittaker
Skelton	Studds	Whitten
Smith, Iowa	Swift	Williams, Mont.
Smith, Nebr.	Tauke	Wilson, Bob
Solomon	Trible	Wolpe
Spellman	Udall	Yates
Spence	Vanik	Young, Fla.
Staggers	Walgren	Zablocki
Stanton	Weiss	

NOES—54

Archer	Frenzel	Petri
Ashbrook	Gephardt	Roth
Bauman	Hance	Rudd
Beilenson	Hansen	Russo
Bereuter	Holt	Satterfield
Burgener	Hubbard	Schroeder
Carney	Hughes	Sriberling
Cavanaugh	Ichord	Shumway
Collins, Tex.	Jeffries	Shuster
Conyers	Jones, Okla.	Simon
Dannemeyer	Kelly	Stangeland
Daschle	Kramer	Steed
Duncan, Oreg.	Leath, Tex.	Symms
Early	Lewis	Taylor
Edwards, Okla.	Luken	Volkmer
English	Marlenee	Weaver
Erlenborn	Moffett	Wirth
Ertel	Pease	

NOT VOTING—159

Albosta	Garcia	Pursell
Alexander	Gibbons	Quayle
Anderson, Ill.	Ginn	Quillen
Anthony	Glickman	Railsback
Applegate	Gradison	Regula
Aspin	Gramm	Reuss
Badham	Gray	Richmond
Barnard	Guyer	Roberts
Beard, R.I.	Harkin	Rodino
Bedell	Harsha	Roe
Biaggi	Hefner	Rose
Bingham	Heftel	Rosenthal
Boggs	Hightower	Rousselot
Boland	Hillis	Runnels
Bolling	Holland	Sabo
Bonior	Hollenbeck	Scheuer
Brinkley	Holtzman	Sebelius
Brooks	Hopkins	Shannon
Brown, Calif.	Horton	Slack
Burton, John	Hutto	Snowe
Butler	Ireland	Snyder
Byron	Jacobs	Solarz
Campbell	Jenkins	St Germain
Chappell	Johnson, Colo.	Steck
Chisholm	Jones, N.C.	Stenholm
Clausen	Kemp	Stewart
Clay	LaFalce	Stump
Cleveland	Latta	Synar
Coelho	Leach, La.	Thomas
Coleman	Lee	Thompson

□ 1920

Mr. SIMON changed his vote from "aye" to "no."

So the bill was passed.

The result of the vote was announced as above recorded.

A motion to reconsider was laid on the table.

Mr. GUDGER. Mr. Speaker, pursuant to the provisions of House Resolution 351, I call up from the Speaker's table

the Senate bill (S. 241), to restructure the Federal Law Enforcement Assistance Administration, to assist State and local governments in improving the quality of their justice systems, and for other purposes, and ask for its immediate consideration.

The Clerk read the title of the Senate bill.

MOTION OFFERED BY MR. GUDGER

Mr. GUDGER. Mr. Speaker, I offer a motion.

The Clerk read as follows:

Mr. GUDGER moves to strike out all after the enacting clause of the Senate bill, S. 241, and to insert in lieu thereof the provisions of the bill, H.R. 2061, as passed, as follows:

That this Act may be cited as the "Justice System Improvement Act of 1979".

SEC. 2. Title I of the Omnibus Crime Control and Safe Streets Act of 1968, as amended, to read as follows:

"TITLE I—JUSTICE SYSTEM IMPROVEMENT

"The Congress finds and declares that the high incidence of crime in the United States is detrimental to the general welfare of the Nation and its citizens, and that criminal justice efforts must be better coordinated, intensified, and made more effective and equitable at all levels of government.

"Congress further finds that juvenile delinquency constitutes a growing threat to the national welfare requiring immediate and comprehensive action by the Federal Government to reduce and prevent delinquency by developing and implementing effective programs to improve the quality of juvenile justice in the United States.

"Congress further finds that there is an urgent need to encourage basic and applied research, to gather and disseminate accurate and comprehensive justice statistics, and to evaluate methods of preventing and reducing crime.

"Congress further finds that although crime is essentially a local problem that must be dealt with by State and local governments, the financial and technical resources of the Federal Government should be made available to support such State and local efforts.

"Congress further finds that the future welfare of the Nation and the well-being of

toward the improvement of civil, criminal, and juvenile justice systems and new methods for the prevention and reduction of crime and the detection, apprehension, and rehabilitation of criminals; (9) encourage the collection and analysis of statistical information concerning crime, juvenile delinquency, civil disputes, and the operation of justice systems; and (10) support manpower development and training efforts. It is further the policy of the Congress that the Federal assistance made available under this title not be utilized to reduce the amount of State and local financial support for criminal justice activities below the level of such support prior to the availability of such assistance.

"PART A—LAW ENFORCEMENT ASSISTANCE ADMINISTRATION

"SEC. 101. There is hereby established within the Department of Justice under the direct authority of the Attorney General, a Law Enforcement Assistance Administration (hereinafter referred to in this title as the 'Administration'). The Administration shall be under the direction of an Administrator, who shall be appointed by the President, by and with the advice and consent of the Senate, and such other Deputy Administrators as may be designated by the Attorney General. The Administrator shall have final authority over all grants, cooperative agreements, and contracts awarded by the Administration.

"SEC. 102. The Administrator shall—

"(a) provide funds to eligible States and units of local government pursuant to part D of this title in order to finance programs approved in accordance with the provisions of this title;

"(b) recognize national criminal justice priorities established by the Office of Justice Assistance, Research, and Statistics in accordance with parts E and F of this title. Inform States and units of local government concerning such priorities and award and allocate funds among the eligible States, units of local government, and public and private nonprofit organizations according to the criteria and on the terms and conditions determined by the Administration to be consistent with parts E and F of this title;

"(c) publish and disseminate information on the condition and progress of the criminal justice system and establish and carry on a specific and continuing program of cooperation with the States and units of local government

their criminal justice and juvenile justice systems; (2) develop and fund new methods and programs to enhance the effectiveness of criminal justice agencies; (3) support the development of city, county, and statewide priorities and programs to meet the problems confronting the justice system; (4) reduce court congestion and trial delay; (5) support community anticrime efforts; (6) improve and modernize the correctional system; (7) encourage the undertaking of innovative projects of recognized importance and effectiveness; (8) encourage the development of basic and applied research directed

Law Enforcement Assistance Administration the Office of Community Anti-Crime Programs (hereinafter in this section referred to as the 'Office'). The Office shall be under the direction of the Administrator and shall—

"(1) provide appropriate technical assistance to community and citizens groups to enable such groups to—

"(A) apply for grants which encourage community and citizen participation in crime prevention and criminal justice activities;

"(B) participate in the formula grant ap-

When a bill has passed one house and is sent to the other house while the latter is still considering a companion bill, the other house may adopt the "Act" and then amend it to contain its language. In this instance, the House amended and then passed S. 241 and then sent it to the Senate with its amendments.

[Illustration 63]

FIRST PAGE OF CONFERENCE REPORT ON S. 241

96TH CONGRESS } *1st Session* }	HOUSE OF REPRESENTATIVES	{ REPORT { No. 96–695

JUSTICE SYSTEM IMPROVEMENT ACT OF 1979

DECEMBER 10, 1979.—Ordered to be printed

Mr. RODINO, from the committee of conference, submitted the following

CONFERENCE REPORT

[To accompany S. 241]

The committee of conference on the disagreeing votes of the two Houses on the amendment of the House to the bill (S. 241) to restructure the Federal Law Enforcement Assistance Administration, to assist State and local governments in improving the quality of their justice systems, and for other purposes, having met, after full and free conference, have agreed to recommend and do recommend to their respective Houses as follows:

That the Senate recede from its disagreement to the amendment of the House, and agree to the same with an amendment as follows:

In lieu of the matter proposed to be inserted by the House amendment, insert the following:

That this Act may be cited as the "Justice System Improvement Act of 1979".

SEC. 2. Title I of the Omnibus Crime Control and Safe Streets Act of 1968 is amended to read as follows:

S. 241 as passed by the House differed from the version as passed by the Senate. In such instances, a joint Conference Committee is appointed. This committee then agrees to new language and issues a Conference Report explaining the changes agreed to. If both houses accept the Conference Report, the "Act" is then sent to the President.

[Illustration 64]

FIRST PAGE OF PUBLIC LAW 96–157

PUBLIC LAW 96-157—DEC. 27, 1979   93 STAT. 1167

Public Law 96-157
96th Congress

An Act

To restructure the Federal Law Enforcement Assistance Administration, to assist State and local governments in improving the quality of their justice systems, and for other purposes.

Dec. 27, 1979
[S. 241]

Be it enacted by the Senate and House of Representatives of the United States of America in Congress assembled, That this Act may be cited as the "Justice System Improvement Act of 1979".

SEC. 2. Title I of the Omnibus Crime Control and Safe Streets Act of 1968 is amended to read as follows:

Justice System
Improvement
Act of 1979.
42 USC 3701
note.

"TITLE I—JUSTICE SYSTEM IMPROVEMENT

"TABLE OF CONTENTS

"Declaration and purpose.

"PART A—LAW ENFORCEMENT ASSISTANCE ADMINISTRATION

"Sec. 101. Establishment of Law Enforcement Assistance Administration.
"Sec. 102. Duties and functions of Administrator.

This is Public Law **96–157**, the product of all of the documents previously illustrated. It consists of 56 pages. Note how citation is given to where it is published in the Statutes at Large, the date it became a law, and the reference to S. 241.

As with many public laws, the various sections of this law will be codified in different titles of the U.S. Code. To locate where a specific section is codified, a Table has to be consulted. See illustration 47.

"Sec. 404. Review of applications.
"Sec. 405. Allocation and distribution of funds.

"PART E—NATIONAL PRIORITY GRANTS

"Sec. 501. Purpose.
"Sec. 502. Percentage of appropriation for national priority grant program.
"Sec. 503. Procedure for designating national priority programs.
"Sec. 504. Application requirements.
"Sec. 505. Criteria for award.

"PART F—DISCRETIONARY GRANTS

"Sec. 601. Purpose.
"Sec. 602. Percentage of appropriation for discretionary grant program.

SECTION G. HOW TO OBTAIN ACCESS TO THE DOCUMENTS OF LEGISLATIVE HISTORIES

After using the indexes previously described, the bills with amendments, the committee reports, the debates on the bills, and the committee hearings now have to be located and consulted. The means of access to these will vary because libraries shelve U.S. government documents in different ways.[18] The various documents that must be consulted, and the tools for gaining access to them are set forth below:

1.   **Bills.** These are usually kept together by Congress, with all different stages of each bill collected together.

2.   **House and Senate Reports** are included as part of the *Serial Set*,[19] and assistance from the library staff is usually needed to locate them. Some law libraries maintain these reports in separate series. Many reports are also reprinted in both the pamphlets and bound volumes of the *United States Code Congressional and Administrative News Service.*[20]

3.   **Transcripts** of debates on the floor of Congress are found in the *Congressional Record.* For each session of Congress, there is an Index volume which contains a *History of Bills Table.* Under the bill number, one is directed to the pages in the *Congressional Record* where the bill was debated.

4.   **Hearings.** The *CCH Congressional Index*, CIS, the *Monthly Catalog of Government Publications*, and *Cumulative Index of Committee Hearings* (issued by the Library of the United States Senate) all indicate when committee hearings have been printed.

[18] If the research for the compilation of a legislative history is being done in a law library, the researcher should ascertain how the law library organizes and indexes government documents. If a researcher is not near a law library, or the law library does not collect government documents, access to needed documents may be had at public or college libraries that are depositories for the publications of the U.S. Government Printing Office. Any such depository collection may be consulted by the public.

Many libraries now receive on microfiche one or more of the items described in this Section, either from the U.S. Government Printing Office or from certain publishing companies.

[19] The *Serial Set* is a bound compilation of *House Documents, Senate Documents, House Reports, and Senate Reports.* They are arranged in numerical sequence.

[20] This set is issued bi-weekly during a session of Congress, and then reissued in bound volumes. It has a section entitled *Legislative Histories.* However, it only reprints either a House Report or a Senate Report, and in some instances, the Conference Report. It does not include all of the other elements which are part of a legislative history.

Senate hearings are now also listed in *United States Senate Publications* [21] which started with the 98th Congress. Senate committees are listed alphabetically with the titles of hearings held.

Hearings are usually shelved according to the Government Printing Office classification scheme. This number is always given in the *Monthly Catalog of United States Government Publications.* In some law libraries hearings are cataloged separately and may be located either through the name of the committee or by subject.

SECTION H. COMPUTER–ASSISTED RESEARCH

1. Congressional Research Service (CIS)

This service, in print format, has been described in Section E–1, *supra.* It is also available through two database vendors: DIALOG Information Retrieval Service and the ORBIT Service of the Systems Development Corporation. The ability to search its abstracts and indexes online may at times allow more access points to the information obtained in them.

2. Other Systems

At present, other available systems allow for getting information on keeping track of legislation pending before Congress or state legislatures.

a. *CCH Electronic Legislative Search System (ELSS).* This system produced by the Commerce Clearing House has a database consisting of bill numbers and titles of pending legislation, as well as information on legislation for the immediate past session. The information for the past session, however, is only kept in the database until the following June. The database can be searched by subject, bill number, bill sponsor, date, or any combination of these.[22]

b. *LEGI–SLATE, INC.* [23] This system provides for the online tracking of federal bills only. Its database includes all bills introduced since the 96th Congress (1979/80). It may be searched by subject, bill number, sponsors, or by date.

c. *Public Affairs Information.* [24] This system's database consists of current and pending legislation for Congress and the fifty state legislatures. It may also be searched by sponsor, subject, or bill number. It includes, however, in addition to bill numbers and titles, abstracts from the *Congressional Record.*

[21] U.S. Government Printing Office, Washington, D.C.

[22] For more detailed information on *CCH ELSS, see* Lawrence, *Electronic Legislative Search System*, DATABASE (Aug. 1983, at 23).

[23] 444 North Capitol Street, N.W., Washington, D.C. 20001.

[24] 1024 Tenth Street, Suite 300, Sacramento, CA 95814.

d. *Individual State Services.* Many states may have a company or state agency providing an online bill-tracking service for its state legislature. For information about such services, consult a state legal research guide (See *Appendix A*) or the state law library.[25]

Computer-assisted research is discussed in more detail in Chapter 20.

SECTION I. SUMMARY

A legislative history of congressional documents for a law passed by Congress consists of all or some of the following:

Bills as introduced, with any amendments

Act with any amendments

Reports of committee to which bill or *Act* was referred

Debates and discussions on floor of Congress, if any

Hearings before committees considering the bill or *Act*

When in need of a legislative history, the following steps should be taken:

1. Check *Sources of Compiled Legislative Histories.* If this gives reference to a compiled legislative history, obtain, if possible, and examine the various documents.

2. If *Sources of Compiled Legislative Histories* is not available, or if the compiled legislative history cited is not available, obtain citations to relevant documents by checking one or more of the following:

CIS Indexes

CCH Congressional Index

History of Bills and Resolutions, Congressional Record Index

Digest of Public General Bills and Resolutions

3. Obtain documents cited in above sources.

[25] For additional information on legislative databases, *see* Skeen, *Legislative Databases—A Review and Evaluation of What is Available*, DATABASE (June 1984, at 13).

Chapter 11

STATE LEGISLATION

There is much similarity between the organization and publication of federal and state statutes. While there are differences between the fifty states, this is mostly in nomenclature rather than substance. Each state has a state legislature and, with the exception of Nebraska, each has an upper and lower house similar to the Senate and the House of Representatives of the United States Congress. In general, the legislative process for the passage of state laws is similar to that previously described for federal laws.

State legislatures meet in either annual or biennial sessions.[1] Information for individual states as to nomenclature, frequency of session, and other pertinent information on state legislatures may be obtained by consulting the latest edition of *The Book of the States.*[2]

SECTION A. SESSION LAWS

Each state publishes all of the laws passed during each session of its legislature in volumes with the generic name, *session laws*, although in some states they may have other names, such as acts and resolves, or statutes or laws. The session laws are published in chronological order comparable to those in the *United States Statutes at Large*. [See Illustrations 65 and 66.] Most states also publish their laws in *slip* form soon after they are passed. In many states current laws are found in the pamphlet or advance sheet services to privately published state codes.

SECTION B. CODIFICATION OF STATE LAWS

Since each volume of the session laws for a state contains the laws passed by the state legislature during an annual, biennial or special session, and since the laws passed are arranged chronologically in each volume, it is necessary to have the laws rearranged by title or subject as they are in the *United States Code*. Each state does, in

[1] The monthly issues of *State Government News*, published by the Council of State Governments, have a section on Legislative Session Dates.

[2] COUNCIL OF STATE GOVERNMENTS, THE BOOK OF THE STATES (biennial). Chapter 11 is devoted to the location of state statutes. It must be noted, however, that after a relevant statute has been located, it is frequently necessary to determine its proper application. For these purposes, consult F. DICKERSON, THE INTERPRETATION AND APPLICATION OF STATUTES (1975); J. SUTHERLAND, STATUTES AND STATUTORY CONSTRUCTION (4th ed. C. Sand 1972–1975).

fact, have a set of statutes which have been extracted from its session laws. The terms *revised, compiled, consolidated,* and *code* are often used indiscriminately to describe such sets of books.[3] In some instances compilations are accomplished under the official auspices of a state, in others by private publishers, and in some states there are both official and unofficial sets of codes. Some are unannotated, while others are fully annotated. Some state codes have been enacted into positive law; others are only *prima facie* evidence of the law with the positive law being in the volumes of the session laws. The important thing to note is that each state has a set of session laws and a current code. The set or sets for the state being used should be carefully examined to note its features, its method of publication, and the way it is kept up to date.

The following features are common to most sets of state statutes:

1. Constitutions

The constitution of the state currently in force as well as the text of previous constitutions.

2. Text of Statutes

Each state code contains the public laws of a general nature and still in force, arranged by subject.

3. Historical Notes

Historical references showing the derivation of each section of the code appear at the end of each statutory section. As many state codes have several completely new codifications during the history of the state, citations are frequently given to the present provision in a previous codification.

4. Annotations

Most state codes have an annotated edition. Some are very similar in appearance to the *U.S.C.A.* or the *U.S.C.S.* Frequently, citations are given to law review articles and to legal encyclopedias.

5. Tables

Each state code will have tables that cross-reference from session law to the code and many will have tables that refer from an

---

[3] Methods of compilation differ from state to state. One state may simply reissue the session laws in chronological order but with temporary and repealed acts not included. A second may arrange the laws still in effect in a classified order but with the text kept intact as originally enacted. A third may rewrite, rearrange, and reenact the laws in a new classified order. *See* Chapter 9, note 12.

older codification to the current one. [See Illustration 69 for examples of a state annotated code.]

SECTION C. INDEXES AND GUIDES TO STATE LEGISLATION

There is no comprehensive indexing service comparable to the *Key Number System* for state statutes. When comparative state statutes are needed, it is necessary at times to consult the indexes to the fifty sets of state codes. As this can be a time-consuming and difficult task, the following sources,[4] which frequently provide citations or digests of all state statutes on a particular subject, should be consulted.

1. Looseleaf Services

These are described in detail in Chapter 13. Many looseleaf services provide either full texts, digests, or tables of citations to state laws on a specific subject. For example, the CCH *All-State Tax Reporter* provides charts and digests of comparative state tax provisions; the Prentice-Hall *Wills, Trusts, and Estates Reporter* reproduces the text of all state laws on these subjects.

2. Martindale-Hubbell Law Directory

This is an annual publication which includes a volume titled *Law Digests* providing a digest of state laws on many subjects.

SECTION D. FINDING STATE LEGISLATION

1. Current State Law

When researching state legislation, one is usually attempting to ascertain if there is a current state statutory provision on a particular legal subject, *e.g.*, at what age may one be issued a driving license? The first step is to examine carefully the code for the state in question and familiarize oneself with the way the code is organized. Consulting the index provided should lead to the citation of a provision in the code which will set forth the current statutory law on the subject. Next, all of the notes set forth below the statutory provision should be consulted. Many annotated codes have references to legislative reports and give citations to law reviews and other secondary sources. The method of supplementation should then be noted (*e.g.*, pocket supplements, bound cumulative supplements, or advance pamphlets). If the set is annotated, the appropriate case annotations

---

[4] For bibliographies listing sources of state statutes by subject, *see* L. FOSTER AND C. BOAST, SUBJECT COMPILATIONS OF STATE LAWS (1981); C. NYBERG AND C. BOAST, SUBJECT COMPILATIONS OF STATE LAWS, 1979–1983: RESEARCH GUIDE AND ANNOTATED BIBLIOGRAPHY (1981 & periodic supp.).

should be checked. Frequently it will also be helpful to use the appropriate *Shepard's Citator*. This will be discussed in Chapter 14.

2. Inoperative State Law

At times the problem being researched may involve an act which has been repealed or is no longer in force. It will then be necessary to consult this law in the code volume that was available when the law was in force, or to consult the session volumes which contain the text of the act as originally passed by the legislature.

SECTION E.　ILLUSTRATIONS

[Illustration 65]

FIRST PAGE OF A 1984 STATE OF WASHINGTON SESSION LAW

1984 LAWS   **Ch. 277**

apply to all executions under chapter 6.24 RCW commenced after the

---

A 1984 session law from Washington State. This illustration is from
West's Legislative Service. After the end of a legislative session, all laws
passed will be published by the state in a bound volume.

ACID RAIN—CURBING SOURCES OF ACID DEPOSITION—MONITORING

CHAPTER 277

HOUSE BILL NO. 1174

AN ACT Relating to acid rain; adding new sections to chapter
70.94 RCW; creating a new section; making appropriations; and
declaring an emergency.

BE IT ENACTED BY THE LEGISLATURE OF THE STATE OF WASHINGTON:

NEW SECTION. Sec. 1. The legislature recognizes that:

(1) Acid deposition resulting from commercial, industrial or
other emissions of sulphur dioxide and nitrogen oxides pose a threat
to the delicate balance of the state's ecological systems,
particularly in alpine lakes that are known to be highly sensitive to
acidification;

Washington is a state that has enacted its codification (Revised Code of
Washington). When adding or amending it, the session law can then cite
directly to the RCW. Note how this is done.

---

(3) There is a direct correlation between emissions of sulphur
dioxides and nitrogen oxides and increases in acid deposition;

(4) Acidification is cumulative; and

(5) Once an environment is acidified, it is difficult, if not
impossible, to restore the natural balance.

It is therefore the intent of the legislature to mitigate or
eliminate the acid deposition problem by curbing sources of acid

Additions in text are indicated by underline; deletions by strikeouts

2279

[Illustration 66]

FIRST PAGE OF A SESSION LAW FROM ILLINOIS LEGISLATIVE
SERVICE

1983 REGULAR SESSION   **P.A. 83-1014**

EDUCATION—COLLECTIVE BARGAINING—
EDUCATIONAL LABOR RELATIONS
BOARD
PUBLIC ACT 83-1014
HOUSE BILL 1530

AN ACT to establish the right of educational employees to
organize and bargain collectively, to define and resolve
unfair practice disputes and to establish the Illinois
Educational Labor Relations Board to administer the Act.

Be it enacted by the People of the State of Illinois,
represented in the General Assembly:

[S.H.A. ch. 48, ¶ 1701]
Section 1. Policy. It is the public policy of this State
and the purpose of this Act to promote orderly and
constructive relationships between all educational employees
and their employers. Unresolved disputes between the
educational employees and their employers are injurious to
the public, and the General Assembly is therefore aware that
adequate means must be established for minimizing them and
providing for their resolution. It is the purpose of this
Act to regulate labor relations between educational employers
and educational employees, including the designation of
educational employee representatives, negotiation of wages,
hours and other conditions of employment and resolution of
disputes arising under collective bargaining agreements. The
General Assembly recognizes that substantial differences
exist between educational employees and other public
employees as a result of the uniqueness of the educational
work calendar and educational work duties and the traditional

> Another typical state session law. Note, however, that this law does not
> make any reference to the Illinois codification as Illinois does not have an
> official one. The bracketed citation to S.H.A., ch. 48, ¶ 1701, has been added
> by the publisher and refers to its unofficial codification. With only a
> citation to an Illinois session law, a transfer table must be used to find
> where the session law has been codified in an unofficial codification. See
> next illustration.

representatives;   (b) requiring educational employers to
negotiate   and   bargain with   employee   organizations
representing educational employees and to enter into written
agreements evidencing the result of such bargaining; and (c)
establishing procedures to provide for the protection of the

[Illustration 67]

PAGE FROM SMITH–HURD ILLINOIS ANNOTATED STATUTES: TABLES VOLUME

TABLE OF SESSION LAWS

Laws 1982				**Laws 1982**			
P.A.	Sec.	Ch.	Par.	P.A.	Sec.	Ch.	Par.
82–1011	2	120	575	82–1040	6	127	40.23
		120	588		7	127	40.23 note
		120	645a	82–1041	—		Appropriation
	2	120	9–917	82–1042	1	111⅔	7a.4
	3	120	450			111⅔	36
	4	120	483.3 note		2	120	467.1
82–1034	1	120	482		3	120	467.16
82–1035	Art. I				4	120	468
	1	121½	1001		5	111⅔	7a.4 note
	2	121½	1002		6	111⅔	7a.4 note
	Art. II			82–1043	1	120	467.3
	1	24	8–11–1		2	120	467.18
		24	8–11–5		3	120	470

> When only a citation to a state session law is available, a transfer table, usually located in a volume of the state's codification, must be consulted to locate where a particular section of a session law may be located within the state's code. For example, Section 15 of Illinois Public Act 82–1039 will be found at Chapter 38, Para. 155–22 of the Illinois Revised Statutes. As an individual session law may deal with several different matters, note how a law may be codified in different parts of a code.

P.A.	Sec.	Ch.	Par.	P.A.	Sec.	Ch.	Par.
	Art. IV			82–1046	1	42	331.1
	1	121½	1001 note			42	331.24
		120	429a note		2	42	323.7
82–1036	1	111	4433			42	323.9
		111	4435			42	328b
		111	4437			42	328bb
	2	111	4433 note			42	323.11
82–1037	1	122	17-2.2a		3	42	331.1 note
	2	122	103-7	82–1047	Art. I		
	3	122	17-2.2a note		1-1	127	133b2
82–1038	—		Special			127	133b4.2
82–1039	1	38	210–1			127	133b10.2
	2	38	210–2			127	133b10.3
	3	38	210–3			127	133b11
	4	38	210–4		1-2		Repeal
	5	38	210–5		Art. II		
	6	38	210–6		—		Appropriation
	7	38	210–7		Art. III		
	8	38	210–8		3-1	127	133b2 note
	9	38	210–9	82–1048	1	111⅔	306.1
	10	38	210–10		2	111⅔	519
	11	38	210–11		3		Repeal
	12	38	210–12		4	111⅔	306.1 note
	13	38	210–13	82–1049	1	95½	1001
	14	38	210–14		2	95½	1002
			Repeal		3	95½	1003
	15	38	155–22		4	95½	1004
		38	155–24		4a	95½	1005
	16	38	209–16		4b	95½	1006
	17	111	2222–1		4c	95½	1007
	18	111	4435		5	95½	1008
	19	38	210–1 note		6	95½	1009
82–1040	—		Special		7	95½	1010
					8	95½	1011
				82–1050	1	67½	701

[Illustration 68]

PAGE FROM INDEX VOLUME, OKLAHOMA STATUTES ANNOTATED

DISCRIMINATION

DISCRIMINATION—Cont'd
Compensation and salaries,
  Employees, 25 § 1302.
  Human relations commissions, of-
    ficers and employees, 25
    § 1704.
Complaints,
  Human relations commission,
    post.
  Referral to local commissions, 25
    § 1705.
  Retaliation, 25 § 1601.
  Transfer to state commission, 25
    § 1706.
Conciliation, 25 §§ 1505, 1602.
  Complaints, human relations com-
    mission, powers, 25 § 1704.
  Discriminatory practices, viola-
    tions, 25 § 1602.
  Powers of local human relations
    commissions, 25 § 1705.
  Violation, discriminatory prac-

DISCRIMINATION—Cont'd
Default, human rights commission
  hearing, 25 § 1503.
Definition, 25 § 1201.
  Discrimination in employment, 25
    § 1301.
  Discriminatory practices, 25
    § 1601 et seq.
  Local commission, 25 § 1701.
  Place of public accommodation,
    25 § 1401.
  Political subdivision, 25 § 1701.
Depositions, human rights commis-
  sion, 25 § 1501.
Determination of discriminatory
  practice, human rights commis-
  sion, 25 § 1505.
Discharge of employees, 25 § 1302.
Discriminatory practice, defined, 25
  §§ 1201, 1601.
Dismissal,

When research involves locating a statute, the search is started in the
index volume of the state code.

Assume the problem under research is whether Oklahoma has a statute
prohibiting discrimination in employment.

This illustration shows how the relevant statute is located in the
Oklahoma Statutes Annotated at Title 25, § 1302.

Conspiracies, discriminatory prac-
  tices, 25 § 1601.
Construction of act, 25 § 1101.
Consumer credit, 14A § 1–109.
Contractors, public works,
  Compliance with act, 25 § 1604.
  Finding of discriminatory prac-
    tices, 25 § 1505.
Cooperation,
  Governmental entities, public con-
    tractors, 25 § 1604.
  Human relations commission,
    state and local agencies, 25
    § 1704.
Copies, proceedings after complaint,
  human rights commission, 25
  § 1502.
Creation of local human relations
  commission, 25 § 1703.
Cross examination of witnesses, hu-
  man rights commission, 25
  § 1503.
Deaf persons, guide dogs, 7 §§ 19.1,
  19.2.
Declaratory judgment action, ex-
  emption from regulations, etc.,
  25 § 1507.

Educational institutions, exemp-
  tions, 25 §§ 1307, 1308.
Employees, human relations com-
  mission, 25 § 1704.
Employer, defined, 25 § 1301.
Employer practices, 25 §§ 1302,
  1306.
Employees fired for making
  claims, damages, reinstate-
  ment, 85 § 5 et seq.
Exceptions, 25 § 1308.
Imbalance, 25 § 1310.
Employment, 25 § 1101 et seq.
Employment agencies, 25 § 1303 et
  seq.; 40 § 55.
  Defined, 25 § 1301.
  Exception, 25 § 1308.
  Imbalance, 25 § 1310.
Employment opportunities, 25
  § 1302.
Enforcement,
  Application,
    District court, 25 § 1506.
    Hardship, resistance, 25 § 1507.
  Human rights commission, duties,
    25 § 1501 et seq.

45

[Illustration 69]

PAGE FROM TITLE 25, OKLAHOMA STATUTES ANNOTATED

25 § 1301   **DEFINITIONS AND GENERAL PROVISIONS**

No-spouse employment policy as constituting marital discrimination. 33 Okl.L.Rev. 636 (1980).

Predecessor labor relations problems in sale of a business. Lynn Paul Mattson. 50 Okl.B.J. 1163 (1979).

> After locating the citation in the Index, the section cited to must be read carefully.
>
> Care must be taken to check any supplement that may have been published. In this set, annual pocket supplements are available.
>
> Note how citations are given to the session laws from which § 1302 was codified.

itics, and Bakke Case. Earl M. Maltz. 30 Okl.L. Rev. 922 (1977).

New rules on age discrimination. Mary T. Matthies. 50 Okl.B.J. 1935 (1979).

Narcotic drug users, blanket exclusion from employment, see New York City Transit Authority v. Beazer, 1979, 99 S.Ct. 1355, 440 U.S. 568, 59 L.Ed.2d 587.

§ 1302. Employers

A. It is a discriminatory practice for an employer:

1. To fail or refuse to hire, to discharge, or otherwise to discriminate against an individual with respect to compensation or the terms, conditions, privileges or responsibilities of employment, because of race, color, religion, sex, national origin, or handicap unless such action is related to a bona fide occupational qualification reasonably necessary to the normal operation of the employer's business or enterprise; or

2. To limit, segregate or classify an employee in a way which would deprive or tend to deprive an individual of employment opportunities or otherwise adversely affect the status of an employee, because of race, color, religion, sex, national origin, or handicap unless such action is related to a bona fide occupational qualification reasonably necessary to the normal operation of the employer's business or enterprise.

B. This section does not apply to the employment of an individual by his parents, spouse or child or to employment in the domestic service of the employer.

Laws 1968, c. 388, § 302. Amended by Laws 1981, c. 231, § 2.

Law Review Commentaries

Civil rights:

Bona fide occupational qualification—Has exception swallowed rule? 31 Okl.L.Rev. 389 (1978).

Insuring against Title VII liability. 31 Okl. L.Rev. 1009 (1978).

No-spouse employment policy as constituting marital discrimination. 33 Okl.L.Rev. 636 (1980).

County of Washington v. Gunther: Movement towards comparable worth? 17 Tulsa L.J. 327 (1981).

Employment discrimination: Gender requirements for labor and delivery room nurses. 34 Okl.L.Rev. 412 (1981).

ERA—Who needs it? Marjorie Downing. 49 Okl.B.J. 1418 (1978).

In defense of employment at will. J. Ronald Petrikin. 53 Okl.B.J. 2209 (1982).

Indian employment preference: Legal foundations and limitations. 15 Tulsa L.J. 733 (1980).

Insurance recovery for Title VII losses. Roger L. Tuttle. 54 Okl.B.J. 843 (1983).

Pregnancy Amendment; Unanswered question of employer responsibility for fetal rights. Lynn Paul Mattson. 52 Okl.B.J. 1232 (1981).

Problems raised by so-called equal rights amendment. Maurice H. Merrill. 49 Okl.B.J. 1421 (1978).

Title VII: Are exceptions swallowing rule? Paula Smoot Ogg. 13 Tulsa L.J. 102 (1977).

Unconstitutionality of Age Discrimination in Employment Act. 17 Tulsa L.J. 782 (1982).

United States Supreme Court

Narcotic drug users, blanket exclusion from employment, see New York City Transit Authority v. Beazer, 1979, 99 S.Ct. 1355, 440 U.S. 568, 59 L.Ed.2d 587.

Notes of Decisions

Age discrimination 7
Compensation and salaries 6

168

[Illustration 69–a]

PAGE FROM TITLE 25, OKLAHOMA STATUTES ANNOTATED

DEFINITIONS AND GENERAL PROVISIONS			**25 § 1303**

Construction and application 1
Education 4
Handicap 5
Insurance 3
Limitation of actions 2

---

1. Construction and application

Const. Art. 23, § 4, which prohibits females as a class from being employed in the underground operation of mines is in conflict with the provisions of Title VII of the Civil Rights Act of 1964, 42 U.S.C.A. § 2000e et seq., which inter alia prohibits discrimination in employment based solely upon sex; therefore by virtue of the Supremacy Clause of the United States Constitution, Const. Art. 23, § 4, as it relates to the employment of females as a class, is preempted by Title VII of the Civil Rights Act of 1964. Op.Atty. Gen. No. 82–162 (Sept. 2, 1982).

Section 86 of title 40, which requires employers

barred by two-year statute of limitations. National Cowboy Hall of Fame and Western Heritage Center v. State ex rel. Oklahoma Human Rights Commission, Okl., 579 P.2d 1276 (1978).

3. Insurance

The provisions of Title VII, § 701(k) of the Civil Rights Act of 1964, 42 U.S.C.A. § 2000e et seq., are not constitutionally applicable to the State of Oklahoma and its political subdivisions and the State as an employer, is not bound to comply with the provisions of subsec..(k) with respect to its employees group health insurance plan. Op.Atty.Gen. No. 79–56 (April 23, 1979).

4. Education

The requirement of a high.school diploma or the equivalent as a condition of eligibility for employment in state government, in the absence of a showing that the requirement is based upon business necessity, constitutes unlawful discrimination under Title VII of the Civil Rights Act of

> At the end of each paragraph of the Code, citations are given to law review articles published in the state and to annotations of all federal and state cases and Attorney General opinions which cited and interpreted this paragraph.
>
> Most annotated state codes are similar to this one.

Oklahoma is eligible for participation in the Firemen's Relief and Pension Fund in that city or town. Op.Atty.Gen. No. 71–371 (Dec. 30, 1971).

2. Limitation of actions

Plaintiff's employment discrimination claim brought under civil rights statute (42 U.S.C.A. § 1981) guaranteeing equal rights under the law was governed by Oklahoma's three-year statute of limitations covering both contract actions and actions on a liability created statute, rather than Oklahoma's two-year statute of limitations for actions for injuries to the rights of another. Shah v. Halliburton Co., C.A.Okl., 627 F.2d 1055 (1980).

Where unsuccessful applicant for employment filed discrimination complaint with Human Rights Commission on or about October 22, 1973, concerning discrimination which allegedly occurred in August of 1973, where meeting was held before majority of members of Commission on October 22, 1975, where, on March 15, 1977, Commission issued order requiring employer to cease and desist from discriminatory hiring practices, and where Commission thereafter instituted action to enforce its order in district court, action was not

ion No. 71–422 is withdrawn to the extent inconsistent herewith. Op.Atty.Gen. No. 80–223 (Sept. 16, 1980).

6. Compensation and salaries

If an employee comes within the group of persons covered by the Fair Labor Standards Act, then that individual is entitled to the minimum wage, regardless of any preexisting agreement entered into between the employee and employer. Op.Atty.Gen. No. 81–41 (April 8, 1981).

School support personnel are not covered by the minimum wage provision of the Fair Wage Labor Standards Act. Id.

7. Age discrimination

The provisions of title 74, § 911, which preclude participants in the Oklahoma Public Employees Retirement System by employees who are 59 years of age or older at the date of their initial employment with the state, are not in violation of the Federal Age Discrimination in Employment Act, 29 U.S.C.A. § 621 et seq., as that Act has been interpreted by federal agencies responsible for its enforcement. Op.Atty.Gen. No. 81–143 (Sept. 16, 1981).

§ 1303. Employment agencies

It is a discriminatory practice for an employment agency to fail or refuse to refer for employment, or otherwise to discriminate against, an individual because of race, color, religion, sex, national origin, or handicap, or to classify or refer for employment an individual on the basis of race, color, religion, sex, national origin, or handicap.

Laws 1968, c. 388, § 303. Amended by Laws 1981, c. 231, § 3.

SECTION F. STATE LEGISLATIVE HISTORIES

Generally, state legislatures do not publish their debates, committee reports, or transcripts of hearings held before legislative committees.[5] It is therefore difficult to compile legislative histories of most state laws such as were described in Chapter 10 for federal laws. Yet the need for them is just as great, since state laws often have provisions which are vague and ambiguous. The most accessible official documents are the Senate and House Journals. These Journals usually contain only brief minutes of the proceedings and the final votes on legislation.[6] A few states may have reports of a State Law Revision Commission or the reports of special committees of the legislature for selected laws. If a state has an annotated code, the notes should be carefully examined to see if reference is made to such documents. Often, guidance for research in state legislative history is available from state legal research guides [7] or from librarians with extensive experience within a state. In many instances, however, extrinsic aids for determining legislative intent are not available and reliance must be made on the language of the act by using the ordinary rules of statutory construction.

[5] To determine those state documents which are available, *see* M. FISHER, GUIDE TO STATE LEGISLATIVE MATERIALS, rev. ed. (AALL Pub.Ser. 15, 1983) (Periodic supplements are issued).

[6] However, Maine and Pennsylvania have legislative journals which record actual legislative debate and parallel the *Congressional Record* in form of content.

[7] See a list of these guides in *Appendix A.*

Chapter 12

ADMINISTRATIVE LAW

SECTION A. FEDERAL ADMINISTRATIVE REGULATIONS AND DECISIONS: INTRODUCTION

Administrative law has been defined as:

[T]he law concerning the powers and procedures of administrative agencies, including especially the law governing judicial review of administrative action. An administrative agency is a governmental authority, other than a court and other than a legislative body, that affects the rights of private parties through either adjudication, rule-making, investigating, prosecuting, negotiating, settling, or informally acting. An administrative agency may be called a commission, board, authority, bureau, office, officer, administrator, department, corporation, administration, division or agency.[1]

The purpose of this chapter is to explain the manner in which the rules and the adjudication of federal administrative bodies are published and how they may be located.

The power of issuing regulations [2] and of adjudication is delegated to administrative bodies by Congress.[3] The increasingly complex problems of security and the economy in the last fifty years have brought about a tremendous increase in the number of administrative agencies and in the documents produced by them for publication. The normal procedure is for Congress to delegate to an administrative office or agency the power to issue rules or regulations, and in some instances the power to hear and settle disputes arising from the statute. Once an administrative body has been established, the issuance of rules or regulations is fairly simple, unlike the enactment of a statute which must go through the legislative process of Congress. Some agencies, such as the National Labor Relations Board, not only promulgate regulations, but are also authorized to adjudi-

---

[1] 1 K. DAVIS, ADMINISTRATIVE LAW AND GOVERNMENT 6 (2d ed. 1978).

[2] For a discussion of Congressional authority to delegate legislative power to administrative agencies, *see* 1 B. MEZINES, J. STEIN, & J. GRUFF, ADMINISTRATIVE LAW § 3.03[1] (1980).

[3] For example, 16 U.S.C. § 1600 *et seq.* (1982 ed.) deals with the nation's Forest Preserves and § 1613 provides that "The Secretary of Agriculture shall issue such regulations as he determines necessary and desirable to carry out the provisions of this subchapter."

cate disputes between management and labor unions; the results of their adjudications are published in a format similar to court reports.

All regulations by administrative agencies are issued either under authority delegated to them by a federal statute or by a Presidential Executive Order.

The types of actions taken by federal agencies may be classified as: (a) rules or regulations, (b) orders, (c) licenses, (d) advisory opinions, and (e) decisions. Each of these may be defined as follows: [4]

a. *Rules or regulations.* These are statements by an agency of general or particular applicability that are designed to implement, interpret, or prescribe law or policy. Properly promulgated rules and regulations have the same legal effect as statutes.

b. *Orders.* These are used to describe the final dispositions of any agency matters (other than rule making but including licensing).

c. *Licenses.* These include any permits, certificates, or other forms of permission.

d. *Advisory opinions.* Although containing advice regarding contemplated action, they are not binding and serve only as authoritative interpretations of statutes and regulations.

e. *Decisions.* Federal agencies authorized by law use decisions to adjudicate controversies arising out of the violation or interpretation of statutes and administrative regulations or rules. This function is performed by special boards of review, hearing examiners, and other officers through administrative decisions.

SECTION B. PUBLICATION OF FEDERAL RULES AND REGULATIONS

1. Federal Register

Before 1936, there was no official source for publication of rules and regulations of federal agencies, nor indeed were such agencies required to make them available to the public. This resulted in much confusion, as there was no way of determining if a proposed action by a person or company was prohibited by some federal agency. In fact, in one well-known instance, the federal government prosecuted a corporation for violations of an administrative regulation. This case [5] reached the Supreme Court of the United States before the Attorney General realized that the action was based on a regulation

---

[4] 5 U.S.C. § 551 (1982 ed.).

[5] Panama Ref. Co. v. Ryan, 293 U.S. 388 (1935).

that had been revoked prior to the time the original action had begun.[6]

As a result of the *Panama* case, Congress passed the Federal Register Act, 49 Stat. 500, 44 U.S.C. § 1504 *et seq.* (1982 ed.). This provided for the publication of the *Federal Register.* It started in 1936 and is published daily (except Saturday, Sunday, or days following official holidays). For any administrative ruling or regulation to be legally effective, it must be published in the *Federal Register.* The definition of what is considered to have general applicability and legal effect is as follows:

> * * * any document issued under proper authority prescribing a penalty or a course of conduct, conferring a right, privilege, authority, or immunity, or imposing an obligation, and relevant or applicable to the general public, members of a class, or persons in a locality, as distinguished from individuals or organizations * * *. 1 C.F.R. § 1.1 (1984).

Thus, since 1936, the *Federal Register* has contained every regulation having legal effect, and amendments thereto, that has been issued by any federal agency authorized by Congress or the President to issue rules or regulations. It now consists of several hundred volumes.

Although the *Federal Register* is the source for publication of regulations, it alone is insufficient to locate the present status of a particular regulation. It is analogous to the *Statutes at Large.* Although the latter contains every law ever passed by Congress, it is not useful in locating a statute on a particular subject. For this, of course, the *United States Code* must be consulted. In order to give subject access to federal regulations in a similar manner, the *Code of Federal Regulations* was also established. This bears the same relationship to the *Federal Register* as the *United States Code* does to the *Statutes at Large.*

a. *Indexes to the Federal Register*

(1) Weekly, quarterly, and annual indexes are issued to the *Federal Register.* These, however, are not too inclusive and, at times, it is difficult to locate a regulation if one does not know the agency that issued it.

(2) CIS *Federal Register Index.* This index started in 1984 and comprehensively indexes each issue of the *Federal Register.* It is issued weekly with periodic cumulative issues. It includes indexes by subject and name, *CFR* number, federal agency docket number, and Calendar of Effective Dates and Current Deadlines.

---

[6] K. DAVIS, ADMINISTRATIVE LAW TREATISE § 2.06 n. 5 (1958); *see also The Federal Register and The Code of Federal Regulations—a Reappraisal,* 80 HARV.L.REV. 439 (1966).

2.   Code of Federal Regulations (CFR) [7]

This set is a codification of the *Federal Register* where all regulations, and amendments, in force, are codified and brought together by subject. It is in fifty titles (similar to the arrangement of the *United States Code*) and published in pamphlet form. Each year, the pamphlet volumes of the *Code of Federal Regulations* are revised at least once and are issued on a quarterly basis approximately as follows:

Title 1 through Title 16 .... as of January 1
Title 17 through Title 27 .... as of April 1
Title 28 through Title 41 ....as of July 1
Title 42 through Title 50 ....as of October 1

Each new volume when issued contains the text of regulations still in force, incorporating those promulgated during the preceding twelve months and deleting those revoked. Through this process, all of the regulations first published chronologically in the *Federal Register* and currently in force are rearranged by subject and by agency in the fifty titles of the *Code of Federal Regulations*. For example, all of the regulations issued by the Federal Communications Commission, and still in force, may be located in Title 47 of the *CFR* and are up to date through October 1. The contents of the *Federal Register* are required to be judicially noticed,[8] while the *Code of Federal Regulations* is *prima facie* evidence [9] of the original documents that were published in the *Federal Register*.

3.   Updating the Code of Federal Regulations

After a title of the *CFR* has been newly published as explained above, an agency may issue new regulations or amend or revoke a regulation. These changes will be published in the *Federal Register*. Thus, whenever using a volume of the *CFR*, it is always imperative to ascertain if the section of the *CFR* being consulted has been changed in any way subsequent to the effective date of the regulations in the particular volume of the *CFR*. To accomplish this, three tables must be consulted:

a.   *LSA: List of CFR Sections Affected*. This is a monthly pamphlet that indicates the changes made since the latest publication of the *CFR* volumes. The December issue cumulates all changes for Titles 1–16, the March issue contains all changes for Titles 17–27, the

[7] For a more detailed history of the publication of the earlier editions of the *Code of Federal Regulations, see* E. POLLACK, FUNDAMENTALS OF LEGAL RESEARCH 366–72 (3d ed. 1967).

[8] 44 U.S.C. § 1507 (1982 ed.).

[9] *Id.* § 1510(e).

June issue, changes for Titles 28–41, and the September issue for Titles 42–50.

There is also available in two volumes a *List of Sections Affected (1964 through 1972)*. This is a cumulation that allows one to find the precise text of *CFR* provisions that were in force on any given date during the years covered.

b. *CFR Parts Affected.* As the list described in 3–a *supra* is issued monthly, a further check must be made for any later changes. This is accomplished by checking in the last issue of each month of the *Federal Register* in *CFR Parts Affected*. [See Illustration 76.] Then check this table in the latest daily issue.

c. *Shepard's Code of Federal Regulations Citations.* This set provides a method for locating citations to court decisions and selected law review articles that have cited a section of the *Code of Federal Regulations*. The use of *Shepard's Citations* is explained in Chapter 14.

SECTION C. FINDING FEDERAL REGULATIONS

1. New Regulations

As has been noted, newly promulgated regulations are first published in the *Federal Register*. There is frequently a period of several months before new regulations may appear in the appropriate volumes of the *Code of Federal Regulations*. These may be located by using the cumulative monthly or the annual indexes to the *Federal Register* or the *CIS Federal Register Index*.

Many current regulations are also published in the *United States Code Congressional and Administrative News Service* and in the Advance Pamphlets to the *United States Code Service*. Each of these sets has its own index.

2. Regulations in Force

a. *Index Method.* A new index volume to the *CFR* is issued annually. This index includes in one alphabet both subject entries and the names of administrative agencies. Consequently, one can consult it either under the name of an agency or under a specific subject heading. Since January 1980, the subject terms used are taken from a thesaurus developed by the Office of the Federal Register. This now assures that the same subject headings will be used in the Index if two or more agencies use different terms covering the same concept. For example, in its regulations, one agency may use the word *compensation*, another *pay*, and a third *salaries*. By the use of the thesaurus, references to all three of

these regulations will appear in the *CFR Index* under the subject heading *Wages*.[10]

The Index always refers to the appropriate Title of the *CFR* and then to the specific Part within the Title. [See Illustration 70.]

b. *Parallel Table of Statutory Authorities and Rules.* If the citation is known to a statute or Presidential Executive Order that authorized an agency or administrator to issue regulations, this Table will indicate where administrative regulations promulgated under such authority will be found in the *CFR*. The 1984 *CFR Index* contains citations from Presidential Executive Orders which authorize the issuance of regulations from 1977 to December 1983. This Table is located in the *Finding Aids* section of the *CFR Index*. [See Illustration 71.] For the parallel table prior to 1977, consult the 1976 *CFR Index—Finding Aids* volume.

It should be noted that as the *CFR* volumes are revised annually on a quarterly schedule, the latest annual *CFR Index* will include reference to some material in the daily issues of the *Federal Register*. The tables described in section B–3, a–b *supra* should always be consulted to bring the *CFR* up to date.

If none of the above techniques is successful in locating a desired regulation, the *Finding Aids Section* in the current *CFR Index* should be consulted for other possibilities.

3. Regulations No Longer in Force

It is often necessary to determine what regulations were in force at some prior date. Where prior editions of *CFR* are available, one can simply consult the edition that was current at the applicable time. Some libraries keep superseded editions of *CFR* either in paper copy or on microform,[11] and recent editions are available on LEXIS and WESTLAW.

One can also begin by locating the applicable subject matter in the current edition of *CFR*, which will give the date and *Federal Register* citation for the adoption of each section, and the same information for each subsequent amendment of that section. This allows the researcher to see if the present language of the section

---

[10] *Thesaurus of Indexing Terms*, 45 Fed.Reg. 2998 (Jan. 15, 1980).

[11] Two private publishing companies have published, in microform, a cumulation of the *CFR* title by title. The Information Handling Services has published the *CFR*, title by title, in microfiche from 1938–76. It also has prepared an extensive paper-bound index of the *CFR* for the years 1977–79. As of June, 1983, the Trans-Media Company has published, in microfilm, the *CFR*, cumulated title by title, for the years 1939–71, and 1972–76. Individual annual supplements for 1977 through 1980 have been published. It also provides its subscribers with a detailed guide to its microfilm edition of the *CFR*.

was in effect at the applicable time, and to find the original language in the *Federal Register* if the section has been amended.

4. U.S. Government Manual

This is an annually published directory of general information about the federal government, with emphasis upon the executive branch and regulatory agencies. Each department and agency is described in concise form with citations to the statutes creating the department or agency, a description of functions and authority, names and functions of major officials and bibliographies of major publications.

Appendix A lists all abolished and transferred agencies with an indication of what has happened to the functions for which they had responsibility. For example, under *United States Civil Service Commission,* it is noted that it has been redesignated as the *Merit System Protection Board* and its functions transferred to the *Board and Office of Personnel Management* by the Reorganization Plan No. 2 of 1978.

Appendix B lists commonly used abbreviations and acronyms.

Appendix C contains Organization Charts.

Appendix D lists the *Standard Federal Regions,* the *Federal Regional Councils,* and the *Federal Executive Board.*

Appendix E lists all agencies, in alphabetical order, that appear in the *CFR.*

There are also separate indexes for names, subjects and agencies.

The *United States Government Manual* is a component unit of the *Federal Register* and the *CFR.* It frequently will be useful to consult this volume before starting research on an administrative law problem.

5. Federal Regulatory Directory [12]

This is an annual publication that is helpful to use in connection with the *United States Government Manual.*

Part I discusses the topic of regulation and the current issues involving federal administrative agencies.

Part II contains extensive profiles of the largest and most important agencies.

Part III contains summary information on most of the other federal agencies.

[12] Published by Congressional Quarterly, Inc., (1980–).

SECTION D.   ILLUSTRATIONS FOR FEDERAL REGISTER AND CODE OF FEDERAL REGULATIONS

Problem: Find regulations for participating in the School Breakfast programs

70.   Page from Code of Federal Regulations Index
71.   Page from Parallel Table of Statutory Authorities and Rules, CFR Index Volume
72.   Pages from Title 7 of CFR
73.   Page from List of CFR Sections Affected Pamphlet—Titles Cumulation Listing
74.   Page from List of CFR Sections Affected Pamphlet
75.   Page from Volume 49, Federal Register—Rules and Regulations
76.   Page from Volume 49, Federal Register—List of CFR Parts Affected

[Illustration 70]

PAGE FROM CODE OF FEDERAL REGULATIONS INDEX

School breakfast and lunch programs	CFR Index

Faculty research abroad fellowship program, 34 CFR 663

National Health Service Corps scholarship program, 42 CFR 62

National Science Foundation, fellowships, applicants for and holders of,

State vocational education programs, 34 CFR 400

Tribally operated previously private schools, school construction contracts or services, 25 CFR 274

School integration

Step 1

Consult the current index to *CFR*. Note the sub-entry *School breakfast program, 7 CFR 220*. This refers to Title 7, Part 220. See next illustration.

---

scholarship program, 28 CFR 545

Public health fellowships, 42 CFR 61

Teachers of handicapped children in areas with a shortage, training program, 34 CFR 322

Veterans Administration, medical, 38 CFR 17

Vocational education, Secretary's discretionary programs, 34 CFR 408

School breakfast and lunch programs

Child nutrition programs

  Cash in lieu of donated foods, 7 CFR 240

  Free and reduced price meals and free milk in schools, determining eligibility, 7 CFR 245

  State administrative expense fund, 7 CFR 235

National school lunch program, 7 CFR 210

School breakfast program, 7 CFR 220

School construction

Areas affected by Federal activities, school construction assistance, 34 CFR 221

Disasters, school expenditures and construction assistance, 34 CFR 219

Federally impacted areas, school construction and financial assistance, hearings, 34 CFR 218

Public schools for Indian education, school construction contracts, 25 CFR 277

Asbestos, friable asbestos containing materials in schools, 40 CFR 763

Asbestos detection and control, local educational agencies, 34 CFR 230

Asbestos detection and State plan, State educational agencies, 34 CFR 231

Aviation maintenance technician schools, 14 CFR 147

Energy conservation grant programs for schools and hospitals and buildings owned by units of local government and public care institutions, 10 CFR 455

Equal employment opportunity, records and reports, 29 CFR 1602

Indians

  Administration policies of all Bureau of Indian Affairs education programs, 25 CFR 32

  Care of Indian children in contract schools, 25 CFR 22

  Federal schools for Indians, 25 CFR 31

  Indian–controlled schools, enrichment projects, 34 CFR 253

  Indian–controlled schools, establishment, 34 CFR 252

  Indian school equalization program, 25 CFR 39

  Maintenance and control of student records in Indian Affairs Bureau schools, 25 CFR 43

  Student rights and due process procedures, 25 CFR 42

  Transfer of Indian education functions in Bureau of Indian Affairs, 25 CFR 33

580

[Illustration 71]

PAGE FROM PARALLEL TABLE OF STATUTORY AUTHORITIES AND RULES, CFR INDEX VOLUME

CFR Index

42 U.S.C.—Continued	CFR
1472	7 Parts 1807, 1822
1480	7 Parts 1804, 1806–1809, 1822, 1823, 1841, 1861, 1863, 1864, 1866, 1872, 1890t, 1900–1902, 1910, 1922, 1924, 1927, 1930, 1933, 1940–1945, 1948, 1951, 1955, 1962, 1965, 1980, 2003, 2012, 2045
1484—1486	7 Part 15
1486	29 Parts 1, 5
1490b—1490d	7 Part 15
1490c	7 Part 1822
1491—1497	24 Parts 1, 2
1500 note	24 Parts 1, 2

42 U.S.C.—Continued	CFR
	44 Part 7
1856	43 Part 28
1856b	36 Part 211
	43 Part 28
1857 et seq	40 Parts 15, 33, 40, 60, 61, 124, 125
1857—1859	40 Part 60
1857—1858	41 Part 101-19
1857	40 Parts 35, 51, 52
1857b	40 Parts 40, 45, 46
	42 Part 61
1857b-1	40 Part 40
1857c-2	40 Part 81

Step 1–A

An alternative method of finding *CFR* regulations

There are times when the U.S.C. citation to the statute that delegated the authority to issue regulations is known. In such instances, the Parallel Table of Statutory Authorities and Rules Section in the Index Volume to CFR can be used to locate citations to regulations in the CFR. For example, one statutory authorization for school breakfast programs is found at 42 U.S.C. § 1776.

	CFR
1754	7 Part 235
1755	7 Parts 15, 240, 250
1756—1757	7 Parts 215, 220
1756	7 Part 235
1758	7 Parts 15, 210, 220, 225, 226, 250
1759—1759a	7 Parts 215, 220, 235
1760	7 Parts 215, 220, 235, 250
1761	7 Parts 15, 210, 215, 225-227, 235, 250
1762a	7 Parts 210, 240, 250
1765	7 Part 240
1766	7 Parts 210, 215, 225, 226, 235, 240, 245, 250
1771—1776	7 Part 235
1771	7 Parts 210, 215, 220, 225
1771 note	7 Part 210
1772—1773	7 Parts 15, 210, 215, 220, 245
1772	7 Part 225
1775	7 Parts 215, 220
→ 1776—1776a	7 Part 220
1776a	7 Part 210
1777—1785	7 Parts 215, 220
1777	7 Part 15
1779	7 Parts 210, 225, 226, 235, 240, 245, 246
1784—1786	7 Part 235
1784—1785	7 Parts 210, 245
1786	7 Parts 15, 246
1788	7 Part 227
1801 et seq	41 Part 20-1
1804	19 Part 161
1807	19 Part 161
1855—1855g	32 Part 736

	CFR
1859	40 Part 52
1859a	7 Part 225
1861—1879	41 Parts 25-1, 25-30, 25-50
1870—1871	45 Part 650
1870	45 Parts 610, 611, 630, 670
1891 et seq	40 Part 40
1891—1893	7 Part 15
	14 Part 1250
	30 Part 651
	32 Parts 272, 273, 736
	43 Part 17
1891—1892	32 Part 300
	33 Part 24
1891	41 Part 23-50
1951	43 Part 17
1961a-4	18 Parts 501-508
1962—1962d-5	18 Part 701
1962c	18 Part 740
1962d-1	18 Parts 704-706, 725
1973c	28 Part 51
	45 Part 801
1973e	45 Part 801
1973g	45 Part 801
1973cc-13—1973cc-14	39 Part 111
1975—1975e	45 Parts 701, 702, 704, 706
1975—1975c	45 Part 705
1979	7 Part 226
1980	7 Part 1980
1981—1982	12 Part 528
1981	12 Parts 531, 701
1996	28 Part 548
	50 Part 12
1997	28 Part 40
2000	23 Part 420

[Illustration 72]

PAGE FROM TITLE 7 OF CFR

Chapter II—Food and Nutrition Service　　　　　　　**§ 220.2**

PART 220—SCHOOL BREAKFAST PROGRAM

Sec.
220.1　General purpose and scope.
220.2　Definitions.
220.3　Administration.
220.4　Payment of funds to States and FNSROs.
220.5　Method of payment to States.
220.6　Use of funds.
220.7　Requirements for participation.
220.8　Requirements for breakfast.
220.9　Reimbursement payments.
220.10　Effective date for reimbursement.
220.11　Reimbursement procedures.
220.12　Competitive food services.
220.13　Special responsibilities of State agencies.
220.14　Claims against school food authorities.
220.15　Management evaluations and audits.
220.16　Procurement standards.
220.17　Prohibitions.
220.18　[Reserved]
220.19　Free and reduced price breakfasts.
220.20　Grant closeout procedures.
220.21　Program information.

APPENDIX A—ALTERNATE FOODS FOR MEALS
APPENDIX B—CATEGORIES OF FOODS OF MINIMAL NUTRITIONAL VALUE

AUTHORITY: Secs. 4 and 10, 80 Stat. 886, 889 (42 U.S.C. 1773, 1779), unless otherwise noted.

§ 220.1　General purpose and scope.

This part announces the policies and prescribes the regulations necessary to carry out the provisions of section 4 of the Child Nutrition Act of 1966, as amended, which authorizes payments to the States to assist them to initiate, maintain, or expand nonprofit breakfast programs in schools.

[Amdt. 25, 41 FR 34758, Aug. 17, 1976]

§ 220.2　Definitions.

For the purpose of this part the term:

(a) "Act" means the Child Nutrition Act of 1966, as amended.

(b) "Breakfast" means a meal which

as determined by the State educational agency, including students who are mentally or physically handicapped as defined by the State and who are participating in a school program established for the mentally or physically handicapped or (2) with the exception of residential summer camps which participate in the Summer Food Service Program for Children, Job Corps centers funded by the Department of Labor and private foster homes, any public or nonprofit private child care institution, or distinct part of such institution, which (i) maintains children in residence, (ii) operates principally for the care of children, and (iii) if private, is licensed to provide residential child care services under the appropriate licensing code by the State or a subordinate level of government. The term "child care institutions" includes, but is not limited to: Homes for the mentally retarded, the emotionally disturbed, the physically handicapped, and unmarried mothers and their infants; group homes; halfway houses; orphanages; temporary shelters for abused children and for runaway children, long-term care facilities for chronically ill children; and juvenile detention centers.

(c-1) "Competitive foods" means any foods sold in competition with the School Breakfast Program. This includes any food that is sold as a separate item even if it is also a component of the breakfast meal.

(c-2) "Competitive foods approved by the Secretary" means all foods sold in competition with the School Breakfast Program to children on school premises from the beginning of the school day until after the last lunch period with the exception of categories of foods of minimal nutritional value as listed in Appendix B of this part.

(d) "CND" means the Child Nutrition Division of the Food and Nutrition Service of the Department.

Step 2

Refer to the Part indicated in the Index. After each *Part* a detailed list of sections is given. In this instance, Section 220.7 seems relevant.

Note how at the end of the listing of the sections, the statutory authorization is given and note after 220.1 the citation to where it had been amended in the Federal Register.

[Illustration 72–a]

PAGE FROM TITLE 7 OF CFR

§ 220.7　　　　　　　　　　　　　　　　　　**Title 7—Agriculture**

(b) Whoever embezzles, willfully misapplies, steals, or obtains by fraud any funds, assets, or property provided under this part, whether received directly or indirectly from the Department, shall—

(1) If such funds, assets, or property are of a value of $100 or more, be fined not more than $10,000 or imprisoned

---

Step 3

Read the specific Section 220.7. This sets forth how applications for a school breakfast program should be made.

When the cover to 7 CFR is examined, it will be seen that it is revised as of January 1. Hence, it must be ascertained if any changes have subsequently occurred. See next illustration.

Amdt. 25, 41 FR 34759, Aug. 17, 1976; Amdt. 28, 44 FR 37899, June 29, 1979]

§ 220.7　Requirements for participation.

(a) The School Food Authority shall make written application to the State agency, or FNSRO where applicable, for any school in which it desires to operate the School Breakfast Program, if such school did not participate in the Program in the prior fiscal year. The School Food Authority shall also submit for approval, either with the application or at the request of the State agency, or FNSRO where applicable, a free and reduced price policy statement in accordance with Part 245 of this chapter. A School Food Authority which simultaneously makes application for the National School Lunch Program and the School Breakfast Program shall submit one free and reduced price policy statement which shall provide that the terms, conditions, and eligibility criteria set forth in such policy statement shall apply to the service of free and reduced price lunches and to the service of free and reduced price breakfasts. If, at the time application is

made for the School Breakfast Program, a School Food Authority has an approved free and reduced price policy statement on file with the State agency, or FNSRO where applicable, for the National School Lunch Program, it need only confirm in writing that such approved policy statement will also apply to the operation of its School Breakfast Program. Applications for the School Breakfast Program shall not be approved in the absence of an approved free and reduced price policy statement.

(a-1) A school which also either participates in the National School Lunch Program or only receives donations of commodities for its nonprofit lunch program under the provisions of Part 250 of this chapter (commodity only school) shall apply the same set of eligibility criteria so that children who are eligible for free lunches shall also be eligible for free breakfasts and children who are eligible for reduced price lunches shall also be eligible for reduced price breakfasts.

(b) Applications shall solicit information in sufficient detail to enable the State agency to determine whether the School Food Authority is eligible to participate in the Program and extent of the need for Program payments.

(c) Within the funds available to them, State agencies, or FNSRO's where applicable, shall approve for participation in the School Breakfast Program any school making application and agreeing to carry out the program in accordance with this part. State agencies, or FNSRO's where applicable, have a positive obligation, however, to extend the benefits of the School Breakfast Program to children attending schools in areas where poor economic conditions exist.

(d) Any School Food Authority may employ a food service management company (or other nonprofit agency or nonprofit organization) in the conduct of its feeding operation in one or more of its schools. A School Food Authority that employs a food service management company shall remain responsible for seeing that the feeding operation is in conformance with its agreement with the State Agency or the FNS Regional Office. The con-

[Illustration 73]

PAGE FROM LIST OF CFR SECTIONS AFFECTED PAMPHLET—
TITLES CUMULATION LISTING

LSA

List of CFR Sections Affected

June 1984

**Save this issue for titles
28–41 (Annual)**

Titles 1–16
Changes January 3, 1984
through June 29, 1984

Titles 17–27
Changes April 2, 1984
through June 29, 1984

Titles 28–41 (Annual)
Changes July 1, 1983
through June 29, 1984

Titles 42–50
Changes October 3, 1983
through June 29, 1984

**Parallel Table of
Authorities and Rules**

Step 4

After reading appropriate regulations in current CFR volume, research has to be made current by checking in this List.

It is issued monthly with the December, March, June, and September issues consisting of an annual cumulation for the titles indicated on the cover.

STANFORD
LAW LIBRARY

[Illustration 74]

PAGE FROM LIST OF CFR SECTIONS AFFECTED PAMPHLET

JUNE 1984   **19**

CHANGES JANUARY 3 THROUGH JUNE 29, 1984

Page

70.77 (a)(4) and (5) revised; in-
terim..2224
Effective date confirmed............10540
75 Revised....................................18724
101.50 Revised................................3640
101.51 Revised................................3640
101.52 Revised................................3640
101.53 Revised................................3640
102.6 (h) added..............................12667
102.13 Revised..............................12667
180.1 (a)(17) revised; interim....... 8234
180.5 (c) revised; interim.............. 8234
180.175 (a) through (m) re-
vised; interim..............................8234

**Chapter II—Food and Nutrition
Service, Department of Agriculture**

201.12a Revised............................. 1172
201.22 Existing text designated
as (a); (b) and (c) added............ 1172
210.4 (a) and (b) amended; (c)
introductory text revised;
(e) removed...............................18985
210.8 (e)(8) revised.......................18985
(f) redesignated from 210.19
(b)..18986
210.13 (b) revised; (b-1) amend-

Page

225.11 (c)(2), (5), and (6) removed; (c)(3), (4), and (7)
through (13) redesignated as
(c)(2), (3), and (4) through
(10); (c)(2), (4), and (5) re-
vised...2464
225.15 (a) revised...........................2465
225.16 (e)(13) added.......................2465
225.19 (e) revised...........................2465
225.21 (b)(6) revised; (c)
amended...................................14078
225 Appendix C added................ 18457
226.6 (d)(2)(i)(B) and (e)(1)
amended...................................14078
(j) introductory text amended;
(j)(11) added...........................18988
226.7 (d) revised........................... 18988
226.10 (c), (d), and (e) revised.....18988
226.18 (b)(10) added...................... 18989
226.23 (b), (c)(5), and (d)
amended...................................14078
226 Appendix C added................. 18457
235.7 (b) amended........................ 18989
235.11 (b)(1) amended;
(b)(2)(v) revised; (b)(3)
through (6) and (d) and (e)
redesignated as (b)(4)
.... f);
.... ed;
.... ic-
.... 18989
.... 26034
.... ed;
.... es-
.... gh

Step 4 (continued)

Note that a subsection of 220.7 has been revised. This revision was first printed at page 18987 of the 1984 Federal Register. This should be read for the text of the revision.

(d)..18987
215.10 (b) revised; (c) re-
moved.......................................18986
215.11 (c) revised..........................18987
215.15 Revised...............................18987
220.4 (a) revised; (d) removed.....18987
220.7 (e)(7) revised........................18987
220.11 (b) revised; (d) re-
moved.......................................18987
220.13 (b) revised; (b-1) re-
moved.......................................18988
220.18 Added.................................18988
220.20 Removed; new 220.20 re-
designated from 220.21.............18988
220.21 Redesignated as
220.20......................................18988
220 Appendix C added...................18457
225.4 (c) revised; (e) amended.......2464
225.9 (h)(1) amended....................14078
225.10 (c) and (d) revised..............2464

(xi); new (a)(1)(iv) added........ 26034
245.6 (a) introductory text, (1)
and (2) amended; (d) re-
moved...................................... 26034
245.6a (a) introductory text
and (3) revised; (a)(2) and
(b) introductory text
amended; (b)(4) removed........ 26034
250.1 (b)(21) revised..................... 25615
250.3 CFR correction................... 19797
250.6 (j) revised........................... 25616
271.2 Amended............... 6302, 22057
272.1 (g)(68) added........................ 6302
(g)(69) added; interim.............. 18462
272.2 (a)(2) amended; (d)(1)(i)
and (ii) and (e)(4), (5), and
(6) redesignated as (d)(1)(ii)
and (iii) and (e)(5), (6), and
(7); new (d)(1)(i) and (e)(4)
added...................................... 6303

[Illustration 75]

PAGE FROM VOLUME 49, FEDERAL REGISTER—RULES AND REGULATIONS

Federal Register / Vol. 49, No. 88 / Friday, May 4, 1984 / Rules and Regulations   18987

corrective action. State agencies may make upward adjustments in Program funds claimed on claims filed within the 60 day deadline if such adjustments are completed within 90 days of the last day of the claim month and are reflected in the final Report of School Program Operations (FNS–10) for the claim month which is required under § 215.11(c)(2). Upward adjustments in Program funds claimed which are not reflected in the final FNS–10 for the claim month shall not be made unless authorized by FNS. Downward adjustments in Program funds claimed shall always be made, without FNS authorization, regardless of when it is determined that such adjustments are necessary.

* * * * *

4. In § 215.11, paragraph (c) is revised to read as follows:

§ 215.11 Special responsibilities of State agencies.

* * * * *

(c) *Records and reports.* (1) Each State agency shall maintain Program records as necessary to support the reimbursement payments made to child care institutions or School Food Authorities under § 215.8 and § 215.10 and the reports submitted to FNS under § 215.11(c)(2). The records may be kept in their original form or on microfilm, and shall be retained for a period of three years after the date of submission of the final Financial Status Report for the fiscal year, except that if audit findings have not been resolved, the records shall be retained beyond the three-year period as long as required fo the resolution of the issues raised by th audit.

(2) Each State agency shall submit to FNS a final Report of School Program Operations (FNS–10) for each month which shall be limited to claims submitted in accordance with § 215.10(b) and which shall be postmarked and/or submitted no later than 90 days following the last day of the month covered by the report. States shall not receive Program funds for any month for which the final report is not submitted within this time limit unless FNS grants an exception. Upward adjustments to a State agency's report shall not be made after 90 days from the month covered by the report unless authorized by FNS. Downward adjustments shall always be made, without FNS authorization, regardless of when it is determined that such adjustments are necessary. Adjustments shall be reported to FNS in accordance with procedures established by FNS. Each State agency shall also submit to FNS a quarterly Financial Status Report

(SF–269) on the use of Program funds. Such reports shall be postmarked and/or submitted no later than 30 days after the end of each fiscal year quarter. Obligations shall be reported only for the fiscal year in which they occur. A final Financial Status Report for each fiscal year shall be postmarked and/or submitted to FNS within 12(ys after the end of the fiscal year. FNS shall not be responsible for reimbursing unpaid program obligations reported later than 120 days after the close of the fiscal year in which they were incurred.

Step 5

The CFR contains all regulations in force up to the date indicated on the cover of each volume. Amendments, revisions, or repeals made after that date are first published in the Federal Register. The previous illustration demonstrated how citations to these changes may be located.

Note the changes to Section 220.7.

---

these provisions to suspension or termination of the Program in School Food Authorities.

PART 220—SCHOOL BREAKFAST PROGRAM

1. In § 220.4, paragraph (d) is removed, and paragraph (a) is revised to read as follows:

§ 220.4 Payments to States and FNSROs.

(a) To the extent funds are available, the Secretary shall make breakfast assistance payments to each State agency for breakfasts served to children under the Program. Subject to § 220.13(b)(2), the total of these payments for each State for any fiscal year shall be limited to the total amount of reimbursement payable to eligible schools within the State under this part for the fiscal year.

* * * * *

2. Section 220.7, paragraph (e)(7) is revised to read as follows:

§ 220.7 Requirements for participation.

* * * * *

(e) * * *

(7) Submit Claims for Reimbursement in accordance with § 220.11 of this part and procedures established by the State agency, or FNSRO where applicable;

3. In § 220.11, paragraph (d) is removed and reserved and paragraph (b) is revised to read as follows:

0.11 Reimbursement procedures.

) Claims for Reimbursement shall ude data in sufficient detail to justify reimbursement claimed and to ble the State agency to provide the orts of School Program Operations iired under § 220.13(b)(2). Unless rwise approved by FNS, the Claim Reimbursement for any month shall ude only breakfasts served in that ith except if the first or last month of ;ram operations for any year ains 10 operating days or less, such ith may be added to the Claim for nbursement for the appropriate cent month; however, Claims for nbursement may not combine rations occurring in two fiscal years. nal Claim for Reimbursement shall)ostmarked and/or submitted to the e agency, or FNSRO where licable, not later than 60 days)wing the last day of the full month ered by the claim. State agencies · establish shorter deadlines at their retion. Claims not postmarked and/ ubmitted within 60 days shall not be i with Program funds unless FNS determines that an exception should be granted. The State agency, or FNSRO where applicable, shall promptly take corrective action with respect to any Claim for Reimbursement as determined necessary through its claim review process or otherwise. In taking such corrective action, State agencies may make upward adjustments in Program funds claimed on claims filed within the 60 day deadline if such adjustments are completed within 90 days of the last day of the claim month and are reflected in the final Report of School Program Operations (FNS–10) for the claim month which is required under § 220.13(b)(2). Upward adjustments in Program funds claimed which are not reflected in the final FNS–10 for the claim month shall not be made unless authorized by FNS. Downward adjustments in Program funds claimed shall always be made, without FNS authorization, regardless of when it is

[Illustration 76]

PAGE FROM VOLUME 49, FEDERAL REGISTER—LISTING OF CFR PARTS AFFECTED

Reader Aids

Federal Register

Vol. 49, No. 127

Friday, June 29, 1984

INFORMATION AND ASSISTANCE

SUBSCRIPTIONS AND ORDERS

Subscriptions (public)	202-783-3238
Problems with subscriptions	275-3054
Subscriptions (Federal agencies)	523-5240
Single copies, back copies of FR.	783-3238
Magnetic tapes of FR, CFR volumes	275-2867
Public laws (Slip laws)	275-3030

PUBLICATIONS AND SERVICES

Daily Federal Register

General information, index, and finding aids	523-5227
Public inspection desk	523-5215
Corrections	523-5237
Document drafting information	523-5237
Legal staff	523-4534
Machine readable documents, specifications	523-3408

Code of Federal Regulations

General information, index, and finding aids	523-5227
Printing schedules and pricing information	523-3419

Laws

Indexes	523-5282
Law numbers and dates	523-5282
	523-5266

Presidential Documents

Executive orders and proclamations	523-5230
Public Papers of the President	523-5230
Weekly Compilation of Presidential Documents	523-5230

United States Government Manual

	523-5230

Other Services

Library	523-4986
Privacy Act Compilation	523-4534
TDD for the deaf	523-5229

FEDERAL REGISTER PAGES AND DATES, JUNE

22751–23018	1
23019–23156	4
23157–23330	5
23331–23596	6
23597–23824	7
23825–24006	8
24007–24106	11
24107–24364	12
24365–24508	
24509–24704	
24705–24872	
24873–24966	
24967–25216	
25217–25420	
25421–25608	
25609–25832	
25833–26022	
26023–26184	
26185–26542	
26543–26696	
26697–27118	

CFR PARTS AFFECTED DURING JUNE

At the end of each month, the Office of the Federal Register publishes separately a List of CFR Sections Affected (LSA), which lists parts and sections affected by documents published since the revision date of each title.

3 CFR

Administrative Orders:
Presidential Determinations:

No. 84–9 of May 31, 1984	24107
No. 84–10 of May 31, 1984	23025
12426 (Amended by EO 12482)	26023
12480	25611
12481	25613
12482	26023

Executive Orders:

11888 (Amended by EO 12483)	26185
12483	26185

Proclamations:

5201	22751
5202	22753
5203	22755
5204	23019
5205	23021
5206	23023
5207	24365
5208	24873
5209	24875
5210	25217
5211	25219
5212	25421
5213	25609
5214	26025

5 CFR

1201	26697

Proposed Rules:

Ch. XIV	25243
831	26746

7 CFR

28	26543
33	23825
825	
825	
1708	
1825	
1331	
1543	
1547	
1221	
1027	
1615	
3187	
1967	
3222	
2758	
3189	
1007	
3192	
3201	
3551	

717	24371
800	26560
810	22761, 24509
900	23825
904	23157
905	23157
908	23158, 24372, 24878, 26035
910	22767, 23826, 24705, 25616, 26708
918	24509
928	24109
930	24510, 26564
953	23333
989	26706
1004	23029
1036	23034
1049	23029
1062	23029
1064	23029
1085	23029
1207	23825, 26202
1250	24009
1421	23597, 23827
1427	25223
1430	26203
1434	24878
1464	23334, 24372
1736	24511
2012	24010

Proposed Rules:

Ch. IX	23186
Ch. X	26239
418	23848
427	23852, 24522
429	23656
430	24528
431	24539
432	24533
435	26238
438	24144
447	24145
504	23651
724	24540
725	26536
810	23651, 25004
911	25243
916	24895
917	24895
989	23193, 25635
991	23061
1006	23653
1007	25879
1012	23653
1093	25879
1094	25879
1139	24736
1765	23860
1872	26072
1900	23359
1901	23359
1951	23359, 26072
1955	23359

> The List of CFR Sections Affected shown in Illustration 73 indicates changes made during the year to the CFR. To ascertain further changes, one should check the CFR Parts Affected Table in the last issues of the month of the Federal Register.

SECTION E. PRESIDENTIAL DOCUMENTS

Although most of the contents of the *Federal Register* and the *Code of Federal Regulations* result from the activities of federal agencies operating under delegated powers from Congress, the President also has the authority to issue regulations that have legal effect. This authority is both constitutional and statutory. Presidential documents are issued in the following forms.

1. Proclamations

While there is no legal difference between Presidential Proclamations and Executive Orders, the former are customarily used for Presidential action that has no legal effect. [See Illustration 77.]

Proclamations appear in:

    a.   *Statutes at Large*

    b.   *Federal Register*

    c.   *Weekly Compilation of Presidential Documents*

    d.   Title 3 *CFR* and compilation volumes of Title 3

    e.   *United States Code Congressional and Administrative News*

    f.   *United States Code Service, Advance Pamphlets*

2. Executive Orders [13]

These are generally used by the President to direct and govern activities of government officials and agencies.

Executive Orders are published in all the sources publishing Proclamations except the *Statutes at Large*.[14]

3. Codification of Presidential Proclamations and Executive Orders

This publication was started in 1979 by the Office of the Federal Register. Its purpose is to provide in one source Proclamations and Executive Orders that have general applicability and continuing effect. This codification has taken all of the previously published Proclamations and Executive Orders that were first separately published as issued and has brought them together by subject. Additionally, in each instance, amendments to the original documents have

---

[13] For a detailed study, *see* HOUSE COMM. ON GOVERNMENT OPERATIONS, 85th CONG., 1st SESS., EXECUTIVE ORDERS AND PROCLAMATIONS: A STUDY OF A USE OF PRESIDENTIAL POWERS (Comm. Print 1957).

[14] To locate Executive Orders issued prior to the publication of the *Federal Register* in 1936, see HISTORICAL RECORDS SURVEY, PRESIDENTIAL EXECUTIVE ORDERS (1944).

been incorporated in the text. This codification is arranged in fifty titles corresponding to those of the *Code of Federal Regulations* and covers the period from January 20, 1961, to January 20, 1981. Annual supplements are planned.

4. Reorganization Plans

By the provisions of 5 U.S.C. § 901 *et seq.* (1982 ed.), the President is authorized to examine the organization of all agencies and make changes that provide for the better management of the executive branch of the government. The President is authorized to submit proposed reorganization plans to both houses of Congress. If after 60 days neither house has passed a resolution opposed to the plan, it goes into effect.

The President issues his proposed changes as *Executive Orders.* In addition to their publication in the sources indicated at 1 *supra,* reorganization plans are published as approved in 5 U.S.C. Appendix.

5. Weekly Compilation of Presidential Documents

This Office of the Federal Register publication is published every Monday and contains statements, messages, and other Presidential materials released by the White House. It includes an Index of Contents at the beginning of each issue for documents in that issue. Each issue also contains a cumulative subject index and name index for the previous issues in that volume. An annual index, divided into names and subjects, is published. Other finding aids are: lists of laws approved by the President, nominations submitted to the Senate, and a checklist of White House releases.

6. Public Papers of the Presidents

This set starts with the administration of President Herbert Hoover. The papers of Franklin Roosevelt and certain earlier Presidents were privately published. Now published annually in one or more volumes, the set includes a compilation of the Presidents' messages to Congress, public speeches, news conferences, and public letters. The final volume of each year contains a cumulative index to the volumes of that year. After all the volumes for an administration are published, a cumulative index for that President is privately published.[15]

Beginning with the 1977 volumes, which cover the first year of President Carter's administration, the set includes *all* of the material printed in the *Weekly Compilation of Presidential Documents.*

[15] The Cumulated Indexes to the Public Papers of the Presidents of the United States (KTO Press 1977–).

7. **Shepard's Code of Federal Regulations Citations**
    See Section B–3–c *supra*.

SECTION F.   ILLUSTRATIONS FOR PRESIDENTIAL DOCUMENTS

[Illustration 77]

PAGE FROM TITLE 3, 1983 CODE OF FEDERAL REGULATIONS

Proclamation 5024 of March 7, 1983

National Children and Television Week, 1983

By the President of the United States of America
A Proclamation

Television has the power to shape thoughts, stir emotions, and inspire actions. It teaches, it sells, it entertains, it informs, and it has the capacity to influence powerfully the lives and values of our children. They learn much from television about the world, our society, and their place in it.

Television can communicate values that are consistent with our heritage and traditions and can portray those actions and attitudes that make for better citizens. It also can depict themes that are destructive of these values. Recognizing that children are at a formative and vulnerable stage in their lives, many individuals and groups have a great interest in television programming. These concerned citizens are working to improve the quality

A Presidential Proclamation issued under the inherent authority of the President.

NOW, THEREFORE, I, RONALD REAGAN, President of the United States of America, do hereby proclaim the week of March 13, 1983, through March 19, 1983, as "National Children and Television Week." I commend all those persons concerned about the quality of children's television programming, and I call upon all government agencies and the people of the United States to observe the week with appropriate activities supporting television programs which are attentive to the needs and interests of children.

IN WITNESS WHEREOF, I have hereunto set my hand this 7th day of March, in the year of our Lord nineteen hundred and eighty-three, and of the Independence of the United States of America the two hundred and seventh.

RONALD REAGAN

17

[Illustration 78]

PAGE FROM TITLE 3, 1979 CODE OF FEDERAL REGULATIONS

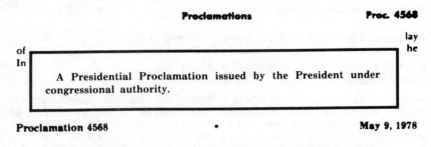

Proclamations   **Proc. 4568**

of

In

A Presidential Proclamation issued by the President under congressional authority.

Proclamation 4568   •   **May 9, 1978**

Application of Certain Laws of the United States to the Northern Mariana Islands

By the President of the United States of America

A Proclamation

The Northern Mariana Islands, as part of the Trust Territory of the Pacific Islands, are administered by the United States under a Trusteeship Agreement between the United States and the Security Council of the United Nations (61 Stat. 3301). The United States has undertaken to promote the political development of the Trust Territory toward self-government or independence and to protect the rights and fundamental freedoms of its people.

In accordance with those obligations, the United States and the Northern Mariana Islands have entered into a Covenant to Establish a Commonwealth of the Northern Mariana Islands in Political Union with the United States of America (Public Law 94–241; 90 Stat. 263). Section 1004(a) of the Covenant provides that if the President finds a provision of the Constitution or laws of the United States to be inconsistent with the Trusteeship Agreement, the application of that provision to the Northern Mariana Islands may be suspended.

Certain provisions of law restrict jury service in Federal District Courts to United States citizens. The vast majority of the inhabitants of the Northern Mariana Islands are not citizens of the United States and consequently may not participate as jurors in proceedings before the United States District Court for the Northern Mariana Islands. They may also be deprived of the right to have their cases heard before juries selected at random from a fair cross-section of their community. These results would be contrary to the obligations assumed by the United States in the Trusteeship Agreement.

NOW, THEREFORE, I, JIMMY CARTER, President of the United States of America, by the authority vested in me by the Constitution and laws of the United States, including Section 1004(a) of the Covenant to Establish a Commonwealth of the Northern Mariana Islands in Political Union with the United States of America, do hereby find, declare and proclaim as follows:

Any provision of the Constitution or laws of the United States which prescribes United States citizenship as a qualification for service on a grand or petit jury in the District Court for the Northern Mariana Islands, including that provision contained in Section 1865(b)(1) of Title 28 of the United States Code, would be inconsistent with the Trusteeship Agreement if applied to a citizen of the Trust Territory of the

25

[Illustration 79]

PAGE FROM TITLE 3, 1983 CODE OF FEDERAL REGULATIONS

Executive Orders   **EO 12420**

to admeasure vessels and issue International Tonnage Certificates, pursuant to the provisions of the Convention.

                                                    RONALD REAGAN

THE WHITE HOUSE,

May 5, 1983.

Executive Order 12420 of May 11, 1983

Incentive Pay for Hazardous Duty

By the authority vested in me as President of the United States of America by Public Law 97–60 and Section 301(a) of Title 37 of the United States Code, and in order to define the scope of two additional categories of hazardous duty, it is hereby ordered as follows:

Section 1. Executive Order No. 11157 of June 22, 1964, as amended, is further amended by adding the following new subsections to Section 109 of Part I:

"(h) The term "duty involving frequent and regular exposure to highly toxic

---

  A Presidential Executive Order issued by the President under Congressional authority.

---

comparable high acute toxicity and hazard potential.

"(i) The term "duty involving laboratory work that utilizes live dangerous viruses or bacteria" shall be construed to mean primary duty performed by members who work with micro-organisms (1) that cause disease (A) with a high potential for mortality, and (B) for which effective therapeutic procedures are not available, and (2) for which no effective prophylactic immunization exists, while such members are assigned by competent orders for a period of 30 consecutive days or more to participate in or conduct applied or basic research that is characterized by a changing variety of techniques, procedures, equipment, and experiments.".

Sec. 2. This Order shall be effective as of October 1, 1981.

                                                    RONALD REAGAN

THE WHITE HOUSE,

May 11, 1983.

189

SECTION G. FEDERAL ADMINISTRATIVE DECISIONS

1. Agency Decisions

Many federal administrative agencies also serve a quasi-judicial function and, in performing this function, issue decisions. The Federal Communications Commission, for example, is authorized by Congress to license radio and television stations. It also has the authority to enforce its regulations covering the operations of these stations. When stations allegedly violate the terms of the statute or the regulations, the Federal Communications Commission will hear the charges and issue decisions.

Decisions of administrative agencies are published, not in the *Federal Register,* but in separately published sets of volumes. They are available in two forms: (1) official publications of the Government Printing Office, and (2) unofficial publications of commercial publishers. The latter will be discussed in Chapter 13.

a. *Official Publications of Federal Administrative Agencies.* These are available in most law libraries, and in public and university libraries that are official depositories of the U.S. Government Printing Office. The format, frequency, and method of publication vary from agency to agency. Generally, they are issued on an infrequent schedule and are poorly indexed. Some sets have separate volumes of indexes and digests, and it is often necessary to check the indexes in the individual volumes of decisions. Some sets of federal administrative agencies do provide an advance sheet service.

2. Judicial Review of Agency Decisions

After an agency has issued a decision, the decision may, in most instances, be appealed to the federal courts. These decisions may be found by consulting the following sets:

a. *West's Federal Practice Digest 3d* and its predecessor sets.

b. *U.S. Supreme Court Digest* or *U.S. Supreme Court Reports Digest.*

c. *American Digest System* if the preceding digests are not available.

d. *Shepard's U.S. Administrative Citations* (discussed in Chapter 14).

e. *Treatises on administrative law* (discussed in Chapter 17).

3. Representative Examples of Currently Published Official Decisions of Federal Administrative Tribunals

a. Interstate Commerce Commission. *Reports,* vol. 1 *et seq.* (1887 to date).

b.   Comptroller General. *Decisions,* vol. 1 *et seq.* (1921 to date).

c.   Federal Communications Commission. *Reports,* vol. 1 *et seq.* (1934 to date).

d.   Federal Trade Commission. *Decisions,* vol. 1 *et seq.* (1915 to date).

e.   National Labor Relations Board. *Decisions and Orders,* vol. 1 *et seq.* (1935 to date).

f.   Securities and Exchange Commission. *Decisions,* vol. 1 *et seq.* (1934 to date).

SECTION H.   FEDERAL REGISTER: OTHER FEATURES

In addition to the publication of the rules and regulations from the Office of the President and the executive agencies, issues of the *Federal Register* contain the following features.

1.   Selected Subjects

On the front page of each issue, broad subject areas are listed along with the involved agency or agencies.

2.   Reader's Aids

This section appears at the end of the *Federal Register* and contains telephone numbers for information and assistance, a parallel table of *Federal Register* pages to dates for the month, a table of *CFR Parts Affected* during the month, and a List of Public Laws, which lists those public bills from the current session of Congress which have recently become Federal law.

3.   Proposed Rules

This section contains notices of proposed issuance of rules and regulations.   Its purpose is to give interested persons an opportunity to participate in the rule-making process prior to the adoption of final rules.

4.   Notices

This section of the *Federal Register* contains documents other than rules or proposed rules that are applicable to the public.

5.   Sunshine Act Meetings

Each Tuesday's *Federal Register* contains an additional section entitled "Sunshine Act Meetings" which are notices of meetings required by the "Government in the Sunshine Act" (Pub.L. No. 94–409), 5 U.S.C. § 552 b(e)(3) (1982).

6. List of Public Laws

Each issue lists those public bills from the current session of Congress that have recently become federal law.

7. Calendar of Federal Regulations

This Calendar is published semiannually. It is produced by the Regulatory Council, and it is designed to be a comprehensive listing of proposed important regulations and will give information on their objectives and benefits, the sectors of the economy affected, the economic implications, and major alternatives under study.

SECTION I. OTHER METHODS OF FINDING FEDERAL REGULATIONS

1. Looseleaf Services

As discussed in the previous sections of this chapter, the rules and regulations and other documents that serve as the written sources for administrative law can all be located through the use of the *Federal Register,* the *Code of Federal Regulations*, and other publications of administrative agencies. But this is frequently an awkward and time-consuming task, necessitating the constant checking of these sources. In the next chapter looseleaf services are discussed. Most of these services consist primarily of documents that appear in the *Federal Register,* or in the publications of administrative agencies. They are usually better indexed and contain other features facilitating the location of information. Consequently, when it is necessary to research a problem of administrative law, it is frequently better practice to ascertain if a looseleaf service covering the topic under research exists and to use that service rather than the official publications discussed above.

2. Computer-Assisted Research

Both LEXIS and WESTLAW have the *Federal Register* and the *Code of Federal Regulations* in full text [16] in their databases. In both instances, the coverage for the *Federal Register* commences with July 1, 1980. In WESTLAW the *Federal Register* and the *Code of Federal Regulations* are searched separately; in LEXIS, they may be searched either separately or in a combined file. WESTLAW has a separate database of *Executive Orders* since 1936 and of *Proclamations, Administrative Orders*, and *Trade Agreements* from the *Federal Register* since January, 1984.

---

[16] Many regulations published in the *Federal Register* or the *Code of Federal Regulations* have tables of statistical information or charts and graphs. This type of information is not included in the databases of either LEXIS or WESTLAW.

Both systems, when available to a researcher, are extremely helpful when there is a need to find all times a *CFR* has been cited, or to locate particular words or phrases that can be found in the *CFR Index*.

More information on computer-assisted research will be found in Chapter 20.

SECTION J. STATE ADMINISTRATIVE REGULATIONS AND DECISIONS

1. State Regulations

The regulations and decisions of state agencies are variously published by the states. In most states [17] the administrative regulations are officially codified and published in sets similar to the *Code of Federal Regulations*. In other states, each agency issues its own regulations, and it is necessary that inquiries be directed to the pertinent agency.

2. State Administrative Decisions

Many state agencies also publish their decisions. These, more commonly, are those of the Unemployment Compensation Commissions, Tax Branches, and Public Utility Commissions.

3. Research in State Administrative Law

a. Check the state code to determine if the state has an Administrative Procedure Act, and if the method of publication for regulations is prescribed.

b. Check the state's organization manual to determine the agencies that issue regulations or decisions.

c. Many states have local legal encyclopedias or local administrative law treatises. These should be consulted.

SECTION K. SUMMARY

1. Federal Register

a. Types of federal documents published in it

(1) Regulations and Rulings of Federal Agencies.

(2) Proposed Regulations and Rules.

(3) Notices of Agencies.

(4) Presidential Executive Orders.

---

[17] Tseng & Pederson, *Acquisition of State Administrative Rules and Regulations—Update 1983*, 25 ADMIN.L.REV. 319 (1983).

   b.   Indexes

(1) Cumulative index published monthly and annually.

(2) *Cumulative List of Parts Affected.*

      This table brings up to date the monthly issues of *Cumulative List of CFR Sections Affected.*

      (3) CIS *Federal Register Index,* 1984–.

   c.   Frequency of Publication.   Began in 1936.   Published Monday through Friday, except on the day following an official federal holiday.

   d.   Publications in the *Federal Register* must be judicially noted.

2.   Code of Federal Regulations

   a.   Contains all regulations that first appeared in the *Federal Register* which are of a general and permanent nature and are still in force.

   b.   Arranged by subject in fifty titles similar to the *U.S. Code.*

   c.   Each title is subdivided into Chapters, Subchapters, Parts, and Sections.   It is cited by title and Section.

   d.   Each title is in separate pamphlets.   Each title is re-published once a year, at which time new material is added, and repealed or obsolete regulations are deleted.

   e.   Regulations published in *CFR* are *prima facie* evidence of the official text.

   f.   *Indexes*

(1) Annual subject and agency index.

(2) *Monthly List of CFR Sections Affected.*

      This list indicates any changes in the annual volumes of the CFR.

   g.   The *Finding Aids* section in the annual index has *Parallel Tables of Authorities or Rules,* and other aids for locating federal administrative documents.

3.   U.S. Government Manual

   a.   Annual Handbook.

   b.   Describes administrative organizations whose regulations are published in the *Federal Register.*

   c.   Information on Congress, the federal judiciary, and important agency personnel.

   d.   Subject index.

4. **Federal Administrative Decisions**

   a. Official publications published by U.S. Government Printing Office.

   b. Unofficially published by commercial publishers.

5. **State Administrative Regulations and Decisions**

   a. Most states have codified their administrative rules.

   b. Some states publish the decisions of administrative agencies.

Chapter 13

LOOSELEAF SERVICES

SECTION A. INTRODUCTION TO LOOSELEAF SERVICES

The rapid growth of statutory and case law has caused a major change in the literature of the law, but it is the expansion of the administrative agency as an arm of the executive branch that has created the greatest obstacle to effective legal research. This is especially true in the area of public law where administrative regulations and rulings play so large a role. Over the past forty years such rules and regulations have shown phenomenal growth, both in numbers and complexity. Thus, while cases and statutes can still be located through the traditional means of digests, annotations and citators, research that involves the publications of administrative agencies demands a broadening of the research focus. For example, to adequately research a problem in the law of taxation, a researcher must locate not only relevant statutes and court decisions, but regulations of the Internal Revenue Service and the Treasury Department, rulings of the Commissioner of Internal Revenue, news releases, technical information bulletins, Tax Court decisions, and other agency documents. A researcher attempting to find the answer to a tax problem using only the *United States Code*, the digests, the *Federal Register*, and the *Code of Federal Regulations* would find it not only cumbersome but, at times, impossible.

It was the inaccessibility, complexity, and bulk of administrative regulations and decisions that prompted the publication of looseleaf services or reporters by private publishers. As the name indicates, looseleaf services consist of separate, perforated pages in special binders that simplify the insertion, removal, and substitution of individual pages. This characteristic allows the publisher to continuously update the material in a process of constant editing, introducing what is new, removing what is superseded. The speed and the accuracy afforded by this on-going revision are two of the looseleaf services' greatest values.[1]

---

[1] Law publishers have always been concerned with keeping their publications current. Traditionally, this has been accomplished by the issuance of pocket supplements, usually on an annual basis. This is still the most common method of keeping sets of statutes, digests, and treatises up to date. More recently, some publishers of these types of law books have begun using looseleaf binders, although still updating on an annual or irregular basis. In this chapter, we restrict our discussion to those

The looseleaf format allows for creativity in organizational approach. Most, however, attempt to consolidate into one source the statutes, court decisions, and commentary on a particular legal topic. By this means a researcher can find all relevant material, both primary and secondary, in one place. Further, most services provide current awareness notices on the topic, which can include news of proposed legislation, pending agency decisions, and even informed rumor.

The convenience, currency, and excellent indexing of looseleaf services make them the best place to begin researching most administrative law problems. It should be noted that in many rapidly developing areas of the law, like privacy, the environment, consumer protection and others, the looseleaf service may be the only research tool available.

Looseleaf services vary in content and coverage, reflecting both the subject area of the service and the editorial policy of the publisher. This chapter can describe only those features that are common to most services. When using any looseleaf service, one should be alert to its individual characteristics, and special attention should be paid to the introductory and prefatory materials supplied by the publisher.[2]

SECTION B.   USING LOOSELEAF SERVICES

1.   In General

Most looseleaf services have the following common elements:

a.   Full text of the statutes on the topic, with significant legislative history.

b.   Full text of administrative regulations, and either full text or digests of relevant court and agency decisions.

c.   Editorial comment and explanatory notes.

d.   Subject or topical indexes.

e.   Tables of cases and statutes.

f.   Indexes to current materials.

g.   Current reports summarizing recent developments. Such reports are issued either weekly, biweekly, or monthly.

sets which are updated weekly, biweekly, or monthly, and in which, in most instances, the new material replaces pages rather than supplements existing pages.

[2] This is particularly necessary when using looseleaf services on taxation or labor law because the magnitude of materials on these subjects makes the looseleaf services very complex. For more detailed information on taxation *see* Chapter 23 in Jacobstein and Mersky, *Fundamentals of Legal Research.* 3d ed. (1985).

**2. Using Commerce Clearing House or Prentice-Hall Looseleaf
Services**

Commerce Clearing House (CCH) and Prentice-Hall (P–H) are
two of the major publishers of looseleaf services. Although their
publications run the full spectrum of form and content, the underlying organizational principles of each publisher are the same. This
allows them to be discussed together.

CCH and P–H services range from those complete in one binder
to those that fill a dozen or more. Regardless of size, they frequently share similar features. They begin with an introductory section
that discusses the use and organization of the service. The importance of this feature cannot be over-emphasized. A careful reading
of it may save the researcher both time and frustration. The
volume(s) will be divided into sections by tabcards. These offer quick
access to major topic headings. Typically, there will be a comprehensive index to the entire service (Topical Index in CCH, Master Index
in P–H). In addition, some services have special indexes to particular
topics or volumes. The quality of the indexing is generally quite
high, and both publishers strive to provide as many access points as
possible.

The indexes are made more useful by the unique, dual numbering system employed in these services. Under this system, in addition to normal pagination, there is a *paragraph* number assigned to
each topic area. These numbers may encompass one textual paragraph or fifty pages. This flexibility of format allows for constant
additions and deletions to the text without a total disruption of the
indexing system. Research can begin by consulting one of the
indexes, which will refer to the appropriate paragraph number. By
turning to the correct paragraph number, one can locate the pertinent
material. In looseleaf services, page numbers are often used only as
guides for filing new pages and removing old ones.

The full texts of new court decisions and agency rulings, often
supplied as part of the looseleaf service, are generally placed in a
separate volume or section. Each case or ruling is commonly assigned its own paragraph number, and can be located in any one of
several ways. Most services have tables of cases, statutes, and
administrative regulations. When a citation to one of these is encountered, research can begin by consulting the appropriate table and
obtaining the paragraph number where the cited material is discussed. Both services have special indexes which cross-reference
from materials found under the paragraph numbers to materials
concerning current developments.

Materials on current developments are generally presented in the
form of weekly bulletins that accompany the pages to be filed.

These bulletins are often retained as part of the service, and constitute valuable research tools in themselves.

In general, the successful use of CCH or P–H looseleaf services requires the following three steps:

a.   Find where the topic or topics under research are dealt with in the service by consulting the Topical or Master Index.

b.   Read carefully all materials under paragraph numbers referred to by the Index.   When digests of cases are given, note citations to cases so that the full text of decisions may be read.

c.   Consult the appropriate index or indexes to current materials.

Illustrations 80–85 demonstrate the use of a CCH service.

3.   Bureau of National Affairs, Inc.

The Bureau of National Affairs (BNA) is the third major publisher of looseleaf services.   Its organizational principles differ from those of CCH and P–H.   BNA's typical format consists of one or more three-ring binders in which periodic issues (or releases) are filed.   Unlike CCH and P–H, the issues do not contain individual pages to be interfiled with existing text, but instead consist of pamphlet-size inserts numbered sequentially and filed chronologically.   Thus, there is no provision for revision of earlier issues.   This format allows for the service to be issued more quickly, at the expense of the comprehensiveness guaranteed by the interfiling system.

Each issue contains several separate components, usually including a summary and analysis of major developments, the text of pertinent legislation, and the text or a digest of court and agency actions.   Such features as important speeches, government reports, book reviews, and bibliographies may also be included.   Each of these components is generally filed behind its own tabcard.   Thus, each issue is an attempt to keep the practitioner fully informed of all developments in the subject area of the service.

BNA services feature cumulative indexes that offer topical access to the material.   Since current issues supplement earlier ones, there is no need for paragraph numbers, and simple pagination is used.   There are also case tables for each service.   BNA periodically supplies special storage binders for old issues, so that the main volumes can always contain current material.

BNA also has one large service that differs in arrangement from its other looseleaf services.   This is its *Labor Relations Reporter*. This set has separate looseleaf volumes for the following areas of labor relations:

Labor Management Relations (Federal)

Labor Arbitration

Wages and Hours

Fair Employment Practices

State Labor Laws

Each of the looseleaf volumes for these units of the *Labor Relations Reporter* contains relevant statutes and regulations and court decisions. Periodically, court decisions are removed from the looseleaf volumes and reprinted in bound series of cases (*e.g., Labor Arbitration, Wage and Hour Cases*).

Each set of cases also has its own index and digest where the cases are classified according to BNA's classification scheme.

The entire set is unified by a *Master Index* looseleaf volume and a *Labor Relations Expediter* looseleaf volume. [See Illustrations 86–88.]

4. Other Features of Looseleaf Services

Looseleaf services aim at providing complete information on a subject. Thus, they frequently contain forms, reports on current congressional activities, summaries of professional meetings, and other news deemed relevant to the researcher or practicing attorney. Those services which include state laws are generally arranged by states, with the same paragraph number being assigned uniformly to the same topic for each state. In some instances, *all-state* charts are published which give citations to the various state codes. [See Illustration 89.]

Many looseleaf services, as already indicated, report the full texts of current court decisions that fall within the scope of a particular service. These are filed in a separate section or volume since they usually arrive with each mailing. In many instances, at the end of the year, the publisher will send to the subscriber a bound volume of the decisions for permanent reference. The looseleaf pages containing the decisions for the year can then be discarded. As an example, subscribers to Commerce Clearing House *Standard Federal Tax Reporter* will receive bound volumes with the title *U.S. Tax Cases.* The latter contain decisions previously sent in looseleaf format. Similarly, subscribers to BNA's *Labor Relations Reporter* will receive bound volumes called *Labor Relations Reference Manual(s),* which contain all cases on federal labor law.

In all cases, headnotes and other editorial aids are prepared by the publishers. Some of these case series have come to be recognized as standard reference units. Of course, the same decisions usually can also be found in official reporters or the *National Reporter System,* but some of these looseleaf sets have become so widely

recognized for their speed, accuracy, and ease of access that they are cited by the courts.[3]

CCH, BNA, and P–H are not the only publishers of looseleaf services, but most services will conform to either the interfiled or supplemented format. If the principles that underlie these formats are understood, any service should be usable. The most vital step will always be a careful reading of the publisher's introductory material. Looseleaf services are listed by subject in Appendix D.

SECTION C. ILLUSTRATIONS

80–85. Illustrations Using CCH Standard Federal Tax Reporter

Problem: May a teacher who used a room in her house for an office and corrected homework papers and prepared lesson plans there deduct this part of her home as a business expense?

86–88. Illustrations Using BNA Fair Employment Practices Division of its Labor Relations Reporter

Problem: When may employers require a high school diploma as a condition of employment?

89.   Page from CCH Food Drug Cosmetic Law Reports

[3] As was noted in Chapter 4, the decisions of the federal district courts are reported selectively. Some decisions not reported in the *Federal Supplement* are published in one or more of the subject looseleaf services. Consequently, it is frequently worthwhile to check the *Table of Cases* of these services for opinions not reported in the *Federal Supplement*.

[Illustration 80]

INDEX PAGE FROM CCH STANDARD FEDERAL TAX REPORTER

Step 1

If the IRC Section Number is known, the research could start in the Finding Aids which would lead to a paragraph number. If Code Section is not known, start in Topical Index. In this instance, looking under Teachers indicates a reference to office in the home.

See next illustration.

TEA

[Illustration 81]

PAGE FROM CCH STANDARD FEDERAL TAX REPORTER

2 7, 7 1 0   **BUSINESS USE OF HOME, ETC.—§ 280A [p. 27,688]**   35 7-27-83

[¶ 2297YT]   **Business Use of Home—Vacation Home**
• • *CCH Explanation*

.001 **Background.**—Ever since the Tax Reform Act of 1976 (P. L. 94-455) enacted Code Sec. 280A, Congress has been dissatisfied with some of the statute's aspects and especially with the proposed regulations (see ¶ 2297YN-2297YP) that the Internal Revenue Service issued in 1980 to implement the statute. This dissatisfaction culminated in legislation (P. L. 97-119) in late December 1981 that restructured the following three areas of Code Sec. 280A:

(1) *Business use of home.* In proposed Reg. § 1.280A-2(b), the IRS states that a taxpayer may have only one principal place of business for purposes of Code Sec. 280A and that, in effect, if the taxpayer's home business is not his principal place of business, no deduction is allowable for the business use of the residence. The Tax Court disagreed with this reasoning in *Curphey* (see .61, below) in which the court allowed deductions to a doctor for a home office from which he managed his rental properties. In P. L. 97-119, Congress adopted the *Curphey* holding by providing that deductions are not to be denied for expenses allocable to a portion of a dwelling unit that is exclusively used on a regular basis as the principal place of business for *any* trade or business carried on by the taxpayer.

(2) *Rental to family member.* Under Code Sec. 280A, as originally

Step 2

Obtain volume that contains Paragraph Number 2297YT. Although the Index referred to 2297YT.67, one should always turn first to the whole number to the left of the decimal point. This usually contains editorial explanatory matter.

dence to a family member, caused a great deal of concern and led to a Congressional ban on the use of the IRS appropriations to implement or enforce regulations in this area. This impasse was finally settled by Congress in P. L. 97-119 which amended Code Sec. 280A to provide that a taxpayer's rental of a dwelling unit to any person (including

¶ 2297YT   Reg. § 1.280A-3

[Illustration 82]

PAGE FROM CCH STANDARD FEDERAL TAX REPORTER

§ 280A [p. 27,688]—BUSINESS USE OF HOME, ETC.   **27,711**

Business Use of Home—Vacation Home

• • *CCH Explanation*

family members) will not constitute personal use by the taxpayer if the dwelling unit is rented at a fair rental for use as the family member's principal residence.

(3) *Repairs and maintenance.* In P. L. 97-119, Congress overruled a portion of proposed Reg. § 1.280A-1(e)(4). The law change agreed with the IRS position that the use of a dwelling unit is to be disregarded for any day on which an individual is engaged in repairs or maintenance work on the unit on a substantially full-time basis. But it overruled that portion of the proposed regulation that provides that if more than one individual is present, all individuals capable of working had to work on a substantially full-time basis in order for that day to be disregarded. Instead, Congress left it to the IRS to prescribe regulations outlining the circumstances under which the use of a dwelling unit for repairs and annual maintenance will not be considered personal use of the unit. However, the regulations may not treat a dwelling unit as used for personal purposes on any day that the taxpayer repairs or maintains the dwelling on a substantially full time bas   ork
on

Step 2 (continued)

acti   tro-
      Additional editorial explanation on the next page.   ode
Sec   ges,
how   imita-
tions. Thus, a taxpayer who may have been denied deductions or failed to claim deductions because of the IRS positions described above has the right to file amended returns for past open years and claim a refund on the basis of the changed law.

.01   **Limitations on office in home.**—Under Code Sec. 280A, a taxpayer is not permitted to deduct any expenses attributable to the use of his home for business purposes except to the extent that they are attributable to the portion of the home used exclusively and on a regular basis as:

(1) The principal place of business of a trade or business of the taxpayer, or

(2) A place of business which is used by patients, clients, or customers in meeting or dealing with the taxpayer in the normal course of business.

As noted at .001, above, the IRS ruled in its proposed regulations (proposed Reg. § 1.280A-2(b)(2)) that a taxpayer may have only one principal place of business for purposes of Code Sec. 280A regardless of the number of business activities in which he or she may be engaged. However, Congress rejected this IRS position by amending Code Sec. 280A(c)(1) to provide that the limitations of Code Sec. 280A do not apply to expenses allocable to a portion of a dwelling unit that is exclusively used on a regular basis as the principal place of business of any trade or business of the taxpayer. This is the same

Reg. § 1.280A-3   ¶ 2297YT.01

[Illustration 83]

PAGE FROM CCH STANDARD FEDERAL TAX REPORTER

§ 280A [p. 27,688]—BUSINESS USE OF HOME, ETC.   **2 7, 7 2 1**

minimum expenses that could have been incurred in using a portion of their home for business purposes were inadequate substantiations.

F. L. Carlson, 41 TCM 1091, Dec. 37,751(M), TC Memo 1981-117.

A home office deduction was disallowed in full where the taxpayer did not establish either that there was gross income attributable to several businesses conducted within his home office or that the home office was the principal place of any of the remaining businesses.

D. A. Roth, 43 TCM 45, Dec. 38,480(M), TC Memo 1981-699.

➤ **.67   Teachers.**—Teachers have been uniformly denied deductions for home office costs by the Tax Court because a home office is not a teacher's principal place of business and because, in those cases where they are provided an office in the school, the home office is not maintained for the convenience of the employer.

G. Kastin, 40 TCM 1071, Dec. 37,187(M), TC Memo 1980-341.

R. Chauls, 41 TCM 234, Dec. 37,355(M), TC Memo 1980-471.

P. W. Cousino, 41 TCM 722, Dec. 37,629(M), TC Memo 1981-19. Taxpayer on appeal to CA-6.

IRS Letter Ruling 7734023, May 24, 1977.

E. R. Strasser, 42 TCM 1125, Dec. 38,261(M), TC Memo 1981-523.

C. Taylor, 43 TCM 727, Dec. 38,840(M), TC Memo 1982-14.

G. H. Storzer, 44 TCM 100, Dec. 39,099(M), TC Memo 1982-328.

L. A. Moskovit, 44 TCM 859, Dec. 39,275(M), TC Memo 1982.

Similarly, as to a principal.

G. Besch, 43 TCM 286, Dec. 38,717(M), TC Memo 1982-15.

➤ *Caution: The following cases involved pre-Code Sec. 280A tax years.* ←

.83 Use of room in a taxpayer's home to read stock market books for the possible initiation of an investment program was insufficient to gain a deduction for part of the home's expenses.

G. D. Hix, 38 TCM 491, Dec. 35,951(M), TC

office expenses. The taxpayer was not required to disclose the names of patients treated at the home office because policies underlying the physician-patient privilege outweighed the Commissioner's need to further verify the evidence submitted.

Wisconsin Psychiatric Services, Ltd., 76 TC 839, Dec. 37,923.

The Commissioner's determination of the amount of a taxpayer's deduction for home office expenses was sustained since his determination of the number of square feet of the taxpayer's bedroom that she used as an office was not unreasonable.

V. Thomas, 42 TCM 328, Dec. 38,042(M), TC Memo 1981-348.

.837   Partial use of apartment or residence for business.—Note: The following cases were decided under the law in effect prior to enactment of Code Sec. 280A. See ¶ 1330.52 and 2297YM et seq.

Harroun, 4 TCM 780, Dec. 14,688(M).

Blanchard, 10 TCM 1036, Dec. 18,631(M).

Chesshire, 11 TCM 146, Dec. 18,792(M).

L. G. Helfrich, 19 TCM 179, Dec. 24,073(M), TC Memo 1960-33.

P. Griswold, 21 TCM 33, Dec. 25,316(M), TC Memo 1962-7.

W. B. Hough, 21 TCM 370, Dec. 25,425(M), TC Memo 1962-70.

W. F. Bolin, 26 TCM 62, Dec. 28,316(M), TC Memo 1967-9.

M. E. Henderson, 27 TCM 109, Dec. 28,837(M), TC Memo 1968-22.

G. H. Newi, (CA-2) 70-2 USTC ¶ 9669, 432 F. 2d 998.

R. K. Johnson, 31 TCM 941, Dec. 31,528(M), TC Memo 1972-192.

F. A. Thomas, 28 TCM 575, Dec. 29,595(M), TC Memo 1969-108.

R. A. Sinskey, 30 TCM 1286, Dec. 31,091(M), TC Memo 1971-302.

J. B. Kasey, 35 TCM 1160, Dec. 33,989(M), TC Memo 1976-266.

O. Grover, 68 TC 598, Dec. 34,527.

P. Monsky, 36 TCM 1046, Dec. 34,563(M), TC Memo 1977-259.

J. H. Barry, 37 TCM 1080, Dec. 35,252(M), TC Memo 1978-250.

W. M. Roberts, 38 TCM 1000, Dec. 36,156(M), TC Memo 1979-250. Taxpayer's appeal to

---

Step 3

Turn to the specific paragraph number indicated in the Index—2297YT.67. This digests and gives citations to rulings and cases dealing with the teacher's right to deduct expenses of maintaining a home office. The full texts of the cases should be read.

A home office maintained by a psychiatrist was his principal place of business, and expenses and depreciation allocable to that portion of his house were deductible home

W. B. Meister, 18 TCM 899, Dec. 23,816(M), TC Memo 1959-202.

X. Deviak, 19 TCM 626, Dec. 24,219(M), TC Memo 1960-118.

[Illustration 84]

PAGE FROM NEW MATTER VOLUME, CCH STANDARD FEDERAL TAX REPORTER

70,332   **Cumulative Index to 1983 Developments**   29 6-15-83
                    (For Reports 1-28)
                See also Cumulative Index at page 70,251.

From Compilation **Paragraph No.**		**To New Development** **Paragraph No.**

Code Sec. 280A—Disallowance of certain expenses in connection with business use of home, rental of vacation homes, etc.

2297YT	.30	*Taylor,,* TCM—Rental expense deduction limited to rental income	7364
	.48	*Baker,* TCM—Allocation of interest and taxes to rental use of property	7397
	.48	*Bolton* aff'd, CA-9 (¶ 9010.1)—Allocation of vacation home expenses. *Rewrite* (¶ 8645).	
	.48	*McKinney*—Gov't on appeal to CA-10.	
	.508	Deductions associated with rental of three bedrooms in personal residence—Letter Ruling	6961
	.51	*Warganz* aff'd, CA-3 (unpublished opinion 10/15/82)	
	.52	*Moller,* ClsCt—Home office expenses were deductible	9009.6
	.52	*Moretti,* TCM—Exclusive use requirement met as to one room	7061
	.52	*Odom,* TCM—Bedroom office	7037
	.52	*Smith,* TCM—No deduction allowed for use of residence	7051
	.54	*Drucker*—Taxpayer on appeal to CA-2.	
	.54	*Warganz* aff'd, CA-3 (unpublished opinion 10/15/82)	
	.57	*Green*—Gov't on appeal to CA-9.	
	.57	*Green* rev'd, CA-9—Client-initiated telephone calls	9387
	.58	*McKinney*—Gov't on appeal to CA-10.	
	.605	*Baker,* TCM—Personal use of property exceeded 14 days	7397
	.605	*Gilchrist,* TCM—Rental property was used for personal expenses	7670
	.61	*Anderson,* TCM—Home was not principal place of business	7113
	.61	*Cally,* TCM—Doctor's home office deduction disallowed	7563
	.61	*Cherry,* TCM (¶ 7115)—Practice room on concert musician. Taxpayer's appeal to CA-4 dismissed 1/21/83.	
	.61	*Cherry,* TCM (¶ 7115)—Practice room of musician. Taxpayer's appeal to CA-2 reinstated.	
	.61	*Cristo,* TCM—Home office deduction disallowed	7010
	.61	*Dempsey,* TCM—Musicians could not deduct the cost of practice room	7116
	.61	*Drucker,* TC—Practice room was not violinist's principal place of business	7090
	.61	*Hauser,* TCM—Public defender's apartment	7250
	.61	*Lopkoff,* TCM—Home office was not administrative assistant principal place of business	7271
	.61	*Perrote,* TCM—Home office deduction was denied	7146
	.61	*Rogers,* TCM (¶ 7114)—Practice room of concert musician. Taxpayer's appeal to CA-2 dismissed.	
	.61	*Trussel,* TCM—Judge's principal place of business	7245
	.61	*Weightman,* TCM—Home office deduction disallowed	7234
	.61	*Wilhelm,* TCM—Nurse's home office not principal place of business	7653
	.617	*Gorod*—Taxpayer on appeal to CA-1.	
	.64	*Druker* aff'd and rev'd, CA-2 (¶ 9116)—Home used as storage facility. Cert. denied taxpayer 5/31/83.	
	.67	*Besch*—Taxpayer on appeal to CA-7.	
→	.67	*Cousino*—Cert. denied taxpayer 11/29/82.	
	.67	*Moskovit*—Taxpayer on appeal to CA-10.	
	.837	*Blackburn,* TCM—No deduction for use of home as office	7029
	.847	*Jackson*—Taxpayer on appeal to CA-9.	

Code Sec. 280B—Demolition of certain historic structures

2297Z	.01	Accrual accounting of Windfall Profit tax—Rev. Rul.	6214
2297ZB	.01	Proposed Reg. § § 1.280A-1 and 1.280A-3	8861

Step 4

After relevant cases have been noted in the Compilation Volumes, a check must be made for new decisions. This is accomplished by checking the Cumulative Index to (year's) Developments (CDI) in the New Matter Volume.

Note the references to Paragraph 2297YT.

		Rul.	6436
	.022	*Terris,* TCM—Bargain purchase of house by shareholder resulted in taxable dividend	7359
	.0615	*Baumer* rev'd and rem'd, CA-11—Law of the case doctrine required lower court to follow prior appellate ruling	9000.7
	.718	*Montpetit,* TCM—Constructive dividend received before close of corporation's tax year	7293

Code Sec. 302—Distributions in redemption of stock

2308	.02	Non-pro rata distribution—Rev. Rul.	6239
2310	.023	*Monson,* TC—Redemption treated as payment in exchange for stock	7213
	.032	*Standard Linen Service*—Acquiescence announced	6355
	.0394	*Hall,* TCM—Stock redemption was essentially equivalent to a dividend	7492

¶ 2297YT   ©1983, Commerce Clearing House, Inc.
                                                   013—32

[Illustration 85]

PAGE FROM NEW MATTER VOLUME, CCH STANDARD FEDERAL TAX REPORTER

70,228   Current Items to Cumulative Index to 1983 Developments   57   12-20-83
                              (For Reports 50-57)
                    See also Cumulative Indexes at pages 70,251 and 70,301.

From Compilation **Paragraph No.**		**To New Development** **Paragraph No.**
2266	.35	*Snyder,* TCM—Tax avoidance was principal purpose for corporate acquisition of department store ... 8138
2267A	.10	*Garbini Electric*—Gov't and taxpayer on appeal to CA-9.
	.10	*Pacella*—Gov't's appeal to CA-2 dismissed.
2296	.11	*Morandini,* TCM—Allocation of foreign travel expenses determined ... 8177
	.176	President's designation udner CBERA ... 6870
	.18	*Frick,* TCM—Entertainment expenses were not substantiated ... 8182
	.18	*Frick,* TCM—Taxpayer failed to substantiate his traveling expenses ... 8182
	.18	*Hawbaker,* TCM—Entertainment expenses disallowed for lack of substantiation ... 8107
	.18	*Nilson,* TCM—Deductions for union dues and meal expenses were not substantiated ... 8165
	.18	*Shantz,* TCM—Business expense deduction for golf club dues was disallowed for lack of substantiation ... 8194
	.23	*Snyder,* TCM—Gifts lacked substantiation ... 8138
	.30	*Astone,* TCM—Unsubstantiated travel expenses ... 8201
	.30	*Caledonian Record Publishing Co., Inc.,* DC—Travel and entertainment expenses were not substantiated ... 9665
	.30	*Fairmont Homes, Inc.,* TCM—Deductions for unsubstantiated travel expenses were disallowed ... 7569
	.30	*Lewis,* TCM—Travel and entertainment expenses disallowed ... 8192
	.30	*Lindsley, Jr.,* TCM—Promotional and public relations expenses were not substantiated ... 8178
	.30	*McCabe,* TCM (¶ 7711)—Unproven expenses. Taxpayer on appeal to CA-10.
	.30	*Snyder,* TCM—Recreational expenses were not substantiated ... 8138
	.60	*Olivares,* TCM—Taxpayers not excused from substantiation rules ... 8089
2297	.58	*McKinney.* CA-10 (¶ 9655)—Tenth Circuit rejects IRS allocation of vacation home expenses—*Rewrite* ... 8478
2297B	.60	*Zwiener,* TCM—No deduction for withheld FICA taxes ... 8101
2297N	.01	Proposed Reg. § 1.278-2 ... 8987E
	.01	Proposed Reg. § 1.278-2—*Rewrite* ... 8481
2297YT	.48	*McKinney.* CA-10 (¶ 9655)—Tenth Circuit rejects IRS allocation of vacation home expenses—*Rewrite* ... 8478
	.52	*Moller,* ClsCt (¶ 9009.6)—Home office expenses were deductible. Rev'd, CA-FC (¶ 9698).
	.52	*Moller,* ClsCt (¶ 9009.6)—Home office expenses were not deductible. Rev'd CA-FC (¶ 9698)—*Rewrite* ... 8476
	.58	*McKinney* aff'd, CA-10 (¶ 9655)—Court of Appeals affirmed Tax Court's allocation of interest and real estate taxes to rental use of home *Rewrite* ... 8478
	.61	*Frick,* TCM—Home office expenses were not deductible ... 8182
	.61	*Weissman,* TCM—College was focal point of professor's business activities ... 8171
	.65	*McCabe,* TCM (¶ 7711)—Unproven expenses. Taxpayer on appeal to CA-10.
→	.67	*Bilenas,* TCM—No home office deduction; college was professor's principal place of business ... 8103
	.67	*Weissman,* TCM—College was focal point of professor's business activities ... 8171
2297ZF		Proposed amendment of Reg. § 1.280-1 withdrawn ... 8987C
2297ZG	.01	Withdrawal of proposed amendment of Reg. § 1.280C-1 ... 8987C
2305	.0245	*Hipp,* TCM—Stock exchanged for property ... 8198
	.042	*Roth,* TCM—Form of cash distribution was not controlling ... 8092
	.0614	*Viereck,* CtCls (¶ 9664)—Corporate distributee received ordinary income—*Rewrite* ... 8486
2308	.01	*Hipp,* TCM—Stock exchanged for property ... 8198
2310	.0315	*Roth,* TCM—Form of cash distribution was not controlling ... 8092
	.059	*Viereck,* CtCls (¶ 9664)—Reduction of net worth did not constitute contraction of business—

Step 4–a

At times during the calendar year, there are supplements to the Cumulative Index to New Developments. Be sure all of them are checked.

---

		dividends to husband ... 8138
	.3245	*Rapoport,* TCM—Dividends were distributed ... 8099
	.394	*Hestnes,* TCM—Sole shareholder's use of corporate funds resulted in constructive dividends ... 8176
	.408	*Astone,* TCM—Constructive dividends ... 8201
	.408	*Snyder,* TCM—Various expenses paid by taxpayer's corporation constituted constructive dividends ... 8138
2442	.053	*Ballou Construction Co., Inc.* rem'd, CA-10—Recognition of income on liquidation distribution of items for which deductions were claimed ... 9677

¶ 2266

[Illustration 86]

PAGE FROM BNA FAIR EMPLOYMENT PRACTICES CUMULATIVE DIGEST AND INDEX VOLUME

FEP Cases OUTLINE OF CLASSIFICATIONS

▶108.00 — Contd.

.0410 Employer status in general
　　　[See also ▶108.0415 et seq.]
.0415 Joint employer
.0420 Successor employer
　　　[For bankruptcy, see ▶108.0422.]
.0422 Bankruptcy
.0425 Size of employer
.0430 Parent-subsidiary relationship
.0440 Employee status
　　　[For standing to file charge see ▶108.543; for standing to sue see ▶108.7441 et seq.]
.0450 Labor organization status
　　　Retroactivity
　　　[See also ▶110.1052.]
.070 —In general
.071 —1964 Act

Step 1

Consult Classification Guide　ral
in latest FEP Cumulative Digest and Index. Note how 　.]
108.1958 appears to be relevant. Consult this paragraph number in the Digest Section of CDI. See next illustration.

(Search could have been started in the Master Index volume using a subject approach rather than a classification approach.)

.1130 Holidays
.1135 Meetings
　　　[For meetings on company premises, see ▶108.1180.]
.1140 Appearance; dress
.1146 Accommodation
.1155 Refusal to work on Sabbath
.1158 Union security agreements
.1160 Promotion; selection
.1162 Transfer
.1164 Wages; salaries; hours of work
　　　[For Sabbath, see ▶108.1155.]
.1170 Work assignments; job classifications
.1180 Harassment; working conditions
.1185 Bona fide occupational qualification

▶108.12 **National Origin Discrimination**
　　　[See also aliens, ▶108.2250 and 110.67; educational and testing requirements, ▶108.1935; and union discrimination, ▶108.2201 et seq. For reverse discrimination, see ▶108.4850. For veterans, see ▶108.3601.]

▶108.12 — Contd.

.1201 In general
.1205 Hiring
.1208 Recruitment
.1210 Discipline; suspension, etc.
.1213 Tenure
　　　[For FEP Volumes 1-20, see ▶108.1215.]
.1215 Discharge; termination; removal
.1220 Demotion
.1223 Layoff; recall
.1225 Experience
.1230 Criminal records
.1235 Garnishment; financial status; credit references
.1238 Appearance; height and weight requirements
.1245 Language; accent
.1248 Working conditions, in general
.1255 Job classifications, assignments
.1260 Harassment; intimidation
　　　[See also retaliation, ▶108.4501 et seq.]
.1262 Wages and salaries
.1268 Hours
.1272 Benefits, in general
.1278 Leave of absence
.1282 Facilities for employees
.1284 Transfer
.1287 Promotion; selection of supervisors
.1290 Training
.1292 Defenses, in general

▶108.15 **Employment Agencies, Discrimination by**
　　　[See also ▶106.1372.]
.1501 In general

▶108.18 **Hiring in General**
　　　[Cases have been reclassified under specific types of discrimination. Consult General Index or Topic Finder.]

▶108.19 **Educational and Testing Requirements**
　　　[See also remedies, ▶230.051 et seq.]
.1901 In general
.1905 EEOC guidelines
.1915 Sex discrimination
.1935 National origin
.1955 Educational requirements, in general
→.1958 High school education
.1960 College education; graduate degrees
.1965 Testing requirements, in general
　　　[See ▶108.1987 for polygraph examinations after FEP Vol. 20.]
.1968 Disproportionate impact
　　　Testing validity; job relatedness
　　　[▶108.1972 was expanded to ▶108.1972 et seq. after FEP Vol. 20.]

54

[Illustration 87]

PAGE FROM BNA FAIR EMPLOYMENT PRACTICES CUMULATIVE DIGEST AND INDEX VOLUME

Ind.-Dig.	EDUCATIONAL AND TESTING REQUIREMENTS	►108.1960

►108.1958 High school education

U.S. Courts of Appeals

Employment discrimination action by black job applicant who obtained high school equivalent educational certificate after he was rejected for lack of high school education is moot insofar as he seeks injunction against educational requirement but is not moot insofar as he seeks damages and related relief —Wilson v. State of Nevada [CA 9 (1982)] 27 FEP Cases 1463

U.S. District Courts

Employer's requirement that job applicants have at least high school education did not discriminate against blacks, where employer made exceptions on basis of applicant's work experience or acquisition of educational credentials equivalent to high school education —Broadnax v. Missouri Pacific RR Co. [DC Ark (1978)] 27 FEP Cases 669

Former use of Wonderlic Test and requirement of high school diploma unlawful —Thomas v. Basic Magnesia, Inc. [DC Fla (1975)] 22 FEP Cases 1277

Statistics showing that employer's hiring rate for whites is approximately three times greater than that for Spanish-surnamed job applicants establish prima facie case that employer's high school education requirement has disparate impact on Spanish-surnamed applicants —Aguilera v. Cook County Police & Corrections Merit Bd. [DC Ill (1979)] 21 FEP Cases 731

Employer's admission that it has never performed validation study on its high school diploma requirement, which has disparate impact on Spanish-surnamed job applicants, is fatal to employer on issue of liability —Ibid.

Government reports that indicate that high school and college graduates should be prime candidates for police recruitment and that 70 percent of country's police forces now require high school education do not justify county police and corrections merit board's requirement of high school education —Ibid.

Bank did not violate Title VII by practice of requiring high school diploma for employment, where EEOC has identified no applicant who was rejected because of requirement —American National Bank; EEOC v. [DC Va (1979) on rem from 17:213, see also 13:572] 21 FEP Cases 1532

EEOC

Employer unlawfully refused to hire black job applicant for brakeman's position because he lacked high school diploma — [EEOC No. 77-30 (Aug. 15, 1977)] 21 FEP Cases 1791

Fire department unlawfully disqualified applicants who lacked high school diploma — [EEOC No. 77-42 (Sept. 29, 1977)] 21 FEP Cases 1826

►108.1960 College education; graduate degrees

U.S. Courts of Appeals

Even assuming that black individual established prima facie case of racial discrimination regarding city's rejection of her application to take civil service examination for position of public health program representative because she failed to satisfy college degree requirement, lower court's finding that degree requirement was justified is not erroneous —Rice v. City of St. Louis [CA 8 (1979) aff 19:197] 21 FEP Cases 81

Court properly found that university's reason for failure to reappoint female mathematics instructor – her lack of Ph.D. degree – was not pretextual and that this requirement is business necessity —Campbell v. Ramsay [CA 8 (1980) aff 22:83] 24 FEP Cases 324

Employer established that college degree requirement for position of trade returns supervisor was justified by business necessity, despite absence of validation study, where witnesses testified at length on reasons why degree requirement was job-related and justified by business necessity —Hawkins v. Anheuser-Busch, Inc. [CA 8 (1983) aff, rvs, rem in part 26:454; 28:1070] 30 FEP Cases 1170

Female employee who was denied promotion to position of trade returns supervisor because she lacked college degree has failed to show that employer had valid and less discriminatory alternative selection method, despite claim based on her on-the-job experience, where she had not

> **Step 2**
>
> Note how 108.1958 digests cases dealing with the question whether the requirement of a high school degree amounts to employment discrimination.
>
> Full texts of the digested cases will be found in the volumes of Fair Employment Practices (FEP) cases.
>
> The search must now be brought up to date.
>
> See next illustration.

Female professor who resigned as humanities division chairman and then reapplied for position failed to establish prima facie case of sex discrimination arising from her nonselection, where she was replaced by another woman, and while professor was only candidate with doctorate in humanities, the other candidates held doctorates in other fields and taught in humanities, and search committee properly concluded that lack of humanities doctorate did not render them less qualified —Taylor v. Southern Univ. of New Orleans [DC La (1983)] 30 FEP Cases 1341

[Illustration 88]

PAGE FROM BNA MASTER INDEX LOOSELEAF VOLUME

Supp. CDI	34 FEP	D-II 305

found it necessary for future of department and university that "a Jesuit presence" in university be maintained and that designated areas of teaching be done by competent Jesuit philosophers [Ibid.]

▶ **108.1287** Finding that Army met rebuttal burden by presenting legitimate reasons for selection of non-Puerto Rican employee to be quality assurance specialist is not erroneous, where selecting official testified that he selected non-Puerto Rican employee because of superior administrative experience and skills [CA 10 (1984)] 34 FEP Cases 1144

Finding that Army official acted properly in subjectively concluding that white equipment repair inspector was more qualified than Puerto Rican equipment repair inspector to be quality assurance specialist by virtue of his strong "administrative" credentials, as opposed to Puerto Rican equipment repair inspector's strong "mechanical or technical" credentials, is not erroneous [Ibid.]

any disparate impact from physical training program and post physical performance test is de minimis [Ibid.]

Fact that only one female police recruit failed academy's self-defense course is not dispositive in action against inclusion of self-defense course in recruit's academic average and requirement of passing grade to graduate, since inquiry is whether course is arbitrary and unnecessary employer-created barrier to competition by female recruits [DC RI (1983) vac TRO 34:1287, see also 34:1274] 34 FEP Cases 1290

Ruling striking down key aspects of police academy's physical training program as being discriminatory against women has no bearing on female recruit's claim that self-defense course violates Title VII [Ibid.]

Police academy's required course in self-defense did not have disproportionately adverse impact on women, unfairly deny them opportunity or access, or have significantly discriminatory impact, since

---

Step 3

Digests of later cases are found in the CDI Supplement located in the Master Index volume under Classification number. Note here the case under 108.1958.

Appellate Review Office's recommendation that commander of military reservation find that Puerto Rican employee was subject to discrimination when he was not selected for position at reservation, despite claim that recommendation established that Army's reason for non-selection was pretextual [Ibid.]

▶ **108.1915** Finding that city that hired man rather than woman as health department code enforcement inspector might reasonably regard man's superior educational qualifications as indicating "self-discipline and an ability to complete tasks and follow instructions" is not clearly erroneous, despite claim that educational qualifications were not reasonably related to requirements of position [CA 1 (1984) aff 32:1611] 34 FEP Cases 1130

Woman who satisfied minimum educational requirements for state agency positions for which she applied has standing to challenge these requirements on behalf of herself and other job applicants, despite claim that her Title VII action never accrued because she was excluded from test in 1971 whereas Title VII became applicable to state in 1972, where she was continuously excluded until she graduated, which was two months after Title VII became applicable [CA 5 (1984) aff, rvs in part 31:1795] 34 FEP Cases 1114

Police academy's physical agility requirements have disproportionately adverse impact on women, where women pass preadmission physical test at 55.6 percent of pass rate for men, and other aspects of physical training program are founded on same components as preadmission test and have even greater adverse impact on women [DC RI (1983)] 34 FEP Cases 1274

Fact that all of women who have entered police academy after institution of post physical performance test have graduated does not refute claim of adverse impact on women from academy's physical agility requirements, nor does claim that

not clearly erroneous [CA 5 (1984) aff, rvs in part 31:1795] 34 FEP Cases 1114

▶ **108.1958** Black unsuccessful job applicants established prima facie case of adverse impact from high school and college educational requirements imposed by state agency on job applicants, where requirements barred more blacks than whites from seeking employment with agency, and over 85 percent of jobs requiring educational minimum were held by whites [CA 5 (1984) aff, rvs in part 31:1795] 34 FEP Cases 1114

▶ **108.1960** Black unsuccessful job applicants established prima facie case of adverse impact from high school and college educational requirements imposed by state agency on job applicants, where requirements barred more blacks than whites from seeking employment with agency, and over 85 percent of jobs requiring educational minimum were held by whites [CA 5 (1984) aff, rvs in part 31:1795] 34 FEP Cases 1114

▶ **108.1968** Job-related explanations, which might be appropriate to rebut prima facie showing that test has adverse impact, do not affect question whether prima facie case has been established, and lower court erred when it found no prima facie showing of adverse impact on ground that previous experience of some minority-group candidates explained differences in score distributions [CA 2 (1984) rvs, rem 34:1050] 34 FEP Cases 1065

Evidence that 49 percent of nonminority-group candidates and 25 percent of minority-group candidates passed promotion test established prima facie case of adverse impact against minority-group candidates, since passing rate of minority-group candidates was approximately 50 percent lower than passing rate of nonminority-group candidates [Ibid.]

Lower court's finding that state agency's written test had discriminatory impact on black job applicants is not clearly erroneous, even though finding is based on single six-month period, where

[Illustration 89]

PAGE FROM CCH FOOD, DRUG, COSMETIC LAW REPORTER

FOOD DEFINITIONS
¶ 10,011

"Food" is defined in most state food laws to mean: (1) articles used for food or drink for man or other animals, (2) chewing gum, and (3) articles used for components of any such article.

A few states impose special restrictions on the use of "food additives," "color additives," and "pesticide chemicals" in or on food and define these terms.

Definitions of "food," "food additive," "color additive," and "pesticide chemical" that appear in the basic laws are referred to in the chart below.

State	"Food"	"Food Additive"	"Color Additive"	"Pesticide Chemical"
Ala.	¶ 11,013			
Alas.	¶ 11,624			
Ariz.	¶ 12,011	¶ 12,011	•¶ 12,011	¶ 12,011
Ark.	¶ 12,512			
Cal.	¶ 13,023	¶ 13,024	¶ 13,015	¶ 13,036
Colo.	¶ 13,512	¶ 13,512	¶ 13,512	¶ 13,512
Conn.	¶ 14,012	¶ 14,012	¶ 14,012	¶ 14,012
Del.				
D. (				
Fla.				
Ga.	Several looseleaf services include coverage for state laws. In some, the sections containing the full text of the state laws are preceded by a chart outlining where the laws on a topic may be found for the various states.			
Hav				
Ida.				
Ill.				;9
Ind.		..	..	..)3
Iowa				
Kan.	¶ 19,012	¶ 19,012	¶ 19,012	¶ 19,012
Ky.	¶ 19,512	¶ 19,512	¶ 19,512	¶ 19,512
La.	¶ 20,012			
Me.	¶ 20,542			

¹ Provisions of the Federal Act also are applicable to commerce within the District of Columbia.

SECTION D. SUMMARY

1.   Each service relates to a special subject.

2.   Includes all relevant sources—both primary and secondary.

3.   Frequent reports keep contents up to date.

4.   Contents.

  a.   Text of statutes on the topic, with significant legislative history.

  b.   Text of relevant administrative regulations as published in the *Federal Register* and the *Code of Federal Regulations.*

  c.   Full texts, or digests, of all court or agency decisions on the subject. Some services also provide permanent bound volumes for decisions.

  d.   Tables of cases, statutes, and regulations.

  e.   Indexes to subjects—including indexes to the most current material.

  f.   Some services cover state law, with comparative analysis.

5.   Best place to start research for subjects governed by administrative regulations and rulings.

6.   Some looseleaf services, in whole or in part, are available for online computer searching. Computer-assisted legal research will be discussed in Chapter 20.

Chapter 14

SHEPARD'S CITATIONS

SECTION A. CASE CITATORS

The previous chapters were directed toward enabling one to locate court decisions relevant to a particular point of law. In most instances, this is a preliminary step toward a more concrete goal—a trial or appellate brief has to be written, or an opinion letter composed, or an article authored. Locating cases is undertaken to find rules of law as determined from the reading of the cases, which can then be cited in another document as authority. But before this can be done with any degree of confidence, one further step must be taken. This is to determine that any given case to be relied on as authority is indeed still good authority. The decision must be checked to make certain that it has not been reversed by a higher court, or overruled by a subsequent decision of the same court. This is accomplished by the use of *Shepard's Citations.*

These sets of law books provide a means by which any reported case (cited decision) may be checked to see when and how another court (the citing decision) has cited the first decision. For example, assume the problem under research is whether a judge could issue a search warrant based on information supplied by an anonymous informer. During the course of the research, the case of *People v. Gates*, 82 Ill.App.3d 749, 403 N.E.2d 77 (1980), has been found. Although this case is exactly on point, it cannot be cited yet as authority. One must first determine if this case has been appealed to the Illinois Supreme Court, and if so, if it has been further appealed to the Supreme Court of the United States, and has been either affirmed or reversed. If it was reversed, it is no longer authority and must not be cited as if it were.

Another factor that must be ascertained is whether the Illinois Supreme Court in a subsequent case overruled its decision in the *Gates* case (assuming it had not been reversed). Again, if it did so, the case no longer can be cited as authority.

This is determined by checking in the *Shepard's Illinois Citations* or *Shepard's Northeastern Citations.* As they list every case subsequently decided in which the cited case was mentioned, it can be determined easily if the cited case has been affirmed, reversed, or overruled.

As *Shepard's Citations* presents all citing cases for a cited case, it is evident that its usefulness goes beyond only checking to see if a cited case has been reversed or overruled. The value of a precedent for any given decision also depends to a large extent on the treatment subsequently given to it by courts deciding whether the cited case is in fact applicable to the case under consideration. Whether a cited case has subsequently been followed, distinguished, limited, or questioned may be of vital importance in determining the present value of the cited case as a precedent. Thus, *Shepard's* may be used to determine how a given case has been treated in subsequent decisions.

The court decisions are listed by volume and page in black letter (bold face) type. Under the citation of the case in point subsequent decisions, which have cited the case, are listed by volume and page with letter-form abbreviations indicating the *judicial history* of the case in point and its *treatment* by subsequent decisions. [See Illustrations 94 and 95.]

The *history of the case* is indicated by abbreviations showing whether the case was affirmed, reversed, dismissed, or modified on appeal. Parallel citations of the cited case in the standard reports are also provided. In like manner, the nature of the *treatment of the case* in point in subsequent decisions is indicated by abbreviations. The introductory pages of each *Shepard's Citations* explain the abbreviations used in the volume. [See Illustration 90.]

[Illustration 90]

PAGE OF ABBREVIATIONS—ANALYSIS, SHEPARD'S NORTHEASTERN CITATIONS

ABBREVIATIONS—ANALYSIS

History of Case

a	(affirmed)	Same case affirmed on appeal.
cc	(connected case)	Different case from case cited but arising out of same subject matter or intimately connected therewith.
D	(dismissed)	Appeal from same case dismissed.
m	(modified)	Same case modified on appeal.
r	(reversed)	Same case reversed on appeal.
s	(same case)	Same case as case cited.
S	(superseded)	Substitution for former opinion.
v	(vacated)	Same case vacated.
*	(certiorari)	Certiorari or appeal denied or dismissed.
US cert den		Certiorari denied by U. S. Supreme Court.
US cert dis		Certiorari dismissed by U. S. Supreme Court.
US reh den		Rehearing denied by U. S. Supreme Court.
US reh dis		Rehearing dismissed by U. S. Supreme Court.

Treatment of Case

c	(criticised)	Soundness of decision or reasoning in cited case criticised for reasons given.
d	(distinguished)	Case at bar different either in law or fact from case cited for reasons given.
e	(explained)	Statement of import of decision in cited case. Not merely a restatement of the facts.
f	(followed)	Cited as controlling.
h	(harmonized)	Apparent inconsistency explained and shown not to exist.
j	(dissenting opinion)	Citation in dissenting opinion.
L	(limited)	Refusal to extend decision of cited case beyond precise issues involved.
o	(overruled)	Ruling in cited case expressly overruled.
p	(parallel)	Citing case substantially alike or on all fours with cited case in its law or facts.
q	(questioned)	Soundness of decision or reasoning in cited case questioned.

NOTES

A superior figure appearing immediately to the left of the page number of any citing reference indicates the particular paragraph of the syllabus or particular headnote of the cited case which states the point of law dealt with in the citing case.

Where the reports of more than one case start on the same page of any volume of reports,

A page similar to this may be found in each unit of _Shepards Citations_. It should always be consulted.

There is a separate set of *Shepard's Citations* for every set of court reports. Consequently, there are sets of *Shepard's* for each of the fifty states, the District of Columbia, and Puerto Rico; separate sets for each of the Regional Reporters of the *National Reporter System*; one set for the *Federal Reporter* and the *Federal Supplement*; and one for the reports of the Supreme Court of the United States.

As most court decisions are reported in both official and unofficial sets of court reports, one has to determine which set of *Shepard's* is to be used in *Shepardizing*[1] a case. For example, the case reported in 82 Ill.App.3d 749 is also reported in 403 N.E.2d 77. It can be *Shepardized* in the *Shepard's Illinois Citations* or the *Shepard's Northeastern Citations.* Which one should be selected will be discussed *infra*.

1. Shepard's State and Territorial Citations

These are used in connection with the state reports. As most reported decisions cover more than one point of law, *Shepard's*, through the use of superscript figures, keys each citing case to the headnotes of the cited case. For example, the case of *People v. Gates* as published in the *Illinois Appellate Reports* has four headnotes, each on a different point of law. A citing case may cite *Gates* only for the point of law in its third headnote. *Shepard's* adds the superscript *3* to the citing case. By this means, one can find in the *Shepard's Illinois Citations* all subsequent cases that cited *Gates* for that point of law. [See Illustrations 91 and 93–95.]

The state *Shepard's* gives citing cases only from courts within the jurisdiction or cases that originated in a federal court within the state.

Additionally, a state *Shepard's* gives citations to any legal periodical published in the state (plus 20 national law reviews) that cite the cited cases. It also gives a citation to the reports of the state Attorney General's opinions that cite the cited cases. State *Shepard's* also have a section or a separate volume arranged by the regional reporter citation. By this means, when only a state unit *Shepard's* is available, the case may be *Shepardized* under the state citation, or the regional reporter citation. In both instances, citing cases are given only for the courts within the state.

2. Shepard's Citations for the Regional Reporters

In the example of *People v. Gates*, this case could also be *Shepardized* in *Shepard's Northeastern Citations* under 403 N.E.2d 77. In such instances, that volume has to be examined to determine

---

[1] The term *Shepardizing* is the trademark property of Shepard's/McGraw-Hill, Inc., and is used here with reference to its publications only and with its express consent.

which headnote or headnotes are of interest. In the *Northeastern Reporter*, there are six headnotes, and each can be followed in citing cases in the same manner as described *supra*. In our example, if the *Shepard's Illinois Citations* is used, all of the citing cases given are to cases in the *Illinois Appellate Reports* or the *Illinois Reports* or to federal cases heard in Illinois. In the *Shepard's Northeastern Citations*, all citations to the same cases are to the *Northeastern Reporter* or to the federal cases. The regional *Shepard's*, unlike the state *Shepard's*, also give citations to any case throughout the *National Reporter System*. Thus, if a Texas case cited *People v. Gates*, it can be found in *Shepard's Northeastern Citations* but not in *Shepard's Illinois Citations*. However, the regional *Shepard's* do not give citations to the national law reviews or to Attorney General's opinions. [See Illustrations 92 and 96–98.]

3. Shepard's Citations for Federal Cases

a. *Shepard's United States Citations.* This unit is divided into four separate parts:

(1) *Cases and Statutes.* The Cases volumes consist of main volumes and bound supplements. The main volumes contain citations to the *U.S. Reports* through 1943 and the history and treatment of the cases appear only under the official (U.S.) citations. The *Lawyers' Edition* and the *Supreme Court Reporter* sections only provide parallel references from their citations to the *U.S. Reports*. The cases must then be *Shepardized* under the official citations.

In all volumes after the 1943 volumes, citations to the citing cases are given under both the official set and the two unofficial sets. It should be noted, however, that when *Shepardizing* under either of the two unofficial sets (*S.Ct.Rep.* or *L.Ed.*), citations are given exclusively to cases from the federal courts. When a state court cites a Supreme Court of the United States decision, it is listed only under the U.S. citation. Where there is no single majority opinion in a case, citing cases are listed separately under the name of the justice whose opinion is being cited in the *U.S. Reports* section, with citations to the syllabus of the case listed under the heading "first." In the *Lawyers' Edition* and *Supreme Court Reporter* sections, citations to all parts of these fragmented decisions are listed together.

(2) *Constitutions, Statutes, Treaties and Court Rules.* These volumes *Shepardize* all cases citing the U.S. Constitution, the U.S. Code, the U.S. Treaties Series, and the court rules of the Supreme Court of the United States.

(3) *Administrative.* These volumes show citations to the decisions and orders of selected federal administrative departments, courts, boards, and commissions.

(4) *Patents and Trademarks.* This unit of the *Shepard's United States Citations* is a compilation of citations to U.S. patents, trademarks, and copyrights.

The patents section lists each patent by number and then lists all citations to a patent by a court or administrative agency.

The copyright section lists titles of copyrighted works and lists citations to all court and administrative decisions involving each title.

The trademark section lists all trademarks alphabetically and then lists all citations to court and administrative decisions involving the trademark.

A separate section contains all citations to decisions published in the *United States Patents Quarterly.*

b. *Shepard's Federal Citations.* These volumes *Shepardize* cases reported in the *Federal Reporter* (F., F.2d); *Federal Supplement* (F.Supp.); *Federal Rules Decisions* (F.R.D.); the *United States Court of Claims Reports*; and *Claims Court Reporter.*

SECTION B. OTHER USES FOR SHEPARD'S CITATIONS— CASES

1. Citations to Articles in Legal Periodicals

The state units of *Shepard's Citations,* in addition to indicating every time a cited case has been cited by a citing case, will also indicate when the cited case has been cited in a legal periodical published within the state or in twenty national legal periodicals.[2]

[2] These are:

American Bar Association Journal

California Law Review

Columbia Law Review

Cornell Law Review

Georgetown Law Journal

Harvard Law Review

Law and Contemporary Problems

Michigan Law Review

Minnesota Law Review

New York University Law Review

Northwestern University Law Review

Stanford Law Review

Texas Law Review

University of California at Los Angeles Law Review

University of Chicago Law Review

University of Illinois Law Review

2. A.L.R. Annotations

When *Shepardizing* a case citation, *Shepard's* will indicate when the case has been cited in the body of an *A.L.R.* annotation.

3. Using Shepard's Citations to Find Parallel Citations

In Chapter 5 it was pointed out how, given a state report citation, the *National Reporter System* regional citations could be found through the use of the *National Reporter Blue Book.* *Shepard's* may also be used for this and, additionally, to find the state citation from the regional reporter citation. It always includes the parallel citation as the first citation under the page number the first time the case is listed.[3] When a case has also been reported in *A.L.R.* that is also listed.

4. Shepard's Citations as a Research Aid

Although *Shepard's Citations* are very useful research aids, they should not be stretched beyond their normal function.

The editors' use of the letter-form abbreviations to indicate the treatment of cases is intelligently conservative. The essence of a citing case may go beyond its expressed language. The inclusiveness of a case is not identified by the abbreviations unless its expression is clearly stated in the opinion. Therefore, a case which implicitly overrules a cited case will not be marked with the symbol *o* for *overruled.* This can be determined only by a careful reading of the case. In other words, although these guides immeasurably facilitate a lawyer's research, there are no substitutes for reading and "squeezing the juices" from cases.

In addition, cases dealing with the same subject matter, which do not cite each other, are not covered by *Shepard's Citations.* Or contrariwise, since the *Shepard's* additions are not selective, the citing cases may be so numerous as to create a formidable research problem. A further limitation is that *Shepard's Citations* perpetuate the inaccuracies created by judges who inappropriately cite cases. But these are minor defects which the general utility, comprehensiveness and accuracy of the *Citators* effectively overbalance.

University of Pennsylvania Law Review

Virginia Law Review

Wisconsin Law Review

Yale Law Journal

[3] As cases are frequently reported earlier in the units of the *National Reporter System* than in the official reports, the parallel state citation frequently is not available at the time a citation first appears in a regional *Shepard's*. When a parallel citation is not the first citation under the page number, check the subsequent issues of the *Shepard's Citations* unit being used. If it still does not appear, it is likely that the state citation is from a state which has discontinued its official state reports.

SECTION C. ILLUSTRATIONS: SHEPARD'S CITATIONS: CASES

SHEPARDIZING PEOPLE v. GATES

[Illustration 91]

FIRST PAGE OF PEOPLE v. GATES IN ILLINOIS APPELLATE REPORTS

82 Ill. App. 3d 749	*People v. Gates*	749

First page of People v. Gates as published in the official Illinois Appellate Reports.

wholly disproportionate to respondent's conduct as to shock the moral sense of the community or the consciences of reasonable men. Therefore, we hold that the Act does not violate the eighth amendment prohibition against cruel and unusual punishment.

For all the foregoing reasons, the judgment of the circuit court of Winnebago County is reversed and the cause remanded for a new hearing to be held at the earliest possible date.

Reversed and remanded.

SEIDENFELD, P. J., and LINDBERG, J., concur.

THE PEOPLE OF THE STATE OF ILLINOIS, Plaintiff-Appellant, *v.* LANCE GATES *et al.*, Defendants-Appellees.

Second District   No. 78-570

Judgment affirmed.

Opinion filed April 1, 1980.

1. SEARCHES AND SEIZURES (§17)—*when reliability of informant must be established*. Whenever search warrant is sought on basis of information supplied by anonymous informant, it is necessary that judge or magistrate issuing warrant be provided with sufficient facts and circumstances from which he can determine reliability of informer and accuracy of his present information so that constitutional requirement of probable cause may be satisfied.

2. SEARCHES AND SEIZURES (§17)—*factors considered in testing sufficiency of affidavit supporting complaint for search warrant*. Judge or magistrate testing sufficiency of affidavit filed in support of issuance of search warrant must be informed of some of underlying circumstances from which informant concluded that defendants were involved in criminal activity, and judge must be informed of some of underlying circumstances from which affiant concluded that informer or his information was worthy of belief.

3. SEARCHES AND SEIZURES (§25)—*search warrant properly quashed as affidavit supporting complaint for warrant was insufficient*. Where affidavit

[Illustration 91–a]

SECOND PAGE OF PEOPLE v. GATES IN ILLINOIS APPELLATE REPORTS

| 750 | *People v. Gates* | 82 Ill. App. 3d 749 |

attached to complaint for search warrant did not reveal manner in which anonymous informer obtained his information, and where anonymous letter from informer contained no more than general allegations that defendants were involved in narcotics sales, and where no details regarding defendant's alleged trip to foreign State were set forth in letter, affidavit failed to meet "basis of knowledge" requirement, therefore, search warrant was properly quashed and evidence seized properly suppressed.

    4. SEARCHES AND SEIZURES (§25)—*evidence properly suppressed as affidavit supporting search warrant was insufficient.* Where allegations set forth in handwritten letter supplied by anonymous informant were partially corroborated by other independent sources, "basis of knowledge test" was not satisfied and quashing of search warrant and suppressing of evidence seized pursuant thereto were proper.

    APPEAL from the Circuit Court of Du Page County; the Hon. WILLIAM V. HOPF, Judge, presiding.

    J. Michael Fitzsimmons, State's Attorney, of Wheaton (Robert L. Thompson, Assistant State's Attorney, of counsel), for the People.

    James W. Reilley, of Chicago, for appellees.

    Mr. JUSTICE LINDBERG delivered the opinion of the court:
    The State appeals an order entered by the Circuit Court of Du Page County which quashed a search warrant and suppressed the evidence seized pursuant to the authority of the warrant. At issue is whether the warrant was sufficient under the standards set forth in *Aguilar v. Texas* (1964), 378 U.S. 108, 12 L. Ed. 2d 723, 84 S. Ct. 1509, and *Spinelli v. United States* (1969), 393 U.S. 410, 21 L. Ed. 2d 637, 89 S. Ct. 584. We affirm.
    The facts are straightforward. On May 3, 1978, the Bloomingdale Police Department received a handwritten, anonymous letter which had no return address. The letter recited as follows:
        "This letter is to inform you that you have a couple in your town
        who strictly make their living on selling drugs. They are Sue and
        Lance Gates, they live on Greenway, off Bloomingdale Road, in the
        condominiums. Most of their buys are done in Florida. Sue his wife

---

There are four headnotes for this case in the Illinois Appellate Reports.

Shepard's will show the treatment of a cited case by a citing case by reference to the headnotes.

[Illustration 92]

FIRST PAGE OF PEOPLE v. GATES IN NORTHEASTERN REPORTER

PEOPLE v. GATES   Ill. **77**
Cite as 403 N.E.2d 77

82 Ill.App.3d 749
38 Ill.Dec. 62

PEOPLE of the State of Illinois, Plaintiff-Appellant,

v.

Lance GATES and Susan Gates, Defendants-Appellees.

No. 78–570.

Appellate Court of Illinois,
Second District.

April 1, 1980.

The case of People v. Gates as published in the Northeastern Reporter.

Defendants, who had been indicted on narcotics and firearms charges, filed a motion to quash the arrest and suppress evidence. The Circuit Court, DuPage County, William V. Hopf, J., granted defendants' motion and the State appealed. The Appellate Court, Lindberg, J., held that information supplied by an anonymous informer, contained in the affidavit filed in support of the search warrant, did not contain sufficient detail to allow the issuing judge to reasonably infer that the informer had obtained his information in a reliable way.

Affirmed.

1. Searches and Seizures ⟢3.6(3)

Whenever search warrant is sought on basis of information supplied by anonymous informant, it is necessary that judge or magistrate issuing warrant be provided with sufficient facts and circumstances from which he can determine reliability of informer and accuracy of his present information so that the constitutional requirement of probable cause may be satisfied. U.S.C.A.Const. Amends. 4, 14.

2. Searches and Seizures ⟢3.6(3)

Two-prong *Aguilar* test, to be applied by judge or magistrate in testing sufficiency of affidavit filed in support of issuance of search warrant, is: first, judge must be informed of some of the underlying circumstances from which informant concluded that defendants were involved in criminal activity (the "basis of knowledge" prong);

[Illustration 92–a]

SECOND PAGE OF PEOPLE v. GATES IN NORTHEASTERN REPORTER

78 Ill.　　　　**403 NORTH EASTERN REPORTER, 2d SERIES**

"veracity" prong). U.S.C.A.Const. Amends. 4, 14.

3. Searches and Seizures ⊖3.6(3)

Veracity prong of *Aguilar* test, testing sufficiency of affidavit filed in support of search warrant, may be satisfied by showing either that informant, whose identity need not be disclosed, is "credible" (the "credibility" spur) or that his information is "reliable" (the "reliability" spur). U.S.C.A. Const. Amends. 4, 14.

4. Drugs and Narcotics ⊖188

Where anonymous letter contained no more than general allegations that defendants were involved in narcotics sales, and although anonymous informer did state that defendants would soon drive to Florida and return with load of drugs no details regarding the trip were set forth in letter, the information supplied by the anonymous informer, contained in affidavit filed in support of search warrant, did not contain sufficient detail to allow issuing judge to reasonably infer that informer had obtained his information in a reliable way. U.S.C.A. Const. Amends. 4, 14.

5. Searches and Seizures ⊖3.6(3)

Partial corroboration of anonymous informant's allegations did not provide a "substantial basis" for crediting information supplied by him in that such corroboration did not establish that informer obtained his information in a reliable manner. U.S.C.A.Const. Amends. 4, 14.

6. Searches and Seizures ⊖3.6(3)

Partial corroboration of informant's story may show his information to be "reliable"; however, such corroboration only satisfies veracity prong of *Aguilar* test and does not establish that informer obtained his information in a reliable manner. U.S.C.A.Const. Amends. 4, 14.

J. Michael Fitzsimmons, State's Atty., Robert L. Thompson, Asst. State's Atty., Wheaton, for plaintiff-appellant.

James W. Reilley, Chicago, for defendants-appellees.

LINDBERG, Justice.

> **Note that there are six headnotes, and these differ from those in the Ill.App.Reports.**
>
> Shepard's Northeastern Citations are keyed to these headnotes.

410, 89 S.Ct. 584, 21 L.Ed.2d 637. We affirm.

The facts are straightforward. On May 3, 1978, the Bloomingdale Police Department received a handwritten, anonymous letter which had no return address. The letter recited as follows:

"This letter is to inform you that you have a couple in your town who strictly make their living on selling drugs. They are Sue and Lance Gates, they live on Greenway, off Bloomingdale Road, in the condominiums. Most of their buys are done in Florida. Sue his wife drives their car to Florida, where she leaves it to be loaded up with drugs, than flys [sic] back after she drops the car off in Florida. May 3, she is driving down there again and Lance will be flying down in a few days to drive it back. At the time Lance drives the car back he has the trunk loaded with over $100,000.00 in drugs. Presently they have over $100,000 worth of drugs in their basement.

"They brag about the fact that they never have to work, and make their entire living on pushers.

"I guarentee [sic] if you watch them carefully you will make a big catch. They are friends with some big drug dealers, who visit their house often.

Lance and Sue Gates
Greenway
In Condominiums"

On the same day the letter was received, Detective Charles Mader of the Bloomingdale Police Department made an inquiry to the Secretary of State's Office regarding the driver's license of one Lance Gates. The computer reply stated that an Illinois

[Illustration 93]

TITLE PAGE: SHEPARD'S ILLINOIS CITATIONS

SHEPARD'S
ILLINOIS CITATIONS
CASES

A COMPILATION OF CITATIONS

TO

ILLINOIS CASES REPORTED IN THE VARIOUS SERIES OF ILLINOIS REPORTS AND IN
THE NORTHEASTERN REPORTER

THE CITATIONS

which include affirmances, reversals, dismissals and denials of certiorari by the Illinois Supreme
Court and the United States Supreme Court

APPEAR IN

ILLINOIS SUPREME COURT REPORTS
ILLINOIS APPELLATE COURT REPORTS
ILLINOIS COURT OF CLAIMS REPORTS
ILLINOIS CIRCUIT COURT REPORTS
NORTHEASTERN REPORTER (Illinois
  Cases)
ILLINOIS DECISIONS
UNITED STATES SUPREME COURT
  REPORTS
LAWYERS' EDITION, UNITED STATES
  SUPREME COURT REPORTS
SUPREME COURT REPORTER
FEDERAL CASES
FEDERAL REPORTER
FEDERAL SUPPLEMENT
FEDERAL RULES DECISIONS
BANKRUPTCY REPORTER
ILLINOIS LAW REVIEW
NORTHWESTERN UNIVERSITY LAW
  REVIEW
UNIVERSITY OF CHICAGO LAW REVIEW
UNIVERSITY OF ILLINOIS LAW FORUM
UNIVERSITY OF ILLINOIS LAW REVIEW
CHICAGO-KENT LAW REVIEW
ILLINOIS BAR JOURNAL
ILLINOIS LAW BULLETIN
ILLINOIS LAW QUARTERLY

DE PAUL LAW REVIEW
JOHN MARSHALL JOURNAL OF
  PRACTICE AND PROCEDURE
JOHN MARSHALL LAW REVIEW
LOYOLA UNIVERSITY OF CHICAGO
  LAW REVIEW
CALIFORNIA LAW REVIEW
COLUMBIA LAW REVIEW
CORNELL LAW QUARTERLY
CORNELL LAW REVIEW
GEORGETOWN LAW JOURNAL
HARVARD LAW REVIEW
LAW AND CONTEMPORARY PROBLEMS
MICHIGAN LAW REVIEW
MINNESOTA LAW REVIEW
NEW YORK UNIVERSITY LAW REVIEW
STANFORD LAW REVIEW
TEXAS LAW REVIEW
UNIVERSITY OF CALIFORNIA AT LOS
  ANGELES LAW REVIEW
UNIVERSITY OF PENNSYLVANIA LAW
  REVIEW
VIRGINIA LAW REVIEW
WISCONSIN LAW REVIEW
YALE LAW JOURNAL
AMERICAN BAR ASSOCIATION JOURNAL

and in annotations of

LAWYERS' EDITION, UNITED STATES SUPREME COURT REPORTS
AMERICAN LAW REPORTS

also, for Illinois cases reported prior to the Northeastern Reporter or prior to their inclusion
in the Northeastern Reporter as cited in all units of the National Reporter System and in Vols.
1–19 Ohio Appellate Reports and Vols. 1–101 Pennsylvania Superior Court Reports

FIFTH EDITION - - - - - Supplement 1966–1984 to Case Edition Part 2, 1966

SHEPARD'S/McGRAW-HILL
COLORADO SPRINGS
COLORADO 80901

[Illustration 94]

PAGE FROM SHEPARD'S ILLINOIS CITATIONS: CASE EDITION

ILLINOIS APPELLATE COURT REPORTS, 3d SERIES								Vol. 82
109IIA⁴973	95IIA²138	cc82IIA490	– 749 –	106IIA¹416	– 863° –	– 937° –	– 990 –	
56Æ1207s	99IIA²290	108IIA¹167	(403NE77)		(403NE475)	(403NE604)	(403NE622)	
1Æ382s	99IIA299		(38IID62)	– 802° –	(38IID244)	(38IID373)	(38IID391)	
	100IIA¹671		a85II2d376	(403NE301)	94IIA716	90IIA¹420	96IIA¹218	
– 578 –	101IIA⁴932	(402NE932)	s454US1140	(38IID213)	100IIA¹928	f107IIA¹1086	98IIA¹959	
(402NE910)	j106IIA1065	(37IID930)	s455US986		107IIA¹463	j107IIA1089	99IIA655	
(37IID908)	107IIA⁴854	s86II2d441	s71LE291	– 807° –				
a85II2d326	107IIA1096		s71LE845	(403NE102)	– 868° –	– 941 –	– 995 –	
	108IIA596	– 689° –	s73LE1398	(38IID87)	(403NE478)	(403NE599)	(403NE631)	
– 581 –	68IBJ702	(402NE915)	s74LE595	105IIA²731	(38IID247)	(38IID368)	(38IID400)	
(402NE912)	69IBJ163	(37IID913)	s75LE426		95IIA⁴440			
(37IID910)	70IBJ629	US cert den	s75LE478	– 814° –	103IIA350	– 949 –	– 1000 –	
	3Æ1170s	in450US915	s102SC997	(403NE287)	30Æ39s	(403NE610)	(403NE678)	
– 586° –		US reh den	s102SC1607	(38IID199)	7Æ336n	(38IID379)	(38IID447)	
(403NE43)	– 630 –	in	f86IIA³561	107IIA²1015		90IIA⁴1148	d92IIA³776	
(38IID28)	(402NE854)	f83II2d129	95IIA²499	108IIA³1041	– 877° –	c99IIA¹74	110IIA²263	
	(37IID852)	87IIA⁹722	97IIA⁴1112		(403NE486)	c99IIA⁷75	110IIA²263	
– 590 –	95IIA¹506	92IIA²1058		– 820° –	(38IID255)			

> This illustration is from the bound 1966–1984 Supplement to the Cases volume of Shepard's Illinois Citations.
>
> Note how the first two citations in parenthesis under 82 Ill.App.3d 749 (the People v. Gates case) are to cases in other sets of court reports.
>
> Note also how this case was appealed to the Illinois Supreme Court which affirmed.
>
> Does this mean that this case may now be cited as good authority? See next illustration.
>
> Also note how the case reported at 86 Ill.App. at page 561 followed the point of law set forth at the third headnote the Gates case.

– 604° –	d108IIA	a86II2d78	99IIA1037		– 839° –	– 906 –	95IIA⁵573	– 1015 –
(403NE57)	[¹⁰1020	87IIA¹722	d99IIA¹1038	(403NE305)	(403NE570)	96IIA⁸501	(403NE694)	
(38IID42)	31Æ1078s		d99IIA⁸1038	(38IID217)	(38IID339)	97IIA³349	(38IID463)	
86IIA¹765		– 710 –	j99IIA1041	US cert den	87IIA983	97IIA⁴990	cc93IIA582	
93IIA⁸750	– 652° –	(403NE33)	f102IIA⁸711	in450US966	102IIA657		f94IIA66	
	(402NE862)	(38IID18)	105IIA1030	cc105IIA175	102IIA⁷657	– 975° –	95IIA⁴506	
– 610 –	(37IID860)		113IIA⁷147	57Æ302s	103IIA537	(403NE662)	101IIA⁴1106	
(402NE847)	f85IIA¹³1136	– 714 –	87Æ624s	34Æ16s	54Æ3612s	(38IID431)	107IIA556	
(37IID845)	89IIA252	(403NE114)				d89II2d296	39Æ840s	
89IIA¹770	90IIA⁸935	(38IID99)	– 781 –	– 916 –	86IIA¹635		
91IIA⁴385	97IIA¹1076	108IIA642	(403NE129)	(403NE583)	d93IIA⁵570	– 1018 –	
103IIA1082	100IIA⁸269	43Æ1128s	(38IID114)	(38IID352)	d93IIA⁵570	(403NE696)	
108IIA295	j102IIA741		90IIA¹979	– 847 –	f110IIA58	(38IID465)	
	6Æ47n	– 719° –	91IIA767	(403NE282)		97IIA²7741	
– 617° –		(403NE90)	e95IIA²884	(38IID194)	– 981 –	110IIA²246	
(402NE831)	– 662° –	(38IID75)	95IIA¹1069	– 922 –	(403NE671)		
(37IID829)	(403NE1)	95Æ3280s	100IIA600	(403NE587)	(38IID440)	– 1024 –	
US cert den	(37IID945)		103IIA1146	(38IID356)		(403NE700)	
in456US905	93IIA⁸772	– 727 –	104IIA188	89IIA¹19	– 984° –	(38IID469)	
US reh den	94IIA¹³606	(403NE108)	104IIA²1127	90IIA589	(412NE554)	f24BRW¹929	
in456US965	95IIA710	(38IID93)	106IIA909	d110IIA¹289	(45IID203)	34Æ1335s	
m87II2d174	98IIA¹³250	s76II2d481	109IIA1062		s71II2d610		
85II2d⁷220	99IIA⁸39	s52IIA442	57Æ302s	– 856° –	d106IIA⁸1091	– 1028 –	
84IIA⁸820	105IIA¹⁴730		6Æ1226n	(403NE470)	s57IIA677	(403NE725)	
d84IIA⁸935	106IIA¹¹1054	– 736 –	7Æ218n	(38IID239)	96IIA²456	(38IID494)	
85IIA⁸781	106IIA¹²1054	(403NE68)	12Æ364n	97IIA⁴352	105IIA¹838	j94II2d274	
f86IIA⁸87	106IIA¹³1054	(38IID53)		100IIA⁴563	96Æ2768s	90IIA⁸526	
87IIA⁴172	107IIA557	34Æ3652s	– 789 –	100IIA⁸809		95IIA⁴600	
87IIA⁸175	110IIA107		(403NE135)	104IIA⁴318	– 987 –		
87IIA²596	17Æ31010s	– 742 –	(38IID120)	104IIA⁸320	(403NE615)	– 1034° –	
89IIA⁴310		(403NE72)	cc58IIA915	105IIA⁴449	(38IID364)	(403NE503)	
89IIA²669	– 681 –	(38IID57)		34Æ1166s	95IIA²25	(38IID272)	
89IIA²968	(402NE440)	82IIA⁷740	– 793° –	35Æ758s	f106IIA²61	85IIA¹808	
90IIA¹³678	(37IID550)	96Æ840s	(403NE83)		40Æ3646s	89IIA¹246	
95IIA⁷10	s66II2d478		(38IID68)			101IIA24	
						101IIA¹929	

°Certiorari or Appeal Denied or Dismissed   459

[Illustration 95]

PAGE FROM SHEPARD'S ILLINOIS CITATIONS: CUMULATIVE SUPPLEMENT

Vol. 81   ILLINOIS APPELLATE COURT REPORTS, 3d SERIES

– 588 – 118II$\mathbf{R}^2$130	– 798 – f125II$\mathbf{R}^4$186	– 1020 – f126II$\mathbf{R}^1$807	– 77 – 121II$\mathbf{R}^1$960	– 297 – d118II$\mathbf{R}^2$1073 120II$\mathbf{R}^4$875	– 569 – 114II$\mathbf{R}^2$129 121II$\mathbf{R}$914	– 763 – 121II$\mathbf{R}^3$888 121II$\mathbf{R}^1$889	123II$\mathbf{R}^1$319 50$\mathbb{A}$3144s
– 596 – 18$\mathbb{A}$5379n 18$\mathbb{A}$5435n	– 808 – d114II$\mathbf{R}^1$437 115II$\mathbf{R}^8$838 116II$\mathbf{R}^3$239	– 1025 – 99$\mathbb{A}$3322s	– 83 – d719F2d [^{2}1330 564FS^{1}979	126II$\mathbf{R}^4$347 d126II$\mathbf{R}^4$348	– 574 – 122II$\mathbf{R}^4$217 125II$\mathbf{R}$56	– 767 – 115II$\mathbf{R}$463	– 963 – 732F2d^{8}89 100$\mathbb{A}$3850s
– 607 – 118II$\mathbf{R}^2$848	116II$\mathbf{R}^2$336 117II$\mathbf{R}^1$596 121II$\mathbf{R}^7$892	– 1031 – 122II$\mathbf{R}^1$1062 124II$\mathbf{R}$308 125II$\mathbf{R}^1$352 15$\mathbb{A}$3899s	– 312 – 32DeP335 16JMR482	– 312 – 98II2d^{4}316 114II$\mathbf{R}^1$692 117II$\mathbf{R}^4$536	– 581 – 711BJ416 59$\mathbb{A}$3152s	– 807 – 125II$\mathbf{R}^2$271	– 968 – cc727F2d656 cc562FS140 65$\mathbb{A}$3705s 2$\mathbb{A}$527s
– 626 – 120II$\mathbf{R}^2$77 121II$\mathbf{R}^2$204 121II$\mathbf{R}^2$207 18$\mathbb{A}$5445n	– 818 – 123II$\mathbf{R}^1$200 719F2d^{8}1331 582FS^{8}549	– 93 – 26$\mathbb{A}$5862n 26$\mathbb{A}$5873n	– 93 – 55$\mathbb{A}$3651s	d121II$\mathbf{R}^7$58 125II$\mathbf{R}^9$1080 125II$\mathbf{R}^7$1080 14$\mathbb{A}$3723s	– 602 – 123II$\mathbf{R}$145	– 814 – 121II$\mathbf{R}^5$5 61$\mathbb{A}$31150s	– 987 – 114II$\mathbf{R}^1$838 121II$\mathbf{R}^1$428
– 641 – 120II$\mathbf{R}$88 6$\mathbb{A}$3604s	– 825 – 117II$\mathbf{R}^1$1081	– 1050 – 115II$\mathbf{R}^3$642 126II$\mathbf{R}^1$781	– 98 – 571FS^{4}1015	– 323 – 115II$\mathbf{R}$682 120II$\mathbf{R}^4$817 120II$\mathbf{R}^3$817	– 610 – 116II$\mathbf{R}^8$26 f120II$\mathbf{R}^3$548	– 832 – 126II$\mathbf{R}^2$415	– 835 – 117II$\mathbf{R}^1$231 d117II$\mathbf{R}^3$294
122II$\mathbf{R}^4$855 126II$\mathbf{R}^1$381	– 838 – 116II$\mathbf{R}^1$182 118II$\mathbf{R}^2$318	– 1067 – 120II$\mathbf{R}^5$504 120II$\mathbf{R}^5$594	– 104 – 6$\mathbb{A}$31197s	– 123 – 717F2d398 567FS^{1}912	126II$\mathbf{R}^1$811 72IBJ626 84$\mathbb{A}$3555s	– 617 – 123II$\mathbf{R}$715 711BJ220	– 847 – 120II$\mathbf{R}^3$526
– 653 – 59CK139 22$\mathbb{A}$51178n	– 843 – 124II$\mathbf{R}^4$742	– 1078 – 114II$\mathbf{R}^9$724 117II$\mathbf{R}$425 121II$\mathbf{R}$728	– 129 – 114II$\mathbf{R}^9$852 115II$\mathbf{R}^1$528	– 328 – 115II$\mathbf{R}$510 115II$\mathbf{R}^4$513	– 639 – e121II$\mathbf{R}^{10}$871 123II$\mathbf{R}^{10}$504	– 856 – 121II$\mathbf{R}$180 122II$\mathbf{R}$523	– 990 – 115II$\mathbf{R}^1$958 116II$\mathbf{R}^1$1015 119II$\mathbf{R}^1$200 734F2d^{1}1270
– 672 – 122II$\mathbf{R}$355 711BJ106 711BJ220 10$\mathbb{A}$3280s 24$\mathbb{A}$5461n	– 866 – d117II$\mathbf{R}^1$80	j122II$\mathbf{R}$434 – 1090 – 125II$\mathbf{R}^1$253	115II$\mathbf{R}^1$840 117II$\mathbf{R}^{10}$30 117II$\mathbf{R}^9$975 16$\mathbb{A}$5362n 16$\mathbb{A}$5378n	115II$\mathbf{R}^4$513 – 338 – 114II$\mathbf{R}^9$912	124II$\mathbf{R}^{10}$155 125II$\mathbf{R}^8$897 2$\mathbb{A}$51173s	– 877 – 117II$\mathbf{R}^1$924	– 1000 – 26$\mathbb{A}$5519n – 1003 – 120II$\mathbf{R}^1$1003 729F2d^{1}1134
– 690 – e102II2d77 115II$\mathbf{R}$599 e115II$\mathbf{R}$599 115II$\mathbf{R}^7$1051 65$\mathbb{A}$3854s	– 894 – 114II$\mathbf{R}^9$1066 118II$\mathbf{R}^9$772 121II$\mathbf{R}^9$39 122II$\mathbf{R}^7$569 56$\mathbb{A}$3300s	– 1102 – 114II – 1 116II 116II 124II 53$\mathbb{A}$ 21$\mathbb{A}$3	– 350 –	– 652 –		– 884 – 99II2d348	

When using Shepard's Citations, one must always be sure to check not only in the bound volumes but also the latest pamphlet supplement or supplements. Here we find that when we check in the latest cumulative paper supplement that the Gates case has been appealed to the Supreme Court of the United States which reversed. Thus, the case in 82 Ill. App.3d 749 cannot be cited as authority!

– 708 – 26$\mathbb{A}$5539n	– 910 – 123II$\mathbf{R}^2$542	– 1 126I				71IBJ534 81McL117	116II$\mathbf{R}^1$175 118II$\mathbf{R}^4$128
– 717 – 115II$\mathbf{R}^2$695 LLP§2.08	– 932 – 67$\mathbb{A}$3442s	– 1 4$\mathbb{A}$				– 937 – 	– 1050 – f564FS^{1}1463 80$\mathbb{A}$2368s
– 729 – 24$\mathbb{A}$5915n	– 944 – 51$\mathbb{A}$38s 96$\mathbb{A}$322s	– 1 f116I 117I				– 949 – 	
– 738 – 17$\mathbb{A}$565n 18$\mathbb{A}$5446n	– 952 – 115II$\mathbf{R}$895 116II$\mathbf{R}^3$1036						
– 759 – 711BJ665 14LoyC452	– 962 – 53$\mathbb{A}$3605s	Vc					
– 764 – 101II2d493 122II$\mathbf{R}$551 125II$\mathbf{R}$158 2$\mathbb{A}$527s	– 966 – 124II$\mathbf{R}^3$167 – 990 – 2$\mathbb{A}$5807s 18$\mathbb{A}$5380n 18$\mathbb{A}$5480n	115I 118I d76L d76L d76L$\mathbf{E}^3$684 d103SC^{1}2480 d103SC^{2}2480 d103SC^{3}2480 713F2d686	– 225 – 7$\mathbb{A}$38s	118II$\mathbf{R}^1$724 f191II$\mathbf{R}^1$130 – 494 – 99II2d^{3}331 46$\mathbb{A}$31393s	– 749 – US reh den in104SC33 r76L$\mathbf{E}$527 r103SC2317 s458US1127	71IBJ534 81McL117 – 937 – f110II$\mathbf{R}^1$12	116II$\mathbf{R}^1$175 118II$\mathbf{R}^4$128
– 776 – 711BJ665 14LoyC474	– 1001 – 16$\mathbb{A}$5827n 16$\mathbb{A}$5859n	– 18 – 116II$\mathbf{R}^2$23	– 252 – 115II$\mathbf{R}^1$270 116II$\mathbf{R}^4$831 117II$\mathbf{R}^2$1036 123II$\mathbf{R}$961	– 516 – 117II$\mathbf{R}^4$803	s459US1028 s459US1194 s460US1009 s103SC10	– 949 – 116II$\mathbf{R}^1$800 118II$\mathbf{R}$760 36BRW^{8}708	– 1054 – 121II$\mathbf{R}^4$321 121II$\mathbf{R}^1$1063 31DeP383
– 784 – 734F2d1269 583FS^{4}256 1COA205§26	– 1005 – 116II$\mathbf{R}^4$296	– 25 – 1$\mathbb{A}$3123s 59$\mathbb{A}$3152s	– 283 – 20$\mathbb{A}$592n	– 530 – 14LoyC701 17$\mathbb{A}$51018n 20$\mathbb{A}$5828n 20$\mathbb{A}$5835n	s103SC436 s103SC1174 s103SC1248	– 956 – 99II2d21 115II$\mathbf{R}^2$37 117II$\mathbf{R}$545 119II$\mathbf{R}^8$443 d119II$\mathbf{R}^3$445	99$\mathbb{A}$3671s 23$\mathbb{A}$51160n 23$\mathbb{A}$51180n
– 794 – 118II$\mathbf{R}$971	– 1012 – 117II$\mathbf{R}^1$366 d121II$\mathbf{R}$498	– 32 – 61$\mathbb{A}$3520s 61$\mathbb{A}$3657s	– 286 – 115II$\mathbf{R}^3$750 115II$\mathbf{R}^3$793 117II$\mathbf{R}^2$632				

114

[Illustration 96]

PAGE FROM SHEPARD'S NORTHEASTERN CITATIONS: ANNUAL CUMULATIVE SUPPLEMENT

Vol. 402		NORTHEASTERN REPORTER, 2d SERIES						
431S2d62	– 1168 –	– 1171 –	– 1192 –	– 1267 –	– 1365 –	cc397NE905	– 142 –	
432S2d157	Case 2	Case 2	(62@S50)	414NE³320	407NE358	f411NE¹1232	US cert den	
433S2d447	(49NY725)	(49NY741)	(16Op3d38)	422NE²703	420NE¹º34	j411NE1234	in449US880	
434S2d65	(426S2d267)	(426S2d270)	e416NE⁴619			412NE¹647		
436S2d829	s392S2d836	s354S2d430		– 1276 –	– 1372 –		– 150 –	
442S2d13	s410S2d679	s411S2d243	– 1196 –	f409NE²697	409NE1343	– 68 –	(49NY429)	
j442S2d13	Nebr	406NE804	(62@S55)	j409NE699	409NE1350	(82IIA736)	(426S2d444)	
	295NW698	428S2d949	(16Op3d41)	411NE¹678	411NE1330	(38IID53)	s411S2d674	
– 1155 –	100A31047n			d425NE¹662	417NE957			
(49NY417)		– 1171 –	– 1201 –	c425NE²667		– 72 –	– 158 –	
(426S2d253)	– 1168 –	Case 3	(62@S62)		**Vol. 403**	(82IIA742)	(49NY446)	
s405S2d127	Case 3	(49NY742)	(16Op3d45)	– 1279 –		(38IID57)	(426S2d452)	
s432S2d852	(49NY729)	(426S2d270)		v420NE1221		.403NE¹71	s415S2d20	
cc364NE1350	(426S2d267)	s414S2d757	– 1203 –		– 1° –			
cc392S2d710	s410S2d312	429S2d243	(62@A1)	– 1284 –	(82IIA662)	– 77 –	– 159 –	
cc396S2d1033			(16Op3d27)	s393NE773	(37IID945)	(82IIA749)	(49NY451)	
409NE840	– 1168 –	– 1171 –		409NE1172	417NE³823	(38IID62)	(426S2d454)	
409NE²926	Case 4	Case 4	– 1211 –	412NE³¹266	418NE⁷998	a423NE887	s426S2d454	
415NE²962	(49NY734)	(49NY744)	419NE¹755		419NE¹³612	f407NE⁴1113	403NE⁸961	
427S2d121	(426S2d267)	(426S2d270)	420NE¹881	– 1285 –	423NE²º1176	420NE²261	414NE⁸391	
427S2d231	s413S2d166	s416S2d860		416NE⁸160	424NE⁸¹296	424NE⁸538	j414NE680	
427S2d910			– 1213 –	422NE³1296			416NE⁴1024	
430S2d562	– 1169 –	– 1172 –	424NE⁸1164		– 169 –	– 82° –	E³¹027	

> **Shepardizing the People v. Gates case in the Shepard's Northeastern Citations. Note the parallel citations and how citations to all citing cases are to the Northeastern Reporter.**

	(426S2d268)	(426S2d271)	US cert den		(38IID15)	(82IIA/96)	d426S2d994	E²671
	s416S2d160	s417S2d307	in449US866	– 1309 –	422NE²951	(38IID80)	j429S2d301	E²356
(49NY720)				f413NE¹563		410NE⁸1050	c430S2d236	JE887
(426S2d259)	– 1169 –	– 1172 –	– 1235 –	419NE¹⁶981	– 33 –		c430S2d237	2d977
s409S2d746	Case 3	Case 3	s406NE641	425NE¹²166	(82IIA710)	– 99 –	430S2d702	2d363
427S2d28	(49NY737)	(49NY750)	424NE³¹087		(38IID18)	(82IIA763)	431S2d603	2d469
	(426S2d268)	(426S2d271)	Tex	– 1324 –		(38IID84)	431S2d908	2d993
– 1162 –	s420S2d243	s409S2d808	618SW360	404NE⁵690	– 36° –		j432S2d384	
(49NY723)		cc401NE410		420NE⁸295	(82IIA505)	– 102° –	432S2d642	
(426S2d261)	– 1169 –	cc425S2d300	– 1239 –		(38IID21)	(82IIA807)	432S2d802	
s412S2d504	Case 4	431S2d891	406NE⁴643	– 1329 –		(38IID87)	e433S2d373	
441S2d617	(49NY737)	442S2d243	406NE1229	402NE³1381	– 43° –		433S2d940	
	(426S2d268)		408NE¹525	402NE⁴1392	(82IIA586)	– 108 –	433S2d¹1010	
– 1163 –		– 1173 –	408NE⁸1265	403NE427	(38IID28)	(82IIA727)	j434S2d180	
(49NY726)	– 1170 –	(49NY752)	408NE⁸1283	403NE¹⁴933	Fla	(38IID93)	434S2d615	
(426S2d262)	Case 1	(426S2d272)	409NE1087	408NE⁷890	399So2d423	s367NE516	434S2d822	
s407S2d826	(49NY738)	s412S2d440	412NE¹739	413NE¹⁷761		s394NE403	435S2d165	
s408S2d793	(426S2d269)		412NE¹769	415NE¹⁷225	– 46 –		435S2d224	
s431S2d989	s422S2d249	– 1175 –	412NE⁴1196	416NE¹516	(82IIA590)	– 114 –	e435S2d421	
405NE¹185		(61@S335)	414NE⁹60	418NE²¹1273	(38IID31)	(82IIA716)	435S2d422	
427S2d¹941	– 1170 –	(15Op3d426)	422NE⁸1183	418NE¹⁶1278		(38IID99)	435S2d⁴688	
623F2d¹201	Case 2		424NE⁸1070	419NE¹⁷1381	– 48 –		435S2d²692	
623F2d¹210	(49NY738)	– 1178 –	425NE⁸674	420NE¹334	(82IIA593)	– 118 –	436S2d382	
	(426S2d269)	(61@S339)		421NE⁸102	(38IID33)	(82IIA767)	437S2d³78	
– 1164 –		(15Op3d428)	– 1244 –	421NE¹⁸765		(38IID103)	440S2d³591	
(49NY730)	US reh den		403NE⁵913	424NE²²501	– 50 –	US cert den	j440S2d593	
(426S2d263)	in448US908	– 1181 –	415NE⁷55	424NE506	(82IIA596)	in449US1101	440S2d³628	
s411S2d543	s446US949	(61@S345)	418NE⁸1157	425NE¹⁷281	(38IID35)	410NE125	f440S2d³879	
	s64LE805	(15Op3d432)		425NE¹⁷290	420NE⁷1102	f411NE⁴135	c441S2d198	
– 1165 –	s100SC2913		– 1248 –	j425NE312		414NE¹286	j441S2d674	
(49NY732)		– 1185 –	408NE⁸¹242	425NE¹387	– 56° –	d418NE¹º964	442S2d171	
(426S2d263)	– 1170 –	(61@S356)	409NE⁴632		(82IIA602)		e442S2d499	
s399S2d795	Case 3	(15Op3d438)	409NE⁴640	– 1346 –	(38IID41)	– 129 –	442S2d658	
	(49NY738)		425NE¹133	420NE²925	422NE⁸1105	(82IIA781)	494FS³1358	
– 1166 –	(426S2d269)	– 1187 –		e421NE⁸¹186		(38IID114)	494FS⁴1358	
(49NY749)		(62@S43)	– 1252 –	e422NE¹²459	– 57° –	414NE⁸¹113	494FS⁵1358	
(426S2d265)	– 1171 –	(16Op3d34)	s389NE723		(82IIA604)	415NE³635		
s420S2d894	Case 1		s393NE208	– 1356 –	(38IID42)	415NE⁵635	– 167 –	
s441S2d969	(49NY739)	– 1189 –		s388NE666	408NE¹485	e420NE⁸861	(49NY465)	
	(426S2d270)	(62@S45)	– 1263 –	cc424NE194	417NE²882	420NE¹877	(426S2d461)	
– 1168 –		D66LE5	406NE1228	411NE469			408NE¹902	
Case 1	D449US801	(16Op3d35)						

[Illustration 97]

PAGE FROM SHEPARD'S NORTHEASTERN CITATIONS: PAMPHLET SUPPLEMENT

Vol. 402 NORTHEASTERN REPORTER, 2d SERIES

– 1285 –
436NE332
545FS[5]243

– 1291 –
440NE[1]511
78A2594s
46A3240s

– 1295 –
434NE[8]597
436NE[13]122
437NE[3]1016
439NE229
446NE[12]15
446NE[3]993
447NE[12]1109
450NE[5]1026
451NE[2]369
452NE[7]417
456NE[7]1071
65A212s
3A3180s

– 1301 –
427NE[7]16
427NE[9]16

– 1309 –
430NE[16]804
432NE[14]424
439NE[14]224
59A21328s
21A3603s
62A3560s

– 1324 –
(380Mas277)
438NE[4]829
445NE1073

– 1329 –
(380Mas220)
426NE[17]1162
428NE[5]834
429NE[1]376
429NE[5]377
433NE[21]457
433NE[22]457
433NE[3]1243
436NE[4]420
437NE[17]1069
443NE1284
444NE[21]1279
444NE[18]1318
d444NE[21]1318
447NE[17]2
447NE[3]1221
448NE[1]403
448NE[21]1139
455NE[20]635
456NE[17]477
2A427s

– 1340 –
(380Mas235)
f440NE[1]1160
f452NE[1]213

– 1346 –
(380Mas246)
d439NE[5]792
448NE[6]379
448NE[7]379
453NE[13]402

531FS[7]1081
531FS[11]1081
531FS[5]1083
AgD§13.27

– 1356 –
(380Mas263)
5A4736n

– 1365 –
(380Mas285)
433NE[11]1265
435NE[10]657
8A2196s

– 1372 –
(9MaA512)
433NE[1]474
436NE[2]408
439NE[1]759
441NE[1]543
441NE[1]561
442NE33

– 1385 –
(9MaA534)
447NE[5]674
ICD§2.24

– 1392 –
(9MaA892)

Vol. 403

– 1 –
434NE[21]792
436NE[19]652
436NE[20]652
437NE882
441NE1176
17A31010s

– 16 –
US cert den
in450US927
428NE[10]905
450NE772
e450NE773
451NE[15]1014
Ala
440So2d1164

– 30 –
23A3932s

– 33 –
448NE560

– 36 –
427NE[3]86
427NE[3]1351

– 43 –
Fla
425So2d1387

– 46 –
438NE1378
438NE[1]1378

– 50 –
428NE[4]687
443NE1179

– 56 –
54ARF495n

– 62 –
US cert den
in454US845

– 68 –
34A3652s

– 72 –
j452NE381
96A3840s

– 77 –
US reh den
in104SC33
r76LE527
r103SC2317
s454US1140
s455US986
s458US1127
s71LE291
s71LE845
s73LE1398
s74LE595
s75LE426
s75LE478
s102SC997
s102SC1607
s103SC10
s103SC436
s103SC1174
s103SC1248
NY
458S2d471

– 83 –
435NE[1]1280

– 90 –
95A3280s

– 95 –
435NE[3]1325
7A4284n

– 102 –
434NE[2]792

– 108 –
454NE[9]759
6A3438s

– 114 –
439NE[4]518
W Va
289SE193
43A21128s

– 118 –
US reh den
in450US989
s435NE226
426NE286
d426NE[9]287
d426NE[12]287
j426NE289
f429NE[9]1328
446NE[11]1233
450NE[6]955
87A2624s

– 129 –
426NE[8]1236
432NE[10]361

432NE1132
433NE[6]1095
436NE[5]743
441NE921
57A2302s
6A41226n
7A4218n
12A4364n

– 142 –
(9MaA892)

– 143 –

– 158 –
456S2d388
52A2437s

– 159 –
j432NE782
e433NE[1]129
433NE1278
441NE[5]1072
443NE944
j447NE715
449NE[4]709
449NE[3]724
449NE[3]1259
449NE[4]1259
453NE[3]544
453NE[4]1082
446S2d58
446S2d466
446S2d690
447S2d71
j447S2d910
e448S2d[1]146
d448S2d909
j448S2d910
449S2d30
450S2d649
450S2d681
f451S2d854
452S2d734
453S2d941
454S2d202
454S2d348
454S2d962
455S2d[5]554
456S2d634
457S2d470
459S2d969
j460S2d772
461S2d198
462S2d670
462S2d[4]815
462S2d[3]830
462S2d943
463S2d112
463S2d[3]181
463S2d[4]181
465S2d307
465S2d522
466S2d142
e466S2d165

466S2d[3]315
466S2d[4]665
466S2d824
466S2d853
467S2d470
467S2d763
469S2d159

– 167 –
430NE[2]883
447NE[1]1278
447NE[2]1278
448NE384

457S2d[3]769
466S2d417

– 170 –
433NE[2]512
446S2d466
448S2d51
448S2d[2]447
450S2d685
j455S2d362
457S2d65
459S2d102
465S2d65

– 178 –
455S2d991

– 179 –
466S2d419

– 182 –
445S2d252
j468S2d893

– 186 –
Case 3
6A4818n

– 189 –
NJ
462A2d173

– 191 –
(15A41153)
j438NE443
e456NE[1]589

– 202 –
456NE1327
63A21393s
79A21028s
88A31008s
90A3775s

– 221 –
427NE[1]144
429NE[6]483
429NE[3]866
431NE[3]370
431NE[4]370
431NE[5]370
433NE[6]680
442NE[2]502

– 225 –
438NE464
446NE259
449NE136
451NE927
456NE120

– 229 –
426NE[4]1137
427NE[4]63
j428NE1194
429NE[1]1291
427NE4806

– 237 –
f432NE[5]322
457NE21
Ariz
660P2d470

– 242 –
j432NE250
453NE944
456NE17
Ind
428NE[6]224
428NE[1]225

– 255 –
454NE269

– 258 –
d449NE1379
457NE[2]15

– 263 –
442NE908

– 266 –
427NE[11]297
435NE[1]218
18A21255s

– 277 –
d435NE851

– 282 –
Vt
439A2d280

– 287 –
438NE[1]543
439NE[2]1276
Ind
427NE[2]1111
Utah
656P2d402
61A31150s

– 291 –
440NE176

– 294 –
d452NE[2]1368
453NE[5]65

Tex
642SW24
17A31010s

– 297 –
d442NE[1]296

– 301 –
Nebr
326NW181

– 305 –
US cert den

– 323 –
429NE[8]1341
441NE[7]341
56A21207s
1A3382s
59A3152s

– 327 –
428NE[2]3
428NE[3]3
j428NE10
428NE[2]244
432NE[3]405
e455NE[3]331

– 330 –
442NE1068

– 331 –
427NE[3]896
436NE[5]309
439NE[5]637
440NE[4]1094
445NE987
451NE306

– 332 –
426NE[3]62
426NE[2]63
j426NE73
434NE[2]92
442NE[4]1054
448NE[2]26
7A4218n
10A471n
12A4364n

– 335 –
e429NE[1]958
429NE[2]1114
j429NE1118
434NE[1]90
448NE[1]1075
453NE349

– 337 –
429NE[5]1116
430NE[4]783
439NE[4]1352
440NE[5]469

– 339 –
e432NE[1]70
443NE1202
447NE[5]1076
98A2726s
4A4147s

– 343 –
f427NE[1]1138
431NE[1]822
431NE[3]822
431NE[4]822
436NE[6]1096
0
18
22
101
074
074
074
97
15

– 345 –
426NE[6]414
426NE[4]1155
f429NE[7]636
430NE422
430NE[7]1149
433NE[7]759
433NE[1]778
437NE[4]54
437NE[7]960
438NE[4]968
440NE[2]1147
444NE[7]847
444NE[8]847
445NE[1]981
450NE[7]526
453NE[7]169
453NE[8]169
453NE[7]199
454NE398
18A3259s

– 348 –
556FS[2]105
Kan
668P2d187
W Va
291SE384
30A39s

– 359 –
455NE[3]1113

– 361 –
443NE[1]316
446NE7

– 363 –
(380Mas314)
426NE[5]1177
433NE[5]429
445NE[11]604
451NE[5]1160
451NE[6]1160
95A3596s
7A4281n

– 370 –
(380Mas326)
442NE[2]1166
Continued

Checking in the latest paper supplement, we note that the Gates case has been reversed by the Supreme Court of the United States.

See note on first page of this division. *Illinois Appellate Court Cases when Certiorari or Appeal Denied or Dismissed

380

[Illustration 98]

PAGE FROM SHEPARD'S NORTHEASTERN CITATIONS

NORTHEASTERN REPORTER, 2d SERIES						Vol. 330
e405S2d296	– 45 –	j333NE²³378	359NE'374	j359NE⁸600	394NE'⁴256	28Æ1115s	392NE²'1220
406S2d1005	(36NY421)	359NE²'369	359NE'1360	360NE³279	397NE⁸645	61Æ996s	412NE²907
407S2d706	(369S2d75)	j372S2d⁵80	364NE²'1125	360NE⁸593	397NE²'646	81Æ31016n	c413NE²721
d409S2d155	s359S2d997	f372S2d985	380NE'176	f364NE⁹1186	400NE802	81Æ31038n	416NE²922
409S2d627	s362S2d513	376S2d1008	380NE²176	371NE⁴707	401NE731		Iowa
409S2d718	cc386S2d441	391S2d²575	384NE'652	372NE⁴194	403NE⁷873	– 134 –	254NW509
410S2d889	cc425S2d122	f396S2d963	393NE'459	377NE⁵423	403NE¹⁰873	(164InA554)	Wash
414S2d347	cc425S2d888	f397S2d501	e402NE'1130	378NE⁴641	404NE'591	392NE²525	554P2d1035
415S2d32	334NE598	398S2d50	414NE'663	378NE⁴865	404NE⁷591	396NE²969	12.Æ3978s
j418S2d617	338NE'599	407S2d416	368S2d635	378NE⁵865	408NE²819	408NE²586	
d418S2d628	338NE'609	d407S2d416	j370S2d743	381NE''464	408NE¹⁰819	413NE987	– 161 –
f418S2d752	344NE⁴406	408S2d592	d372S2d881	382NE'902	409NE⁷1267		(367Mas849)
419S2d79	351NE'654	411S2d166	e376S2d'88	384NE⁴1040	413NE³566	– 137 –	s311NE52
419S2d964	f351NE655	422S2d349	e376S2d³88	386NE⁹1190	417NE¹⁴1192	(164InA565)	330NE6477
j419S2d965	j351NE'659	432S2d145	j376S2d²92	391NE'²808	III	375NE⁵622	340NE²⁵866
420S2d20	366NE²856	433S2d561	376S2d273	393NE'²139	365NE²²1086	c393NE⁴'783	343NE²⁵881
424S2d205	j378NE87	e438S2d969	382S2d²741	393NE'²139	365NE²³1086		363NE²⁴241
424S2d491	380NE'198	430US³337	384S2d³110	399NE⁸363	Nev	– 140 –	363NE²⁵241
426S2d788	380NE⁴201	51LE²386	386S2d'396	399NE⁸363	574P2d1014	(164InA674)	j363NE²⁴244
427S2d344	385NE⁵1229	97SC²1218	387S2d³106	403NE⁵1380	98.Æ3682n	381NE1273	372NE²245
427S2d685	390NE''1167	Alk	389S2d41	408NE⁵1235			372NE²⁵245
428S2d706	393NE'452	598P2d900	390S2d'864	416NE''468	– 102 –	– 141 –	372NE²⁰'287
430S2d933	397NE'719	Me	391S2d'567	418NE⁸223	(164InA443)	(164InA638)	378NE²⁵955
432S2d335	412NE'379	414A2d238	j394S2d986	419NE'²149	339NE⁴90	330NE⁸390	389NE'⁴74
432S2d957	371S2d378	Okla	396S2d122	419NE⁵1295	342NE'652	330NE⁸390	389NE²575
436S2d18	372S2d651	563P2d142	396S2d³354	73Æ1187s	393NE'195	330NE⁵781	391NE'937
438S2d851	376S2d'83	Ore	j396S2d442	7.Æ38s	f399NE'806	330NE⁶781	j394NE1124
440S2d234	376S2d'97	604P2d394	397S2d895	33.Æ3335s	399NE⁸808	f332NE²247	396NE³728
440S2d289	376S2d985	85.Æ3985n	403S2d561		407NE⁸292	f332NE⁴247	396NE¹⁰730
d440S2d389	378S2d547		403S2d564	– 88 –	412NE⁸807	f335NE⁴826	396NE'⁷731
f441S2d177	380S2d985	– 68 –	406S2d62	(263Ind297)	25.Æ3951s	f335NE⁵826	396NE'⁷731
d441S2d179	381S2d⁴474	(36NY457)	406S2d1022	348NE⁴400		336NE⁴416	396NE²³999
j441S2d245	385S2d669	(369S2d108)	407S2d888	375NE1068	– 113 –	336NE⁴416	396NE'⁹1002
d441S2d390	f386S2d8	s354S2d197	408S2d290	386NE⁸204	(164InA583)	336NE⁷417	396NE'⁰1004
441S2d391	386S2d'8	368S2d916	408S2d'345	390NE⁵992	358NE'146	336NE⁴417	397NE²⁵1120
j441S2d394	j386S2d'13	390S2d957	408S2d²345	391NE³1173	358NE'156	338NE⁵511	400NE'851
442S2d700	386S2d949	482FS⁷460	412S2d'105	f405NE⁴64	c370NE'971	338NE⁵511	f406NE'⁹737
440US⁴651	388S2d624	71.Æ382s	417S2d1004	408NE³531	o375NE594	338NE⁶665	406NE²²738
59LE⁴666	389S2d159		419S2d'463	417NE⁷1131	375NE'594	338NE⁸666	417NE'⁷1240
99SC⁴1394	391S2d315	– 72 –	423S2d214	e421NE³24	376NE1192	338NE717	534F2d'⁴408
528F2d²714	392S2d162	(36NY462)	e426S2d'228	Tex		f358NE210	455FS⁵412
561F2d884	f393S2d598	(369S2d113)	434S2d'163	571SW879	– 116 –	385NE⁸454	486FS²⁰15
f417FS⁴82	395S2d214	s354S2d207	432FS⁷817	41.Æ227s	(164InA558)	97.Æ549s	502FS⁴1056
443FS²142	d396S2d771	347NE²579	Wash	14.Æ3831s	366NE'⁰1197		508FS1075
III	397S2d²768	348NE³877	632P2d75		367NE⁵1139	– 147 –	III
358NE⁵91	401S2d16	393NE²445		– 92 –	377NE⁶674	(29IIÆ12)	340NE⁷299
358NE⁶91	404S2d243	409NE⁷891	– 79 –	(263Ind282)	405NE'93	354NE³398	Ariz
358NE292	j406S2d723	422NE²539	(36NY473)	s310NE877	415NE'145	f361NE⁴1173	547P2d1082
358NE696	408S2d'368	367S2d981	(369S2d123)	333NE⁵107	417NE'1144		560P2d1221
386NE⁷132	408S2d⁴371	376S2d60	(88.Æ3697)	333NE⁵793	419NE⁸1041	– 149 –	Conn
Calif	413S2d⁵299	381S2d333	s352S2d633	f334NE⁷696	13.Æ355s	(28IIÆ906)	368A2d134
149CaR592	414S2d709	383S²d²719	405NE'685	335NE⁸224		s303NE443	DC
585P2d214	417S2d'243						408A2d47
Del	417S2d512						4G8A2d60
382A2d1364	419S2d'456						424A2d94
Haw	j421S2d694						La
577P2d785	422S2d'28						355So2d891
Kan	f422S2d956						Md
576P2d1100	432S2d'693						350A2d697
587P2d888	442S2d574						413A2d177
Md							Tenn
398A2d805	– 48 –						569SW417
Minn	(36NY427)						Tex
232NW910	(369S2d80)						541SW819
241NW477	s352S2d719						Utah
257NW308	380S2d523						626P2d973
290NW783	384S2d298						Va
294NW699	421S2d645						224SE134
NH	10BRW'⁵598						19.Æ31361s
358A2d663	Wyo						20.Æ3988s
NJ	576P2d463						75.Æ3625n
414A2d977							75.Æ3633n
Ore	– 53 –						
554P2d195	(36NY433)						
	(369S2d87)						
	s356S2d733	354NE²846	j359NE²599	394NE⁵197	411NE⁴652	392NE'1188	

The regional Shepard's not only gives citations to citing cases within the state of the cited case, but also picks up citations from any other state which cite the cited case.

Note, e.g. the various states citing 330 N.E.2d 161, a Massachusetts case.

These other state citations do not appear in the Shepard's Massachusetts Citations.

*illinois Appellate Court Cases when Certiorari or Appeal Denied or Dismissed

[Illustration 99]

PAGE FROM SHEPARD'S CITATIONS: PAMPHLET SUPPLEMENT

VOL. 76	APRIL, 1985	NO. 11

CUMULATIVE SUPPLEMENT

Shepard's
NORTHEASTERN
REPORTER
Citations

(USPS 605390)

The latest paper-back supplement always has this box that indicates all of the units of a particular Shepard's Citations.

It should always be checked and your *Sheparding* should include using all the volumes and supplements relevant to your search.

AN

**FOR YOUR
SHEPARD'S
REPRESENTATIVE
SEE BACK
COVER**

What Your Library Should Contain

1945 Vol. 1	1974 Vol. 2
1945-1982 Supp.	1974-1982 Supp.
to Vol. 1	to Vol. 2

Supplemented with
April, 1985 Annual Supplement Vol. 76 No. 11

Destroy All Other Issues

SEE "THIS ISSUE INCLUDES" ON PAGE THREE

SECTION D.   STATUTE CITATIONS

Statutes are dealt with by *Shepard's Citations* in a manner similar to cases.   The notations cover the form and operation of the law by the legislature and the courts.   Its operation is identified by abbreviations denoting legislative changes (amendments, repeals, revisions, reenactments, etc.) and judicial interpretations (constitutional, unconstitutional, invalid, etc.).

The form of statutes vary, depending on the plan adopted by a jurisdiction.   The Table of Abbreviations in each unit of *Shepard's Citations* should be examined specifically to determine the local scheme.   [See Illustration 100.]

The Citations to Statutes units of *Shepard's Citations* cover the following areas: citations to the United States Constitution and state constitutions; the *United States Code* and Acts of Congress (not included in the *United States Code*); the various state codes, legislative enactments, and court rules; and various municipal charters and ordinances.

The information contained in the statutes units is presented in accordance with this arrangement: statutory amendments, repeals, etc., are listed first, followed by state and federal court citations and citations in the attorneys general opinions, legal periodicals, and acts of the legislature.

1.   Constitutions

The federal and state constitutions are covered by the *Statute Editions* to *Shepard's Citations*.   A constitution section in a *Statute Edition* is arranged under the articles and amendments to the constitution.   Citing sources are listed under these provisions.   [See Illustration 102.]

2.   City Charters and Ordinances

The municipal charters and ordinances are part of the *State Citations*.   Reference should be made to the citator of the state in which the city is located for citations to the city's charter or ordinances.

The section under *Municipal Charters* in the *Statute Citations* is arranged alphabetically by cities in many state editions and subdivided by topics.   The unit may have a separate *Index to Municipal Charters*.   The *Ordinances* section also may be arranged alphabetically by cities and subdivided by topics.   It, too, may have a separate *Index to Ordinances*.   In some citators, the citations to the ordinances of the larger cities are arranged separately.   To meet editorial

requirements, the citations to ordinances may be indexed by section numbers as well as topically.

3. Shepard's Ordinance Law Annotations

This six-volume set is actually a digest rather than a citator. It is arranged under broad subjects, with each subject subdivided into sub-entries. Under each sub-entry, annotations of court decisions are listed. This set is useful when legal research requires the locating of cases on the same aspect of local government law in different cities.

4. Court Rules

Citations to court decisions interpreting court rules are also covered by *Shepard's Citations.* The Court Rules section is arranged by courts (final, intermediate, and original jurisdiction), and is subdivided by rule numbers.

[Illustration 100]

ABBREVIATIONS—ANALYSIS TABLE FROM SHEPARD'S NEW YORK CITATIONS—STATUTES: PAMPHLET SUPPLEMENT

ABBREVIATIONS—ANALYSIS

History of Case

a	(affirmed)	Same case affirmed on appeal.
cc	(connected case)	Different case from case cited but arising out of same subject matter or intimately connected therewith.
D	(dismissed)	Appeal from same case dismissed.
m	(modified)	Same case modified on appeal.
r	(reversed)	Same case reversed on appeal.
s	(same case)	Same case as case cited.
S	(superseded)	Substitution for former opinion.
v	(vacated)	Same case vacated.
US cert den		Certiorari denied by U. S. Supreme Court.
US cert dis		Certiorari dismissed by U. S. Supreme Court.
US reh den		Rehearing denied by U. S. Supreme Court.
US reh dis		Rehearing dismissed by U. S. Supreme Court.

Treatment of Case

c	(criticised)	Soundness of decision or reasoning in cited case criticised for reasons given.
d	(distinguished)	Case at bar different either in law or fact from case cited for reasons given.
e	(explained)	Statement of import of decision in cited case. Not merely a restatement of the facts.
f	(followed)	Cited as controlling.
h	(harmonized)	Apparent inconsistency explained and shown not to exist.
j	(dissenting opinion)	Citation in dissenting opinion.
L	(limited)	Refusal to extend decision of cited case beyond precise issues involved.
o	(overruled)	Ruling in cited case expressly overruled.
p	(parallel)	Citing case substantially alike or on all fours with cited case in it law or facts.
q	(questioned)	Soundness of decision or reasoning in cited case questioned.

NOTES

A superior figure immediately to the left of the page number of any New York or federal court citing reference indicates the particular paragraph of the syllabus or particular headnote of the cited case which states the point of law dealt with in the citing case.

Where the reports of more than one case start on the same page of any volume of reports,

---

As the **ABBREVIATIONS-ANALYSIS** may vary from state to state, this Table for the state Shepard's being used should be consulted.

---

that page.

11

SECTION E. ILLUSTRATIONS: STATUTE CITATIONS

[Illustration 101]

PAGE FROM SHEPARD'S U.S. CITATIONS—STATUTES SECTION

UNITED STATES CODE '76 Ed. & '81 Supp.   T. 26 § 6416

§ 6323	Subsec. c	Subd. 2	Subsec. a	Subsec. d	Subd. 9	→ § 6402
et seq.	711F2d684	566FS1510	A96St638	Rs96St639	22BRW916	Up560FS
570FS852	712F2d260	Subd. 4	PMTP§7.94	Subsec. d	Subsec. c	[1103
	569FS952	721F2d169	Subsec. b	(96St639)	76LE257	688F2d754
§ 6323	35BRW612	721F2d169	PMTP§7.94	Subd. 1	103SC2146	717F2d772
76LE246	Subd. 1	21BRW862	PMTP§7.94	32BRW187	51USLW	555FS1053
103SC2136	711F2d686	23BRW1021	Subd. 3	Subsec. e	[4628	557FS732
51USLW	35BRW612	Subd. 6	558FS155	RnSubsec f	USDk	575FS1306
[4623	¶A	721F2d169	Subsec. d	[96St639	81-1476	22BRW729
USDk	Cl. 1	546FS53	PMTP§7.94	Ad96St639	711F2d95	26BRW600
81-1476	569FS957	554FS587	Subd. 3		573FS884	28BRW1019
711F2d687	35BRW613	Subsec. i	PMTP§7.98	§ 6332	35BRW43	31BRW451
712F2d263	Cl. 3	721F2d1099	Subd. 1	76LE525	Subsec. d	1COA683
721F2d166	711F2d685	548FS174	Subsec. e	77LE791	559FS174	IIT§3.01
539FS103	¶B	Subd. 2	PMTP§7.94	103SC2316	22BRW916	Subsec. a
553FS16	711F2d685	709F2d519	Subsec. f	103SC3168	Subd. 1	717F2d772
554FS571	569FS957	32BRW95	28BRW402	51USLW	A96St638	570FS177
554FS585	Subd. 2			[4709	USDk	575FS1306
556FS199	712F2d264	§ 6324	§ 6331	51USLW	81-1476	21BRW925
556FS711	¶A	76LE245	et seq.	[5076	§ 6335	26BRW600
565FS390	35BRW613	103SC2136	21BRW860	USDk	76LE519	28BRW86
565FS854	Cl. 1	51USLW	29BRW366	81-1938	103SC2311	29BRW55
570FS852	569FS957	[4623		USDk	51USLW	31BRW451
21BRW859	¶B	USDk	§ 6331	82-215	[4706	36BRW963
24BRW991	569FS957	81-1476	76LE246	707F2d20	76LE519	IEP§3.44
26BRW80	¶C	705F2d1490	76LE519	721F2d166	103SC2311	Subsec. b
27BRW715	569FS957	729F2d501	77LE791	726F2d1296	51USLW	574FS593
31BRW963	Subsec. d	PMTP§6.188	103SC2137	554FS112	[4706	575FS1306
32BRW187	711F2d689	Subsec. a	103SC2311	566FS1013	USDk	Subsec. c
33BRW917	Subsec. f	IEP§11.31	103SC3168	568FS1199	82-215	557FS733
94Æ748s	691F2d833	PMTP§7.94	51USLW	32BRW192	103SC2317	574FS587
30Æ39s	711F2d684	Subd. 1	[4623	35BRW655	51USLW	575FS1306
IEP§11.32	545FS798	705F2d1488	51USLW	35BRW798	[4709	22BRW730
Subsec. a	561FS638	IEP§11.33	[4706	Subsec. a	USDk	31BRW451
691F2d833	565FS390	PMTP§7.94	51USLW	711F2d687	82-215	§ 6403
705F2d1489	565FS853	Subd. 2	[5076	726F2d1294	562FS596	31BRW451
711F2d687	569FS959	729F2d498	USDk	566FS1013	32BRW188	PMTP§5.07
712F2d261	26BRW79	IEP§11.33	81-1476	35BRW798	35BRW798	§ 6405
545FS798	29BRW850	PMTP§7.94	USDk	Subsec. c	Subsecs.	574FS1429
545FS1095	31BRW732	Subd. 3	81-1938	36BRW827	b to d	Subsec. a
546FS53	32BRW94	IEP§11.33	USDk	Subsec. b	726F2d1300	574FS1428
554FS587	PMTP§6.188	PMTP§7.94	82-215	76LE526	Subd. 3	§ 6412
561FS638	Subd. 1	Subsec. b	711F2d683	103SC2317	76LE255	Subsec. a
565FS63	23BRW1021	457US197	721F2d1100	568FS1199	103SC2144	Subd. 1
565I			726F2d1293	576FS794	51USLW	A96St2183
569I			544FS90		[4627	Subsec. b
570I					USDk	→ § 6413
574I					81-1476	A96St590
22BI						712F2d285
24BI				.Dk		Subsec. a
29BI				82-215	§ 6362	712F2d285
29BI				2FS596	Subsec. b	Subd. 1
31BI				BRW828		A96St589
32BI				Subsec. d		Subsec. b
33BI				BRW828		A96St590
35BI				Subsec. e		712F2d285
Su				Subd. 1		Subsec. c
711F				5F2d1322		Subd. 1
565F				§ 6337		A96St586
21BI				5F2d1323	§ 6365	Subd. 2
32BI				4FS114	Subsec. c	A97St120
S				BRW611	Subd. 2	¶C
21BI				BRW667	A96St589	A97St120
23BI				BRW188		→ § 6416
721F				BRW188		Subsec. a
S				Subsec. a		714F2d1196
570F				5F2d1490		Subd. 1
S				BRW618		A96St2177
691F				BRW818		¶D
24BI				Subsec. b		555FS1101
				5F2d1490		
				BRW716		
				Subd. 1		
				6St639		
				5F2d1322		
				557FS734		
				31BRW451		

Note 1

Note 2

Note 3

> **Shepardizing a U.S. Code section.**
>
> This unit gives citations to each court decision citing the U.S. Code. It also indicates when a code section has been amended, repealed, or held constitutional or unconstitutional.
>
> Notes:
>
> 1. 26 U.S.C. § 6402 held unconstitutional in part in 560 F.Supp. 1103.
>
> 2. 26 U.S.C. § 6413 amended by 96 Statutes at Large at page 590.
>
> 3. 26 U.S.C. § 6416 Subd. 1 amended by 96 Statutes at Large at page 2177.

227

[Illustration 102]

PAGE FROM SOUTH CAROLINA CONSTITUTION IN THE SHEPARD'S SOUTH CAROLINA CITATIONS—STATUTES SECTION

SOUTH CAROLINA CONSTITUTION   Art. 8-A

§ 13	88CQ 12	1966p2233	170SE273	211SoC144	Florence	**§ 11**
211SoC113	12SCQ127	1966p2706	172SE699	213SoC428	145SoC449	1966p2808
44SK105	133CQ300	1966p3059	174SE919	232SoC546	143SE166	1972p3189
4SCQ385	13SCQ371	1967p76	5SK573	234SoC 559	Georgetown	A1973p67
§ 15	158CR187	1967p1074	9SK785	234SoC 506	229SoC 67	A&Rn
1968p3186	168CR121	LJ1967p1541	24SK365	236SoC 137	91RK 887	[ArtVIII
1970p2079	23SCR654	1968p2523	40SK684	237SoC 356	Marion	[A§1
Ad1971p72	32SCR481	[§4	44SK187	239SoC 187	213SoC428	[1973p146
	§ 2	A1973p67	49SK720	243SoC 497	49SK721	179SoC219
Art. 8	1972p3191	130SoC131	53SK316	245SoC 198	Orangeburg	249SoC271
1972p3184	A1973p67	172SoC118	59SK638	250SoC85	205SoC228	183SE765
A1973p67	174SoC35	219SoC322	87SK587	251SoC227	217SoC65	1538E001
123SoC281	186SoC290	125SE297	1278E 631	C254SoC535	31SK385	C1898E7
156SoC157	213SoC231	173SE72	1308E 573	256SoC411	59SK639	198CR169
160SoC169	221SoC440	65SK236	156SE117	257SoC223	143SE166	20SCR750
214SoC473	223SoC472	**§ 5**	160SE600	258SoC487	145SoC449	**§ 12**
221SoC447	232SoC 553	1963 p 1150	181SK664	116SE277	143SE166	A1973p67
236SoC566	C253SoC210	A1973p67	186SK239	130SE873	Spartan-	**§ 13**
240SoC 508	258SoC524	146SoC473	3SCQ309	130SE876	burg	A1973p67
115SE599	176SE870	149SoC236	98CQ110	133SE340	130SoC434	**§ 14**
152SE813	195SE539	154SoC350	128CQ127	134SE390	132SoC487	A1973p67
158SE147	49SK1	159SoC496	26SCR438	141SE265	126SE336	216SoC350
53SK325	76SK612	174SoC35	32SCR479	150SE270	129SE833	58SK93
71SK5	103SB 33	177SoC144	**§ 7**	151SE469	Water-works	
1158K 276	C1698B617	181SoC353	1960 p 2221	151SE576	139SoC188	**Art. 8**
1268E 560	1808K827	203SoC446	1964 p 2603	161SE454	147SoC498	(1973p67)
118CQ 12	445F2d835	221SoC418	A1965 p 13	170SE435	159SoC496	**§ 8**
§ 1	482F2d580	223SoC254	1966p2110	174SE461	160SoC406	261SoC267
1908p3408	22SCR646	236SoC 174	1966p2116	175SE821	137SE597	261SoC269
L1969p3	**§ 3**	245SoC 428	1966p3018	176SE870	145SE412	262SoC568
A1973p67						
126SoC160						
148SoC229						

> Each State Shepard's has a part for statutes which includes a section on the state constitution.
>
> Note how Article 8, Section 7 of the South Carolina constitu- has been amended several times and has also been held constitutional.
>
> The amending citations are to the South Carolina session laws.

		A1973p67	1971p1343	C176SE290	176SE870	449FS993	282SK852
	1963 p 246	127SoC158	A1973p67	182SK744	47SK728		**§ 16**
119SE378	1963 p 258	138SoC187	A1973p74	185SK306	65SK667	261SoC267	262SoC565
146SE12	1963 p 519	170SoC262	123SoC334	189SK284	93SK 20	262SoC565	267SoCR1
152SE701	1963 p 642	172SoC26	133SoC156	95F2d774	4SCQ413	264SoC512	268SoC403
158SE147	1963 p 652	173SoC94	133SoC189	95F2d777	26SCR443	267SoC335	206SK75
158SE235	1963 p 1206	192SoC112	136SoC345	138F2d739	**§ 9**	273SoC643	226SK36
195SE539	1964 p 1751	194SoC339	143SoC120	10FS859	A1973p67	275SoC22	234SK226
42SK534	1964p1757	202SoC236	152SoC458	19FS933	**§ 10**	199SK542	287SK479
53SK317	1964 p 1766	209SoC456	154SoC257	3SCQ315	A1973p67	206SK75	**§ 17**
58SK93	1964 p 1773	211SoC144	154SoC350	4SCQ382	126SoC24	216SK181	262SoC565
58SK334	1964 p 1858	213SoC428	163SoC243	9SCQ28	149SoC449	228SK94	267SoC330
71SK1	1964 p 1892	214SoC452	170SoC362	17SCR 31	177SoC428	255SK340	275SoC23
71SK8	1964 p 2348	217SoC62	172SoC478	23SCR662	192SoC112	259SK107	206SK875
85SK194	1964 p 2429	227SoC163	173SoC333	Boganville	227SoC539	267SK84	228SK94
108SB 29	1965 p 20	241SoC 195	174SoC35	129SoC189	119SE784	449FS992	267SK84
113SE 535	1965 p 204	242SoC 238	177SoC82	123SE823	147SE438	**§ 6**	**Art. 8-A**
121SE 910	1965 p 261	250SoC137	177SoC382	Camden	181SE482	32SCR499	Ad1973p146
126SE 554	1965 p 523	253SoC196	178SoC69	122SoC213	5SK573	**§ 7**	**§ 1**
130SE 573	1965 p 670	256SoC178	183SoC52	115SE251	88SK684	261SoC267	1973p865
181SB672	1965 p 767	257SoC433	188SoC378	Charleston	238SK210	262SoC565	A1975p35
204SE377	1965p1287	120SE717	194SoC339	123SoC92		264SoC510	
7SCQ156	1966p2170	136SE393	198SoC82	116SE104			

41

[Illustration 103]

PAGE FROM SHEPARD'S SOUTH CAROLINA CITATIONS—STATUTES SECTION

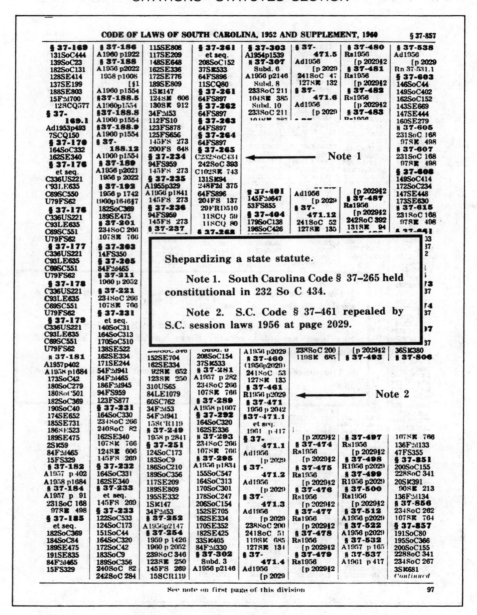

SECTION F.   KEEPING SHEPARD'S CITATIONS CURRENT

1.   Supplements

As with any set of law books, there must be a method of keeping the set up to date. Since *Shepard's Citations* are used to determine current status of a case or statute or an administration regulation or ruling, the method of supplementation is of utmost importance. Nearly every unit of *Shepard's* is available in at least one bound volume; many units have one or more bound supplement volumes. Additionally, each unit receives a cumulative paper supplement that covers all changes since the date of the latest bound volume. The frequency of the issuance of the paper supplements varies among the different units. Some units are updated monthly; others, three times a year; still others, quarterly. Consequently, it is extremely important to ascertain that all bound volumes and paper supplements of the unit being used are at hand. The latest paper supplement usually contains a box entitled *What Your Library Should Contain.* This should be examined carefully, and all of the indicated bound volumes and paper supplements should be consulted. [See Illustration 99.]

2.   Shepard's Special Citation Service

A special updating service is now available to subscribers to any unit of *Shepard's Citations*. By writing or calling the publisher, information to citing cases subsequent to the latest supplement may be obtained. Detailed information about this service is available upon request.

SECTION G.   COMPUTER–ASSISTED RESEARCH

Both LEXIS and WESTLAW provide access to *Shepard's Citations*. However, neither system has the Statutes sections and each lacks other units. The list of *Shepard's Citations* available on each system should be checked upon use.

An advantage of using *Shepard's Citations* in an online format is that it is possible to bring up immediately on the screen the text of a citing case.

OTHER UNITS OF SHEPARD'S CITATIONS. See Jacobstein and Mersky, *Fundamentals of Legal Research*, 3d ed., Chapter 15, Sections F and G.

Chapter 15

LEGAL ENCYCLOPEDIAS

SECTION A. INTRODUCTION

In the previous chapters, we have discussed the primary sources of the law: court decisions; constitutions; statutes; legislative histories; court rules; and the indexes, digests, and other sets of law books that enable a researcher to find both the source and status of the law. In the remaining chapters, we shall discuss the secondary sources of the law. The mass of primary source materials has reached such voluminous proportions that secondary publications have assumed significant roles in identifying and explaining the law. As will be pointed out, it is frequently much better practice to start one's research with secondary publications rather than with the sets containing the primary sources that were studied in the previous chapters. The secondary sources to be discussed consist of legal encyclopedias, treatises, periodicals, restatements, and other miscellaneous sets of law books.

Legal encyclopedias are written in narrative form, arranged by subject and containing supporting footnote references to cases in point. In most instances, they are noncritical in approach and do not attempt to be analytical or evaluative. Instead, they simply state the propositions of law, with introductory explanations of an elementary nature. The legal encyclopedia, because of these features, is a popular and useful research tool. Its utility, however, as a secondary source has frequently been abused by both courts and attorneys. In particular, it is often cited as a final authoritative source rather than as an expository introduction to case authority.

In many research problems, it is necessary to go beyond such rudimentary sources. It is not wise to stop one's research without reading the cases cited in the footnotes because cited references frequently will not fully reflect the propositional ramifications for which they stand, or because the facts of the immediate problem will be distinguishable and different from those in the cited cases.

This criticism should not be interpreted as being directed at the function of the encyclopedia. It is an excellent index and introductory guide to the law. As long as this is kept in mind, and it is not relied upon as the final authority for a proposition of law, it is a valuable publication to be consulted initially. In most instances, the cases cited will have to be read, analyzed, and *Shepardized;* statutory

264

sources must be checked to ascertain whether the rules of law have changed in any particular jurisdiction.

SECTION B.   CURRENT GENERAL ENCYCLOPEDIAS

1.   Corpus Juris Secundum (C.J.S.)

Corpus Juris Secundum, published by the West Publishing Company, attempts to restate the entire body of American law in encyclopedic form—from the first reported case to the present. It includes both procedural and substantive law and aims at citing all reported cases in its footnotes. *Corpus Juris Secundum* contains 101 volumes (or about 150 actual volumes counting supplements) and supersedes its predecessor, *Corpus Juris.*[1]

Cross-references from *C.J.S.* titles and sections to corresponding West Topics and Key Numbers are provided also, permitting easy entry to the *American Digest System.* The West Topics and Key Numbers and other secondary authority sources are noted under *Library References,* which precede the texts of the sections in the *C.J.S.* replacement volumes published since 1961 and in the annual cumulative pocket supplements.

C.J.S. has a five-volume general index. Each volume also has a separate index to the topics contained in it. Where the topic is covered in more than one volume, the Topic Index appears in the concluding volume of the topic.

The set is kept up to date by replacement volumes and annual cumulative pocket supplements. Replacement volumes appear when significant sections of the text require rewriting or when the recent pocket supplements become very extensive and unwieldy. The pocket supplements may cover rewritten text, citations to cases rendered since the publication of the original volume, and secondary sources.

Judicial and other definitions of *words and phrases* and *legal maxims* are interfiled alphabetically with the essay topics. They also are listed in each appropriate volume preceding the index, with references to the pages containing the definitions. *Corpus Juris Secundum* provides some discussion of federal and local statutory law, including court interpretation of these enactments.

A *List of Titles in Corpus Juris Secundum* precedes the text in each volume. At the beginning of each Topic, there is an outline and classification for the organization of the Title. This may be used when using the topical approach. [See Illustrations 104–106.]

---

[1] Although *Corpus Juris Secundum* supersedes *Corpus Juris,* occasionally the footnotes in *Corpus Juris Secundum* will refer to *Corpus Juris* rather than repeating the citations that appeared in that set.

2. American Jurisprudence 2d (Am.Jur.2d)

Am.Jur.2d is published by the Lawyers Co-operative Publishing Company and the Bancroft-Whitney Company. It is a textual statement of substantive and procedural law, arranged alphabetically under 400 topics. It contains 82 volumes plus an eight-volume index and supersedes *American Jurisprudence.*

This set differs from *Corpus Juris Secundum* in that it does not cite all reported decisions in support of its textual statements of the law. Rather, *Am.Jur.2d* cites only selected decisions in its footnotes but does give citations to *A.L.R.* annotations. In using *Am.Jur.2d,* reported cases may be located through its footnotes and by consultation of the cited *A.L.R.* annotations.

Am.Jur.2d also gives in its footnotes references to treatment of a topic in the other sets of the *Total Client-Service Library.* Since *Am.Jur.2d* has a detailed multi-volume index, it is much more inclusive in entries than are the indexes to *A.L.R.* It is frequently easier to locate an *A.L.R.* annotation by starting in the *Am.Jur.2d* index, reading the section cited to, and then locating the appropriate *A.L.R.* citation in *Am.Jur.2d*'s footnotes.

The publishers describe *Am.Jur.2d* as giving the law in breadth and *A.L.R.* as the law in depth. The former is very useful to obtain a quick answer to a problem that then may be explored in-depth through the use of *A.L.R.* In use, one may go directly to the volume containing the topic being researched. For example, if one is interested in the law of *Copyright,* the index volumes may be by-passed and the search started immediately by consulting the volume that contains the title *Copyright.* If the broad topic of the law under which the subject is included is not familiar to the researcher (e.g., restrictive covenants), the search should start first in the index volumes.

Some features of *Am.Jur.2d* are:

a. Greater emphasis is placed on statutory law, federal procedural rules, and uniform state laws. The federal statutory law germane to a topic is covered, while state statutory law is covered in general but without reference to the specific laws of each state. There is a separate volume of *Table of Statutes and Rules Cited.* This *Table* covers the *United States Code Service,* the Federal Rules of Procedure, the Federal Rules of Evidence, and the Uniform Laws. When a citation to one of these is at hand, this *Table* may be consulted to find where the subject matter of such citations is discussed in *Am.Jur.2d.*

b. Federal tax laws are covered in volumes 33 and 34, which are replaced annually. The volumes contain substantially the same text found in the current edition of the Research Institute of America

(RIA) *Tax Guide*, a looseleaf service with weekly supplements. The volumes as printed in *Am.Jur.2d* are supplemented during the year only for major federal tax law changes. As rules, regulations, and new court decisions occur so frequently in tax law, the user of these *Am.Jur.2d* volumes should always check for the most current materials in the RIA *Tax Guide* or in the other taxation services described *supra* in Chapter 13, Section B.

c.   *Am.Jur.2d New Topic Service*, a looseleaf volume started in 1973, covers (1) new topics of the law which have developed after the printing of the main volumes and (2) new and substantial changes in already published articles. For example, this *Service* contains articles on *No-Fault Divorce* and *Right to Die*. The pocket supplements to the multi-volume index includes references to this *Service*.

d.   The *Am.Jur.2d Desk Book* is another feature of *Am.Jur.2d*, which functions as a *legal* almanac of miscellaneous data and information. The *Desk Book* is divided into seven main categories: (1) governmental documents and historical matters, (2) the courts (the canons of judicial ethics and the business and organization of the courts), (3) lawyers and the legal profession, (minimum requirements for admission to legal practice in the United States and professional data), (4) statutes and statutory material (text of the ancient statutes and tabulated statutory material—*e.g.*, marriage laws, record of passage of Uniform and Model Acts), (5) statistical matters (*e.g.*, financial and mathematical tables), (6) tables of law reports (abbreviations), and (7) miscellaneous information (*e.g.*, selected legal [Latin] maxims and phrases, freely translated).

e.   *Am.Jur.2d* is kept up to date by annual pocket supplements.

[See Illustrations 107–109.]

3.   American Jurisprudence: Related Encyclopedias

These sets are part of what the publishers call their *Total Client-Service Library*. Once a lawyer has determined the state of the substantive law related to the problem under research, these related sets will provide the information required to prepare the case for trial. The sets are:

a.   *American Jurisprudence Proof of Facts*. This set is now in its second series. Its purpose is to provide a guide for a lawyer in the organization and preparation of materials for trial and in the examination of witnesses. It is designed to assist lawyers in obtaining information from clients, in the taking of depositions, in the preparing of briefs, and in other steps necessary in preparing for trial.

b.   *American Jurisprudence Trials*. This set of over 230 volumes is essentially a treatise on trial practice. The first six

volumes cover matters that are common to all types of problems in trial practice. The remaining volumes are called *Modern Trials* and deal with the handling of trials for a specific topic. Unlike *Am.Jur. 2d* and the other related sets, *American Jurisprudence Trials* is not written by the editorial staff of the publishers. Rather, each topic included in the set is written by an experienced trial lawyer.

c. *American Jurisprudence Legal Forms 2d* and *American Jurisprudence Pleading and Practice Forms.* These two sets contain forms needed in the conduct of a trial and for other aspects of a lawyer's practice. Form books will be discussed in more detail in Chapter 18.

4. The Guide to American Law: Everyone's Legal Encyclopedia

As the title indicates, this encyclopedia, published by West Publishing Company, is directed toward the non-lawyer. It is in twelve volumes and contains over 5,000 topics. It is a useful set to consult when a non-technical explanation of a point of law is desired.

SECTION C. ILLUSTRATIONS: ENCYCLOPEDIAS

In Chapters 6 and 7, we discussed the use of the *Key Number System* of the *American Digest System* and the *American Law Reports, Annotated* for finding cases. We used as an example the finding of cases dealing with damages done to a car left at a parking lot.

Another approach would have been to start the search in either *Corpus Juris Secundum* or *American Jurisprudence 2d.*

Corpus Juris Secundum

104. Page from Analysis to Topic: Motor Vehicles
105. Page from Volume 61A
106. Page from Pocket Supplement, Volume 61A

Am.Jur.2d

107. Page from General Index
108. Page from Volume 38
109. Page from Pocket Supplement, Volume 38

[Illustration 104]

PAGE FROM TOPIC OUTLINE: MOTOR VEHICLES

MOTOR VEHICLES 61A C. J. S.

XI. OFFENSES AND PROSECUTIONS—Continued

B. PARTICULAR OFFENSES—Continued

The most common method of locating the relevant paragraphs in C.J.S. is by consulting the General Index. Sometimes it may be easier to take a topical approach. In this instance, by consulting the Topic outline for Motor Vehicles, it quickly becomes evident that the matter under research is covered in paragraphs 726 or 727.

[Illustration 105]

PAGE FROM TOPIC: MOTOR VEHICLES, VOLUME 61A C.J.S.

---

§ 727 MOTOR VEHICLES   61A C. J. S.

allege facts showing that he has an interest in prosecuting the action.[46]

b. Evidence

In an action against a garage keeper to recover for loss of, or damage to, a motor vehicle left with him for storage, a presumption of negligence arises and a prima facie case of negligence is established when the plaintiff proves that he delivered his motor vehicle in good condition to the garage keeper and that the latter returned it in a damaged condition or failed or refused to return it on demand.

In an action against a garage keeper to recover for loss of, or damage to, a motor vehicle left with him for storage, plaintiff has the burden of establishing his contentions[47] by a preponderance of the evidence.[48] While it has been held that proof by plaintiff that he left his motor vehicle in good condition in defendant's garage and that it was in a damaged state the next morning does not make out a prima facie case[49] or cause the burden of proof to shift to defendant,[50] according to the weight of authority a presumption of negligence arises, and a prima facie case of negligence is established, where plaintiff proves delivery of his motor vehicle in good condition to the garage keeper and that the latter failed to produce it in a similar condition,[51] or that the garage keeper failed or refused to return it on demand,[52] or that the vehicle or merchandise in it was stolen while in his care.[53]

In such cases, defendant, to counteract the presumption and rebut the prima facie case, has the burden of going forward with evidence of due care and lack of negligence on his part,[54] or, if there be any negligence, of establishing that such negligence was not the proximate cause of the damages of the automobile owner;[54.5] and where defendant

---

46. La.—Douglas v. Haro, App., 32 So.2d 387.

47. Mo.—Stines v. Dillman, App., 4 S.W.2d 477.

Plaintiff must prove negligence where his vehicle was lost by fire. Ohio.—Blackburn v. Norris, 189 N.E. 262, 46 Ohio App. 469.

Negligence in lack of supervision In action against garage owner by

52. Conn.—Anderson v. Gengras Motors, 109 A.2d 502, 141 Conn. 688.
Ill.—Byalos v. Matheson, 159 N.E. 242, 328 Ill. 269.
Ind.—Employers' Fire Ins. Co. v. Consolidated Garage & Sales Co., 155 N.E. 533, 85 Ind.App. 674.
N.Y.—**Corpus Juris Secundum quoted in** Guild v. Atlantic-Third Corp., 186 N.Y.S.2d 77, 81, 18 Misc.2d 635.
Ohio.—North River Ins. Co. of New

54. Mich.—Loving v. Howard Lare, Inc., 73 N.W.2d 290, 344 Mich. 97.
N.Y.—**Corpus Juris Secundum quoted in** Guild v. Atlantic-Third Corp., 186 N.Y.S.2d 77, 81, 18 Misc.2d 635—Hobbie v. Ryan, 223 N.Y.S. 654, 130 Misc. 221.
Ohio.—Dietrich v. Peters, 162 N.E. 753, 28 Ohio App. 427.
38 C.J. p 89 notes 15, 17.

> A discussion of cases dealing with cars damaged after being left in a garage or parking lot. Note the relationship of text to footnotes. C.J.S. claims to include all reported cases.

---

ment, 119 N.Y.S.2d 924, 202 Misc. 586.

48. Mo.—Stines v. Dillman, App., 4 S.W.2d 477.

49. Mass.—Hanna v. Shaw, 138 N.E. 247, 244 Mass. 57.

50. Mass.—Hanna v. Shaw, supra.

51. Ill.—Hollingshead Motors Co. v. Crogan, 84 N.E.2d 440, 336 Ill.App. 423—Black v. Downtown Parking Stations, 75 N.E.2d 395, 332 Ill.App. 418.
La.—Standard Motor Car Co. v. State Farm Mut. Auto. Ins. Co., App., 97 So.2d 435.
N.Y.—**Corpus Juris Secundum quoted in** Guild v. Atlantic-Third Corp., 186 N.Y.S.2d 77, 81, 18 Misc.2d 635.
38 C.J. p 89 note 10.

Proof of damage by fire to stored automobile raises prima facie presumption of garage keeper's negligence.
N.Y.—Hobbie v. Ryan, 223 N.Y.S. 654, 130 Misc. 221.
38 C.J. p 89 note 10 [a] (2).

under care of owner, his agent or servants, or keeper of public garage where vehicle has been accepted for hire or gain, proof of damage shall be prima facie evidence that damage resulted from negligence of such owner or keeper, and under the common law of bailments.
Mich.—Loving v. Howard Lare, Inc., 73 N.W.2d 290, 344 Mich. 97.

53. Colo.—Cascade Auto Co. v. Petter, 212 P. 823, 72 Colo. 570.
Mich.—Tatro v. Baker-Fisk-Hugill Co., 184 N.W. 449, 215 Mich. 623.
N.Y.—Merchants Auto Delivery Corp. v. Terminal Garage, Inc., 168 N.Y. S.2d 374, 4 A.D.2d 1015.

Corpus Juris Secundum quoted in Guild v. Atlantic-Third Corp., 186 N.Y.S.2d 77, 81, 18 Misc.2d 635.

Doctrine of res ipsa loquitur is, however, inapplicable to action by bailor, where bailee's failure to return automobile was due to employee's theft.
Ill.—Rhodes v. Warsawsky, 242 Ill. App. 101.

C.Wash., 1 F.Supp. 589.
La.—Gulf & S. I. R. Co. v. Sutter Motor Co., 126 So. 458, 12 La.App. 495.

(2) On proof of theft, defendant's burden was not merely the burden of going forward with proof or a shifting burden, but the burden of proving to the jury that the loss did not arise from his negligence.
Minn.—Harding v. Shapiro, 206 N.W. 168, 165 Minn. 248.
38 C.J. p 89 note 18.

(3) Also, it has been held that garage proprietor had burden, in action by owner for damages resulting to automobile when it was delivered by proprietor's employee to unauthorized person, contrary to special contract for storage, to prove that person who took automobile had express or implied authority to receive it.
Mont.—Montana Leather Co. v. Colwell, 30 P.2d 473, 96 Mont. 274.

54.5 Mich.—Loving v. Howard Lare. Inc., 73 N.W.2d 290, 344 Mich. 97.

[Illustration 106]

PAGE FROM ANNUAL CUMULATIVE POCKET SUPPLEMENT, VOLUME 61A

61A CJS 57   **MOTOR VEHICLES § 730**
Page 660

30.5. Lessee not agent of lessor
Mass.—Fairfield's Motors, Inc. v. Fitz-Inn Auto Park, Inc., 297 N.E.2d 514, 1 Mass App. 833

Lessor negligent
S.C.—Collins Cadillac, Inc. v. Bigelow-Sanford, Inc., 279 S.E.2d 611, 276 S.C. 465

24. Mo.—Bewley v. Allright Carpark, Inc., App. 617 S.W.2d 547

N.Y.—General Motors Acceptance Corp. v. Grafinger, 306 N.Y.S.2d 606, 61 Misc.2d 670

Tex.—Ampco Auto Parks, Inc. v. Williams, Civ App. 517 S.W.2d 401, err ref no rev err

26. La.—U.S. Fidelity & Guaranty Co. v. Dixie Parking Service, Inc., 262 So.2d 345, 262 La. 45

N.Y.—General Motors Acceptance Corp. v. Grafinger, 306 N.Y.S.2d 606, 61 Misc.2d 670

page 650

27. N.Y.—General Motors Acceptance Corp. v. Grafinger 306 N.Y.S.2d 606, 61 Misc.2d 670

31. Mo.—Progressive Mut. Ins. Co. v. Avis Ford, Inc., 166 N.W.2d 622, 15 Mich App. 49

page 654

60. Award sustained by evidence
Ind.—Hendrickson & Sons Motor Co. v. Osha, 331 N.E.2d 743, 165 Ind.App. 185

page 655

72. Mass.—Hale v. Massachusetts Parking Authority, 265 N.E.2d 494, 358 Mass. 470

77.5. Mo.—Bewley v. Allright Carpark, Inc., App. 617 S.W.2d 547

78. S.C.—Collins Cadillac, Inc. v. Bigelow-Sanford, Inc., 279 S.E.2d 611, 276 S.C. 465

page 656

80. Miss.—City of Meridian v. Webb, 387 So.2d 85

Exemplary damages not recoverable
Ga.—Brown v. Five Points Parking Center, 175 S.E.2d 901, 121 Ga.App. 819

Attorneys fees not recoverable
Ga.—Brown v. Five Points Parking Center, 175 S.E.2d 901, 121 Ga.App. 819

An owner of a motor vehicle who

page 658

86. Colo.—Budwell v. German Motors, Inc., 586 P.2d 1003, 41 Colo.App. 284

Ind.—Deck v. Jim Harris Chevrolet-Buick, App., 386 N.E.2d 714, 5 A.L.R. 4th 305

Automobile repair statute
Cal.—Parada v. Small Claims Court of Los Angeles Judicial Dist., 139 Cal.Rptr. 87, 70 C.A.3d 766

87. La.—Classic Car Imports, Inc. v. Martin, App., 395 So.2d 1390

90. Agreement to do less than provided for in written estimate
Cal.—Parada v. Small Claims Court of Los Angeles Judicial Dist., 139 Cal.Rptr. 87, 70 C.A.3d 766

page 659

95. Setting of prices
Ariz.—Bishop v. Department of Public Safety, App., 596 P.2d 38, 122 Ariz. 512

The authority of a police officer to authorize the removal of a disabled

---

As with all sets of law books, one's research must always be made current. In C.J.S. this is accomplished by checking in the cumulative pocket supplement.

Note here the reference to the case of *Garlock v. Multiple Parking Services, Inc.,* the case previously located by using the *American Digest System* and A.L.R.

---

page 652

47. N.Y.—Garlock v. Multiple Parking Services, Inc., 427 N.Y.S.2d 670, 103 Misc.2d 943, 13 A.L.R. 4th 428

51. N.J.—McGlynn v. Parking Authority of City of Newark, 432 A.2d 99, 86 N.J. 551

Doctrine of res ipsa loquitur applicable
Ark.—Megee v. Reed, 482 S.W.2d 832, 252 Ark. 1016

Res ipsa loquitur inapplicable
N.Y.—Board of Ed. of Ellenville Central School v. Herb's Dodge Sales & Service, Inc., 435 N.Y.S.2d 179, 79 A.D.2d 1049

52. Mich.—Flynn v. Libkie, 300 N.W.2d 560, 101 Mich.App. 331, remanded 308 N.W.2d 98, 411 Mich. 942

54. N.J.—McGlynn v. Parking Authority of City of Newark, 432 A.2d 99, 86 N.J. 551

N.Y.—Motors Ins. Corp. v. American Garages, Inc., 614 N.Y.S.2d 841, 98 Misc.2d 887

page 653

58.10. Testimony of other garage owners as to general custom etc.
(f) Other matters
Mich.—Flynn v. Libkie, 300 N.W.2d 560, 101 Mich.App. 331, remanded 308 N.W.2d 98, 411 Mich. 942

Evidence held sufficient
(5) Fla.—Crippen Oldsmobile, Inc. v. Brabec, App., 244 So.2d 554

Effect of finding of consumer affairs department
N.Y.—Hippodrome Garage v. Myerson, 331 N.Y.S.2d 206, 69 Misc.2d 831

N.C. 301

Contract with insurer
(3) Other matters
Kan.—Branner v. Crooks, 635 P.2d 1265, 6 Kan App.2d 813

Mortgagee-loss payee who received checks from mortgagor's collision insurer not liable
La.—Lott & Sons, Inc. v. Strahan, App., 236 So.2d 577, writ ref 239 So.2d 361, 256 La. 861

page 657

84.60. La.—Alexander v. Qwik Change Car Center, Inc., 352 So.2d 188

N.H.—Brooks v. R.A. Clark's Garage, Inc., 378 A.2d 1144, 117 N.H. 770

Sequestration of automobile held premature
La.—McCann v. George, App., 238 So.2d 197, writ ref 239 So.2d 541, 256 La. 883

What law governs
D.C.—O'Donnell v. S. & R., Inc., App., 369 A.2d 168

85. La.—Colhns v. Wright, App. 2 Cir., 412 So.2d 659

N.C.—Anderson Chevrolet/Olds, Inc. v. Higgins, 292 S.E.2d 159, 57 N.C.App. 650

Out-of-pocket expenses recovered for unauthorized repairs
N.Y.—Hammerstein v. Potamkin Cadillac Corp., 412 N.Y.S.2d 337, 97 Misc.2d 786

Stolen car
Kan.—United States Fidelity & Guaranty Co. v. Marshall, 601 P.2d 1169, 4 Kan App.2d 9

Suspension of registration
N.Y.—Massaro Detroit Diesel Allison, Inc. v. Fotchko, 453 N.Y.S.2d 798, 89 A.D.2d 685

Falls Ins. Co. 276 A.2d 386, 114 N.J.Super. 350

4 N.C.—Terrell v. H & N Chevrolet Co., 181 S.E.2d 124, 11 N.C.App. 310

Ohio—Aetna Cas. & Sur. Co. v. Woody Sander Ford, Inc., 254 N.E.2d 700, 21 Ohio App.2d 62

§ 730. Care as to Repairs, Services, or Supplies

page 660

7. Cal.—Pearson Ford Co. v. Ford Motor Co., 78 Cal.Rptr. 279, 273 C.A.2d 269

La.—Patton v. Precision Motors, Inc., App., 352 So.2d 341, 1 A.L.R.4th 339

Mo.—Fancher v. Southwest Missouri Truck Center, Inc., App., n18 S.W.2d 271

N.Y.—Tobey v. Melton, 426 N.Y.S.2d 110, 74 A.D.2d 708

Wash.—Myers v. Ravenna Motors, Inc., 468 P.2d 1012, 2 Wash.App. 613

Duty to inspect
N.Y.—McGeraid v. Mobil Service Center, 431 N.Y.S.2d 313, 106 Misc.2d 133

N.C.—Stilley v. Automobile Enterprises of High Point, Inc., 284 S.E.2d 684, 55 N.C.App. 33, review den 290 S.E.2d 708, 305 N.C. 307

Okl.—Stuckey v. Young Exploration Co., 586 P.2d 726

8. Vt.—Thurber v. Russ Smith, Inc., 260 A.2d 390, 128 Vt. 216

Brakes
La.—Metrailer v. F & G Merchandising, Inc., App., 230 So.2d 395

Automobile repainting
Ill.—Jeffreys v. Hickman, 269 N.E.2d 110, 132 Ill.App.2d 272

[Illustration 107]

PAGE FROM INDEX TO AMERICAN JURISPRUDENCE 2d

GENERAL INDEX

PARKING PLACES AND LOTS—Cont'd
Limitation of liability, Garages §§ 28, 33, 34
Location, Garages § 20
Master and servant, Garages §§ 36, 42, 91, 104
– invitees, employees as, Garages § 96
– labor and labor relations, supra
– workmen's compensation, Workm C § 268
Mechanics' liens, Mech L § 90
Meters. **Parking Meters** (this index)
Misdelivery, liability for, Garages §§ 33, 40, 72
Moving vehicles, injuries or damage caused by, Garages §§ 44, 91, 104
Municipal corporations
– bonds. **Public Securities and Obligations** (this index)
– delegation of power, Mun Corp § 196
– licenses and permits, Garages §§ 14, 17-19
– police power, infra
– posting of rates, Garages § 25
– public utility, defined, Mun Corp § 561
– regulations, generally, Garages §§ 14, 20, 22; Mun Corp § 481
– specific performance requiring enactment

The General Index to *Am.Jur.2d* will lead the researcher to where the topic under research is covered in *Am.Jur.2d.*

– taxation, Garages § 20
– tort liability, generally, Mun Tort Liab §§ 123, 124
– **Zoning and Planning** (this index)
Negligence liability, Garages §§ 27-34, 81-106, 136; and see appropriate lines in this topic
Noise as nuisance, Garages § 8
Nonresident motorist statute, place of accident as affecting applicability of, Courts § 862
Notice
– contents of vehicles, Garages §§ 31, 71
– limitation of liability, Garages § 33
Nuisances, Garages §§ 8, 11; Nuis § 70
Obstructions, injuries caused by, Garages § 90
Off street parking, see lines throughout this topic
Oil causing slippery conditions, Garages §§ 100, 101
Ordinary care. Standard of care, infra
Overnight parking, Auto § 231
– zoning ordinance, Zoning § 136
Parks and playgrounds, Parks § 32
Passengers as invitees or licensees, Garages §§ 83, 85, 96, 98
Permits. Licenses and permits, supra
Personal injuries, Garages §§ 81-106, 136; and see appropriate lines in this topic
Picketing, Labor § 1395
Pits, personal injuries caused by, Garages §§ 88, 93, 99
Pleading in tort actions, Garages §§ 70, 136

PARKING PLACES AND LOTS—Cont'd
Police power, Garages §§ 14, 20, 25; Mun Corp § 442
– pledge of municipal parking meter revenues to build parking facilities as abandonment of, Mun Corp § 214
Posting of rates, Garages § 25
Premises liability, Garages §§ 81-106; and see appropriate lines in this topic
Presumptions and burden of proof, Garages §§ 71-74, 136
Price signs, Garages § 25
Property damage, Garages §§ 27-34, 42; and see appropriate lines in this topic
Proximate cause, Garages §§ 29, 136
– fire damage, Garages § 43
– theft, Garages § 35
Public funds
– diversion of, Pub F § 4
– municipal police power, pledge of parking meter revenues to build parking facilities as abandonment of, Mun Corp § 214
– **Public Securities and Obligations** (this index)
Questions of law and fact, Garages §§ 78, 87, 99, 103
Railroads, rights of, RR § 113
Rates and charges
– license fees and taxes, License & P § 116
– liens for parking charges, Garages § 144
– meters. **Parking Meters** (this index)
– posting of rates, Garages § 25
Reasonable care. Standard of care, infra
Records of vehicles, keeping of, Garages § 30
Residential districts, nuisances in, Garages § 8
Revocation of licenses and permits, Garages § 19
Schools, liability for injuries in parking lots, Sch § 325
Self-park garages or lots, Garages §§ 28, 31
Shops, parking lots and garages used by customers of, Garages §§ 82, 83, 96
Sidewalks (this index)
Signs, Garages § 25
Slippery conditions, injuries caused by, Garages §§ 89, 92, 100, 101
Snow or ice, injuries caused by, Garages §§ 89, 92
Special assessments, Spec A § 29
Stairways, falls on, Garages § 101
Standard of care, Garages §§ 29, 30
– fires, Garages § 43
– invitees or licensees, Garages §§ 82-85, 95-98
– theft, Garages §§ 35, 37
– trespassers, Garages § 86
Stolen property. Theft, infra

203

[Illustration 108]

PAGE FROM VOLUME 38, AMERICAN JURISPRUDENCE 2d

---

§ 42   GARAGES, ETC.   38 Am Jur 2d

in the garage.[13] But a garageman has been held not liable for the loss of
a motor vehicle where the evidence showed that keys to the garage had been
furnished to the plaintiff and other customers, in order that they might
enter the garage after midnight to put away their cars; that neither the
garageman nor his employee remained at the garage after midnight; that the
plaintiff's car was driven off by a man resembling the plaintiff's chauffeur;
and that the plaintiff's chauffeur was not called as a witness nor his absence
explained.[14]

3. Other Causes or Circumstances of Loss or Damage

§ 42. Generally.

Recovery may be had against a garage keeper for damage to a bailed
motor vehicle while being lowered in the garage elevator by a garage employee,
where the latter may be presumed to have acted with the garage keeper's

> Note how *Am.Jur.* has more text and fewer footnotes than *C.J.S.*.
> But note also the references to *A.L.R.* citations where additional
> cases can be located. *Am.Jur.* is a useful way to find *A.L.R. Annota-*
> *tions.*
>
> Now the annual cumulative pocket supplement must be checked.

the garage at the owner's request, has been held liable for the damage to the
vehicle resulting from the employee's negligence while bringing the vehicle
to the garage, although at the time of the accident the employee had deviated
from the regular route between the garage and the owner's house.[17] In some
cases, an operator of a garage or parking lot has been held liable where the
engine, transmission, or clutch of a bailed motor vehicle was damaged as a
result of the negligent driving of the vehicle by a parking attendant,[18] but
the operator has been held not liable where the evidence of the attendant's
alleged negligence was insufficient to show that the damage had actually
been caused by the attendant's conduct.[19] He has also been held not liable
for damage to a bailed vehicle caused by its being run 5 minutes without oil
and water by an employee of the garage, who was changing the position of

---

13. Meine v Mossler Auto Exch., Inc. 10 La
App 65, 12 So 533, holding, where the plaintiff's car was stolen while standing on the
street, unlocked, rather than in the defendant's
garage, that the defendant was negligent and
therefore liable for the loss of the car.
Annotation: 7 ALR3d 974, § 12; 43 ALR2d
426, § 10.

14. Hogan v O'Brien, 212 App Div 193, 208
NYS 477, where the court stated that no evidence pointed to the guilt of the defendant in
removing the car with any more certainty than
it did to the guilt of any of the others who also
had keys to the garage, and with far less certainty than it did to the guilt of the plaintiff's chauffeur.
Annotation: 7 ALR3d 979, § 13; 43 ALR2d
436, § 14.

15. Einhorn v West 67th Street Garage, 191
App Div 1, 180 NYS 704.
Annotation: 7 ALR3d 988, § 15.

16. Union Indem. Co. v Blaise Downtown
Storage, 18 La App 295, 138 So 226.
Annotation: 7 ALR3d 988, § 15.

17. Southern Garage Co. v Brown, 187 Ala
484, 65 So 400.
Annotation: 15 ALR 690, s. 42 ALR 141,
65 ALR 436.

18. Michaels v Gravier Improv. Co. (La
App) 158 So 2d 260; Butler v Bowdoin
Square Garage, 329 Mass 28, 105 NE2d 838;
Mervine v Sley System Garages, Inc. 193 Pa
Super 394, 164 A2d 59; Carothers v Moore
(Tex Civ App) 183 SW2d 987.
Annotation: 7 ALR3d 982, § 14.

19. Hanna v Shaw, 244 Mass 57, 138 NE
247, disapproved on other grounds Bean v
Security Fur Storage Warehouse, 344 Mass
674, 184 NE2d 64; Rea v Grant-Long Co.
(CP) 79 Ohio L Abs 357, 155 NE2d 724.
Annotation: 7 ALR3d 987, § 14.

[Illustration 109]

PAGE FROM POCKET SUPPLEMENT TO VOLUME 38, AM.JUR.2d

GARAGES, ETC.   § 42

immaterial to creation of bailment for hire that car was locked and keys taken was proper. Richard v Massachusetts Port Authority (**Mass** App) 1974 Adv Sheets 451, 310 NE2d 146.

The owner of a parking lot was not liable for the unexplained disappearance of plaintiff's automobile in the absence of proof that he was negligent, where plaintiff took a parking ticket from a machine, parked her automobile, locked it and took the keys prior to leaving the parking lot. Ellish v Airport Parking Co., 42 App Div 2d 174, 345 NYS2d 650, app dismd 33 NY2d 764, 350 NYS2d 411, 305 NE2d 490 and affd 34 NY2d 882, 359 NYS2d 280, 316 NE2d 715.

Parking lot management was not liable for loss of automobile parked overnight in lot, where owner left keys at nearby Greyhound station extinguishing parking lot's control and custody of vehicle. Mobile Parking Stations, Inc. v Lawson, 53 **Ala** App 181, 298 So 2d 266.

No bailment was created, and parking lot owner was not liable for theft of plaintiff's car where plaintiff did not surrender keys to parking lot attendant, whose role was confined to collecting uniform 25-cent fee from motorists as they entered own lot and directing them to parking spaces. Sewall v Fitz-Inn Auto Parks, Inc. (**Mass** App) 1975 Adv Sheets 934, 330 NE2d

things, keys to owner's car were not placed in dealer's safe as was case with all other cars in garage. Leatherman v Miller's Mut. Fire Ins. Co. (**La** App) 297 So 2d 540.

§ 40. Misdelivery or unauthorized delivery

Practice aids: Liability for loss of automobile left at parking lot or garage, 13 ALR4th 362, superseding in part 7 ALR3d 927.

§ 41. Other particular circumstances

Additional case authorities for section:

In action by corporation officer against parking garage operator for loss of officer's personal property while such property was in automobile owned by corporation and parked in garage, parking garage operator, as bailee, was subject to no liability for loss of such property, where bailment contract stated that garage was not responsible for articles left in car, where bailment contract, although between garage and corporation, was signed by officer as president, and where such signature was a descriptio personae rather than a signing as agent for corporation. White v Atlanta Parking Service Co., 139 **Ga** App 243, 228 SE2d 156.

Defendant municipal parking garage was lia-

> **Check the same section in the pocket supplement. Note under Paragraph 42, the digest of the *Garlock v. Multiple Parking Service* case.**

---

place, had locked his car and had taken his keys with him, and had obtained a ticket from an automatic machine for the purpose of determining time in computing the fee rather than for the purpose of identifying the automobile; thus, there was no presumption of negligence on the part of the parking lot operator and such operator could not be held liable for the theft of the car in the absence of proof that it had been affirmatively negligent. Allright Auto Parks, Inc. v Moore (1977, **Tex** Civ App) 560 SW2d 129.

Garage was not bailee and therefore was not liable to car owner for theft of wire wheels absent proof of specific acts of negligence where garage was of type where person parks car by receiving ticket from machine, chooses own parking space, and retains own keys. Central Parking System v Miller (1979, **Ky**) 586 SW2d 262.

Owner of self-service "lock and park" lot was not liable for theft of plaintiff's automobile since defendant had never exercised custody and control over vehicle. Rhodes v Pioneer Parking Lot, Inc. (1973, **Tenn**) 501 SW2d 569.

§ 39. Thief breaking into garage

Additional case authorities for section:

Automobile dealer was liable to owner of automobile, left with dealer for repairs, which was stolen from dealer's garage when thieves broke in during night, where, among other

street before regular closing time. Meridian v Webb (1980, **Miss**) 387 So 2d 85.

§ 42. Generally

Practice aids: Liability for damage to automobile left in parking lot or garage, 13 ALR4th 442, superseding in part 7 ALR3d 927.

Additional case authorities for section:

Operator of parking lot was liable for damages done to lid of trunk of plaintiff's car when someone had attempted to pry trunk open, notwithstanding fact that car owner parked his car and kept car keys, where there was evidence that five employees were present to service customers in enclosed parking area of hotel and where supervisor of parking area acknowledged that watching for theft and for tampering with vehicles was part of employee's job. Parking Management, Inc. v Gilder (**Dist Col** App) 343 A2d 51.

In action against corporation operating parking lot brought by owner of automobile, which was damaged and from which tape deck and tapes were stolen while parked there, evidence showed that acts of omission of defendants were, as matter of law, negligence, where it had failed to fence or provide guard and thus had failed to protect properly plaintiff's vehicle from damage through acts of vandal, and where possibility of such acts were clearly foreseeable considering parking lot's location, size and general accessibility. Garlock v Multiple

SECTION D.   STATE ENCYCLOPEDIAS

Some states have encyclopedias devoted to their own laws. Five states have encyclopedias published by the Lawyers Co-operative Publishing Company/Bancroft-Whitney Company, and they follow the format of *Am.Jur.2d* while covering only the laws of a specific state.   These are:

California Jurisprudence 3d

Florida Jurisprudence 2d

New York Jurisprudence 2d

Ohio Jurisprudence 3d

Texas Jurisprudence 3d

Three states have encyclopedias published by the West Publishing Company, and these follow the format of *Corpus Juris Secundum*.   These are:

Illinois Law and Practice

Maryland Law and Practice

Michigan Law and Practice

A few other states have sets by other publishers.

Common Features of State Encyclopedias

1.   *Scope:* case and statutory law (substantive and procedural). The cases include both state and federal courts interpreting state law.

2.   *Arrangement:* alphabetically by topics.

3.   *Index:* general index and individual volume indexes.   In some local encyclopedias, the titles included in a volume are separately indexed in the volume.

4.   *Supplementation:* cumulative annual pocket parts and replacement volumes.

5.   *Table of Statutes:* shows where code sections are cited in the local encyclopedia.

6.   *Words and Phrases:* definitions of words and phrases are indexed.

7.   *Research aids:* references to other secondary aids, such as *A.L.R.* annotations and periodical articles, are often provided.

Chapter 16

LEGAL PERIODICALS

Legal periodicals are an important secondary source in legal research. During the nineteenth century, they greatly contributed to improving the image of the legal profession in America.[1] With the ever-increasing proliferation of legislation and court decisions, legal periodicals in the twentieth century play an increasingly important role in keeping lawyers current in developing areas of law and in providing information on the specialized areas of the law. The function of a legal periodical may be described as "recording and critici[zing] of doings of legislators and judges, discussion of current case law, narration of lives of eminent lawyers, and the scientific study of * * * jurisprudence."[2] Legal periodicals may be classified into three groups: (1) law school publications, (2) bar association publications, and (3) special subject and interest periodicals.

SECTION A. LEGAL PERIODICALS

1. Law School Reviews

The periodical publications of law schools are generally called *reviews* (as the *Harvard Law Review* or *Michigan Law Review*). Law school reviews play a unique role in legal research. One distinctive feature of law school reviews is the control of editorial policy and management by student editors. As one legal scholar has noted:

> There is not so far as I know in the world an academic
> faculty which pins its reputation before the public upon the

[1] M. BLOOMFIELD, AMERICAN LAWYERS IN A CHANGING SOCIETY 1776–1876, at 142–43 (1976). For a brief account of legal periodicals in nineteenth-century America, *see* L. FRIEDMAN, A HISTORY OF AMERICAN LAW 546–48 (1973). Some additional references that deal with the early history of legal periodicals in the United States are as follows:

Brainerd, *Historical Sketch of American Legal Periodicals*, 14 LAW LIBR.J. 63 (1921).

Pound, *Types of Legal Periodicals*, 14 IOWA L.REV. 257 (1929).

Digest of American Reports and American Law Periodicals, 23 AM.JURIST 128 (1840).

A complete list of legal periodicals of the last century and their dates of publication may be found in L. JONES, INDEX TO LEGAL PERIODICALS TO 1886, at vii-xiii (1888), and 1887–1899, at vii-xii.

[2] F. HICKS, MATERIALS AND METHODS OF LEGAL RESEARCH 210 (3d rev.ed. 1942).

work of undergraduate students—there is none, that is, except in the American law reviews.[3]

The students forming the board of editors are chosen on the basis of their scholarship record or through a writing competition. Each year a new board is chosen and has the responsibility for the publication of the next volume.

The typical law review is in two or more sections. The first consists of solicited leading articles on various legal topics, usually written by law professors. These articles are usually scholarly in nature and frequently have a substantial impact in changing the law or in charting the course for newly developing fields of law.[4] The second section is written entirely by the students and is devoted to surveys of selected subjects and critical analyses of current court decisions. In many law reviews the former are called *comments* and the latter *notes*. Many reviews also publish book reviews. There are now published more than 200 law school reviews. The majority of law reviews are general in nature with no emphasis placed on any specific subjects, but some continue to stress only the law of the state where they are published. A new trend in law schools is to publish more than one review; in such instances, the additional publications are on specialized subjects, such as civil rights, constitutional law, environmental law, or international law. A representative listing is set forth in Section H *infra*.

The law school reviews have had a high degree of success in meeting these goals.[5] The foremost legal scholars of this century have written for law reviews, and their articles have been instrumental in molding the course of many legal doctrines. Increasingly, courts have cited law review articles and student comments.[6] It is interesting to note that only as recently as the 1920's did the Supreme Court of the United States begin citing law review articles

[3] K. LLEWELLYN, THE BRAMBLE BUSH 105 (2d ed. 1951).

[4] Warren & Brandeis, *The Right to Privacy*, 4 HARV.L.Rev. 193 (1890); Robinson, *Private Management and Operation of the Space Shuttle: Some Legal Problems Related to Market Entry*, 13 AKRON L.REV. 601 (1980).

[5] *See, e.g.*, Douglas, *Law Reviews and Full Disclosure*, 40 WASH.L.REV. 227 (1965); Warren, *Upon the Tenth Anniversary of the UCLA Law Review*, 10 U.C. L.A.L.REV. 1 (1962); Hughes, *Forward*, 50 YALE L.J. 737 (1940); Edmunds, *Hail to Law Reviews*, 1 JOHN MAR.J.PRAC. & PROC. 1 (1967); M. HALL, SELECTED WRITINGS OF BENJAMIN NATHAN CARDOZO 190–92 (1947).

[6] For a scientific study of the citation patterns of the *major* law reviews, *see* Maru, *Measuring the Impact of Legal Periodicals*, 1 A.B.F.RES.J. 227 (1976). *See also* Johnson, *Legal Periodical Usage Survey: Method and Application*, 71 LAW LIBR.J. 177 (1978).

in its opinions,[7] while presently many decisions of the Court cite or quote from law review articles.

But law school reviews have not been without their critics.[8] The substance of the criticism is aimed at their pedantic style and their similarity to each other. Indeed, some members of Congress have even attacked law reviews as having an insidious influence on the Supreme Court of the United States.[9]

Law school reviews do, however, play a significant role in the growth of the law and remain important to legal research. The typical review may be summarized as being subsidized by its parent institution, with its circulation usually limited to law libraries, its alumni, and members of the bar within the jurisdiction where it is published.[10] It is edited by a select group of law students and serves as an important vehicle for the publication of significant legal research as well as an incisive and effective teaching tool.

2. Bar Association Periodicals

All fifty states and the District of Columbia have bar associations. In some states, membership is voluntary; in other states, it is a prerequisite to the practice of law within the state. The latter have what is called an *integrated bar*. [11] In addition, many counties and larger cities have their own local bar associations. Most of the state bar associations and many of the local ones publish periodicals. They vary in scope from such distinguished periodicals as the *American Bar Association Journal* or the *Record of the Association of the Bar of the City of New York*, to those that are little more than newsletters. The primary purposes of bar association publications are to inform the membership of the association's activities, to comment on pending and recent legislation, and to review current local court decisions. When they do publish articles, they tend to stress the more practical aspects of the law, with emphasis upon problem-solving, rather than the theoretical ones. They are concerned more with the law as it is rather than with what it should be. Thus, they perform different functions than the law school reviews, where the emphasis is upon reform and scholarly legal research. As a consequence, bar association publications have less historical value

[7] Newland, *The Supreme Court and Legal Writing: Learned Journals as Vehicles of an Anti-Trust Lobby?*, 48 GEO.L.J. 105, 127 (1959).

[8] *See, e.g.,* Rodell, *Goodbye to Law Reviews,* 23 VA.L.REV. 38 (1936), and *Goodbye to Law Reviews—Revisited,* 48 VA.L.REV. 279 (1962); Miller, *The Law Journals,* 5 CHANGE 64 (1973).

[9] 103 CONG.REC. 16159–16162 (1957) (remarks of Representative Patman). *See also* Douglas, *supra* note 5.

[10] The *Harvard Law Review* has the largest circulation at over 10,000.

[11] For a complete list *see* latest American Bar Association Directory.

but are more useful when researching subjects of current interest to practitioners.

3. Subject and Interest Legal Periodicals

As the literature of the law grows and reflects the increasing complexity of society, it has become ever more difficult for lawyers to keep current not only with the general development of the law, but also with their particular legal interests. Concurrent with this law explosion, there has been developing a movement in the legal profession toward the publication of periodicals of interest to one particular sub-group within the legal profession. Some are published by law schools, edited by students, and follow the format of the traditional law review; others are published by non-profit Associations; and still others are published by private publishing companies. Another recent development has been the publication of periodicals devoted to law and its interaction with another discipline. These reflect the increasing emphasis many law schools and legal scholars are placing on integrating the findings of the social and behavioral sciences with the legal process.

a. *Subject Journals.* Journals devoted to one area of law vary in scope from the very practical to the very scholarly.[12] *Insurance Law Journal* or *Trusts and Estates*, both published by private companies, are examples of periodicals aimed primarily at the practicing attorneys specializing in particular fields of law. They contain articles written by well-known practitioners interpreting the impact of recent legislation and court decisions and may contain reviews of books within their subject area. The *Law and History Review* and the *American Journal of Comparative Law* are examples of periodicals published under the auspices of learned societies, while the *Ecology Law Quarterly*, published at the University of California, Berkeley, School of Law, and the *Urban Law Review*, published at the University of Texas School of Law, are typical of subject journals that are similar to law school reviews.

b. *Special Interest Periodicals.* These periodicals are aimed at those members of the bar who have similar interests and serve as means to encourage writing and research within the special area of interest. They include such journals as *Black Law Journal*, the *Women Lawyers Journal*, the *Catholic Lawyer*, the *Christian Lawyer*, and the *Judges' Journal.*

c. *Interdisciplinary Journals.* Perhaps the most distinguished of this group is the *Journal of Law and Economics*, published by

[12] A few publishers have begun the practice of collecting the best articles written and published over the course of each year, and combining them into a single volume which measures the development of the law in a particular subject area over the period. *Advertising Law* is an example of one such annual.

the faculty of the University of Chicago School of Law. Other representative titles are the *University of Michigan Journal of Law Reform*, the *Journal of Psychiatry and Law, Law and Society Review*, and the *Journal of Legal Medicine*.

4. Legal Newspapers

In many larger cities [13] there are newspapers devoted to legal affairs of their metropolitan area. Most are published daily, Monday through Friday, and primarily contain information on court calendars and dockets, changes in court rules, news about recent changes in legislation, new administrative rules, and stories about local judges and lawyers. Some of the larger ones, such as the *New York Law Journal* or the *Los Angeles Daily Journal*, also publish current court opinions and articles on various legal topics.

There are also two weekly legal newspapers that are national in scope. These are the *Legal Times* and the *National Law Journal*. A monthly legal newspaper, *The American Lawyer*, contains similar national coverage and features.

SECTION B. COMPREHENSIVE PERIODICAL INDEXES

As described in Section A, the usefulness of legal periodicals to legal research depends almost entirely on the researcher's ability to find what articles have been written and where they have been published. Generally, it is necessary to rely on indexes to legal periodical literature for this purpose.

1. Jones-Chipman Index to Legal Periodicals, 1888–1937, 6 volumes

This was the first index that attempted to provide a comprehensive and systematic index to English language legal periodicals. It is still necessary to consult this set to locate articles published prior to 1908.

2. Index to Legal Periodicals (I.L.P.)

This index, first published in 1908 by the American Association of Law Libraries, was purchased in 1961 by the H.W. Wilson Company. From 1961 until 1979, the Committee on the *Index to Legal Periodicals* of the American Association of Law Libraries served in an advisory capacity to the publisher on indexing and editorial policy. This *Index* includes legal periodicals published in the United States, Canada, Great Britain, Ireland, Australia and New Zealand, if they regularly publish legal articles of high quality and of permanent

---

[13] A complete list of legal newspapers is available in the annual *Ayer Directory of Publications*, One Bala Avenue, Bala Cynwyd, Pennsylvania 19004.

reference value. It includes only articles which are at least five ordinary pages or two folio pages in length. Case notes, bibliographies, biographies, and book reviews must be at least two ordinary pages or one folio page in length. Over five hundred periodicals are included, with new titles added when they meet the criteria for inclusion in this *Index.*

Until 1983, authors were listed only as cross-references to subjects under which their articles were entered. Currently, authors and subjects are in one alphabet with full title and citation under each. The *Index* is published monthly, except during September, with an annual cumulation.

In addition to the Author/Subject Index, there are the following sections:

a. *Table of Cases Commented Upon.* This lists the names of cases (for the time period of the issue) that have had a note or comment written on them.

b. *Table of Statutes Commented Upon.* This lists statutes by subject under each jurisdiction.

c. *Book Review Index.* This lists by authors all books reviewed in the periodicals indexed by the *Index to Legal Periodicals.*

An Advisory Committee of Law Librarians and Practicing Lawyers serves as consultant to the publisher on the selection of subject headings and periodicals for inclusion.

[See Illustrations 110–112 for sample pages from the *Index to Legal Periodicals.*]

3. Current Law Index and Legal Resource Index

Information Access Corporation began publication of these two indexes in 1980. Both are published under the auspices of the American Association of Law Libraries. They are computer-produced, and each has the following features:

Author/Title Index: This section lists all articles by author with full title and periodical citation given. It also lists all articles by title giving the periodical citation.

Book Reviews: Book reviews that appear in the periodicals covered by the Indexes are listed under both the author and title of the book in the *Author/Title Index* section. An interesting feature is the rating of books from A–F, recording the opinion of the reviewer.

Indexing Policy: Titles to be included are selected by An Advisory Committee of the American Association of Law Libraries. All titles are in the English language (except for a few in French from Canada) and are published throughout the world. All materials of

value are indexed without limitation as to the number of pages. Coverage begins with the 1980 imprint for each periodical. Subject headings are selected from the Library of Congress *Subject Headings* as augmented by additional or alternative terms as recommended by the Advisory Committee.

Table of Cases: Cases that are the subject of case notes are listed under the names of both plaintiff and defendant.

Table of Statutes: Lists all statutes cited in articles, both by official and popular citation.

a. *Current Law Index (CLI).* This is a printed index issued monthly with quarterly and annual cumulations. It indexes over 700 periodicals, and each issue contains a list of periodicals indexed with addresses.

b. *Legal Resource Index (LRI).* This index includes all of the titles and all of the features of *Current Law Index.* It has, in addition, the following features:

(1) It is produced on microfilm and read on a specially designed automated microfilm reader.

(2) Each month a cumulated reel of microfilm is sent to subscribers. Thus, it is never necessary to examine several separate issues, as when using a printed index.

(3) In addition to including all of the titles that are in the *Current Law Index,* it indexes many more titles such as the more important legal newspapers and some newsletters of the American Bar Association and selected state bar associations.

(4) It includes articles of legal interest from:

Magazine Index, which indexes nearly 400 popular periodicals;

National Newspaper Index, which indexes the *Christian Science Monitor,* the *Los Angeles Times,* the *New York Times,* the *Wall Street Journal,* and the *Washington Post.*

(5) It includes under each subject heading selected entries for books and government documents on legal subjects.

(6) Computer searching: Since the *LRI* is produced by computer, its information is available in machine-readable form. It may be computer-researched through the DIALOG Information Systems.[14]

[See Illustrations 113–115 for sample pages of *Current Law Index.*]

---

[14] Lockheed Missiles & Space Company, Inc., Palo Alto, CA.

SECTION C.   ILLUSTRATIONS FOR LEGAL PERIODICALS

[Illustration 110]

PAGE FROM INDEX TO LEGAL PERIODICALS

> **Articles are listed alphabetically under headings.**
>
> **Note how authors are listed. One has to refer to the subject headings indicated to locate the articles. The letter in the parenthesis refers to the first letter of the title of the article. However, starting with the 1983–84 issues, full titles are listed under authors.**

Justice Holmes ——— [?]
27 Am J Juris 32–45 '82
Natural law of administrative law. W. H. Rodgers, jr. 48 Mo L Rev 101–11 Wint '83
"Natural" law revisited. R. A. Dworkin. 34 U Fla L Rev 165–88 Wint '82
Obedience to the law in Plato's Crito. E. J. Weinrib. 27 Am J Juris 85–103 '82
On the difference between wealth and liberty. D. Glasner. 2 Int'l Rev L & Econ 227–33 D '82
Separation of powers: introduction to the study of executive agreements. G. J. Schmitt. 27 Am J Juris 114–38 '82
What price "natural law"? G. Niemeyer. 27 Am J Juris 1–13 '82

NATURAL resources
See also
Energy resources
Environmental law
Environmental protection
Marine resources

Anticipating transboundary resource needs and issues in the U.S.–Mexico border region to the year 2000: a symposium. 22 Nat Resources J 729–1174 O '82
Beyond Commonwealth Edison Co. v. Montana (101 S Ct 2946)—direct congressional limitations on state taxation of natural resources. J. T. Bradford. 9 J Corp Tax 253–69 Aut '82
Bringing people back: toward a comprehensive theory of taking in natural resources law. W. H. Rodgers, jr. 10 Ecology L Q 205–55 '82
Commerce clause and federalism: implications for state control of natural resources. 50 Geo Wash L Rev 601–26 My '82
Conserving natural resources: toward a comprehensive state solid waste recycling program under the Federal Resource Conservation and Recovery Act. 10 N Y U Rev L & Soc Change 469–501 '80/'81
Countryside conservation and the Wildlife and Countryside Act 1981. H. McCoubrey. 132 New L J 826–8 S 2 '82
Enforcing property rights: extending property rights theory to congestible and environmental goods. D. W. Barnes. 10 B C Envt'l Aff L Rev 583–638 '82/'83
Federalism and natural resources: a symposium. Prologue. J. H. Goetz; Reflections on Commonwealth Edison Co. v. Montana (101 S Ct 2946) M. McGrath. W. Hellerstein; The new federalism of the Supreme Court: diminished expectations of National League of Cities (National League of Cities v. Usery. 96 S Ct 2465) J. J. Lopach; The effect of federal legislation on historical state powers of pollution control: has Congress muddied state waters? J. T. Renz. 43 Mont L Rev 155–216 Summ '82
Foreign investment in United States energy and mining: crossroads for policy. 8 Colum J Envt'l L 237–67 '82
Good old American permits: Madisonian federalism on the territorial sea and continental shelf. M. S. Ball. 12 Envtl L 623–76 Spr '82
Ilegalidad de la proyectada explotacion de los recursos naturales de Puerto Rico bajo el actual regimen colonial. Olivero Barreto. 43 Rev C Abo P R 435–48 Ag '82
Interstate resource conflicts: the role of the federal courts. R. B. Stewart. 6 Harv Envtl L Rev 241–61 '82
Limitations on state power to tax natural resource development on Indian reservations. 43 Mont L Rev 217–34 Summ '82
Mitigating fish and wildlife impacts of nonfederal resource development: flexibility, intimidation or congressional uncertainty? J. M. Morgan. 29 Fed B News & J 347–52 S/O '82
Protecting a natural treasure: Michigan's Upper Peninsular. D. S. Favre. 62 Mich B J 304–7 My '83
Public trust totem in public land law: ineffective—and undesirable—judicial intervention. S. M. Jawetz. 10 Ecology L Q 455–95 '82
Symposium on the taxation of natural resources. Editors' note. A. M. Church. A. E. Utton; Variable rate severance taxes: impact and incidence. R. F. Conrad; The incidence of coal severance taxes: political perceptions and economic realities. R. B. Shelton. D. P. Vogt;

NATURALIZATION
Fedorenko v. United States (101 S Ct 737): a new test for misrepresentation in visa applications. 7 N C J Int'l L & Com Reg 129–41 Wint '82
Immigration—naturalization—"good moral character" requirement is a question of federal law. Nemetz v. INS. 647 F 2d 432. 6 Suffolk Transnat'l L J 383–94 Fall '82

NAVAL LAW. SEE MILITARY LAW

NAVE, David R.
Bonds (I)
Inc tax: deductions—US (I)

NAVY. SEE ARMED FORCES

NAWAZ, Mohammad
Int Fund for Agricultural Development (L)
Loans (L)

NEATE. Graeme J.
Australian aborigines (L)
Language (L)
Title to land (L)

NEBRASKA
Annual survey of Nebraska law. 16 Creighton L Rev 239–440 '82/'83

NEELEMAN, Stanley D.
Blog (Crapo)

NEELEY-KVARME, Michael
Medicare (A)

NEELY, David H.
Attorneys (H)
Handicapped (H)   ←

NEGLIGENCE
See also
Air law
Comparative negligence
Contributory negligence
Maritime law
Motor vehicles
Personal injuries
Products liability
Proximate cause
Wrongful death

Accountants' liability to third parties for negligently prepared financial statements. S. Gosnell. 40 U Toronto Faculty L Rev 35–48 '82
Administering the tort of negligent infliction of mental distress: a synthesis. 4 Cardozo L Rev 487–518 Spr '83
Akins v. Glenns Falls City School District 424 N E 2d 531 (NY)]: a crack in the wall of comparative negligence. 46 Alb L Rev 1533–53 Summ '82
Applying negligence doctrine to the teaching profession. T. P. Collingsworth. 11 J L & Educ 479–505 O '82
Attorney accountability in Kentucky—liability to clients and third parties. G. P. Johnston. 70 Ky L J 747–805 '81/'82
Attorney negligence in real estate title examination and will drafting: elimination of the privity requirement as a bar to recovery by foreseeable third parties. 17 New Eng L Rev 955–98 '81/'82
Automobile "ownership, maintenance, and use"—a driver's liability for injuries to alighting passengers in North Carolina. 18 Wake Forest L Rev 537–54 Je '82
Bulk buyers and economic loss. P. N. Todd. 1983 J Bus L 42:54 Ja '83
Common law liability of the certified public accountant for negligent misrepresentation. H. B. Wiener. 20 San Diego L Rev 233–63 Mr '83
Compensating the child's loss of parental love, care, and affection. 1983 U L Rev 293–316 '83
Contracts—exculpatory provisions—a bank's liability for ordinary negligence: Lynch v. Santa Fe National Bank [627 P 2d 1247 (N M)] 12 N M L Rev 821–31 Spr '82

[Illustration 111]

PAGE FROM INDEX TO LEGAL PERIODICALS, 1982–1983 VOLUME

TABLE OF CASES COMMENTED UPON

A. Gay Jenson Farms Co. v. Cargill, Inc. 309 N W 2d 285 (Minn)
  58 N D L Rev 835-49 '82
AARON v. SEC, 100 S Ct 1945
  27 N Y L Sch L Rev 211-23 '81
ABC Builders, Inc. v. Phillips, 632 P 2d 925 (Wyo)
  17 Land & Water L Rev 467-85 '82
ABELE, In re, 214 USPQ 682
  64 J Pat Off Soc'y 531-5 S '82
ACHIRO v. Commissioner [1981] Tax Ct Rep (CCH) (77 T C) 38,351
  14 Conn L Rev 819-41 Summ '83
ACKER v. Guinn, 464 S W 2d 348 (Tex)
  33 Oil & Gas Inst 193-223 '82
ACLU v. Rabun County Chamber of Commerce, Inc. 698 F 2d 1098
  34 Mercer L Rev 1603-18 Summ '83
ACTING Special Counsel v. Paul D. Sullivan, ---- MSPB ---- (1981)
  34 Ad L Rev 593-608 Fall '82
ACTION for Children's Television (ACT) v. FCC, 564 F 2d 458
  3 Comm/Ent L J 701-17 Summ '81
ADAMS v. Peck, 415 A 2d 292 (Md)
  11 U Balt L Rev 344-56 Wint '82
ADAMS v. Texas, 100 S Ct 2521
  10 Am J Crim L 47-63 Mr '82
ADOUE v. State, 408 So 2d 567 (Fla)
  10 Fla St U L Rev 290-300 Spr '82
ADULT Anonymous II, In re 452 N Y S 2d 198
  21 J Fam L 551-2 My '83
ADVANCE Business Sys. and Supply Co. v. SCM Corp. 287 F Supp 143

ALLDERS Int'l Ltd. v. Parkins [1981] I R L R 68
  11 Indus L J 192-7 S '82
ALLEN v. McCurry, 101 S Ct 411
  5 Crim Just J 149-73 Fall '81
ALLEN, In Re Marriage of, 626 P 2d 16 (Wash)
  58 Wash L Rev 111-28 D '82
ALLISON v. United States, 82-1 US T C ¶ 9163
  31 Oil & Gas Tax Q 106-19 S '82
ALLNATT London Properties Ltd. v. Newton (1983) 45 P & C R 94
  1983 Conv 158-60 Mr/Ap '83
ALLSTATE Ins. Co. v. Hague, 101 S Ct 633
  10 Hofstra L Rev 973-1071 Summ '82
ALLSTATE Ins. Co. v. Inversiones Navieras Imparca, 646 F 2d 169
  7 Mar Law 109-19 Spr '82
  56 Tul L Rev 1409-20 Je '82
ALVIS v. Ribar, 421 N E 2d 886 (Ill)
  1982 S Ill U L J 89-110 '82
ALYUCAN Interstate Corp. In re. 12 Banker 803
  1982 Utah L Rev 383-99 '82
Les AMBASSADEURS Club v. Bainda [1982] I R L R 5
  11 Indus L J 192-7 S '82
AMENDMENT of the Constitution of Canada, Reference Re (1981) 125 D L R (3d) 1
  23 Harv Int'l L J 395-404 Wint '83
AMERICAN Civil Liberties Union of Georgia v. Rabun County Chamber of Commerce, Inc. 678 F 2d 1379
  6 Am J Trial Advocacy 337-9 Fall '82
  35 U Fla L Rev 188-94 Wint '83

> When it is known that a particular case deals with the subject under
> research, law review citations on the subject can be located in the Table
> of Cases section of the Index to Legal Periodicals. Later issues of the
> I.L.P. should be consulted for later law review citations.

  48 Brooklyn L Rev 1027-51 Summ '82
AGUILAR v. Texas, 84 S Ct 1509
  14 Loy U Chi L J 57-77 Fall '82
A.H. Belo Corp. v. Sanders, 632 S W 2d 145 (Tex)
  14 Tex Tech L Rev 523-30 '83
AILSA Craig Fishing Co. Ltd. v. Malvern Fishing Co [1983] 1 All E R 101
  99 Law Q Rev 163-5 Ap '83
  45 Mod L Rev 322-9 My '82
AIR New Zealand v. Mahon (No. 2) [1981] 1 N Z L R 618
  4 Auckland U L Rev 328-33 Je '82
AIRCRASH in Bali, Indonesia on Apr. 22, 1974, In re. 684 F 2d 1301
  77 Am J Int'l L 153-5 Ja '83
AKBARIN v. Immigration and Naturalization Serv. 669 F 2d 839
  20 San Diego L Rev 11-36 D '82
AKINS v. Glens Falls City School Dist. 424 N E 2d 531 (NY)
  46 Alb L Rev 1533-53 Summ '82
ALADDIN'S Castle, Inc. v. City of Mesquite, 630 F 2d 1029
  12 Stetson L Rev 207-35 Fall '82
ALBALA v. City of New York, 429 N E 2d 786 (NY)
  15 Conn L Rev 161-81 Fall '82
  50 Tenn L Rev 195-211 Fall '82
ALBEMARLE Paper Co. v. Moody, 95 S Ct 2362
  8 J Corp L 565-76 Spr '83
ALBERTA Gas Chem. Ltd. v. Celanese Corp. 650 F 2d 9
  12 Ga J Int'l & Comp L 231-9 Spr '82
ALBERTSON'S, Inc. v. Workers' Compensation Appeals Bd. of State of California, 182 Cal Rptr 304
  29 Med Trial Tech Q 424-33 Spr '83
ALCOHOLIC Beverage Control Bd. v. Taylor Drug Stores, Inc., 635 S W 2d 319 (Ky)
  71 Ky L J 703-25 '82/'83
ALFRED L. Snapp and Son, Inc. v. Puerto Rico. 102 S Ct 3260
  68 ABA J 1492 N '82
ALICEA v. Gagnon 675 F 2d 913
  52 U Cin L Rev 267-76 '83

P 2d 899 (Cal)
  14 Pac L J 835-67 Ap '83
AMERICAN Paper Inst. v. Environmental Protection Agency, 16 E.R.C. 1252 (4th Cir 1981)
  22 Nat Resources J 455-65 Ap '82
AMERICAN Radio Ass'n v. Mobil Steamship Ass'n, Inc. 95 S Ct 409
  15 N Y U J Int'l L & Pol 395-434 Wint '83
AMERICAN Soc'y of Mechanical Eng'rs v. Hydrolevel Corp. 102 S Ct 1935
  68 ABA J 846-7 Jl '82
  1983 B Y U L Rev 483-97 '83
  64 Chi B Rec 356-8+ My/Je '83
  87 Dick L Rev 465-75 Wint '83
  13 Seton Hall L Rev 354-73 '83
  60 Wash U L Q 1487-504 Wint '83
AMERICAN Spring Wire Corp. v. United States, 16-49 Cust. B. & Dec. 56 (1982), 4 Int'l Trade Rep. Dec. (BNA) 1308 (1982)
  24 Harv Int'l L J 219-25 Summ '83
AMERICAN Textile Mfr. Inst. Inc. v. Donovan, 101 S Ct 2478
  34 Ad L Rev 483-94 Summ '82
  47 Alb L Rev 975-1018 Spr '83
  12 Golden Gate U L Rev 449-72 Spr '82
  17 New Eng L Rev 1345-72 '81/'82
  35 Rutgers L Rev 133-62 Fall '82
  56 St John's L Rev 537-57 Spr '82
  49 Tenn L Rev 365-88 Wint '82
  4 Whittier L Rev 275-312 '82
AMERICAN Tobacco Co. v. Patterson, 102 S Ct 1534
  96 Harv L Rev 278-88 N '82
  33 Lab L J 409-16 Jl '82
  36 Sw L J 1039-53 N '82
  14 U Tol L Rev 433-68 Wint '83
AMOCO Prod. Co. v. Alexander, 622 S W 2d 563 (Tex)
  14 Tex Tech L Rev 459-93 '83
AMOCO Prod. Co. v. North Dakota Indus. Comm'n, 307 N W 2d 839 (ND)
  58 N D L Rev 675-87 '82
AMSTAR Corp. v. S/s Alexandros T. 664 F 2d 904
  14 J Mar L & Com 281-8 Ap '83
ANDERSON v. Celebrezze, 103 S Ct 1564
  69 ABA J 824 Je '83

[Illustration 112]

PAGE FROM INDEX TO LEGAL PERIODICALS

Each issue has a separate Book Review Section. All books that have been reviewed in the periodicals indexed in an issue are listed alphabetically by author.

[Illustration 113]

PAGE FROM ANNUAL ISSUE—CURRENT LAW INDEX

[Illustration 114]

PAGE FROM ANNUAL ISSUE—CURRENT LAW INDEX

AUTHOR/TITLE INDEX

BRAGOLI, J.E.R.
Gaming cheats and chesting. (paper presented at Autumn Symposium of Forensic Science Society, London, Nov. 7-8, 1980) (transcript)
21 J. For. Sci. Soc'y 251-257 July '81

BRAHAMS, Diana

BRAITHWAITE, William J.
Derivative works in Canadian copyright law.
20 Osgoode Hall L.J. 191-231 June '82
Developments in criminal law and procedure: the 1978-79 term. (Canada Supreme Court)
1 Sup. Ct. L. Rev. 187-248 Ann '80

BRANNON, GERARD M.
by Bruce Allen Murphy rev by Judith Resnik grade C
71 Calif. L. Rev. 776-794 March '83
by Bruce Allen Murphy rev by Myron H. Bright and David T. Smorodin grade D
16 Loy. L.A. L. Rev. 205-226 Wntr '83

A typical page from the Author-Title Section of Current Law Index. Note the following:

1. **Authors are listed alphabetically with complete title and citation.**

2. **Articles are also listed under title.**

3. **Book reviews are included in this section under both the author and title of the book. Books are rated A–F according to the opinion of the reviewer.**

---

51 Medico-Legal J. 181-182 Summ '83
Informed consent does not demand full disclosure of risks. (Great Britain - Lancet Reprints)
51 Medico-Legal J. 185-186 Summ '83
Sex change is no change. (Lancet Reprints)
51 Medico-Legal J. 179 Summ '83
The postcoital pill and intrauterine device: contraceptive or abortificient? (Great Britain - Lancet Reprints)
51 Medico-Legal J. 180-181 Summ '83
The morning-after pill: contraception or abortion?
133 New L.J. 417-418 May 6 '83
R. v. MacKenny and Pinfold: rules governing admissibility of psychiatric evidence definition of medical evidence - distinguishing a psychologist from a psychiatrist. (Great Britain) (includes bibliography)
51 Medico-Legal J. 100-103 Spr '83
R. v. Sullivan: epilepsy, insanity and the common law. (from The Lanceiot) (Great Britain)
51 Medico-Legal J. 112-115 Spr '83
What damages should be payable for the birth of an unplanned baby? (Great Britain) (editorial)
51 Medico-Legal J. 65-66 Spr '83
R. v. Sullivan: epilepsy, insanity and the common law. (Great Britain)
133 New L.J. 137-138 Feb 11 '83
Extension of time limit in a medical negligence action. (reprinted from The Lancet)
50 Medico-Legal J. 171-172 Wint '82
Inquest to be held into the death of Helen Smith. (reprinted from The Lancet, death of British nurse in Saudi Arabia under questionable circumstances)
50 Medico-Legal J. 172-174 Wint '82
Wasting medical experts' time. (Great Britain, reprinted from The Lancet)
50 Medico-Legal J. 174-175 Wint '82
Coroner's jurisdiction extends to deaths while abroad - inquest into the death of Helen Smith. (Great Britain)
132 New L.J. 750-751 Aug 5 '82

BRAHE, Cec
The ABC of evidence. by Reg Bartley and Cec Brahe rev by Frank Bates grade B
56 Austl. L.J. 498 Sept '82

BRAIN, Elizabeth Devin
Recent developments in RICO.
52 U. Cin. L. Rev. 464-502 Spr '83
Use of collateral estoppel in private civil actions under RICO: the procedural benefits of Parklane Hosiery v. Shore.
52 U. Cin. L. Rev. 490-502 Spr '83
Federal civil procedure - class actions - limitations of actions - after class certification has been denied for lack of numerosity, a putative class member cannot claim the statute of limitations was tolled while the certification determination was pending so that she might file an independent suit. (case note)
52 U. Cin. L. Rev. 225-238 Wntr '83

BRAIOTTA, Louis, Jr
Audit committees: a checklist review of documents, procedures, and events.
7 Corp. L. Rev. 56-63 Wntr '84
The audit director's guide. by Louis Braiotta Jr. rev by Linda B. Samuels grade B
6 Corp. L. Rev. 95-96 Wntr '83

BRAITHWAIT, Steven
Econometric and end-use models are not dichotomous. (critique of John C. Sawhills and Lester P. Silverman - Do utilities have strategic options.)
111 Pub. Util. Fort. 6(2) June 9 '83

BRAITHWAITE, John
Asbestos and health: a case of informal social control. (Australia) by John Braithwaite and Brent Fisse
16 Austl. & N.Z.J. Criminology 67-80 June '83
Prisons, education and work. by John Braithwaite rev by Tony Parlett grade B
24 Can. J. Criminology 465-467 Oct '82

Tax aspects of the Colorado Program. (Colorado Lawyer Trust Account Foundation.)
12 Colo. Law. 582-583 April '83

BRAME, J. Robert, III
Antitrust liability of local governments: the effect of City of Boulder. by J. Robert Brame III and Howard Feller
9 Va. B.A.J. 14-18 Wntr '83
The immunity of local governments and their officials from antitrust claims after City of Boulder. by J. Robert Brame III and Howard Feller
16 U. Rich. L. Rev. 705-729 Summ '82

BRAMER, Randall J.
Insurance law - emotional distress damages in commercial contract action - emotional distress damages are not recoverable by insured for breach of disability insurance contract absent proof that damages for emotional distress were contemplated by the parties at the time of contract formation. (case note)
60 U. Det. J. Urb. L. 120-136 Fall '82

BRAMS, Steven J.
Biblical games: a strategic analysis of stories in the Old Testament. by Steven J. Brams rev by Nicholas R. Miller grade B
92 Ethics 397 Jan '82

BRANA-SHUTE, Gary
Crime and punishment in the Caribbean. by Rosemary Brana-Shute and Gary Brana-Shute rev by Paul Gendreau grade B
25 Can. J. Criminology 131-133 Jan '83

BRANCATELLI, Joe
The ties that bind (choke).
12 Perspectives: Civ. Rights Q. 38-43 Spr '80

BRAND, C.M.
The caravan as a home: planning aspects - II. (Great Britain) by C.M. Brand and D.W. Williams
127 Solicitor's J. 721-722 Nov 4 '83
The caravan as a home: planning aspects - I. (Great Britain) by C.M. Brand and D.W. Williams
127 Solicitor's J. 703-704 Oct 28 '83
House conversion - operational change of use? (Great Britain) by C.M. Brand and D.W. Williams
133 New L.J. 509-510 June 3 '83
Third parties and development control - a better deal for Scottish neighbours? by C.M. Brand and Brian Thompson
J. Plan. & Envt'l L. 743-762 Dec '82

BRAND, Horst
Productivity improvements in two fabricated metals industries. by Horst Brand and Clyde Huffstutler
v106 Monthly Labor Review p18(7) Oct '83
The evolution of fair labor standards: a study in class conflict.
v106 Monthly Labor Review p25(4) Aug '83
Productivity in commercial banking: computers spur the advance. by Horst Brand and John Duke
v105 Monthly Labor Review p19(9) Dec '82
Productivity in the pump and compressor industry. by Clyde Huffstutler and Horst Brand
v105 Monthly Labor Review p38(8) Dec '82

BRAND, Sharon Elaine
Parental termination proceedings and the requirement of clear and convincing evidence. (case note)
24 S. Tex. L.J. 390-399 Wntr '83

Brandeis.
by Lewis J. Paper rev by Gerald T. Dunne grade A-
69 A.B.A.J. 1270-1271 Sept '83
Brandeis: an intimate biography of one of America's truly great Supreme Court justices.
by Lewis J. Paper grade B
57 Fla. B.J. 562 Oct '83
by Lewis J. Paper grade A.
88 Com. L.J. 528 Oct '83
The Brandeis-Frankfurter connection.
by Bruce Allen Murphy rev by Mark B. Rotenberg grade B
83 Colum. L. Rev. 1863-1878 Nov '83
by Bruce Allen Murphy grade B
19 Cal. W.L. Rev. 407 Spr '83
by Bruce Allen Murphy rev by Russell H. Wheeler grade B-
81 Mich. L. Rev. 931-945 March '83

11 Legal Aspects Med. Prac. 1-8 May '83
Electronic fund transfers and the New Payments Code. (annual survey of consumer financial services law) by Roland E. Brandel and Jay N. Soloway
39 Bus. Law. 1355-1370 May '83
Introduction to the annual survey of consumer financial services law. by Roland E. Brandel and Ralph J. Rohner
39 Bus. Law. 1267-1269 May '83

BRANDELL, Roland St. John
The law of the straits settlements: a commentary. by Roland St. John Brandell rev by R.H. Hickling grade A
32 Int'l & Comp. L.Q. 1043-1045 Oct '83

BRANDON, Michael
UK accession to the Convention on the establishment of a scheme of registration of wills and of the Convention providing a uniform law on the form of an international will.
32 Int'l & Comp. L.Q. 742-747 July '83

BRANDT-CASADEVALL, C.
Experimental evaluation of rigor mortis, VI. Effect of various causes of death on the evolution of rigor mortis. (Switzerland) by T. Krompecher, C. Bergerioux, C. Brandt-Casadevall and H.-R. Gujer
22 For. Sci. Int'l 1-9 July '83

BRANDT, G.J.
The Quebec veto reference: a constitutional postscript.
21 U.W. Ont. L. Rev. 163-171 May '83
Canadian Charter of Rights and Freedoms - right to property as an extension of personal security - status of undeclared rights.
16 Can. B. Rev. 398-406 March '83

BRANDT, T.J.
Procedure for objections to the determination of state death taxes and valuation. (report of Committee on State Death Tax Problems of Estates and Trusts) by Phyllis K. Fairbanks, Richard G. Bacon, George T. Bogert, T.J. Brandt, Richard F. Edwards, William D. Haught, Robert C. Lovejoy, F. Edmund Lynch, Lloyd Leva Plaine, Archie W. Service, L. Franklin Taylor, James H. Thompson and Howard Van Antwerp III
18 Real Prop. Prob. & Tr. J. 34-50 Spr '83

BRANDZEL, Jacob R.
Payment of expenses by lessee may subject lessor to Sec. 163(d) limitation on investment interest. by Jacob R. Brandzel and Mark J. Blumenthal
14 Tax Adviser 596-597 Oct '83
Some tax traps under few Sec. 338 rules. by Eileen D. Suffian and Jacob R. Brandzel
14 Tax Adviser 601-602 Oct '83

BRANIT, Thomas J.
Contributory infringement liability in Universal City Studios, Inc. v. Sony Corp.: the one and only pays for our sins.
14 Loy. U. Chi. L.J. 79-103 Fall '82

BRANN, Andrew R.
Use of legislative histories by the United States Supreme Court. by Andrew R. Brann. by Jorge L. Carro and Andrew R. Brann
9 J. Legis. 282-303 Summ '82

BRANNIGAN, Augustine
The legal framework of plea bargaining. (includes bibliography) (Canada)
25 Can. J. Criminology 399-419 Oct '83

BRANNIGAN, Vincent
Open discussion. (Symposium on law-science cooperation under the National Environmental Policy Act) (transcript) by Vincent Brannigan, Howard T. Markey, Robert Ketcham and Jeffrey Lubbers
15 Nat. Resources Law. 625-627 Summ '83

BRANNIGAN, Vincent M.
Applying new laws to existing buildings: retrospective fire safety codes. (Symposium: Code Enforcement: Issues and Answers for the 80's)
60 U. Det. J. Urb. L. 447-472 Spr '83

BRANNON, Gerard M.
The fiscal policy issues in the 1984 budget.
18 Tax Notes 571-574 Feb 14 '83

[Illustration 115]

PAGE FROM ANNUAL ISSUE—CURRENT LAW INDEX

> **The Table of Cases in the Current Law Index lists all cases commented on in articles indexed and gives citation of the case, and full title of the casenote. A similar cumulative Table is available in the Legal Resources Index.**

A.B. v. Wiltshire County Council,
Fam. July 12, 1983 Paying for independent social work reports. (Great Britain)   *L.A.G. Bull. 112 Sept '83*

A. Bourjois & Co. v. Katzel,
274 F. 856 (S.D.N.Y. 1920) Preventing the importation and sale of genuine goods bearing American-owned trademarks: protecting an American goodwill.
35 Maine L. Rev. 315-340 Spr '83

A.E. Dorsett (Aimar Dolls Ltd.), Daley v,
1981 I.R.L.R. 385 (E.A.T.) Unfair dismissal: the compensatory award. (Recent Cases) (Great Britain)
11 Indus. L.J. 123-124 Ann '82

A.G. Becker, Inc. v. Board of Governors of the Federal Reserve System,
693 F.2d 136 (D.C. Cir. 1982) Banks and banking - securities - prime quality commercial paper of less than nine month maturity issued by third parties and sold by commercial banks in denominations of over $100,000 to financially sophisticated customers who are neither fiduciary accounts over which the bank has discretion nor the general public is not a security within the prohibitions of the Glass-Steagall Act. (case note)
52 U. Cin. L. Rev. 618-636 Spr '83

A. Gay Jenson Farms Co. v. Cargill, Inc.,
309 N.W.2d 285 (Minn. 1981) Principal and agent - an agency relationship exists between a large corporate grain dealer and a local grain elevator when the dealer exercises de facto control over the operations of the elevator. (case note)
58 N.D.L. Rev. 835-849 Fall '82

A.H. Belo Corp. v. Sanders,
632 S.W.2d 145 (Tex. 1982) Proof of loss of a specific sale is required to recover on a slander of title action in Texas. (case note)
14 Tex. Tech. L. Rev. 523-530 April '83

A.H. Robins Co., Dortch v,
650 P.2d 1046 (Or. 1982) Oregon's limitations statute for products cases strictly construed. (case note)
19 Willamette L. Rev. 322-325 Spr '83

A.L.A. Schechter Poultry Corp. v. United States,
295 U.S. 495 (1935) Schechter and the FTC: a roving commission.   *39 Bus. Law. 153-170 Nov '83*

A.M. Pullen & Co., Travelers Indemnity Co. v,
289 S.E.2d 792 (Ga. Ct. App. 1982) An overview of the liability of the contractor's accountant to third parties in the construction industry.
4 Construction Law. 1(5) Spr '83

A.P.E.X., Cheall v,
(1982) 3 W.L.R. 685 (C.A.) The closed shop and the Bridlington agreement. (Great Britain)
99 Law Q. Rev. 19-22 Jan '83
(1983) 2 W.L.R. 679 Bridlington agreement in the House of Lords. (Great Britain)
99 Law Q. Rev. 337-338 July '83

A.R.O.W.-B.N.I.C.,
(1983) 2 Common Mkt. L.R. 240 (Eur. Comm. Comm'n Dec. 15, 1982) Competition and industrial property: voluntary price fixing extended by order of government commissioner. (European Economic Community)
8 European L. Rev. 259-262 Aug '83

A.S.L.E.F. (No. 2), Secretary of State for Employment v,
(1972) 2 Q.B. 455 Nature of industrial action. (Great Britain)   *99 Law Q. Rev. 340-341 July '83*

A.V.G. Management Science Ltd. v. Barwell Developments Ltd.,
(1979) 2 S.C.R. 43 Developments in contract law: the 1978-79 term. (Canada Supreme Court)
1 Sup. Ct. L. Rev. 137-186 Ann '80

A. v. X,
641 P.2d 1222 (Wyo. 1982) Constitutional law - putative biological father is not denied due process or equal protection by state statute which denies him standing to establish his paternity to a child born in wedlock to mother and her husband, the presumed father. (case note)   *21 J. Fam. L. 349-353 Jan '83*

A., Z. Ltd. v,
(1982) 1 All E.R. 556 Mareva injunctions: the third party problem. (Great Britain)
10 Austl. Bus. L. Rev. 375-390 Dec '82

A-Z, Z Ltd. v,
(1982) 2 W.L.R. 288 Position of banks under the Mareva injunction (1). (international business) (Great Britain)   *4 Company Law. 87-89 March '83*

AARON v. SEC,
446 U.S. 680 (1980) Corporate legal ethics - an empirical study: the Model Rules, the Code of Professional Responsibility, and counsel's continuing struggle between theory and practice.
8 J. Corp. L. 601-724 Summ '83

ABADOM, R. v,
(1983) 1 W.L.R. 126 (C.A.) Admissibility of statistical scientific material. (Great Britain)
47 J. Crim. L. 86-88 May '83

ABBEY Films v. Attorney-General,
(1981) I.R. 158 Obstruction of officer investigating fair trading. (Ireland)   *46 J. Crim. L. 235-237 Nov '82*

ABBOTT & Associates, Illinois v,
103 S. Ct. 1356 (1983) Federal grand jury file not open to state.   *69 A.B.A.J. 814(2) June '83*

ABBOTT, In re,
(1982) 3 All E.R. 181 Matrimonial property and bankruptcy - a sequel. (Great Britain)
N.Z.L.J. 231 Aug '83
Matrimonial property and bankruptcy. (New Zealand)   *N.Z.L.J. 2-3 Jan '83*

ABBOTT Laboratories, Jefferson County Pharmaceutical Ass'n v,
103 S. Ct. 1011 (1983) Price discrimination law applies to states.   *69 A.B.A.J. 656-657 May '83*

ABBOTT Laboratories, Payton v,
437 N.E.2d 171 (Mass. 1982) Tort law - begetting a cause of actions for those injured by a drug prior to birth. (case note)   *17 Suffolk U.L. Rev. 257-268 Spr '83*

ABBOTT Laboratories, Sindell v,
26 Cal. 3d 588 (1980) Beyond Sindell: relaxation of cause-in-fact rules for indeterminate plaintiffs. (from 1982 California Law Review 881)
Pers. Inj. Ann. 339-374 Ann '83
Torts - market share liability - the California roulette of causation eliminating the identification requirement. (case note)
11 Seton Hall L. Rev. 610-628 Spr '81
607 P.2d 924 (Cal. 1980) Bichler and Sindell: generic drug products and liability without causation.
33 Fed'n Ins. Counsel Q. 315-335 Summ '83
DES and the identification problem.
16 Akron L. Rev. 447-470 Wntr '83
Punitive damages in DES market share litigation.
23 Santa Clara L. Rev. 185-210 Wntr '83
Market share liability: a plea for legislative alternatives.   *1982 U. Ill. L. Rev. 1003-1043 Fall '82*
Cause in fact in tort law - a philosophical and historical examination.
31 De Paul L. Rev. 769-817 Summ '82
National product liability legislation: in search for the best of all possible worlds.
18 Idaho L. Rev. 411-508 Summ '82
A new avenue for DES litigation. (Women's Law Forum) (case note)
11 Golden Gate U.L. Rev. 917-943 Summ '81
Market share liability adopted to overcome defendant identification requirement in DES litigation. (case note)   *59 Wash. U.L.Q. 571-584 Summ '81*
Industry-wide liability and market share allocation of damages.   *15 Ga. L. Rev. 423-450 Wntr '81*

[Illustration 116]

PAGE FROM 68 VIRIGINIA LAW REVIEW

VIRGINIA LAW REVIEW

VOLUME 68 APRIL 1982 NUMBER 4

MULTIPLE CAUSATION IN TORT LAW: REFLECTIONS ON THE *DES* CASES

*Glen O. Robinson**

AS every freshman student of tort law soon learns to his discomfort, "causation" is an inscrutably vague notion, susceptible to endless philosophical argument, as well as practical manipulation. This is evident most notoriously in the case of "proximate cause," that uniquely legal concept of causal responsibility whose protean puzzles have tangled the heads of generations of law students, scholars, and judges. The problems of what lawyers misleadingly call "actual causation" or "causation-in-fact" have been somewhat less preoccupying. Perhaps this is because actual causation typically has been regarded as predominantly a factual matter
an   y.[1]
P   ise
th   A typical leading article in a typical law review.   al-
le   ual
an   ot-

* John C. Stennis Professor of Law, University of Virginia. I have benefited from comments by friends and colleagues too numerous to list, but I would specially like to thank David Kaye, Saul Levmore, Stephen Saltzburg, Alan Schwartz, and Gary Schwartz. I am also indebted to two of my students, John Cassidy and Lynn Stofan, for research and assistance.

[1] See, e.g., W. Prosser, Handbook of the Law of Torts 237, 244 (4th ed. 1971). H. Hart & A. Honore, Causation in the Law 83-102 (1959), discusses, but does not appear to endorse, the distinction. In fact, its analysis of causation suggests that the authors regard both actual and proximate causation as presenting similar, essentially factual questions. See id. chs. II, VI. Admittedly, actual and proximate causation are similar in regard to the purpose they serve. See infra text accompanying notes 143-44. It is questionable whether either concept can be accurately labeled as merely "factual."

[2] "[Public policy] is a very unruly horse, and when once you get astride it you never know where it will carry you." Richardson v. Mellish, 2 Bing. 229, 252, 130 Eng. Rep. 294, 303 (1824) (opinion of Burrough, J.).

[Illustration 117]

PAGE FROM 69 CALIFORNIA LAW REVIEW

Sindell v. Abbott Laboratories: A Market Share Approach to DES Causation

In *Sindell v. Abbott Laboratories*,[1] the California Supreme Court allowed a cause of action against a group of manufacturers of the drug diethylstilbestrol (DES)[2] even though the plaintiff was unable to identify which manufacturer had supplied the drugs that plaintiff's mother had taken to prevent a miscarriage.[3] The decision is an attempt by the court to provide victims of latent product defects a means of recovery where they would otherwise be unable to establish causation because of prolonged delay in injury manifestation.[4] In doing so, *Sindell* departs from traditional common law recovery requirements and raises numerous problems in its application.

Part I of this Note briefly describes the case. Part II discusses existing tort theories which the *Sindell* court could have adopted to allow a cause of action for DES induced injuries and explains why these theories were not suitable. Part III analyzes the market share cause of action created by the court, examining problems in defining the essential requirements of the theory and potentially faulty factual assump-

---

A typical law review student note. The purpose of student notes or comments is to provide critical analyses of recent cases or topics of law.

Most notes or comments are from two to twelve pages in length.

---

2. DES is a synthetic compound of the female hormone estrogen used as a miscarriage preventive from 1947 until 1971.

3. DES may cause adenocarcinoma in the daughters exposed to it before birth. The heretofore rare disease is a rapid-spreading cancer of the vagina and uterus with a current incidence of between 1 in 250 to 1 in 10,000. DES also causes adenosis, an abnormality of the vaginal and cervical tissue which affects between 30% to 90% of postpubertal girls exposed to DES in utero. Comment, *DES and A Proposed Theory of Enterprise Liability*, 46 FORDHAM L. REV. 963, 964-67 (1978).

DES is still marketed for treatment of menopausal disturbances, senile vaginitis, relief of breast engorgement during lactation suppression, and cancer of the prostate in men. It is also used in animal feed and drugs as a growth promoter. *Id.* at 963 n.2.

4. The disease has a minimum latent period of ten to twelve years. 26 Cal. 3d at 594, 607 P.2d at 925, 163 Cal. Rptr. at 133. For many women it may be twenty years before the carcinogenic effects of the drug appear. Comment, *supra* note 3, at 970 n.23.

SECTION D. OTHER INDEXES TO PERIODICAL LITERATURE

There are other periodical indexes less comprehensive than those discussed in Section B that may be useful in legal research.

1. Index to Periodical Articles Related to Law [15]

This publication is issued quarterly and indexes all articles of a legal nature in English that, in the judgment of the editors, are of research value and appear in periodicals that are not covered by the *Current Law Index*, the *Index to Foreign Legal Periodicals*, or the *Index to Legal Periodicals*. It is arranged in three parts: an *Index to Articles*, an *Author Index*, and a *List of Journals Indexed*. The last issue of each volume is a cumulative one. There is a ten-year cumulative volume covering the years 1958–68, followed by five-year cumulative volumes.

Since legal subjects are assuming greater prominence in a variety of non-legal journals, this *Index* is particularly useful in locating timely articles on newly developing areas which often first appear in non-legal periodicals. With fifteen or more different periodical indexes being brought together in this publication, it is a useful tool as a companion to the comprehensive legal periodical indexes.

2. Index to Foreign Legal Periodicals

Since 1960, the American Association of Law Libraries has published an *Index to Foreign Legal Periodicals*. It covers a wide range of journals dealing with international law (public and private), comparative law, and the municipal law of all countries of the world, other than the United States, the British Isles, and nations of the British Commonwealth whose legal systems are based on the common law.

The *Index to Foreign Legal Periodicals* is published quarterly with triennial cumulations. Articles and book reviews of two or more pages in length are indexed in this publication. Titles of articles are given in the language of publication, transliterated for those languages not using the Roman alphabet.

The publication is divided into the following units: (1) subject index; (2) geographical index, grouping—by country or region—the topics of the articles listed in the subject index; (3) book review index; and (4) author index. The author index entries refer to the subject index where the notations are complete.

[15] INDEX TO PERIODICAL ARTICLES RELATED TO LAW, Glanville Publishers, Inc., Dobbs Ferry, N.Y. 10522. Edited by R.M. Mersky and J.M. Jacobstein, this index started publication in 1958.

3. Index to Indian Legal Periodicals

Since 1963 the Indian Law Institute (New Delhi, India) has issued this publication which indexes periodicals (including yearbooks and other annuals) pertaining to law and related fields published in India. Articles, case comments, notes, and other material are included irrespective of the length of the material. Unbound issues appear semiannually with bound, annual cumulations.

4. Index to Canadian Legal Periodical Literature

This Index was started by the Canadian Association of Law Libraries in 1961 to cover the growing number of Canadian legal journals and to give access to two systems of law, civil and common, in two languages, English and French. This is published in quarterly and annual cumulative volumes.

5. Index to Commonwealth Legal Periodicals

This index is published bimonthly with annual cumulations by the Sir James Dunn Law Library, Dalhousie University, Halifax, Nova Scotia, Canada.

6. Current Australian and New Zealand Legal Literature Index

This is a quarterly non-cumulating index of Australian and New Zealand legal periodicals. It contains subject, name, and case indexes.

7. Contents of Current Legal Periodicals

Published by the Corporation Services Company, this monthly service reprints the table of contents for most currently issued legal periodicals and includes an index of articles by field of law.

8. Law Review Ink

This weekly list copies contents pages of major law reviews and annuals, as well as selected edited books.

9. Legal Information Management Index (vol. 1, no. 1, 1984–)

This index is published bimonthly with an annual cumulation. It indexes over 125 periodicals published in the United States and abroad, including journals, newsletters, newspapers, and annuals. Substantive English-language articles, bibliographies, surveys, and reviews relating to legal information management and law librarianship are covered. There are key word, author, and review indexes. The Index is available from Fox Information Consultants, Inc., Newton Highlands, Massachusetts.

SECTION E.   INDEXES TO SPECIAL SUBJECTS

1.   Index to Federal Tax Articles

This index, published by Warren, Gorham, and Lamont, is a computer-produced bibliography first published in 1975. It covers the literature on federal income, estate, and gift taxation contained in legal, tax, and economic journals, as well as non-periodical publications. Consisting of separate subject and author indexes, all of the entries are arranged in reverse chronological order. It is kept current by quarterly supplements.

2.   Commerce Clearing House, Federal Tax Articles

This monthly looseleaf reporter of the Commerce Clearing House, Inc., which began publication in 1962, contains summaries of articles on federal (income, estate, gift and excise) taxes appearing in legal, accounting, business, and related periodicals. Proceedings and papers delivered at major tax institutes are also noted. The contents are arranged by Internal Revenue Code section numbers.

Articles may also be located by subject by consulting the *Index to Subjects* and by author in the *Index to Authors.*

As the looseleaf volume becomes full, material is removed and placed in bound volumes for permanent reference.

3.   Criminal Justice Periodical Index

This quarterly index, published by University Microfilms International, covers approximately 100 criminal justice and law enforcement periodicals published in the United States, England, and Canada. There is an author index and a subject index, which includes case names.

4.   Kindex

Subtitled, *An Index to Legal Periodical Literature Concerning Children, Kindex* is published six times each year with annual cumulations by the National Center for Juvenile Justice. The indexers emphasize practical information for those involved in the juvenile justice system.

SECTION F.   PERIODICAL DIGESTS AND ABSTRACTS

1.   Criminology and Penology Abstracts

Formerly *Excerpta Criminologica* (Volumes 1–8, 1961–68), this is an international abstracting service covering the etiology of crime and juvenile delinquency, the control and treatment of offenders, criminal procedure, and the administration of justice. It is prepared

by the Criminologica Foundation in cooperation with the University of Leiden, The Hague, Netherlands.

2. Law Review Digest

This bi-monthly digest contains selected, condensed articles from the legal periodical literature.

3. Monthly Digest of Legal Articles

Selected legal articles from 200 periodicals are condensed and published monthly, closely following the words and style of the original writers.

4. Monthly Digest of Tax Articles

This monthly periodical presents significant current tax articles in abridged form.

5. National Law Review Reporter

This started in 1980 and reprints in their entirety articles selected from currently published law reviews. It is issued six times a year.

SECTION G. OTHER SOURCES

References to periodical articles may frequently be found in other reference books. Many state codes and the annotated editions of the *United States Code* will cite relevant articles in the notes preceding the annotations. Additionally, many of the West digests will, under each Topic and Key Number, give citations to pertinent law review articles.

1. Shepard's Law Review Citations

This citator lists, since 1957, over 180 law reviews and legal periodicals. It is arranged similarly to other units of *Shepard's Citations*. By using the *Shepard's Law Review Citations*, a researcher may *Shepardize* a periodical article and find citations to it by courts or in other articles. A footnote reference is given for periodicals added more recently and indicates the year the coverage begins. [See Illustration 118.]

2. Federal Law Citations in Selected Law Reviews

This unit of *Shepard's* indicates when the *United States Supreme Court Reports, Federal Reporter 2d, Federal Supplement, Federal Rules Decisions*, the United States Constitution, and the *United States Code* have been cited in the twenty national law reviews. [See Illustration 119.]

3. Legal Periodical Citations in Other Units of Shepard's Citations

As indicated in Chapter 14, the state units of *Shepard's Citations* indicate when a case or statute has been cited in a legal periodical published in the state or the twenty law reviews covered by all of the state *Shepard's Citations.*

4. Computer-Assisted Research

As indicated in B–3 *supra,* the *Legal Resource Index* is available online. Both LEXIS and WESTLAW now have selected legal periodicals online in their databases. LEXIS, at present, only has several of the leading law reviews available. WESTLAW lists several hundred titles, but only selected articles are included. When using either service, the list of periodicals included should be consulted to obtain the latest information as to the periodicals available.

[Illustration 118]

PAGE FROM SHEPARD'S LAW REVIEW CITATIONS

BOSTON UNIVERSITY LAW REVIEW							Vol. 62

Vol. 58	–733–	Vol. 59	Vol. 60		–815–	Vol. 61	Vol. 62
	11Pcf762			14SMJ837	52USLW		
	14Tol29			34StnL747	[4630		

Vol. 58

- 1 -
485FS1214
29WAp441
Wash
628P2d1340
60DJ621
27EmJ1116
48FR149
37MiL80
28StlJ88
17WFL927

- 165 -
53SCL808
31StnL858

- 199 -
518FS429
20BCR499
71CaL349
71CaL646
81CR1553
31HLJ371
12LoyC312
30SR614
80ULR¶132

- 337 -
62BUR1128
67Cor1047
93HLR310
40MdL246
60NCL326
77NwL496
128PaL92
26VR1127
60WLQ44
82WLR494
90YLJ492

- 391 -
69CaL932
28DR322
128PaL1039

- 527 -
599F2d1078
1BRW678
2BRW299
14BRW669
94HLR325
66ILR843
16JMR518
62NCL697
76NwL901
33RLR302
32StnL1146
34VLR1221

- 685 -
623F2d857
30CLA691
33FLR357
69Geo20
67KLJ895
66MnL14
70VaL71
34VLR280
22W&M50
60WLQ1324
92YLJ411

–733–
11Pcf762
14Tol29

Vol. 59

- 1 -
83AzS384
59BUR226
59BUR837
50ChL1066
29CLA361
9Hof45
18HUL268
35StnL182
92YLJ249

- 55 -
21BCR391
28CM596
50FR369
10GGU1057
93HLR1148
96HLR1546
36StnL300
12UCD220
26VR307
26WnL1300

- 209 -
83DuL92
9Hof45
18HUL268

- 257 -
69CaL73
90YLJ495

- 433 -
61BUR5
61BUR1141
56NYL20
13Pcf60

- 452 -
66Cor310
68Cor533
15UCD44
70VaL454

- 597 -
731F2d1177
69CaL199
16Suf362

- 811 -
18HUL271
43LJ665
44LJ32
35StnL207
12Tol310
27WnL602

- 857 -
60BUR512

Vol. 60

- 1 -
45Alb309
66Cor332
56ILJ52
57NDL299
93YLJ285

- 46 -
30AU979

- 204 -
554FS1126
192Ct78
Conn
469A2d1216
36AkL218
16Akr582
23AzL585
30Buf463
62BUR871
63BUR812
64BUR120
49ChL421

14SMJ837
34StnL747
35SMJ215
35StnL1037
56TLQ298
60TxL418
61TxL1428
52UCR7
52UCR691
70VaL109
38W&L39
24W&M411
28WnL4
22Wsb257
90YLJ1020
90YLJ1064

- 239 -
638F2d906
662F2d44
23AzL132
60BUR480
81ILR39
59TxL845
68VaL39

18GaL170
71Geo1524
51GW550
34HLJ1033
95HLR813
96HLR796
67ILR726
42LJ4
42LJ88
42LJ189
42LJ211
42LJ265
42LJ292
42LJ337
42LJ394
42LJ466
42LJ877
43LJ315
44LJ98
44LJ612
80McL463
82McL211
82McL319
40MdL1
41MdL214
42MdL430
56NYL280
56NYL360
56NYL471
57NYL364
35OR5
131PaL1356
132PaL446
12Pcf626
56SCL884
32SCR428

568FS1560
36BL1024
37BL1258
38BL437
62BUR147
81CR1660
83CR250
30EmJ223
94HLR1164
66ILR496
37MiL316
56NDL907
58NDL197
58NYL947
33StnL880
34StnL788
49TnL53

- 473 -
643F2d875
95HLR949
16UCD896
16UCD967
16UCD978
34VLR43

- 542 -
25AzL72
68CaL1132
82DuL996
95HLR617
42MdL222
56NDL850
67VaL575
60WLQ349
90YLJ496

–815–
52USLW
[4630
USDk
82-940
514FS819
28C3d888
Calif
172CaR684
625P2d227
23AzL109
62BUR869
63BUR3
57CK1030
31CLA362
95HLR954
77NwL776
16UCD987

Vol. 61

- 1 -
61BUR318
48ChL656

- 90 -
14EnL257

- 132 -
67Cor914
82CR1393
33FLR347
34FLR502
51GW390
76NwL415
56SCL47
68VaL958
30WnL2

- 271 -
61BUR563
60TxL40

- 563 -

- 823 -
71CaL385
95HLR1541
80McL1591
129PaL860

- 885 -
49ChL987
35FLR261
9Hof1423
82IILR857
67MnL1128
130PaL1299
44PitL188
35StnL90
35StnL243
60TxL879
51UCR742
93YLJ67

- 1099 -
700F2d382
702F2d545
82CR1330
57StJ275
69VaL627

Vol. 62

- 1 -
63BUR36
63BUR413

- 385 -
62NCL462
60TxL732

- 443 -
75LR158
103SC1153
85WVL618

- 661 -
80LR14
104SC1559
71CaL443
32DR883
69VaL1405
36VLR223

- 701 -
32Em1146

> This unit of Shepard's provides a means for "Shepardizing" law review articles cited since 1957. Through its use, one can find every time a law review article has been cited by another law review or in a court decision.

[Illustration 119]

PAGE FROM SHEPARD'S FEDERAL LAW CITATIONS IN SELECTED LAW REVIEWS

FEDERAL REPORTER, 2d SERIES **Vol. 600**

-1173- 66MnL446

-1185- 57NYL516

-1195- 64MnL813

-1202- 82IlLR414 64MnL896 57NYL238

-1214- 34StnL1166

-1231- 57NYL505

Vol. 597

-13- 28CLA722

-46- 47ChL723 65Cor26

-57- 93YLJ45

-63- 58NYL18

-133- 81CR480 82CR1341 131PaL134

-220- 67MnL948 55NYL1081

-295- 74NwL388

-306- 69CaL1357 81CR797 94HLR492

-314- 34StnL397 34StnL398

-337- 29CLA85 65MnL263 93YLJ56

-377- 78McL187 128PaL1441 129PaL1079

-436- 58NYL837

-453- 76NwL877

-474- 81McL18

-535- 94HLR426

-564- 79McL65

-596- 75NwL345

-635- 76NwL577 129PaL288

-667- 68CaL316 80CR1199

-676- 48ChL18

-693- 69CaL748

-789- 70CaL37 79CR99 94HLR1034 95HLR601 81IlLR640 75NwL124 76NwL564 129PaL288 61TxL1275

-798- 69Geo1176

-814- 71CaL357 65VaL961 81WLR31

-840- 132PaL1357

-897- 65Cor26

-927- 1979LF569

-936- 55NYL802

-946- 82CR120 58NYL18

-958- 70Geo1149 79McL1514

-1138- 80WLR253

-1170- 93HLR419

-1237- 69CaL754

-1240- 78NwL798

-1273- 64Cor909 68Geo198 76NwL564 129PaL265 61TxL1253 61TxL1274

-1348- 61TxL610

Vol. 598

-1- 64MnL607 62TxL875 66VaL622

-37- 67CaL1142 47ChL673 127PaL86 60TxL217 64VaL240 88YLJ737 93YLJ100

-62- 81CR777 97HLR853 46LCP(3)207 78NwL584

-91- 48ChL205 80CR970 81CR778 71Geo23 94HLR494 46LCP(3)207 78NwL587 128PaL1462 84WLR419 92YLJ1136

-176- 69Cor2 80CR1645 96HLR381 64MnL622 66MnL21 55NYL1076 81WLR229

-216- 80CR903

-228- 46ChL859

-321- 64MnL107

-349- 59TxL281

-363- 80LF973 55NYL1070

-381- 55NYL1056

-408- 80WLR263

-432- 68Geo1009 77NwL514 128PaL1236 35StnL912 69VaL23 93YLJ715

-450- 82IlLR899

-535- 64MnL242 59TxL512 62TxL212

-558- 67MnL1097

-564- 78NwL1370

-637- 46LCP(3)212

-663- 82CR310

-666- 82CR310

-705- 70Geo20 42LCP(4)9 92YLJ632

-722- 78McL555

-759- 94HLR492 129PaL305

-839- 69Geo25

-995- 66VaL463

-1002- 78McL1018

-1017- 66Cor40 67Cor590 76NwL610 56NYL961 60TxL751 61TxL1248 61TxL1281

-1033- 68Geo827 83WLR86

-1064- 65MnL183

-1079- 66Cor409 83IlLR591

-1110- 81CR1383

-1221- 94HLR492

-1244- 70Geo266 81WLR124

-1253- 58NYL18

-1264- 67MnL618

-1273- 80WLR267

-1345- 95HLR978

-1357- 93YLJ704

Vol. 599

-17- 91YLJ684

-32- 80CR320 72Geo55

-34- 58TxL1216

-56- 67Cor1065

-91- 81CR503 68VaL1478

-120- 81IlLR632 55NYL1083 80WLR263

-151- 81CR976

-193- 77McL1722 75NwL998

-196- 68CaL41 76NwL372

-262- 57NYL878

-269- 56NYL76

-274- 66Cor576 74NwL743

-310- 70Geo1119

-335- 129PaL134

-504- 69Geo16 71Geo922 57NYL452

-582- 31CLA317

-599- 69CaL213

-622- 81McL1428

-685- 58NYL18

-707- 47ChL740

-745- 69VaL314

-770- 69Geo88

-787- 69Geo911 57NYL892

-893- 78McL549

-1074- 94HLR332 80WLR723

-1094- 58NYL285

-1098- 81CR753

-1126- 131PaL204

-1140- 50ChL542 132PaL680

-1160- 67MnL608

-1190- 70CaL26 80LF399 60TxL751 83WLR547

-1203- 62TxL885

-1224- 69Geo14 71Geo924 57NYL451 66VaL611

-1247- 29CLA18 69Cor414 95HLR1306 81McL1440

-1286- 132PaL1415

-1299- 47ChL471

-1378- 58NYL18

-1387- 56NYL1006

Vol. 600

-1- 67CaL1273 69Cor236

-5- Case 1 66MnL644

-11- 69Cor240

-12- 129PaL305

-22- 43LCP(3)45

-24- 71Geo863

-35- 69VaL305

-45- 58TxL343

-70- 65Cor40

-120- 77NwL756

-124- 43LCP(3)47

-211- 65Cor46 84IlLR13 55NYL799

-219- 30CLA893

-238- 68VaL797

-313- 77NwL766 131PaL34

-335- 71Geo120

-355- 76NwL932 91YLJ708

-448- 94HLR322

-458- 78NwL785

-470- 69VaL80

-498- 66VaL623

-502- 82IlLR905

-563- 93YLJ220

-671- 68Cor527

-681- 65Cor449

-693- 66MnL766 35StnL424

-710- 79CR1285

-754- 71Geo120

-765- 78McL553

-815- 58NYL19

-844- 68CaL57 129PaL1075

-1003- 31CLA334 65Cor5 82CR311 71Geo134 129PaL811 32StnL1138 81WLR677

-1027- 81IlLR627 55NYL1045

-1043- 91YLJ1102

-1069- 128PaL506

-1070- 69CaL207 43LCP(3)42 132PaL298 35StnL1114 66VaL1109 68VaL453 91YLJ1329

-1148- 50ChL668 80CR1628 71Geo831 128PaL270 60TxL683 81WLR185

323

SECTION H.   LISTS OF SUBJECT LEGAL PERIODICALS

1. **Representative Subject Periodicals from American Law Schools**

Columbia University Law School:

Art and the Law

Columbia Human Rights Law Review

Columbia Journal of Environmental Law

Columbia Journal of Law and Social Problems

Columbia Journal of Transnational Law

Harvard University Law School:

Harvard Civil Rights-Civil Liberties Law Review

Harvard Environmental Law Review

Harvard International Law Journal

Harvard Journal of Law and Public Policy

Harvard Journal on Legislation

Harvard Women's Law Journal

University of California, Hastings College of Law:

COMM/ENT: A Journal of Communications and Entertainment Law

Hastings Constitutional Law Quarterly

Hastings International and Comparative Law Review

University of California School of Law (Berkeley):

Ecology Law Quarterly

Industrial Relations Law Journal

International Tax and Business Lawyer

La Raza Law Journal

University of Michigan Law School:

Michigan Yearbook of International Legal Studies

University of Michigan Journal of Law Reform

University of Texas School of Law:

American Journal of Criminal Law

Review of Litigation

Texas International Law Journal

Urban Law Review

Yale University Law School:

Yale Law and Policy Review

Yale Studies in World Public Order

2. International Legal Periodicals from American Law Schools

Arizona Journal of International and Comparative Law

Boston College International and Comparative Law Review

Brooklyn Journal of International Law

Boston University International Law Journal

California Western International Law Journal

Case Western Reserve Journal of International Law

Columbia Journal of Transnational Law

Cornell International Law Journal

Denver Journal of International Law and Policy

Dickinson International Law Annual

Fordham International Law Forum

Georgia Journal of International and Comparative Law

Harvard International Law Journal

Hastings International and Comparative Law Review

Houston Journal of International Law

International Trade Law Journal (University of Maryland)

Journal of International Law and Economics (George Washington University)

Journal of Space Law (University of Mississippi)

Law and Policy in International Business (Georgetown University)

Lawyer of the Americas (University of Miami)

Loyola of Los Angeles International and Comparative Law Journal

Michigan Yearbook of International Legal Studies

New York Law School Journal of International and Comparative Law

New York University Journal of International Law and Politics

North Carolina Journal of International Law and Commercial Regulation

Northwestern Journal of International Law & Business

Stanford Journal of International Law

Suffolk Transnational Law Journal

Syracuse Journal of International Law and Commerce

Texas International Law Journal

Vanderbilt Journal of Transnational Law

Virginia Journal of International Law
Wisconsin International Law Journal
Yale Studies in World Public Order

Chapter 17

TREATISES, RESTATEMENTS, MODEL CODES, AND UNIFORM LAWS

SECTION A. TREATISES

Legal treatises are another important category of the secondary sources of the law. Treatises or textbooks are usually able to treat a subject in greater depth and with more analysis than a legal encyclopedia or periodical article. The first treatises were written by legal scholars during the early development of the common law. As there were few court decisions available as precedent, the early text writers such as Lord Coke or William Blackstone played a significant role in the development of the law. As the growth of the law resulted in an ever-increasing number of law reports, treatises were needed to organize the diffuse principles of case law. As one commentator has noted, treatises were first written because of the lack of precedents and then subsequently because there were too many precedents.[1]

During the eighteenth and the early nineteenth centuries in the United States, English treatises were an integral part of an American lawyer's library. But, gradually, American lawyers and legal scholars began publishing treatises devoted entirely to American law.[2] Moreover, the American system of federalism has resulted in an increasing number of published treatises dealing with the law of a particular state.

1. Nature of Treatises

Treatises may be defined as expositions by legal writers on case law and legislation. Generally, treatises are more exhaustive in their coverage of particular fields of law than are legal encyclopedias. Treatises may be broadly classified into five types: (1) critical; (2) interpretative; (3) expository; (4) textual (for law students); and (5) educational (for practitioners keeping up in their fields). In most instances, however, particular treatises do not fall neatly into such a

---

[1] G. PATON, A TEXTBOOK OF JURISPRUDENCE 231–32 (3d ed. 1964); see also Simpson, The Rise and Fall of the Legal Treatise: Legal Principles and the Form of Legal Literature, 48 U.CHI.L.REV. 632 (1981).

[2] For a discussion of the development and influence of treatises on American law, see L. FRIEDMAN, A HISTORY OF AMERICAN LAW 538–46 (1973).

classification, and they frequently may include some features of all five types.

    a. *Critical Treatises.* These examine an area of law in depth and constructively criticize, when necessary, rules of law as presently interpreted by the courts. They often include historical analyses in order to show that current rules actually had different meanings or interpretations from those presently given by the courts. The author may include a thoughtful examination of the policy reasons for one or more such rules.[3] Critical treatises are not common, but their numbers are increasing.

    b. *Interpretative Treatises.* These provide an analysis and interpretation of the law. Authors of such works do not attempt to evaluate rules in relation to underlying policy but rather to explain the terminology and meaning of the rules as they exist. Emphasis is placed upon understanding the law and not upon proposing what the law should be.

    c. *Expository Treatises.* These exist primarily as substitutes for digests and are principally used as case finders. They consist primarily of essay paragraphs arranged under conventional subject headings with profuse footnote citations. Usually minimal analysis and synthesis of conflicting cases are the most a researcher can expect to find in them.

    A real danger exists if one relies exclusively upon the expository treatise or encyclopedia article without verifying the writer's synopsis of the cases.

    d. *Student Textbooks.* These may also be classified expository because they are usually elementary treatments and omit comprehensive and critical features of other works. In fact, the term *hornbook*[4] *law,* frequently used by a judge to describe simple and well-settled points of law, comes from the *Hornbook* series of student treatises published by the West Publishing Company.

    Student hornbooks, however, are useful as case finders as their references are usually selective and limited to landmark cases.

    e. *Continuing Legal Education Handbooks.* In recent years, continuing education for lawyers has become increasingly important. The American Law Institute, American Bar Association Joint Com-

---

    [3] For example, Professor Richard Powell in his treatise on real property in discussing the interests of a lessor and lessee in a condemnation proceeding criticizes the current rule as follows: *"This is the regrettable position taken by the majority of the jurisdictions* (Emphasis ours). It is a regrettable position because it embodies a rigidly conceptualistic survival of the historical idea that the lessee 'owns the land for his term' * * *. It would be more businesslike and reasonable to hold * * *." R. POWELL, 2 POWELL ON REAL PROPERTY ¶ 247[2], at 372.144 (1977)

    [4] For the derivation of the word *hornbook, see* THE NEW ENCYCLOPAEDIA BRITANNICA, 5 MICROPAEDIA 135 (1975).

mittee on Continuing Legal Education, and the Practising Law Institute hold seminars and symposiums on many current subjects which are directed toward practicing lawyers to keep them up to date on new developments in the law. Many states have their own continuing legal education institutes.[5] It is quite common for such institutes to publish handbooks and texts in connection with their programs. These volumes usually furnish analyses of the law, practical guidance, forms, checklists, and other time-saving aids. Very frequently, these publications deal with such subjects as business transactions, personal injuries, commercial and corporate practice, trial practice, and other subjects of primary interest to practicing attorneys.

2. The Characteristics of Treatises

The fundamental characteristics of treatises are essentially the same. They contain the following elements:

a. *Table of Contents.* The table of contents shows the topical division of the treatise, which is usually arranged by chapters and subdivisions thereof.

b. *Table of Cases.* The table of cases provides references as to where decisions discussed by the author are cited in the text.

c. *Subject Matter.* The subject matter of the text is contained in the main body of the publication.

d. *Supplementation.* The current trend is to provide pocket parts at the back of the volumes to supplement the text and indicate recent statutory and case developments.

Some current treatises are looseleaf in format, providing for the addition of current material, usually by interfiling.

e. *Index.* The index, embodying an alphabetical arrangement of the topics, sub-topics, and descriptive words, and cross-references, is the last feature.

SECTION B. ILLUSTRATIONS: TREATISES

[5] For a listing of Continuing Legal Education courses, *see* the monthly issues of the CLE REGISTER, published by the ALI/ABA Committee on Professional Education.

[Illustration 120]

INDEX PAGE FROM BLASHFIELD, AUTOMOBILE LAW AND PRACTICE, THIRD EDITION

PARKING LOTS

PARKING LOTS—Continued
Liability insurance,
    Attendant moving vehicle, business use, § 317.4, n. 49.
    Omnibus clause, § 315.16.
Licenses and permits, municipal police power, § 470.13.
Lookout, § 181.4.
Naval air base, governmental immunity, § 256.5, n. 36.
Negligence in maintaining, existence of condition as proximate cause, § 53.6,

---

Problem:

Finding cases involving theft of articles from automobile left in a parking lot.

Step 1.   Check index of treatise chosen in this case, Blashfield, Automobile Law and Practice, which indicates that discussion will be found at § 476.4.

Public policy, willful misconduct, § 476.4.
Repairs, municipal immunities, § 256.12, n. 22.
Restaurant liability, stolen automobile, negligent operation, § 251.3, n. 15.
Run away vehicle, § 251.3, n. 15.
School districts, immunities, § 256.16, n. 63.
Shopping centers,
    Defects, instructions to jury, standards of care, § 463.10, n. 96.
    Safe condition, § 181.6, n. 66.
Signs, limitation of liability, § 476.4.
Speed limitations, § 105.20.
Store's, injuries to patron, § 251.3, n. 15.
Theft,
    Burden of proof, § 476.4.
    Goods from vehicle, liability of bailee, § 476.4.
    Unlawful acts, anticipation, § 116.46.
Traffic rules and regulations, §§ 470.1, n. 7, 470.13.
Tripping over cement bumper, contributory negligence, § 145.1, n. 9.
Turning, § 120.21, n. 14.
Vehicle left for sale, stolen vehicle, owner liability, § 254.4, n. 46.
Vicarious liability, duty of care, pleading, § 457.12, n. 19.
Wearing apparel, bailment, § 476.4, n. 59.
Willful misconduct, bailment, § 476.4.

PARKING METERS
    Generally, § 470.12.
Adjoining landowners, § 470.14.
Burden of proof, revenue measure, § 470.12.
Counterfeit coins, use in, criminal liability, § 490.99, n. 95.
Criminal liability, ordinance violation, § 490.99.
Constitutional law, § 470.12, n. 25.
Evidence, violations, § 470.12.
Fees, § 470.12.
    Disposition, § 470.12.
Fines and penalties, authority to impose, § 490.2, n. 20.
Installation, delegation of power, § 470.5.
Municipalities, conflict with state laws, §§ 471.1, 471.4.
Nuisance, obstruction of streets, § 470.12, n. 25.
Ordinance violation, criminal liability, § 490.99.

214

[Illustration 121]

PAGE FROM BLASHFIELD, AUTOMOBILE LAW AND PRACTICE, THIRD EDITION

---

§ 476.4   BAILMENT RELATIONSHIPS   **Ch. 476**

Circumstances existing and known to the automobile owner when he leaves his car on the lot are not, in themselves negligence.[57]

If the lot owner permits an automobile owner to park free of charge there is at most a gratuitous bailment, and the parking lot owner is liable for theft only if guilty of gross negligence akin to fraud.[58]

Liability for loss of articles

In the absence of notice or a special agreement, it has been held that a parking lot proprietor cannot be held liable for the loss of articles left in a parked automobile other than the usual ordinary equipment of the automobile,[59] but, with regard to

---

, **A typical treatise will contain text and then footnote references to cases and other relevant materials.**

While not illustrated, pocket supplement should be checked.

---

on did not constitute negligence rendering operator liable for damage to automobile stolen from lot, but were merely pre-existing circumstances known to automobile owner and bearing on question of care necessitated thereby on operator's part. Ramsden v. Grimshaw, 162 P.2d 901, 23 Wash.2d 864.

58. Va.—Dawson v. Fusco's Auto Service, 17 S.E.2d 364, 178 Va. 350.

59. D.C.—Lucas v. Auto City Parking Co., Mun.App., 62 A.2d 557.

La.—Lee v. New Orleans Roosevelt Corp., App., 106 So.2d 855 (in action by owners of automobile for loss of personalty missing from the trunk of their automobile when delivered to them by parking lot owner, evidence that plaintiff removed his luggage from the trunk of the car in the presence of a doorman wearing a "maroon coat uniform" did not establish such notice to the proprietor as to make it responsible for the loss of the luggage).

for loss of wallet which plaintiff left on seat of her automobile which was parked in parking lot when there was no showing that operator had knowledge that wallet was left on seat of automobile).

Ohio.—Giles v. Meyers, Com.Pl., 107 N.E.2d 777 (suitcases); Palotto v. Hanna Parking Garage Co., App, 68 N.E.2d 170.

W.Va.—Barnette v. Casey, 19 S.E.2d 621, 124 W.Va. 143.

Medical bag and instruments

A medical bag containing medical instruments cannot be considered the usual ordinary equipment of an automobile for which a garage or parking lot would normally be expected to answer in case of loss. Lucas v. Auto City Parking Co., D.C.Mun. App., 62 A.2d 557.

Wearing apparel

Where owner of parking lot had no knowledge, either actual or constructive, of fact that baggage containing wearing apparel was left in the rear compartment of automobile which was delivered to attendant at

[Illustration 122]

PAGE FROM PROSSER AND KEETON ON THE LAW OF TORTS, FIFTH EDITION

Chapter 5

NEGLIGENCE: STANDARD OF CONDUCT

Table of Sections

§ 28. History

Although the strands of fault and carelessness may be traced in accident law back for centuries, negligence took shape as a separate t... the ninet... the word ... sense to c... ligation, c... to designate a mental element,

usually one of inadvertence or indifference, entering into the commission of other torts.[2] Some writers, in fact, once maintained that negligence was merely one way of commit-...ticu-...urts, ...negli-...cen-...tury, it has received more or less general

Page from a treatise written primarily for law students.

§ 28

1. Winfield, The History of Negligence in the Law of Torts, 1926, 42 L.Q.Rev. 184; Gregory, Trespass to Negligence to Absolute Liability, 1951, 37 Va.L.Rev. 359; Malone, Ruminations on the Role of Fault in the History of the Common Law of Torts, 1970, 31 La.L. Rev. 1; Arnold, Accident, Mistake, and Rules of Liability in the Fourteenth-Century Law of Torts, 1979, 128 U.Pa.L.Rev. 361; Rabin, The Historical Development of the Fault Principle: A Reinterpretation, 1981, 15 Ga. L.Rev. 925; Schwartz, Tort Law and the Economy in Nineteenth-Century America: A Reinterpretation,

1981, 90 Yale L.J. 1717; Roberts, Negligence: Blackstone to Shaw to? An Intellectual Escapade in a Tory Vein, 1965, 50 Cornell L.Q. 191; Donnelly, The Fault Principle: A Sketch of its Development in Tort Law During the Nineteenth Century, 1967, 18 Syr.L.Rev. 728.

2. Wigmore, Responsibility for Tortious Acts: Its History, 1894, 7 Harv.L.Rev. 315, 441, 453.

3. Salmond, Law of Torts, 6th ed. 1924, 21–26; Jenks, History of English Law, 1934, 319, 320.

4. See supra, § 6.

160

[Illustration 122-a]

PAGE FROM PROSSER AND KEETON ON THE LAW OF TORTS, FIFTH EDITION

164 **NEGLIGENCE: STANDARD OF CONDUCT** **Ch. 5**

case.[20] Persuaded by arguments such as these, many courts have emphasized that the instruction should be reserved for exceptional situations where called for by the unique facts of a particular case,[21] and some have more generally disapproved the una-voidable accident instruction for use in negligence cases altogether.[22] Probably a majority of jurisdictions still permit the instruction in appropriate cases, however, and the instruction is still stoutly defended as helpful in focusing the issues in proper cases.[23] Neither the unavoidable accident doctrine nor instructions thereon should be expected to wither away completely any time soon because of the notion's underlying logical simplicity and because such instructions, properly applied, may usefully serve to translate the arcane words and concepts of the law into a common sense perspective of everyday life and experience that jurors can readily understand.[24]

WESTLAW
REFERENCES ←

272k140 /p "unavoidable accident"
heart coronary epilep! faint! /10 seizure* attack* & "unavoidable accident"

20. See, e.g., Butigan v. Yellow Cab Co., 1958, 49 Cal.2d 652, 320 P.2d 500, 65 A.L.R.2d 1; Graham v. Rolandson, 1967, 150 Mont. 270, 435 P.2d 263, 273.

21. See, e.g., Del Vecchio v. Lund, S.D.1980, 293 N.W.2d 474; Damron v. Hagy, 1979, 220 Va. 455, 258 S.E.2d 517, 518 (occasion for use of instruction "rare"

the evid
held to
Kalamat

22. G
P.2d 26:
N.E.2d 6
1977, 25:
1964, 15(
1964, 23:
1968, 92 Idaho 332, 442 P.2d 742; Camaras v. Moran, 1966, 100 R.I. 717, 219 A.2d 487; George v. Guerette, Me.1973, 306 A.2d 138; Alexander v. Delgado, 1973, 84 N.M. 717, 507 P.2d 778 (summarizing arguments); Vespe v. DiMarco, 1964, 43 N.J. 430, 204 A.2d 874. See also Deskin v. Brewer, Mo.App.1979, 590 S.W.2d 392, 402 (at least in auto collision cases, per M.A.I. 1.01 (2d ed.1969)); Maxwell v. Olsen, Alaska 1970, 468 P.2d 48 (semble); City of Phoenix v. Camfield, 1965, 97 Ariz. 316, 400 P.2d 115 (semble); Cox v. Vernieuw, Wyo. 1980, 604 P.2d 1353 (Act of God defense not appropriate in negligence cases).

§ 30. Elements of Cause of Action

Negligence, as we shall see,[1] is simply one kind of conduct. But a cause of action founded upon negligence, from which liability will follow, requires more than conduct. The traditional formula for the elements necessary to such a cause of action may be stated briefly as follows:[2]

1. A duty, or obligation, recognized by the law, requiring the person to conform to a certain standard of conduct, for the protection of others against unreasonable risks.[3]

2. A failure on the person's part to conform to the standard required: a breach of the duty. These two elements go to make up what the courts usually have called negligence; but the term quite frequently is applied to the second alone. Thus it may be said that the defendant was negligent, but is not liable because he was under no duty to the plaintiff not to be.

23. See, e.g., Anderton v. Montgomery, Utah 1980, 607 P.2d 828, 835 (in light of instructions on res ipsa loquitur, it was "not only permissible but indeed proper that the need to find negligence, by one means or another, be reemphasized"); Butigan v. Yellow Cab Co., 1958, 49 Cal.2d 652, 320 P.2d 500, 508 (dissenting opinion) (instruction "can lead only to *better understand-*

s have
rnst v.
.271.

).Mich.
West-
ern Railroad, 1980, 99 Wisc.2d 514, 299 N.W.2d 615; Arneson v. City of Fargo, N.D.1981, 303 N.W.2d 515; ABC Builders, Inc. v. Phillips, Wyo.1981, 632 P.2d 925; Lawyers Surety Corp. v. Snell, Tex.Civ.App.1981, 617 S.W.2d 750; Quillen v. Quillen, Ala.1980, 388 So.2d 985; Beauchene v. Synanon Foundation, Inc., 1979, 88 Cal. App.3d 342, 151 Cal.Rptr. 796; Strother v. Hutchinson, 1981, 67 Ohio St.2d 282, 423 N.E.2d 467 (including element of plaintiff's freedom from contributory negligence). See generally Second Restatement of Torts, § 281.

3. See infra, ch. 9.

> Note footnote references to court decisions. This treatise happens to be published by the West Pub. Co. Note its indication on how to frame a search in WESTLAW, its online computer database.

SECTION C. THE RESTATEMENTS OF THE LAW

In the 1920's, concern was being shown by prominent American judges, lawyers, and law professors over two main defects in case law—its growing uncertainty and undue complexity. Finally, in 1923, the American Law Institute was founded by a group of these leaders to overcome such weaknesses.[6] The objectives of the Institute were focused on the reduction of the mass of legal publications which had to be consulted by the bench and bar, on the simplification of case law by a clear systematic restatement of it, and on diminishing the flow of judicial decisions. It was feared that the increasing mass of unorganized judicial opinions threatened to break down the system of articulating and developing case law.[7]

To remedy this, the American Law Institute undertook to produce a clear and precise restatement of the existing common law that would have "authority greater than that now accorded to any legal treatise, an authority more nearly on a par with that accorded the decisions of the courts." [8]

Procedurally, this was accomplished by the engagement of eminent legal scholars to be Reporters for the various subjects that were to be restated. Each Reporter prepared tentative drafts, which were then submitted to and approved by the members of the Institute.

Between 1923 and 1944, Restatements were adopted for the law of agency, conflict of laws, contracts, judgments, property, restitution, security, torts, and trusts. Since 1952, Restatements, Second Series, have been adopted for agency, contracts, conflict of laws, foreign relations law, judgments, property, landlord and tenant, torts, and trusts.

[6] This discussion of the Restatements is based on the following sources: Lewis, *History of the American Law Institute and the First Restatement of the Law,* in AMERICAN LAW INSTITUTE, RESTATEMENT IN THE COURTS (Permanent ed. 1945); Goodrich, *The Story of the American Law Institute,* 1951 WASH.U.L.Q. 283; H. GOODRICH & P. WOLKIN, THE STORY OF THE AMERICAN LAW INSTITUTE, 1923–1961 (1961); THE AMERICAN LAW INSTITUTE 50th ANNIVERSARY (1973); AMERICAN LAW INSTITUTE ANNUAL REPORTS. *See also* M. PIMSLEUR, CHECKLISTS OF BASIC AMERICAN LEGAL PUBLICATIONS, AALL PUBLICATIONS SERIES NO. 4, § 5: AMERICAN LAW INSTITUTE, RESTATEMENTS OF THE LAW (1976). This checklist updates all previous checklists and lists all Restatements, including preliminary and tentative drafts.

[7] Lewis, *supra* note 6, at 1.

[8] *Report of the Committee on the Establishment of a Permanent Organization for the Improvement of the Law Proposing the Establishment of an American Law Institute,* February 23, 1923, in THE AMERICAN LAW INSTITUTE 50th ANNIVERSARY 34 (1973).

The current status of the revision of specific Restatements and of proposed new Restatements may be ascertained from the latest *Annual Report* of the American Law Institute.

There are two aspects of the Restatements that limit their scope and function. First, they lack legislative sanction. It has been recommended that state legislatures be required to approve the Restatements, not as formal legislative enactments, but as aids and guides to the judiciary so that they would feel free to follow the "collective scholarship and knowledge of our profession." [9] But this proposal was not adopted by the Institute. Nevertheless, many courts began to give greater authority to the Restatements than that accorded to treatises and other secondary sources. In many instances, an authority is given to the Restatements nearly equal to that accorded to court decisions.[10]

The First Series of the Restatements reflected the desire of the American Law Institute founders that the Restatements would be admired and adopted by the courts. To this end they deliberately omitted the Reporters' citations and tentative drafts upon which the Restatement rules were based.

With publication of the Second Series of the Restatements, it was decided to abandon the idea of the Restatements serving as a substitute for the codification of the common law. The Second Series will also at times indicate a new trend in the common law and attempt to predict what a new rule will or should be.[11] This change in policy is also reflected in the appearance of citations to court decisions and to the Notes of the Reporters.

Further debate over the value of the Restatements may be left to others.[12] As a legal researcher, however, one must be familiar with the publications of the American Law Institute and their method of use.

1. The Features of the Restatements

The frequency with which the Restatements are cited by the courts merit their study in legal research. As of April 1, 1984, the

---

[9] Mason, *Harlan Fiske Stone Assays Social Justice, 1912–1923*, 99 U.PA.L.REV. 887, 915 (1951).

[10] For a discussion of the precedential authority of the Restatements, *see* Byrne, *Reevaluation of the Restatements as a Source of Law in Arizona*, 15 ARIZ.L.REV. 1021, 1023–26 (1973).

[11] *Id.*

[12] An exhaustive list of articles on all aspects of the work of the American Law Institute may be found in each ANNUAL REPORT in a section entitled *The Institute in Legal Literature, A Bibliography*.

Restatements have been cited by the courts 85,618 times.[13] There-fore, they not only provide clear statements of the rules of the common law which are operative in the great majority of the states but also provide very valuable sources for finding cases in point. Moreover, a comparison of the texts of the Restatements and the case law of the several states revealed that there were surprisingly few deviations from the common law as expressed in the Restate-ments. It has been suggested, therefore, that there is in fact a common law which transcends state lines and prevails throughout the nation.[14] But the legal rules may at times be inaccurately and confusingly stated by the various courts. Thus, the objective of the Restatements is to clear away much of the verbal debris and bring the accepted rules to the forefront. To this extent, the Restatements are useful research aids in the law.

The following features are included in the Restatements, Second Series:

a. Reporters' Notes.

b. Citations to the Restatements that the courts have made to the First Series of the Restatements.

c. Cross-references to West's *Key Number System* and to *American Law Reports Annotated.*

2. Indexes

a. *Restatements, First Series.* A one-volume index to all of the Restatements has been published. Each Restatement also has its own index.

b. *Restatements, Second Series.* Each Restatement has its own index.

3. Restatements in the Courts

The purpose of this set is to record each time a court cites a section of a Restatement. Each such case is digested at length under the appropriate section. The Permanent Edition covers the years 1932–1944. There are bound supplements to the Permanent Edition for the years 1945–1975. For the years since 1975, pocket supple-ments have been issued separately for each of the subject Restate-ments.

---

[13] AMERICAN LAW INSTITUTE, ANNUAL REPORT 24 (1984). For the years between April 1, 1980 and April 1, 1984, this represents an average of 4440 times per year.

[14] Goodrich, *Restatement and Codification,* in DAVID DUDLEY FIELD CENTE-NARY ESSAYS, 241–50 (1949).

4. Shepardizing the Restatements

Starting in 1976, *Shepard's Citations* has published a new unit devoted entirely to the *Restatements of the Law.* This set gives citations to all federal reports, all units of the *National Reporter System,* and all state reports that cite a Restatement. It also includes citations that appear in the leading law reviews. [See Illustration 126.]

5. State Annotations

Many states have prepared annotations to court citations to the Restatements, *e.g., California Annotations to the Restatement of the Law of Torts * * *.* The catalog in local law libraries should be consulted to ascertain if such annotations exist for a particular state.

SECTION D. ILLUSTRATIONS: RESTATEMENT OF THE LAW OF TORTS

Problem: **A, an inmate in a state prison, had suffered a severe toothache. The Warden waited three days before taking A to a dentist. As a result of the delay, A had to have all of his teeth removed. Is the Warden subject to liability to A?**

123–123–c.   **Pages from the Restatement of the Law of Torts, Second**

124.   **Page from Appendix Volume, Restatement of the Law of Torts, Second**

125–125–a.   **Pages from the Restatement in the Courts, Cumulative Annual Supplement to the Restatement of the Law of Torts, Second**

126.   **Page from Shepard's Restatement of the Law Citations**

[Illustration 123]

PAGE FROM RESTATEMENT OF THE LAW OF TORTS, 2d

TABLE OF CONTENTS

The Section of the Restatement of Torts 2d covering the problem under research may be located by consulting the Index or by the Table of Contents as in this illustration.

VIII

[Illustration 123-a]

PAGE FROM RESTATEMENT OF THE LAW OF TORTS, 2d

§ **314**   TORTS, SECOND   Ch. 12

is subject to liability for permitting the train to continue in motion with knowledge of A's peril.

e. Since the actor is under no duty to aid or protect another who has fallen into peril through no conduct of the actor, it is immaterial that his failure to do so is due to a desire that the other shall be harmed.

Illustration:

4. A, a strong swimmer, sees B, against whom he entertains an unreasonable hatred, floundering in deep water and obviously unable to swim. Knowing B's identity, he turns away. A is not liable to B.

f. Except as stated in §§ 335, 337, and 339, it is immaterial that the other's peril and need of aid or protection is due to the condition of land or chattels owned or in the possession or custody of the actor, unless he stands in some relation to the other which carries with it the duty of preparing a safe place or thing for the other's reception or use, or of warning him of its dangerous condition. (See §§ 342–350.)

§ **314 A.** Special Relations Giving Rise to Duty to Aid or Protect

(1) A common carrier is under a duty to its passengers to take reasonable action

(a) to protect them against unreasonable risk of ~~physical harm, and~~

> The Restatement's "Black Letter" Rules immediately follow the Paragraph Number.

(2) An innkeeper is under a similar duty to his guests.

(3) A possessor of land who holds it open to the public is under a similar duty to members of the public who enter in response to his invitation.

(4) One who is required by law to take or who voluntarily takes the custody of another under circumstances such as to deprive the other of his normal opportunities for protection is under a similar duty to the other.

See Reporter's Notes.

See Appendix for Reporter's Notes, Court Citations, and Cross References

[Illustration 123-b]

PAGE FROM RESTATEMENT OF THE LAW OF TORTS, 2d

Ch. 12   **STANDARD OF CONDUCT**   **§ 314 A**

Caveat:

The Institute expresses no opinion as to whether there may not be other relations which impose a similar duty.

Comment:

a. An additional relation giving rise to a similar duty is that of an employer to his employee. (See § 314 B.) As to the duty to protect the employee against the conduct of third persons, see Restatement of Agency, Second, Chapter 14.

b. This Section states exceptions to the general rule, stated in § 314, that the fact that the actor realizes or should realize that his action is necessary for the aid or protection of another does not in itself impose upon him any duty to act. The duties stated in this Section arise out of special relations between the parties, which create a special responsibility, and take the case out of the general rule. The relations listed are not intended to be exclusive, and are not necessarily the only ones in which a

Following the "Black Letter" Rule or Rules are comments explaining the purpose of the Rules.

tween husband and wife for personal injuries are permitted. The question is therefore left open by the Caveat, preceding Comment *a* above. The law appears, however, to be working slowly toward a recognition of the duty to aid or protect in any relation of dependence or of mutual dependence.

c. The rules stated in this Section apply only where the relation exists between the parties, and the risk of harm, or of further harm, arises in the course of that relation. A carrier is under no duty to one who has left the vehicle and ceased to be a passenger, nor is an innkeeper under a duty to a guest who is injured or endangered while he is away from the premises. Nor is a possessor of land under any such duty to one who has ceased to be an invitee.

d. The duty to protect the other against unreasonable risk of harm extends to risks arising out of the actor's own conduct, or the condition of his land or chattels. It extends also to risks arising from forces of nature or animals, or from the acts of third persons, whether they be innocent, negligent, intentional, or even criminal. (See § 302 B.) It extends also to risks arising from pure accident, or from the negligence of the plaintiff himself, as

See Appendix for Reporter's Notes, Court Citations, and Cross References

[Illustration 123-c]

PAGE FROM RESTATEMENT OF THE LAW OF TORTS, 2d

Ch. 12　　　　　**STANDARD OF CONDUCT**　　§ **314 A**

over at a station to those who will do so. A continues to ride on the train in an unconscious condition for five hours, during which time his illness is aggravated in a manner which proper medical attention would have avoided. B Railroad is subject to liability to A for the aggravation of his illness.

3. A is a guest in B's hotel. Without any fault on the part of B, a fire breaks out in the hotel. Although they could easily do so, B's employees fail to call A's room and warn him to leave it. As a result A is overcome by smoke and carbon monoxide before he can escape, and is seriously

---

Frequently the Comment Section is followed by examples.

---

on the part of B, A runs and falls, and gets his fingers caught in the mechanism of the store escalator. B's employees see what has occurred, but unreasonably delay in shutting off the escalator. As a result, A's injuries are aggravated in a manner which would have been avoided if the escalator had been shut off with reasonable promptness. B is subject to liability to A for the aggravation of his injuries.

5. A, a patron attending a play in B's theatre, suffers a heart attack during the performance, and is disabled and unable to move. He asks that a doctor be called. B's employees do nothing to obtain medical assistance, or to remove A to a place where it can be obtained. As a result, A's illness is aggravated in a manner which reasonably prompt medical attention would have avoided. B is subject to liability to A for the aggravation of his illness.

6. A is imprisoned in a jail, of which B is the jailor. A suffers an attack of appendicitis, and cries for medical assistance. B does nothing to obtain it for three days, as a result of which A's illness is aggravated in a manner which proper medical attention would have avoided. B is subject to liability to A for the aggravation of his illness.

7. A is a small child sent by his parents for the day to B's kindergarten. In the course of the day A becomes ill with scarlet fever. Although recognizing that A is seriously ill, B does nothing to obtain medical assistance, or to take the child home or remove him to a place where help can be obtained. As a result, A's illness is aggravated in a manner which proper medical attention would have avoided.

See Appendix for Reporter's Notes, Court Citations, and Cross References

121

ILLUSTRATIONS

317

[Illustration 124]

PAGE FROM APPENDIX VOLUME, RESTATEMENT OF THE LAW OF
TORTS, 2d

§ 314   **TORTS, SECOND**   **Ch. 12**

Duty of motor vehicle driver to sound warning in approaching place
where children are playing or gathered. 30 A.L.R.2d 40.
Unsignaled stop or slowing of motor vehicle as negligence. 29 A.L.R.
2d 5.
Liability growing out of pulling out of parked motor vehicle as affected
by signals or warnings. 29 A.L.R.2d 116.
Duty as to signaling driver approaching from opposite direction or on
intersecting highway to pass or proceed. 90 A.L.R.2d 1431.
Duty of airplane owner or operator to furnish aircraft with naviga-
tional and flight safety devices. 50 A.L.R.2d 898.
Duty and liability of one who voluntarily undertakes to care for injured
person. 64 A.L.R.2d 1179.
Liability of one undertaking to care for child for injury to child. 27
A.L.R. 1018.

§ 314 A. Special Relations Giving Rise to Duty to Aid or Protect.

REPORTER'S NOTES

This Section has been added to
the first Restatement.

Illustration 1 is based on Yazoo
& M. V. R. Co. v. Byrd, 89 Miss.
308, 42 So. 286 (1906); Layne v.
Chicago & Alton R. Co., 175 Mo.

Co., 145 Conn. 451, 144 A.2d 56
(1958).

Compare, as to the duty of a
carrier to protect its passengers
from dangers arising from the
conduct of third persons: Hill-

**The Appendix volumes contain most useful information such as citations to
cases upon which the text was based, references to relevant A.L.R. Annotations,
and to West Key Numbers.**

(1958); Continental Southern
Lines, Inc. v. Robertson, 241
Miss. 796, 133 So. 2d 543, 92
A.L.R.2d 653 (1961), passenger
injured through his own negli-
gence.

Illustration 2 is taken from
Middleton v. Whitridge, 213 N.Y.
499, 108 N.E. 192, Ann. Cas.
1916C, 856 (1915). Cf. Kambour
v. Boston & Maine R. Co., 77 N.H.
33, 86 A. 624, 45 L.R.A. N.S. 1188
(1913); Jones v. New York Central R. Co., 4 App. Div. 2d 967,
168 N.Y.S.2d 927 (1957), affirmed, 4 N.Y.2d 963, 177 N.Y.S.
2d 492, 152 N.E.2d 519 (1958);
Yu v. New York, N. H. & H. R.

193 Mass. 341, 79 N.E. 815, 7
L.R.A. N.S. 729, 118 Am. St. Rep.
516 (1907); Exton v. Central R.
Co. of New Jersey, 62 N.J.L. 7, 42
A. 486, 56 L.R.A. 508 (1898), af-
firmed, 63 N.J.L. 356, 46 A. 1099,
56 L.R.A. 512; Kinsey v. Hudson
& Manhattan R. Co., 130 N.J.L.
285, 32 A.2d 497, 14 N.C.C.A. N.S.
692 (Sup. Ct. 1943), affirmed, 131
N.J.L. 161, 35 A.2d 888 (Ct. Err.
& App.); Harpell v. Public Serv-
ice Coordinated Transport, 20
N.J. 309, 120 A.2d 43 (1955);
Mulhause v. Monongahela St. R.
Co., 201 Pa. 237, 50 A. 937
(1902); St. Louis, I. M. & S. R.
Co. v. Hatch, 116 Tenn. 580, 94

See also cases under division, chapter, topic, title, and subtitle
that includes section under examination.

16

[Illustration 125]

PAGE FROM THE RESTATEMENT IN THE COURTS,
ANNUAL SUPPLEMENT

**Place this Supplement next to Volume 2, Appendix, §§ 310–402, of the
Restatement of the Law, Second, Torts 2d (1966)**

RESTATEMENT IN THE COURTS

Cumulative Annual Supplement
For Use In 1984–1985

Reporting Cases From January 1976
Through June 1983 that cite

Restatement of the Law of Torts (4 Vols.)
and
Restatement of the Law, Second
Torts 2d (4 Vols.)

The Restatements are kept up-to-date by either pocket Supplements or pamphlet Supplements.

For citations prior to January 1976, reference should be made to
Appendix Volume 2, §§ 310–402, of the Restatement of the Law,
Second, Torts 2d (1966) and to subsequent Restatement in the Courts
Supplements, except where a section of title in this Pocket Part contains
the notation *No earlier citations.*

Editor: Violet H. Meehan
The American Law Institute
4025 Chestnut Street
Philadelphia, PA 19104

ST. PAUL, MINNESOTA
AMERICAN LAW INSTITUTE PUBLISHERS
1984

ALI–Torts 2d (§§ 310–402)—1
1985 Supp.

21

[Illustration 125-a]

PAGE FROM RESTATEMENT IN THE COURTS, ANNUAL SUPPLEMENT TO RESTATEMENT OF TORTS, 2d

§ 314A RESTATEMENT IN THE COURTS

condition. Thus, the issue before the court was whether the relationship between the decedent and the defendant was a special relationship such that defendant had a duty to warn or otherwise insure the safety of decedent. In deciding the issue, the court relied upon the Restatement. The trial court granted defendant's motion to dismiss, holding that, under Illinois law, there was no duty to warn or otherwise insure against criminal acts of third parties arising solely from business relations between a travel agent and a corporation who invited the agent to visit its properties, and, therefore, no cause of action was stated for the wrongful death of an agent who was killed in Mexico by unknown assailants. Semmelroth v. American Airlines, 448 F.Supp. 730, 732, 733.

N.D.Ill.1982. Cit. in sup., com. (a) cit. in sup. Three former state prison officials, one of their wives, and three administrators of the estates of correctional officers who had died in an inmate riot brought this action under the Civil Rights Act of 1866 against the director of the state department of corrections, the warden, the assistant warden, and former correctional officers of the prison, seeking redress for alleged failure to take steps to control inmate riots. The plaintiffs alleged that the defendants failed to warn the plaintiffs of an impending prison disturbance, failed to operate, equip, and maintain the prison in a safe

between an employee and his superior imposed on the superior an affirmative duty to protect the employee from the reasonably foreseeable attacks of third persons. Whether the assistant warden satisfied such an obligation or whether his alleged inaction was so egregious that this claim rose to the level of a constitutional deprivation were factual issues that were better resolved on a motion for summary judgment or at trial; therefore the assistant warden's motion to dismiss was denied. Walker v. Rowe, 535 F.Supp. 55, 59.

E.D.Pa.1983. Cit. in sup., Caveat cit. in sup., com. (b) cit. in sup. (Erron. cit. as § 314(a).) A police informant and the executor of the informant's girlfriend's estate brought an action against the United States to recover under the Tort Claims Act when the informant and his girlfriend were ambushed, allegedly be those against whom the informant had testified. This court denied the defendant's motion for summary judgment as to the police informant and granted the defendant's motion for summary judgment as to the executor of the girlfriend's estate. The Good Samaritan Rule, which imposed liability on a person for a negligent performance of an act which the actor had voluntarily undertaken, was not applicable. An FBI agent's statement that the informant should call if he wanted protection was, at best, a gratuitous promise, where the informant's testimony was of-

---

This set indicates each time a Restatement rule has been cited by a court, and further indicates whether the court supported, or did not support the rule.

The Restatement in the Courts was published in separate volumes until 1976. Since then, pocket supplements have been issued every two years and placed in the subject Restatement volumes.

---

fellow correctional officers because they had no affirmative duty to warn all the other correctional officers every time a rumor of disturbance arose in the prison. The court stated that a relationship which did not support a tort claim under state law, as here, could not support a civil rights claim, either. As to the assistant warden, the court stated that the special relationship

wanted his cooperation. The informant gave the government officials valuable information and testified before the grand jury. The informant notified an FBI agent of his fear of his father. The FBI had no duty to the girlfriend resulting from a special relationship between her and the FBI, nor from her association with the informant, since her relationship with the infor-

See also cases under division, chapter, topic, title and subtitle that includes section under examination. For earlier citations· see Restatement of the Law, Second, Torts 2d Volume 2 Appendix and Restatement In The Courts 1967, 1968–1969, 1970–1971, 1972–1973, 1974–1975 and 1976 Supplements.

[Illustration 126]

PAGE FROM SHEPARD'S RESTATEMENT OF THE LAW CITATIONS

§ 313				TORTS, SECOND			
313NE442	664P2d139	Ill	603P2d122	Comment a	Illustra-	441FS1216	148CaR808
Comment c	Fla	419NE571	Calif	535FS59	tion 7	497FS188	151CaR731
533F2d400	390So2d156	Minn	134CaR32	70CA3d779	153CA3d382	510FS1128	152CaR231
365Mas518	428So2d376	323NW25	144CaR799	107IIR352	6MaA555	541FS1007	159CaR847
Mass	429So2d1325	NJ	157CaR824	Calif	Calif	555FS374	167CaR75
313NE442	Haw	403A2d509	190CaR314	139CaR86	200CaR262	561FS1134	169CaR284
Mo	649P2d1119	Comment e	199CaR189	Ill	Mass	566FS1419	169CaR372
646SW770	Ill	Calif	200CaR783	437NE934	379NE1114	570FS1335	176CaR470
Comment d	371NE70	664P2d142	Fla	Comment b		124Az230	176CaR499
572FS1203	Ind	Illustra-	372So2d1147	70CA3d779		136Az509	185CaR255
193Su255	433NE49	tion 4	401So2d1137	79CA3d159	§ 314B	63CA3d541	185CaR398
Iowa	Mass	Ky	401So2d1367	104CA3d811	596F2d560	74CA3d33	187CaR631
300NW107	449NE334	566SW775	421So2d195	153CA3d	65H188	75CA3d480	187CaR794
NJ	Minn	Comment f	429So2d1326	[1143	107IIR352	112CA3d209	188CaR212
473A?d545	289NW483	30C3d367	Haw	34C3d31	129McA543	112CA3d476	191CaR710
	Mo	Calif	592P2d825	Calif	Haw	123CA3d257	199CaR189
	648SW885	178CaR788	604P2d1202	139CaR86	649P2d1119	123CA3d332	199CaR527
§§ 314	650SW297	636P2d1126	549P2d1119	144CaR799	Ill	135CA3d537	200CaR783
to 324A	ND		Idaho	164CaR269	437NE935	137CA3d	539P2d41
721F2d869	349NW642		659P2d139	192CaR241	Mich	[1011	551P2d343
45LCP(3)75	Nev	§ 314A	Ill	200CaR783	342NW604	138CA3d318	560P2d749
	580P2d483	545F2d283	344NE538	664P2d145	77McL1593	138CA3d621	602P2d767
	NJ	573F2d435	367NE281	Comment c		143CA3d308	614P2d733
§§ 314	403A2d509	592F2d46	393NE584	722F2d222		151CA3d	649P2d897
to 320	NY	680F2d1260	395NE185	448FS732	§ 315	[1098	Fla
56NYL1244	426S2d934	721F2d869	419NE571	153CA3d	et seq.	152CA3d446	390So2d156
	443S2d143	722F2d220	435NE188	[1143	73CA3d706	153CA3d	-Ga
	Ohio	727F2d954	437NE934	200CaR783	Calif	[1143	287SE720
§ 314	458NE1263	448FS732	441NE370	Tex	141CaR193	15C3d42	296SE696
588F2d928	Pa	535FS59	441NE390	652SW569		17C3d435	Haw
590F2d763	428A2d1357	566FS1231	461NE619	Comment e		19C3d47	602P2d536
596F2d560	Vt	124Az230	Iowa	573F2d438	§§ 315	25C3d727	632P2d660
709F2d709	433A2d273	63CA3d542	294NW561	63CA3d542	to 320	27C3d751	Ill
721F2d869	Wis	79CA3d159	334NW759	107IIR352	78CA3d313	32C3d203	371NE70
727F2d954	270NW426	96CA3d522	Ky	386Mas887	104CA3d819	250Ga201	374NE1058
448FS871	45LCP(3)87	141CA3d448	566SW775	Calif	123CA3d257	61Ga.A580	393NE583
508FS934	77McL1593	151CA3d	La	134CaR33	135CA3d537	61H257	406NE20
561FS1134	124PaL1034	[1098	439So2d564	437NE935	138CA3d621	2HA362	437NE934
565FS647	70A31130n	153CA3d	446So2d1249	Iowa	143CA3d308	55IIR410	456NE366
63CA3d541	83A31202n	[1143	Mass	294NW561	152CA3d446	58IIR1034	Ind
79CA3d159	Comment a	60H564	438NE349	Mass	17C3d435	74IIR925	314NE774
141CA3d446	15C3d49	61H376	449NE334	438NE349	27C3d751	84IIR574	411NE414
148CA3d942	30C3d367	65H188	Mich	Comment f	168Su483	107IIR352	431NE537
150CA3d862	Calif	104Ida385	258NW545	386Mas887	Calif	119IIR342	432NE50
151CA3d	123CaR473	36IIR969	308NW693	85Wis2d305	131CaR23	161InA117	462NE250
[1102	178CaR788	52IIR200	339NW217	Fla	144CaR188	162InA528	463NE1094
157CA3d144	539P2d41	74IIR925	342NW606	401So2d	148CaR808	234Kan493	Iowa
15C3d49	636P2d1126	76IIR697	345NW688	[1137	151CaR731	234Kan559	304NW295
30C3d367	Comment b	95IIR154	Nev	Iowa	152CaR231	3MaA753	Kan
34C3d23	56!FS1134	105IIR920	580P2d483	294NW561	164CaR268	400Mch608	673P2d94
65H188	Comments	107IIR352	NJ	Mass	167CaR75	278Mdi67	675P2d62
55IIR410	c to f	109IIR886	403A2d509	438NE349	176CaR470	53MdA482	La
103Msc2d583	364Mas709	109IIR980	359NE392	Wis	185CaR398	94Nev403	446So2d1250
110Msc2d926	Comment c	122IIR408	161NE305	270NW427	188CaR212	89NJ277	Md
3MaA753	135CA2d527	106Msc2d818		191CaR710	30NW660		?d552
389Ma							?d418
94Nev							lich
90S79							W411
286Pa							linn
168Su							W804
139Vtt							W886
85Wis							W484
Ca							W25
123CaR473	Calif	191McA279	Wash	77McL1268	tion 1	603P2d122	338NW255
134CaR32	131CaR23	94Nev403	562P2d267	Illustra-	69Cor210	667P2d209	343NW288
144CaR799	148CaR808	41NY82	Wis	tion 5		673P2d952	Mo
178CaR787	151CaR731	59NY258	270NW426	153CA3d382	§§ 315	Calif	648SW885
190CaR312	152CaR231	43OrA507	345NW448	Calif	to 319	123CaR473	ND
192CaR235	178CaR788	88SD25	W Va	200CaR262	Minn	130CaR107	349NW642
196CaR304	185CaR398	269SoC482	271SE338	Illustra-	338NW255	131CaR23	Nev
197CaR923	188CaR212	168Su484	67Cor940	tion 6		134CaR32	580P2d483
199CaR192	190CaR312	17WAp242	45LCP(3)75	153CA3d382	§ 315	136CaR860	NJ
203CaR580	191CaR710	85Wis2d302	77McL1268	Calif	573F2d435	141CaR94	445A2d1144
539P2d41	199CaR527	117Wis2d683	77McL1593	200CaR262	590F2d763	141CaR219	NY
636P2d1125	551P2d343	Alk	79A31214n	Fla	612F2d140	141CaR269	
Colo	636P2d1126	627P2d628	Caveat	429So2d1326	727F2d901	142CaR204	*Continued*
		Ariz	168Su484				

> "Shepardizing" § 314A of the Restatement of Torts, 2d, in Shepard's Restatement of the Law Citations.

114

SECTION E.   UNIFORM LAWS AND MODEL CODES

1.   Uniform Laws

The Restatements, as mentioned, have as their aim the restating of the common law as developed by the courts. The movement for law reform has also focused on statutory law and the need, in many instances, for similar statutes among the states. Toward this aim, the American Bar Association passed a resolution recommending that each state and the District of Columbia adopt a law providing for the appointment of Commissioners to confer with Commissioners of other states on the subject of uniformity in legislation on certain subjects. By 1912, each of the states, the District of Columbia, and Puerto Rico had passed such a law, and the National Conference of Commissioners on Uniform State Laws was formed. Its object is to "promote uniformity in state laws where uniformity is deemed desirable and practicable." [15]

The National Conference meets once a year and considers drafts of proposed uniform laws. When such a law is approved, it is the duty of the Commissioners to try to convince their state legislatures to adopt it. The National Conference has approved over two hundred acts.

A complete list of acts approved by the National Conference of Commissioners on Uniform State Laws appears each year in the Appendices in its annual *Handbook*. These tables also list which states have adopted each uniform law.

Laws approved by the National Conference of Commissioners on Uniform State Laws are published in the following forms.

(a) Separate pamphlet form.

(b) In the annual *Handbook of the National Conference.*

(c) *Uniform Laws Annotated, Master Edition*, 1969—.

The Uniform Laws Annotated, Master Edition, published by the West Publishing Company, replaces all former editions. After each section of a uniform law, pertinent official comment of the Commissioners is given. This is followed by a list of law review commentaries and then by digests of federal and state court decisions citing the particular section of the uniform law. It is kept up to date by annual pocket supplements.

2.   Model Acts

The National Conference of Commissioners on Uniform State Laws has determined that it will designate an act as a *Uniform Act*

[15] NATIONAL CONFERENCE OF COMMISSIONERS ON UNIFORM STATE LAWS, HANDBOOK 269 (1978).

when it has a reasonable possibility of ultimate enactment in a substantial number of jurisdictions.[16]   Acts which do not have such possibility are designated as *Model Acts*.   As a general rule, *Model Acts* embrace subject areas that do not have substantial interstate implications.

The American Law Institute also occasionally will draft and approve a Model Act,[17] and will participate jointly with the National Conference of Commissioners on Uniform State Laws as it did in the compilation of the *Uniform Commercial Code.*

3.   Indexes to Uniform Laws and Model Acts

a.   *Handbook of the National Conference of Commissioners on Uniform State Laws.*   A complete list of acts appears in the annual *Handbook.*   Information is given for all of the Acts and Model Acts promulgated by the National Conference.   There are also charts showing which states have adopted specific Acts, and the date of adoption.

b.   *Directory of Acts and Table of Adopting Jurisdictions.* This is a pamphlet, frequently reissued, which is published as part of the *Uniform Laws Annotated.*   It lists all Acts in alphabetical order and indicates where they are printed in *Uniform Laws Annotated.* There is also a table for each state listing all of the Acts adopted.

SECTION F.   ILLUSTRATIONS: UNIFORM LAWS

127–127–b.   **Pages From Uniform Laws Annotated, Master Edition**
128.   **Page from Uniform Laws Annotated—Directory of Uniform Acts**
129.   **Page from Uniform Laws Annotated—Table of Adopting Jurisdictions**

[16.] *Id.* at 302–304.

[17] *See* AMERICAN LAW INSTITUTE, ANNUAL REPORTS.

[Illustration 127]

PAGE FROM VOLUME I, UNIFORM LAWS ANNOTATED, MASTER EDITION

§ 2—609   UNIFORM COMMERCIAL CODE

> **Typical Uniform Law adopted by the National Conference of Commissioners on Uniform State Laws.**

buyer to provide cash or satisfactory security ; however seller's dissatisfaction with defendant's financial standing must not be false or arbitrary. James B. Berry's Sons Co. v. Monark Gasoline & Oil Co., C.C.A.8, 1929, 32 F.2d 74 (cited in Official Comment, supra).

Where a vendor contracts to deliver goods, and allows a buyer credit for with the buyer's financial responsibility is to be settled by the seller before he parts with the goods ; but there must be a real want of satisfaction with the buyer's financial responsibility, and the refusal to ship without payment or security must be based on that reason alone. Corn Products Refining Co. v. Fasola, 1920, 100 A. 505, 94 N.J.Law 181 (cited in Official Comment, supra).

§ 2—610.   Anticipatory Repudiation

When either party repudiates the contract with respect to a performance not yet due the loss of which will substantially impair the value of the contract to the other, the aggrieved party may

     (a) for a commercially reasonable time await performance by the repudiating party; or

     (b) resort to any remedy for breach (Section 2—703 or Section 2—711), even though he has notified the repudiating party that he would await the latter's performance and has urged retraction; and

     (c) in either case suspend his own performance or proceed in accordance with the provisions of this Article on the seller's right to identify goods to the contract notwithstanding breach or to salvage unfinished goods (Section 2—704).

          ——————▶ **Action in Adopting Jurisdictions**

Variations from Official Text:

   Kentucky. In paragraph (b), should refer to 2—703, not to 7—703.

|Official Comment|

Prior Uniform Statutory Provision: See Sections 63(2) and 65, Uniform Sales Act.   *For text of prior provision, see Appendix in end volume.*

400

[Illustration 127-a]

PAGE FROM VOLUME I, UNIFORM LAWS ANNOTATED, MASTER EDITION

SALES   **§ 2—610**

Purposes: To make it clear that:

1. With the problem of insecurity taken care of by the preceding section and with provision being made in this Article as to the effect of a defective delivery under an installment contract, anticipatory repudiation centers upon an overt communication of intention or an action which renders performance impossible or demonstrates a clear determination not to continue with performance.

> After each Section the official comment of the Commissioners explaining the Section is given.

he cannot recover resulting damages which he should have avoided.

2. It is not necessary for repudiation that performance be made literally and utterly impossible. Repudiation can result from action which reasonably indicates a rejection of the continuing obligation. And, a repudiation automatically results under the preceding section on insecurity when a party fails to provide adequate assurance of due future performance within thirty days after a justifiable demand therefor has been made. Under the language of this section, a demand by one or both parties for more than the contract calls for

in the way of counter-performance is not in itself a repudiation nor does it invalidate a plain expression of desire for future performance. However, when under a fair reading it amounts to a statement of intention not to perform except on conditions which go beyond the contract, it becomes a repudiation.

3. The test chosen to justify an aggrieved party's action under this section is the same as that in the section on breach in installment contracts—namely the substantial value of the contract. The most useful test of substantial value is to determine whether material inconvenience or injustice will result if the aggrieved party is forced to wait and receive an ultimate tender minus the part or aspect repudiated.

4. After repudiation, the aggrieved party may immediately resort to any remedy he chooses provided he moves in good faith (see Section 1—203). Inaction and silence by the aggrieved party may leave the matter open but it cannot be regarded as misleading the repudiating party. Therefore the aggrieved party is left free to proceed at any time with his options under this section, unless he has taken some positive action which in good faith requires notification to the other party before the remedy is pursued.

Cross References:

Point 1: Sections 2—609 and 2—612.

Point 2: Section 2—609.

Point 3: Section 2—612.

Point 4: Section 1—203.

[Illustration 127-b]

PAGE FROM VOLUME I, UNIFORM LAWS ANNOTATED, MASTER EDITION

§ 2—610   UNIFORM COMMERCIAL CODE

Definitional Cross References:

"Aggrieved party". Section 1—201.

"Contract". Section 1—201.
"Party". Section 1—201.
"Remedy". Section 1—201

Cross References

Assurance of performance, see section 2—609.
Good faith, enforcement of contracts, see section 1—203.
Installment contracts, defective delivery, see section 2—612.
Letters of credit
    Anticipatory repudiation for wrongful disposition of, see section 5—115.
    Application of remedies under this section for wrongful repudiation, see section 5—115.
Recovery of damages by seller for wrongful repudiation, see section 2—708.

Law Review Commentaries

Anticipatory breach of contract: a comparison of the Texas law and the Uniform Commercial Code. 30 Tex. L.Rev. 744 (1952).

Remedies under law of sales in the proposed Commercial Code. Samuel Williston. 63 Harvard L.Rev. 584 (Feb. 1950).

Remedies under this title. William C. Jones. 30 Mo.L.Rev. 212 (Spring 1965).

Repudiation of a contract under the Code. Arthur Anderson. 14 DePaul L.Rev. 1 (Autumn-Winter 1964).

Sales: "from status to contract". Howard L. Hall. 1952 Wis.L.Rev. 209.

Library References

Sales ⬦84, 98, 116, 370, 405.

C.J.S. Sales §§ 79, 98-100, 464, 520.

Notes of Decisions

Construction with other laws 1
Executory contracts, limitation to 2
Insolvency of parties 4
Remedies available on breach 5
Suspension of performance 3
Tender of delivery 6

----

1. Construction with other laws

This section and sections 2—700, 2—718 and 2—719 relating to anticipatory repudiation of a sales contract, and action for price, liquidation or limitation of damages, and modification or limitation of remedy, must be read and interpreted together, and unconscionable modification or limitation of remedial provisions must be deleted. Denkin v. Sterner, 1956, 10 Pa.D. & C.2d 203, 70 York Leg.Rec. 105.

2. Executory contracts, limitation to

Theory of an anticipatory breach cannot be invoked where contract, at

time of fraud claimed as basis for re-

> At the end of each Section, references to additional research aids are given.
>
> Also, annotations to all court decisions citing the Section are indicated.
>
> Pocket supplement should also be checked.

402

[Illustration 128]

PAGE FROM UNIFORM LAWS ANNOTATED—DIRECTORY OF
UNIFORM ACTS

DIRECTORY OF UNIFORM ACTS

List of Uniform Acts or Codes, in alphabetical order,
showing where each may be found in Uniform Laws Annotated, Master Edition.

The designation "Pocket Part" under the page column
indicates that the particular Act or Code is complete in the
Pocket Part. The user should always, of course, consult
the Pocket Part for changes and subsequent material when
an Act or Code appears in the main volume.

	Uniform Laws Annotated	
Title of Act	**Volume**	**Page**
Abortion Act, Revised (1973 Act)	9	1
Absence as Evidence of Death and Absen-		
tees' Property Act	8	1
Acknowledgment Act	12	1
Administrative Procedure Act, State (Model)	14	357
Adoption Act	9	11
Aircraft Financial Responsibility Act	12	21

This Table lists all Uniform Acts and shows where the
text may be found in the Uniform Laws Annotated. Similar information may also be found in the annual Handbook
of the National Conference of Commissioners on Uniform
State Laws.

Certification of Questions of Law Act	12	49
Child Custody Jurisdiction Act	9	111
Children and minors,		
Abortion Act, Revised (1973 Act)	9	1
Adoption Act	9	11
Child Custody Jurisdiction Act	9	111
Civil Liability for Support Act	9	171
Gifts to Minors Act (1966 Act)	8	181
Gifts to Minors Act (1956 Act)	8	225

[Illustration 129]

PAGE FROM UNIFORM LAWS ANNOTATED—TABLE OF
ADOPTING JURISDICTIONS

TABLE OF JURISDICTIONS LISTING
UNIFORM ACTS ADOPTED

List of jurisdictions, in alphabetical order, listing the
Uniform Acts or Codes adopted by that particular jurisdiction, and where each may be found in Uniform Laws Annotated, Master Edition.

Each Uniform Act or Code in the Master Edition contains
a Table showing the statutory citations of each of the
adopting jurisdictions.

ALABAMA

Title of Act	Uniform Laws Annotated Volume	Page
Anatomical Gift Act	8	15
Brain Death Act	12	Pocket Part
Certification of Questions of Law Act	12	49
Commercial Code	1 to 3	
Common Trust Fund Act	7	83
Controlled Substances Act	9	187
Criminal Extradition Act	11	51
Declaratory Judgments Act	12	109

This Table lists all of the states alphabetically and
then indicates whether uniform acts or codes have been
adopted by the individual states.

Motor Vehicle Certificate of Title and Anti-Theft Act	11	421
Partnership Act	6	1
Photographic Copies of Business and Public Records as Evidence Act	14	145
Principal and Income Act (1931 Act)	7A	461
Reciprocal Enforcement of Support Act (1950 Act)	9A	747
Securities Act	7A	561
Simplification of Fiduciary Security Transfers Act	7A	709
Simultaneous Death Act	8	605
Testamentary Additions to Trusts Act	8	629

9

SECTION G. INTERSTATE COMPACTS

The United States Constitution provides that "No state shall, without the consent of Congress * * * enter into any Agreement or Compact with another state * * *." [18]

In an early interpretation of this clause, the Supreme Court of the United States held that it prohibited all agreements between states unless consented to by Congress.[19] But, in a subsequent decision,[20] the Court changed its position and held that Congressional consent was not necessary for agreements or compacts which did not increase the political powers of the states or interfere with the supremacy of the United States. Normally, interstate agreements or compacts are formally enacted by the legislatures of the states involved, and are then submitted to Congress for its consent.[21]

Until about 1900, most interstate compacts dealt with boundary disputes between states. Since then, the compacts have more commonly been used as a means of cooperation for solving problems common to two or more states, such as flood control, control of pollution, or the establishment of a port authority.

1. Publication of Interstate Compacts

As interstate compacts ordinarily do not come into effect until agreed to by the states involved, and with the consent of Congress, the text of agreements or compacts will be found in the session laws of the respective states and in the *United States Statutes at Large.*[22]

A complete listing of compacts may be found in *Interstate Compacts and Agencies*, published periodically by the Council of State Governments. It contains the following information:

List of compacts involving boundaries;

Subject arrangement of all other compacts, with short annotations;

---

[18] U.S. Const. Art. I, § 10, cl. 3.

[19] Holmes v. Jennison, 14 Pet. (39 U.S.) 540 (1840).

[20] Virginia v. Tennessee, 148 U.S. 503, 518 (1893). *See also* U.S. Steel Corp. v. Multistate Tax Commission, 434 U.S. 452 (1978).

[21] Interstate agreements do not have to be formally enacted. *See* the annotation to Art. I, § 10, cl. 3, in THE CONSTITUTION OF THE UNITED STATES OF AMERICA, ANALYSIS AND INTERPRETATION 419–23 (Lib. of Cong. ed. 1973). *See also* F. ZIMMERMAN & M. WENDELL, THE LAW AND USE OF INTERSTATE COMPACTS (2d ed. 1976); Comment, *Federal Question Jurisdiction to Interpret Interstate Compacts*, 64 GEO.L.J. 87 (1975); P. HARDY, INTERSTATE COMPACTS: THE TIES THAT BIND (1982).

[22] E.g., The North Dakota-Minnesota Boundary Agreement is published in 1961 Minn.Sess.Laws, ch. 236; 1961 North Dakota Sess.Law, ch. 319, and Congressional consent is given in Pub.Law No. 87–162, 75 Stat. 399.

Index of defunct or dormant compacts;

Index to compacts.

Each biennial edition of the *Book of States* has a chapter on current developments in interstate compacts, and a selective listing of the more significant ones.

2. Locating Court Decisions on Interstate Compacts

a. *Digests.*   Cases involving interstate compacts are digested under *States* ☜6 in the *Key Number* digests and under *States* § 52 in the *Digest of the U.S. Supreme Court* (Lawyers' Edition).

b. *Annotated Statutes.*   The practice of including the text of compacts in state codes varies. The indexes to the codes of the states concerned should be checked.

c.   *Citators.*   The Statutes section of the appropriate *Shepard's Citations* may be used to *Shepardize* the state code or session law citation, or the *United States Statutes at Large* citation.

Chapter 18

OTHER RESEARCH AIDS

Attorneys General Opinions, Dictionaries, Directories, Form Books, Briefs and Records on Appeal, and Ethics Opinions

This chapter covers sets of law books that are useful in legal research but which fit into none of the categories previously discussed. They are: (1) attorneys general opinions; (2) law dictionaries; (3) directories; (4) form books; (5) briefs and records; and (6) opinions on legal ethics.

SECTION A. OPINIONS OF THE ATTORNEYS GENERAL

The opinions of the attorneys general have the characteristics of both primary and secondary authority.[1] As the legal advisor to the executive officials of the government, the attorney general renders requested legal advice to them, generally in the form of written opinions. Although these opinions are the official statements of an executive officer, issued in accordance with his authority, they are merely advisory statements and are not mandatory orders. Therefore, the inquirers and other officials are not bound to follow such recommendations and conclusions. However, the opinions are strongly persuasive and are generally followed by executive officers. Also, they have significant influence on the courts in their deliberations.

The opinions, as a general rule, relate to: (1) the interpretations of statutes or (2) general legal problems. Some attorneys general limit their advice and will not render opinions as to the constitutionality of proposed legislation.

1. Attorney General of the United States

The opinions of the Attorney General have been published in forty-two volumes covering the years 1789–1974.[2] Each volume contains the opinions covering several years. In between the publication of the bound volumes, opinions are made available in slip-opinion

---

[1] For more detailed information on the role of Attorneys General, see Thompson, *Transmission or Resistance: Opinions of State Attorneys General and the Impact of the Supreme Court*, 9 VAL.U.L.REV. 55 (1974). See also NATIONAL ASSOCIATION OF ATTORNEYS GENERAL, THE OFFICE OF ATTORNEY GENERAL (1974), and POWERS, DUTIES, AND OPERATIONS OF STATE ATTORNEYS GENERAL (1977); Heiser, *The Opinion Writing Function of Attorneys General*, 18 IDAHO L.REV. 9 (1982).

[2] For a history of the publications of U.S. Attorney General opinions, see Rhodes, *Opinions of the Attorney General Revived*, 64 A.B.A.J. 1374 (1978).

format.   There are also digest volumes to the bound volumes of the U.S. Attorney General's opinions.

The *United States Code Annotated* and *United States Code Service* include digests of U.S. Attorney General opinions in their annotations.   They are also included in the United States and federal *Shepard's Citations* when cited in a court decision.

2.   State Attorneys General Opinions

Nearly every state publishes the opinions of its attorney general.[3]   They are included in the annotations of many state annotated codes, and *Shepard's Citations* (state units) indicate when an attorney general's opinion has been cited by a court.

LEXIS and WESTLAW also include attorneys general opinions for selected states.   Their listings should be checked for coverage.

SECTION B.   LAW DICTIONARIES

Law dictionaries are useful for locating the definition of words in their legal sense or use.   For each word or phrase a short definition is given.   Most legal dictionaries also provide a citation to a court decision or other reference tracing the source of the word or phrase. In Chapter 6, Section G, the set entitled *Words and Phrases* was discussed.   This set includes digests from all court decisions in which a word or phrase has been interpreted.   *Words and Phrases* may also be used as a dictionary; but as it is limited to those words which were involved in litigation, it is not a true dictionary.   Moreover, most dictionaries are much more compact and are published in one or two volumes.   Listed below are some of the more commonly used American and English law dictionaries.

1.   American Law Dictionaries

a.   *Ballentine's Law Dictionary*, with Pronunciations, 3d ed., Lawyers Co-operative Publishing Company, 1969, 1429 p.

b.   *Black's Law Dictionary*, 5th ed., West Publishing Company, 1979, 1511 p.   Includes: *Guide to Pronunciation of Latin Phrases* and a *Table of Abbreviations*.

c.   Bouvier, *Law Dictionary* (3rd revision), 8th ed., West Publishing Company, 1914, 3 Volumes.

This edition is now out of date in some respects.   It is a particularly scholarly work, however, and many of its definitions are

[3] A checklist of published opinions of state attorneys general may be found in M. PIMSLEUR, CHECKLISTS OF BASIC AMERICAN LEGAL PUBLICATIONS sec. III (1962).   For the availability of individual states' attorney general opinions, *see* M. FISHER, GUIDE TO STATE LEGISLATIVE MATERIALS (AALL Pub.Ser. No. 15, 1979).

encyclopedic in nature. It still is very useful for many historical terms.

    d. *Cochran's Law Lexicon: Pronouncing Edition*, 4th ed. (rev. by Gilmore), W.H. Anderson, 1973, 428 p.

    e. Redden and Veron, *Modern Legal Glossary*, Michie Company, 1980, 576 p.

2. English Law Dictionaries

    a. Jowitt, *Dictionary of English Law*, 2d ed., Sweet & Maxwell, 1977, 2 vols.

    b. Mozley and Whitley, *Law Dictionary*, 8th ed., Butterworths, 1970, 389 p.

    c. *Stroud's Judicial Dictionary*, 4th ed. (J.S. James), Sweet & Maxwell, 1971, 5 vols., with second cumulative supplement, 1982.

    d. Walker, *The Oxford Companion to Law*, Clarendon Press, 1980, 1366 p.

3. Special Law Dictionaries

    There are also dictionaries devoted to specific subjects, such as labor law or taxation. These may be located by checking the catalog of a library under the subject and then subdivision—*e.g.*, Taxation—U.S.—Dictionaries.

4. Legal Abbreviations

    a. *Current American Citations with Examples.* Edited by D. Bieber, 1983.

    b. Law dictionaries and books on legal research. Most legal dictionaries and manuals of legal bibliography have tables of abbreviations.

SECTION C. LAW DIRECTORIES

    Law directories vary in the scope of their coverage. Some attempt to list all lawyers; others are limited to a region, state, municipality, or to a specialty. Law directories are useful in locating information about a particular lawyer and are used by many lawyers when they have to refer a case to a lawyer in another city.

    In 1935 the American Bar Association appointed a *Special Committee on Law Lists* to investigate the law list business. This Committee developed *Rules and Standards as to Law Lists*, [4] which were adopted by the American Bar Association in 1937. The American Bar Association has taken the position that " * * * A law list is conclusively established to be reputable if it is certified by the

    [4] The text may be found in the *Martindale-Hubbell Law Directory*.

American Bar Association as being in compliance with its rules and standards." [5]   As a result, nearly all lists and directories now seek to receive the certification of the American Bar Association.

1. General Directories

a. *Martindale-Hubbell Law Directory.* This multi-volume annual publication is the most comprehensive directory of lawyers. All lawyers admitted to the bar of any jurisdiction are eligible for listing without cost. The volumes are arranged alphabetically by state. Each of these volumes is in two parts. The first part consists of two alphabetical lists, one of the cities within each state, and a second of the lawyers within each city. For each listed attorney, information is given for date of birth, date of admission to the bar, college and law school attended, American Bar Association membership, and specialty. Confidential ratings [6] are also given which estimate legal ability, recommendations, and promptness in paying bills. The second part is another double alphabetic arrangement, this time done by cities within the state and law firms within each city. This entry may include the address and telephone number of the firm, names, and short biographies of its members, representative clients and areas of practice. Since this form of advertising carries a charge, the list is not complete.

The following items are also included. As their location may change from year to year, the Table of Contents pages should be consulted for their location.

List of Canadian Lawyers

Government Lawyers Roster

Patent Lawyers Roster

Foreign Lawyers Section

Law digests of the statutory law for the fifty states, Canada, and over fifty foreign countries

American Bar Association Information

Corporate Law Department Biographical Section

b. *The Lawyers Directory. The Lawyers Directory* is an annual publication which lists the following:

Part I: Leading lawyers and law firms in the United States and Canada and a list of foreign lawyers; Part II: Corporate law department counsel roster: Part III: Complete list of foreign embassies and legations in Washington, D.C., and U.S. embassies, legations and consular offices throughout the world.

---

[5] CODE OF PROFESSIONAL RESPONSIBILITY DR 2–102–A–6 (1979).

[6] A *Confidential Key* to their ratings is included in the inside covers of the volumes.

c. *Who's Who in American Law.* This biannual compilation contains biographical information on approximately 34,000 attorneys selected for their prominence as judges, educators, or practitioners. Despite the large number of entries, there is no claim to comprehensiveness in any of the above areas of the profession. The format is similar to that used in other Marquis *Who's Who* publications.

d. *The American Bar, The Canadian Bar, The International Bar.* This is an annual biographical directory of ranking United States and foreign lawyers. It provides sketches of the North American law offices listed and individual biographical data. The third unit is a professional international directory of "the finest lawyers in the world."

e. *Other International Directories.* Many other companies publish directories that are to be used to locate a *recommended* attorney in a particular country and city to deal with any general legal questions. Included in this group are *The International List, The International Laywers,* and Kime's *International Law Directory.*

f. *Law & Legal Information Directory.* This is a guide to national and international organizations and contains other information about the legal profession.

g. *Directory of the Legal Profession* (1984). This publication of the *National Law Journal* covers nearly 600 of the nation's most important law firms and a sampling of the largest legal departments at big corporations. This directory includes such items as billing rates, clients, starting salaries for associates, and names of managing partners.

2. State and Regional Directories

The Legal Directories Publishing Company, Inc.,[7] produces 25 directories that are approved by the American Bar Association and list attorneys in specific states or regions. Examples of the state directories are the *Florida Legal Directory,* the *Illinois Legal Directory,* and the *Texas Legal Directory.* The regional directories include the *Mountain States Legal Directory,* the *New England Legal Directory,* and the *Virginias, Maryland, Delaware, and District of Columbia Legal Directory.* Each of these directories contains sections on:

a. Federal and state officials (including members of the state legislatures).

b. Federal, state and local courts.

[7] Legal Directories Publishing Co., Inc., 2122 Kidwell Street, P.O. Box 140700, Dallas, TX 75214.

c. Attorneys practicing in the state (arranged by county and city). This section also contains some biographical data on law firms and their members.

3. Specialty Directories

Some directories have been published that contain only the attorneys who practice law in a particular specialty. These are useful for one who wishes reference to a lawyer in a specific city on a legal problem common to the specialty. Examples of such directories include: *The Probate Counsel, American Bank Attorneys,* and *Markham's Negligence Counsel.* Specialty directories may be located by consulting a library catalog under the heading of *Lawyers— Directories.*

4. Judicial Directories and Biographies

a. Directories

(1) *Federal Court Directory* (Lawyer's Diary & Manual, Newark, NJ)

(2) *Federal Court Directory* (sometimes entitled *United States Court Directory*) (Legal Reporters, Associates, Washington D.C.)

(3) *United States Court Directory* (Administrative Office of the United States Courts)

b. Biographical Directories

(1) *Biographical Dictionary of the Federal Judicary, 1789– 1974* (Gale Research Company, based on materials from *Who's Who in America* and *Who Was Who in America*)

(2) *Federal Judiciary Almanac, 1984* (John Wiley & Sons)

(3) *Judges of the United States,* 2d ed., 1982 (Bicentennial Committee of the Judicial Conference of the United States; covers the years 1780–1982)

(4) *The Almanac of the Federal Judiciary,* 1984 (Chicago: Law Letters, Inc.)

5. Academic Directories

Certain directories are compiled to serve the academic world and provide a ready reference to those wishing to make use of the law schools' facilities. The *Directory of Law Teachers* [8] allows one to find biographic information on law school faculty, as well as indexing by subject or specialty. Law libraries of the United States and Canada are indexed geographically in the *Directory of Law Librar-*

[8] Directory of Law Teachers, West Publishing Company, 50 West Kellogg Blvd., St. Paul, MN 55102.

ies. [9] An alphabetical listing of library personnel is also provided in this directory.

SECTION D. FORM BOOKS

Form books are used as aids in drafting legal documents. Much of a lawyer's time is spent in drafting forms. To assist lawyers in this aspect of their practice, there are available many different types of form books. When using form books, it should be kept in mind that they are all general in nature and that before using a form, extreme care should be exercised to make sure that the language is entirely suitable for the purpose for which it is to be used. Books of forms may be classified as follows:

1. General Form Books

This type provides forms for all aspects of legal practice and varies from one volume to multi-volume sets. They generally are annotated, and each form contains references to cases that have favorably construed provisions within the form. Editorial comment is also frequently given. Examples are:

> *American Jurisprudence, Legal Forms 2d,* 1971–74, 20 volumes with pocket supplements.

> *West's Legal Forms, 2d* (West Publishing Company).

> Nichols, *Cyclopedia of Legal Forms, Annotated,* 1955–1964, 14 volumes with pocket supplements.

> Rabkin and Johnson, *Current Legal Forms with Tax Analysis,* 1968, 22 volumes. Looseleaf.

> Warren, *Forms of Agreement,* 1966, one volume. Looseleaf.

Most large states also have general form books that are keyed to local practice. These are published both by commercial publishers and state bar association programs. They contain the same features as the form books discussed above, but are designed for local use, and hence may be more useful to the practitioner. Examples are:

> *California Legal Forms, Transaction Guide* (Matthew Bender). One volume. Looseleaf.

> *Legal Form Manual for Real Estate Transactions* (State Bar of Texas). One volume.

2. Subject Form Books

Many form books are devoted to a special subject. These are similar in format to the general form books but contain more forms

---

[9] Directory of Law Libraries, Commerce Clearing House, Inc., 420 Lexington Ave., New York, NY 10017.

on the aspect of the subject covered than will usually be found in the general ones. Examples are:

> H. Lavien, *Bankruptcy Forms* (West Publishing Company) (with supplements).
>
> M. Melville, *Forms and Agreements on Intellectual Property* (Clark Boardman). One volume.
>
> A. Arnold, *Modern Real Estate and Mortgage Forms* (Warren, Gorham, and Lamont). Looseleaf.

3. Other Sources of Forms

a. *Forms in Treatises.* Many multi-volume sets of treatises will include forms, either integrated with the text, or in separate volumes.

b. *State Codes.* Some state codes include both substantive and procedural forms. For any particular state code, consult the general index under *Forms*.

c. *Procedural Forms.* These are discussed in Chapter 12, Jacobstein and Mersky, *Fundamentals of Legal Research*, 3d ed. (1985).

SECTION E. BRIEFS AND RECORDS ON APPEAL

After a case has been decided by a trial court or an intermediate court of appeal, the case may be appealed to a higher court. When this happens, the attorneys for each side submit written briefs in which they set forth the reasons why the appellate court should either affirm or reverse the decision below. Such briefs contain the theories upon which arguments hinge and a discussion and analysis of the law, with citations to the authorities. Where available, the record of trial court action is submitted with the brief. This record usually contains forms of the preliminary motions and pleadings in the case; examination and cross-examination of witnesses; the instructions to the jury; the opinion of the lower court; and various other exhibits.

Briefs and records provide an attorney who has a similar case with much of his research and a list of arguments that have or have not impressed an appellate court.

1. Briefs and Records of the Supreme Court of the United States

A small number of libraries receive copies of the briefs and records that are submitted to the Supreme Court.[10] Most law school libraries and larger bar association libraries also have these briefs and records available on microform.

---

[10] *See* Charpentier, *Appellate Records—A Beginning Union List*, 62 LAW LIBR.J. 273 (1969).

Oral arguments presented before the Court have been tape-recorded since 1955. They are available for purchase after three years have elapsed and must be used for scholarly or instructional purposes. Further information may be obtained from the Office of the Marshal of the Supreme Court of the United States.

Starting with the 1980 term, oral arguments are being made available by University Publications of America.

2. Federal Courts of Appeals

Most large law libraries receive the briefs and records for the federal court of appeals for the circuit in which they are located. Others may frequently be obtained from a local law library on interlibrary loan.

SECTION F. PROFESSIONAL RESPONSIBILITY

The national standard of conduct for lawyers is set forth in the *Model Rules of Professional Conduct* promulgated by the American Bar Association in 1984.[11]

The American Bar Association, as a voluntary association, has no means for enforcing its Code. Only the state legislature or the highest court of each state has the power to discipline lawyers. Each state has adopted either its own code or that of the American Bar Association.

In August 1983, the American Bar Association adopted the new *Model Rules of Professional Conduct* which are intended to replace the *Code of Professional Responsibility*. These rules are available in a variety of sources, including the last volume of *Martindale-Hubbell*. Note that it is up to each individual state to adopt the *Model Rules* as its state standard.

1. Discipline of Lawyers

The procedure for the discipline of lawyers varies from state to state. The rules governing discipline may be located by consulting the indexes of the state codes. The common practice is for the highest court of the state to appoint a committee of lawyers to hear complaints and make recommendations to the court.

2. Opinions on Legal Ethics

The American Bar Association has a *Committee on Legal Ethics*. Lawyers may submit to this Committee a situation they are facing and request an opinion as to whether or not their suggested action may be a breach of the *Model Rules of Professional Conduct*.

---

[11] The *Model Rules* replace the *Code of Professional Responsibility* adopted in 1970, which in turn replaced the 1908 *ABA Code of Professional Ethics*.

The opinions of this Committee are published in two series: *Formal Opinions* and *Informal Opinions*.

Most state bar associations have similar committees. Until recently, the opinions of their *Committees on Legal Ethics* were not published in any systematic method. They may now be located in the following sets:

a. *ABA/BNA Lawyer's Manual on Professional Conduct.* Two volumes. Looseleaf. This set contains a wide range of material dealing with the legal profession. Volume 2 contains court decisions on the discipline of lawyers and the text of state legal ethics opinions.

b. *National Reporter on Legal Ethics and Professional Conduct.* This multi-volume looseleaf set reprints digests of court decisions and texts of state legal ethics opinions.

c. Wypski, *Opinions Committees of Professional Ethics.* Volumes 1–3 contain the opinions of the Association of the Bar of the City of New York and New York County Bar Association; Volume 4, the opinions for other states.

3.   Shepard's Professional Responsibility Citations

This citator is devoted to the coverage of citations to the *Code of Professional Responsibility* by both the federal and state courts.

Chapter 19

INTERNATIONAL LAW

SECTION A. INTRODUCTION

Research in international law is neither esoteric nor limited to the practice of the specialist. American treaties, as primary law,[1] are frequently determinative of the rights and duties of Americans. To illustrate this point, a resident of one state may leave a will devising her property to a relative in a foreign country. The state may have a statute prohibiting an alien from taking property by succession or testamentary disposition. The United States Supreme Court has held that such a state statute must give way when it conflicts with the terms of a United States treaty.[2] Similarly, another court has held that a Washington state statute regulating the fishing rights of certain Indian tribes is not enforceable when the statute is in violation of a treaty between the United States and the Indian tribes.[3]

These are not isolated illustrations, for they occur more frequently than is generally realized. It is essential, therefore, for the legal researcher to have some knowledge of the sources of international law and the tools available for locating them.

International law has been defined as

[A] body of rules governing the relations between states * * *. Customary, as distinguished from conventional, international law is based upon the common consent of the nations extending over a period of time of sufficient duration to cause it to become crystalized into a rule of conduct. When doubt arises as to the existence or nonexistence of a rule of international law, or as to the application of a rule to a given situation, resort is usually had to such sources as pertinent treaties, pronouncements of foreign offices, statements by writers, and decisions of international tribunals

[1] "[A]ll Treaties made, or which shall be made, under the Authority of the United States, shall be the supreme Law of the Land." U.S. Const. Art. VI, cl. 2.

[2] Zschernig v. Miller, 389 U.S. 429 (1968).

[3] United States v. Washington, 520 F.2d 676 (9th Cir.1975). A brief survey of the annotations in either *U.S.C.A.* or *U.S.C.S.* under Art. VI, cl. 2, will indicate both the amount and currentness of litigation arising from this article.

and those of prize courts and other domestic courts purporting to be expressive of the law of nations.[4]

Another international law scholar has defined international law in terms of how it is made.

When contrasted with national or *domestic* law, we think of international law as that which is created by two or more states, whether such action is in the form of treaty-making or the formation of international customs.[5]

International law as so stated is usually known as *public* international law as distinguished from *private* international law, which is defined as:

[T]hat branch of municipal law which determines before the courts of what nation a particular action or suit should be brought, and by the law of what nation it should be determined.[6]

This chapter will focus on public international law, but will be devoted primarily to the researching of the conventional international law of the United States as represented in the treaties and other international agreements entered into between the United States and other countries.[7]

SECTION B.   RESEARCH IN INTERNATIONAL LAW IN RELATION TO THE UNITED STATES

1.   Treaties and International Agreements Between the United States and Other Countries

Under the Constitution of the United States, the President "* * * shall have Power, by and with the Advice and Consent of the Senate, to make Treaties, provided two-thirds of the Senators present concur; * * *."[8] An international agreement is one that the President may enter into under his constitutional power as

---

[4] 1 G. HACKWORTH, DIGEST OF INTERNATIONAL LAW 1 (1940); *see also* The Paquette Habana, 175 U.S. 677, 700 (1899).

[5] H. KELSEN, PRINCIPLES OF INTERNATIONAL LAW 300 (2d ed. R. Tucker 1966).

[6] 1 JOWITT'S DICTIONARY OF ENGLISH LAW 999–1000 (2d ed. J. Burke 1977). In the United States the term *conflict of laws* is generally used rather than private international law.

[7] For additional information on the substantive aspect of international law, *see* the latest editions of J. BRIERLY, THE LAW OF NATIONS, or C. FENWICK, INTERNATIONAL LAW. For bibliographies *see* Marke, *International Law: An Annotated Bibliography,* in 1978 ANN. SURVEY AM.L. (Supp.55–159) and PUB. INT'L L.: A CURRENT BIBLIOGRAPHY (semiannual).

[8] U.S. Const. Art. II, § 2, cl. 2. The Constitution does not mention how a treaty may be terminated, and whether the advice and consent of the Senate is needed. For a detailed study of this question, *see* SENATE COMM. ON FOREIGN RELATIONS,

President or as authorized by an act of Congress and which does not need the consent of Congress.[9] The actual power of the President to enter into international agreements rather than treaties is not entirely clear and has long been a matter of dispute.[10] But nevertheless, international agreements are entered into by Presidents much more frequently than are treaties.

2. Restatement (Second) of Foreign Relations Law of the United States

This Restatement was adopted by the American Law Institute in 1962. Its purpose, as stated in the introduction, is to set forth the foreign relations law of the United States, which consists of those rules the United States conceived to be established by international law and those parts of the domestic law which give effect to rules of international law. It is a useful place to start research for matters involving the interpretation of U.S. treaties or statutes and for cases interpreting them. Note that this Restatement is currently undergoing revision, and that parts of this revision may be available in *tentative draft* form.

SECTION C. SOURCES FOR UNITED STATES TREATIES

1. Current Publications

a. *Prior to Ratification by the Senate.* After the President has negotiated and signed a treaty, it has to be submitted to the Senate for advice and consent. The text of the treaty along with the presidential message and other documents are published in the *Senate Executive Documents* series. Prior to 1945, these were almost always printed as confidential documents and were not generally available. Since 1946, the Senate has ordered them printed without the confidential classification.

Treaties submitted to the Senate by the President are assigned to the Committee on Foreign Relations. This committee may hold hearings and then after consideration issue a report recommending that the treaty be or not be ratified. These reports are published in

95TH CONG., 2D SESS., TERMINATION OF TREATIES; THE CONSTITUTIONAL ALLOCATION OF POWER (Comm.Print 1978).

[9] RESTATEMENT (SECOND) OF FOREIGN RELATIONS LAW OF THE UNITED STATES § 115(a) (1965). *See also* A. GILBERT, EXECUTIVE AGREEMENTS AND TREATIES, 1946–1973 (1973).

[10] For an excellent discussion and bibliography of executive agreements, *see* Leary, *International Executive Agreements: A Guide to the Legal Issues and Research Sources,* 72 LAW LIBR.J. 1 (1979). *See also* Schmitt, *Separations of Powers: Introduction to the Study of Executive Agreements,* 27 AM.J.JURIS. 114 (1982); Lesser, *Superseding Statutory Law by Sole Executive Agreements: An Analysis of the American Law Institute's Shift in Position,* 23 VA.J.INT'L L. 6 (1983).

the *Senate Executive Reports* series and may be located through either the *Monthly Catalog* or the *CIS Index*. [11]

b. *After Ratification.* Since December 27, 1945, all treaties and international agreements are first published in pamphlet form in the *Treaties and Other International Acts Series* (T.I.A.S.). This Series starts with Treaty Number 1501, since it combines and continues the numbering of two previous publications of treaties and international agreements, *i.e.,* 994 numbers of the *Treaty Series* and 506 numbers of the *Executive Agreement Series*. [12] It contains all treaties which have been proclaimed during the calendar year to which the United States is a party, and all international agreements other than treaties to which the United States is a party that have been signed, proclaimed, or with reference to which any other final formality has been executed during that calendar year.[13] The documents are literal prints of the originals with marginal notes and footnotes.

c. All of the pamphlets issued in the *Treaties and Other International Acts Series* since 1950 are published in bound volumes under the title *United States Treaties and Other International Agreements* (UST). By statute,[14] the treaties contained in the *Statutes at Large* and *United States Treaties and Other International Agreements* are evidence admissible in all federal courts, state courts, and courts of the territories and insular possessions of the United States.

d. *Status of Pending Treaties.* The *CCH Congressional Index* has a section which contains a status table for all treaties which have

---

[11] These Documents and Reports are collected in M. MABRY, CHECKLIST OF SENATE EXECUTIVE DOCUMENTS AND REPORTS ∗ ∗ ∗ 1947–AUGUST 1970 (1970), and since 1969 in each annual volume of *CIS–Abstracts*, under *Senate Committees—Foreign Relations—Executive Reports and Executive Documents* (S384 & S385).

[12] The T.I.A.S. replaces the *Treaty Series*, 1908–45, and the *Executive Agreement Series*, 1929–45. The *Treaty Series* consists of separate treaty prints in pamphlet or slip form, arranged numerically in chronological order of proclamation or publication. The publication of this Series was commenced in January 1908 with Treaty Number 489 by the Department of State. Prior to October 1, 1929 (Treaty Number 813) the *Treaty Series* included both treaties and executive agreements. From October 1, 1929 (Treaty Number 813) to the end of the publication in December 1945 (Treaty Number 994), however, the *Treaty Series* is limited to treaties and international agreements submitted to the Senate. Another series, also by the Department of State, called the *Executive Agreement Series*, started its publication on October 1, 1929, and ended on March 16, 1945. This series contains 506 numbers and picks up the executive agreements, exchanges of notes, etc. excluded from the *Treaty Series* for that period. For a fuller explanation of these two series and for the treaties prior to Number 489, see H. MILLER, I TREATIES AND OTHER INTERNATIONAL ACTS OF THE UNITED STATES OF AMERICA 35–38, 99–135 (1931).

[13] 1 U.S.C. § 112a (1982 ed.)

[14] *Id.*

been submitted to the Senate Committee on Foreign Relations and are awaiting action by the committee or the full Senate.

e. *Commerce Clearing House, Tax Treaties.* This service provides looseleaf reporting on income and estate tax treaties between the United States and foreign countries. The Reporter contains interpretative regulations, news on treaties in preparation, significant court decisions and editorial comment. A special section of the publication features *CCH Treaty Charts* which show in graphic style the contents of each treaty relating to some 200 major tax aspects.[15]

2. Collections of United States Treaties

U.S. treaties have from time to time been published in separate sets. These are:

a. *Treaties, Conventions, International Acts, Protocols, and Agreements Between the U.S.A. and Other Powers,* 4 vols. (often called *Malloy's Treaties* after the compiler of the first two volumes. Volumes 3 and 4 are sometimes cited by the names of their compilers, Redmond and Trenwith). This set contains all treaties, etc., between 1776 and 1937 with some annotations. Volume 4 includes an index to the set and a chronological list of treaties.

b. *Treaties and Other International Acts of the United States,* edited by Hunter Miller. This is a more recent compilation of treaties. However, only 8 volumes covering the years 1776 to 1863 were published.

c. From 1789 to 1950, many treaties were published in the *Statutes at Large,* but until volume 32 (1903) their publication in this set had been irregular. With volume 47 (1931–32),[16] the *Statutes at Large* started to include international agreements as well.

d. *Treaties and Other International Agreements of the United States,* 1776–1949, edited by C.E. Bevans, and published by the Department of State. It includes the English text, or in cases where no English text was signed the official United States Government translations, of all treaties and international agreements which were published in the *Statutes at Large* between 1776 and 1949. The first four volumes contain multilateral treaties and agreements, arranged chronologically according to date of signature. The next eight volumes (volumes 5–12) list bilateral treaties and agreements arranged alphabetically by country. Each volume includes a brief index which is consolidated into volume 13, a cumulative analytical index arranged in one alphabet by country and subject. Although the set is annotated, its essential value rests in its collection of

---

[15] A similar service is published by Prentice-Hall.

[16] For a detailed study of the inclusion (and exclusion) of treaties in the *U.S. Statutes at Large, see* Miller, vol. 1, at 33–35.

documentary texts. The current status of a treaty or an agreement in this set may be determined by consulting the latest annual volume of *Treaties in Force* and the monthly *Department of State Bulletin.*

e. *Unperfected Treaties of the United States,* 1776–1976,[17] edited by C. Wiktor. This multi-volume set is an annotated collection of the texts of all treaties to which the United States was signatory but which never went into force.

f. *Extradition Laws and Treaties of the United States,* [18] edited by I. Kavass and A. Sprudzs. This set, published in looseleaf volumes, contains all operative extradition treaties arranged in alphabetical sequence of countries with which the United States entered into extradition arrangements.

g. *Indian Affairs, Laws and Treaties,* compiled and edited by C. Kappler. This set has been recently reprinted by the U.S. Government (1976), and the treaties volume (volume 2) has been separately reprinted as *Indian Treaties* 1778–1883 (Interland Publishing, Inc. 1972). Though the last treaty with an Indian tribe was ratified in 1868, this volume cannot be considered comprehensive because the U.S. Government continued to sign *Agreements* (which have the same force as treaties) with Indian tribes until 1909. Earlier compilations of Indian treaties, such as the one found in volume 7 of the *Statutes at Large,* are not as comprehensive or well indexed as *Kappler.* Agreements not found in *Kappler* can usually be found in the *Statutes at Large* using the sources described below in Section C–4. For treaties concluded with Indian tribes prior to the formation of the United States, *see* A. Vaughan (ed.), *Early American Indian Documents: Treaties and Laws* 1607–1789 (1979).

3. Indexes to U.S. Treaties

a. *Treaties in Force.* This is an annual publication of the U.S. Department of State, listing all treaties and agreements, by country and by subject, that are still in force.

b. *A Guide to the United States Treaties in Force* (edited by I. Kavass and A. Sprudzs). This annual publication supplements *Treaties in Force* by providing additional access points. Part 1 contains numerical lists and a subject reference index, and part 2 indexes multilateral treaties and agreements.

c. *United States Treaties and Other International Agreements Cumulative Indexes,* 1776–1949.[19] This 4-volume set indexes all treaties and international agreements from 1776 to 1949 that were published in the *Statutes at Large,* the *Malloy's,* the *Miller's,* the

---

[17] Oceana Publications, Dobbs Ferry, N.Y. (1976–).

[18] W.S. Hein, Buffalo, N.Y. (1979).

[19] Edited by I. Kavass and M. Michael.

Bevans's, and other relevant sources. Arrangements are numerical by treaty number, chronological by date of signature, by country, and by topic.

(1) *United States Treaties and Other International Agreements Cumulative Index,* 1950–1975.[20] This four-volume set and Supplement indexes all treaties and international agreements published in the *United States Treaties and Other International Agreements.* This set is kept current by looseleaf supplement volumes.

(2) *Current Treaty Index: A Cumulative Index to the United States Slip Treaties and Agreements.* [21] This annual pamphlet indexes slip treaties and agreements and is useful as there are frequently long delays before the bound volumes of the *United States Treaties and Other International Agreements* are published.

d. *Statutes at Large,* Vol. 64, pt. 3, at B 1107 *et seq.* This section lists alphabetically by country all treaties and agreements that were included in volumes 1–64, 1789–1949, except those treaties signed with Indian tribes.

e. *Department of State Bulletin.* This is a monthly publication of the Department of State. Each issue has a section entitled *Treaty Information* which gives current information on treaties. This should be used to supplement *Treaties in Force.* There are monthly and annual indexes to the *Department of State Bulletin* which may be used to locate current information either by subject or country.

4. Special Subject Indexes—American Indians

A checklist and bibliography of Indian treaties appears in *List of Indian Treaties,* House Committee on Interior and Insular Affairs, 88th Cong., 2d Sess. (Comm. Print No. 33, 1964). This print consists of a chronological list of all ratified Indian treaties from 1778 to 1868, a list of treaties and agreements alphabetically by tribe from 1778 to 1881, and the index to the *Kappler* collection of Indian treaties (2–g *supra*). The first two lists cite to the *Statutes at Large.*

A *Chronological List of Treaties and Agreements Made by Indian Tribes with the United States* (Institute for the Development of Indian Law, 1973) attempts to list all treaties and agreements between 1778 and 1909 whether ratified or unratified. For each ratified treaty or agreement, a citation to the *Statutes at Large* is given. Also, the uncodified volume of the *United States Code Service* lists, by year, Indian treaties which have been cited or construed by the courts, with digests of the decisions.

[20] Edited by I. Kavass and A. Sprudzs.

[21] *Id.*

5. Interpretations of Treaties

a. Digests. These are more than case digests and include excerpts from treaties, periodical articles, and court decisions from various countries, and documents of the various international organizations. These digests have been published by the Department of State and the editors have all been distinguished scholars: [22]

(1) *Wharton's Digest of International Law.* 3 vols. 1886.

(2) *Moore's Digest of International Law.* 8 vols. 1906.

(3) *Hackworth's Digest of International Law.* 8 vols. 1940–1944.

(4) *Whiteman's Digest of International Law.* 15 vols. 1963–1973. Supplements *Hackworth's.*

(5) *Digest of United States Practice in International Law.* This is an annual publication which started in 1973.

(6) *Contemporary Practice of the United States Relating to International Law.* This appears in each quarterly issue of the *American Journal of International Law.* It digests current materials under the same headings as are used in the *Digest of United States Practice in International Law.*

6. Citators for Treaties

After the text of a treaty or agreement has been located, steps should be taken to ascertain the interpretations given to it by the courts. The language of treaties, as that of statutes, may not be clear in meaning, or there may be doubt if it was the intent of the treaty to cover certain situations. Two methods of locating court decisions involving treaties are:

a. *Shepard's United States Citations—Statutes Volumes.* Treaties entered into before 1950 may be *Shepardized* in the usual manner in the section for *Statutes at Large (not in United States Code).* Treaties entered into after 1950 may be *Shepardized* in the section for *United States Treaties and Other International Agreements.*

b. *United States Code Service.* The unnumbered volume for uncodified laws and treaties lists treaties by year of ratification and gives annotations to court decisions.

---

[22] *See* Rovine, *U.S. International Law Digests: Some History and a New Approach,* 67 AM.J.INT'L L. 314 (1973), for a discussion of these digests.

SECTION D.   ILLUSTRATIONS: UNITED STATES TREATIES AND INTERNATIONAL AGREEMENTS

Illustrations

[Illustration 130]

TITLE PAGE FROM ANNUAL ISSUE OF TREATIES IN FORCE

TREATIES IN FORCE

A List of Treaties

and Other International Agreements

of the United States

This publication is reissued each year. It lists treaties and other international agreements of the United States on record in the Department of State on January 1, which had not expired by their terms or which had not been denounced by the parties, replaced or superseded by other agreements, or otherwise definitely terminated.

It is in two sections: Part 1 lists all countries for which the U.S. has bilateral agreements; Part 2 is arranged alphabetically by subject and lists all multilateral agreements to which the United States is a signatory.

Compiled by the Treaty Affairs Staff,
Office of the Legal Adviser,
Department of State.

[Illustration 131]

PAGE FROM ANNUAL ISSUE OF TREATIES IN FORCE

56   **TREATIES IN FORCE**

FRANCE (Cont'd)

OCEANOGRAPHY

Memorandum of understanding on the participation of France in the international phase of ocean drilling of the deep sea drilling project. Signed at Paris January 15, 1976; entered into force January 15, 1976. 28 UST 5026; TIAS 8610.

Amendment:
October 12 and 26, 1978 (30 UST 2180; TIAS 9323).
October 27, 1981 and February 19, 1982.

PACIFIC SETTLEMENT OF DISPUTES

Treaty to ... disputes. S ... 15, 1914; ... 1915. 58 Stat. II ...

Treaty of a ... dated Mar ... Washingto ... force April ... 46 Stat. 2 ... LNTS 5 ...

PATENTS

Agreement ... rights and technical information for defense purposes. Signed at Paris March 12, 1957; entered into force March 12, 1957. 8 UST 353; TIAS 3782; 279 UNTS 275.

Agreement approving the procedures for reciprocal filing of classified patent application in the United States and France. Exchange of notes at Paris May 29 and July 10, 1959; entered into force July 10, 1959. 10 UST 2151; TIAS 4386; 367 UNTS 336.

POSTAL MATTERS

Postal money order convention. Signed at Washington August 19, 1931; operative February 1, 1932.

Convention relative to the exchange of parcel post. Signed at Paris December 7 and at Washington December 30, 1935; operative August 1, 1935. 49 Stat. 3322; Post Office Department print; 171 LNTS 117.

International express mail agreement, with detailed regulations. Signed at Washington and Paris March 17 and April 15, 1981; entered into force May 18, 1981. TIAS 10115.

PUBLICATIONS

Agreement relating to exchange of official publications. Exchange of notes at Paris August 14, 1945; entered into force January 1, 1946. 60 Stat. 1944; TIAS 1579; 7 Bevans 1095; 73 UNTS 237.

RELIEF SUPPLIES AND PACKAGES

Agreement for free entry and free inland transportation of relief supplies and packages. Signed at Paris December 23, 1948; entered into force December 23, 1948. 62 Stat. 3587; TIAS 1873; 7 Bevans 1296; 67 UNTS 171.

Amendments:
January 31, 1950 (1 UST 224; TIAS 2043; 67 UNTS 171).
August 3, 1950 (1 UST 597; TIAS 2107; 93 UNTS 567).
July 2 and August 5, 1952 (3 UST 5039; TIAS 2684; 181 UNTS 345).

SATELLITES

Agreement on cooperation in intercontinental testing in connection with ... a cooperative program in science and technology, with appendices. Signed at Paris May 30, 1978; entered into force May 30, 1978. TIAS

Memorandum of understanding covering cooperation in the field of geological sciences. Signed at Orleans and Reston July 8 and 23, 1982; entered into force July 23, 1982. TIAS 10422.

SMUGGLING

Convention for prevention of smuggling of intoxicating liquors. Signed at Washington June 30, 1924; entered into force March 12, 1927. 45 Stat. 2403; TS 755; 7 Bevans 938; 61 LNTS 415.

TAXATION

Agreement relating to relief from double income tax on shipping profits. Exchange of notes at Washington June 11 and July 8, 1927; entered into force July 8, 1927; operative from January 1, 1921. 47 Stat. 2604; EAS 12; 7 Bevans 955; 114 LNTS 415.

Agreement relating to relief from taxation of United States Government expenditures in France in the interests of common defense. Exchange of notes at Paris June 13, 1952; entered into force June 13, 1952. 3 UST 4828; TIAS 2655; 181 UNTS 3.

Amendment:
November 27, 1956 (7 UST 3405; TIAS 3712; 265 UNTS 356).

Agreement relating to the payment by the United States of taxes on electricity provided the surplus commodity housing units in France. Exchange of notes at Paris August 1, 1963; entered into force August 1, 1963. 15 UST 727; TIAS 5595; 527 UNTS 89.

Convention with respect to taxes on income and property with exchange of notes. Signed at Paris July 28, 1967; entered into force August 11, 1968. 19 UST 5280; TIAS 6518; 719 UNTS 31.

Protocol to the convention of July 28, 1967 with respect to taxes on income and property with exchange of notes. Signed at Washington October 12, 1970; entered into force February 21, 1972. 23 UST 20; TIAS 7270.

... respect to ... f July 28, ... f October ... Signed at ... ; entered ... effective ...

... f double ... al evasion ... heritances ... November ... r 1, 1980.

TELECOMMUNICATION

Agreement relating to the reciprocal granting of authorizations to permit licensed amateur radio operators of either country to operate their stations in the other country.[1] Exchange of notes at Paris May 5, 1966; entered into force July 1, 1966. 17 UST 719; TIAS 6022; 595 UNTS 279.

Amendment:
October 3, 1969 (20 UST 2398; TIAS 6711).

NOTES:
[1] Applicable to all territories.

TERRITORIAL ACQUISITION

Treaty for the cession of Louisiana. Signed at Paris April 30, 1803; entered into force October 21, 1803. 8 Stat. 200; TS 86; 7 Bevans 812.

TRADE AND COMMERCE (See COMMERCE)

VISAS

Reciprocal agreement relating to visa fees for nonimmigrants.[1] Exchanges of notes at Washington August 19 and September 4, 5, and 16, 1947; entered into force September 16, 1947; operative October 1, 1947. 61 Stat. 3776; TIAS 1721; 7 Bevans 1210; 84 UNTS 19.

FINDING BILATERAL TREATIES

Problem: Does the United States have a treaty agreement with France in regard to smuggling?

Answer: Use Part 1 of latest edition of *Treaties in Force*. All treaties or international agreements which the U.S. has entered into with other countries are listed, by subject, under the name of the other country.

Note citation where text may be found.

[Illustration 132]

PAGE FROM PART 2, ANNUAL ISSUE OF TREATIES IN FORCE

---

284   TREATIES IN FORCE

SATELLITE COMMUNICATIONS SYSTEMS (Cont'd)

States which are parties:
Canada
France
United States

Understanding concerning cooperation in a joint experimental satellite-aided search and rescue project. Signed at Leningrad November 23, 1979; entered into force for

Dominican Rep.
Ethiopia
Finland
German Dem. Rep.
Germany, Fed. Rep.[4]
Ghana
Grenada[1]
Guinea-Bissau
Hungary
Iceland
India[2]
Iran
Iraq
Ireland
Italy[2]

Agreement concerning interim arrangements relating to polymetallic nodules of the deep sea bed. Done at Washington September 2, 1982; entered into force for the United States September 2, 1982.
TIAS
States which are parties:
France
Germany, Fed. Rep.
United Kingdom
United States

SEALS

Interim convention on conservation of North Pacific fur seals. Signed at Washington February 9, 1957; entered into force for the United States October 14, 1957.
8 UST 2283; TIAS 3948; 314 UNTS 105.
States which are parties:
Canada
Japan
Union of Soviet Socialist Reps.[1]
United States[1]

Amendment and extension:
October 8, 1963 (15 UST 316; TIAS 5558; 494 UNTS 303).
September 3, 1969 (20 UST 2992; TIAS 6774; 719 UNTS 313).
May 7, 1976 (27 UST 3371; TIAS 8368).
October 14, 1980 (TIAS 10020).

NOTES:
[1] With understanding to the October 14, 1980 amendment.

Convention for the conservation of Antarctic seals, with annex and final act. Done at London June 1, 1972; entered into force for the United States March 11, 1978.
29 UST 441; TIAS 8826.
States which are parties:
Argentina
Belgium
Chile
France
Japan
Norway
Poland
South Africa
Union of Soviet Socialist Reps.[1]
United Kingdom[2]
United States

NOTES:
[1] With statement.
[2] Extended to Channel Islands and Isle of Man.

SHIPPING (See under MARITIME MATTERS; RULES OF WARFARE)

> ## FINDING MULTILATERAL TREATIES
>
> **Problem: Is the United States a signatory to an international convention on the conservation of seals?**
>
> **Answer: Check in Part 2 of *Treaties in Force* under subject: Seals.**
> Note citations to where text may be located. As additional countries become signatories, they are listed in the *Department of State Bulletin* and then included in the next edition of *Treaties in Force*.

United States

SEA, LAW OF (See under FISHERIES; MARITIME MATTERS)

SEABEDS

Treaty on the prohibition of the emplacement of nuclear weapons and other weapons of mass destruction on the seabed and the ocean floor and in the subsoil thereof. Done at Washington, London and Moscow February 11, 1971, entered into force for the United States May 18, 1972.
23 UST 701; TIAS 7337.
Ratification, accession or succession deposited by:
Afghanistan
Antigua & Barbuda[1]
Australia
Austria
Belgium
Botswana
Bulgaria
Byelorussian Soviet Socialist Rep.
Canada[2]
Cape Verde
Central African Rep.
China (Taiwan)[3]
Congo
Cyprus
Czechoslovakia
Denmark
Dominica[1]

Qatar
Romania
Rwanda
St. Lucia[1]
Sao Tome & Principe
Saudi Arabia
Seychelles
Singapore
Solomon Is.[1]
South Africa
Swaziland
Sweden
Switzerland
Togo
Tunisia
Turkey
Ukrainian Soviet Socialist Rep.
Union of Soviet Socialist Reps.
United Kingdom[6]
United States
Vietnam, Socialist Rep.[2]
Yemen (Aden)
Yugoslavia
Zambia

NOTES:
[1] See under country heading in the bilateral section for information concerning acceptance of treaty obligations.
[2] With declaration.
[3] See note under CHINA (Taiwan) in bilateral section.
[4] Applicable to Berlin (West).
[5] Extended to Netherlands Antilles.
[6] Extended to Brunei, St. Christopher-Nevis-Anguilla, and territories under the territorial sovereignty of the United Kingdom.

[Illustration 133]

PAGE FROM GUIDE TO TREATIES IN FORCE, PART 2

GUIDE TO TREATIES IN FORCE
SUBJECT REFERENCE INDEX

353

SEABEDS - STOLEN PROPERTY

SEABEDS
See also ARMS LIMITATION and
RULES OF WARFARE
Multilateral
Polymetallic nodules Unnumbered:
Sept. 1982
Prohibition of nuclear weapons
emplacement on the
seabed   TIAS 7337

SEALS
Multilateral
Antarctic, conservation TIAS 8826
North Pacific, conser-
vation   TIAS 3948
TIAS 5558
TIAS 6774
TIAS 8368
TIAS 10020

SEISMIC OBSERVATIONS
See also SEISMOLOGICAL
RESEARCH
Bilateral
Australia   TIAS 8995
Thailand   TIAS 8774

SEISMOLOGICAL RESEARCH
See also SEISMIC OBSERVATIONS
Bilateral
Norway   TIAS 6526

SEWAGE DISPOSAL SYSTEM
Bilateral
Canada   TIAS 6037

SHELLFISH
Bilateral
Canada   TIAS 1747
Iceland   TIAS 9368
Japan   TIAS 5207
Korea, Republic of   TIAS 7516
Mexico   TIAS 10433
New Zealand   TIAS 9968

SHIPPING
See also CUSTOMS, MARITIME
MATTERS and RULES OF
WARFARE
Bilateral
Brazil   TIAS 8981
TIAS 9923
Denmark   TIAS 9278
Finland   Unnumbered:

SLAVERY
See also AFRICA and TRAFFIC IN
WOMEN AND CHILDREN
Multilateral

This unofficial Guide may also be used to
locate treaties in force.
Note how in its subject Index, it not only
lists multilateral treaties and agreements for
which the United States is a signatory, but also
lists bilateral treaties between the United
States and another country.

France   TS 755
Greece   TS 772
Japan   TS 807
Netherlands   TS 712
Norway   TS 689
Panama   TS 707
Poland   TS 821
Spain   TS 749
Sweden   TS 698
United Kingdom   TS 685

SOCIAL SECURITY
Bilateral
Argentina   TIAS 7458
Bahamas   TIAS 8946
Canada   TIAS 6254
Gabon   TIAS 6999
Germany, Federal Republic
of   TIAS 7326
TIAS 9542
Ghana   TIAS 7734
Italy   TIAS 9058
Japan   TIAS 8452
Kenya   TIAS 8847
Liechtenstein   TIAS 7476
Mali   TIAS 6961
Mexico   TIAS 7620
Niger   TIAS 8194
Panama   TIAS 10492
Philippines   TIAS 5452
TIAS 6663
Poland   TIAS 7200
Singapore   TIAS 8190
Switzerland   TIAS 9830
Togo   TAS 7094
United Kingdom   TIAS 7619

SOUTHEAST ASIA TREATY
ORGANIZATION (SEATO)
See DEFENSE

1967   TIAS 6347
Registration of objects
launched   TIAS 8480
Research using sounding
rockets   TIAS 7830
Space laboratory and space
shuttle system   TIAS 7722
Bilateral
Botswana   TIAS 9943
Mexico   TIAS 5783

SPACE COOPERATION
See also SPACE and SPACE
RESEARCH
Bilateral
Brazil   TIAS 9403
TIAS 10419
Unnumbered:
May 1982
Canada   TIAS 8400
TIAS 9601
Japan   TIAS 6735
TIAS 9915
TIAS 9940
USSR   TIAS 8732

SPACE LIABILITY
Bilateral
Canada   TIAS 8005

SPACE RESEARCH
See also SPACE and SPACE
COOPERATION
Bilateral
Germany, Federal Republic
of   TIAS 10286
Spain   TIAS 5992

[Illustration 134]

PAGE FROM MONTHLY ISSUE OF THE DEPARTMENT OF STATE BULLETIN

Treaties

Satellite Communications System
Agreement relating to the International Telecommunications Satellite Organization (INTELSAT), with annexes. Done at Washington Aug. 20, 1971. Entered into force Feb. 12, 1973. TIAS 7532.
Accession deposited: Niger, Apr. 14, 1980.

Operating agreement relating to the International Telecommunications Satellite Organization (INTELSAT), with annex. Done at Washington Aug. 20, 1971. Entered into force Feb. 12, 1973. TIAS 7532.
Signature: Niger, Apr. 14, 1980.

Sugar
International sugar agreement, 1977, with annexes. Done at Geneva Oct. 7, 1977. Entered into force provisionally, Jan. 1, 1978; definitively Jan. 2, 1980. TIAS 9664.
Notification of provisional application deposited: Colombia, Apr. 14, 1980.
Ratification deposited: Costa Rica, Mar. 27, 1980.

Terrorism
International convention against the taking of hostages. Adopted at New York Dec. 19, 1979.[1]
Signatures: Bolivia, Mar. 25, 1980; Haiti, Apr. 21, 1980; Italy, Apr. 18, 1980; Lesotho, Apr. 17, 1980.

Trade
Protocol extending the arrangement regarding international trade in textiles of Dec. 20, 1973 (TIAS 7840). Done at Geneva Dec. 14, 1977. Entered into force Jan. 1, 1978. TIAS 8939.

Acceptance deposited: Argentina, Feb. 18, 1980.

Agreement on trade in civi[...]
at Geneva Apr. 12, 1979. E[...]
force Jan. 1, 1980. TIAS 9[...]
Ratification deposited: Swi[...]
Apr. 2, 1980.

U.N. Industrial Developm[ent]
Organization
Constitution of the U.N. Ir[...]
velopment Organization, w[...]
Adopted at Vienna Apr. 8, [...]
Ratification deposited: Nic[...]
1980.
Signatures: Malaysia, Apr. 10, 1980; Somalia, Mar. 21, 1980; Trinidad and Tobago, Apr. 14, 1980.

Wheat
Protocol modifying and further extending the wheat trade convention (part of the international wheat agreement), 1971 (TIAS 7144). Done at Washington Apr. 25, 1979. Entered into force June 23, 1979, with respect to certain provisions, July 1, 1979, with respect to other provisions.
Ratification deposited: Egypt, Apr. 22, 1980; Guatemala, Apr. 28, 1980.

Food aid convention, 1980 (part of the International Wheat Agreement), 1971, as extended (TIAS 7144). Done at Washington Mar. 11, 1980. Enters into force July 1, 1980, if by June 30, 1980 the governments

referred to in paragraph (3) of Article III have deposited instruments of ratification, acceptance, approval or accession, or declarations of provisional application, and provided that the 1979 protocol for the fifth extension of the Wheat Trade Convention, 1971, or a new Wheat Trade Convention replacing it, is in force.
Signatures: Argentina, Australia, Belgium, Canada, Denmark, European Economic Community, France, Federal Republic of Germany, Ireland, Italy, Luxembourg, Netherlands, U.K., Apr. 30, 1980; Austria, Switzerland, U.S., Apr. 29, 1980; Finland, Japan, Apr. 22, 1980; Norway, Apr. 24, 1980; Sweden, Apr. 9, 1980.

BILATERAL

Bangladesh
Agreement amending the agreement for sales of agricultural commodities of Aug. 2, 1978 (TIAS 9389), with agreed minutes. Effected by exchange of notes at Dacca Mar. 7, 1980. Entered into force Mar. 7, 1980.

Botswana
Agreement providing for a radio facility for the purpose of relaying Voice of America programs to areas in Africa. Signed at Gaborone Mar. 28, 1980. Entered into force Mar. 28, 1980.

Canada
Protocol to amend the convention for the protection, preservation, and extension of the sockeye salmon fisheries in the Fraser River System of May 26, 1930, as amended (50 Stat. 1355, TIAS 3867). Signed at [...]

President: Mar. 31, 1980.

Colombia
Agreement amending the agreement of Aug. 3, 1978, as amended (TIAS 9515, 9645), relating to trade in cotton, wool, and manmade fiber textiles and textile products. Effected by exchange of letters at Bogota Jan. 2 and 31, 1980. Entered into force Jan. 31, 1980.

Cyprus
Convention for the avoidance of double taxation and the prevention of fiscal evasion with respect to taxes on income, with related exchange of notes. Signed at Nicosia Mar. 26, 1980. Enters into force upon the exchange of instruments of ratification.

Haiti
Agreement amending the agreement of Aug. 17, 1979 (TIAS 9595), relating to trade in cotton, wool, and manmade fiber textiles and textile products. Effected by exchange of notes at Port-au-Prince Jan. 28 and Mar. 3, 1980. Entered into force Mar. 3, 1980.

Indonesia
Agreement for sales of agricultural commodities, with agreed minutes. Signed at Jakarta Mar. 6, 1980. Entered into force Mar. 6, 1980.

Kenya
Agreement for sales of agricultural commodities, with minutes of negotiation. Signed at Nairobi Mar. 6, 1980. Entered into force Mar. 6, 1980.

Malaysia
Agreement amending the agreement of May 17 and June 8, 1978, as amended (TIAS 9180, 9602), relating to trade in cotton, wool, and manmade fiber textiles and textile products. Effected by exchange of letters at Washington and New York Jan. 8 and Mar. 27, 1980. Entered into force Mar. 27, 1980.

Malta
Agreement with respect to taxes on income, with related exchange of notes. Signed at Valletta Mar. 21, 1980. Enters into force upon the exchange of instruments of ratification. Provisions shall have effect in respect of income or profits arising on or after the first day of January of the year in which the agreement enters into

Pakistan
Agreement for sales of agricultural commodities, with minutes. Signed at Islamabad Mar. 25, 1980. Entered into force Mar. 25, 1980.

Poland
Agreement amending the agreement of Jan. 9 and 12, 1978, as amended (TIAS 9064, 9213, 9640), relating to trade in cotton, wool, and manmade fiber textiles and textile products. Effected by exchange of notes at Warsaw Jan. 22 and Mar. 17, 1980. Entered into force Mar. 17, 1980.

Agreement amending the agreement of Jan. 9 and 12, 1978, as amended (TIAS 9064, 9213, 9640), relating to trade in cotton, wool, and manmade fiber textiles and textile products. Effected by exchange of

---

The Department of State Bulletin is published monthly. Each issue has a section on Treaty Information which serves as "advance sheets" to Treaties in Force.

[Illustration 135]

PAGE FROM TREATY STATUS TABLE—CCH CONGRESSIONAL
INDEX

---

70 7-12-84   **Treaties**   **7059**

96-2, Executive R (7-17-80)—Civil rights—discrimination—women

The Convention on the Elimination of All Forms of Discrimination
Against Women was adopted by the United Nations General Assembly on
December 18, 1979 and signed by the United States on July 17, 1980. It calls
for States Parties to "take all appropriate measures" to eliminate discrimination against women in such diverse fields of human endeavor as politics, law,
employment, education, health care, commercial transactions, and domestic
relations.

   Injunction of secrecy removed: 11/12/80
   In Foreign Relations Committee: 11/20/80

96-2, Executive T (9-26-80)—Income taxes—Canada

The Convention between the United States and Canada with respect to
Taxes on Income and Capital replaces an existing convention and is based on
the United States and OECD model conventions. It provides that the business
profits of a resident of one Contracting State will not be subject to tax by the
other state except to the extent that they are attributable to a permanent
establishment which the resident has in the other state. The definition of
"permanent establishment" is broader than in the existing convention. The
Convention establishes maximum reciprocal rates of withholding at source
for dividends, interest and royalties.

   Injunction of secrecy removed: 11/12/80.
   In Foreign Relations Committee: 11/12/80.
   Reported: S. Ex. Rept. No. 98-22, 5/21/84
   Ratified: 6/28/84

96-2, Executive V (11-13-80)—Education—post-secondary—degrees—recognition

The Convention on the Recognition of Studies, Diplomas and Degrees
Concerning Higher Education in the States Belonging to the European Region
establishes a mechanism to achieve international and domestic cooperation and
coordination in facilitating the recognition of academic credentials and to
improve the mobility of students, teachers and scholars.

   **After the President has signed a treaty, it must be ratified by the Senate. This
Table lists treaties awaiting ratification by the Senate.**

   **It is arranged by Number of Congress and gives information as to the present
status of such pending treaties. Weekly supplements are issued to this Service.
Treaties not ratified in one Congress are held over for subsequent Congresses.**

---

needs and to establish hunting seasons.

   Injunction of secrecy removed: 11/24/80
   In Foreign Relations Committee: 11/24/80

96-2, Executive Y (12-2-80)—Income tax—exemptions—Bangladesh

The Convention on the Avoidance of Double Taxation with Bangladesh
differs in one major respect from other recent U. S. tax treaties. In most of
these treaties a source country tax exemption is provided for shipping and
aircraft operating income. The convention with Bangladesh provides exemption for aircraft income only; shipping income is taxable under the internal
laws of the two states.

   Injunction of secrecy removed: 12/2/80
   In Foreign Relations Committee: 12/2/80

Congressional Index—1983-1984   **96-2**

[Illustration 136]

PAGE FROM SHEPARD'S U.S. CITATIONS—STATUTES VOLUME

UNITED STATES STATUTES AT LARGE (Not in United States Code)   1946

§ 5 70St116	Art. 1 158F867	Art. 5 A6UST6157		6UST645 8UST69 11UST32 UST1690
Aug. 14 41 St. 1912		Sept. 25 41 St. 2479	Oct. 9	Oct. 30	

After locating a treaty or other agreement, it may be Shepardized to find subsequent amendments, other changes, or court decisions which have cited or interpreted the treaty or agreement.

For treaties or agreements entered into before the publication of the United States Treaties Series, the "Shepardizing" is done under the U.S. Statutes at Large citation.

Aug. Ch. 5 60 St. 1					Art. 2 ¶ 2 8T507 ¶ 3
329US- 91LE2 67SC17 329US9 91LE6 67SC3 329US6 91LE6 67SC36					UST963 Art. 5 8T507 18T2999 8T645 UST331 UST33 UST494 ¶ 1
§ 2 152FS8 70St54					UST963 ¶ 3 8T509 8T658 UST331 UST33 UST494

Aug. Ch. 9oz 60 St. 1057	5UST2493	[1022	[1376	¶ 4 10UST961	Annex ¶ 2	13UST497 14UST112
Rs70A St1 61St798	Aug. 24 Ch. 210	Art. 11 R14UST [1022	Sept. 25 61 St. 3524	Art. 11 10UST745 Art. 12 10UST745	A12UST847	14UST1690 Art. 7 8UST70
§§ 1 to 20 Rs70A St1	60 St. 121	78St1248 Art. 12	Oct. 1 61 St. 1222	Art. 13 10UST745	Nov. 16 61 St. 2479	Art. 11 3UST3003
	79St285	R14UST [1022	Rs2UST [1423	Art. 14 62St1659 10UST745	62St3023	Schedule A13UST493
Aug. 14 Ch. 963 60 St. 1062	Aug. 30 61 St. 1236	78St1248 ¶ 1 158F864	Sept. 25 61 St. 3540	Art. 15 10UST745 Oct. 7 61 St. 2398 Art. 17	Annex to Air Transport	A13UST497 A14UST112 A14UST
		¶ 2		10UST745	Agreement	[1691
§ 1 R74St726 61St214	64St B33 3UST3922 3UST3927	158F864 Art. 15 ¶ 1	Rs2UST [1458	E3UST351 Sg11UST [1982 Art. 19	§ B A62St3023	A15UST [2547 ¶ 1
	4UST2058	A13UST409	Sept. 30	6UST3771 15UST2489		Subd. a
Aug. 14 Ch. 964 60 St. 1062	Protocol Art. 1 Sg1UST626	A14UST [1023 Art. 17	61 St. 2495 A6UST6157	Art. 3 3UST352 Art. 9	Nov. 20 61 St. 2795	A11UST32 A14UST [1691
	62St1654 Art. 2	A14UST [1022	Art. 2 A6UST6157	6UST3771 Art. 10	A61St3777	4UST2184
68St526 § 2	Sg1UST626 62St1654 3UST3922	78St1248 ¶ 2 13UST410	¶ 3 Rn ¶ 4	6UST3771 Art. 12	Dec. 2 61 St. 2475	¶ 4 A4UST2181 A6UST647
Subd. a ¶ 3	3UST3927	Schedule 1	10UST966 ¶ 3	11UST1982 Art. 14	Oct. 18	¶ 4
61St955		R14UST [1022	Ad10UST [966	11UST1982 Art. 15	64 St. B3 Sg8UST843	E62St3645 Sg1UST540 (6UST645)
Subd. d A618t55 61St694	Sept. 6 61 St. 4121	78St1248 Schedule 2	¶ 4	11UST1982 Art. 16	Art. 7	109FS343 Cl. 1 A11UST33
Subd. f R64St100	2UST460 Art. 8	R14UST [1022	Rn ¶ 5 10UST966	11UST1982 Art. 17	Subd. a A8UST847	Cl. 2 62St3600 63St2630	R7UST657
§ 3	9UST1468	78St1248	Art. 4	11UST1982	Art. 17	63St2654	¶ 5 A4UST2181
Subsec. 44 60St1099	Schedule 1 Rs9UST	Notes Rp14UST	¶ 2 A10UST969	Art. 20 11UST1982 Art. 21	A8UST848 Protocol E8UST843	64St B84 A61St3614	8d7UST657 A8UST2204 A11UST33
	[1468 Schedule 2	[1022	¶ 3 Rs10UST	11UST1982 Art. 22	Art. 1 Subd. 3	¶ 5 A61St3614	A14UST [1691
Aug. 14 Ch. 966 60 St. 1082	Rs9UST [1468	Sept. 13 61 St. 3750	[969 A10UST970 ¶ 8	11UST1982 Art. 24 11UST1982	A8UST845	¶ 6 Sub ¶ e Sg1UST541	¶ 6 A1UST506 A2UST11
Title 1 § 11 A61St694	Sept. 12 61 St. 2688	Art. 3 A62St1889	A10UST963 ¶ 9 Rs10UST	Art. 25 11UST1982 Art. 29	Oct. 23 61 St. 2876	¶ 8 A61St3614 ¶ 12	A3UST3001 A3UST5094 A4UST2180
	E13UST [2266	Sept. 23	[970 ¶ 10	11UST1982 Art. 33	13UST1918	61St3606	A6UST647 ¶ 6
	E14UST359 158F864 78St1248 13UST408	61 St. 2903 62St3575	A10UST959 ¶ 14 Ad10UST [961	11UST1982	Oct. 25 61 St. 1044 A61St1073	Dec. 2 62 St. 1716 3UST3001	(6UST645) A10UST330 A13UST498 Continued

[Illustration 137]

PAGE FROM SHEPARD'S U.S. CITATIONS—STATUTES VOLUME

UNITED STATES TREATIES AND OTHER INTERNATIONAL AGREEMENTS   Vol. 8

-597-	**Art. 3**	¶ 7	10UST200	**Art. 14**	**-1421-**	**-1633-**	First
11UST388	12UST1045	Rn¶8	10UST1033	A10UST	8UST869	A13UST	Memo-
-600-	**-721-**	[12UST	10UST1638	[1818	10UST2049	[1482	randum of
13UST268	E8UST1392	[2947	11UST2515	**-1265-**	**-1425-**	**-1725-**	Under-
-617-	**Art. 1**	**-859-**	12UST728	A10UST	10UST2081	Sg12UST	standing
A12UST240	A8UST1392	9UST397	**-1063-**	[1659	**-1427-**	[904	**§ 1**
¶ 4	**Art. 2**	**-863-**	8UST1069	8UST213	8UST821	**-1741-**	A9UST1355
A12UST240	¶ 1	12UST1195	**-1069-**	8UST1225	8UST866	Sg11UST	E10UST150
-625-	Cl. c	**-866-**	8UST1063	**Art. 6**	**-1431-**	[1405	9UST1003
8UST26	A9UST1167	A8UST1427	**-1073-**	13UST1770	8UST367	**Art. 2**	**-1903-**
8UST77	**-738-**	8UST821	8UST1063	¶ A	9UST237	¶ 7	13UST2645
-637-	A12UST155	**-869-**	8UST1069	A10UST	12UST3176	11UST1406	14UST1424
8UST279	**Art. 4**	10UST2050	**-1093-**	[1659	**-1435-**	**-1757-**	**-1937-**
-657-	¶ A	**-890-**	7l8t454	**Art. 8**	A11UST	11UST1405	10UST2208
8UST680	A12UST155	7l8t C51	10UST1425	¶ A	[1783	**-1757-**	**-2021-**
22UST508	**Art. 7**	76St1468	14UST1265	A10UST	A13UST	15UST167	A15UST289
13UST2650	A12UST156	77St972	14UST1489	[1660	[1484	**-1767-**	**-2043-**
Art. 1	**-753-**	**-894-**	**Art. 6**	13UST1770	A15UST	77St971	186FS300
A9UST1416	14UST2222	13UST2178	¶ A	¶ B	[2007	10UST272	46ABA24
¶ 1	**-764-**	¶ 3	Cl. 3	A10UST	**-1442-**	13UST2757	**Art. 1**
A9UST1417	E10UST25	13UST2178	A14UST135	[1660	Sg10UST	13UST2823	186FS320
Art. 2	A10UST	**Annex A**	**Art. 12**	¶ C	[1997	13UST2801	**Art. 5**
A9UST1417	[1383	A9UST1334	10UST87	A10UST	**-1445-**	15UST2580	288F2d375
¶ 1	E11UST	**-899-**	13UST416	[1660	A15UST	¶ 1	**Art. 6**
Cl. d	[1455	11UST2165	¶ A	A13UST	[1539	13UST2679	¶ 2
A14UST	¶ 6	**Art. 8**	Cl. 1	[1770	**-1457-**	¶ L	186FS320
[1066	10UST25	11UST2165	**-1289-**	10UST1182	13UST2606	**-2205-**
Art. 3	**-771-**	**-933-**	A11UST	**-1534-**	¶ N	Sg8UST967
12UST508	9UST1264	7l8t C50	¶ C	[1872	8UST1629	13UST2679	13UST2068
¶ 1	**-773-**	76St1468	14UST1269	8UST799	9UST1416	¶ R	**Art. 1**
A9UST1419	R10UST	77St972	**Art. 14**	9UST1	21UST508	13UST2678	13UST2070
¶ 2	[1418	**Schedule**	9UST1	10UST1049	**-1537-**	¶ W	¶ 1
A9UST1419	797	¶ 907	7l8t454	¶ D	A13UST	76St1469	A9UST305

Treaties and other agreements that are published in the United States Treaties Series may be Shepardized under those citations in this section of Shepard's U.S. Citations.

9UST1379	**Art. 3**	[1074	**Art. 12**	**-1363-**	Cl. e	13UST879	A9UST305
11UST401	¶ 2	**-957-**	¶ C	15UST2209	R13UST	13UST898	9UST868
-680-	Cl. d	8UST963	15UST1459	**-1367-**	[1878	13UST907	9UST1343
8UST657	A8UST1289	**Art. 1**	**-1225-**	A13UST	Cl. f	13UST1037	**-2213-**
-683-	A11UST	¶ 3	A13UST	[1486	R13UST	13UST1218	9UST1113
Sg11UST	[1872	8UST963	[1486	**Art. 6**	[1878	13UST1818	**-2283-**
[1982	**-821-**	**Art. 5**	8UST213	A13UST	¶ 10	13UST2989	A15UST317
-691-	8UST866	11UST2362	**Art. 4**	[1812	Cl. b	¶ Z	8OSt1091
E10UST22	**Art. 1**	**-963-**	¶ 3	**Art. 8**	A13UST	**Art. 35**	**Art. 2**
E11UST210	A8UST866	8UST957	A13UST	A13UST	[1878	11UST1543	Rn¶3
15UST1523	A8UST1427	**-965-**	[1486	[1813	Cl. d	**-1862-**	15UST317
¶ 6	**-832-**	A13UST	**Art. 5**	**Art. 10**	A13UST	Sg11UST	Cl. g
10UST22	A11UST	[1033	A13UST	¶ B	[1878	[2249	15UST317
-697-	[1874	10UST3185	[1487	A13UST	**-1561-**	10UST1730	Ad15UST
A10UST	13UST1776	**-970-**	**Art. 11**	[1815	10UST1620	**Art. 1**	[317
[1233	**-835-**	8UST721	A13UST	**Art. 12**	**-1567-**	A10UST	Cl. h
Art. 2	A12UST	**-973-**	[1487	A13UST	9UST1379	[1733	Ad15UST
¶ 1	[2947	9UST1444	[1487	[1816	**-1593-**	**-1869-**	[317
Cl. a	E14UST	**-1245-**	**-1386-**	E10UST	¶ 3	A15UST317
A10UST	[1178	9UST131	A10UST	12UST1659	14UST1210	A15UST317
[1233	¶ 4	9UST1073	[1815	[3026	**-1879-**	**Art. 3**
Cl. b	A9UST1547	9UST1075	**Art. 4**	**-1391-**	**-1604-**	10UST385	A15UST318
A10UST	¶ 6	**-993-**	¶ A	8UST721	11UST2337	**-1885-**	8OSt1092
[1233	Rn¶7	A11UST	A10UST	8UST970	**-1626-**	A9UST1003	**Art. 5**
-715-	[12UST	[2632	[1815	**-1395-**	12UST718	13UST1953	8OSt1093
A9UST1025	[2947	A11UST	**Art. 7**	10UST970	13UST2598	**Art. 1**	¶ 2
12UST1044	¶ 6	[2559	A10UST	**-1410-**	**-1629-**	13UST1953	Cl. e
Art. 1	Ad12UST	9UST1015	[1815	14UST337	8UST1534	**Art. 3**	A15UST318
12UST1045	[2947	9UST1474		**-1413-**	9UST1416	13UST1953	Continued
				E9UST1146	12UST508		

SECTION E.   UNITED STATES COURT DECISIONS ON INTERNATIONAL LAW

Litigation frequently arises involving the principles and rules of international law, including the effect and interpretations of treaties to which the United States is or was a signatory. These decisions are reported in the standard sets of court reports discussed in previous chapters. All cases published in the various sets of the *National Reporter System* have been reprinted in the *American International Law Cases*, 1793–.[23]

SECTION F.   SOURCES OF INTERNATIONAL LAW FOR COUNTRIES OTHER THAN THE UNITED STATES

Most countries have collections of their treaties and indexes to them, but their description is beyond the scope of this book. There are, however, more general works published by international organizations which are useful when searching for information on treaties to which the United States is not a signatory. These are briefly discussed below: [24]

1.   Multinational Collections of Treaties [25]

a.   *The Consolidated Treaties Series.*[26] This series is a reproduced collection of world treaties in their original languages and existing translations in English or French from the foundation of the modern system of states, 1648, to the date of the commencement of the *League of Nations Treaty Series* (approximately 1918–1920). This set contains 231 volumes plus Index volume.

b.   *League of Nations Treaty Series.* This set covers the period of 1920 to 1945, and contains treaties of member and nonmember nations registered with the Secretariat.

c.   *United Nations Treaty Series*, 1946 to date. This set contains the text of all treaties registered with the Secretariat by its member states, or filed and recorded by nonmember states or international organizations. Each volume also includes a list of notifications of ratifications, accessions, successions, extensions, and denuncia-

---

[23] Oceana Publications (1971–).

[24] For a detailed discussion of locating treaties between countries for which the United States is not a signatory, *see* Parry, *Where to Look for Your Treaties*, 8 INT'L J.L.LIBR. 8 (1980). *See also* A. SPRUDZS, TREATY SOURCES IN LEGAL AND POLITICAL RESEARCH: TOOLS, TECHNIQUES, AND PROBLEMS—THE CONVENTIONAL AND THE NEW (1971).

[25] For difficulties in searching for multilateral treaties, *see* Sprudzs, *Status of Multilateral Treaties: Researcher's Mystery, Mess or Muddle?*, 66 AM.J.INT'L L. 365 (1972).

[26] C. Parry, ed. (1969–1983). Oceana Publications.

tions concerning published treaties. The *Series* is published in accordance with Article 102 of the United Nations Charter. The texts are given in their original language with English and French translated editions. Cumulative Indexes to the *United Nations Treaty Series* are published. Each Cumulative Index covers from 50 to 100 volumes and consists of three sections: (1) chronological index of all treaties; (2) chronological index of multilateral treaties; and (3) alphabetical index by country and subject.[27]

   d.   United Nations, Office of Legal Affairs, *Multilateral Treaties in Respect of Which the Secretary-General Performs Depository Function*. This is an annual publication started in 1968, which covers all multilateral treaties which have been concluded under the auspices of the United Nations and which have been deposited with the Secretary-General.

   A looseleaf volume (Annex) contains final clauses of the treaties deposited. It serves as a reference bank to the annual volumes.

   e.   *Keesing's Treaties and Alliances of the World*, 3d ed. This single-volume publication is designed to present the state of affairs with regard to groupings of states and their important treaties with each other, noting treaties in force as of early 1980. It covers several thousand agreements, mainly bilateral, which deal with trade, economic and technical aid, cultural relations and extradition.

   f.   *Major Peace Treaties of Modern History, 1648–1967*. This is the first comprehensive collection of peace treaties to appear in English. It consists of four volumes and is edited by Fred L. Israel. The official English translations, prepared by the British Foreign Office, were used whenever available. When such English documents were nonexistent, private translations were used. The first document in the series is the peace treaty of Westphalia, concluded in 1648, and the last document in the set is the peace settlement concluded at Tashkent in 1966 between India and Pakistan through the intercession of the Soviet Union. The treaties are chronologically arranged, with a subject index in volume 4.

   g.   *Organization of American States Treaty Series* (formerly *Pan American Union Law and Treaty Series*). The General Secretariat of the Organization of American States is responsible not only for the receipt and custody of the instruments of ratification but also

---

[27] The official index to the UNTS is supplemented by *Cumulative List and Index of Treaties and International Agreements Registered and Recorded with the Secretariat of the United Nations*, December 1969 to December 1974, 2 vols. (J. & R. Vanberry eds. 1977). Oceana Publications. This index contains information not included in the official index. For the difficulties and lacunae in the *League of Nations Treaty Series* and the *United Nations Treaty Series*, *see* Parry, note 24 *supra*, at 15–16.

for the preparation and publication of the official texts of the Organization.

Since 1957, these texts, in English and Spanish, have been issued by the General Legal Division as part of its Treaty Series. The Series includes Organization treaties and other significant instruments. Treaty Series No. 1 covers the Charter of the Organization of American States, signed at the Ninth International Conference of American States, March 30–May 2, 1948.

No. 5 is a useful chart, revised at regular intervals, showing the Status of Inter-American Treaties and Conventions.

h. Harvard Law School Library, *Index to Multilateral Treaties* (1965 and Supps.). This is a chronological list of multi-party, international agreements from the sixteenth century (1596) through 1963, with citations to their text. A subject and regional guide is also provided. The subject analysis does not include specific sections of a treaty; nor is the current status of each treaty given. Supplements were issued for 1964–1966.

i. *International Legal Materials: Current Documents.* This bi-monthly publication of the American Society of International Law is a collection of current official foreign and United States documents relating to international legal affairs. It began publication in 1962. The documents include: (1) current materials that may not become available in more permanent collections until a later date and (2) recent materials that are not readily accessible in any other form in most law libraries.

j. *World Treaty Index* and *Treaty Profiles, 2d ed.* [28] The *Index* is a computerized index in five volumes of the *League of Nations Treaty Series*, the *United Nations Treaty Series*, and over 6000 other treaties assembled from forty-two national collections from 1920 to 1972 which were not included in these two series. The database for this index is in machine-readable form and the volumes are printed from it. *Treaty Profiles* is a companion volume with statistical analyses of the treaties in the database.

Standard information given for each treaty includes: (1) parties; (2) date of signature; (3) topic; (4) citation; and (5) treaty number.

2. Yearbooks of International Law

Many countries now publish annual publications which usually contain articles on international law and international relations, decisions or digests of decisions from both international courts [29] and

---

[28] Edited by P. Rohn (1983), American Bibliographical Center—Clio Press, Santa Barbara, CA.

[29] For information on international courts, *see* items listed in bibliographies cited in note 7 *supra*.

domestic courts, and other material relevant to the practice of international law.[30]

SECTION G.   INTERNATIONAL LAW: RESEARCH PROCEDURE

Research methodology relating to treaties can be reduced to these steps: (1) identify a problem as being within the scope of a treaty and determine whether a treaty covers the problem, (2) if there is a treaty in point, ascertain its present status, and (3) elicit interpretations of the treaty.   The following procedure encompasses these steps.

Some individuals begin their research by checking a status table immediately to determine both the scope and the status of a treaty. Others start with a descriptive publication, such as *Whiteman's Digest*.   Still others commence their research with a treaty collection or an index.   The nature of the problem also influences research procedure.   To facilitate our explanation of methodology, we will follow a conventional procedure.

1.   Determination of the Existence or the Status of an American Treaty

a.   *Treaties in Force* and *Guide to Treaties in Force*.   Check the most recent edition of these annual publications for information as to the existence and status of an American treaty.

b.   *Department of State Bulletin*.   The current issues of the *Bulletin* provide information as to recent developments of important pending treaties.   This supplements *Treaties in Force*.

2.   Location of the Treaty Text

Besides the authoritative lists mentioned above, which cite to the sources below, most of these compilations have their own indexes.

a.   *United States Treaties and Other International Agreements* (UST).   This is the official source for treaties and agreements entered into since 1949.   There is an exhaustive, privately published index.   Prior to the publication of this set, the official source for this material was either the *Executive Agreement Series* (1929–1945), the *Treaty Series* (1908–1945) or the *Statutes at Large*.

b.   *Treaties and Other International Acts Series*.   This is the slip form in which treaties appear prior to their compilation in the UST.   They are numbered in a single numerical series.   Prior to their appearance in this series, the text of the treaties might be found in

[30] For a complete listing, *see* Stepan & Chapman, *National and Regional Yearbooks: A Brief Survey*, 8 INT'L J.L.LIBR. 19 (1980).

the *Department of State Bulletin* or in the Senate Executive Documents.

    c.   *Treaties and Other International Agreements of the United States of America, 1776–1949.* This 13-volume set, edited by C. Bevans, collects all United States Treaties prior to the initiation of the UST series. Volume 13 is a country-subject index. This set supersedes *Treaties, Conventions, International Acts, Protocols, and Agreements Between the U.S.A. and Other Powers* (Malloy) and *Treaties and Other International Acts of the United States* (Miller).

    The privately published *United States Treaties and Other International Agreements Cumulative Index* covers all of the sets above, as well as citing to the *Statutes at Large,* the *Executive Agreement Series,* and the *Treaties and Other International Acts Series.*

    d.   C. Wiktor, *Unperfected Treaties of the United States, 1776–1976.* This is the only collection of treaties which never went into force. For more recent and current treaties under consideration consult the *Department of State Bulletin* and the *CCH Congressional Index.*

3. Interpretations of Treaties

    Judicial and other interpretations of treaties may be located through the following publications:

    a.   *United States Code Service, Uncodified Laws and Treaties Volume*

    b.   *Shepard's United States Citations*

    c.   *Shepard's State Citations*

    d.   *Wharton's Digest*

    e.   *Moore's Digest*

    f.   *Hackworth's Digest*

    g.   *Whiteman's Digest*

    h.   *Digest of the United States Practice in International Law* (annual)

    i.   *American International Law Cases, 1793–1978*

    j.   *U.S. Supreme Court Digests*

4. Treaties by Popular Names

    When the popular name of a treaty is known, the following publications provide references from that name to the *Statutes at Large* or *Treaties and Other International Agreements* citation:

    a.   *Malloy's Treaties,* Index in vol. 4 (Trenwith).

    b.   *Shepard's Federal Acts and Cases by Popular Names.*

5. Foreign Treaties

Treaties between foreign countries may be found in a number of publications. The most exhaustive sources for such materials are the *Consolidated Treaty Series,* the *League of Nations Treaty Series* and the *United Nations Treaty Series.* There may also be specialized collections of treaties such as the *International Tax Treaties of All Nations.* [31] It may also be useful to check the *United Nations List of Treaty Collections* for a list of treaty collections since the 18th century.

SECTION H. SUMMARY

1. Treaties between the United States and other countries are published in:

a. 1789–1949—*Statutes at Large;* reprinted in *Treaties and Other International Agreements of the United States,* 1776–1949.

b. 1950–date—*United States Treaties and Other International Agreements* (UST); published first in slip format in *Treaties and Other International Acts Series* (T.I.A.S.).

c. Indian treaties—Kappler, *Indian Affairs, Laws and Treaties* (1903–1941, 5 vols.). Indian treaties are compiled in vol. 2.

d. *Malloy's Treaties,* 1776–1937.

e. *Miller's Treaties,* 1776–1863.

f. *Treaty Series,* 1908–1945; replaced in 1945 by *Treaties and Other International Acts Series.*

g. *Executive Agreement Series,* 1929–1945; replaced by *Treaties and Other International Acts Series.*

h. *Tax Treaties.* Looseleaf volumes published by Commerce Clearing House and Prentice-Hall.

2. Indexes to United States Treaties

a. *Treaties in Force.* Issued annually by U.S. Department of State.

b. I. Kavass and M. Michael, *United States Treaties and Other International Agreements Cumulative Index,* 1776–1949.

c. I. Kavass and A. Sprudzs, *UST Cumulative Indexes,* 1950–1979 and supplements.

d. I. Kavass and A. Sprudzs, *Guide to Treaties in Force.*

---

[31] W. Diamond (ed.), Oceana Publications (1975).

3. Interpretations of United States Treaties

a. *United States Code Service,* Uncodified Laws and Treaties Volume.

b. *Shepard's Citations.*

(1) *United States Citations,* for federal cases construing or mentioning the treaties.

(2) *State Citations,* for state cases pertaining to treaties.

c. *Wharton's Digest.*

d. *Moore's Digest.*

e. *Hackworth's Digest.*

f. *Whiteman's Digest.*

g. *Digest of United States Practice in International Law.*

An annual digest which started publication in 1973. Serves as a supplement to *Whiteman's.*

h. *International Legal Materials: Current Documents.*

(1) Collection of current official foreign and United States documents relating to international legal affairs, which are otherwise unavailable.

(2) 1962 to date; bi-monthly.

i. *American International Law Cases,* 1793–1978. This set collects state and federal cases interpreting U.S. treaties.

4. Status of United States Treaties

a. *CCH Congressional Index: Treaty Section.*

b. *Department of State Bulletin: Treaties Section.*

5. Multinational Collections of Treaties

a. *Consolidated Treaty Series,* 1648–1919

b. *League of Nations Treaty Series,* 1920–1945

c. *United Nations Treaty Series,* 1946–date

6. Latin American Treaty Collections

a. *Pan American Union Law and Treaty Series,* succeeded *Organization of American States Treaty Series.*

7. Indexes to Multinational Treaties

a. *United Nations List of Treaty Collections,* 1956. List of some 700 treaty collections published since the latter part of the 18th century.

b. *World Treaty Index,* 2d ed. 5 vols.

c. Harvard Law School Library, *Index to Multilateral Treaties,* 1965 and Supps.

d. United Nations, Office of Legal Affairs, *Multilateral Treaties in Respect of Which the Secretary-General Performs Depository Function.*

Chapter 20

COMPUTERS AND MICROTEXT IN LEGAL RESEARCH

New technology is playing an increasingly important role in legal research. This chapter will discuss two important developments in the way legal information is stored, retrieved, and used: computer-assisted research and microtext.

SECTION A. INTRODUCTION TO COMPUTER-ASSISTED LEGAL RESEARCH

Many of the legal materials described in the preceding chapters of this book have been made available to the researcher in machine readable form. The tremendous speed and manipulative power of computers make it possible to find and use these sources in new and more powerful ways. In order to get the maximum benefit from computer-assisted legal research it is necessary to understand its strengths and limitations. Computer research is not a substitute for manual research, but a method that can supplement and enhance the results of manual research.

1. Equipment

To use computer-assisted legal research services, one needs only a terminal capable of communicating over telephone lines with a central computer. The terminal has a typewriter keyboard and a screen upon which the requested information is displayed. Most terminals are attached to a printer that can be used to make paper copy of search results. The large central computer contains the information and does the actual search processing.

2. Databases

Both of the two widely-marketed computer-assisted legal research services, WESTLAW and LEXIS, contain the full texts of over a million documents. Similar documents, such as cases from the same jurisdiction or sections from the same code, are gathered together into databases that can be searched with a single search request. Effective searching begins by choosing the database or group of databases that contain the sort of authority one wishes to find.

Both WESTLAW and LEXIS contain hundreds of different databases, many of which include or overlap others. Early databases

tended to gather together documents that would be found in the same set of books, such as cases that are published in the same reporter. Many newer databases are organized by subject, such as admiralty law or labor law. The oldest and most frequently used databases contain case law, but many other kinds of documents are now included in the services. Both WESTLAW and LEXIS have databases containing statutes, Attorney General opinions, regulations, law review articles, treatises, administrative announcements and decisions, and citation indexes.

Individual documents are divided into *segments* or *fields*. Court decisions, for example, are typically divided into sections for the name of the case, its date, the name of the judge who wrote the opinion, and the body of the decision. Each of these parts of a case can be searched separately, and searches on the parts can be combined.

In the case law databases there is an important difference between WESTLAW and LEXIS. LEXIS loads cases just as they are received from the courts, including official summaries and headnotes only for the few jurisdictions in which they are officially prepared. WESTLAW adds to this the editorial material that appears with the case in the *National Reporter System*, including the synopsis, the West *Key Numbers*, and the headnotes. These additional materials are included in separate fields, and they can be searched separately or together with the rest of the case.

3. Searching the Databases

Both WESTLAW and LEXIS use the same basic technique for retrieving documents. The rest of this section and the following section on search formulation discuss this technique in the context of searching for case authority, but the same considerations apply to searching for any other sort of document.

Every word of every case covered by the services is a part of the WESTLAW and LEXIS databases, and every word (except for a few very common *noise words* like *of*, *the*, and *to*) is a point of access for the case. The computer retrieves cases by searching for words and combinations of words specified by the user. This way of searching is known as *key word* searching.

The ability to find every word in a case can be remarkably useful. To find a case by its docket number, for example, one can search for that number (numbers are *words* as far as computers are concerned) in the field that contains the captions of all of the cases in the database. Similarly, one can quickly retrieve all of the cases argued by a certain attorney, written by a certain judge, decided after a certain date, involving a certain defendant, or citing a certain case. In some cases this information is virtually unavailable except

for the computer. For example, there is no published docket number listing for the decisions of most courts, and it would be very time-consuming to look through the reporters for a case with a given docket number.

The most common need of legal researchers, however, is not to find a case that contains a given number, date, or name; it is to find cases by subject, to find cases about a particular topic or relevant to a given situation. Computer-assisted legal research is not as efficient or reliable for this purpose.

The reason that a key word approach does not work particularly well for subject searching is that there is not a perfect correspondence between the words used in a case and what the case is about. This lack of correspondence manifests itself in three forms: synonymous words, ambiguous words, and complex expressions. The researcher should be aware of all of these problems when deciding whether or not a particular research question is suitable for computer searching.

a. *Synonymous Words.* Many words can be used to refer to the same thing. A court discussing a ten-year-old boy might refer to him by any one of a number of words, including:

boy	child	youth	infant
minor	juvenile	ten-year-old	young man

The court could also refer to him by using words showing his relationship to something else, including his connection to the case itself:

son	brother	ward	student
pupil	victim	witness	plaintiff
defendant	appellant	petitioner	patient

and many others too numerous to list. Cases relevant to the same issue might refer to other people who have the same legal standing:

girl	daughter	ten-and-a-half-year-old

The court might also refer to the boy with a pronoun or by his proper name.

To retrieve as many relevant cases as possible, it is important to include as search terms as many synonyms as possible. Consulting a thesaurus is helpful, and it is often wise to look in a legal encyclopedia or a treatise to learn the nomenclature used in the area of law being researched. Both WESTLAW and LEXIS allow the searcher to list different words for the same idea so that the search will retrieve a case with any of the listed words, and both provide some assistance in finding synonyms by automatically searching for many plurals and other equivalent expressions. Even with these features, however, many relevant cases are missed in computer searches because the

searcher did not list all of the possible synonyms for the basic search terms.

b. *Ambiguous Words.* The converse problem is that one word can mean several different things depending upon context. For example, a search for Iowa cases discussing the drug diethylstilbestrol should certainly include the common abbreviation *DES* as an alternative search term, but this also causes the search to retrieve all of the cases in which the city of Des Moines is mentioned. To choose a more common example, a search on some aspect of criminal assault will also retrieve civil assault cases.

In most cases the searcher must read through all of the retrieved cases and sort out the relevant cases from those selected by the computer because they contain a search term in some irrelevant meaning. In other cases, it is possible to reduce the number of *false drops* by using other search terms to provide some context for the ambiguous word, for example, by adding words conveying the idea of pregnancy and drug to the search for DES.

c. *Complex Expressions.* A more difficult and pervasive problem is that much of the meaning of a case is not captured in individual words but in whole sentences and paragraphs. WESTLAW and LEXIS allow the searcher to require that certain terms occur in the same document, or within a certain number of words of each other, but these rough relationships between words do not capture the subtleties of the English language.

When the words of the search are very distinctive words it is usually possible to ignore the problems of complex expressions, but where the search contains only very common words, the effectiveness of the search diminishes dramatically. For example, consider this research question:

If a person waives his or her right to trial by jury in one trial, can a jury trial still be demanded in a subsequent new trial of the same matter?

The words needed to describe the main points of this question are *trial, jury, waiver,* and various words meaning *new trial.* All of these words are so common in reported cases that any search that retrieved a substantial proportion of the relevant cases would also retrieve thousands of irrelevant cases.

Certain kinds of cases tend to use more distinctive words than others. Fact patterns, for example, tend to be better for computer searching because they use words that do not appear in many cases. Procedural questions, in contrast, are difficult to search because they tend to use words like *trial* and *motion* that occur very often.

The combined effect of these various kinds of error is to make computer searching much less effective than one would wish. Expe-

rience has shown that thorough manual research usually turns up more relevant cases than computer-assisted research.

The superiority of manual research derives from the fact that it relies on intelligent human judgment rather than simple word-matching. In conventional research, an indexer reads each document and then assigns to it index terms that describe what the document is about. These index terms are usually chosen from a controlled vocabulary so that the same idea is always listed under the same index term. For example, cases about ten-year-old boys might be listed under *children* or *minors* or *youths*, but all of the cases should be under the same term in any given index, and cross-references should be given from the terms not used to the terms that are. The user of the service looks in the index under the index terms that seem to apply to the facts at hand, and finds all of the cases listed there by the indexer. Indexers make mistakes, but they can make much more accurate and sophisticated judgments as to the relevance of a given document to a particular topic than a computer can. Thus, when a printed index that covers the desired sources can be found, it is usually more productive to use the printed index than to use computer-assisted research.

Computer-assisted legal research is, however, very helpful for subject searching in certain situations where good human subject indexing is not available. Human indexing is not useful where the indexer has not anticipated the need of the researcher. For example, most cases are much more thoroughly indexed with respect to the legal theories they discuss than the fact patterns that gave rise to them, and so computer searching is comparatively good at turning up cases with particular facts. Computer searching is also very effective in discovering cases that discuss an unusual combination of factors that are individually very common. Full text searching can be used to search for new ideas that have not yet been added to the controlled vocabularies used by indexers. Finally, full text searching is a good way to find cases that are too new to be reflected in the available indexes and cases that have been badly indexed in printed sources.

Computer searching is a good way to find a few cases on point to use as starting points for other sorts of research. Many of the research techniques discussed elsewhere in this book work better if the researcher already knows of some relevant authority.

Thus, while computer searching does not ordinarily find as many relevant cases as manual searching does, the two systems can work together to produce better results than either does by itself. Judicious use of computer-assisted legal research will enhance the researcher's effectiveness in many instances.

SECTION B. FORMULATING A COMPUTER
SEARCH REQUEST

Formulating a good computer search request is a complex operation, and is a little different in each service. It is beyond the scope of this book to give detailed instructions for either WESTLAW or LEXIS, but the following four-step approach can be used to help formulate key word searches generally:

1. Identify the elements of the problem

2. Select the elements to be searched

3. Express the elements in key words

4. Join the key words with connectors

This section will discuss each of these steps and follow a sample problem through the entire process.

1. Identify the Elements of the Problem

To prepare a good computer search, one must first break the problem at hand into its elements. This process is discussed in detail in Chapter 2 of this book.

Consider the following research problem: a client is a high school student who is on trial for possession of marijuana after the police used a specially trained German shepherd to sniff out a cache of the drug in his school locker. Find cases that discuss whether this was an illegal search.

The elements of the problem should be expressed in general terms. It really does not matter that the dog was a German shepherd; the same legal issues would be raised no matter what the breed of the dog. Also, it probably does not matter that marijuana was found in the search; the issues might be the same if the contraband discovered was heroin, alcohol, or stolen property. The list of elements chosen depends on the researcher's view of the case, but one possible list of elements for the problem is this:

student	*school*	*police*
dog	*sniffing*	*search*
contraband	*hidden*	*locker*

2. Select the Elements to Be Searched

The next step in formulating a search request is deciding which of the elements should be included. Both WESTLAW and LEXIS contain well over a million cases, so it is essential to include elements that will distinguish the few relevant cases from the mass of irrelevant ones. This is best done by beginning with the most distinctive element of the problem, and then adding as many additional elements

as necessary to limit the search result to a reasonable number of cases. Once the query has enough required parts to return a manageable number of cases, however, no additional elements should be added. Each new element risks the loss of relevant cases.

The most distinctive part of the sample problem is the *sniffing dog*, and so the search should be based on those two elements. To distinguish relevant cases from the rest of the sniffing dog cases in the database, we can specify the additional element *school*. Now we have the following three search elements:

dog   *sniffing*   *school*

At this point it is reasonable to suppose that the search is specific enough. There are probably only a few cases in the reporters that discuss sniffing dogs in schools, and the searcher can pick the relevant cases out of this small group without wasting a great deal of time on the others.

There are, of course, several other elements that could be added to this search, but it would be a mistake to add them. Each time another element is added to the search there is a risk that relevant cases will be excluded because the words used for that element in the search do not appear in the case. For example, one could add the element of *contraband* to this search, but it is impossible to anticipate all of the words that might be used in a case to describe things that students are not allowed to have in their lockers. The element *locker* could be used, but one would risk missing analogous cases in which the sniff search was performed on the student's car or backpack.

When in doubt, searches should err on the side of having too few elements rather than too many. If, after looking at the first few documents retrieved, it appears that the first search found too many irrelevant documents, additional elements can be added to make the search narrower.

3. Express the Element in Key Words

Once the elements of the search have been identified, the next step is to select the key words that will embody those elements in the search query. The searcher must guess which words were used in the relevant cases to express each element.

Much of the difficulty of formulating search requests is encountered in this stage. As discussed in the preceding section, there is only an imperfect correspondence between words and ideas, and the searcher has to grapple with the problems of synonymity, ambiguity, and complex expression. Often an element of a search simply cannot be adequately represented by key words. When this happens, the searcher should return to the preceding step and select different elements as the search elements. If the problem element is essential

to the subject of the search, computer research may not be an appropriate research technique. One should not, however, abandon an element just because it cannot be perfectly embodied in key words. It is unrealistic to expect computer searches to find every relevant case.

The first element of the search in the example, *dog*, can be reasonably well represented by the word *dog*. It is possible that a court would refer to a dog by its breed, calling it, for example, a *German shepherd*, but it would be impractical to list all of the possible breeds of dog as search terms.

The second element, *sniffing*, is well represented by the various forms of the word *sniff*. By using the search term SNIFF!, the search will retrieve *sniff, sniffs, sniffed,* and *sniffing* (as well as the unwanted forms *sniffle* and *sniffy*).

The third element, *school*, can be represented by the words *school* and *student*. These words are not equivalent, one representing the place of the occurrence and the other the status of one of the people involved, but the presence of either would suggest that the case is likely to be relevant.

Representing the elements of the sample search by the selected terms, we now have:

DOG   SNIFF!   SCHOOL or STUDENT

4. Join the Key Words with Connectors

The final step in formulating a search is to join the selected search terms together with appropriate connectors. WESTLAW and LEXIS use somewhat different connectors and so will be discussed separately.

a. *WESTLAW connectors.* WESTLAW searches use slightly different connectors. Only a space is needed to connect alternative key words in an element. In addition to the AND and W/n connectors used in LEXIS, WESTLAW permits search elements to be joined by /P and /S, which require that the search terms be found in the same paragraph or the same sentence, respectively. The /P connector is especially useful because it makes use of the natural organization of the text. Words used by the author in the same paragraph are more likely to be related to the same point than are words that are close together but occur in different paragraphs or even different sections of the case.

Applying these considerations, we form the following WESTLAW query:[1]

DOG /P SNIFF! /P SCHOOL STUDENT

[1] These sample searches, when run in the WESTLAW and LEXIS databases that contain federal cases on November 19, 1984, retrieved the same 12 cases. Eleven of

b. *LEXIS connectors.* In LEXIS, alternative key words representing one element of the search are joined by the connector *OR*. Key words representing different elements of the search may be joined with a variety of connectors, the most common being *AND* and *W/n*. AND requires that the different elements occur anywhere in the same case. W/n requires that the terms representing the elements be found within some number of significant words of each other in the opinion. For example, using a *W/5* between elements of a search would require that the key words be found within 5 words of each other, excluding the very common *noise* words. Since reported decisions are often very long and discuss many different and often unrelated points of law, W/n is usually preferred because it tends to retrieve cases in which the search terms are more closely related.

The W/n connector can be made tighter or looser by changing the number used for *n*. Many searchers try to specify a number close to the length of a short paragraph, reasoning that words occurring within a paragraph or so of each other are probably related to the same point.

Using these considerations in the example, we arrive at the following LEXIS query:[2]

DOG   W/30   SNIFF!   W/30   STUDENT or SCHOOL

Carefully preparing a search request before sitting down to a WESTLAW or LEXIS terminal saves computer time and ordinarily leads to better results, but it is no guarantee of a successful search. The searcher should always examine the first few cases retrieved to see if the query is finding the right sort of cases. Often, problems with a search will become apparent only at this stage.

SECTION C. OTHER DATABASES USEFUL IN LEGAL RESEARCH

There are many computer databases other than WESTLAW and LEXIS that are useful in legal research. Lawyers often need access to information that is not strictly legal: information about current events, corporate disclosures, patent filings, and a host of other topics. A growing information industry supplies this material to the public.

1. Databases

Thousands of databases are available to the public. It is beyond the scope of this book to mention all of those that might be of

---

these cases were either relevant themselves or were selected because they discussed relevant cases. WESTLAW and LEXIS each retrieved two other cases; both of these were relevant in the LEXIS search and one was relevant in the WESTLAW search.

[2] *See* Note 1, *supra.*

interest to attorneys, but the following examples show some of the resources available: The Electronic Legislative Search Service (ELSS), a service of Commerce Clearing House (CCH), provides very current information about legislative activity in Congress and all 50 states. Data Courier's ABI/INFORM indexes over 500 journals in the field of business management and administration. Dow Jones News/Retrieval provides current information about financial markets and business news. DISCLOSURE gives access to reports filed with the Securities and Exchange Commission by thousands of publicly traded companies. In addition, many individual publications are available online, from the very general (*e.g., Encyclopedia Britannica*) to the very specialized (*e.g., Genetic Technology News*).

There is an online service available for virtually any sort of information need. John Schmittroth's *Encyclopedia of Information Systems and Services*, 6th ed. (Detroit: Gale Research, 1984) describes over 3000 organizations involved in the production and distribution of electronic information.

Most online databases differ from WESTLAW and LEXIS in that they cannot search on the full text of the documents they index. What is contained in the computer is not the document itself, but a record containing roughly the same information one finds on a library catalog card, including author, title, subject headings, date, and any other information necessary to find the document in printed form. Many databases also have an abstract of the document, which might be a few lines or several hundred words depending upon the database.

Searching these databases is different from searching WESTLAW and LEXIS in several important respects. Key word subject searching can be done by matching words in the title (and in the abstract for the databases that have them), but the most effective subject searches are performed by matching key words in subject headings. Since the subject headings are assigned by human indexers from a controlled vocabulary, many of the problems associated with full-text searching are avoided.

To make effective use of these services, however, it is important to find the right words from the controlled vocabulary to use as search terms. For example, if the index term used in a database is *children*, using *minors* as a search term would not find the relevant documents. Many databases publish lists of the subject headings used by their indexers, which are called *thesauri*. Other databases use the standard Library of Congress subject headings found in most library catalogs. Many have some provision for finding proper search terms online.

The databases contained in Mead Data Central's NEXIS system, and some others, have the full text of documents online and use the

same sort of search logic as do WESTLAW and LEXIS. Other databases contain both human subject indexing and full text capability.

2. Database Vendors

Many of the most popular non-legal databases are made available through database vendors. These organizations provide a common search logic and central billing for a group of databases. NEXIS, Lockheed's DIALOG, Bibliographic Retrieval Service (BRS), and Systems Development Corporation's ORBIT, are examples of these services. Each of these vendors publishes instructions for use of its system and a catalog of the databases it provides. Often the same database is available from more than one vendor, frequently at different prices.

3. Help in Accessing These Databases

Each of the thousands of available databases differs from the others in the information it contains, and databases often differ in their format, search logic, thesauri, accessibility, and costs. Selecting the right database, getting access to it through the right vendor, and formulating an effective search request can be very difficult.

Most large law firms, government agencies, and educational institutions employ librarians who have special training and experience in online searching. Many public libraries also provide this service, often with no extra charge for the services of the librarian. Other people with this training have gone into business as *information brokers*, providing online searching and other information services to their clients.

SECTION D. CITATION FORM

The thirteenth edition of *A Uniform System of Citation* (or *Bluebook*) has made an initial attempt to address computer-assisted legal research citation needs. The general philosophy of citation form requires a citation to clearly identify the cited source, distinguish that source from similar sources, and provide assistance to the reader in locating the source. Additionally, any information conveyed through a citation should be expressed in the minimum number of necessary characters. The *Bluebook* is designed for law review citation style. Law review footnotes are more costly to typeset than is the textual portion of the review. Therefore, citation form attempts to provide the most information in the minimum amount of space.

Rule 10.8.1 on special citation forms for pending and unreported cases includes the application of computer-assisted legal research sources. There are several ways by which this rule can be located.

Both WESTLAW and LEXIS are indexed in the *Bluebook* index, with reference to page 52 on which Rule 10.8.1 appears. Also, the table of contents for case citation form indicates the page on which special citation form is explained.

The *Bluebook* limits the application of WESTLAW/LEXIS citation to unreported cases. By inference, reported decisions should not be cited to computer services. A reported decision is one that appears in an official or commercially prepared reporter or service.

Notice that page 52 only provides an example of a LEXIS citation form. Since WESTLAW and LEXIS are both indexed to this page, one must assume that the exampled form is appropriate to both services, so long as the correct service is parenthetically noted. The apparent philosophy of the *Bluebook* editors is that availability of the case on WESTLAW and LEXIS is better than none at all. However, the citation form still requires all components for citing to an unreported decision—case name, docket number, parenthetically noted court, and complete date. For example, an unreported opinion should be cited as follows:

Smith v. Jones, No. 52–1234 (Mass.Dist.Ct. July 31, 1952).

In an additional parenthetical note, information as to the availability on a particular computer service must be noted. Since it is impossible to know when an unreported case will be available on a computer-assisted legal research service, the portion of the parenthetical requiring notation of an availability date is unnecessary. A case may be available in different databases in WESTLAW, or in different libraries or files in LEXIS. The *Bluebook* does not address this discrepancy; therefore, any correct designation of a database on WESTLAW, or combination of libraries and files on LEXIS should be appropriate. For example an unreported decision on WESTLAW should be cited as follows:

Smith v. Jones, No. 52–1234 (Mass.Dist.Ct. July 31, 1952) (on WESTLAW, Allstates database).

On LEXIS, an unreported decision should be cited:

Smith v. Jones, No. 52–1234 (Mass.Dist.Ct. July 31, 1952) (on LEXIS, States library, Mass. file).

The *Bluebook* editors recognized the developing nature of the electronic information technology. In their preface to the thirteenth edition, *How to Use This Book*, the editors note that citations to information available in alternative formats (*e.g.*, microforms, computer tape, and computer databases) should be noted parenthetically. In effect, the editors provide a great deal of latitude in developing a citation format for these unique materials.

Citation form for computer-assisted legal research databases continues to develop as electronic formats expand the breadth of

materials available online. Innovative citation approaches must be developed to accommodate the new medium. Once a universal standardized citation form is available, citation directly to the electronic format will be possible. For the time being, a patchwork of ad hoc citation forms must suffice.

SECTION E. MICROTEXT

Microtext is the generic term for bibliographic materials that have been photographically reduced in size and which require magnification on a microtext reader or video display terminal for normal use. Various ratios of reduction are used, varying from 8X to 90X or higher.[3] The most common reduction used for printed materials varies from 18X to 42X. Microtext publication has increased dramatically in the last five years. Libraries have found microtexts to be economical as well as a solution to space and preservation problems.

1. Microtext Format

There are many different formats used for microtext publications. Those generally used for printed and bibliographic materials are:

a. *Microfilm.* Microfilm is a roll of film packaged in either reels, cartridges, or cassettes. Microfilm is either 16mm or 35mm wide, with 35mm being the preferred standard. Material normally microfilmed includes long runs of newspapers, periodicals or archival documents and papers.

b. *Computer Output Microfilm* (COM). COM is produced directly in the form of microfilm or microfiche from information stored on computer. It is economical and gaining widespread use as more information is computerized. Examples of its use are the production of *Current Law Index* and *Legal Resource Index* (described in Chapter 16). The indexing for these publications is done on a computer terminal which produces a computer tape. Using a COM recorder, information on the computer tape is transferred to either microfilm or microfiche which is used to print the issues of *Current Law Index* and to cumulate the monthly microfilm issues of the *Legal Resource Index*. Many libraries are now substituting COM-produced catalogs, either in book form or microfiche, for their card catalogs.

c. *Microfiche.* Microfiche is fast becoming the most common form of microtext. It is a sheet of film varying in size from 3 x 5 inches to 6 x 9 inches, with 4 x 6 inches being the standard size for

---

[3] The reduction ratio is a measure of the number of times a given linear dimension of an object is reduced when photographed. The larger the *X*, the smaller the reduction.

materials on microfiche for libraries. Depending on the reduction ratio used, up to 98 normal size printed pages, arranged in rows and columns, can be placed on one standard size microfiche. Microfiche is especially favored for, but not limited to, publications or documents which contain from one to several hundred pages.

d. *Ultrafiche.* Ultrafiche is sheet film with the same standards and arrangement as microfiche, but which has a much higher reduction ratio—as much as 150X. As many as 2380 pages can be placed on a single sheet. Ultrafiche is expensive to produce and is generally used for commercial catalogs such as *Sears and Roebuck Catalog.* West's *National Reporter System,* which is reproduced on ultrafiche from the printed *Reporters,* is an example of its use in law libraries.

e. *Micro-opaques.* Micro-opaques are similar to microfiche in size; however the printed text is reproduced on opaque card stock rather than on transparent film. They require special reading machines and are more difficult to read than microfilm or microfiche. Micro-opaques are not now generally produced.[4]

2. Microform Equipment

Due to the miniaturization process, special reading machines are needed to read microtexts. Frequently, separate machines must be used for each type of format, although some machines will adjust to two or more types of microtext format. Readers come in varying sizes, with various options available. One of the most useful microtext readers is the reader-printer. The reader-printer magnifies the microtext on the display screen and is capable of producing a full-size photocopy of the page. Advances in technology have also made it possible for some microtext readers to transfer a microtext page to a slide format. Many libraries now have microtext reading rooms in which microtexts are stored and various types of reading equipment are available. Some libraries also have portable microtext readers which may be borrowed and used elsewhere in the library or at home.

3. Legal Materials Available on Microtext

There is an increasing amount of legal materials available on microtext.[5] Some, which are more useful for legal research, are:

a. *Briefs and Records.* The briefs and records of the United States Supreme Court, some of the federal courts of appeals, state supreme courts and appellate courts are available on microtext.

---

[4] The micro-opaques' sizes vary by their trade names: *Microcard* (3 x 5 inches and 4 x 6 inches); *Microprint* (6 x 9 inches); *Microlex* (6½ x 7½ inches); *Mini-Print* (6 x 9 inches).

[5] For a comprehensive bibliography of legal materials available on microtext, *see* H. TSENG, COMPLETE GUIDE TO LEGAL MATERIALS IN MICROFORM (1976 and supplements).

b. *Congressional Documents*. Nearly all of the congressional bills, committee reports and hearings are now available in some form of microtext. The U.S. Government Printing Office is also publishing an increasing number of government documents and reports on microtext. Approximately 64% of the titles published by the U.S. Government Printing Office in 1982 were in microtext, with the percentage expected to increase in subsequent years.

c. *Legislative Histories*. Both the U.S. Government Printing Office and private publishing companies are reprinting legislative histories in microtext.

d. *State Documents*. Statutes, codes, registers, Attorney General opinions and other state documents are now available on microtext. Many libraries are now purchasing state documents on microtext to save money and facilitate storage.

e. *Foreign Documents*. Statutes, official gazettes and court reports of many foreign countries are becoming available in microtext editions. Many libraries are now able to make this previously unavailable or hard to acquire material available to the academic and legal communities.

4. Microtext Summary

Microtext materials are playing an increasingly important role in legal research. Due to the availability of microtext almost any law library may have in its collection research materials such as briefs and records, legislative histories, out-of-print treatises and important but scarce periodicals which have been available only at the largest law libraries. The rising cost of printed materials has led to even greater availability and use of microtexts. Some publications, particularly government publications, are now only available on microtext. Microfacsimile transmission, the electronic transmission of microtexts over telephone lines or other communication devices, will become increasingly important as libraries expand their efforts to provide legal research materials for the academic and legal communities. In the future, many more types of legal materials will be reproduced or published exclusively on microform as the microtext explosion continues.

Chapter 21

A GENERAL SUMMARY OF RESEARCH
PROCEDURE

SECTION A. RESEARCH PROCEDURE

Legal research is as much an art as it is a science. There are as many approaches to legal research as there are problems to be solved. Each of the various types of research tools available for resolution of legal problems has been discussed in the previous chapters. The final measure is to develop a systematic approach to using the research tools that have been described. It should also be noted that the approach to legal research may be determined by where the research is occurring. Not all law libraries will have all of the sets described, and a detailed knowledge of each research tool will assist in formulating the research problem. Methods of approach will be suggested in this chapter; but, in the end, each researcher must develop a system which best suits his or her needs.

No matter how sophisticated one becomes in any particular field of law, there will always be problems calling for research into areas of the law with which one is utterly unfamiliar. It is at these moments that the basic approach developed as a novice becomes the artful technique of a trained professional.

A worthwhile system of legal research can be broken down into five basic steps. These are:

STEP 1. Identify the legally significant facts.

STEP 2. Frame the legal issues to be researched.

STEP 3. Identify the relevant sources of law.

STEP 4. Research the issues presented.

STEP 5. Communicate the solution of the problem.

The discussion herein will focus on each of these steps individually; however, it is to be remembered that each step is closely interrelated with all the others. In the actual process of executing any one of the steps it may be necessary simultaneously to refine the work done under all of the previous steps.

STEP 1. Identifying Facts of Legal Significance

The first task of a researcher is to isolate the facts surrounding the particular problem to be solved. Some facts have legal signifi-

cance; others do not. The task of legal research begins with the compiling of a descriptive statement of legally significant facts. As one gains expertise in a particular field of law, one becomes more skilled in the process of isolating facts which have legal significance. It is, however, often difficult for a beginner to identify the significant facts and to discard the insignificant ones. Consequently, when researching a problem in an unfamiliar area of the law, it is usually best to err on the side of over-inclusion rather than on the side of exclusion.

It must also be kept in mind that the words used to describe a particular problem or fact situation may both assist and hinder the research process. Many research tools are indexed by a set of descriptive words, although this is not a hindrance with LEXIS and WESTLAW where literal searching is permissible. Failure to describe the fact situation in sufficient detail can sometimes cause one to overlook important legal issues because of the failure to find the right words in the index or database.

STEP 2.   *Framing the Legal Issues to Be Researched*

Writing a clear, concise statement of each legal issue raised by the significant facts is undoubtedly the most important and usually the most difficult task associated with legal research. Failure to frame all of the issues raised by a particular set of facts can and often will lead to an erroneous solution.

It is better, when framing the issues, for a beginner to err on the side of too many issues. Insignificant ones can always be eliminated after they have been thoroughly investigated, and overlapping ones can be consolidated. As a particular issue is researched, it is often discovered that it is overly broad and it becomes evident that the statement of the issue should be narrowed. It may also be necessary at times to split an issue into two, or to divide it into two sub-issues. Similarly, it may develop that the original issue is too narrow and as a result is not leading to any relevant authority. In such instances, the issue should then be broadened. Many times, during the course of one's research, it becomes apparent that other issues not originally thought of are relevant.

It is for this reason that the task of framing issues may not be completed until the research project is finished.

Once statements of each issue raised by the significant facts have been drafted, they should be arranged in a logical pattern which will provide continuity and preserve the integrity of the thought process during the course of the legal research. Logically related issues may be combined as sub-issues under a broader main issue. Issues which depend upon the outcome of more major issues should be arranged accordingly.

When arranging the issues, one should keep in mind that it is usually best to exhaust all relevant legal authority on one issue before going on to research another issue. This technique is more methodical than an approach which exhausts a given legal authority on all the issues raised by the facts before moving on to the next source of law.

The technique of exhausting all relevant authorities on a particular issue before going on to the next issue also serves other practical purposes. It allows one to focus on a fairly narrow area of the law, thus avoiding the temptation to stray into interesting but irrelevant areas. It also allows one to quickly gain some knowledge of the time required to complete the project so that one can accurately schedule each step of the process, ensuring that it will be completed on time.

For these reasons, it is always advisable to frame the issues so that they can be researched independently and to arrange these issues and sub-issues into a logically progressive pattern.

STEP 3. *Identifying the Relevant Sources of Law*

Once Steps 1 and 2 have been completed, the next and equally important step is to decide for each issue to be researched which sources to use, which sources not to use, and the order in which these sources should be examined. Failure to give thought to the precise sources to be used before beginning the research on a particular issue may result in omitting a vital source of law. More importantly, it may cause the research to start from the wrong end, unnecessarily increasing the difficulty of the task. For these reasons, the researcher should always prepare a list of sources arranged in the order they will be used for each issue to be researched.

One notable exception to this process involves the use of legal database searching. Depending on the level of one's skill and the availability of LEXIS and/or WESTLAW, it may be worthwhile to the researcher to do both a preliminary search and a follow-up search as the first and last steps in the research process. Because of the speed and comprehensiveness of both LEXIS and WESTLAW, a *quick and dirty* search in the beginning may prove to be a far more efficient means of turning up relevant cases than doing the manual research alone. Doing a final search on LEXIS and WESTLAW serves to verify what has been found and should produce very few cases, regulations, or other sources which are not yet available in hard copy.

It is convenient to classify general legal problems into four categories: (1) constitutional law; (2) statutory law; (3) case law; and (4) administrative law. Each of these categories is generally divided into federal, state, and local law. In actual practice, most legal problems are interrelated and concern two or more of the above categories, since they may involve both federal and state law. Legal

issues cannot really be compartmentalized. This is one reason why it is usually advisable to research each issue separately and completely before turning to the next issue.

Notwithstanding the interrelationship of legal issues, it is still best to list relevant sources of legal authority as separate, independent units. In Section B, a list of sources is suggested, and order of use is given. The sources cover constitutional, statutory, case, and administrative law. It should be kept in mind that if a particular issue overlaps more than one category, one must prepare a list of sources containing authorities drawn from all the applicable categories. In addition, thought must be given as to how to coordinate the use of the relevant sources in obtaining a rapid, accurate solution of the issues being researched. Following the list of sources is a *Chart on Legal Procedure* which summarizes the information previously presented in narrative form.

STEP 4. Researching the Issues Presented

Once the issues have been framed and the sources of legal authority listed in the order in which they are intended to be used, it is time to begin researching the first issue. The first issue should be completed, exhausting all relevant authorities on point, before progressing to the second issue. The first source on the list after WESTLAW and/or LEXIS is entered through its index, using the descriptive words developed by applying the TARP method discussed in Chapter 2. The contents of the first source should be thoroughly exhausted and a list of statutes, cases, and other relevant authorities should be compiled. If the first source is covered by *Shepard's Citations*, it is *Shepardized*, either manually or through the use of the *Shepard's* file in WESTLAW and/or LEXIS. The first source for all materials on point should be exhausted so that there will be no need to return to this source again during the research of the first issue.

The next step is to read all the authorities cited by the first source. These authorities should be consulted in the following order: (1) constitutions; (2) statutes and local ordinances; (3) cases; (4) administrative materials, and, finally, (5) secondary authorities. As each of these cited authorities is read, a list of authorities which they cite should be compiled, checking to eliminate duplicates. Each cited source should be *Shepardized* before moving on to the next cited source. The second source on the original list is then consulted and the same process repeated. This pattern continues until all sources on the original list and the authorities they cite are fully researched.

As each new source is evaluated for its relevance, further sources can be developed and pursued in the same two-pronged fashion: consult sources in the text and footnotes for materials the

source in hand relied upon, and *Shepardize* for sources which cite to it. For each relevant source located, no matter how far down the chain from the starting point, the same checking should be done.

It may be helpful to think of the process as doing further research on a subject on point by consulting both recent and less recent published sources. Beyond simply giving the researcher different sources for points of law, this process should show the development of a legal idea over time and give indications of the trend in the law. But judgment must be exercised at each step of the process or the research will become sidetracked on irrelevant issues. In some instances this developmental model of legal research is very obvious. For instance, one may research a constitutional or statutory provision by searching for preceding provisions and legislative history and the most recent judicial interpretations as well as the actual text. All may be useful persuasive authority, but the real value of such a thorough research is the view it affords of the development and trend of the provision in question.

At this point it is worth noting that as one moves down the original list of sources, the frequency of repetitive citations begins to increase rapidly. This means that the available sources in point are beginning to be exhausted. Near the end of the list of sources, it will usually be found that all of the citations are repetitive, indicating that the research is both thorough and complete. Citations should be placed on note cards, organized according to the type of source involved. Failure to maintain an accurate list of citations will result in wasted time and may cause crucial sources of authority to be overlooked.

The following is a quick example of the process just described. Suppose that the problem being researched involves state law. The first source on the list is the local encyclopedia (or a general encyclopedia if a state encyclopedia is not available). The index is checked using the TARP method, the text is read, and a list is developed containing, for example, citations to the state annotated statutes and to several cases.

Since an encyclopedia cannot be *Shepardized,* the cited authorities, starting with the annotated statutes, are read. The appropriate sections of the annotated statutes are then *Shepardized.*

The next step is to read and *Shepardize* all of the cases cited by the encyclopedia and the citations obtained from the annotated statutes and from *Shepard's Citations.* From this process any additional relevant cases are listed and then *Shepardized.*

Then, go back to the original list of sources and exhaust the second source contained on the list. This will probably be the state annotated statutes. Although this source has already been investigated, this time it is entered through the index using the TARP

method. At this point it will usually be discovered that, in exhausting the citations obtained from an encyclopedia, all or most of the statutory provisions located by the use of the index have already been read. One now begins to develop a sense that the statutory authority in point has been exhausted.

The third source on the original list of sources should now be consulted. Suppose that this is the state digest. This is entered through the descriptive word index. Again, it will most likely be discovered that all of the relevant cases in the digest have been previously read, since they were cited by the local encyclopedia. Once any additional cases found in the state digest have been exhausted, the next source on the original list is consulted. This process is continued until the original list of authorities is completed. At this point the research of the first issue is completed, and one can begin the research of the second issue.

As one gains increased expertise in the process of executing legal research, one begins to develop certain shortcuts which increase the researcher's speed without sacrificing accuracy. For example, one may begin to use a host of abbreviations such as those used by *Shepard's Citations.*

Skilled researchers can rapidly evaluate the potential value of a case without reading the entire reported decision. One such technique is as follows: (1) read the headnotes, selecting those which bear on the issue being researched; (2) read that portion of the text relating to the headnotes selected; (3) read the facts of the case and as much of the opinion as is necessary to understand the point of law involved; (4) jot down the headnote numbers for *Shepardizing* if the textual material is in point; (5) jot down every important citation to authority made by the textual material in point; (6) then, read the entire case *only if* it is a vital link in the chain of case law authority in point. Of course, if the skilled researcher discovers at any point in the above process that the case adds nothing to the point of law being researched or that it is of little value for some other reason, the researcher will discard the case and mark it off the list of cases.

Skilled researchers also develop insight into knowing when they can safely terminate their research without exhausting every source on their list of authorities. There is no uniform rule which tells one how extensive the research should be in solving a legal problem. The extensiveness of research is often influenced by extraneous factors such as limitations of time and compensation; the nature of the problems; the legal measures being adopted; and the research habits and attitudes of the researcher.

The preceding discussion in this chapter describes an exhaustive system of legal research; however, such complete procedures are not always necessary. Carrying a problem through all the sources can

be needless, unwarranted or repetitious. Common sense and professional insight, therefore, play a significant role in research procedure.

Obviously, there is no pat answer to the question which we, as
researchers, ask every time we investigate a legal problem: "Can I
safely stop here?"

In the last analysis, the skills of sophisticated researchers are
measured as much for the knowledge of what can be omitted as for
what and how research materials are used to solve legal problems.
In some instances, a skilled researcher merely spot-checks a *single*
publication, *e.g.*, a general encyclopedia. A skilled researcher usually
does not consult duplicative sources of the same type, *i.e.*, *Am.Jur.2d*
and *CJS*. The researcher's stock in trade is *time*; a skilled researcher knows how to use it wisely. On the other hand, the researcher
must always solve the problem accurately. For this reason, the
novice is cautioned to always err on the side of over-inclusion,
duplication, and excessive time, because the work product expected of
the novice is no different from that expected of the skilled professional—an accurate solution to the problem.

STEP 5. *Communicating the Solution of the Problem*

The final step of the research process is somewhat outside the
scope of this work, being reserved for individualized instruction at
the classroom level. Nevertheless, the true test of the capacity to
research legal issues is found in the capacity to communicate the
results to other persons.

The notes which were prepared during Step 4, above, should be
in a form which can easily be organized and presented orally or in
written form. If the research is to be reduced to written form,
usually a memorandum of law, there are several techniques which
can be used to ensure that the written words accurately convey the
results of the research. The most important rule to follow is that the
words selected must be objective in nature, avoiding an adversary
approach. One must always evaluate the merits of both sides of each
legal issue.

The key elements of a well-drafted memorandum of law are: (1)
a title identifying the nature of the writing; (2) a statement of the
issues presented in the order they are to be discussed; (3) a brief
answer for each of the issues presented; (4) a statement of the
operative facts; (5) a discussion of each issue presented; and (6) a
conclusion (optional). It should be noted that in executing Steps 1
and 2 of the research process, the second and fourth elements of a
memorandum of law were completed.

One should begin writing the memorandum by refining the
statement of the issues and by reducing the statement of facts to
eliminate all irrelevancies. The next step is to outline and then

carefully write the discussion section. The brief answer section is then prepared, stating, in as few words as possible, the conclusions drawn in the discussion section of the memorandum. A conclusion section should be used only in complex memoranda when the reader requires a more detailed summary of the problem than is provided by the conclusory statements contained in the brief answer. The entire memorandum should then be given a short, highly descriptive title, and edited for citation errors, literary style, and, most importantly, for brevity.

The discussion section is the heart of the memorandum and deserves a bit more explanation. It should be organized issue by issue. Each issue and sub-issue should be discussed completely before progressing to the next issue. The most widely accepted method of discussing an issue of law employs the following format: (1) state the issue; (2) state the law which applies to the issue; (3) apply the law to the relevant operative facts; and (4) draw a conclusion. This format can be repeated for each issue and sub-issue in the memorandum.

Finally, there are a few common errors which must be avoided if a memorandum is to be a professional document. Backtracking or excessive interplay of issues is to be avoided. Each issue and sub-issue should be distinct and logically complete. Excessive overlapping of thought in the discussion section usually indicates that the issues have not been drafted with sufficient precision.

When an authority is cited, it must stand for the proposition asserted. If a citation is to dictum in a case, it must be so identified. One must avoid excessive citation to authority. String citations are rarely appropriate. Try to cite only the leading authority or authorities in point. Do not use quotations as a substitute for analysis and use quotations only where they add to, rather than supplement, the body of the memorandum.

Never give the appearance of avoiding resolution of a problem by pleading the need for additional facts. On the other hand, a memorandum should deal with potentially variant outcomes by assuming the existence of any facts which are clearly within the ambit of and which have not been negated by the given fact complex.

The greatest temptation of the novice is to include information which the researcher has spent many hours developing but which were later discovered to be wholly irrelevant to a proper analysis of the issues presented. A novice should expect to investigate a host of irrelevant leads during the research process. Avoid the burning temptation to include this information in the memorandum, as it detracts from and often masks the legal analysis which is directly in point.

It must always be remembered that a memorandum is objective in nature. It is not intended to be an adversary document. The presentation of analysis in adversary form casts grave doubt in the mind of the reader as to the objective validity of the memorandum. The task is to explore both the strengths and the weaknesses of each conclusion drawn. The task of the writer is to evaluate, not to persuade.

The first exposure to the mechanics of executing a legal research project from its beginning to its end has now been completed. The system we have discussed is one of the many possible approaches. The ultimate objective of the researcher is to develop the capacity to solve legal problems rapidly and accurately. That capacity can only be developed by constructing a basic, systematic approach to legal research. Therefore, it is now the task of the researcher to synthesize the materials contained in this chapter and to fashion a system of legal research which is commensurate with the researcher's existing professional skills and which assures the researcher of a professional work product each time the system is utilized.

SECTION B. SUGGESTED LIST OF SOURCES [1]

1. Constitutional Law Problem

a. *Federal Constitution*

(1) General Background. For a general discussion of a federal constitutional law question, consult a general legal encyclopedia (*CJS* or *American Jurisprudence 2d*). More critical and detailed studies may be found in the periodical literature by examining the *Current Law Index*, the *Index to Legal Periodicals* or the *Legal Resource Index*. The latter is also available online as a *Dialog* database. A recent treatise may be consulted to explore the area. Several other interpretative sources are discussed in Chapter 8.

Examine the *American Law Reports* and the *United States Supreme Court Reports* (L.Ed.) for possible annotations. A good annotation found early in the research can save the researcher a great deal of time.

(2) Text and Interpretation. If the matter is a recognizable federal constitutional problem, consult the following sources:

For the text of the Constitution and its interpretation, *see*:

United States Code Annotated

United States Code Service

[1] This section and Section C were authored by Jenni Parrish, Assistant Professor of Law and Law Librarian, University of Pittsburgh.

Constitution of the United States (Library of Congress ed.
        1984; updated by a biennial pocket supplement)

(3) *Shepard's Citations. Shepardize*: (a) several important
cases and (b) the applicable provision of the Constitution in *Shepard's
United States Citations* and in the appropriate *Shepard's State
Citations*. Use *Shepard's Federal Citations* when given an intermediate or lower federal court decision. Numerous case citations
under a provision of the Constitution in *Shepard's United States
Citations* may make the Constitution section in *Shepard's* unwieldy
and unusable.

(4) Additional Cases. Check a United States Supreme Court
digest, the *Federal Practice Digest, 3d* (and its earlier editions), or
the *American Digest System* for additional judicial interpretations.
Not to be overlooked, when available, are the LEXIS and WESTLAW
databases as sources of additional cases.

(5) Intent. In the absence of adequate judicial interpretation or
to re-examine the meaning given to the Constitution by its framers,
the historical source materials cited at footnote 5 in Chapter 8 should
be consulted.

b. *State Constitutions*

(1) General Background. For a discussion of a state constitution, consult a local encyclopedia, if one is published for the state,
e.g., Texas Jurisprudence 2d and *Illinois Law and Practice*.

In the absence of a local encyclopedia, a general encyclopedia
(*CJS* or *American Jurisprudence 2d*) may provide a helpful general
discussion of the question. An *American Law Reports* annotation or
a periodical article may also treat the constitutional issue.

(2) Text and Interpretation. The text and case interpretations of
a state constitution are included in the appropriate annotated state
code. Additional cases may be located through the state digest.

The state Attorney General's opinions should be consulted as a
possible source of interpretation of the state constitution. These are
now available for selected states in the LEXIS and WESTLAW
databases. See also Chapter 18, Section A.

(3) *Shepard's Citations. Shepardize*: (a) several leading cases
and (b) the provision of the state constitution in the appropriate
Shepard's State Citations.

(4) Additional Cases. For cases of other states, consult the
American Digest System.

The *Constitution of the United States* (Columbia University,
1980, updated with pocket supplements) cites comparative state constitutions. Through these references, the annotated constitutions of
other states may be examined, evaluated and compared. This proce-

dure is useful in citing persuasive decisions from another state whose provision was copied, or where the provision, situation and setting are comparable or where there is a dearth of judicial interpretation of the provision by a particular state court.

Comparative constitutional study may also be pursued by *Shepardizing* cases under their citations in the appropriate *Shepard's Citations*.

(5) Intent. Examine the proceedings, reports and other documents relating to state constitutional conventions for the meaning given the provision by its draftsmen.

2. Statutory Problem

a. *Federal Statute*

(1) General Background. Treatises are available for a number of federal statutory laws, *e.g.*, R. Callman, *Law of Unfair Competition, Trademarks and Monopolies* (4th ed., 1981, 4 vols.). They provide not only background but also detailed subject information. Thus they are valuable not only for their informational content but also as casefinders. Check the subject section of the law library's catalog to locate citations.

Annotations in the *American Law Reports* and the *United States Supreme Court Reports* (L.Ed.) and periodical literature are additional useful secondary aids.

(2) Text and Interpretation. For the text and interpretation of a federal statute which is in force, use the *United States Code Annotated* or the *United States Code Service*. The amendatory history of the act is included in these annotated codes. They will also include annotations of relevant United States Attorney General's opinions.

For the legislative history (intent of the draftsmen) of the act, consult the congressional bills, reports, hearings and debates. *See* Chapter 10. As explained there, *Congressional Information Service* (CIS) provides these documents on microfiche for legislation passed in 1970 and thereafter. Prior to 1970, finding the relevant documents is more difficult.

(3) *Shepard's Citations*. *Shepardize*: (a) the provision in *United States Code* or *Statutes at Large* for the history and the treatment of the act and (b) several significant cases in *Shepard's United States Citations*. Consult *Shepard's Federal Citations* to *Shepardize* intermediate *and* lower federal court cases.

State court decisions which cite federal statutes are listed in *Shepard's State Citations* or the regional *Shepard's Citations*.

(4) Additional Cases. Where there are meager case interpretations, examine the United States Supreme Court digests, the *Federal Practice Digest, 3d* or the *American Digest System*.

(5) Other. Where available to the researcher, a LEXIS or WESTLAW terminal can retrieve the text of the *United States Code* as well as the texts of federal and state cases in which federal laws have been cited.

b. *State Statutes*

(1) General Background. The local encyclopedia is helpful in providing information about, and interpretations of, a state statute. Local treatises and periodical articles, having more detailed bearing on the act, are equally useful references.

Where there is no local encyclopedia, *American Jurisprudence 2d* and *Corpus Juris Secundum* may give general information on some topics. Annotations in the *American Law Reports* cover statutory law of the several states.

(2) Text and Interpretation. Unannotated state codes provide the texts of the statutes. Annotated state codes give both the texts of the statutes and case interpretations.

The codes provide the amendatory history of the state acts. Legislative histories for state legislation are usually difficult or impossible to compile because of the dearth of published debates, committee reports, hearings, and other legislative actions. For further comment, see Chapter 11.

Shepard's Law Locators, where available, can also be a helpful interpretative source. See Chapter 14.

If the state's Attorney General has addressed the interpretation of this statute in an opinion, it is certainly worth noting. For a discussion of state Attorneys General opinions, see Chapter 18.

(3) *Shepard's Citations*. Shepardize: (a) the provision of the state statute and (b) several important cases in the applicable *Shepard's State Citations*.

(4) Additional Cases. For additional cases interpreting the statute, examine the state or regional digest.

If there is a dearth of statutory interpretation in the state, consult the annotated codes of other states for those states' interpretations. Such interpretations can be very persuasive. Some codes list comparative legislation of representative and neighboring states. Consultation of *Uniform Laws Annotated* (discussed in Chapter 18) may also be worthwhile in finding additional cases and commentary.

(5) Other. A number of research guides geared to particular state jurisdictions have appeared in recent years. Where available they should be consulted. See those listed in Appendix A.

c. *Local Ordinances and Codes*

(1) Text and Interpretation. The texts of city ordinances are included in city codes. Generally, city codes are not annotated.

Treatises can sometimes be the source of interpretative commentary and case law relevant to municipal legislation. The appropriate state digest is useful in providing interpretations of the city ordinance, but the problem must be approached by subject or topic.

In the absence of a current city code, check the ordinances in the office of the city counsel, city clerk, or other local official whose duties include the maintenance of a current file of city laws.

(2) *Shepard's Citations. Shepardize*: (a) the provision of the city code and (b) several significant cases, if existing, in the applicable *Shepard's State Citations*.

(3) Other. *Shepard's Ordinance Law Annotations* provide annotations on court decisions pertaining to city charters and ordinances.

The LEXIS and WESTLAW databases, where available, should not be overlooked as a source of pertinent case law.

3. Case Law Problem

a. *Federal Cases*

(1) General Background. For background information on federal case law, one of the two standard legal encyclopedias, *CJS* or *American Jurisprudence 2d*, should be consulted. For further information, go to a treatise on the particular topic or a relevant law review article. The American Law Institute's *Restatements* can also be valuable aids in finding case law on particular topics (see Chapter 17). The annotations found in *American Law Reports* are good secondary research aids as well.

(2) Texts of Cases. The texts of United States Supreme Court cases may be found in the official *United States Reports*, in *United States Supreme Court Reports* (Lawyers Co-operative Publishing Company), and in *Supreme Court Reporter* (West Publishing Company).

Federal circuit courts of appeals decisions are found in *Federal Reporter*, first and second series.

Decisions of federal district courts are selectively reported in *Federal Supplement* and in some subject reporters.

Full discussions of all these reporters are found in Chapter 4.

The LEXIS and WESTLAW databases can also be sources of the text of federal court cases.

(3) *Shepard's Citations. Shepardize* the significant cases in *Shepard's Federal Citations* (*i.e.*, circuit courts of appeals and district court decisions) and *Shepard's United States Citations* (Supreme Court decisions).

(4) Additional Cases. Additional cases may be found in (a) the *U.S. Supreme Court Digest*, (b) *Federal Practice Digest*, *2d* and *3d*, *Modern Federal Practice Digest*, and *Federal Digest*, and (c) looseleaf services on the particular topic.

(5) Other. Records and briefs of federal court cases may be of assistance in interpreting the decisions. Such records and briefs for the United States Supreme Court are commercially published in microform (see Chapter 20), and are also available on LEXIS. Where such documents are not published, the clerk of the court should be contacted to ascertain the availability of these materials.

b. *State Cases*

(1) General Background. For background information on state case law, the local encyclopedia, if available, may be a good source for a discussion of the topic. In the absence of a local encyclopedia, *American Jurisprudence 2d* or *Corpus Juris Secundum* may be consulted for an exposition of the case law.

American Jurisprudence 2d may give specific references to *American Law Reports* annotations, eliminating the use of *A.L.R.* indexes or regional digests. In some fields of the law, the researcher might begin with a local treatise or periodical article.

(2) Interpretation. References to state court cases may be found in the appropriate state or regional digest.

(3) *Shepard's Citations*. *Shepardize* several of the significant cases in *Shepard's State Citations* or in the appropriate regional *Shepard's Citations*.

(4) Additional Cases. Other state digests, the regional digests, and the *American Digest System* provide judicial decisions of other states on the point of law. There may also be a looseleaf service on the topic that will provide abstracts or full text of relevant court decisions, (*e.g.*, CCH's *Labor Law Reporter*).

Shepard's Citations give additional references to cases from other states which have cited an applicable state case.

(5) Other. The LEXIS and WESTLAW databases can provide state court decisions.

4. Administrative Law Problem

a. *Federal Administrative Law*

(1) General Background. *Corpus Juris Secundum* and *American Jurisprudence 2d* discuss federal administrative law. Pike and Fischer, *Administrative Law*, treatises (*e.g.*, K. Davis, *Administrative Law*), and periodical literature provide more detailed studies of administrative law.

Annotations on the subject are included in the *American Law Reports* and the *United States Supreme Court Reports* (L.Ed.).

(2) Text and Interpretation. The texts of federal administrative regulations are contained in: (a) looseleaf services, (b) the *Code of Federal Regulations* and the *Federal Register*, and (c) the LEXIS and WESTLAW databases.

The decisions of federal administrative agencies are included in: (a) looseleaf services, (b) agency reports, (c) the LEXIS and WESTLAW databases.

Interpretative sources of federal administrative law are: (a) looseleaf services, (b) U.S. Supreme Court digests and (c) *Federal Practice Digest, 2d* and *3d*, the *Modern Federal Practice Digest* and the *Federal Digest*.

(3) *Shepard's Citations*. Rules and regulations found in the *Code of Federal Regulations* can be *Shepardized* in *Shepard's Code of Federal Regulations Citations*.

Cases of certain agencies (*e.g.*, Federal Trade Commission, Securities and Exchange Commission) may be *Shepardized* in *Shepard's United States Citations* and *Shepard's Federal Citations*.

b. *State Administrative Law*

(1) General Background. Refer to a local encyclopedia for a discussion of state administrative law.

Other secondary aids, such as local treatises, periodical articles and *American Law Reports* annotations are also helpful sources.

(2) Text and Interpretation. If a state has a current administrative code, check it for state regulatory material. In the absence of an administrative code, inquiry should be directed to the appropriate agency for its regulations.

If a looseleaf service covers the state law, it can be consulted for agency rules and decisions (*e.g.*, BNA's *Environmental Reporter*).

Some states publish a work comparable to the *Federal Register* (*e.g.*, *Texas Register*, *Oklahoma Gazette*), in which recent state agency regulations are discussed. Where available, such a publication should be consulted.

Where the state's Attorney General has analyzed an agency ruling or regulation in an opinion, this should be sought for its interpretative value.

The accessibility of agency decisions should be determined by inquiry at the appropriate state agency.

Interpretative cases are covered by the state or regional digest.

(3) *Shepard's Citations*. *Shepardize* applicable court cases in *Shepard's State Citations* or the regional *Shepard's Citations*.

(4) Additional Cases.   Court decisions of other states relating to a comparable administrative law problem may be located in (a) other state digests, (b) regional digests, and (c) the *American Digest System*.

Shepard's Citations also provide citations to cases of other states which cited a state court decision on point.

   c.   *Local Administrative Law*

(1) Text and Interpretation.   If available, city administrative regulations generally are published separately as pamphlets for each body.   Information regarding these rules, such as regulatory and licensing provisions, should be obtained directly from the local administrative department.

Cases pertaining to local administrative law are included in the state digest.

(2) *Shepard's Citations*.   *Shepardize* cases on the problem by using *Shepard's State Citations* or a regional *Shepard's Citations*.

SECTION C. CHART ON LEGAL RESEARCH PROCEDURE

CHART ON LEGAL RESEARCH PROCEDURE

RESEARCH PROBLEM	GENERAL BACKGROUND	MORE CRITICAL & DETAILED STUDIES	ANNOTATIONS	TEXT OF LAW	LEGISLATIVE HISTORY	INTERPRETATION	SHEPARDIZING	ADDITIONAL CASES	OTHER
CONSTITUTIONAL LAW									
1. Federal	1. C.J.S. 2. Am Jur 2d	1. Treatises 2. Periodicals: Index Leg Per. Legal Resource Index (Current Law Index)	1. A.L.R. Fed. 2. U.S. Sup. Ct. Repts. L. Ed. 3. L.C. Constitution	1. U.S.C. 2. U.S.C.A. 3. U.S.C.S.	1. Citations: U.S.C.A., U.S.C.S., Shep. U.S., U.S.C., Stat. at Large 2. Intent: Federalist Papers, etc.	1. U.S.C.A. 2. U.S.C.S. 3. L.C. Constitution 4. U.S. Atty. Gen. ops.	1. Provisions: U.S., State 2. Cases: Fed. U.S., State	1. U.S. Sup. Ct. Digs. 2. West's Fed. Prac. Dig. 2d & 3 d., Mod. Fed. Prac. Dig., Fed. Dig. 3. Am. Dig. System	1. LEXIS 2. WESTLAW
2. State	1. Local Ency. 2. C.J.S. or Am. Jur 2d	1. Periodicals: Index Leg Per. Legal Resource Index (Current Law Index)	A.L.R.	1. State Code 2. State Code Annotated	1. State Const. Convention a. Proceedings b. Reports 2. Locally pub'd Legislative reporters, House and Senate Journals, etc. 3. Local newspapers 4. Local experts	1. State Code Annotated 2. State Dig. 3. State Atty. Gen. ops.	1. Provisions: State Cit. 2. Cases: State Cit. or Regional Cit.	1. Am. Dig. System 2. Constitution of the U.S. National and State; Index	1. LEXIS 2. WESTLAW
STATUTORY LAW									
1. Federal	C.J.S. or Am. Jur 2d	1. Treatises 2. Periodicals: Index Leg Per. Legal Resource Index (Current Law Index)	1. A.L.R 2. L. Ed.	1. U.S.C. 2. U.S.C.A. 3. U.S.C.S.	1. Pre-1970—see Chap. 10 2. Post-1970—C.I.S. 3. Published Legis. Histories	1. U.S.C.A. 2. U.S.C.S. 3. U.S. Atty. Gen. ops.	1. Provisions & Cases: U.S. 2. Cases: Fed. 3. Provisions: State or Regional Cit.	1. U.S. Sup. Ct. Digs. 2. West's Fed. Prac. Dig. 2d & 3 d, Mod. Fed. Prac. Dig., Fed. Dig.	1. LEXIS 2. WESTLAW
2. State	1. Loc. Ency. 2. C.J.S. or Am. Jur 2d	1. Treatises 2. Periodicals: Index Leg Per. Legal Resource Index (Current Law Index)	A.L.R.	1. State Code 2. State Code Annotated	1. Citations: State Code 2. Intent: See Chap 11	1. State Code Annotated 2. Shepard's Law Locator where available	Provisions & Cases: State or Regional Cit.	1. State or Regional Dig. 2. Other States Codes Annot. 3. Uniform Laws Annotated	Legal research guide for the state, where available
3. Local		Treatises		1. Mun. Code 2. Mun. Ordinances 3. Appropriate city official		State Dig.	Provisions & Cases: State Citator	Shepard's Ord. Law Annotations	1. LEXIS 2. WESTLAW

CHART ON LEGAL RESEARCH PROCEDURE

RESEARCH PROBLEM	GENERAL BACKGROUND	MORE CRITICAL & DETAILED STUDIES	ANNOTATIONS	TEXT OF LAW OR CASE	LEGISLATIVE HISTORY	INTERPRETATION	SHEPARDIZING	ADDITIONAL CASES	OTHER
CASE LAW									
1. Federal	1. C.J.S. 2. Am. Jur. 2d	1. Treatises 2. Periodicals: Index Leg. Per. Legal Resource Index (Current Law Index) 3. ALI Restatements	A.L.R.	1. S. CT.: U.S. Reports (L.Ed.) Supreme Ct. Reporter (West) 2. Fed. Reporter & Federal Reporter, 2d 3. Fed. Supp.			Shepard's U.S. & Fed. Cit.	1. U.S. Sup. Ct. Digs. 2. West's Fed. Prac. Dig. 2d&3d, Mod. Fed. Prac. Dig., Fed.Dig. 3. Looseleaf Services	1. LEXIS 2. WESTLAW 3. Records and Briefs, if available
1. State	1. Local Ency. 2. C.J.S. or Am. Jur. 2d	1. Treatises 2. Periodicals: Index Leg. Per. Legal Resource Index (Current Law Index)	A.L.R.	1. National Reporter System 2. State Reports			1. Shepard's State or Regional Cit. 2. National Reporter Blue Book	1. Am. Dig. System 2. Looseleaf Services	1. LEXIS 2. WESTLAW 3. Records and Briefs, if available 4. Restatements of the Law
ADMINISTRATIVE LAW									
1. Federal	C.J.S. or Am. Jur.	1. Pike & Fischer 2. Treatises 3. Periodicals: Index Leg. Per. Legal Resource Index (Current Law Index)	1. A.L.R. 2. L. Ed.	1. Fed. Reg. & CFR: Rules & Decisions 2. Agency Reps: Decisions 3. Looseleaf Services: Rules & Decisions		1. Looseleaf Services 2. U.S.S. Ct. digs. 3. West's Fed. Prac. Dig. 2d&3d, Mod.Fed. Prac. Dig., Fed. Dig.	1. CFR: Cit. 2. Agency Cases: U.S. Admin. Cit. 3. Ct. Cases: U.S. & Fed. Cits.		1. LEXIS 2. WESTLAW
2. State	Local Ency	1. Local Treatises 2. Periodicals: Index Leg. Per. Legal Resource Index (Current Law Index)	A.L.R.	1. Ad. Code, if pub. 2. Register of agency regulations and rulings, if pub. 3. Agency: Rules & Decisions 4. Looseleaf service, if available		1. State or Regional Dig. 2. State Atty. Gen. ops.	Cases: State Cit. or the regional cit.	1. Other state or regional digs. 2. Am. Dig. System	
3. Local				1. Local Adm. Dept. 2. Pamphlets		State Dig.	Cases: State Cit.	Other state digests	

Appendix A

STATE GUIDES TO LEGAL RESEARCH

As discussed in Chapter 1, the United States consists of 51 major legal systems, one for each state and the federal government. While the state systems have much in common, each is the product of a unique history and legal background. Methods of legislating, codifying, and court reporting vary from state to state. Where possible, a researcher should take the time to learn the unusual aspects of legal research in each state's materials in which extended research is conducted.

In many states, law librarians who are familiar with legal research have published guides detailing the legal history and organization of their states. The list below is a compilation of such guides. A researcher contemplating or beginning anything more involved than preliminary research in one of the states listed below would be well advised to consult the guides first. Such a first step could save much time and effort in the endeavor.

California	D. Henke, *California Law Guide* (2 ed. 1976).
Colorado	Weinstein, Colorado Legal Source Materials, 7 COLO.LAW. 2084 (1978).
Florida	R. Brown, *Guide to Florida Legal Research* (1980).
	H. French, *Research in Florida Law* (2d ed. 1965).
	B. Girtman, *Courts, Reports, and Digests: Girtman's Compendium of Federal and Florida Case Law, Where to Find It and How to Cite It* (1979).
Georgia	L. Chanin, *Reference Guide to Georgia Legal History* (1980).
Illinois	B. Davies, *Research in Illinois Law* (1954).
	R. Jacobs et al., *Illinois Legal Research Sourcebook* (1977).
	Wendt, Researching Illinois Legislative Histories—a Practical Guide, 1982 S.ILL.U.L.J. 601.
Indiana	S. Taylor & K. Welker, *1978 Model Bibliography of Indiana Legal Materials*.
Louisiana	K. Wallace, *Louisiana Legal Research Manual* (1972).

Massachusetts	M. Botsford & R.G. Matz, *Handbook of Legal Research in Massachusetts* (1982).
Michigan	R. Beer, *An Annotated Guide to the Legal Literature of Michigan* (1973).
Mississippi	C.S. Bunnell, *Mississippi Legal Research Bibliography* (1983).
Nebraska	P. Hill, *Nebraska Legal Research and Reference Manual* (1983).
New Jersey	P. Axel-Lute, *New Jersey Legal Research Handbook* (1984).
	N.J. Law and Legislative Reference Bureau, *Legal Research Guide for the New Jersey State Library* (1957).
New Mexico	A. Poldervaart, *Manual for Effective New Mexico Legal Research* (1955).
New York	Brown, An Annotated Bibliography of Current New York State Practice Materials, 73 LAW LIBR.J. 28 (1980).
North Carolina	I. Kavass & B. Christensen, *Guide to North Carolina Legal Research* (1973).
Pennsylvania	E. Surrency, *Research in Pennsylvania Law* (2d ed. 1965).
South Carolina	R. Mills & J. Schultz, *South Carolina Legal Research Handbook* (1976).
Tennessee	L. Laska, *Tennessee Legal Research Handbook* (1977).
Texas	M. Boner, *A Reference Guide to Texas Law and Legal History* (1976).
Washington	University of Washington Law School, *Legal Research Guide* (1980).
Wisconsin	D. Danner, *Legal Research in Wisconsin* (1980).
	W. Knudson, *Wisconsin Legal Research Guide* (2d ed. 1972).

Appendix B

LEGAL RESEARCH IN TERRITORIES OF THE UNITED STATES

The United States has sovereignty over a relatively small number of territories which are not among the fifty states. Each of these territories enjoys some degree of local autonomy, and researchers interested in the law of any of these areas must examine certain locally-originated materials as well as those portions of the general body of federal law that apply to the territory. The following is a listing of the more important local sources of law in these territories.

AMERICAN SAMOA

American Samoa was annexed by the United States pursuant to a treaty with Britain and Germany in 1899. It has a popularly-elected governor and a bicameral legislature. It is administered under the United States Department of the Interior, which publishes the annual reports of the governor and other information about the territory.

Statutes

American Samoa Code Annotated, Book Publishing Company, Seattle, Wash., 1981–.

The code is in looseleaf format, updated annually by replacement pages. It has a general index and tables showing the location of sections by legislative act and from the 1949, 1961, and 1973 codifications of American Samoa statutes.

Legislative Material

Fono Journal, American Samoa Legislature, Pago Pago, American Samoa, 1948–1952.

The annual Fono was a predecessor of the present legislature. It began as an advisory board made up of selected Samoa title holders who met once a year to discuss items placed on its agenda by the government.

House Journal, American Samoa Legislature, 1953–; *Senate Journal*, American Samoa Legislature, 1953–.

The official journals of the legislature.

Session Laws and Digest, American Samoa Legislature, 1976–.

This service contains most of the available material for legislative history as well as the text of new statutes.

Court Reports

American Samoa Reports, the Government of American Samoa, Equity Publishing Corporation, Orford, N.H.

There are presently only four volumes in this set, covering the period from the beginning of American sovereignty in 1900 until 1974. Each volume contains headnotes and a digest, and has tables of lands and Matai titles considered as well as the more common tables of cases and of statutes and regulations cited or construed.

Administrative Rules and Regulations

American Samoa Administrative Code, Book Publishing Company, Seattle, Wash., 1981–.

The administrative code is in looseleaf format, updated annually by replacement pages. It has a general index.

Law Review

The Samoan Pacific Law Journal, American Samoa Bar Association, Pago Pago, American Samoa, 1973–1981.

In addition to the more usual law review articles, this journal published case summaries and digests for recent cases that are not yet contained in the *American Samoa Reports.*

GUAM

Guam, like Puerto Rico, was ceded to the United States by Spain in the 1898 Treaty of Paris. It has a popularly-elected governor and a unicameral legislature, and it sends one non-voting delegate to the United States House of Representatives. Guam is under the jurisdiction of the Department of the Interior, which publishes annual reports of the Governor and other information on the island.

Statutes

Guam Code Annotated, Guam Law Revision Commission, Agana, Guam, 1980.

Since 1975 Guam has undertaken a comprehensive review and recodification of its statutory law. The new code is published in looseleaf format, but it is updated irregularly and has no general index.

Legislative Materials

> *Public Laws and Executive Orders*, Guam Law Revision Commission, Agana, Guam, 1975–.
>
> > This service is published as a looseleaf.

Court Reports

> *Guam Reports*, Equity Publishing Corporation, Orford, N.H., 1979–.
>
> > The one bound volume of this set is supplemented by a looseleaf service.

Administrative Rules and Regulations

> *Administrative Rules and Regulations of the Government of Guam*, Secretary of the Legislature, Agana, Guam.
>
> > A looseleaf set with annual supplementation.

Journal

> *Guam Bar Journal*, Guam Bar Association, Agana, Guam, 1981–.

PUERTO RICO

Puerto Rico was ceded by Spain to the United States under the 1898 Treaty of Paris. Since 1917 its citizens have been citizens of the United States, and since 1952 it has had approximately the same control over its internal affairs as do states of the United States, exercised through a governor and a bicameral legislature. Puerto Rico currently has *commonwealth status* with only non-voting representation in the United States Congress.

Statutes

> *Laws of Puerto Rico*, 1900–, Equity Publishing Corporation, Orford, N.H.
>
> > The session laws are published in bound volumes, but not until a few years after the close of a session. They are also available on microfiche in the William Hein & Company series of state session laws.
>
> *Laws of Puerto Rico Annotated*, Equity Publishing Corporation, Orford, N.H., 1965–, 12 vols.
>
> > This set is updated annually by pocket parts which are quite slow (they are usually at least a year behind). The annotations include not only court cases but also cross-references to *Rules and Regulations of Puerto Rico*. There are historical notes to trace the development of var-

ious sections. *Laws of Puerto Rico Annotated* is published in separate English and Spanish editions, as both languages are official.

Court Reports

Puerto Rico Reports, Equity Publishing Corporation, Orford, N.H., vols. 1–100.

    This English-language set includes all cases from the Supreme Court of Puerto Rico from 1900–1972. The English version suspended publication with volume 100.

Decisions de Puerto Rico, Equity Publishing Corporation, Orford, N.H., vols. 1–.

    The Spanish version of the reports of the Supreme Court of Puerto Rico continues to be published, but there is approximately a two-year delay before a volume of decisions is published.

Administrative Rules and Regulations

Rules and Regulations of Puerto Rico, Commonwealth of Puerto Rico, Department of State, San Juan, Puerto Rico, 1957–1972.

    A looseleaf service which contained the codification of all regulations adopted by the executive branch of Puerto Rico. This set is no longer kept current.

Puerto Rico Register, Commonwealth of Puerto Rico, Department of State, San Juan, Puerto Rico, 1957–1982.

    This looseleaf service was published periodically (about seven times a year), and contained new regulations and amendments to existing regulations, thus keeping the *Rules and Regulations of Puerto Rico* up to date.

    In 1975 Escrutinio Legislative, Inc. entered the field of Puerto Rico's regulations and began publishing a weekly description of those promulgated during the previous seven days, including register number, date of issuance, promulgating agency and a brief description.

    The publisher has also added executive orders to the weekly listing. The service is called *Escrutinio Ejecutivo* and is available in both English and Spanish, with a quarterly cumulative index, arranged alphabetically by agency name. This service is unique to Puerto Rico.

    On February 28, 1979, Escrutinio published a *Catalog of Regulations.* This reference manual includes a description of every regulation promulgated since January 1972 (the last update of *Rules and Regulations*), and is cross-indexed by

promulgating agency and by the law under which the regulation is promulgated. It is updated annually, and is designed as an interim measure until *Rules and Regulations* can be brought up to date. The weekly regulations service is designed to keep the subscriber up to date between recompilations of the *Catalog*.

Executive Opinions

Informes del Secretario, Puerto Rico Department of Justice, San Juan, Puerto Rico, 1903–.

The *Informes* are more or less equivalent to attorney general's opinions. They come out irregularly but are kept up to date.

Law Reviews

Revista De Derecho Puertorriqueno. Quarterly publication of the Universidad Catolica de Puerto Rico, School of Law, Ponce, Puerto Rico, 1961–.

Revista del Colegio de Abogados de Puerto Rico. Quarterly publication of the Colegio de Abogados de Puerto Rico, San Juan, Puerto Rico, 1939–. Recently publication has been suspended.

Revista Juridica de la Universidad de Puerto Rico. Quarterly publication of the Escuela de Derecho de la Universidad de Puerto Rico, Rio Piedras, Puerto Rico, 1932–.

Revista Juridica de la Universidad Interamericana de Puerto Rico. A triannual publication of the Universidad Interamericana de Puerto Rico, Santurce, Puerto Rico, 1964–.

Citation Index

Shepard's Puerto Rico Citations, Shepard's/McGraw-Hill, Colorado Springs, Colo., 1968–.

This is a complete citation system showing all citations by the Puerto Rico and federal courts to the Puerto Rico cases reported in the various series of Puerto Rico reports and all citations by the Puerto Rico and federal courts to the Constitution of the Commonwealth of Puerto Rico, the Organic Acts, and codes and laws, acts, ordinances, and court rules. All citations by the Puerto Rico courts to the United State Constitution and federal statutes are also shown.

VIRGIN ISLANDS

Formerly the Danish West Indies, the Virgin Islands of the United States were purchased by the United States in 1917. A local

government consisting of a governor and a 15-member unicameral legislature has existed since 1954. The territory sends a non-voting delegate to the United States House of Representatives. Past efforts to draft a formal constitution securing a greater measure of self-government have been unsuccessful.

Statutes

Session Laws of the Virgin Islands, Office of the Government Secretary, Charlotte Amalie, Saint Thomas, Virgin Islands: Equity Publishing Corporation, Orford, New Hampshire, 1955–.

Published annually, this publication contains the complete text of all laws and resolutions enacted by the legislature and approved by the governor. It also contains a resume of legislative activities, which gives a short summary of action taken on every bill introduced in the legislature for that year. The messages of the governor (mainly veto messages) can be found in the appendix of each volume. Each volume contains a table showing bill numbers of acts and resolutions, a table showing the corresponding sections of the *Virgin Islands Code* to the new acts, and a topical index. The Session Laws of the Virgin Islands are also contained in the series of state session laws published in microfiche by William Hein & Company.

Virgin Islands Code Annotated, Office of the Government Secretary, Charlotte Amalie, Saint Thomas, Virgin Islands, Equity Publishing Corporation, Orford, N.H., (3d ed.), 1970–.

Annotated and updated annually with pocket parts, this set contains the complete text of documents and acts having historical and current significance to the Virgin Islands (*i.e.,* the Danish Colonial Law of 1906; the 1916 Convention between the United States and Denmark providing for the cession of the Danish West Indies; and the Organic Acts). There are distribution tables showing where provisions of prior laws were carried into the *Code.* An index is also included.

Court Reports

Virgin Islands Reports, the Government of the Virgin Islands, Equity Publishing Corporation, Orford, N.H., 1959–.

Beginning in 1917, the *Reports* contain opinions of the District Court of the Virgin Islands, and of the United States Court of Appeals for the Third Circuit and the Supreme Court of the United States in cases originating in the Virgin Islands. Also included are opinions of the District Court

Commissioners (if not reversed), opinions of the police (now municipal) courts if they discuss questions of the law, opinions of the Tax Court of the United States in Virgin Islands cases, and opinions of the Attorney General of the United States with respect to matters concerning the Virgin Islands. Each opinion has headnotes, and each volume has a table of cases reported and tables of statutes, treaties, executive orders, court procedural rules, and other resources cited or construed, and a topical digest of the cases found in that volume.

The *Reports* are kept up to date by a looseleaf service containing current cases, but the update service is more than a year behind.

Administrative Rules and Regulations

Virgin Islands Rules and Regulations, Government Secretary for the Government of the Virgin Islands, Equity Publishing Corporation, Orford, N.H., 1959–.

Contained in looseleaf binders for easy updating, this service provides an official record of all departmental regulations filed with the Government Secretary. The regulations have been classified by subject matter and arranged and numbered to correspond to the pertinent titles and chapters of the *Virgin Islands Code*. A source note under the first section of each regulation or group of regulations shows the office or agency that issued it, and the approval and effective dates. The set contains a topical index and a table of agencies showing which regulations have been adopted by each agency or department. The *Virgin Islands Rules and Regulations* are kept up to date by the *Virgin Islands Register*.

Virgin Islands Register, Government Secretary for the Government of the Virgin Islands, Equity Publishing Corporation, Orford, N.H., 1960–.

Each issue of the *Register* is published in two parts. Part 1 (called *Temporary and Special Materials*) contains gubernatorial proclamations, executive orders and reorganization plans, documents, or classes of documents that the governor determines to have general applicability and legal effect, and documents required by the legislature to be published. Part 2 (called *Amendments and Additions to Rules and Regulations*) contains supplementary looseleaf pages that are interfiled into the *Virgin Islands Rules and Regulations* to keep it current. Volumes for 1960–1970 were issued by the Government Secretary for the Govern-

ment of the Virgin Islands; those for 1971 to the present are issued by the Lieutenant Governor of the Virgin Islands.

Attorney General Opinions

Opinions of the Attorney General of the Virgin Islands, the Lieutenant Governor for the Government of the Virgin Islands, Equity Publishing Corporation, Orford, N.H., 1965–.

This service contains all important opinions of general significance rendered from 1935 by the chief legal officer of the Government of the Virgin Islands, variously designated as Government Attorney, the District Attorney, the United States Attorney, and the Attorney General of the Virgin Islands. Each volume contains headnotes at the beginning of the opinions (summarizing the legal points therein) and a digest of legal points at the end of the volume. Also included are tables listing federal, and local laws; federal, state and local judicial opinions; and regulations and executive orders cited throughout the opinions.

Appendix C

STATE REPORTS

A. YEAR OF FIRST REPORTED CASE DECIDED IN THE STATES' APPELLATE COURTS

Many of the states were territories or colonies at the time of their first appellate decision. Pennsylvania was a commonwealth. In 1840, what is now the state of Texas was an independent republic.

While printing began in the Colonies in 1638, the first case reported appears to be the *Trial of Thomas Sutherland* for murder, printed in 1692. About 30 of the 150 English reports were being used in this country prior to the American Revolution as the written case law, because only about 35 to 40 legal books or pamphlets had been printed here.

Connecticut was the first state to publish an official law report after a 1784 statute entitled *An Act Establishing the Wages of the Judges of the Superior Court* was passed which required judges of the supreme and superior courts to file written opinions. The first volume, known as *Kirby's Reports,* was published in 1789 by Ephraim Kirby in Litchfield, Connecticut. In 1790 came Dallas' *Pennsylvania cases* ; in 1792 followed Hopkinson's *Admiralty Reports* ; and Chipman's *Vermont Reports* in 1793. Through the early 1800's reports followed in North Carolina, Virginia, Kentucky, New Jersey, Maryland, Louisiana, New York, and Tennessee.

State	Date	State	Date
Alabama	1820		
Alaska	1869	Nebraska	1860
Arizona	1866	Nevada	1865
Arkansas	1820	New Hampshire	1796
California	1850	New Jersey	1789
Colorado	1864	New Mexico	1852
Connecticut	1764	New York	1791
Delaware	1814	North Carolina	1778
District of Columbia	1801	North Dakota	1867
Florida	1846	Ohio	1816
Georgia	1805	Oklahoma	1890
Hawaii	1847	Oregon	1853
Idaho	1866	Pennsylvania	1754
Illinois	1819	Philippine Islands	1901
Indiana	1817	Puerto Rico	1899
Iowa	1839	Rhode Island	1828
Kansas	1858	South Carolina	1783
Kentucky	1785	South Dakota	1867
Louisiana	1809	Tennessee	1791
Maine	1820	Texas	1840
Maryland	1658	Utah	1855
Massachusetts	1786	Vermont	1789
Michigan	1836	Virginia	1729
Minnesota	1851	Washington	1854
Mississippi	1818	West Virginia	1864
Missouri	1821	Wisconsin	1839
Montana	1868	Wyoming	1870

B. STATES THAT HAVE DISCONTINUED PUBLISHING OFFICIAL STATE REPORTS

State	Last Published Volume	Year	First Volume Only in National Reporter System
Alabama	295	1975	331 So.2d
Ala.App.	59	1975	331 So.2d
Colorado	200	1981	616 P.2d
Colo.App.	43	1981	616 P.2d
Delaware	59	1965	220 A.2d
Florida	160	1947	37 So.2d
Iowa	261	1967	158 N.W.2d
Kentucky	314	1950	237 S.W.2d
Louisiana*	263	1971	270 So.2d
Maine	161	1964	215 A.2d

State	Last Published Volume	Year	First Volume Only in National Reporter System
Minnesota	312	1976	254 N.W.2d
Mississippi	254	1965	183 So.2d
Missouri	365	1955	295 S.W.2d
Mo.App.	241	1951	274 S.W.2d
North Dakota	79	1953	60 N.W.2d
Oklahoma	208	1953	265 P.2d
Okla.Crim.	197	1953	265 P.2d
South Dakota	90	1975	245 N.W.2d
Tennessee	225	1971	476 S.W.2d
Tenn.App.	63	1971	480 S.W.2d
Tenn.Crim.App.	4	1970	475 S.W.2d
Texas*	163	1961	358 S.W.2d
Tex.Crim.App.*	172	1961	363 S.W.2d
Tex.Civ.App.*	63	1910	134 S.W.
Utah* (2d Series)	30	1973	519 P.2d

* These states have discontinued their official reports, but have not adopted the *National Reporter System* Reports as official.

Appendix D

COVERAGE OF THE NATIONAL REPORTER SYSTEM

The entire system, with its coverage, is outlined below:

Reporter	Began in	Coverage
Atlantic Reporter	1885	Conn., Del., Me., Md., N.H., N.J., Pa., R.I., Vt., and D.C.
California Reporter	1959	Calif. Sup. Ct., District Courts of Appeal and Appellate Department of the Superior Court.
New York Supplement	1888	N.Y. (all state courts). Since 1932, the N.Y. Court of Appeals opinions are published here as well as in the North Eastern Reporter.
North Eastern Reporter	1885	Ill., Ind., Mass., N.Y., and Ohio.
North Western Reporter	1879	Iowa., Mich., Minn., Neb., N.D., S.D., and Wis.
Pacific Reporter	1883	Alaska, Ariz., Cal. to 1960, Calif.Sup. Ct. since 1960, Colo., Hawaii, Idaho, Kan., Mont., Nev., N.M., Okla., Or., Utah, Wash., and Wyo.
South Eastern Reporter	1887	Ga., N.C., S.C., Va., and W.Va.
South Western Reporter	1886	Ark., Ky., Mo., Tenn., and Tex.
Southern Reporter	1887	Ala., Fla., La., and Miss.
Supreme Court Reporter	1882	Supreme Court of the United States.
Federal Reporter	1880	From 1880 to 1932: Circuit Courts of Appeals and District Courts of the U.S., U.S. Court of Customs and Patent Appeals, Court of Claims of the U.S., and Court of Appeals of the District of Columbia. From 1932 to date: U.S. Courts of Appeals, and U.S. Court of Customs and Patent Appeals.[1]

1. Since 1983, jurisdiction of the U.S. Court of Customs and Patent Appeals and the appellate division of the U.S. Court of Claims transferred to U.S. Court of Appeals for the Federal District.

Reporter	Began in	Coverage
		From 1942 to 1961: U.S. Emergency Court of Appeals.
		From 1969 to 1982: U.S. Court of Claims Temporary Emergency Court of Appeals since 1972.
Federal Supplement	1932	U.S. District Courts, U.S. Court of Claims to 1960, U.S. Customs Court since vol. 135 (1949). Special Court, Regional Rail Reorganization Act since 1974. Judicial Panel on Multidistrict Litigation since 1969.
United States Claims Court Reporter	1983	Decisions from U.S. Claims Court and appellate decisions which review Claims Court decisions.
Federal Rules Decisions	1940	District Courts of the United States.
Military Justice Reporter[2]	1975	U.S. Court of Military Appeals and the Courts of Military Review for the Army, Air Force, Navy, and Coast Guard.
West's Bankruptcy Reporter	1979	Bankruptcy decisions from the U.S. Bankruptcy Courts, U.S. District Courts, U.S. Courts of Appeals, and the U.S. Supreme Court.

2. This set replaces the U.S. Court of Military Appeals, *Decisions*, and *Court-Martial Reports*, which have ceased publication.

SELECTED LISTING OF REPORTER SERVICES BY LAW SCHOOL COURSE

Note: This selected listing of looseleaf reporting services and specialized newsletters has been prepared as an aid to students wishing to see the types of information available for some law school courses.

---

1. **Accounting**
   a. *Accountancy Law Reports* (CCH) monthly

2. **Administrative Law**
   see also: Regulated Industries
   a. *Administrative Law Service* (P & F) second series; bimonthly
   b. *United States Law Week* (BNA) weekly, Supreme Court decisions when rendered

3. **Admiralty**
   a. *Benefits Review Board Reporters* (MB) biweekly
   b. *Federal Maritime Commission Service* (Hawkins) periodically supplemented
   c. *Shipping Regulation* (P & F) periodically supplemented

4. **American Indian Law**
   a. *Indian Law Reporter* (American Indian Lawyer Training Program, Inc.) monthly

5. **Antitrust**
   includes: Unfair Competition; Trade Regulation
   see also: Regulated Industries
   a. *Antitrust & Trade Regulation Report* (BNA) weekly
   b. *FTC: Watch* (Wash. Regulatory Reporting Group) biweekly
   c. *Trade Regulations Reports* (CCH) weekly

6. **Arbitration**
   see: Labor Law

7. **Aviation Law**
   a. *Aviation Cases in the Courts* (Hawkins) periodic supplementation
   b. *Aviation Law Reports* (CCH) semimonthly

c. *Civil Aeronautics Board Service* (Hawkins) monthly

d. *National Transportation Safety Board Service* (Hawkins) 8–10 times per year

8. **Banking**

see: Regulated Industries

9. **Bankruptcy**

a. *Bankruptcy Court Decisions* (CRR) semimonthly

b. *Bankruptcy Law Reports* (CCH) biweekly

10. **Civil Procedure**

a. *Class Action reports* (Class Action Reports) quarterly

b. *Federal Rules of Evidence News* (CAL) monthly

c. *Federal Rules Service* (CAL) monthly

d. *United States Law Week* (BNA) weekly; Supreme Court decisions when rendered

11. **Civil Rights**

includes: Employment Discrimination; Fair Housing; Sex-Based Discrimination

see also: Constitutional Law; Poverty Law; Women and the Law

a. *Civil Rights Actions* (MB) periodic supplementation

b. *EEOC Compliance Manual* (BNA) periodic supplementation

c. *EEOC Compliance Manual* (CCH) periodic supplementation

d. *The Equal Employer* (FP) biweekly

e. *Fair Employment Practice Series* (BNA) weekly

f. *Housing & Development Reporter* (BNA) weekly

g. *Mental Disability Law Reporter* (ABA) periodic

h. *United States Law Week* (BNA) weekly; Supreme Court decisions when rendered

12. **Collective Bargaining**

see: Labor Law

13. **Commercial Law**

a. *Secured Transactions Guide* (CCH) biweekly

b. *United States Law Week* (BNA) weekly; Supreme Court decisions when rendered

c. *Uniform Commercial Code Law Letter* (WGL) monthly

d. *Uniform Commercial Code Reporting Service* (CAL) monthly

14. **Communications Law**

see: Regulated Industries

15. Computers

see: Law and Science

16. Constitutional Law

a. *Federal Immigration Law Reporter* (CCH) monthly

b. *Media Law Reporter* (BNA) weekly

c. *United States Law Week* (BNA) weekly; Supreme Court decisions when rendered

d. *U.S. Supreme Court Bulletin* (CCH) monthly and on each decision day while court is in session

17. Consumer Law

a. *Consumer & Commercial Credit* (P–H) monthly

b. *Consumer Credit & Truth-in-Lending Compliance Report* (WGL) monthly

c. *Consumer Credit Guide* (CCH) biweekly

d. *Consumer Protection Report* (National Association of Attorneys General) monthly

e. *Consumer Protection Reporting Service* (CSG Press) monthly

f. *Fair Credit Reporting Manual* (WGL) annual supplements

18. Corporations

includes: Business Planning; Corporate Finance

a. *Business Strategies* (CCH) monthly

b. *Corporate Acquisitions, Mergers and Divestitures* (P–H) monthly

c. *Corporate Practice Series* (BNA) portfolios and weekly newsletter

d. *Corporation Law Guide* (CCH) biweekly

e. *Corporation Service* (P–H) biweekly

f. *Professional Corporation Guide* (P–H) biweekly

19. Creditors' Rights

see: Bankruptcy; Commercial Law

20. Criminal Law and Procedure

a. *Arrest Law Bulletin* (Quinlan) monthly

b. *Criminal Law Advocacy Reporter* (MB) periodic supplementation

c. *Criminal Law Monthly* (National College for Criminal Defense) monthly

d. *Criminal Law Reporter* (BNA) weekly

e. *The Law Officers Bulletin* (BNA) biweekly

f. *Narcotics Law Bulletin* (Quinlan) monthly

g. *National Verdict Survey* (National Verdict Survey) weekly

h. *Search & Seizure Law Report* (CB) monthly

21. Domestic Relations

includes: Family Law; Juvenile Law

a. *Family Law Reporter* (BNA) weekly

b. *Juvenile Law Newsletter* (Nat'l Juvenile Law Center) bimonthly

c. *Juvenile Law Reports* (Knehans-Miller) monthly

22. Education Law

a. *College & University Reports* (CCH) weekly

b. *Education for the Handicapped Law Report* (CRR) biweekly

c. *Nolpe School Law Reporter* (Nat'l Organization on Legal Problems in Education) monthly

d. *School Law Bulletin* (Quinlan) quarterly

23. Election Law

a. *Federal Election Campaign Financing Guide* (CCH) periodic supplementation

b. *Campaign Practices Reports Newsletter* (Plus Publications) biweekly

24. Energy Law

see: Environmental Law

25. Entertainment Law

includes: Sports Law

see also: Patents, Copyrights and Trademarks

a. *Entertainment Law Reporter* (E.L.R. Publishing Company) monthly

26. Environmental Law

see also: Land Use Planning

a. *Chemical Regulation Reporter* (BNA) weekly

b. *Energy Management* (CCH) weekly

c. *The Energy Regulation Manual* (Aspen) quarterly

d. *Energy Resources Tax Reporter* (CCH) monthly

e. *Energy Users Report* (BNA) weekly

f. *Environmental Law Reporter* (Environmental Law Institute) monthly

g. *Environment Reporter* (BNA) weekly

h. *Hazardous Materials Transportation* (BNA) monthly

i. *International Environment Reporter* (BNA) monthly

j. *International Hazardous Materials Transport Manual* (BNA) monthly

k. *Natural Gas Handbook* (FPAS) monthly

l. *Natural Gas Policy Act Information Service* (Federal Programs Advisory Service) biweekly

m. *Noise Regulation Reporter* (BNA) biweekly

n. *Pollution Control Guide* (CCH) weekly

27. Estate Planning

see also: Taxation

a. *Estate Planning & Taxation Coordinator* (RIA) biweekly

b. *Successful Estate Planning* (P–H) semimonthly

c. *Inheritance, Estate & Gift Tax Reports* (CCH) weekly

d. *Tax Management: Estates, Gifts, Trusts* (BNA) bimonthly journal and portfolio supplements

28. Family Law

see: Domestic Relations

The Family Law Reporter (BNA) weekly

29. Government Contracts

a. *Contract Appeals Decisions* (CCH) biweekly

b. *Extraordinary Contractual Relief Reporter* (FP) periodic supplementation

c. *Federal Contracts Report* (BNA) weekly

d. *The Government Contractor* (FP) biweekly

e. *Government Contracts Reports* (CCH) weekly

30. Insurance

a. *Automobile Law Report* (CCH) biweekly

b. *Fire & Casualty Insurance Law Reports* (CCH) biweekly

c. *Insurance Guide* (P–H) monthly

d. *Life, Health & Accident Insurance Law Reports* (CCH) periodic reports

e. *Loss Prevention and Control* (BNA) biweekly

f. *Social Security Coordinator* (RIA) monthly

g. *Unemployment Insurance—Social Security* (CCH) weekly

31. International Law

a. *International Environment Reporter* (BNA) monthly

b. *International Law Perspective* (International Law Perspective) monthly

32. International Transactions

a. *Common Market Reports* (CCH) biweekly

b. *International Trade Reporter* (BNA) weekly

c. *Tax Management: Foreign Income Series* (BNA) portfolios and journal supplemented monthly

33. Juvenile Law

see: Domestic Relations

34. Labor Law

includes: Arbitration; Collective Bargaining; Economic Controls; Occupational Safety and Health; Pensions; Public Employment

a. *Benefits Today* (BNA) biweekly

b. *Collective Bargaining, Negotiations & Contracts* (BNA) biweekly

c. *Construction Labor Report* (BNA) weekly

d. *Daily Labor Report* (BNA) daily

e. *Employee Benefits Cases* (BNA) weekly

f. *Employee Relations Weekly* (BNA) weekly

g. *Employment Coordinator* (RIA) looseleaf service, monthly supplement, biweekly newsletter

h. *Employment & Training Reporter* (BNA) weekly

i. *Employment Practices Guide* (CCH) semimonthly

j. *Employment Safety & Health Guide* (CCH) weekly

k. *Fair Employment Practice Series* (BNA) weekly

l. *Government Employee Relations Report* (BNA) weekly

m. *The Government Manager* (BNA) biweekly

n. *Health Care Labor Manual* (Aspen) bimonthly

o. *Human Resources Management* (CCH) monthly

p. *Job Safety & Health* (BNA) biweekly

q. *Job Safety & Health Report* (Business Publishers, Inc.) biweekly

r. *Labor Arbitration Awards* (CCH) weekly

s. *Labor Arbitration Information System* (Labor Relations Press)

t. *Labor Arbitration Reports* (BNA) weekly

u. *Labor Law Reports* (CCH) weekly

v. *Labor Relations Reporter* (BNA) weekly

w. *Occupational Safety & Health Reporter* (BNA) weekly

x. *Pension & Annuity Withholding Service* (RIA) monthly

y. *Pension Plan Guide* (CCH) weekly

z. *Pension Reporter* (BNA) weekly

aa. *Policy and Practice Series* (BNA) weekly

bb. *Public Employee Bargaining* (CCH) biweekly

cc. *Public Personnel Administration* (P–H) biweekly

dd. *Retail/Services Labor Report* (BNA) weekly

ee. *Termination of Employment* (P–H) monthly

ff. *Union Labor Report* (BNA) weekly

gg. *White Collar Report* (BNA) weekly

35. Land Use Planning

see also: Environmental Law

a. *Housing & Development Reporter* (BNA) weekly

b. *Land Development Law Reporter* (Land Development Institute, Ltd.) monthly

c. *Land Use Law & Zoning Law Digest* (American Planning Association) monthly

d. *Zoning and Planning Law Report* (CB) monthly

36. Law and Science

includes: Computers

a. *Computer Law Reporter* (Computer Law Reporter) bimonthly

b. *Bioethics Reporter* (UPA) monthly

37. Legal Profession

includes: Professional Responsibility

a. *ABA/BNA Lawyer's Manual of Professional Responsibility* (BNA) bi-weekly

b. *Ethics in Government Reporter* (Washington Service Bureau) monthly

c. *National Reporter on Legal Ethics & Professional Responsibility* (UPA) monthly

d. *Professional Liability Reporter* (Prof. Liability Reporter Co.) monthly

38. Legislation

a. *Congressional Index* (CCH) weekly while Congress is in session

b. *Daily Report for Executives* (BNA) daily

39. Military Law

a. *Military Law Reporter* (Public Law Education Institute) bimonthly

40. Natural Resources

see: Environmental Law

41. Occupational Safety and Health

see: Labor Law

42. Patents, Copyrights, and Trademarks

see also: Entertainment Law

a. *Copyright Law Reporter* (CCH) monthly

b. *Patent, Trademark & Copyright Journal* (BNA) weekly

c. *United States Patents Quarterly* (BNA) weekly

43. Pensions

see: Labor Law

44. Product Liability

includes: Consumer Product Safety

a. *Consumer Product Safety Guide* (CCH) weekly

b. *Products Liability Reports* (CCH) biweekly

c. *Product Safety & Liability Reporter* (BNA) weekly

45. Professional Responsibility

see: Legal Profession

46. Public Employment

see: Labor Law

47. Public Utilities

see: Regulated Industries

48. Real Property

see also: Land Use Planning

a. *National Property Law Digest* (NPLD, Inc.) monthly

b. *Timesharing Law Reporter Briefs* (Land Development Institute) monthly

49. Regulated Industries

includes: Banking; Communications; Energy; Food, Drug & Cosmetics; Public Utilities; Transportation

see also: Administrative Law; Aviation Law

a. *Cable Television Law* (MB) biannual

b. *Energy Users Report* (BNA) weekly

c. *F–D–C Reports* (FDC Reports) weekly

d. *Federal & State Carriers Reports* (CCH) biweekly

e. *Federal Banking Law Reports* (CCH) weekly

f. *Federal Carriers Reports* (CCH) biweekly

g. *Federal Power Service* (MB) biweekly

h. *Food Drug Cosmetic Law Reports* (CCH) weekly

i. *Medical Devices Reports* (CCH) periodic supplementation

j. *Motor Carrier—Freight Forwarder Service* (Hawkins) monthly

k. *Media Law reporter* (BNA) weekly

l. *Nuclear Regulation Reports* (CCH) weekly

m. *Radio Regulation, 2d* (P & F) weekly

n. *Rail Carrier Service* (Hawkins) monthly

o. *Utilities Law Reports* (CCH) weekly

p. *Washington Financial Reports* (BNA) weekly

50. Securities Regulation

a. *Blue Sky Law Reports* (CCH) semimonthly

b. *Commodities Futures Law Reports* (CCH) semimonthly

c. *Corporate Capital Transactions Coordinator* (RIA) biweekly

d. *Federal Securities Law Reports* (CCH) weekly

e. *Mutual Funds Guide* (CCH) biweekly

f. *SEC Compliance Manual* (P–H) biweekly

g. *SEC No-Action Letters* (WSB) weekly

h. *Securities & Federal Corporate Law Report* (CB) monthly

i. *Securities Regulation* (P–H) monthly

j. *Securities Regulation & Law Report* (BNA) weekly

k. *Securities Regulation Law Alert* (WGL) biweekly

51. Taxation

see also: Estate Planning

a. *Daily Tax Report* (BNA) daily

b. *Divorce Taxation* (P–H) monthly

c. Energy Resources Tax Reporter *(CCH) monthly*

d. *Federal Taxes Citator* (P–H) monthly

e. *Federal Tax Compliance Reporter* (CCH) monthly

f. *Federal Tax Coordinator, 2d* (RIA) biweekly

g. *Federal Tax Guide* (CCH) weekly

h. *Federal Taxes* (P–H) weekly

i. *Individual Retirement Plan Guides* (CCH) monthly

j. *Interest & Dividends* (CCH) monthly

k. *IRS Positions Reports* (CCH) weekly

l. *Standard Federal Tax Reports* (CCH) weekly

m. *Tax Court Reported Decisions* (P–H) weekly

n. *Tax Court Reports* (CCH) weekly

o. *Tax Management: Primary Sources* (BNA) monthly

p. *Tax Management: U.S. Income* (BNA) portfolios supplemented biweekly; biweekly memorandum

q. *Taxes Interpreted* (Philips Publishing) biweekly

r. *Tax Notes* (Tax Analysts) weekly

s. *Weekly Tax Report* (BNA) weekly

t. *West's Federal Tax Guide* (West) biweekly

52. Torts

a. *Civil Trial Practice Manual* (BNA) biweekly

b. *Hospital Law Manual* (Aspen) bimonthly

c. *Personal Injury Newsletter* (MB) biweekly

53. Trade Regulation

see: Antitrust; Consumer Law; Regulated Industries

54. Unfair Competition

see: Antitrust

55. Urban Law

    a. *Housing & Development Reporter* (BNA) weekly

    b. *Urban Affairs Reports* (CCH) weekly

56. Wills

    see: Estate Planning

57. Women and the Law

    Women's Rights Law Reporter (Rutgers Law School) quarterly

58. Workers' Compensation

    a. *Worker's Compensation Law Bulletin* (Quinlan) monthly

    b. *Workmen's Compensation Law Reports* (CCH) biweekly

59. Zoning

    see: Land Use Planning

Abbreviations	Major Publishers
ABA	American Bar Association
BNA	The Bureau of National Affairs, Inc.
CAL	Callaghan & Company
CB	Clark Boardman Company, Ltd.
CCH	Commerce Clearing House, Inc.
CRR	Corporate Reorganization Reporter, Inc.
EIC	Environment Information Center, Inc.
FP	Federal Publications, Inc.
MB	Matthew Bender
P & F	Pike & Fischer
P–H	Prentice-Hall, Inc.
RIA	Research Institute of America, Inc.
UPA	University Publications of America
WSB	Washington Service Bureau, Inc.
WGL	Warren, Gorham & Lamont, Inc.

INDEX

References are to Pages, italic type indicates Titles of Publications

APPEAL PAPERS
See Briefs and Records.

APPELLATE BRIEFS
See Briefs and Records.

APPELLATE COURTS, 13–14

ATTORNEYS GENERAL OPINIONS, 330–
331
In *Lexis* and *Westlaw,* 331.
State, *Shepard's Citation* to, 240.

AUTO–CITE, 60, 116
For parallel citations, 58.

BAR ASSOCIATIONS
See Legal Periodicals.

BILLS
See Legislative Histories.

BIOGRAPHY
See Directories.

BLUE AND WHITE BOOK, 57

BLUEBOOK
See Citation Form.

BOOK REVIEWS
See Legal Periodicals.

BRIEFS AND RECORDS, 337
In microform, 379.
United States Supreme Court, 337–338.

**BUREAU OF NATIONAL AFFAIRS,
LOOSELEAF SERVICES,** 223–224
Illustrations of, 232–234.
List of, Appendix E.

CANADA
Directory of lawyers in, 333.
*Index to Canadian Legal Periodical
Literature,* 293.

CASES, COURT
See Court Reports.

CASES BY POPULAR NAME
See Popular Names, Tables of.

CENTURY DIGEST, 64–65

CHAMBER OPINIONS
U.S. Supreme Court, 34.

CITATION
Parallel citations, 57–58.
Auto-Cite or *Insta-Cite* for, 61.

CITATION FORM
Court reports, 27, 55–57.
Uniform System of Citations, 27.

CITATORS
See *Shepard's Citations.*

CIVIL LAW, 5–6

CIVIL PRACTICE
See Court Procedure.

CODE OF FEDERAL REGULATIONS, 195–
196
Citator for, 295.
Cumulative list of changes, 195–196.
Executive orders in, 208.
Illustrations of, 199–207.
In *Lexis* and *Westlaw,* 216–217.
In looseleaf services, 216.
Presidential documents in, 208–209.
Publication of, 193.
Updating of, 195–196.

**CODE OF PROFESSIONAL RESPONSIBIL-
ITY (ABA),** 338
See also Model Rules of Professional
Conduct.

CODES
See also Legislation.
Defined, 131–134.

CODIFICATION
Civil law, 5–6.
Federal statutes, 131–137.
State, 181–182.

COM
See Computer Output Microfilm.

**COMMERCE CLEARING HOUSE,
LOOSELEAF SERVICES**
Illustrations of, 226–231.
List of, Appendix E.
Use of, 222–223.

COMMITTEE HEARINGS
See Congressional Hearings.

COMMITTEE REPORTS, 155–156

COMMON LAW
Definition, 1.
Sources of, 2, 3.

**COMPUTER ASSISTED LEGAL RE-
SEARCH,** 365–377
Citation form for, 375–377.

COMPUTER OUTPUT MICROFILM, 377

†